Profiling and Serial Crime

Theoretical and Practical Issues

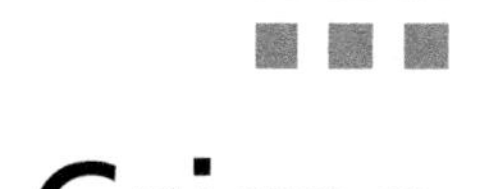

Profiling and Serial Crime

Theoretical and Practical Issues

Third Edition

Wayne Petherick

AMSTERDAM • BOSTON • HEIDELBERG • LONDON • NEW YORK • OXFORD
PARIS • SAN DIEGO • SAN FRANCISCO • SINGAPORE • SYDNEY • TOKYO

Academic Press is an imprint of Elsevier

Academic Press is an imprint of Elsevier
225 Wyman Street, Waltham, MA 02451, USA
The Boulevard, Langford Lane, Kidlington, Oxford, OX5 1GB, UK

Notices

Knowledge and best practice in this field are constantly changing. As new research and experience broaden our understanding, changes in research methods, professional practices, or medical treatment may become necessary.

Practitioners and researchers must always rely on their own experience and knowledge in evaluating and using any information, methods, compounds, or experiments described herein. In using such information or methods they should be mindful of their own safety and the safety of others, including parties for whom they have a professional responsibility.

To the fullest extent of the law, neither the Publisher nor the authors, contributors, or editors, assume any liability for any injury and/or damage to persons or property as a matter of products liability, negligence or otherwise, or from any use or operation of any methods, products, instructions, or ideas contained in the material herein.

Library of Congress Cataloging-in-Publication Data
Application submitted.

British Library Cataloguing-in-Publication Data
A catalogue record for this book is available from the British Library.

ISBN: 978-1-4557-3174-9

Table of Contents

Preface: The More Things Change, the More They Stay the Same

Another three years have passed since the publication of the second edition of *Serial Crime*, and this new third edition sees not only a new title, but a new publisher, having moved to an imprint of Elsevier. A lot has changed in this time, with an increased focus on certain behavior types such as bullying (most notably where this bullying involves the use of physical force), with governments, administrators, behavioral scientists, and others acknowledging that the push-and-shove of the school yard can have significant lifelong impacts on both offenders and bullies. Changes in the availability of, and access to, technology have likely heralded an increase in the surveillance activities of stalkers and other serial pests, while some countries around the world are struggling with outlaw motorcycle gangs, and the trouble they often bring.

But this time has been about more than change in the outside world; it has also been a time for introspection, change, and growth among myself and the contributors to this work. We have all continued to blaze ahead in our own ways, and to continue down our own paths. But these paths change, as they often do, and so too must the professional directions we travel. Exposure to and experience with particular situations, coupled with an insatiable interest, have led me to investigate self-esteem and personality disorder, and their relationship to both crime and victimization. Not only that, but this has also been in an attempt to better understand the crimes and criminal behavior being examined, and in an effort to better educate our students when they see it.

The field of profiling is a contentious one. Just spend a short amount of time with the literature, and this will become painfully evident. There is little consensus, and little uniformity. What's more, in an attempt to grab celebrity, some may be more concerned with gratuitous self-promotion and the personal advancement this may bring. There is little concern for who is trodden on, or in what way, just as long as personal agendas are met. Sadly, here the field and its advancement will take a sorry second or third place.

There is no time like the present for a refocus of efforts. For anyone who is truly passionate about the field, it is time to make a commitment to advance applied crime analysis in general (of which profiling is one specific type), and the understanding of serial crime to a level beyond the personalities involved, to acknowledge that these personalities are just one part of a very small machine, and that the pursuit of personal agendas and celebrity set us back, not drive us forward.

As part of this commitment, this third edition will expand the focus from previous editions with the inclusion of entirely new chapters, and the modification of some of the existing chapters to reflect time- or location-based changes impacting on content. The discussions of profiling have also been extended to include chapters on staging and case linkage. In addition, this work has increased content on serial crime, from specific instances (the inclusion of a chapter on serial bullying and harassment) to general matters surrounding crime and victimization (as can be found in the final chapter on motivation).

As such, the work is comprised of two conceptual divisions. The first revolves around a type of applied crime analysis, most usually referred to as criminal profiling (though behavioral profiling and simply profiling are also common terms). This section includes the history, theoretical background, profiling types (including a new discussion on geographic profiling), research on profiling, and the more philosophical debates regarding where we should be heading. The second conceptual section involves serial crimes, including arson, murder, rape, stalking, and the new chapter on bullying and harassment. As a capstone, the final chapter examines motivation, from both victim and offender perspectives, including a suggested pathways model to offending, and the psychopathological backdrop that may accompany either offending or victimization.

To begin, Chapter 1 by Norris provides a history of profiling that contains all the major landmarks in its most recent history, from the work of medical men during the "Jack the Ripper" inquiry in England, circa 1888, through the development of the first serious attempts by mental health professionals to provide a "profile" of unknown offenders for crimes still under investigation. This would also include the psychological profile done of Adolf Hitler for a US intelligence agency during World War II. From here, Norris chronicles the development of each of the major schools of thought, starting with the Criminal Investigative Analysis (CIA) of the Federal Bureau of Investigation (FBI). Far from being just a history, this chapter also briefly discusses the state of flux of the field, and suggests future directions.

Next, Petherick provides an overview to logic, and the role of induction and deduction in profiling. More than just of peripheral relevance to the subject, the application of logic and reasoning is central to the differences between profiling methods, with some relying on statistical assumptions to provide a composite of the crime, and others relying more strictly on crime scene information, such as physical evidence, and what this can tell us about what happened. Examples are provided where relevant throughout to show the application of the logic.

As an extension to Chapter 2, Chapter 3, "Behavioral Consistency, the Homology Assumption, and the Problems of Induction," takes some of the problems of inductive logic and transposes them directly onto the area of profiling. For example, inductive profiling approaches rely on both consistency—that an offender will behave the same way across offenses—and homology—that two different offenders who do similar things will have similar background characteristics. Yet research has failed to show that either of these two propositions are valid, or in the best case, that they may be valid, but only in certain crime types. This would, at the very best, limit their generalizability.

Having set the stage for logic and reasoning, which comprise the most broad theoretical differences between profiling approaches, Petherick then goes on to detail each of the schools of thought, including their genesis, theoretical assumptions, and the results of research into the types; that is, the type of characteristics they offer, on what each bases their inference or assumption of offender characteristics, and how common this reasoning is within each method. For this edition, geographic profiling now has its own chapter.

Norris, in Chapter 5, takes us through geographic profiling, from its historical roots to the current theoretical propositions and practical applications. From the development and theoretical roots, such as theories of spatial behavior and main protagonists, Norris discusses whether geographic profiling is a method in its own right, or whether it forms part of an overall investigative strategy.

Chapter 6 then moves onto the fallacy of accuracy in criminal profiling; that is, while accuracy is cited as one yardstick of whether a profile is useful, it may in fact be the worst predictor of the utility of a profile. For example, what happens if a profile is accurate on 10 characteristics, but none of them actually helps police identify any suspect pools? What about in another instance where the profile gives 10 characteristics, is accurate on three of them, and one of those three helps identify a suspect who turns out to be the killer? Which has the right to claim accuracy? Which on utility? These issues are discussed in detail.

Following this, Michael McGrath, a forensic psychiatrist, provides an overview of case linkage, where attempts are made to link multiple crimes back to an offender(s) through a behavioral examination of the act. McGrath will cover not only the theory and underlying assumptions behind case linkage, but will also look in depth at the case of *New Jersey v. Fortin*, which has come and gone from legal scrutiny over the years. This case is of particular relevance, because not only has it seen considerable legal attention in the original trials and appeals, but also because the central issue has been the failure of case linkage attempts at multiple levels.

From here, Ferguson presents the concept of staging, wherein offenders attempt to obscure links between themselves and the crime in an attempt to mislead investigators. This chapter will not only discuss staging conceptually, but will also present some of the results of Dr. Ferguson's PhD, which was the first work of its kind to present staging as a form of deception.

The next chapter, also written by Dr. Ferguson, is the result of previous research she has conducted into investigative relevance. Here, the idea that profiles should be relevant to the police who are most often consumers is presented (something that should not be foreign but an examination of content suggests it is), as well as examining which particular profile characteristics have this relevance, and which may not. Criteria for inclusion and exclusion to investigative relevance are also provided.

In this next chapter on metacognition, Woodhouse and Petherick present the results of Barry's Master of Psychology (Forensic) thesis that sought to determine whether those given a basic level of profiling education were better at discriminating between a good profile and a bad profile. Results suggest that, even with a basic level of education, individuals rated a poor (and fictional) account of profiling as being of poorer quality than the other profile presented in the experiment. The theory behind metacognition, knowing when you don't know, is provided, and discussed within the context of the experiment.

In Chapter 11, Petherick and colleagues look at profiling as expert evidence. While not allowed in many jurisdictions, others have been more receptive to this type of expert testimony. As a result, the rules of expert evidence in Australia and elsewhere are discussed, along with those areas in which profiling may be able to assist in the legal process. This chapter will also discuss in some detail relevant cases where profiling evidence has been offered, including the outcome of the cases where known.

Chapter 12, the last in the profiling section, looks at the future of profiling, and what can still be done to make the field more valid (measuring what it claims to measure) and reliable (being able to measure consistently across time and situations). This chapter looks specifically at research, ethics, accountability, and education and training. For example, there is no unified ethical canon by which profilers live, and there are no universal training standards. Far be it from the authors to suggest that this chapter offers this; rather, these issues are discussed in a general sense, including what makes their unification across methods and practitioners difficult, if not impossible.

This first chapter in the serial crimes section discusses the highly relevant and problematic issues of serial bullying and harassment. While not always rising to the levels of criminal behavior (because of the age of the offenders or the nature of behavior itself), these often set the stage for future victimization or criminal behavior. For example, many bullies are victims, and many perpetrators rise to the level of adult criminal. These and other issues are discussed, including school-based practices, prevalence and incidence, and outlooks for bullies and victims.

The chapter on serial stalking contains the same case studies as the previous version, but with updates to the literature and theory when required. For example, new research on serial stalking is incorporated, which discusses how many stalkers may be serial offenders, in addition to base issues such as the definition of stalking, and how often it occurs as a base behavior.

Then Jenkins and Petherick provide a fresh perspective on serial rape, looking not only at base definitions of rape and sexual assault, but also at victim and offender characteristics, typologies of rape, and also the variety of criminological theories that have been, or can be, used to explain rape and serial rape. These include psychodynamic theories and evolutionary theories; the latter sees rape as an attempt by males to ensure the survival of their blood line. This chapter concludes with a discussion of various forensic techniques that may be useful during the investigation of serial rape.

A direct incarnation of the serial murder chapter from the second edition, Dan Kennedy and Robert Homant provide a detailed overview of serial murder from a variety of facets. This includes the diathesis-stress model of the development of serial murder and the trauma control model of serial murder. In addition, a variety of other serial murder theories are discussed with a detailed case study included to highlight the major features and points as relevant throughout.

In the next chapter, Brogan discusses the issue of serial arson. While this chapter is written by an Australian author, aspects of serial arson are discussed from an international perspective, drawing on information from the United States and United Kingdom as related to the issue of serial arson. Best practice with arson investigations is discussed at length, along with other aspects of serial arson that are relevant to investigator, student, and academic alike. Ross provides a number of case studies of some of Australia's worst serial arsonists. The issues they highlight are global in nature.

Finally, Petherick and Sinnamon provide a comprehensive overview of motivations, from the perspective of both the offender and the victim. This includes a developmental view of the pathways that lead to the development of certain motivations, for both offenders and victims, and details the role of self esteem, personality, and personality disorder. The authors feel that this holistic treatment provides a never-before-seen treatment of the issue. As noted, this chapter serves as the capstone to both conceptual sections of this book, both from the perspective of criminal profiling and serial crime, of all sorts.

As with all previous editions of this text, it has been a pleasure to work with all of these authors. Their combined passion, intellect, and desire to advance their particular fields is inspiring and encouraging. They serve as a base from which to further and better not only the field, but our individual selves. They remind us that we don't know all we need to know, and that the pursuit of knowledge never ends, as long as we don't become complacent. More importantly, we should never stop reading, learning, or trying to know, because there is always someone out there who will read more, learn more, or know more than you. The goal is to know as much as you can, and to do the best you can with what you know. Read on.

Wayne Petherick, PhD

Digital Assets

Thank you for selecting Academic Press's *Profiling and Serial Crime.* To complement the learning experience, we have provided a number of online tools to accompany this edition. Two distinct packages of interactive digital assets are available: one for instructors and one for students.

Please consult your local sales representative with any additional questions.

For the Instructor

Qualified adopters and instructors need to register at the this link for access: http://textbooks.elsevier.com/web/manuals.aspx?isbn=9781455731749

- **Test Bank** Compose, customize, and deliver exams using an online assessment package in a free Windows-based authoring tool that makes it easy to build tests using the unique multiple choice and true or false questions created for *Profiling and Serial Crime.* What's more, this authoring tool allows you to export customized exams directly to Blackboard, WebCT, eCollege, Angel and other leading systems. All test bank files are also conveniently offered in Word format.
- **PowerPoint Lecture Slides** Reinforce key topics with focused PowerPoints, which provide a perfect visual outline with which to augment your lecture. Each individual book chapter has its own dedicated slideshow.
- **Lesson Plans** Design your course around customized lesson plans. Each individual lesson plan acts as separate syllabi containing content synopses, key terms, content synopses, directions to supplementary websites, and more open-ended critical thinking questions designed to spur class discussion. These lesson plans also delineate and connect chapter-based learning objectives to specific teaching resources, making it easy to catalogue the resources at your disposal.

For the Student

Students will need to visit this link in order to access the ancillaries below. http://www.elsevierdirect.com/companion.jsp?ISBN=9781455731749

- **Self-Assessment Question Bank** Enhance review and study sessions with the help of this online self-quizzing asset. Each question is presented in an interactive format that allows for immediate feedback.
- **Case Studies** Apply what is on the page to the world beyond with the help of topic-specific case studies, each designed to turn theory into practice and followed by three interactive scenario-based questions that allow for immediate feedback.

About the Authors

Wayne Petherick, PhD

Wayne Petherick is currently Associate Professor of Criminology at Bond University on Queensland's Gold Coast. Wayne teaches in the areas of Alcohol, Drugs, and Crime, Criminal Profiling, Applied Crime Analysis, Criminal Motivations, Crime and Deviance, Forensic Victimology, and Forensic Criminology. Wayne is currently author, editor, or coeditor of three textbooks including this work, *Forensic Victimology*, and *Forensic Criminology*.

His research areas of interest include criminal profiling, with his doctoral thesis *Criminal Profiling: A Qualitative and Quantitative Analysis of Methods and Content* examining profiles to better understand the nature of logic employed and the types of characteristics offered by the different approaches. Other areas include stalking, where he is developing a Response-Outcome model to understand the response style of victims and how this may perpetuate the harassment. In other work, Wayne is examining the relationship between self-esteem, personality disorder, crime, and criminal (and victim) motivations, and in bullying and harassment.

In addition to his teaching and research work, Dr. Petherick also works on a variety of cases including homicides, threat and risk cases, and stalking. He can be contacted via email at wpetheri@staff.bond.edu.au or wpetheri@me.com.

Ross Brogan, MA (Fire Investigation)

Ross joined the New South Wales (NSW) Fire Brigades, in Australia, in 1970 and worked as a firefighter and officer throughout NSW during that period. Ross was awarded the Australian Fire Service Medal in 2005 for his contribution to fire investigation with the NSW Fire Brigades. He retired in December 2007 after serving the community of NSW for more than 37 years. In June 1987, he successfully completed the Arson Awareness section of NSW Police Detective training course; in August he was appointed to NSW Fire Brigades Fire Investigation Unit as an investigator, a position he held until 2003. In January 1999, Ross was awarded a Graduate Certificate in Fire Investigation; in 2004, he graduated with a Graduate Diploma of Fire Investigation; and in 2008, he graduated with a Master of Arts (Fire Investigation). Since March 2003, Ross has co-presented a 6-day practical fire investigation course for Charles Sturt University to students from the police, the fire service, private investigators, insurance investigators, and forensic science students. Ross continues to teach for Charles Sturt University. Ross is currently a member of the International Association of Arson Investigators, NSW, Victoria, and Queensland chapters; a USA International member; and a member of the Australian & New Zealand Forensic Science Society. He has been qualified by voir dire in both the criminal and the civil jurisdiction of the Supreme Court in NSW to give opinion evidence as an expert witness in fire matters. In all, Ross has attended and given evidence in excess of 100 matters throughout Australia.

Nathan Brooks, GradDip Psych, MPsych (Forensic), BPsychSc

Nathan holds a Postgraduate Diploma in Psychology and a Masters of Psychology (Forensic) from Bond University. He is currently a doctoral candidate in the Psychology Department at Bond University, where he is studying psychopathy in the community and business setting. Nathan has worked with a variety of offenders and his areas of interest include, sexual and violent offenders, personality disorders and risk assessment. Nathan works as a Psychologist in private practice and at Bond University as an Adjunct Teaching Fellow in the Psychology Department. Nathan can be contacted at nbrooks@bond.edu.au.

Claire Ferguson, PhD

Claire Ferguson holds her Bachelor of Arts degree in honours Psychology from the University of Western Ontario in Canada, her Masters degree in Criminology, and her PhD in Criminology, both from Bond University in Australia. Dr. Ferguson has worked for St. Leonard's Society, as well as interned with Queensland Fire and Rescue services (Fire Investigation Unit). She also undertook an internship with Forensic Solutions in 2008. She is a Lecturer, researcher and consultant in forensic criminology, and her expertise surrounds Forensic Criminology. Dr. Ferguson's doctorate (2010) was an analysis of staged crime scenes in homicide cases internationally. This project was the only systematic review of these types of cases to ever be conducted and was viewed with great esteem in the criminological community inside and outside of Bond University.

Dr. Ferguson has been nominated for the 'Excellence in Teaching and Learning' award and the 'UniJobs Lecturer of the Year' award by her students. Along with teaching, she has also participated in several large scale research ventures involving teams of researchers, complex methodologies and competitive national grants. Two involving the law school at Bond have led to significant policy implications in Queensland. In 2009, she received both the 'Bond University Research Candidate of the year' and the 'Faculty of HSS research Candidate of the year'. Claire is currently doing research and is a project manager for The Australian Centre for Arson Research and Treatment at Bond University.

Elizabeth Fry, MCrim

Elizabeth completed a Joint Honours degree in Criminology and Sociology including a thesis on Education in a Young Offender Institute in the United Kingdom. She has also completed a Master of Criminology which included a thesis on Consistencies in Crime Scene

Characteristics and Offender Behaviour in Intimate Partner Homicide in Queensland, Australia. Elizabeth's current interests include criminal profiling, forensic criminology and juvenile homicide.

Elizabeth is currently working with young offenders and chaotic, homeless youths in a residential setting supporting them to get into education, training and employment and live successfully in the community.

David Field, LLB

David Field is an Associate Professor of Law at Bond University in Gold Coast, Australia. Former Solicitor for Prosecutions for Queensland, stipendiary magistrate for Glasgow, also former prosecutor and defense trial attorney in both Scotland and Australia (Qld and NSW). Author of *Evidence Law in Queensland*, as well as numerous textbook chapters relating to law end evidence.

Kind to children, considerate towards animals, and environmentally friendly. Available for funerals and bah mitzvas. Happily married, although my wife may not be.

Robert Homant, PhD

Robert has a PhD in Clinical Psychology. After 4 years as a staff psychologist at Michigan State Prison where he was director of the Sex Offender Program, he moved to Wisconsin State Prison as Chief Psychologist. He is currently full professor and chair of the Department of Sociology and Criminal Justice at the University of Detroit Mercy, where he teaches courses in deviant behavior, psychology and law, and corrections. His research interests include workplace violence and suicide by cop, and he has written a number of articles on criminal profiling and factors affecting criminally deviant behavior.

Yolande Huntingdon, BSocSci (Criminology)

Yolande Huntingdon completed Bachelor of Social Science degree (double major Criminology, major Psychology) degree at Bond University, achieving top of class in Australian Criminal Justice System, Forensic Victimology, Applied Behavioural Evidence Analysis and Crime and Deviance in Australia and is currently embarking on her Master of Arts (by Research), with the intention of commencing her PhD endeavours within the next 12 months.

Yolande is on the Board of Directors as criminological consultant for At The Ark, a not-for-profit registered charity dealing with childhood sexual assault victim and family support and has initiated and overseen the commencement of a friendship and focus group for adult survivors of child sexual abuse, now being administered and coordinated by a qualified counsellor.

Furthermore, Yolande has completed a report addressing Australian urban transport crime prevention; this report now having been distributed to unions, transit and government authorities and key stakeholders nationwide. The Minister for Transport has requested that Yolande present these findings at a public forum into the issue of Queensland urban transit safety.

Yolande is a regular speaker, having addressed many groups and organisations on issues such as crime and deviance, crime in the community, the overrepresentation of victims of child abuse in the criminal justice system, crime prevention strategies and online sexual predation of children via social networking sites.

Alicia Jenkins BPsychSci (Hons), PhD Candidate

Alicia Jenkins has Certificate 4 in Justice Administration from the Tafe of South Australia, she also holds her Bachelor of Psychological Science and a Bachelor of Health Science Honours from The University of Adelaide, South Australia. Her Honours thesis evaluated the effectiveness of an Australian Government program 'We are Family', aimed at reducing companion animal attacks on babies and children. Her research made suggestions to the state Government of Victoria and South Australia for program and delivery improvements.

She is currently a PhD candidate in the Faculty of Humanities and Social Science at Bond University, Gold Coast, with her studies focusing on self-esteem and criminal behaviour. Ms Jenkins has worked as a research assistant for the Commonwealth Scientific & Industrial Research Organisation (CSIRO), The University of Adelaide and the Royal Adelaide Hospital and is also a tutor in the Criminology Department at Bond University.

Ms Jenkins areas of interest include forensics, serial criminals, personality traits related to different types of criminals, the role of upbringing on individuals, self esteem and personality disorders.

She can be contacted at alicia.jenkins@student.bond.edu.au

Daniel B. Kennedy, PhD

Daniel B. Kennedy began his career in criminal justice and security administration as a civilian crime analyst with the Detroit Police Department in 1966. Over the next decade, Dr. Kennedy also served as a counselor for the Federal Bureau of Prisons, as a probation officer in Detroit, and as a senior administrator of two police academies in southeastern Michigan. While serving in these capacities, he studied sociology and criminology at Wayne State University, earning B.A. (1967), M.A. (1969), and Ph.D. (1971) degrees along the way.

Since completing his formal education, Dr. Kennedy has had extensive specialized training in various aspects of criminal behavior, policing operations, corrections operations, and private sector security management. He successfully tested for the Certified Protection Professional designation in 1983 and has been recertified every three years since. For the past several years, he has also studied terrorism, antiterrorism, and counterterrorism through participation in focused training at the Naval Postgraduate School and other locations across the U.S., Israel, and Dubai. After spending a year teaching at the College of the Virgin Islands in St. Thomas, USVI, Dan returned to his hometown and accepted a faculty position at the University of Detroit in 1977. In June of 2008, he was honored with the title Professor Emeritus by the President and Deans of the University of Detroit Mercy.

For the past twenty-five years, Dr. Kennedy has developed expertise in forensic criminology: the application of criminological knowledge to matters of immediate concern to various courts of law. Dan practices this specialty in three ways: academic publication, participation in litigation as an expert, and teaching. He is widely published in such journals as *Journal of Police Science and Administration, Journal of Criminal Justice, Justice Quarterly, Crime and Delinquency, Professional Psychology, Journal of Social Psychology, Criminal Justice and Behavior, FBI Law Enforcement Bulletin, Police Quarterly, The Police Chief, Security Journal, Security Management, Journal of Security Administration, Journal of Homeland Security and Emergency Management, American Jails*, and a host of others.

In addition, Dr. Kennedy frequently is called to court to testify in cases involving state police agencies, municipal police departments, and county sheriffs' departments. His testimony generally involves explaining to jurors the appropriate standards of care for the use of deadly force, vehicle pursuits, emergency psychiatric evaluations, prisoner health care, prevention of prisoner suicide, positional asphyxia/excited delirium, and "suicide by cop." Also, Dr. Kennedy evaluates numerous lawsuits concerning premises liability for negligent security in the private sector involving properties both in the U.S. and overseas. He specializes in crime foreseeability issues, appropriate standards of care in the security industry, and analyses of the behavioral aspects of proximate causation.

Although Dr. Kennedy taught forensic criminology for several years, he is currently teaching as an adjunct at Oakland University in Rochester, Michigan. He offers courses in profile and threat assessment and in homeland security through the university's criminal justice program. Also active as a trainer, he frequently provides specialized seminars on related topics for a variety of justice agencies and attorneys' associations.

Andrew Lowe, BSocSci (Criminology)

Andrew is a police officer with the Queensland Police Service. He holds a Bachelor of Social Science (Criminology) qualification, and has published in the area of stalking. His interests include stalking, criminal profiling and forensic science. Andrew currently works in child protection as a detective and is pursuing advanced education in criminology and public safety.

Michael McGrath, MD

Michael McGrath, MD is a board certified forensic psychiatrist, licensed in the state of New York. He is a clinical associate professor in the Department of Psychiatry, University of Rochester School of Medicine and Dentistry, Rochester, NY, and medical director and chair of the Department of Behavioral Health, Unity Health System, Rochester, NY.

Dr. McGrath divides his time between clinical, teaching, research and administrative activities. He has published peer reviewed articles and chapters in texts on subjects such as false reports, sexual asphyxia, Internet harassment and child pornography, criminal profiling, eyewitness testimony, codependence, etc. He has lectured on three continents and is a founding member of the International Association of Forensic Criminologists (formerly the Academy of Behavioral Profiling). He can be contacted at: mmcgrath@profiing.org.

Gareth Norris, PhD

Dr Gareth Norris is a lecturer in the Department of Law and Criminology at Aberystwyth University, Wales, UK. He is a graduate of the MSc Investigative Psychology degree from the University of Liverpool and continues to research in forensic and investigative psychology. More recently he has focused on legal issues relating to the interpretation of evidence and the psychology of jury decision making. Recent publications include an assessment of the acceptance of profiling evidence in court and the use of technology in legal contexts. He was part of a special panel on 'The Psychology of the Courtroom' at the American Bar Association's annual conference and continues to lecture to student and professional audiences in legal psychology

Grant Sinnamon, BPsych (Hons), PhD (Candidate)

Grant Sinnamon has an academic background in adult education, psychology, counselling, and medicine. Grant's interest in criminology stems from an interest in the impact of early-life adversity on neurobiological developmental trajectories and personality formation and the consequences for adult neuropsychological, behavioural and physiological function. Professionally, Grant divides his time between research, teaching, private practice and delivering consulting and professional development services to a diverse range of clinicians and service providers in the areas of mental health, education, child development, child safety, and family & community services. Grant's professional passion has a dual focus. The first is his work in childhood onset autoimmune disease. In this area Grant's work is in the area of understanding the psychoneuroimmunology of autoimmune type 1 diabetes. Grant's second passion is in the field of developmental neurobiology and both understanding and treating the neurological deficits that can occur as a result of early-life adversity such as abuse, neglect and trauma as well developmental disorders such as autistic spectrum disorder, processing disorders, attention deficit disorders, and other conditions that impact learning, behaviour, emotion, and physical and psychological development. Grant is married to Natalie and together they have four children.

Barry Woodhouse MPsych (Forensic)

Barry is a registered Psychologist and holds a Masters Degree in Forensic Psychology from Bond University on the Gold Coast, Australia. He has worked in a variety criminal justice settings, including with victims and perpetrators of sexual abuse, drug and alcohol rehabilitation, other areas of forensic psychology, and in sentencing policy. Barry currently works for the Australian Government as part of a team administering a large program of research aimed at improving retention amongst Defence Force personnel. His current research interests include transnational organised crime, international security policy, and the psychological aspects of intelligence collection.

PART 1

Profiling

PART I

Profiling

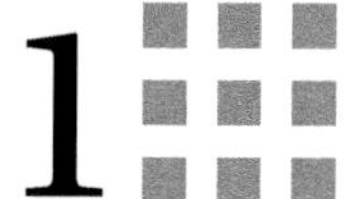

The Evolution of Criminal Profiling: From Whitechapel to Quantico and Beyond

Gareth Norris

Introduction

Criminal profiling, also known as offender profiling, psychological profiling, offender analysis, behavioral profiling, or just profiling, is an investigative practice that was initially developed to provide behavioral advice to police investigations and has become synonymous with the crimes of the serial killer. Likewise there exist numerous definitions of what actually constitutes a profile, and what the overriding aims of this advice are deemed to be. Geberth (1996, p. 492) suggests that it is "[...] an educated attempt to provide investigative agencies with specific information as to the type of individual who would have committed a certain crime." Whereas numerous variations exist in form and content, the general aim of a profile is to provide the police with a composite "sketch" of the likely offender(s). This usually includes common demographic variables, such as age, ethnicity, and marital status, and the more specific considerations of past criminal history, possible motivation, and likely area of residence (Ault & Reese, 1980). The level of detail, and indeed the overall style of a profile, will depend not just on the actual technique being utilized but also very much on the individual who is creating it. With a range of often conflicting schools of thought providing the theoretical paradigm on which profiling is based, there are often contradictory accounts of the various elements, from evidence examination to the nature of investigative advice. Depending on who is consulted to provide such a profile, therefore, could have a profound influence on the investigation of a crime—should it rely on the profile for guidance.

In the screen version of Thomas Harris's fictional tale, *The Silence of the Lambs*, there is an interesting exchange between the FBI agent, Clarice Starling, and the incarcerated psychiatrist-cum-serial-killer, Hannibal Lecter. During one of these encounters, Lecter advises Starling on how to decipher the behavior of "Buffalo Bill"—he suggests:

> *First principles, Clarice. Simplicity. Read Marcus Aurelius. Of each particular thing ask: What is it in itself? What is its nature? What does he do, this man you seek?*

However interesting these musings are, there is somewhat a giant leap to extrapolate motivations through to investigative priorities. The majority of profiling knowledge is gleaned from the myriad of TV shows and movies that have its core principles intertwined within the plot. Additionally, the central characters are often the profilers themselves, and the cat-and-mouse game of power between investigators and the offender provides a ready-made script with which to satisfy our curiosity with the criminal mind. Numerous accounts of the accurate representation of profiling and its depiction in mainstream media precede this writing (Alison & Canter, 1999; Petherick, 2003); however, many of these fictional accounts bear little resemblance to actual practice in live investigations. Similarly, the knowledge and procedures imparted to the viewer are often lacking in scientific rigor and provide a rather skewed account of the abilities eschewed to these fictional professionals. It is hoped this chapter will provide some background to the field and a chronological account showing the reader how the context and development of these endeavors has led us up to the present day.

Early Beginnings

One of the earliest examples of profiling comes from the infamous case of Jack the Ripper, who terrorized the streets of Whitechapel, London, in the late 1800s. Police pathologist Dr. Thomas Bond was to infer that the offender may have been suffering from a condition known as *satyriasis*—excessive and uncontrollable sexual desire in males (Rumbelow, 1988, p. 140). Contrary to popular belief, Bond also cast doubt on previous speculation that the offender was a surgeon or butcher, allegedly due to the deft use of his weapon of choice. Whereas some had speculated over the proficiency of dismemberment, the physical evidence suggested to Bond that the offender did not have particularly specialized anatomical knowledge. Unfortunately, and in a similar vein to many modern attempts at profiling, the offender in this case has never been identified, and people still speculate as to the likely perpetrator to this day. A similar case involving early manifestations of profiling—the Dusseldorf Vampire, Peter Kurten—also included a number of psychological considerations by pathologist Dr. Karl Berg in 1929. In this case, Berg believed the offender to be a narcissistic psychopath due to the degrading treatment of his victims (Berg, 1945). Both of these examples demonstrate how the two pathologists speculated as to the *type* of individual who was likely to have committed these crimes. As medical personnel, their remit was to determine the cause of death and, somewhat unintentionally, the opinion served to indicate who the authorities should be looking for, even though these affirmations may have been uninformed.

Although doctors and other professionals (including coroners and police officers) made what we identify as the first criminal profiles,[1] as a branch of medicine, *psychiatrists* have also engaged in various forms of assessment of unknown suspects. Whereas pathologists and other medical specialists are occasionally involved in criminal investigations, psychiatrists are more often frequently found in forensic settings, primarily in the assessment of mental illness and fitness to plead/stand trial. Similarly, military psychiatrists/psychologists are more often employed in the assessment of personnel; however, one other aspect of their work may involve the creation of propaganda materials, such as creating information for leaflet drops behind enemy lines. Judging the opinions of those involved in a conflict has often been used to guide strategy, and there are numerous accounts of German psychologists who were involved (involuntarily or otherwise) in the Nazi war effort (Billig, 1978). Recent claims were made against the use of psychologists in the designing of torture techniques following the September 11, 2001 attacks and the apprehension of terrorism suspects (see APA, 2007/8).[2]

The use of behavioral theories by the military is well documented in relation to strategy and related concepts, such as morale. However, in 1943 a psychiatrist named Walter Langer[3] was asked to provide a more specific psychological profile by the US Office of Strategic Services.[4] With psychodynamic theory being at the forefront of behavioral analysis at the time, the resulting assessment indicated the individual to be a *neurotic psychopath* in dire need of expressing his manliness to his mother. He predicted that at the ultimate climax to conflict, the individual would most likely commit suicide. The focus of this profile was Adolf Hitler, and although a thorough comparative clinical examination could not be performed, Langer was at the very least correct about Hitler committing suicide, who did so in his Berlin bunker two years later. Interestingly, commentators place much emphasis on the suicidal realization of Hitler when, in fact, the prediction was the most probable in a list of eight such scenarios:

1. *Hitler may die of natural causes*—deemed to be a remote possibility because he was in good health aside from a stomach ailment, probably linked to a psychosomatic disturbance.
2. *Hitler might seek refuge in a neutral country*—unlikely because it would cast doubt on his myth of immortality by fleeing at the critical moment.
3. *Hitler might be killed in battle*—a possibility because he may desire to expose himself as a fearless leader and may have the adverse effect of binding the German people to his legend.
4. *Hitler might be assassinated*—another plausible outcome, which he himself had speculated over.

[1] Interestingly, Arthur Conan Doyle's fictional detective Sherlock Holmes was based on one of Doyle's instructors, a doctor, at the Edinburgh Royal Infirmary.

[2] http://www.apa.org/about/policy/torture.aspx

[3] The actual document was authored with the collaboration of Henry Murray, Ernst Kris, and Bertram Lawin.

[4] The Office of Strategic Services was a part of the US Army in charge of gathering intelligence during the war effort. It disbanded in 1945, and many of its functions were taken over by the Central Intelligence Agency.

5. *Hitler may go insane*—he was believed to exhibit many characteristics of a borderline schizophrenic, and if faced with defeat, it was likely his psychological structure would collapse.
6. *German military might revolt and seize him*—an unlikely event due to the unique position he enjoyed in the eyes of the German people, but he may be confined in secret should he become unstable.
7. *Hitler may fall into our hands*—the most unlikely eventuality because this would be the scenario he personally would do his utmost to avoid.
8. *Hitler might commit suicide*—the most conceivable conclusion due to his inordinate fear of death, which he had already envisaged, stating, "Yes, in the hour of supreme peril I must sacrifice myself for the people."

What is important to understand at this period in time is that although clinical assessment was becoming an important and emerging field, seldom was any evaluation conducted with the person not *in situ*. What Langer was attempting to provide was a psychological picture of someone whom he had not physically examined and also to provide some indication of his likely future actions. Indeed, Langer was to comment that such as study "was a far cry from the firsthand data with which a psychoanalyst usually works" (Langer, 1972, p. 26). Langer's eventual profile was exhaustive and included a number of sections on how the German people viewed Hitler, the way in which his associates regarded him, and the way Hitler believed himself to be. The overall aim was to both tentatively guide future dealings with him and, specifically, to aid in the propaganda effort against him.

Although Langer documents each circumstance and its likelihood of occurrence, a more detailed review of the text indicates the tenuous nature of the profile in general. There is some level of psychiatric assessment—for example, that he could be a borderline schizophrenic or a hysteric—but significant interpretation on his actual behavior relies on Hitler's own assertions, gleaned primarily from his writings and speeches. Nevertheless, Langer's work led the way for others to analyze "unknown" individuals based on the observation of their behavior. Similar evaluations of major political leaders have also been constructed; Freud's seldom-cited psychological profile of former US President Thomas Woodrow Wilson (Freud & Bullitt, 1966) is another similar example.

James Brussel and Forensic Psychiatry

Following the work of Langer, the New York-based psychiatrist James Brussel provided a profile of the "Mad Bomber," who had been terrorizing the city for a number of years (Brussel, 1968). The apprehension of George Metesky in 1956, being almost the mirror image of Brussel's prediction, right down to the legendary double-breasted suit Brussel predicted he would be wearing,[5] was to guide profiling into a new era. Whereas Langer had information on his subject and was aware of him as a person in the physical sense, Brussel had been able to provide

[5]Contrary to popular belief, Metesky was apprehended at his home and answered the door to the police wearing his pajamas. He requested he be allowed to change, and he emerged wearing a buttoned double-breasted suit.

his assessment on the basis of other information and with no prior knowledge of the actual offender. From his examination of the crime scene actions and other materials (e.g., the letters sent to the police), Brussel suggested that the offender was suffering from paranoia and most probably held a grudge against the Edison Electrical Company (the organization was defamed in numerous letters discovered at the bomb sites and also the target of the first bomb). In particular, the letters written by Metesky to the police contained numerous phrases that were uncommon among the colloquial language of resident Americans and led to the (correct) assumption that the bomber was therefore more likely an overseas immigrant. Geographically, Brussel also examined the locations where the letters were posted and determined that the bomber most likely commuted to Manhattan by train and therefore could quite probably live somewhere in Connecticut. According to Brussel, when apprehended and taken in for questioning, Metesky appeared almost relieved that his vendetta could now come to an end (Brussel, 1968). Confined to a secure facility, Brussel would sporadically come into contact with Metesky, who he described as a gentleman and model patient.

Criminal profiling was now becoming largely the property of a number of leading psychiatrists, who through relative genius, educated guesswork, or just plain luck were assisting the police in some high-profile cases. This method of profiling has since been termed *diagnostic evaluation* (Wilson, Lincoln & Kocsis, 1997), and it is essentially the psychologist's or psychiatrist's evaluation of the offender based on, for example, developmental and/or clinical issues (Badcock, 1997). Developmental (the personal needs and life experiences) and clinical (patterns of offending associated with mental illness) analyses are the cornerstone of forensic practitioners, enabling their expertise and training to be utilized in identifying possible aspects of the offender's psyche. Aside from theorizing over these developmental, clinical, and other related issues, forensic consultants have also attempted to marry theories of personality with those of the likely individual involved in a crime (Boon, 1997; Copson, Badcock, Boon & Britton, 1997). Personality theories provide a framework for assessing what are commonly regarded as relatively consistent patterns of behavior present in an individual that cause him or her to behave in certain ways in certain situations. Therefore, theoretically at least, their application to criminal profiling would seem pertinent.

The forensic practitioner's main strengths perhaps lie in providing insight into the more bizarre cases. Indeed, some believe profiling should be undertaken only when there are signs of psychopathology (Pinizzotto, 1984), or else support the work of nonforensic profilers by providing them with insights into personality and abnormal psychology (McGrath, 2000). Liebert (1985, p. 294) is critical and suggests that "if investigative personnel believe that a serial murderer is basically a bad person who behaves offensively because he has chosen a particularly nefarious habit, the psychiatrist can be of little assistance." The general consensus appears to be that although most crimes can be profiled, it is the more atypical and disturbing ones that hold a place for the opinion of the forensic clinician. Their understanding of psychopathology gleaned from clinical assessment of their patients, coupled with their extensive training in abnormal psychology, is unparalleled in assessing the behavior of such criminals. Although other methods may have a more practical application within the investigative process, the consultation with forensic psychologists and psychiatrists still has a valuable role.

The Federal Bureau of Investigation and Crime Scene Analysis

When in 1964 Albert DeSalvo was apprehended and charged with being the "Green Man" rapist, it was largely Brussel's profile that provided the police with the confidence to also charge him with being the Boston Strangler, following his confession to his psychiatrist, because he was so similar to the profile (Brussel, 1968).[6] Additional cases such as the Son of Sam[7] also indicated that profiling had a lasting utility in the investigation of many serious criminal episodes. Brussel was involved in the advent of what is regarded by many as the first serious attempt to standardize and validate the profiling process and provide some theoretical and empirical base for its predictions. Collaboration between Brussel and two members of the newly emerging Federal Bureau of Investigation (FBI) Academy, Special Agents Howard Teten and Pat Mullany, led the organization to create a systematized basis for the understanding of criminal behavior in the early 1970s (Turvey, 2008). Teten and Mullany established the Behavioral Science Unit (BSU)—immortalized in the movie *The Silence of the Lambs*—at Quantico, Virginia. The unit still exists as the National Center for the Analysis of Violent Crime.

Although it would still be some years before the term *profiling* would be officially accepted into wider discourse, Teten and Mullany essentially instructed new recruits at the academy about profiling, under the banners of *applied criminology* and *abnormal psychology*. Although these two individuals were the forefathers of this program, credit for the program usually falls to a number of other members of the unit. The initial results of the first main study on profiling, with the aid of a grant from the National Institute of Justice, were published in May 1985 (Ressler & Burgess, 1985). The original document is a relatively technical script, complete with pages devoted to statistical analysis; however, included within is a separate section titled *Crime Scene and Profile Characteristics of Organized and Disorganized Murderers*. The edited report was later published as the text *Sexual Homicide: Patterns and Motives* (Ressler, Burgess & Douglas, 1988). Primarily, it is the significance of the organized/disorganized dichotomy that is of particular importance in understanding the history of this branch of profiling.

Now termed *Criminal Investigative Analysis*, the technique has transformed from humble beginnings as an exploratory study of incarcerated offenders to using this information as a base for inferring characteristics of past offenders. In 1979, the BSU began the Criminal Personality Research Project, which was a precursor to the larger Institute of Justice-funded study (Ressler et al., 1988, p. 104). Eventual data collection took four years (1979–1983) and involved, by its eventual completion, 36 individuals, including a number of professional staff from Boston City Hospital (Ressler & Burgess, 1985). Interviews were conducted with 36 incarcerated sexual killers,[8] and revealed a number of generalizable patterns of behavior. These were subsequently separated by what was perceived at the time to be a function of the level

[6] DeSalvo was never actually tried for the Boston murders, due to his violent death at the hands of another inmate while on remand. Some controversy still surrounds whether he was actually the culprit.

[7] Profiled by Dr. Murray Miron (from Geberth, 1996).

[8] Although legend has it that 36 of the United States' most prolific serial murderers were examined, there were in fact only 36 multiple killers, and not all the sample agreed to be interviewed; instead, their data were gleaned from official documents.

of organization that had been extended to the commission of the crime by the offender. The approach resulted in a checklist of behaviors, each categorized as being associated with an organized or a disorganized offender. These crime scene behaviors were then mapped onto the list of characteristics of that particular style of offender. It is documented that as early as 1978, BSU agents were profiling not only murders but also rape, arson, extortion, and a range of other violent and nonviolent offenses (Ressler et al., 1988, p. 104). Although in 1978 the actual organized/disorganized system had not been formally confirmed, its practical application had already been firmly established.

Their work also spawned many interesting concepts, including the *Crime Classification Manual* (CCM; Ressler, Douglas, Burgess & Burgess, 1992). Another FBI agent, Roy Hazelwood, later developed a categorization system for rapists, classifying them as being either selfish or unselfish according to their level of interaction with the victim (Hazelwood, 1987). Within this classification, Hazelwood further categorized them into a number of more detailed typologies[9] that were believed to reveal significant clues as to the type of offender concerned. The CCM set about providing detailed characteristics of offenders who committed various subtypes of behaviors (e.g., anger excitation) within the more general crime type (e.g., rape). Whereas the original study had focused on sexual murderers, there was now an attempt to give a more comprehensive understanding to many other types of criminal behavior. This has been likened by some to what the *Diagnostic and Statistical Manual* did for the assessment and treatment of clinical patients in psychology and psychiatry (McGrath, 2000). The CCM aimed to allow investigators to look up the behaviors of a particular crime and then map these onto the type of offender they were looking for. The FBI's study was one of the most innovative and pioneering approaches to the study of crime at the time, and credit should be awarded to the collaborators on the project. Agents from the FBI have consulted on major crimes throughout the world, and many past agents have attained almost celebrity status in the field of crime analysis, producing many semiautobiographical accounts of their cases. In addition to these memoirs, they are often available for comment on many high-profile incidents for which their expert opinion is still widely sought.

David Canter and Investigative Psychology

In November 1985, Professor David Canter, from the University of Surrey, England, was contacted by two senior detectives from New Scotland Yard to discuss the viability of adopting the new method of criminal detection being developed by the FBI in the United Kingdom.[10] According to Canter (1994), these meetings were fairly casual from their outset until concern rose over a spate of violent rapes and murders in Greater London. The media had coined the name "Railway Rapist" to describe John Duffy, who was later apprehended with the assistance of the profile created by Canter. In particular, the locations of Duffy's offenses,

[9]Labeled as power reassurance, power assertive, anger retaliatory, and anger excitation (developed from Groth, 1979).

[10]The FBI prior to this had been consulted by the Metropolitan Police on a number of rapes in the Surrey district of Guildford.

being near railway lines and stations, enabled a reasonably accurate prediction of his home location. Other features of the profile—that Duffy would be in a troubled marriage, would be interested in martial arts, and would collect pornography—proved similarly accurate, but with perhaps less direct practical investigative utility. While on trial for an assault on his wife, the police brought a previous victim to the court in an attempt to identify Duffy. Realizing the victim may have recognized him, Duffy's behavior escalated and he began to murder his future victims to hinder subsequent identifications. It was at this point, armed with forensic evidence and the information from Canter's profile, that Duffy was arrested. This early success led to further explorations into this emerging field, which was named Investigative Psychology (IP) and taught as a postgraduate course at the University of Surrey.[11]

The profile that Canter constructed of Duffy was, by his own admission, a very rudimentary document; as an environmental psychologist, Canter was at this time not fully acquainted with the workings of the criminal mind (Canter, 1994). Despite obvious apprehension, Canter, with the aid of two seconded police officers, began a systematic review of past cases in order to analyze them and provide a logical pattern. Although taken for granted in the age of the Internet, Canter used computer technology available at the time to search for patterns in the offender's behavior, revealing a subset of practically identical indicators. One important feature to emerge was that it appeared the individual in question was learning from his mistakes as the crime series progressed. The most striking aspect, however, was that although descriptions of offenders usually include height and hair color and are notoriously inaccurate (as in this case), a composite sketch of the *type* of person who was committing these rapes and murders was beginning to emerge. The main tenet of Canter's theory was that offenders do not live and operate in a vacuum but, rather, their criminal behavior mirrors their noncriminal behavior. This led to what Canter referred to as a "criminal shadow." Canter's theory of criminal narratives, as explained by his five-factor model of interpersonal coherence, time and place, criminal career, forensic awareness, and criminal characteristics, has a strong psychological basis and is regarded as being a relatively robust and viable way of classifying offenders (West, 2000). As the more academic of the three disciplines discussed so far, IP has a continually evolving theory base, and research continues on its applicability and utility in investigations.

Kim Rossmo and Geographic Profiling

Although Canter's explorations into spatial behavior form a major part of the overall profiling process within the five-factor model of offending behavior he proposed (Canter, 1994), others have further developed an almost separate branch of the profiling tradition. In particular, Kim Rossmo advocates his technique of *geographical profiling* as a distinct subdiscipline of profiling (Rossmo, 2000). The use of crime mapping in the more general sense has become a prominent tool in the police arsenal. Emanating from environmental criminology, and with particular reference to the work of Brantingham and Brantingham (1982), the majority of

[11]The Master's of Science in Investigative Psychology program ran from 1992 to 1994 at the University of Surrey before moving to its current base at the University of Liverpool. Courses in IP are now taught throughout the world.

spatial theories share the same theoretical underpinning, namely that the farther an offender is away from his or her home location, the less likely he or she is to offend. This is commonly referred to as *distance decay*, and relies on the assumption that not only do criminals prefer to operate in areas that they are familiar with, but also the areas where they offend share distinct overlap with the places they attend as noncriminals. Rossmo's Criminal Geographic Targeting computer simulation uses an algorithm based on the Brantinghams' notion of distance decay and buffer zones. Indeed, comparative analysis of a number of such systems revealed a surprising similarity in their levels of accuracy (Levine, 1999). Geographic profiling has developed out of a distinct psychological theory base, and it is incorrectly considered by some to be the most "scientific" of the methodologies in that it relies on a number of mainstream psychological and behavioral principles, such as routine activity theory (Rossmo, 2000).

Prior to these computer simulations, Kind (1987) reported his retrospective prediction of the home location of the Yorkshire Ripper, Peter Sutcliffe. Navigational techniques, particularly the notion of a center of gravity, enabled Kind to accurately calculate Sutcliffe's home location. The accuracy of geographical profiling, however, is in some instances less impressive. For this reason, it is seldom used in isolation, instead frequently forming a subsection of an overall profile. Cases such as the "Beltway Sniper" in Washington, DC (see Chapter 5), are useful illustrations of the limitations of this particular method; in many instances, the crime is so unusual that nobody could realistically predict the spatial behavior of the offender(s) (Canter, 2003). Rossmo and Canter have been at the forefront of geographical profiling research, and their consultation with law enforcement agencies has helped to bring this technique into the public eye. Other applications of geographical profiling are regularly used by crime analysts and others interested in geographical crime trends (Ainsworth, 2001). Although it is unlikely that such a profile would be sufficient to apprehend a suspect in its own right, some continue to argue that it is a particularly useful way of prioritizing suspects through geographic location rather than through more subjective personal characteristics.

Brent Turvey and Behavioral Evidence Analysis

Concerned that these relatively reductionist methods of analyzing criminal behavior were largely based on biographical narratives of a small number of incarcerated offenders, forensic scientist Brent Turvey created another addition to the profiling portfolio. In the mid-1990s, following an interview of convicted murderer Jerome Brudos, Turvey rejected statistical evaluations on the basis that the accounts on which they were largely based could not be accurately relied on (Turvey, 2008). Reviewing the interview material from Brudos, Turvey discovered some major discrepancies in comparison with the police case files. This led him to the conclusion that it was inappropriate to accept the premises on which the profiles were usually based because the data analyzed were equivocal at best and, more often than not, factually incorrect. The method that arose from these concerns was termed *Behavioral Evidence Analysis* (BEA). It is distanced somewhat from the other methods in that it is viewed as deductive rather than inductive, the distinction being the specificity of the former and the generalizability of the latter (and the subsequent "certainty" with which the premises of any prediction can be made). Whereas diagnostic evaluations, CSI, and IP aim to provide guidance and focus to police investigations, BEA purports to be more of a holistic philosophy of criminal investigation (Turvey, 2008).

Regardless of its philosophy or content, BEA embraces a comprehensive and methodological approach to profiling, alongside the forensic science backdrop on which it is based. Particular emphasis is placed on such facets of the criminal event as victimology and motivation, which run parallel to such features of the BEA profile as wound pattern analysis and crime scene reconstruction. The cornerstone of this approach is not only the desire to give the police some guidance in their investigation or to narrow suspect pools, but also to provide a comprehensive reconstruction of each criminal event. In contrast, CSA or IP, for example, provide a more general picture of the likely offender based on the analysis of past cases and assume to a large degree that the police and forensic experts have made available all the information relating to the investigation. Although this reconstruction process should not be overlooked, BEA is still a relatively new concept; however, a fourth edition of the popular *Criminal Profiling* text and other publications continue to add to its theoretical foundation (Chisum & Turvey, 2007; Petherick, Turvey & Ferguson, 2009; Turvey, 2011). Courses in BEA are also taught to students and professionals in a range of jurisdictions, including the United States, China, Singapore, and Australia.

Conclusion

For a historical review to be of any practical utility, the conclusion to it must provide a snapshot of not only the current position but also likely future directions. The four main methodologies documented currently operate in relative isolation from each other; indeed, much acrimony exists between the many proponents from each camp as to who has constructed the most valid and reliable technique. As has been illustrated, each theory has developed in part by drawing upon each other in at least one respect, if only to capitalize on the inherent weaknesses present in each. The early explorations into the criminal mind by forensic practitioners such as Brussel paved the way for the agents from the FBI to develop these principles into a more structured and systematized approach to classifying criminals and identifying their likely attributes. The studies conducted by David Canter have further refined these early explorations into a rigorous and comprehensive methodology that has been applied to many different crime types and situations. Canter has been a strong proponent of the importance of time and space, and these ideas resonate in the work on geographical profiling by Kim Rossmo. Although the work of Brent Turvey somewhat distances itself from these methods, it was born of the concern that the generalizations on which they are based may be the result of inaccurate data, and it provides a healthy warning on the nature of being too complacent in the profiling process.

The term profiling has been extended into other areas of the legal system, has become increasingly linked with the notions of "jury" and "racial" profiling, and is now almost synonymous with terrorism. The methodologies involved can also take on the form of data-driven, statistical generalizations or the hunches of the individuals believing themselves to be gifted in such perceptions (Wrightsman, Greene, Nietzel & Fortune, 2002). For the profiling of suspects in criminal cases, attempts to evaluate such approaches for their validity or accuracy have been largely inconclusive (Copson, 1995). One reason for this has been a general reluctance by most practitioners to reveal their methods, let alone their results. Comparisons between the different methods in experimental situations have been rare, if not nonexistent, but evaluations between trained profilers, detectives, psychologists, and other groups have met with unconvincing results (Kocsis, Irwin, Hayes & Nunn, 2000; Norris, Rafferty & Campbell, 2010; Pinizzotto & Finkel, 1990). Some high-profile cases have highlighted other issues with profiling that have cast their own limitations on such practices. In particular, ethical and legal concerns have been prominent in shaping the direction of professional profiling practice (see Norris & Petherick, 2010). As noted by Alison, McLean, and Almond (2007), there has been a general reluctance by both the British Psychological Society and the American Psychological Association to devote attention to profiling as a specific subdiscipline of forensic psychology, with the exception of the usual cursory note regarding members engaging in activities outside of their training or expertise. However, in the United States, the FBI has its own training program, and in the United Kingdom, the National Police Improvement Agency (NPIA) holds lists of accredited profilers and is home to the Serious Crime Analysis Section (SCAS). Other organizations, such as the Academy of Behavioral Profiling, also seek to add some level of professionalism and accountability to the work of its members.

However, one of the biggest shifts in recent years has been the relative departure of the term profiler in both popular and professional discourse. The former has been in relation to the explosion in popular media of forensic science and, in particular, television dramas such as *CSI*. Whereas the psychological inputs to the investigation still fascinate audiences, the visual impact of evidence analysis makes for equally if not more compelling viewing. The latter has been a direct result of the recognition of the limitations of profiling as an investigative technique and undoubtedly some of the errors that have resulted from these broad-based approaches to the investigation of serious crime. Although the term profiling may have suffered a crisis of confidence in professional circles and fallen out of vogue with the general public also, there is still a place for these techniques in modern policing. What has become known as the *Behavioural Investigative Advisor* (BIA) has emerged from the shadows and essentially represents a specific form of the more traditional crime analyst, who is charged with providing support and advice to investigative teams during major and serious inquiries. In contrast to the traditional vision of the profiler, these professionals—of whom only five are employed full time in the United Kingdom based at the NPIA headquarters—provide a range of services, including offense linkage, risk assessment, interview/media advice, and familial DNA prioritization (Rainbow, 2007). An additional area of development is in relation to supporting the actual decisions made by SIOs during major cases. Rainbow, Almond, and Alison (2011) highlight that the cognitive biases can serve to severely limit the use of all available evidence—including profiling advice—to provide the optimal investigative strategy.

It seems that profiling has evolved progressively through the decades and the current state-of-play is a mixture of individual theories alongside a more dedicated and applied service provided to the police. Because of the complex nature of these investigations, it is difficult to ascertain with any degree of conviction what the most appropriate situation would be.

Certainly, the nature and style of advice given to police has developed since the early days, although it appears that the nature of these propositions has done little to actually prove its overall utility. Academic research in this area has a major input, but the police now appear to be developing their own in-house activities in the form of dedicated BIAs and analysts, alongside specific training for detectives. Whereas these endeavors were traditionally separate domains, they have now evolved into the recognition that they provide complementary support in the apprehension of some of the most complicated investigations in modern police work.

Questions

1. One of the earliest examples of criminal profiling was:
   a. Peter Kurten (The Dusseldorf Vampire)
   b. Jack the Ripper
   c. Adolf Hitler
   d. Woodrow Wilson
   e. None of the above
2. The criminal profiling program in the FBI was primarily started by:
   a. John Douglas and Robert Ressler
   b. Robert Ressler and Roy Hazelwood
   c. Howard Teten and Pat Mullany
   d. Jack Kirsch and Brent Turvey
   e. Maurice Godwin and David Canter
3. The terms offender profiling, behavioral profiling, offender analysis, and psychological profiling have all been used interchangeably over time. *True or false?*
4. The Washington, DC, sniper case is a useful illustration of the utility of geographic profiling. *True or false?*
5. Provide a brief overview of each of the major profiling paradigms presented in this chapter.

References

Ainsworth, P. B. (2001). *Offender profiling and crime analysis.* Cullompton, UK: Willan.

Alison, L., & Canter, D. (1999). Profiling in policy and practice. In D. Canter & L. Alison (Eds.), *Profiling in policy and practice* (pp. 3–22). Aldershot, UK: Dartmouth.

Alison, L., McLean, C., & Almond, L. (2007). Profiling suspects. In T. Newburn, T. Williamson, & A. Wright (Eds.), *Handbook of criminal investigation.* Cullompton, UK: Willan.

Ault, R., & Reese, J. (1980). A psychological assessment of crime profiling. *FBI Law Enforcement Bulletin,* 49.

Badcock, R. (1997). Developmental and clinical issues in relation to offending in the individual. In J. L. Jackson & D. A. Bekerian (Eds.), *Offender profiling: Theory, research and practice* (pp. 9–42). Chichester, UK: Wiley.

Berg, K. (1945). *The sadist: An account of the crimes of a serial killer.* London: Heineman.

Billig, M. (1978). *Fascists: A social psychological view of the national front.* London: Academic Press.

Boon, J. C. W. (1997). The contribution of personality theories to psychological profiling. In J. L. Jackson & D. A. Bekerian (Eds.), *Offender profiling: Theory, research and practice* (pp. 43–60). Chichester, UK: Wiley.

Brantingham, P. L., & Brantingham, P. J. (1982). Mobility, notoriety and crime: A study of crime patterns in urban nodal points. *Journal of Environmental Systems, 11*, 89–99.

Brussel, J. (1968). *Casebook of a crime psychiatrist.* New York: Bernard Geis.

Canter, D. (1994). *Criminal shadows.* London: HarperCollins.

Canter, D. (2003). *Mapping murder: The secrets of geographical profiling.* London: Virgin Books.

Chisum, W. J., & Turvey, B. E. (2007). *Crime reconstruction.* London: Academic Press.

Copson, G. (1995). *Coals to Newcastle? Part 1: A study of offender profiling (Police Research Group Special Interest Series No. 7).* London: Home Office.

Copson, G., Badcock, R., Boon, J., & Britton, P. (1997). Articulating a systematic approach to clinical crime profiling. *Criminal Behaviour & Mental Health, 7*, 13–17.

Freud, S., & Bullit, W. C. (1966). *Thomas Woodrow Wilson: A psychological profile study.* Boston: Houghton.

Geberth, V. J. (1996). *Practical homicide investigation* (3rd ed.). New York: CRC Press.

Groth, A. N. (1979). *Men who rape: The psychology of the offender.* New York: Plenum.

Hazelwood, R. R. (1987). Analyzing the rape and profiling the offender. In R. R. Hazelwood & A. W. Burgess (Eds.), *Practical aspects of rape investigation: A multidisciplinary approach.* New York: Elsevier.

Kind, S. (1987). Navigational ideas and the Yorkshire Ripper investigation. *Journal of Navigation, 40*, 385–393.

Kocsis, R. N., Irwin, H. J., Hayes, A. F., & Nunn, R. (2000). Expertise in psychological profiling: A comparative assessment. *Journal of Interpersonal Violence, 15*(3), 311–331.

Langer, W. (1972). *The mind of Adolf Hitler.* New York: Basic Books.

Levine, N. (1999). *Crimestat: A spatial statistics program for the analysis of crime incident locations.* Washington, DC: National Institute of Justice.

Liebert, J. (1985). Contributions of psychiatric consultation in the investigation of serial murder. *International Journal of Offender Therapy and Comparative Criminology, 29*(3), 187–199.

McGrath, M. G. (2000). Criminal profiling: Is there a role for the forensic psychiatrist? *Journal of the American Academy of Psychiatry and Law, 28*(3), 315–324.

Norris, G., & Petherick, W. (2010). Criminal profiling in the courtroom: Behavioural investigative advice or bad character evidence? *Cambrian Law Review, 41*, 40–55.

Norris, G., Rafferty, E., & Campbell, J. (2010). An analysis of content preference in offender profiles. *International Journal of Offender Therapy and Comparative Criminology, 54*, 412–429.

Petherick, W. (2003). Criminal profiling: What's in a name? Comparing applied profiling methodologies. *Journal of Law and Social Challenges, 5*(1), 173–188.

Petherick, W., Turvey, B., & Ferguson, C. (2009). *Forensic criminology.* Boston: Academic Press.

Pinizzotto, A. J. (1984). Forensic psychology: Criminal personality profiling. *Journal of Police Science and Administration, 12*(1), 32–39.

Pinizzotto, A. J., & Finkel, N. J. (1990). Criminal personality profiling: An outcome and process study. *Law and Human Behavior, 14*, 215–233.

Rainbow, L. (2007). The role of behavioral science in criminal investigations. *Forensic Update, 88*, 44–48.

Rainbow, L., Almond, L., & Alison, L. (2011). BIA support to investigative decision making. In L. Alison & L. Rainbow (Eds.), *Professionalising offender profiling: Forensic and investigative psychology in practice.* Oxford: Routledge.

Ressler, R. K., & Burgess, A. W. (1985). *Sexual homicide crime scenes and patterns of criminal behavior [Final Report].* Boston: National Institute of Justice.

Ressler, R. K., Burgess, A. W., & Douglas, J. E. (1988). *Sexual homicide: Patterns and motives.* New York: Lexington Books.

Ressler, R. K., Douglas, J. E., Burgess, A. W., & Burgess, A. G. (1992). *The crime classification manual.* New York: Simon & Schuster.

Rossmo, K. (2000). *Geographic profiling.* Boca Raton, FL: CRC Press.

Rumbelow, D. (1988). *The complete Jack the Ripper.* London: Penguin Books.

Turvey, B. (2011). *Criminal profiling: An introduction to behavioral evidence analysis* (4th ed.). Burlington, MA: Academic Press.

West, A. (2000). Clinical assessment of homicide offenders: The significance of crime scene in offence and offender analysis. *Homicide Studies, 4*(3), 219–233.

Wilson, P., Lincoln, R., & Kocsis, R. (1997). Validity, utility and ethics of profiling for serial violent and sexual offenders. *Psychiatry, Psychology and Law, 4*, 1–12.

Wrightsman, L. S., Greene, E., Nietzel, M. T., & Fortune, W. H. (2002). *Psychology and the legal system* (5th ed.). Belmont, CA: Wadsworth.

Induction and Deduction in Criminal Profiling

Wayne Petherick

Introduction

Literature on criminal profiling has reached a considerable volume, including not only a quantity of true crime works but also numerous scholarly texts and articles. The casual reader will be familiar with some aspects of profiling, with the more discerning reader being familiar with the steps involved in the profiling process (Holmes & Holmes, 2002; Ressler, Burgess & Douglas, 1988; Turvey, 2011), the so-called "inputs" and "outputs" of a criminal profile (Davis, 1999; Egger, 1999; Geberth, 1996; Ressler & Burgess, 1985; Ressler, Burgess & Douglas, 1988), and the personality and grandiosity of profilers (see a variety of memoirs, such as Canter, 1994; Ressler & Shachtman, 1992; Douglas & Olshaker, 1996, 1997, 1998).

However, beyond a few works (Petherick, 2006; Turvey, 2011) there has been less written in any valid way about the logical processes employed by the profiler when drawing conclusions about the offender.[1] This chapter provides an in-depth examination of the two main approaches used by profilers to arrive at their conclusions: induction and deduction. First, a general commentary on the logic of criminal profiling is provided, followed by a detailed discussion of induction and deduction, illustrating the fundamental differences between the two

[1]There has actually been quite a lot written on logic in profiling, but much of it relies on subjective or personal accounts with little recourse to foundational theoretical works on the subject. This results in a skewed, often biased, and largely invalid account of logic and reasoning.

forms of reasoning. Finally, a hypothetical case scenario highlights the procedural aspects of how hypotheses are generated and a deductive conclusion is drawn.

Logic and Criminal Profiling

This section begins by providing an introduction to logic and continues with the application of logic in criminal profiling. This is based largely on Petherick (2007, 2008).

Logic may be defined as the process of argumentation or as a "unified discipline which investigates the structure and validity of ordered knowledge" (Farber, 1942, p. 41). Bhattacharyya (1958) suggests that logic is the science of valid thought, and Stock (2004) claims that logic is both science and art. More than simply providing a theoretical foundation on which to structure arguments, the basic principles and precepts of logic allow for a more thorough and rigorous testing of any argument put forth in a profile. In short, we can establish the veracity of a conclusion by juxtaposing the theory of logic onto that conclusion to determine whether it complies with good reasoning.

As a good starting point, McInerney (2004) provides three basic principles of logic that all profilers should avail themselves of. In this author's experience of peer review and examination of written profiles, many errors of logic fall into at least one of the following categories:

The principle of identity: A thing is what it is. Existing reality is not a homogeneous mass, but it is composed of a variety of individuals. In profiling, this argument may be best used to argue for the independence of thought in regard to profiling particular crimes. That is, each case should be treated as an individual rather than a simple extension of other similar crimes. In other words, each crime represents its own universe of evidence, behavior, and victim–offender interactions.

The principle of the excluded middle: Between being and nonbeing, there is no middle state. Perhaps the best way to view this in the context of profiling is "either a crime (or an action/behavior) has occurred, or it hasn't." The key to establishing the validity of this premise is in carrying out a detailed and complete reconstruction to establish exactly what has occurred and what has not. Only through a proper forensic evaluation can the true nature and quality of the thing being examined be gauged.

The principle of sufficient reason: There is sufficient reason for everything. This may also be called the principle of causality. This principle states that everything in the known universe has an explanation for its existence. Implied here is that nothing is self-explanatory or the cause of itself, and perhaps most important, that all instances of a known thing must have an explanation that is realistic within an accepted body of knowledge. Farber (1942) suggests that knowledge in its primary sense means true knowledge, in that it conforms to established facts of reality. In short, any argument put forth must not be sensational or rely on phenomenological explanations for cause or existence.

It would not be an understatement to claim that there is confusion surrounding logic within profiling. This goes far beyond a lack of theoretical understanding and extends into a total lack of regard for the practical implications of sound logic and reasoning. Before further considering the differences between the two main types of logic, it is necessary to first understand the confusion and its subsequent impact.[2] This confusion is not peculiar to initiates in the profiling community but is also prevalent among practicing profilers.

Deduction, a specific type of reasoning, has taken on a casual meaning, with the majority treating it as synonymous with a conclusion, thereby believing that any conclusion is a deduction. For example, the following extract provides a profile and a brief commentary boldly claiming the conclusion is deductive, when in fact it is not (Klump, 1997, p. 123):

> *"You didn't have a burglary," I told the caller. "It was an employee, a man who has worked for you about 4 months. He's an assistant manager or a shift leader, probably between the age of 25 and 30, a loner and a quiet person. He's usually broke, but does not borrow money from other employees. He probably drives an older car that doesn't run very well; he may have trouble getting to work on time because of it. He's probably married and has young children. Do you have anyone like that?"*
>
> *"Yes we do," the owner answered, "The assistant manager. He closed on Friday night. How do you know all this?"*
>
> *"Well, actually, you told me."*
>
> *Deduction is a mental art investigators should cultivate. When they are evaluating a business crime, deducing the meaning of seemingly insignificant verbal or physical clues can trigger a chain of insights that lead directly to the perpetrator.*

Even Brussel, the famous psychiatrist who profiled the Mad Bomber, adopts a rather casual usage (Brussel, 1968, p. 44):

> *Next I risked a deduction about the Bomber's age. I said, "He's middle aged." The plainclothes detectives looked dubious again.*
>
> *Inspector Finney asked, "How do you figure that?"*
>
> *"Well," I said, "Paranoia develops slowly. It doesn't usually erupt in its full force before the person is 35. This man has been making and planting his devices for 16 years."*

If this were a valid deduction, the development of paranoia would have to follow such a predictable course that the age of onset occurred so often, and had been studied so extensively, that it had become law or principle (the age of onset may differ depending on the severity of the condition, whether medication is involved, and the biochemistry of the individual). Furthermore, it must have been unequivocally established that the offender produced no bombs prior to those showing up in New York (so that the spree could not predate the 16-year mark). Even then, the nature of the deduction would be dubious (it would actually be a nondemonstrative inference or false deduction because many of the premises could not be reliably

[2]This section is adapted from Petherick (2007, 2008).

established). Therefore, the argument is non sequitur, meaning the conclusion does not necessarily follow logically from the premise.

In *Hunting Serial Predators*, Godwin (1999, p. iii) provides his view on induction and deduction:

> *Profiles constructed by the FBI profilers, clinical psychologists, criminologists, and the police routinely draw inferences about, for example, serial murderers and their behaviors based solely on work experience, gut feelings, and the motivation of the offender. This form of deductive profiling is where the profiler assumes one or more facts as self-evident about a crime or offender and then, following work experience and hunches, arrives at other facts commonly called conclusions. Hence, the FBI profiles are deductive rather than inductive. However, some argue that the FBI profiling method is inductive. Broadly, the argument put forward for the FBI method being inductive is since the FBI relies on data collected from interviews with serial murderers, as a foundation for developing their profiles, then their reasoning must be inductive. The basis for this argument is flawed, because the data collected by the FBI has never been empirically analyzed, nor has it been properly organized in a systematic manner so that profilers could refer to it in the future.*

Godwin suggests that the Federal Bureau of Investigation's (FBI) method is deductive, and the basis for this seems to be because the FBI relies on experience and "gut feelings." He also notes that profilers using deduction make assumptions about facts as being self-evident, even though such assumptions are contradictory to both theoretical and applied logic. Godwin, like Canter (1995), goes on to explain how others consider the FBI to be deductive because it relies on data collected from interviews with offenders. He notes that this is incorrect because the data have never been empirically analyzed or organized in such a way that it could be referred to in the future. This is incorrect on two fronts. First, the data were statistically analyzed and presented by Burgess and Ressler (1985) in their NIJ-funded report. Second, inductive analyses need not be subjected to any high-level statistical procedures. A conclusion is inductive, at the most basic level, because it is probabilistic and uncertain, representing only one possibility of many. However, at the most basic level, a deduction is not a matter of statistical probability but, rather, a certain conclusion based on the established validity of the premises.

In 2002, Godwin published "Reliability, Validity, and Utility of Criminal Profiling Typologies." This article seeks to address the problems with a number of profiling methods, including those prescribed by the FBI (2002), Holmes and Holmes (2002), and Hickey (2002). Therein, he provides a number of critiques of what is referred to erroneously as "deduction." For example (Godwin, 2002, p. 13),

> *As previously discussed, the reliability, validity, and utility of deductive profiles generally offered to police investigations are weak and have met with continual criticisms. For example, Godwin (1978) argues that profilers are playing blind man's bluff, groping in all directions in the hope of touching a sleeve. Levin and Fox (1985) point out that offender profiling as we know it today is vague and general and basically useless in identifying a killer.*

As discussed in Chapter 3, there are very few criticisms of deductive (rational/concrete/case-oriented) profiling methods in the literature. Godwin, in fact, appears to be referring to profiling methods, such as those taught by the FBI, which are not actually deductive. This is a case of mistaken identity on Godwin's part because FBI methods are inductive (statistical/abstract/group-oriented). Subsequently, his claims of their weakness and other criticisms are misdirected.

It is also useful to note that Godwin's critique of profiles, which references material that dates back to 1978, predates the development of literature and theoretical foundation for the current application of deductive logic to profiling (Petherick & Turvey, 2011). As such, his use of Godwin (1978) is entirely misplaced and all but moot. Levin and Fox's (1985) claim is similarly dated in light of modern developments. It would seem that these researchers would do well to invest in updated reference material in that regard.

However, all of these critiques could be legitimately levied at inductive profiling approaches, even those in use today. To do this, however, authors would need to correctly identify the differences, advantages, and disadvantages of each. This has yet to occur in the literature.

Interestingly, Godwin (2002) goes on to cite a number of other problems, including bias, selective thinking, and a particular logical fallacy—post hoc ergo propter hoc (it is actually cited as post hoc ergo proper hoc, which is incorrect). Of bias and selective thinking, Godwin is actually referring to adductive reasoning. This is a well-known concept in the science of logic, wherein a conclusion is developed without a full appreciation of the facts, and the reasoner then seeks out only confirmatory evidence. An example is the case in which a female homicide victim is found and the police believe it is a domestic homicide. The husband cannot provide an alibi, which the police believe "proves" their theory. This despite the fact that the victim was in a relationship with another male and has been receiving threatening and abusive e-mails and telephone calls and has been the subject of physical stalking. This information is ignored because it does not conform to the prevailing theory. Such reasoning, again, is emblematic of inductive profiling methods.

Of additional concern in this article is Godwin's constant reference to psychics and visions. In the discussion on the post hoc fallacy, Godwin (2002, p. 14) suggests that:

> *This form of reasoning in profiling is the basis for many erroneous conclusions. For example, you have a "vision" that a body is going to be found in the water near a tree and later a body is found in the water near a tree.*

I do not disagree at all with the first assertion, that the post hoc fallacy is a problem in the profiling community, but to suggest that deductive reasoning is in any way associated with psychics or visions is an error of considerable note.

The safeguard against all this is a thorough application of the scientific method. It is the cornerstone of deductive profiling and by nature devoid of weak or biased inductive profiling conclusions. However, the problem does not end there, and things definitely do not get any better.

Godwin is not alone in claiming that deduction revolves around experience, and Canter (2000, p. 24) also uses this as the basis to determine whether something is inductive or deductive. For example, "deduction is a form of implicit reasoning in which whatever experience or logic the reasoner can draw upon will be used to derive inferences about the culprit from aspects of the crime." This will be faulty in part because of the failure to subject theories to falsification, a core component of any deductive argument.[3] As a form of personally experienced average such conclusions are actually inductive, with experience failing to meet the threshold of a deductive conclusion. Canter (2000, p. 24) also supplies the following:

> *An example that illustrates this well is a case in which the victim of an unidentified assailant noticed that the offender had short fingernails on his right hand and long fingernails on his left hand. Somebody with specialist knowledge suggested that this was a characteristic of people who are serious guitar players. It was therefore a reasonable deduction that the assailant was somebody who played the guitar.*

As with Godwin's argument about reasoning, Canter is simply providing one explanation out of any possible number of offender characteristics. This example is actually using Holmesian logic to draw conclusions about what is inductive and deductive, and this is perhaps not the best position from which to argue the point. Despite the prima facie validity of some of Holmes's arguments, many of his assertions were inductive hypotheses awaiting testing and are not deductions in their own right (the style of logic employed by Sherlock Holmes is referred to as hypothetico-deduction). Another discussion given on this case shows a further lack of understanding regarding proper logic (p. 24):

> *This example shows the fundamental weaknesses of the deductive approach. Without clear empirical evidence about the prevalence of this particular pattern of nail length it is difficult to know whether the claim that it is unique to guitar players is valid. It may not be true of many guitar players and it may be a pattern that exists in many other individuals. In fact, in the case in question, the offender who was eventually identified had no contact with guitars and had this peculiar pattern of nail length because of his job in repairing old tires.*

By Canter's own admission, there are other possibilities, one of which was discovered after the apprehension of the offender. For this to be a proper deduction, there would have to be a universal law or principle governing the situation in which someone's fingernails were shorter on one hand than on the other, as well as the subsequent reason for this. Furthermore, it would have to be established that this is true in every single case. Even carrying out research on this particular constellation of nail length, as suggested, would not make the conclusion deductive because other possibilities may explain the difference.

[3] There is nothing inherently wrong with using experience to inform opinions because it is intuition and experience that may tell a detective what question to ask or where to look for evidence. However, when conclusions are based only on experience, the process, regardless of good intent, will likely be flawed.

In an earlier piece, Canter (1995, p. 343) likens deduction to common sense reasoning as if the employment of common sense is a sufficient condition to meet the strict requirements of putting forward a deductive argument:

> *Although the inference processes on which the FBI agents drew were illuminated by interviews they themselves had conducted with a few dozen convicted offenders, and by their own experiences of investigating many crimes, their processes of inference derivation were broadly deductive, being based upon common sense as might be the basis of judicial decisions. In the tradition of the detective novel, and other less fictional accounts of the solving of crimes, the processes that the FBI agents used focused on the clues derived directly from the crime scene. They drew upon general principles, drawn from everyday experience, to deduce the implications that the internal logic of a crime might have.*

It seems that a good deal of the confusion comes from the definitions of induction and deduction used (if any), or indeed, whether one simply makes up his or her own as is often the case. It is worth noting that very few authors operationalize their terminology, with most relying on an idiosyncratic interpretation of what induction and deduction mean. This need to operationalize definitions is more than a simple academic exercise. It avoids ambiguity, communicates meaning, and enables the end user to understand exactly how the conclusion arose from the available evidence. As stated by McInerney (2004, p. 37):

> *The most effective way to avoid vagueness or ambiguity in logical discourse is to define one's terms. We speak of defining terms, but actually what we are defining is the objects to which terms (words) refer. The process of definition, the mechanics of it, is the way we relate a particular object (the object to be defined) to other objects and thereby give it a precise "location." In defining a term or word, we relate it as rigorously as possible to the object to which it refers. There are two immediate practical benefits of carefully defining terms. Our own ideas are clarified, and, as a result, we can more effectively communicate them to others.*

Strano (2004) shows similar confusion in his understanding of induction and deduction. Although accurately identifying that the criminal profile should be deduced from a forensic examination and behavioral reconstruction of the criminal event, Strano falls back into statements of probability where it is suggested that (p. 497):

> *From the combination of these data, a profiler attempts to deduce the characteristics of an offender who most likely* [italics added] *has committed a specific crime, with a specific victim, and under the distinctive conditions that characterize a particular crime scene.*

Perhaps Strano's misunderstanding comes from the fact that he cites Godwin (1999), who is himself unaware of the finer points of logic:

> *The criticisms of the deductive profiling model underline the fact that a deductive profiler's inferences about crime scene behavior may produce conclusions without any scientific basis. Occasionally, a profiler's deductive opinions about what may have happened at a*

> *crime scene are theoretically or empirically driven by research activity and hypothesis testing, but in many cases, they are based on personal experiences, a small number of cases (often closed, confidential information), and personal hunches.*

It is true that a deductive process employs rigorous theory building and testing, and deductive conclusions are usually premised on inductively derived knowledge. However, the position that a deduction is based on personal experience belies a greater misunderstanding. Strano (2004) accurately suggests that the strength of the deductive method lies in the fact that if the premises are true, then the conclusions will also be true. However, he goes on to suggest that this is not always the case, which means the conclusion would not actually be deductive. This becomes a fault in understanding and application, not method.

In perhaps the most confusing discussion in the literature to date, Kocsis and Palermo (2007) discuss only some of the methods of profiling, without any discussion at all of others, but of most concern is their take on deduction. They state the following (pp. 336–337):

> *One recent development has been the suggestion that two distinct forms of profiling exist. The premise for this distinction is based on differing reasoning processes (i.e., inductive or deductive) that are argued to be in use by an individual when composing a profile. Inductive criminal profiling uses inductive reasoning, which in this context is defined as "reasoning involving broad generalizations or statistical reasoning, where it is possible for the premises to be true while the subsequent conclusion is false" (89, p. 686). Deductive criminal profiling, on the contrary, involves deductive reasoning, which is defined as "an argument where, if the premises are true, then the conclusions must also be true. In a deductive argument, the conclusions flow directly from the premises given" (89, p. 682). These distinctions form the basis of a method of profiling, referred to as behavior evidence analysis (BEA), which exclusively favors the use of deductive reasoning in combination with an understanding of the forensic sciences for the composition of a competent profile (90).*
>
> *The problem with such distinctions is that it transposes philosophical paradigms onto the functional processes of the mind. Although the distinction between inductive or deductive reasoning is a well-established concept in the literature pertaining to critical thinking (91), there is debate in the cognitive psychology/psychiatry literature as to whether the mind functions in such a categorical fashion—that is, whether cognitive functions akin to inductive or deductive reasoning can be undertaken to the exclusion of one another (92, 93). Unlike the autonomic functions of a computer, it is unlikely that the human mind is truly capable of engaging in such a discrete process of reasoning. Indeed, the brain itself, as a complex and highly active neuronal synaptic system, may subconsciously process diverse and/or intrusive thoughts that may increase the difficulty of full engagement in one or the other method. If the cognitive processes of the mind are incapable of engaging in this fashion, the suggestion of a method of profiling premised on the issue of one form of reasoning to the exclusion of the other is rendered highly problematic.*

This provides yet another example of how these concepts get more than a little lost, with the most confusing assertion being that the human mind is not capable of thinking in such a discrete way. Readers should by now be more than familiar with, and critical of, the problem of taking such a position on the issue of induction and deduction.

Regardless of what profiling method is used, all approaches use logic to reach conclusions, with the logical structure of profiles being based on two components: premises and conclusions. The premises are the reasons that support the main claim of an argument (Alexandra, Matthews & Miller, 2002), whereas the conclusions are what is inferred from them. For example, if a profiler argued that an offender was a male, there should be some support for that claim. This support may rely on physical evidence—semen found inside a sexual assault victim is a premise that supports such a conclusion—or the victim or a passerby may have identified the offender as a male. It is mainly in the strength of the link between premises (reasons) and conclusions (claims) that profiling methods significantly differ.

The reasons offered in support of the argument must directly contribute to strengthening the conclusion, and those reasons must be true. That is, the argument must link logically, and the arguments made must be true of the world (the principle of sufficient reason). For example, if the examination of a sexual assault victim did not yield any pubic hair, it is not logical to immediately argue that the offender did not have any pubic hair because other considerations and possible links should be explored. Also, if there is semen inside the vaginal vault, it is not sound reasoning to argue that women have semen, so it must have been a woman (because this would be unsupported by what is known to be true). What needs to be established is that the argument is valid (linkage) and sound (true of this world). Establishing the veracity of each component ensures that one's judgment has logical foundation.

As noted previously, an argument can be either inductive or deductive. Inductive arguments are likely, whereas sound deductive arguments are certain. These forms of reasoning are best thought of as representing different points of certainty along the same continuum. Although distinguishable along a continuum, both generally have, in their own right, an equally important function contingent on context.[4] Induction has a place in logical argumentation, but its place within the process of profiling is questionable beyond a certain point. In other words, a statistical probability is not a conclusion and should never be offered up as one.

Inductive Criminal Profiling

An inductive argument is one in which the conclusion is made likely by the supporting reasons or premises. A good inductive argument provides strong support for the conclusion, though the argument is not infallible. For example, U.S. crime statistics indicate that 90% of people who committed murder in 2002 were male (FBI, 2002). This does not guarantee the conclusion that an unknown offender for any given murder case will be a male; therefore, inductive

[4] Induction is used to structure arguments typically concerning future events.

premises provide varying degrees of certainty. In an inductive profile, the characteristics put forth in the profile are projective or predict some future event; they state what the offender will be like when he or she is found. As such, profile characteristics are a determination of offender traits evidenced at the crime scene and are assumed to be relatively stable over time. For example, an offender who displays anger at the crime scene may be assumed to be a generally angry person in everyday life. An offender who treats his or her victims with care and attention may also be thought to exhibit these characteristics as part of his or her personality.

Inductive profiles rely on statistical and/or correlational reasoning (Petherick & Turvey, 2011); thus, the information rendered in an inductive profile is based on probabilities. Induction is "a type of inference that proceeds from a set of specific observations to a generalization, called a premise, and this premise is a working assumption" (Thornton, 1997, p. 13).[5] Specific observations in a case are compared to the differences or similarities in past cases of the same or similar nature, and these past cases serve as a generalization of typical offender characteristics. In terms of application, induction is also the simplest method to use.

It is the simplicity of this method that makes it more widely used in the profiling community because a vast amount of knowledge is not required in any one area. Instead, requisite skills include the ability to analyze statistics and prior crimes information as well as knowledge of where to find research when required. These two components are often an attribute of any profiling approach in which induction features prominently, as discussed by Kocsis (2001, p. 32):

> *To use this model to produce a psychological profile, behaviors from any of the [behavior] patterns are compared and matched with those of the unsolved case. Once a behavior pattern has been matched with the unsolved case it can be cross-referenced with offender characteristics.*

As illustrated by the sample size in the original FBI study of 36 offenders (Burgess & Ressler, 1985) and Hickey's (2002) study of serial murderers (62 women and 337 men over a period of 195 years), access to a large number of offenders or cases may not be possible, depending on the type of crime. Thus, the sample size of these studies is generally small, limiting studies to exploration, not explanation. Other authors are also concerned about the issue of sample size. For example, Canter (2004) notes that the FBI agents who conducted the study did not use a random or even a large sample of offenders. One can never be certain, therefore, that the studies used as a point of reference are indeed reflective of the circumstances of a given case. Other factors may further hamper the application of generalizations, and Turvey (2011) identifies five scenarios in which averaged offender characteristics may not apply. The following are relevant to all inductive efforts:

- Anger retaliatory offenders who do not suffer from any kind of mental illness
- Domestic-violence-related offenses
- Staged offenses
- Interrupted offenses
- Offenses involving controlled substances

[5] Induction is not always identifiable, however, by whether the argument moves from the specific to the general.

Thus, although inductive generalizations may be true in some (even many) cases, there is no guarantee that they will apply in the current case, and before the offender is caught there is no real way to determine if they do apply.

Applied Inductive Profiling

The following inductive profile was presented to a Coroner's Court in Australia in 2003. The testimony was offered by a state police profiler trained under the International Criminal Investigative Analysis Fellowship. When questioned on the racial extraction of the offender, the profiler reasoned as follows (p. 37):

> *The likely characteristics of the person responsible are that he would be a male and [he] would be of white European racial extraction. That is based on the victim being white European and generally these crimes are committed intraracially and also you have the demographics of the area which was also predominately white European.*

The logic of this style of profiling can be broken down as follows:

Premise 1: The victim was a white European.
Premise 2: Generally these crimes are committed intraracially.
Premise 3: The demographics of the area are predominately white European.
Conclusion: The likely person responsible is of white European racial extraction.

The conclusion is only probable because the profiler's primary source of guidance when determining the offender's racial or ethnic identity is Premise 2. This profiler has examined the case, referred to the research, and subsequently found that there is a general pattern of intra-racial comparability, giving an opinion based on that comparability. Premise 3 is a supportive inference because presumably the demographics of a given geographical location are also indicative of offender racial extraction. Overall, the strength of the conclusion is contingent on the term generally in Premise 2. Thus, it should be clear how inductive reasoning guides the formulation of a profile.

Furthermore, if inductive arguments are linked together to support a conclusion, then one must be sure of the reliability of each premise. This is because a faulty chain of reasoning can lead from case observations to offender characteristics in a less than reliable manner. The following example illustrates how delicate final conclusions can be when contingent on a chain of probable reasoning. This example shows how age was reasoned in the same case (to reproduce the passage in its entirety would be awkward; see Coroner's Court [2003] for full details):

Premise 1: During the course of the abduction, the victim was able to scream out twice, the second time longer and louder.
Premise 2: The victim's property was left behind at the scene.
Premise 3: There was a tearing of the shopping bag.
These indicate,
Premise 4: The victim was able to struggle and resist up to a point.
also,

Premise 5: There were two male offenders.[5] Incidentally, the number of offenders in this case was not fully established, so this remains an assumption and any subsequent conclusions drawn are questionable.
This suggests,
Premise 6: Their execution plan was somewhat sloppy.
in turn,
Premise 7: This reflects some inexperience in this area.
because,
Premise 8: If the offenders had more experience in their backgrounds, one would not expect to see the victim scream and resist in this way.
Therefore,
Premise 9: It appears that they were inexperienced, probably immature.
Premise 10: These things contribute to the youthful age.
Conclusion: The (dominant) offender is most likely in his early twenties.

At first glance, the premises may appear to logically support the opinion. Yet, each step in the chain of reasoning weakens the strength of the overall conclusion because not every argument is deductive in its own right. Premises 1, 2, and 3 work to support Premise 4, and there are no obvious problems with the initial premises (unless the claims are rejected outright). However, Premises 4 and 5 argue that because the victim was able to struggle and resist against the offender(s), this supports Premise 6—that the offense plan was sloppy. This is questionable logic because the claim that the offenders insufficiently planned an abduction is reasoned on the basis of how the victim reacted at the time of the offense. This argues that such an interaction is indeed predictable. In turn, the assumption of predictability supports Premise 7 that the offenders were inexperienced, and Premise 8 states that experienced offenders do not allow Premise 4 to happen. Because the offenders are deemed to be inexperienced, they are probably immature. Premise 9 argues that experiential immaturity equals a youthful age, as stated in Premise 10. From this chain of causal reasoning, the conclusion is reached that the dominant offender is most likely in his early twenties. If any premise within the argument is found to be incorrect at any point (e.g., Premise 6), then the characteristic becomes questionable. This is because the conclusion is reliant on the entire chain of reasoning.

Any lack of certainty should be reflected in the end product by the language used to portray any thoughts the profiler has about the likely offender. Such statements as "the offender usually," or "it would be typical to find," and "it is my belief that" must accompany inductive profiles in order to articulate the lack of certainty the profiler has about the conclusions. For example, if one were to assert that most murderers are male and, therefore, an unknown murderer is male, this is presenting an inductive argument as certain—the offender is—rather than a statement of probability—the offender is likely to be. It should be clear then that the principal purpose of inductive reasoning is the development of hypotheses and not conclusions.

Deductive Criminal Profiling

Deductive profiling involves a more scientific approach and is a rational or logical process in which offender characteristics are a direct extension of the physical evidence (Petherick & Turvey, 2011). Thus, if the premises are true, then the conclusions must also be true (Bevel & Gardiner, 1997). Neblett (1985, p. 114) goes further, stating that "if the conclusion is false, then at least one of the premises must be false." For this reason, it is incumbent on the profiler to establish the validity of each and every premise before drawing conclusions.

Because deductive arguments are structured so that the conclusion is implicitly contained within the premises, unless the reasoning is invalid, the conclusion follows as a matter of course. For example, if police enter a domestic dispute and find the husband in the process of stabbing his wife and she later dies from the severity of these stab wounds, it is valid to deductively reason that the husband killed his wife. One may argue that in fact the wife died as a result of blood loss or through the hemorrhaging of a vital organ and, therefore, not as a result of the husband's actions per se. However, as long as it can be proven that the husband's actions directly contributed to the death of his wife, one is entitled to deduce from the premises that the husband killed his wife.

Deductive arguments are designed to take us from truth to truth. That is, an argument is valid if (Alexandra, Matthews & Miller, 2002, p. 65)

- It is not logically possible for its conclusion to be false if its premises are true.
- Its conclusion must be true, if its premises are true.
- It would be contradictory to assert its premises yet deny its conclusion.

Applying this rationale to the prior example, it is not logically possible for the conclusion (that the husband killed his wife) to be false if the premises (the police caught the husband in the act and the wife died from the severity of the stab wounds) are true. Second, that the husband is responsible for the act of killing his wife must be true if one accepts the premises (that the police walked in on the husband stabbing his wife and she died as a result of these injuries). Third, it would be contradictory to assert that the police caught the husband in the process of stabbing his wife and she later died from the stab wounds, and then deny that the husband is the person who killed his wife. Thus, the argument is deductive.

Deductive profiling draws on the scientific method, which involves the testing of hypotheses through observation and experimentation. When a hypothesis has consistently withstood falsification, it can be presented using the appropriate deductive structure. In exactly the same manner, deductive profiling develops particular hypotheses about a case and then attempts to rule out competing hypotheses on the basis of the available physical evidence. However, simply submitting a hypothesis to falsification does not make it deductive. For this to happen, the certainty of the argument must be rationally unquestionable. This means that any subsequent falsification of the conclusion must not be undertaken with reference to the fantastical or phenomenological. In addition, the structure of the argument is critical and should conform to a specific standard. This can be found in any introductory text on logic and is also covered briefly next.

The Logic of Deductive Profiling

A scientific profiling paradigm develops hypotheses about a case from which attempts are made to falsify competing hypotheses on the basis of the available physical evidence. The end result is a set of conclusions that is, on the basis of all available physical evidence, deductive. However, the resulting profile is by no means static, with new developments in logic challenging currently held hypotheses. A deductive profile will attempt to ascertain how this evidence fits the profile. That is, does this new knowledge change the current hypothesis? If so, the profile is updated to fit this new paradigm of understanding. If not, it is categorized as a weaker hypothesis but not discarded (an example of this process is provided at the end of this chapter).

An example of how a deductive profile is reasoned can be found in Turvey (2011). On the basis of the physical evidence, Turvey reasons from the hypothesis that if an offender carefully disarticulates a victim, that he or she has demonstrated some degree of medical knowledge to the conclusion that the crime evidences an offender with medical knowledge:

> **Premise 1**: If an offender carefully disarticulates a victim, then he or she has demonstrated some degree of medical knowledge.
> **Premise 2**: The victim was not dismembered with commonly associated chopping instruments such as a hatchet, cleaver, or machete applied to areas of bone (such as a butcher might use).
> **Premise 3**: There is no evidence that a sawing instrument such as a hacksaw, band saw, skill saw, or radial saw was used.
> **Premise 4**: There is evidence that the offender(s) separated the victim's head, arms, legs, and feet at their respective joints with the utmost deliberation, precision, and care using a very sharp cutting instrument not unlike a scalpel.
> **Conclusion**: The crime evidences an offender with medical knowledge.

The conclusion is a direct extension of the available physical evidence and does not make any conclusions outside the physical evidence, nor does it claim what level of medical knowledge the offender must have—only that the offender's behavior suggests that he or she has the requisite skill to perform the disarticulation. To reject the argument as deductive would require that the conclusion is not true due to rejection of the premises on which it is based. By extension, rejection of the premises would require rejection of the physical evidence. Because no interpretation has been placed on the evidence, this is not logical (the scalpel is an example of what tool may have been used to obtain that kind of precision). Second, one would have to argue that the conclusion could be false even on the acceptance of the premises. Because the argument leads directly from the physical evidence to the conclusion, any argument would have to suggest that the disarticulation of human joints with the utmost precision does not logically suggest (in any way) some degree of medical knowledge. Third, one would have to explain why it is not contradictory to assert the premises and subsequently deny the conclusion.

As a result, deductive profiling is typically less adventurous with its determinations, with Turvey (2011) citing four characteristics that can be deductively inferred.[6] These are knowledge of the victim, knowledge of the crime scene, knowledge of methods and materials, and criminal skill. Although it may appear at first to be a shortcoming, it must be remembered that a deductive profile works with physical evidence and will not venture into the unknown with supposition and assumption. To have four points about which one can be certain is better than having 40, the bases of which are questionable. It is also worth noting that the utility of a profile is largely a consequence of the surety of its conclusions. A profiler who is willing to venture into the unknown with his or her analysis runs the very real risk of leading investigations astray and wasting valuable time.

Practical Application of Deductive Profiling

The following is a scenario that illustrates how deductive profiling is applied. This example is not meant to be exhaustive, nor will it include every possibility from the evidence presented, but it is designed to be procedurally instructive. Note that more detail has been provided in this chapter regarding deduction because, comparatively speaking, deduction is far more complex than the application of statistical generalizations and therefore warrants greater explanation.

Consider the following crime scene behavior:

> *During an anal sexual assault, an offender approaches the victim from the front, allowing her to get a good look at him. He then wraps a belt around her neck, pulls down his pants before pulling her shirt up over her head, thereby revealing her breasts, which he manipulates. After completing the sodomy, the offender leaves the victim with her shirt in place, which covers her face.*

Analyzing the case from a deductive perspective presents one with a number of hypotheses that can be measured against the evidence, including the following:

- The offender is a male.
- The belt was brought to the crime scene by the offender.
- The offender pulled the shirt up over the victim's head to help him believe the victim was somebody else.
- The offender pulled the shirt up over the victim's head to obscure identification.
- The offender pulled the shirt up to provide access to the victim's breasts.

These await testing against the available evidence and show the development of theories and, in the first instance, a deductive conclusion. Some of the hypotheses may or may not be

[6]It is possible to infer other offender characteristics deductively, such as the sex of the offender, if there is physical evidence, as will be shown. However, if physical evidence is present, one may not need a profile to state it.

borne out by further examination of the physical and behavioral evidence. These are considered in turn:[7]

1. The offender is a male. Following evidence at the crime scene and provided by the victim, it could be said that this hypothesis has been established. However, the ways in which this may be established through physical evidence include, for example, an examination that yields sperm in and around the victim's anus. This can be reasoned as follows:
   Premise 1: The victim was subjected to an anal sexual assault.
   Premise 2: The victim reports seeing the offender's penis.
   Premise 3: Semen was found around the victim's anus and vagina.
   Conclusion: The offender is a male.
2. The belt was brought to the crime scene by the offender. This can be reasoned as follows:
   Premise 1: The belt did not belong to the victim.
   Premise 2: The victim stated that the belt was not at the crime scene prior to the assault.
   Premise 3: The victim reported seeing the offender remove the belt from around his waist.
   Conclusion: The belt was brought to the crime scene by the offender.
3. The offender pulled the victim's shirt over her head to assist with the fantasy that the victim was someone else. This hypothesis can be reasoned as follows:
   Premise 1: The offender did not call the victim by another name.
   Premise 2: The offender did not engage in any other fantasy-related behavior.
   Conclusion: At this point in time, there is no evidence to suggest that the offender pulled the victim's shirt over her head to assist with the fantasy that she was someone else.
4. The offender pulled the shirt up over the victim's head to obscure identification.[8] This hypothesis can be reasoned as follows:
   Premise 1: The victim saw the offender on initial approach and a number of times before the shirt was pulled up.
   Premise 2: The offender made no attempt to stop the victim from seeing him.
   Premise 3: The offender did not engage in any other precautionary acts.
   Premise 4: The offender left the victim alive and made no threats to her safety should she contact police.
   Conclusion: The shirt was not pulled up over the victim's head to obscure identification.
5. The offender pulled the shirt up over the victim's head to provide access to the victim's breasts. This hypothesis can be reasoned as follows:
   Premise 1: The offender did not pull the shirt up over the victim's head to assist with the fantasy that she was someone else.

[7] Although this is how a deductive argument is structured in theory, it would not be usual to find the logic outlined in such a detailed way. To present each characteristic in this way may be cumbersome, and providing the argument is supported in a logical way, it may not be necessary to provide the full and complete logic for a given characteristic. However, there must be a minimum threshold providing support for the argument.

[8] As with everything in profiling, context is critical, and a determination of exactly when during the assault this was done would help discover the reason behind the action.

Premise 2: The offender did not pull the shirt up over the victim's head to obscure his identification.

Premise 3: Once the shirt was raised over the victim's head, the offender immediately started fondling her breasts.

Conclusion: The offender pulled the shirt up to provide access to the victim's breasts.

Restated for absolute clarity, determining offense-related characteristics is about asking the right questions of offense-related behavior (Turvey, 2011). The first part of this process is defining the characteristic we are arguing, and the second part involves determining which physical or behavioral evidence supports this. If the reconstruction of the offense includes those behaviors, then they can be argued. Considering and ruling out competing hypotheses is also important, as these examples and discussion have shown.

It should be apparent that this process is very systematic and thorough in developing knowledge about a particular case. Deduction utilizes a scientific approach for examining competing hypotheses and identifies certain arguments from the available physical evidence. In this way, not only can voids in knowledge be identified but also we can provide investigative strategies to overcome these voids. This leads to a more complete approach, leaving little to guesswork. Verifying the validity of the physical evidence also helps determine the veracity of the subsequent behavioral evidence and its interpretation, which is an extension of hypothesis generation.

Conclusion

This chapter has examined the logical structure of criminal profiling. Inductive profiling involves the application of statistical and probabilistic knowledge to a current case, and the source of this information is usually criminological studies, the profiler's own experience, intuition, bias, stereotypes, and generalizations. The strength of the conclusion reached through inductive profiling is contingent on the probability of the knowledge or research that has been utilized. Although useful in developing hypotheses, induction is not well suited to the final determination of offender characteristics. Conversely, deductive profiling involves the assessment of the physical material relating to the current case. Deductive profiling analyzes the evidence in the context of the case. Sound reasoning and critical thinking skills are applied to thus arrive at a logical conclusion.

Criminal profilers should not attempt to formulate a hypothesis about a case until they have examined all the physical evidence. Once the case has been thoroughly examined and hypotheses have been generated, then the profiler can attempt to provide a behavioral interpretation of the physical evidence. Apart from the practical implications, through an increased awareness of the logic and reasoning employed in the profiling process, we will also be better able to understand the individual methods and the utility they offer.

Questions

1. The two main types of logic used in criminal profiling are __________ and __________.
2. Explain the difference between inductive and deductive logic.

3. What are the five scenarios provided by Turvey that will affect the application of generalizations in a given case?
4. The argument that follows the format "If P then Q, P, therefore Q" is known as __________.
5. In deductive logic, if the premises are true, then the conclusion will be true. *True or false?*

References

Alexandra, A., Matthews, S., & Miller, M. (2002). *Reasons, values and institutions.* Melbourne: Tertiary Press.

Bevel, T., & Gardiner, R. (1997). *Bloodstain pattern analysis: With an introduction to crime scene reconstruction.* Boca Raton: CRC Press.

Bhattacharyya, S. (1958). The concept of logic. *Philosophy and Phenomenological Research, 18*(3), 326–340.

Brussel, J. A. (1968). *Casebook of a crime psychiatrist.* New York: Dell Books.

Burgess, A. W., & Ressler, R. K. (1985). *Sexual homicides crime scene and patterns of criminal behavior.* National Institute of Justice Grant. 82-IJ-CX-0065.

Canter, D. (1994). *Criminal shadows: Inside the mind of the serial killer.* London: Harper Collins.

Canter, D. (1995). Psychology of offender profiling. In R. Bull & D. Carson (Eds.), *Handbook of psychology in legal contexts.* New York: Wiley.

Canter, D. (2004). The organized/disorganized typology of serial murder. *Psychology, Public Policy, and Law, 10,* 293–320.

Canter, D., Alison, L. J., Alison, E., & Wentink, N. (2000). Offender profiling and criminal differentiation. *Legal and Criminological Psychology, 5,* 23–46.

Coroner's Court. (2003). *Transcript of Evidence: K. Illingsworth N.S.W. Coroner's Court*: 5th March.

Davis, J. (1999). Criminal personality profiling and crime scene assessment: A contemporary investigative tool to assist law enforcement public safety. *Journal of Contemporary Criminal Justice, 15*(3), 291–301.

Douglas, J. E., & Olshaker, M. (1996). *Mindhunter: Inside the FBI elite serial crime unit.* London: Mandarin Books.

Douglas, J. E., & Olshaker, M. (1997). *Journey into darkness: How the FBI's premier profiler penetrates the minds of the most terrifying serial criminals.* London: Arrow Books.

Douglas, J. E., & Olshaker, M. (1998). Obsession: The FBI's legendary profiler probes the psyche of killers: *Rapists, and stalkers and their victims and tells how to fight back.* New York: Pocket Books.

Egger, S. (1999). Psychological profiling: Past, present and future. *Journal of Contemporary Criminal Justice, 15*(3), 242–261.

Farber, M. (1942). Logical systems and the principles of logic. *Philosophy of Science, 9*(1), 40–54.

Federal Bureau of Investigation.(2002). *Uniform Crime Report.* Available at <http://www.fbi.gov/ucr/cius_02/html/web/index.html> Accessed 23.09.04.

Geberth, V. J. (1996). Practical homicide investigation: Tactics: *Procedures and forensic techniques* (3rd ed.). Boca Raton: CRC Press.

Godwin, G. M. (1999). *Hunting serial predators: A multivariate approach to profiling violent behavior.* Boca Raton: CRC Press.

Godwin, G. M. (2002). Reliability, validity, and utility of criminal profiling typologies. *Journal of Police and Criminal Psychology, 17,* 1–18.

Hickey, E. (2002). *Serial murderers and their victims* (3rd ed.). Belmont: Wadsworth.

Holmes, R., & Holmes, S. (2002). *Profiling violent crimes: An investigative tool* (3rd ed.). Thousand Oaks: Sage.

Klump, C. S. (1997). Taking your cue from the clues. *Security Management, 41*(9), 123–126.

Kocsis, R. N. (2001). Serial arsonist crime profiling. Firenews: Winter.

Kocsis, R. N., & Palermo, G. B. (2007). Contemporary problems in criminal profiling. In R. N. Kocsis (Ed.), *Criminal profiling: International theory, research, and practice.* New York: Humana Press.

McInerney, D. Q. (2004). *Being logical: A guide to good thinking.* Westminster: Random House.

Neblett, W. (1985). *Sherlock's logic: Learn to reason like a master detective.* New York: Barnes and Noble Books.

Petherick, W. A. (2006). *Serial crime: Theoretical and practical issues in behavioral profiling.* Boston: Academic Press.

Petherick, W. A. (2007). *Criminal profiling: A qualitative and quantitative analysis of methods and content.* Gold Coast: Bond University. Unpublished doctoral dissertation.

Petherick, W. A. (2008). Offender profiling in Australia. In K. Fritzon & P. Wilson (Eds.), *Forensic psychology and criminology: An Australasian perspective.* North Ryde: McGraw Hill.

Petherick, W. A., & Turvey, B. E. (2011). Criminal profiling, the scientific method, and logic. In B. E. Turvey (Ed.), *Criminal profiling: An introduction to behavioral evidence analysis* (4th ed.). Boston: Academic Press.

Ressler, R. K., & Burgess, A. W. (1985). Crime scene and profile characteristics of organized and disorganized murderers. *FBI Law Enforcement Bulletin, 54*(8), 18–25.

Ressler, R. K., Burgess, A. W., & Douglas, J. E. (1988). *Sexual homicides: Patterns and motives.* New York: Lexington Books.

Ressler, R. K., & Shachtman, T. (1992). *Whoever fights monsters: The brilliant FBI detective behind the Silence of the Lambs.* New York: Simon & Schuster.

Stock, G. W. J. (2004). *Deductive logic.* Oxford: Project Guttenberg Press.

Strano, S. (2004). A neural network applied to criminal psychological profiling: An Italian initiative. *International Journal of Offender Therapy and Comparative Criminology, 48*(4), 495–503.

Thornton, J. (1997). The general assumptions and rationale of forensic identification. In D. L. Faigman, D. H. Kaye, M. J. Saks, & J. Sanders (Eds.), *Modern scientific evidence: The law and expert testimony.* Minnesota: St. Paul.

Turvey, B. E. (2011). *Criminal profiling: An introduction to behavioral evidence analysis* (4th ed.). Burlington: Academic Press.

3

Behavioral Consistency, the Homology Assumption, and the Problems of Induction

Wayne Petherick and Claire Ferguson

Introduction

The ultimate goal of profiling is to identify the major behavioral and personality characteristics to narrow the suspect pool. Inferences about offender characteristics can be accomplished deductively, based on the analysis of discrete offender behaviors established within a particular case. They can also be accomplished inductively, involving prediction based on abstract offender averages from group data (these methods and the logic on which they are based is detailed extensively in Chapters 2 and 4). As discussed, these two approaches are by no means equal.

The reliability and validity of inductive profiling rest almost exclusively on two weak theories: behavioral consistency and the homology assumption. Behavioral consistency posits that the same offender will do the same thing across the span of time during different offenses. The homology assumption suggests that, generally, there will be a similarity between different offenders who commit similar crimes. Without either of these theories, comparing the current offender(s) to past offenders is essentially futile.

Although some in the profiling community understand the importance of these theories to actual casework, many do not. Either way, most are unaware of their limitations, which causes serious implications for the legitimate role of inductive profiling when providing investigative or forensic inferences regarding behavioral evidence.

This chapter provides an in-depth discussion of both behavioral consistency and the homology assumption, outlining some of the research that has been done in the area. The purpose is to educate students and professionals regarding what these concepts are, why they are important, and the consequences to casework in light of their limitations. It builds on the discussion of inductive methods presented in Chapter 2.

Behavioral Consistency

There are essentially two types of consistency that are important to the application of profiling knowledge. The first is that an offender will show consistency between his or her non-criminal and criminal actions. This has been referred to as interpersonal coherence (Canter, 1994), and although discussed further, it is not the type of consistency that is the focus of this chapter. The second type of consistency, and the subject of considerably more study in criminal profiling, is that a criminal will behave consistently across the offenses he or she commits.

The importance of consistency is related by Canter (1995, p. 347), who notes that:

> *...one hypothesis central to profiling is that the way an offender carries out a crime on one occasion will have some characteristic similarities to the way he or she carries out crimes on other occasions. If the inherent variations between contexts, for any aspect of human behavior, are greater than the variations between people then it is unlikely that clear differences between individuals will be found for those behaviors. This hypothesis is applicable to the situation in which a person has committed only one crime. Even in that case a "profile" has to be based upon the assumption that the criminal is exhibiting characteristics that are typical of that person, not of the situation in which the crime was committed.*

Canter (2004, p. 4) also provides the following commentary:

> *One aspect of these salient features that also needs to be determined as part of scientific development is that they are consistent enough from one context, or crime, to another to form the basis for considering those crimes and comparing them with other offenses. This issue of consistency turns out to be a complex one. Part of this complexity comes from weaknesses in the sources of data.*
>
> *A more conceptual challenge to determining consistency, as in all human activity, is that some variation and change is a natural aspect of human processes. There therefore will be criminals who are consistently variable or whose behavioral trajectories demonstrate some form of career development, as well as those whose criminal behavior will remain relatively stable over time. These questions are very similar indeed to those discussed in the more general personality literature about what is constant about people and what is*

> *variable, as Youngs (2004) explores. Research around all these possibilities of consistency is therefore central to any development of a scientific basis for offender profiling.*[1]

Woodhams and Toye (2007, p. 3) provide the following discussion with regard to determining whether different crimes have been committed by the same individual. This process is known as case linkage, and is discussed by McGrath in Chapter 7:

> *A second hypothesis of offender profiling is the offender (behavioral) consistency hypothesis (Canter , 1995). This hypothesis predicts that an offender will show consistency (or similarity) in their criminal behavior across their series of crimes. As explained by Mokros and Alison (2002), this hypothesis is necessary for offender profiling to work because "one person has to remain rather consistent in his or her actions if the correspondence of similarity associations holds between a person's characteristics and behavior" (p. 26).*
>
> *The offender behavioral consistency hypothesis also underlies the practice of case linkage. If offenders were not consistent in their criminal behavior, it would be impossible to assign crimes to a common offender on the basis of their behavioral similarity.*

Holmes and Holmes (2002) make this same assumption in *Profiling Violent Crimes*. Here, they suggest that not only does the crime scene reflect the personality (interpersonal coherence) but also the personality will stay the same (behavioral consistency), and the manifestation of the behavior at the crime (in both modus operandi and signature) will stay the same. It is necessary to provide their discussion in near fullness (Holmes & Holmes, 2002, pp. 41–44):

> *Several assumptions can be made regarding psychological profiling. These assumptions are important to consider because they deal directly with the reasons why profiles are important and the manner in which certain information can be obtained and used to formulate a credible criminal investigative assessment. These assumptions are detailed next.*
>
> ***The Crime Scene Reflects the Personality***[2]
>
> *The basic assumption of psychological profiling is that the crime scene reflects the personality of the offender. After all, how effective would profiling be if the crime itself was not indicative of the pathology assessment?*[3] *The assessment will aid in the direction and scope of the investigation of the crime.*
>
> *Not only is the manner in which the victim was fatally dispatched important, but the physical and nonphysical evidence will also lend, to some degree, an assessment of the type of personality involved in a particular murder. The amount of chaos, for example, might indicate that a disorganized personality was involved in this crime. If this is true, then we can make certain assumptions about particular social core variables of the*

[1] Canter is intimating that the "science" of profiling will come from the numbers. As with all endeavors, the science is in the interpretation, not the statistics.

[2] Although this is generally referred to as interpersonal coherence, the reader will recall that it is a form of behavioral consistency that occurs between the noncriminal and criminal behavior of the offender.

[3] It should be restated for clarification that this is the central question of this chapter. However, Holmes and Holmes's (2002) position appears to be at odds with our own. They suggest, with little qualification or clarification, that these theoretical assumptions be accepted uncritically. There is no discussion of how emotion, drugs, alcohol, staging, interruption, or anything else affect either behavior or personality in a given crime. It would seem that these things would need to be considered before any discussion of the temporal stability of personality could be embarked upon.

unknown perpetrator. On the other hand, if the crime scene is "neat and clean" or thoroughly chaotic, then other assumptions might lead us to an offender who possesses a different set of social core variables.

The focus of the attack may also indicate certain information that aids in the apprehension of the unknown offender. For example, in a Midwestern state, an elderly woman was killed in her own home. She was stabbed repeatedly and suffered multiple deep wounds to the upper legs and genital area. For reasons that we will further detail in a later chapter, the profile offered an assessment of the crime itself that, in part, resulted in the arrest of a man who was considered a suspect at the beginning stages of the law enforcement investigation.

...

The Method of Operation Remains Similar

The behavior of the perpetrator, as evidenced in the crime scene and not the offense per se, determines the degree of suitability of the case for profiling (Geberth, 1983, p. 401). The crime scene contains clues that experienced profilers determine to be signatures of the criminals. Because no two offenders are exactly alike, it is equally true that no two crime scenes are exactly alike.[4] *As certain as a psychometric test reflects psychopathology, the crime scene reflects a person with a pathology.*[5]

Many serial offenders themselves are very aware of the nonphysical evidence that is present at a crime scene. One murderer remarked,

First of all, any investigative onlooker to my crime scene would have immediately deduced that the offender was extremely sadistic in nature. The visible markers of bondage, nature of the victims' wounds and evidence of unhurried, systematic abuse should have indicated that these sadistic acts were not new to me. And that I had committed such brutal crimes in the past and would likely do so again (Author's files).

...

The remarks from this killer show the one dimension of personality—the conscious dimension—that profiling often neglects. This murderer and rapist illustrates by his remarks the elements within his crime scenes that truly reflect his personality. The method of operation, the M.O., was repeated many times in the course of his rapes and murders.[6]

Addressing the stability of an individual's behavior across situations, Shoda, Mischel, and Wright (1994) delved into the behavior of schoolchildren in a summer camp setting. Although

[4]This alone questions the application of arbitrary generalizations when the crime itself has not come to be understood as its own universe. Furthermore, it appears that the authors of the text are getting confused about the concepts they are arguing: This section is about modus operandi (MO), yet they are arguing that an experienced profiler will be able to determine the signature. Nor will the MO always remain the same, which also seems to be a point of confusion.

[5]It is also prudent to discuss the issue of pathology. This word is derived from the Greek word pathos, meaning illness or sickness. However, it is more likely that in a crime involving true pathology, aspects of the offender's personality are likely to be obscured. This issue has not been significantly discussed in the literature.

[6]Refer to footnote 4. The case study as presented discusses the sadistic aspect of the offender's crimes, which is in turn more aligned to notions of signature. Why this is used as an example here is confusing and misleading.

not examining criminal behavior, the opening paragraphs of their article are relevant to the current discussion. Not only do they suggest that idiographic analysis is of utmost importance in understanding a single case, they also highlight the importance of considering person–situation interactions (p. 674):

> *Allport (1937) introduced the concept of idiographic analyses half a century ago, urging personologists to understand each individual deeply in terms of how that person functions, instead of just studying "operations of a hypothetical 'average' mind" (p. 61). Nonetheless, the idiographic focus has been bypassed by mainstream personality psychology. Probably this neglect reflects not a lack of interest but an absence of appropriate methods and theory for studying individual functioning in ways that are objective and scientific rather than intuitive and clinical. In our view, understanding individual functioning requires identifying first the psychological situations that engage a particular person's characteristic personality processes and the distinctive cognitions and affects that are experienced in them. Then, an individual's functioning should become visible in the distinctive or unique ways the person's behavior changes across situations, not just in its overall level or mean frequency. For example, a person may often behave in a warm and empathic way with her colleagues at work but almost always in a very critical manner with her family. Another person may show the opposite pattern so that he is warm and empathic with his family but critical with his professional colleagues. If two people are similar in their behaviors averaged across situations, but differ in the situations in which they display those behaviors, are these differences merely a reflection of momentary situational influences? Or do such differences reflect differences in enduring and meaningful aspects of their personality?*

To reiterate and expand on some of the issues this passage raises as relevant to profiling, consider the following:

1. Idiographic analysis provides a more thorough description and explanation of an individual situation compared to that afforded through hypothetical averages.
2. When considering the actions of one individual, situational variables play a pivotal role.
3. In profiling, the person–situation interactions must be accounted for in a detailed reconstruction of the criminal event. Without this, situational variables may not, or will not, be accounted for, rendering any conclusions about the offender potentially incorrect.
4. We cannot rely on the notion of behavioral consistency, given the differences between the public and private faces of individuals over time. That is, what we see of a person in one environment will differ greatly from what we see of that person in another, and the behavior of an individual in one crime may differ greatly from that in another crime.

The main problem with consistency is that without performing a complete crime reconstruction, we cannot assume that there has been any level of consistency in the offender's behavior, either in single instances or across multiple offenses. Furthermore, we cannot assume that even though there may be consistency between two different crimes committed by the same offender, that this will always be true. Consistency is a nice theory, but in practice, it will not be suitably or reliably predictive.

To round out this discussion, the variety of influences on consistency must be noted. These influences will be different across crimes and situations, and will depend to a great deal on the emotional context under which the crime takes place, victim behaviors, and biochemical influences. These would include, but are by no means limited to, the following:

- The influence of alcohol or other drugs.
- Crimes with a high emotional content, such as some stalking offenses and certain homicides, including domestic homicide and domestic violence.
- Crimes involving mental illness.
- Crimes involving other psychopathology such as personality disorder.
- Staged crime scenes (see Chapter 8).
- Targeting different victim types.
- Offender development over time.
- Crimes involving multiple offenders where this is unknown.

A relevant case example showing the fallibility of consistency is that of Louis Peoples. This was outlined by Petherick (2005, pp. 92–95) and was chronicled in the first instance with permission:

> *On the 16th of September, 1997, an unknown offender went onto the grounds of California Spray Dry Company, vandalizing vehicles parked in the employee lot and shooting at employees. Thomas Harrison, shot in the stomach and thigh, described the offender as a white adult male, 5 feet 9 inches tall, about 160 pounds in weight. He was wearing a dark baseball cap and dark clothes.*
>
> *Approximately 5 weeks later, at 4:12 pm, the Stockton Branch of the Bank of the West was held up at gunpoint. A white male entered the bank wearing a black hat, black jacket, and dark glasses, approaching the teller at position 1, who was handed a note which read "give me all of your 100s, 50s, 20s, 10s and nobody will get shot." He took a small handgun from his jacket while the teller got the notes before fleeing the bank.*
>
> *Five days later, a telephone call was made to Charter Way Tow of Stockton, California. Tow driver James Loper attended the scene. No reports of trouble were mentioned during the 3:30 am radio call to the dispatcher. Loper was later found by sheriff's deputies at 3:48 am. He had been shot 10 times.*
>
> *The body of Stephen Chacko was found on the 4th of November 1997 in front of Mayfair Discount Liquors and Tobacco. Mr. Chacko was employed as the cashier at Mayfair, and was taken to St. Joseph's Medical Center where he was pronounced dead 20 minutes later from five gunshot wounds. It was found that during the robbery the offender fired at the cash register in a attempt to open it, but these attempts failed.*
>
> *About a week later, Besun Yu and Jun Gao were shot and killed during a robbery at the Village Oaks Market, again in Stockton. Both victims were working in front of the store at the time of the robbery. The offender came in through the front door, shot Besun Yu at the*

cash register, and then shot Jun Gao in the aisle. The offender took the cash register out of the checkout stand and left the store.

The collection of facts in this case suggested to Turvey that the offender was becoming more desperate in their attempts. He had tried to open a cash register unsuccessfully by shooting at it, had stolen another cash register which he also couldn't open, and had shot staff at the places he had taken them from (when the simplest thing would be to get them to open the cash registers).

The offender took precautions in all of the above cases, such as wearing hats, sunglasses, and a jacket. In some cases he had a healthy knowledge of the layout of the premises and in some cases prepared an escape plan (such as cutting through chain link fences).

Oddly enough, despite the preparation evident in many of the cases, the offender did a number of things that seemed a contradiction to those precautionary acts intended to help him get away with his offenses. In the first case at Cal-Spray, he spent considerable time at the scene, thereby increasing his chances of apprehension. Also, the repeated use of a firearm, and a big one at that (.40 caliber), further increased his chances of getting caught owing to the noise it would generate. During the bank robbery, he waited in line to be seen by a teller, also increasing the risk of apprehension. If not for the severe nature of his act and the fact that someone died at his hand, his actions in relation to James Loper would have been comical: Shortly after shooting Mr. Loper, the offender rang Charter Way Towing looking for work claiming he had heard they were "short a man."

The cases were linked through the use of ballistics but the bank and Cal-Spray were not linked to the crime series until other ballistics tests tied them in just prior to Turvey's involvement. Looking back at the series of crimes, Turvey believed that the offender's actions at Cal-Spray provided the greatest insight into the crimes. Turvey suggested to investigators that the amount of time spent at Cal-Spray, the damage to cars, familiarity of the location, and ingress and egress routes all meant they should look for a former employee. When approached with this information, managers of the company informed police that they should seek out a former employee: Louis Peoples.

Peoples was a methamphetamine addict (which affected his behavior during the offense) and when arrested, he led police to the .40 caliber handgun used in the crimes which he had buried. He had also kept a diary of the media coverage of his crimes in the form of a scrapbook titled "Biography of a Crime Spree."

As can be noted from this example, it is both dangerous and inaccurate to assume behavioral consistency between a person's criminal behavior in one instance and his or her static personality and behavioral characteristics. There are too many factors that may be acting on the offender at the time of the crime, which are unknown to the investigator, that will influence the behavior of that offender. If these are not recognized and accommodated for, the inductive profiler will likely render an inaccurate assessment. That is, the behavior of an individual in one state cannot and should not be used to determine or predict trait characteristics.

The Homology Assumption

The homology assumption, put simply, refers to whether there is a concordance between the behavior of two offenders and their subsequent background characteristics. It could be argued that this is also a form of consistency—that is, consistency between the behaviors and backgrounds of different criminals. As stated by Mokros and Alison (2002, pp. 25–26):

> *Offender profiling involves the process of predicting the characteristics of an offender based on information available at the crime scene. Decisions about the likely sociodemographic characteristics of that person are made on the basis of behavior. If it is possible to infer something about the person from what happened at the crime scene then any two persons who commit a particular type of crime in roughly the same way should be rather similar to each other.*
>
> *As a consequence, offender profiling in its conventional form is a nonconditional, linear process. If conditional "if ... then" rules were included to accommodate for individual peculiarities, situational influences or nondeterministic relations, the resulting profiles would contain "either ... or" predictions. To give an example: If excessive violence in cases of sexual assault could be associated with antisocial personality disorder or intoxication of the offender, the profile for a given case where increased levels of violence are present could predict either an antisocial perpetrator or a person with proneness to substance abuse or a combination of those two.*

The homology assumption, as it stands, is not unique to the profiling approach known as Investigative Psychology. All inductive (trait) methods of profiling rely on concordance between the current offender and those characteristics of past offenders. Mokros and Alison (2002, p. 26) suggest that it is a "condition for the process of offender profiling to be feasible." In addition (p. 26):

> *With respect to the assumptions that underlie offender profiling, this means that the degree of similarity in the offense behavior of any two perpetrators from a given category of crime will match the degree of similarity in their characteristics. In other words, there is an assumed sameness in the similarity relations between the domains of crime scene actions and demographic features. The more similar two offenders are, the higher the resemblance in their crimes will be.*

This proposition extends beyond the degree of similarity between behaviorally similar offenders: The assumption holds not only that two offenders who are behaviorally similar will be demographically similar but also that offenders who behave similarly will be demographically similar to future offenders who exhibit this same behavior. Otherwise, the homology assumption would only be true of one group at one time, rendering the theory redundant. The authors suggest that (p. 26):

> *The assumption of behavioral consistency does not subsume the second assumption (i.e., that of a correspondence in similarity of offense behavior and characteristics between*

> *offenders). If, however, the homology assumption is found to be valid, the assumption of behavioral consistency must be valid as well. The reason for this is the self-similarity of individuals. One person has to remain rather consistent in his or her actions if the correspondence of similarity relations holds between a person's characteristics and behavior.*

To state the previous proposition another way, it could be argued that if the homology assumption does not hold, behavioral consistency will not either. As discussed later, research has largely failed to find support for the homology assumption.

This is not the last of the problems with the homology assumption, however. It also presupposes to a degree that the behavior of one offender that is similar to that of another will have a similar origin. That is, the cognition or motivation for the behavior is assumed to be similar given that the behavior is similar. This assumption is flawed because different offenders will do similar things for different reasons at different times. Possible reasons for these changes, as outlined by Bandura and Cervone (1983, p. 1018), are changes in our perceived abilities, "the self-efficacy mechanism also plays a central role in human agency and motivation … It is partly on the basis of self-percepts of efficacy that people choose what to do, how much effort to mobilize for given activities, and how long to persevere at them." So our perceived ability will alter over time based on both internal and external conditions, such as our state and trait self-esteem, and the perceived difficulty of the task at hand.

Furthermore, this assumption, and those made by Holmes and Holmes (2002) discussed previously, violates a basic principle of criminal profiling—that modus operandi behavior is not static, with Douglas and Munn (1992) suggesting that it is both dynamic and malleable, and Hazelwood and Warren (2003) suggesting that:

> *In serial sexual crimes, the MO evolves quite rapidly over time and can present significant changes in a period of only weeks or months. This evolution manifests itself as a result of experience, the natural process of maturation, and the education, criminal or otherwise, of the offender.*

Mokros and Alison (2002) tested the homology assumption with a sample of 100 male stranger rapes. The results were presented across three domains: age, sociodemographic features, and criminal history. The results show the following (pp. 37–39):

> *Test of the homology assumption with respect to age*
>
> *If the homology assumption is correct, two offenders with close centroids will be within a similar age range. To test whether there is a positive correlation between centroid distance and age difference, two matrices were calculated. One contained the Euclidean distances between the centroids for each offender; the other comprised the age differences of all offenders.*
>
> …

> *The comparison of the two matrices yielded a Spearman's rho rank-ordered correlation of $r_s = -0.01$ ($p < 0.001$). Hence, there is no linear relationship between age and offense behavior: In the sample, offenders with smaller age differences did not have closer centroids. With respect to age, the null hypothesis must be retained.*
>
> *Test of the homology assumption for sociodemographic features*
>
> *Concerning sociodemographic features, the list of variables is limited to the following: non-European ethnic background, unemployment, unskilled labor, living circumstances (scored if the offender lived alone), and previous imprisonment/detention. This yields 48 offenders for whom information on all five variables was available.*
>
> . . .
>
> *Analogously, the same 48 offenders were compared with respect to their crime scene actions.... [This means that] there is no positive linear relationship between the five sociodemographic features analyzed and offense behavior. In the sample, offenders who are more similar with respect to sociodemographic features do not display any significant similarity in their style of offending. With respect to sociodemographic features, the null hypothesis must be retained.*
>
> *Test of the homology assumption for previous convictions*
>
> *The previous convictions were examined in 12 categories: theft, burglary (both dwelling and/or nondwelling), violence minor, violence major, criminal damage, damage endanger life, public order/drunkenness, motor vehicle crime, drugs (both possession and/or supply), indecent exposure, indecent assault, and rape of a female. They were coded as present if an offender had at least one conviction in a given category, either as a juvenile and/or as an adult.*
>
> . . .
>
> *In the sample, there is no positive linear relationship between the 12 previous conviction variables and the offender's crime scene actions. Offenders who display some resemblance in their criminal histories do not commit their rape offenses in similar ways. As is the case for the sociodemographic variables, the small correlation observed in the sample is in the direction opposite to the one predicted by the hypothesis. For previous convictions the null hypothesis cannot be refuted (i.e., there is no positive linear relationship with the domain of offense behavior).*

Retaining the null hypothesis means that rapists who display a similar style of offending are not similar with respect to their background characteristics. In other words, there is no support for the homology assumption.

Woodhams and Toye (2007) also considered the homology assumption as part of their study on serial commercial robberies. As did Mokros and Alison (2002), Woodhams and Toye failed to find support for the homology assumption on the offender characteristics of age, ethnicity, employment status, criminal history, and distance traveled from home to the offense location. Woodhams and Toye suggest that it is possible that this relates to the three different robbery styles that share some offense characteristics, a result of the offense characteristics included, and the selection of just one offender from a team to represent the offense. Despite noting these possible reasons for the lack of support, it is also possible that there is another reason: The homology assumption is nothing more than a nice theory.

This all reduces to the following: Inductive methods rely almost exclusively on the comparison of a crime to other similar crimes. This must occur both within the offender's crimes (consistency) and between this offender's crimes and those of like offenders (homology). Without either two conditions, inductive profiling simply cannot be upheld. This chapter demonstrates the following in this regard: (1) Consistency simply cannot be assumed, especially in the absence of a thorough crime reconstruction, and (2) homology cannot ever be assumed, especially in light of the findings of Mokros and Alison (2002), Woodhams and Toye (2007), and an array of other research.

The Problems of Induction

Inductive profiling as a means of forming theories is both necessary and useful, but using it as the sole basis for developing conclusions is improper. This section deals with the problems of induction as they relate specifically to consistency and homology.

The Problem of Reliability

The general "problem of induction," as Karl Popper (2003) put it, is that we can never know if we are dealing with a statistical average or a statistical anomaly (reliability). In reality, any inductive inference is an untested theory based on what has happened in the past; it may or may not have been studied or recalled properly, and it may or may not happen again. Hoping does not make it so.

Unfortunately, inductive profiling is easier and less time-consuming than its deductive counterpart. This makes it a more attractive prospect for anyone who prefers to expend little effort. Little to no examination of the physical evidence in a case need be conducted and subsequently less analyst training is required. In practice, the specific behavioral evidence in a particular case is often assumed by inductive analysts based on their research or experience rather than established by any scientific examination of case facts.

The inductive profiler also relies heavily, and even blindly, on the interpretations of others, which is a practice historically fraught with peril. The following provides one such case.

The USS Iowa

In 1989, an explosion aboard the USS *Iowa* prompted the Naval Investigative Service (NIS; now NCIS) to call for assistance from the Federal Bureau of Investigation (FBI). Roy Hazelwood and Richard Ault of the Behavioral Analysis Unit were sent to conduct an Equivocal Death Analysis of Clayton Hartwig who, it was assumed, caused the blast as a result of a rebuffed homosexual advance.

In this case, the Investigations Subcommittee and Defense Policy Panel of the Committee on Armed Services House of Representatives (1990, p. 39) found that the base investigation conducted by the Naval Investigative Service was lacking:

The criminal investigation conducted by the NIS agents was a key part of the Navy's overall investigation of the USS Iowa *explosion. The subcommittee staff investigation and our three days of hearings raised a number of important concerns relating to the conduct of the NIS investigation.*

The subcommittee believes the scope of the NIS investigation was too quickly narrowed to focus on Clayton Hartwig. This might have caused the NIS to miss evidence that would have implicated other individuals as suspects. Every one of the 1,000 crewmen had access to the turret and could have planted an explosion there. In addition, NIS agents seemed to focus almost exclusively on Hartwig's explosives knowledge and suicidal tendencies.

This narrow focus became crucial to making the Navy's case that Hartwig committed suicide and murder.

Given that this criticism brings the known facts of the case into question, it would seem problematic to proceed with a profile on the basis of it. However, this is exactly what was done, and not surprisingly it brought scorn from the Committee (1990, p. 42):

Because the FBI's psychological profile was key to making the Navy's case, the subcommittee examined the process used by the FBI to reach its conclusion. The two chief areas of concern were the quality of the material upon which the analysis was based and the degree of certainty of the opinion.

To begin with, the profile was prepared by two FBI Special Agents assigned to the FBI National Center for the Analysis of Violent Crime.

An equivocal death is a death whose manner (i.e., homicide, suicide, or accident) has not been resolved through normal investigative activities. While these two Special Agents have experience working with such profiles, having compiled some 30 analyses in the last several years, neither of them are licensed psychologists with experience dealing with the multitude of behavior that may be manifest in an individual's personality. Both Special Agents have advanced degrees in counseling.

This lack of licensing is especially crucial when the material that they analyze becomes suspect. In this case the preponderance of the material came from interviews conducted and provided to the FBI by the NIS. As the subcommittee found earlier, serious questions were raised about the leading nature or bias introduced in the interviews by the NIS interviewing agents. Some witnesses denied making statements to NIS that are significant to the profile, chiefly that concerning Hartwig's alleged teenage suicide gesture. We know that, in at least one instance, the witness recanted several portions of his testimony, but was still considered as a reliable witness. The NIS inquiry was a criminal inquiry focused on some very specific aspects of Hartwig's and Kendall Truitt's personalities.[7] *These interviews in no way serve as a collection of clinical information on which a reliable analysis may be based.*

[7] Hartwig was the sailor accused of causing the explosion, whereas it was Truitt's alleged rebuff that led Hartwig to cause the explosion.

> *This leads to the second concern of the subcommittee—the degree of certainty of the opinion. Given the questionable nature of material upon which the analysis was based—and that FBI personnel in cases like these do not conduct an active investigation of themselves—it seems to the subcommittee that some caveats on the FBI's conclusion should have been made clear to the Navy, even if only that certain significant information, such as prior counseling and school records, interviews with teachers, parents and friends, was not available to the FBI for review.*

In his excellent review of the case, Thompson (1999, p. 356) provides a similarly scathing account of the inductive Equivocal Death Analysis in this case and the lack of effort made to substantiate or corroborate witness statements and evidence:

> *On December 21, the third and final day of the hearings held in the Rayburn House Office Building, FBI psychological profiler Richard Ault was asked by Representative Mavroules if he had discussed the case with Dr. Froede. Ault said he had not. Had he even examined the autopsy reports? He hadn't done that, either. Mavroules told Ault that the medical examiner had ruled that all 47 deaths were accidental. "That is his opinion, and we have our opinion," Ault said, somewhat churlishly. Mavroules asked Hazelwood if he were sure that the material NIS had provided him was factual. "No, sir," Hazelwood replied, adding that it wasn't his job to corroborate information.*

In fact, Hazelwood's specific justification for not questioning the evidence he and Ault were given was that when getting involved in an investigation with an outside agency, FBI profilers assume that they are working with professionals who have done their job. Therefore, no evaluation of the information coming from another agency is made.

The danger of relying blindly on information collated by others should be perfectly clear. In fact, it violates the very standards of practice that dictate evidence-based profiling. As this approach is based on physical evidence, considerations of physical evidence should be paramount. As discussed by Thornton (2006, p. 37):

> *We are interested in physical evidence because it may tell a story. Physical evidence—properly collected, properly analyzed, and properly interpreted—may establish the factual circumstances at the time the crime occurred. In short, the crime may be reconstructed. Our principal interest is ultimately in the reconstruction, not the evidence per se ... Also, along with this ethos is an ethic—a moral obligation to maintain the integrity of the processes by means of which the reconstruction is accomplished ... "Getting it right" involves more than guessing it correctly. It necessitates a systematic process. It involves the proper recognition of the physical evidence, the winnowing of the relevant wheat from the irrelevant chaff, and the precise application of logic, both inductive and deductive. The process is not trivial.*

The uncritical reliance on this, or any information from others, is a potentially dangerous practice. It is incumbent on the profiler, not the client, to establish the veracity of the information they work with and from. For some, questioning the work product of others may be considered professionally impolite, but for the analyst passing on the information who has actually done the work, or performed a competent analysis, they will be more than happy to show their workings. If the opposite proves true, and they get angry at any request to prove their work, suspicions should be raised as the fear of discovery of ineptitude may be the basis for their anger.

Without a competent investigation and forensic analysis to establish the facts of a case, and an evaluation of the quality of any evidence provided, it is not possible for the profiler to accurately infer related behavioral evidence. Conclusions about the meaning of behaviors in this context will be irrelevant when it cannot be reasonably established that anything actually occurred. Such a context also makes comparisons between cases irrelevant because the analyst cannot be certain whether the behavior he or she is comparing from one case to another did in fact occur. In short, profilers have a duty to evaluate the quality of what they are given so any conclusions that follow will be based on accurate information and, therefore, relevant. They are admonished not to assume reliability, facts, or behaviors for the purposes of their analysis—an all too common practice.

If a profiler is unable to assess the quality of the evidence he or she has been given, then this identifies an important training need. The profiler should remove himself or herself as inexpert from any case when confronted with evidence that he or she is unfamiliar with or cannot evaluate with respect to quality, or the profiler should seek the advice of colleagues who are able to make such a determination.

The Problem of Relevance

A second major problem with inductive methods, and one that is directly aligned to notions of consistency and homology, is the relevance of the literature providing the average for reference. For a better understanding, consider the following example from Alison, Goodwill, and Alison (2005, p. 257):

> *Offender's age The offender is likely to be within an age range of 28 to 35 (CATCHEM). However, age has proven an extremely difficult variable to "profile." No suspect should be eliminated solely on the basis that he does not fall within the profiled age range.*
>
> *Although the average age of child sexual murderers in Boudreaux, Lord, and Dutra's (1999) study was 27 years old with the great majority under 30, the CATCHEM data indicates that when the victim's body is transported from the scene of the murder the offender's likely age group is around 30 to 35 years old. Offenders who do not transport their victims tend to be younger, around age 18 to 25 years old.*

Here, the CATCHEM database is used as the standard for reference from which offender comparisons are drawn. These comparisons provide the basis for the offender characteristics given in the profile, which is simply a reiteration of past research findings. As seen, there is little reference to the evidence or victim in the case at hand, with much of the report being no more than a general summary of research conducted on similar crimes or crime in general. This is clearly problematic in that it presents this offender not as an individual but as an assembly of averages. This is especially apparent when it is noted that for each crime of a similar type, the profile offered using this method would be (and often is) virtually identical, regardless of case specifics. Perhaps most troubling is the authors' own admission that the research is drawn from jurisdictions different than that in which the crime being profiled was committed. This raises the question of cross-cultural validity and reliability.

The Problem of Trait Reliance

Another major problem with induction related to consistency and homology is the reliance on trait descriptions of the offender. What this means is that the behaviors of the offender at the time of the crime are believed to represent the offender's general personality, not only now but also at some time in the future (Petherick, 2008; see Chapter 2). In other words, an offender who displays anger at the crime scene is believed to be generally angry in his or her daily life, as suggested by the theory of interpersonal coherence. The link between personality and profiling is made clear in Kocsis (2006, p. xii):

> *Today, with the luxury of hindsight, the development of profiling can be seen as akin to the field of personality theory. Within the disciplines of psychology and psychiatry, there exists an accepted consensus in the existence of a conceptual construct known as the mind. Although there is agreement in the concept of the mind, there are numerous rival approaches or theories that attempt to explain the nature and operation of the mind. A few examples of these differing approaches or "personality theories" include the psychoanalytic, behaviorist, and biological theories. The work and research into profiling can be viewed in an analogous fashion. There appears to be a general consensus that profiling is a concept whereby crime behaviors can be interpreted for the purpose of making predictions concerning the probable offender's characteristics. Akin to the varying personality theories, differing approaches have evolved over time that propose how crime behaviors are interpreted or profiled.*

The association between studies of criminal groups and the inference of the characteristics of one offender can be seen in Canter (1995, p. 344), where it is stated that "by considering empirical results from the study of actions of a large number of criminals it has been possible to propose both theories and methodologies that elaborate the relationship between an offender's actions and his or her characteristics." The problem inherent in this assumption is best stated by Theodore Reik in *The Unknown Murderer* (1945, p. 42): "It is still not sufficiently realized that the criminal at the moment of the act is a different man from what he is after it—so much so that one would sometimes think them two different beings."

The Relevance of Risk Assessment Research

The problem of relying too heavily on statistical averages is not peculiar to profiling, and one of the most damning indictments on using a statistical average comes from the domain of risk assessment. A prediction of whether someone poses a risk of violence in the future is not a far cry from the predictive analysis made by inductive profilers, who argue for the traits a person will exhibit at some point in the future. Risk assessment tools have come and gone, and like many areas of social science inquiry, this field has seen revision, evolution, and revolutions in the practices that are endorsed and applied.

Three generations of risk assessment practices have been identified (Ogloff & Davis, 2005), which have presumably come about because of changes in the way the risk assessment process is perceived and practiced. The first of these involved relatively unstructured assessments of an individual made by the clinician. These clinical assessments of risk have great similarity to diagnostic evaluations in criminal profiling, a method in which clinicians bring their experience with personality and psychopathology to bear in determining the profile of the current offender (Badcock, 1997; Boon, 1997; Wilson, Lincoln & Kocsis, 1997). The second generation of risk assessment, brought about largely by dissatisfaction with previous idiosyncratic appraisals, utilized statistical models for risk assessment, which also considered situational factors in the determination of risk. The third generation saw a more critical application of risk assessment appraisals, moving beyond dichotomous classifications of "dangerous" or "not dangerous" to include risk factors for violence, harm, and risk level (Ogloff & Davis, 2005). Similar to the previous generation, predictive statistical models are employed to maintain an objective assessment of risk; however, these are balanced with the clinical judgment of the analyst. Thus, statistical assessments and clinical judgment work in concert to give an overall determination of a person's risk, providing a balance between clinical and statistical models.

This historical examination of risk assessment provides us with an enlightening view on modern practice and serves as more than a lesson in the determination of risk. This illustrates that, over time, an opinion developed entirely through the experiences of an individual (the knowledge of one) was deemed to be inaccurate, and so debate turned to the suitability of research (the knowledge of many) for answers. However, years of practice also found that the knowledge of many was largely unsuited to predicting individual behaviors, and so the field turned to a combination of knowledge between one and many, weighing actuarial predictors against individual experiences. From this example, it can be suggested that idiosyncratic models provide for more bias and therefore more error. However, of greatest importance here is the recognition also of the dangers of actuarial judgment on its own, despite the fact that introducing this method was likely based on the goal of increased objectivity into the process as a whole. Most notably, the problem with actuarial methods lies in acknowledging the degree to which group studies can be used to predict the behavior of individuals.

This problem is best articulated by Arthur Conan Doyle through his fictional character Sherlock Holmes in *The Sign of Four* (Doyle, 2002, p. 60): "You can, for example, never foretell what any one man will do, but you can say with precision what an average number will be up to."

The relevance of group predictions to individual cases was put to the test by Hart, Michie, and Cooke (2007), who assessed two widely used and accepted actuarial instruments for the assessment of risk: the Violence Risk Appraisal Guide (the VRAG) and the Static-99. Hart et al.

provided in their literature review a summary of the risks posed by generalizing from the population to the individual (p. 61):

> *Suppose a public opinion survey of 500 eligible voters found that 54% expressed their intent to cast ballots for candidate Smith in an upcoming election. This information allows one to forecast with reasonable confidence that candidate Smith will be elected by another group-namely, the general electorate. However, this same information does not allow one to predict the behavior of a randomly selected voter with great confidence. Even though, in the absence of other relevant information, the most rational prediction is that every single voter will cast a ballot for candidate Smith, these individual predictions frequently will be wrong. So, to return to the ARAI example above, we need to know the margin of error for predictions made using Test X that a given person, such as Jones, will commit violence.*

It was these margins of error that Hart and colleagues examined. Without delving into the specific statistical results of the study, the confidence intervals of both instruments were examined. The results of the study and the suitability of group estimates to individual cases are best summarized in their discussion (p. 63):

> *Our analyses indicated that two popular ARAIs used in risk assessment have poor precision. The margins of error for risk estimates made using the tests were substantial, even at the group level. At the individual level, the margins of error were so high as to render the test results virtually meaningless. Our findings are consistent with Bohr's conclusion that predicting the future is very difficult.*
>
> *Our findings likely come as no surprise to many people. The difficulties of predicting the outcomes for groups versus individuals—whether in the context of games of chance or of violence risk assessments—are intuitively obvious.*

In line with the findings of Hart, Michie, and Cooke (2007), Meloy (1998, p. 8) provides a similar warning with regard to stalking that applies equally to the current discussion:

> *Nomothetic (group) studies on threats and their relationship to behavior are not necessarily helpful in ideographic (single case) research on risk management, beyond the making of risk probability statements if the stalker fits closely into the reference group. Such studies may overshadow the commonsense premise that threats have one of three relationships to subsequent violence in single stalking cases: They exhibit violence, they disinhibit violence, or they have no relationship to the individual's violence. Careful scrutiny of the subject's threat/violence history should be the investigative focus when this relationship is analyzed in an individual stalking case; and the importance, or weight, of threats in a risk management situation should be determined by searching for the presence of other factors that may aggravate or mitigate violence (Monahan & Steadman, 1994).*

The relevance of this passage to the current discussion on profiling is evident. However, to avoid any confusion, the following conclusions are restated:

1. Nomothetic knowledge is not necessarily helpful in understanding individual cases.
2. Probability statements can really only be made if the subject falls within the reference group; however, we can never know the degree to which the subject fits within the reference group in profiling until after the offender is caught.
3. A careful scrutiny of the individual case should be the investigative focus.

The Problem of Case Linkage

Although case linkage will be discussed at length in Chapter 7, this practice is directly influenced by considerations of consistency and homology, so it is worthy of some separate treatment here.

With inductive methods, case linkage rests almost entirely on the assumption of behavioral consistency—that is, offenders who commit two or more crimes will behave similarly, or consistently, between the various offenses. In fact, this is absolutely necessary in the statistical assessment of crimes to determine whether the same offender or group of offenders is responsible. However, the practice is also problematic on a number of fronts.

The following discussion is by no means exhaustive, but it rounds out the discussion of consistency and homology. A number of factors need to be considered. First, although research has shown some evidence for consistency (see Woodhams & Toye, 2007; Salfati & Bateman, 2005; Santilla, Fritzon & Tamelander, 2005, among others), there are a number of methodological and practical problems that may render the research invalid. These include the type of crime involved, the target (property or personal), the inaccurate recording of information in police offense databases (e.g., the recording of preliminary, unverified data instead of established case facts), the use of controlled substances by offenders making their behavior more unpredictable, or the staging of crime scenes to mislead or hamper investigative efforts.

Perhaps most notable among the problems with extant research are the domains on which consistency has been found. To date, consistent offender behaviors are assessed or found on the basis of congruence in their modus operandi. These behaviors include anything that is done for the successful completion of the crime, such as disguising one's appearance or voice, cleaning up the crime scene and/or removing evidence, and planning. It is not a long bow to draw that the behavior of serial offenders will be more similar across offenses in those elements that allow them to successfully complete their crimes.

However, the cautious profiler will know that this cannot be assumed but must be investigated and established until all probabilities are exhausted. In other words, behaviors that help the offender evade capture are more likely to be repeated, whereas those that increase the offender's exposure to harm will be less likely to recur. Thus, using these behaviors as the basis for whether a series of crimes are linked borders on circular reasoning: Serial offenders are more likely to learn and adopt behaviors that are successful, behaviors that are successful are most predictive of case linkage, the crimes of serial offenders can be predictive of a given offender if measured on behaviors that are successful.

Grubin, Kelly, and Brundson (2001, p. 39) provide the following less than encouraging commentary on the issue of consistency and case linkage:

> *While the preceding chapters have demonstrated that behavioral consistency can be described across serial sexual attacks, it remains to be seen whether this can be translated into a methodology to identify linked offenses which can act as a screening procedure for offenses.*
>
> *The methodology developed is based on the fact that the frequency with which each of the 256 possible combinations of domain types occurs can be easily determined. This allows a probability for each combination to be calculated. If the number of cases in the database was sufficiently large, then this probability would approach the actual rate that occurs in rape generally. Unfortunately, although large, data sets of this type, both in the UK and ViCLAS databases, are small in relative terms; many of the 256 possible combinations simply do not occur, while random fluctuations may mean that others are overrepresented.*

The authors go on to note that to account for this, they employed a statistical technique to smooth out the data. Having to potentially manipulate the data is one thing, but the larger problem that potentially leads to this manipulation is another. It is possible that, for logistical, political, or other reasons, crime data may simply not be presented to those agencies charged with its collation and distribution. This is problematic in those cases in which local, state, or federal databases are the basis for crime data on which a profile is based. One potentially concerning example is provided by Harwood (2012) who found:

> *In January, a 20-year-old Brazilian man named Luis Scavone and a teenage accomplice allegedly raped a 15-year-old girl on a Royal Caribbean holiday cruise. You'll find no mention of the crime, however, in the FBI and Coast Guard's database of cruise ship crime. Nor will you find mention of the other rape that allegedly happened on that same cruise. In fact, as Cruise Law News points out, you won't find a single instance of rape or sexual assault reported on any Royal Caribbean cruises this year.*
>
> *It's not as though such crimes are uncommon on cruises. In fact, sexual assaults on cruise ships have been such a problem that in 2010 Congress passed the Cruise Vessel Security and Safety Act of 2010 to increase regulation of the cruise industry, including a requirement that companies create policies to protect rape victims. It also required cruise lines to report serious crimes and missing persons to the FBI when they involved a U.S. citizen, a tally of which would be reported online quarterly on a website maintained by the U.S. Coast Guard. Within the reports, crimes would be broken down by cruise line, the type of offense and whether the perpetrator was a crew member or passenger. Previously, cruise ships voluntarily provided crime statistics to the FBI, but they weren't made public.*
>
> *But inexplicably, the FBI inserted language into the bill when it was in committee that has undermined the reporting requirement, raising uncomfortable questions of whether the Bureau is too close to an industry it now has jurisdiction over. The reporting change is all the more peculiar because it flies in the face of how law enforcement has recorded and reported crimes for almost a century.*
>
> ...

As the law took effect, the ICV began to notice that the number of crimes reported onboard cruise ships had all but vanished. For instance, in between December 2007 and October 2008, cruise lines voluntarily reported 363 crimes to the FBI, according to FOIA requests from South Florida's Sun Sentinel. But only 54 crimes were reported publicly between 2010 and the first quarter of 2012 under the FBI's new mandatory reporting methodology. In the third quarter of 2011, zero crimes were reported, even though the FBI admitted that alleged crimes had occurred.

In a late 2011 letter to the FBI, ICV president Jaime Barnett, who lost her daughter on a Carnival Cruise Line ship, decried the criminal reporting stats listed on the Coast Guard website. "We believe and firmly assert that the FBI reports, which are published by the USCG, are not in compliance with the actual reporting requirements as outlined in the law which clearly indicates that all alleged crimes recorded in each report, that are not under investigation by the FBI, be reflected," she wrote.

However, this problem is not confined to the UCR or any other single database for that matter. Woodhams and Toye (2007) also note a number of problems with extracting data from such databases. ViCLAS (Violent Crime Linkage Analysis System), an adaptation of the FBI's Violent Criminal Apprehension Program system, despite being widely adopted, has also been criticized (McKenna, 2005):

A national system to catch serial killers, rapists, and extortionists by "profiling" and comparing crimes across states has been slammed as ineffective because police in all but two states refuse to share information.

Senior Queensland police have complained that the Violent Crime Linkage Analysis System—set-up in 1997 after several high-profile serial killer cases—is not being supported by law enforcement across Australia.

The system, modeled on a hugely successful FBI program in the US, is coordinated by the Australian Crime Commission and involves an automated database that finds patterns between violent crimes.

It is the only behavioral analysis carried out on crimes in Australia and focuses on cases of rape, murder, attempted murders, extortions, and sexual offenses.

Each state police service, as well as the Australian Federal Police, is supposed to file detailed information on violent crime, which is then analyzed for similarities to other cases around the country.

But a federal parliamentary inquiry into the ACC has been told that the system is not working to its potential because of a lack of police cooperation.

Detective Superintendent Stephan William, head of the Intelligence Support Group of the Queensland Police Service, told a parliamentary hearing that the ACC needed to take charge and overhaul the system. "The database is not well supported uniformly across Australia," he said.

"I think it is fair to say that some jurisdictions make no contributions at all, and it will never reach its full potential while that occurs."

> *"We need to have that addressed at a national level one way or another so that we can decide how we are going to take it forward."*
>
> *Senior police told The Australian yesterday that only Queensland and Western Australia were "taking the database seriously."*
>
> *Under the system, an investigator fills out a 140-strong questionnaire, covering all details of the method of the crime and any detected links between the offender and victim.*
>
> *The ACC and NSW and Victorian police were yet to respond to the claims last night.*
>
> *But it is understood many jurisdictions are not cooperating because of a perception that the ACC is not properly analyzing the case information because of their focus on tackling organized crime.*
>
> *Superintendent William indicated to the inquiry that some of the blame could be directed to the ACC. "It is a difficult problem for them (ACC) because it does not really fit within their charter, but they have inherited it," he said.*
>
> *"But we, as a jurisdiction which has committed fairly heavily towards it, would like to see some sort of resolution on what is going to happen."*
>
> *At the time of the system's implementation, senior police said the high-profile cases of serial backpacker killer Ivan Milat and Sydney "granny killer" Kevin Glover had highlighted that Australian law enforcement lacked a capability for behavior analysis.*
>
> *In Queensland, the system was first used to track and convict "granny rapist" Gilbert Atwell.*

Atwell was sentenced to life imprisonment in 2000 for attacks on 11 elderly Brisbane women.

However, the problem starts long before the database is scoured for information or similarities. As with any research endeavor, the initial information must be collected and classified correctly (including being accurately recorded initially, in this context, the crime scene). Then the information must be passed along to be entered into the database, where it must be correctly entered by an analyst. That information must then be searched, usually through an assembly of algorithms or search strings, in a meaningful way. Once mined, the data may then be passed along to a researcher who may also have to impart some level of interpretation during the coding that provides the data for analysis. The whole process is ripe for human error.

As with so many areas of criminal profiling, these problems could be overcome by discarding statistical averages and generalizations and conducting thorough analyses of the current case through the employ of critical thinking, analytical logic, and the scientific method. Being able to reconstruct a crime and therefore to become intimate with its peculiarities will not only answer investigative and forensic questions but also prove to be a more valid basis on which to determine those crimes in a series that are the work of the same offender.

Conclusion

In light of the problems discussed in this chapter, there can be no question that continued reliance on consistency and homology, and by extension inductive profiling, is an error of considerable proportions. That such practices continue unabated is a testament to the low quality of training available to profilers, to the absence of behavioral scientists engaged in casework, to entrenched mind-sets and affiliations, and to the failure of those in the community to understand what they have read.

For behavioral consistency and the homology assumption to be even useful theories, a number of things must occur. First, a full and thorough reconstruction of the evidence must be undertaken to ensure that the behaviors being examined for consistency are valid. Similarly, one cannot assume that others are trained professionals who have done their jobs professionally. This is too often not the case. One also cannot assume that available research is representative or reflective of a particular offender or offender populations. For example, would research on single homicides be a suitable standard from which to assess the behavior of a serial murderer? Would general research on homicide, including domestic homicides, be a suitable standard from which to assess the behavior in a stranger killing? But this too is really only one problem among many, and speaks to nothing of the problem of criminal diversity, wherein one offender may be committing multiple crime types either at the same time or across a criminal career. In just one study, Smallbone and Wortley (2004) identified 362 adult males serving sentences for sexual offenses against children. The results of the study reveal a surprisingly high level of criminal diversity (p. 179):

> *Two hundred three offenders (64.4%) had previous convictions recorded in their criminal histories. Of these, 70 (34.5%) had previous convictions for sexual offenses and 187 (92.1%) had previous convictions for nonsexual offenses. Table 1 shows the percentages of the total sample of offenders with at least one recorded previous conviction for each offense type. Previous convictions were most common for theft (30%), traffic and motor vehicle offenses (24%), sexual offenses (22%), justice offenses (21%), and personal injury offenses (19%). Nonsexual offenses accounted for 86.3% of all criminal history offenses, with the full range of nonsexual offense categories represented. At least in terms of official convictions, the present sample was indeed criminally diverse.*

Another problem is the assumption that the way an offender behaves at a crime scene is reflective of his or her general personality traits. The presence of extreme emotions, alcohol, or drugs, among others (as discussed previously) can obscure an offender's personality, either at the time of the crime or at some time in the future. The severity of mental illness may wax and wane, individuals can vary their medication regime, or what led an offender to be angry at the crime may be fleeting or enduring.

It would seem that after reviewing the literature in the previous discussions, continued use of inductive methods may be a function of (1) the seemingly "scientific" status of inductive methods (Hicks & Sales, 2006) afforded by the use of numbers, in no small way a view continually peddled by those who employ them, and (2) the ease with which these methods can be taught and applied, noting that no real expertise in the behavioral or forensic sciences is necessary to use them. Neither argument on its own or combined provides a sufficient reason for their continued use.

It should be clear at this point that inductive methods are not only incorrect in their presentation of nomothetic research as relevant to individual cases but also misleading in that they present each individual offender as a hypothetical average offender from previous crimes, where these characteristics may have little to do with the crime at hand. Undoubtedly, profilers should all endeavor to be more selective in their approach to the way offender characteristics in criminal profiles are derived.

Despite these limitations, there continues to be a proliferation of methods relying on both consistency and homology in determining the characteristics of an unknown offender. Until this practice stops, profiling as a whole will continue to be viewed with skepticism and maintain its position as an underutilized investigative tool.

As for change, there is no time like the present.

Questions

1. The theory that the same offender will do the same thing across the span of time during different offenses is known as:
   a. Behavioral homology
   b. Behavioral consistency
   c. Homology assumption
   d. Interpersonal consistency
   e. None of the above
2. The study conducted by Mokros and Alison (2002) on 100 male stranger rapes found:
   a. Support for the homology assumption with respect to age
   b. Support for the homology assumption for sociodemographic features
   c. Support for the homology assumption for previous convictions
   d. Limited support for the homology assumption
   e. No support for the homology assumption
3. The problem of relevance relates to the relevance of the literature used in providing an average for reference. *True or false*?
4. The only profiling method that relies on the homology assumption is investigative psychology. *True or false*?
5. Discuss some general problems with crime data.

References

Alison, L., Goodwill, A., & Alison, E. (2005). Guidelines for profilers. In L. Alison (Ed.), *The forensic psychologist's casebook: Psychological profiling and criminal investigation.* Devon: Willan.

Badcock, R. (1997). Developmental and clinical issues in relation to offending in the individual. In J. L. Jackson & D. A. Bekerian (Eds.), *Offender profiling: Theory, research and practice.* Chichester: John Wiley and Sons.

Bandura, A., & Cervone, D. (1983). Self-evaluative and self-efficacy mechanisms governing the motivational effects of goal systems. *Journal of Personality and Social Psychology*, *45*(5), 1017–1028.

Boon, J. (1997). The contribution of personality theories to psychological profiling. In J. L. Jackson & D. A. Bekerian (Eds.), *Offender profiling: Theory, research and practice.* Chichester: John Wiley and Sons.

Canter, D. (1994). *Criminal shadows: Inside the mind of the serial killer*. London: Harper Collins.

Canter, D. (1995). In R. Bull & D. Carson (Eds.), *Psychology of offender profiling*. London: Handbook of Psychology in Legal Contexts Wiley.

Canter, D. (2004). Offender profiling and investigative psychology. *Journal of Investigative Psychology and Offender Profiling, 1*, 1–15.

Douglas, J., & Munn, C. (1992). The detection of staging and personation at the crime scene. In A. Burgess, A. Burgess, J. Douglas, & R. Ressler (Eds.), *Crime classification manual*. San Francisco: Jossey-Bass.

Doyle, A. C. (2002). *The complete sherlock holmes*. New Lanark, UK: Geddes & Grosset.

Grubin, G., Kelly, P., & Brundson, C. (2001). *Linking serious sexual assault through behavior home office*. London: Research Development and Statistics Directorate.

Hart, S. D., Michie, C., & Cooke, D. J. (2007). Precision of actuarial risk assessment instruments: Evaluating the "margins of error" of group v. individual predictions of violence. *British Journal of Psychiatry, 190*(49), 60–65.

Harwood, M. (2012). *Erasing cruise ship crime: Why did the FBI gut a bill requiring the cruise industry to report sexual assaults and rapes?* Salon. Retrieved 27 June 2012 from <http://www.salon.com/2012/06/25/erasing_cruise_ship_crime/singleton/>.

Hazelwood, R. R., & Warren, J. J. (2003). Linkage analysis: Modus operandi, ritual, and signature in serial sexual crime. *Aggression and Violent Behavior, 8*, 587–598.

Hicks, S. J., & Sales, B. D. (2006). *Criminal profiling: Developing an effective science and practice*. Washington, DC: American Psychological Association.

Holmes, R. M., & Holmes, S. T. (2002). *Profiling violent crimes: An investigative tool*. Thousand Oaks, CA: Sage.

Investigations Subcommittee and Defense Policy Panel of the Committee on Armed Services, (1990). *USS* Iowa *tragedy: An investigative failure*. Washington DC: US Government Printing Office.

Kocsis, R. N. (2006). *Criminal profiling: Principles and practice*. Totowa, NJ: Humana Press.

McKenna, M. (2005). States refusing to share crime data. *The Australian, November 8*

Meloy, J. R. (1998). *The psychology of stalking: Clinical and forensic perspectives*. Boston: Academic Press.

Mokros, A., & Alison, L. J. (2002). Is offender profiling possible? Testing the predicted homology of crime scene actions and background characteristics in a sample of rapists. *Legal and Criminological Psychology, 7*, 25–43.

Ogloff, J. R. P., & Davis, M. R. (2005). Assessing risk for violence in the Australian context. In D. Chappell & P. Wilson (Eds.), *Issues in Australian crime and criminal justice*. Sydney: Butterworths.

Petherick, W. A. (2005). *Serial crime: Theoretical and behavioral issues in behavioral profiling*. Boston: Academic Press.

Petherick, W. A. (2008). Criminal profiling. In P. R. Wilson & K. Fritzon (Eds.), *Forensic and criminal psychology: An Australian perspective*. Melbourne: McGraw-Hill.

Popper, K. (2003). *The logic of scientific discovery*. London: Routledge Classics.

Reik, T. (1945). *The unknown murderer*. New York: Prentice Hall.

Salfati, G., & Bateman, A. L. (2005). Serial homicide: An investigation of behavioral consistency. *Journal of Offender Psychology and Offender Profiling, 2*, 121–144.

Santilla, P., Fritzon, K., & Tamelander, A. L. (2005). Linking arson incidents on the basis of crime scene behavior. *Journal of Police and Criminological Psychology, 9*, 1–16.

Shoda, Y., Mischel, W., & Wright, J. C. (1994). Personality processes and individual differences. *Journal of Personality and Social Psychology, 67*(4), 674–687.

Smallbone, S. W., & Wortley, R. K. (2004). Criminal diversity and paraphilic interests among males convicted of sexual offenses against children. *International Journal of Offender Therapy and Comparative Criminology, 48*(2), 175–188.

Thompson, C. C. (1999). *A glimpse of hell: The explosion aboard the USS* Iowa *and its cover up*. New York: W. W. Norton and Co.

Thornton, J. I. (2006). The general assumptions and rationale of forensic identification. In D. Faigman, D. Kaye, M. Saks, & J. Sanders (Eds.), *Modern scientific evidence: The law and science of expert testimony* (Vol. 2). St. Paul: West Publishing.

Wilson, P. R., Lincoln, R., & Kocsis, R. N. (1997). Validity, utility and ethics of profiling for serial violent and sexual offenders. *Psychiatry, Psychology and Law, 4*(1), 1–12.

Woodhams, J., & Toye, K. (2007). An empirical test of the assumptions of case linkage and offender profiling with serial commercial robberies. *Psychology, Public Policy, and Law, 13*(1), 59–85.

4 Criminal Profiling Methods

Wayne Petherick

Introduction

As an investigative aid, criminal profiling has received a great deal of attention from academic audiences and popular culture (Petherick, 2003), and significant advances have been made in both practical and theoretical terms. Even though our collective knowledge of this area has grown, there is still much about the process that remains a mystery. For example, there is little acknowledgment or understanding of the logic or reasoning employed within the profiling process (see Chapter 2), or that there are indeed different methods employed within the profiling community. Of more concern is the fact that many practitioners continue to confuse these issues even in the face of overwhelming contradictory evidence. Just as serious is when practitioners cannot distinguish between methods, or when they practice one but pass it off as another.

It is the aim of this chapter to provide a theoretical and practical overview of the main criminal profiling methods in use. This includes a detailed analysis of the Federal Bureau of Investigation's (FBI) *Criminal Investigative Analysis*, Canter's *Investigative Psychology*, Rossmo's *Geographic Profiling*, and Turvey's *Behavioral Evidence Analysis*.[1]

[1]Although the individual proponents would probably argue that the individual methods do not "belong" to them, those listed are considered the primary or leading practitioners of each method and are generally accredited with their development. In addition, the generic method employed by mental health professionals known as *diagnostic evaluations* is also addressed. Each section provides not only a comprehensive review of the theoretical and practical underpinnings of each approach but also a summary of critiques.

Criminal Profiling: What Is It?

In a broad sense, a *criminal profile* is an attempt to provide personality and behavioral clues about offenders based on their behavior and the evidence they leave behind. "It is an inferential process that involves an analysis of … their interactions with the victim and crime scene, their choice of weapon and their use of language among other things" (Petherick, 2003, p. 173).

According to Geberth (1996, p. 710), "a criminal personality profile is an educated attempt to provide investigative agencies with specific information as to the type of individual who would have committed a certain crime." Holmes and Holmes (2002) simply cite this definition from Geberth. Bennett and Hess (2001), in their textbook on criminal investigation, do not specifically define profiling; instead, they classify it according to its goal: identifying an individual's mental, emotional, and psychological characteristics.

The FBI and its associates no longer use the term *criminal profiling* to describe their method of offender behavior analysis. This term and others (e.g., psychological profiling and behavioral profiling) have been replaced by the blanket term *Criminal Investigative Analysis* (CIA), which covers not only profiling but also other services such as indirect personality assessment, equivocal death analysis, and trial strategy. Criminal profiling under this paradigm is aimed at (Hazelwood, Ressler, Depue & Douglas, 1995, p. 116):

> *Providing the client agency with the characteristics and traits of an unidentified offender that differentiate him from the general population. These characteristics are set forth in such a manner as to allow those who know and/or associate with the offender to readily recognize him.*

Thus, it should be apparent that despite the differences in approach or author, there is a degree of unanimity in the ways profiling is defined. Generally, any attempt to interpret an offender's actions to suggest features of his or her personality and behavior constitutes criminal profiling. There is less agreement, however, about who may be a criminal profiler.

One need not call oneself a criminal profiler to offer profile characteristics. In fact, a number of other professions have trodden into areas that have historically been the province of criminal profilers. Consider the following example from Thomas Noguchi, MD, Chief Medical Examiner (reproduced exactly as per the original document):

> *Medicolegal Opinion*
>
> *For the purpose of assisting the investigation of law enforcement agencies on the death of Janine Katherine Kirk, I submit the following opinions.*
>
> *My opinions were based on injury pattern, the circumstances surrounding the death, information during the discovery and the recovery of the body at the scene. The following observations were made to predict certain characteristics of the assailant involved in the case. This type of work has been known in a field of forensic sciences as a profiling of the assailant.*

Physical Characteristics of the Assailant

1. *The person is a male, strong and much taller than that of the decedent. In order to deliver a concentrated blunt force to a small target area, above mentioned physical characteristics would be required.*
2. *The person would be right-handed, thus, he would be able to deliver blows to the left side of the victim. The blows were delivered from his right to left direction.*
3. *The person delivered his blows to the face of the victim as he was facing the decedent.*
4. *Severe blows to the back of the neck causing severe bruises to the skin and underlining muscles.*

Psychological Characteristics

1. *The person would be acquainted with and known by a decedent, thus, the assailant was able to approach her without difficulty.*
2. *The person had ability to plan in advance and execute his plan, including the disposition of the body.*

Furthermore, one need not be a capable or competent profiler to use the label. As in many areas of endeavor, this has led to a distinct stratification of skills and abilities. Unfortunately, a substandard practitioner in this area has the very real capacity to ruin not only his or her own reputation but also that of other practitioners and the field in general. One bad experience may lead all profilers to be tarred with the same brush and probably contributes to a great deal of the skepticism voiced by a number of critics. For instance, Godwin (1985, p. 276), in one widely cited criticism, believes that profilers "play a blind man's bluff, groping in all directions in the hope of grabbing a sleeve. Occasionally they do, but not firmly enough to seize it, for the behaviorists producing them must necessarily deal in generalities and types." Liebert (1985) is also critical, stating that superficial behavioral profiling that rigidly reduces serial murder to a few observable parameters has the potential to lead an investigation astray.

The previous chapter discussed how a profile can be inductive or deductive, and it should be noted that the style of reasoning employed in a process can be identified even before the individual methods discussed next are considered. A method is identified as inductive or deductive based on the primary style of logic or reasoning employed in developing offender characteristics, with most methods being inductive. The first four methods presented here employ inductive reasoning. The last, behavioral evidence analysis, employs deductive reasoning.

Criminal Investigative Analysis

Perhaps one of the best known methods is that devised by the FBI. The method chiefly arose out of one core study conducted between 1979 and 1983, for which federal agents interviewed offenders about their crimes. The goal was to determine whether there are any consistent features across offenses that may be helpful in classifying these offenders, with a number of publications arising directly from this study (Burgess, Hartman, Ressler, Douglas & McCormack, 1986; Douglas, Ressler, Burgess & Hartman, 1986; Ressler & Burgess, 1985; Ressler, Burgess & Douglas, 1988; Ressler, Burgess, Douglas, Hartman & D'Agostino, 1986; Ressler, Burgess, Hartman, Douglas & McCormack, 1986).

A mainstay of the FBI approach has been the organized/disorganized dichotomy, which distinguishes offenders by virtue of the sophistication of their offenses. Because this system was in use before the research was conducted, this is perhaps best thought of as a validation study with the terminology first appearing in *The Lust Murderer* in 1980 by Hazelwood and Douglas. The researchers state that one of the quantitative goals of the study was to "identify the differentiating characteristics used by the BSU [Behavioral Sciences Unit] agents to classify sexual murderers and determine whether or not these variables were valid statistically" (Burgess & Ressler, 1985, p. 4).

An *organized offender* is often said to be psychopathic and is literally organized in most facets of his or her life, cleaning up his or her crime scenes, removing weapons and evidence, and even attempting to hide the body. *Disorganized offenders* are often said to be psychotic and make no such attempt to clean up their crime scenes, remove evidence, or hide the body. Although the association has been discarded in most publications on the subject, some authors continue to associate organized crimes with psychopathic offenders and disorganized crimes with psychotic offenders (Geberth, 1996; Holmes & Holmes, 2002), although whether this holds true in practice is contended. Ressler and Shachtman (1992, pp. 113–114) note that the terminology had to be "dumbed down" for the police, who typically lacked training in psychology and psychiatry:

> *To characterize the types of offenders for police and other law enforcement people, we needed to have terminology that was not based on psychiatric jargon. It wouldn't do much good to say to a police officer that he was looking for a psychotic personality if that police officer had no training in psychology.... Instead of saying that a crime scene showed evidence of a psychopathic personality, we began to tell the police officer that such a crime scene was "organized" and so was the likely offender, while another and its perpetrator might be "disorganized," when mental disorder was present.*

At its simplest, the model works by associating factors from the crime scene (Table 4.1) with a criminal's personality (Table 4.2).

Thus, if the crime scene appeared planned and controlled with restraints used, where there were aggressive acts with the body prior to death, and the weapon or evidence was absent (ergo, an organized crime scene), it could be said that the offender would be of above-average intelligence, socially competent, with a controlled mood during the crime, and so forth (ergo, an organized offender).

Confusingly, although the original sample was composed of offenders in sexual homicides, the terminology of the original FBI study has been adopted in the classification of other crimes.

Table 4.1 Crime Scene Characteristics of the Organized and Disorganized Offender

Psychopathic (Organized) Crime Scene Characteristics	Psychotic (Disorganized) Crime Scene Characteristics
Offense planned	Offense spontaneous
Victim is a targeted stranger	Victim or location known
Personalizes victim	Depersonalizes victim
Controlled conversation	Minimal conversation
Crime scene reflects overall control	Crime scene random and sloppy
Demands submissive victim	Sudden violence to victim
Restraints used	Minimal restraints used
Aggressive acts prior to death	Sexual acts after death
Body hidden	Body left in plain view
Weapon/evidence absent	Weapon/evidence often present
Transports victim	Body left at death scene

From Ressler and Burgess (1985)

Table 4.2 Offender Characteristics of the Organized and Disorganized Offender

Psychopathic (Organized) Offender Characteristics	Psychotic (Disorganized) Offender Characteristics
Average to above-average intelligence	Below-average intelligence
Socially competent	Socially inadequate
Skilled work preferred	Unskilled work
Sexually competent	Sexually incompetent
High birth order	Low birth order
Father's work stable	Father's work unstable
Inconsistent childhood discipline	Harsh discipline as a child
Controlled mood during crime	Anxious mood during crime
Use of alcohol with crime	Minimal use of alcohol
Precipitation situational stress	Minimal situational stress
Living with partner	Living alone
Mobility with car in good condition	Lives/works near the crime scene
Follows crime in news media	Minimal interest in the news media
May change jobs or leave town	Minimal change of lifestyle

Despite the limitations of the original study, organized and disorganized labels have also appeared in the area of stalking (Wright, Burgess, Laszlo, McCrary & Douglas, 1996; implied in Geberth, 1996) and arson (Douglas, Burgess, Burgess & Ressler, 1992; Kocsis, Irwin & Hayes, 1998).

According to Ressler et al. (1988), the CIA process is composed of six steps (ultimately five, with the final [ideal] stage being the apprehension of the offender).

Stage 1, profile inputs, involves the collection and integration of all the known material relating to the criminal offense, including but not limited to the physical evidence, police reports, and photographs/videos. In addition to autopsy photographs, aerial photographs and pictures of the crime scene are also needed, along with crime scene sketches with distances, directions, and scale (Douglas et al., 1986). Also during this stage, the victim is examined, including his or her "domestic setting, employment, reputation, habits, fears, physical condition, personality, criminal history, family relationships, hobbies, and social conduct" (p. 405).

Decision process models, the second stage, involves the integration of the various profiling inputs into patterns that may assist in determining the homicide type and style, intent, victim and offender risk, escalation, and time and location factors. Although not specifically discussed, it is likely that much of this information was drawn on for the *Crime Classification Manual*, a tool designed to "make explicit crime categories that have been utilized informally" (Douglas et al., 1992, p. 6). These include the following (Ressler et al., 1988, pp. 138–142):

> *Homicide Type and Style: A single homicide involves one victim and one homicidal event. A double homicide is two victims, with one event and one location, and a triple homicide is three victims in one location during one event. More than three victims is classified as a mass homicide.*
>
> *Primary Intent of the Murderer: The killer's primary intent could be criminal enterprise, emotional, selfish, cause specific, or sexual. Murder may not be the primary intent of the offender but may be engaged in to meet one of the above goals.*
>
> *Victim Risk: The victim risk is determined by looking at the victim's age, occupation, lifestyle, and the physical stature of the victim. Low-risk victims include those whose daily lives do not usually put them in harms' way, whereas a high-risk victim is targeted by a murderer who knows where they can find victims. Information about the victim can provide insight into the type of offender sought.*
>
> *Offender Risk: Like victim risk, the actions of the offender that may place them at risk are also of interest. The risks an offender places themselves at may indicate emotional maturity, personal stress, or confidence in the police.*
>
> *Escalation: This refers to the propensity of an offender to increase the nature of their criminal behavior, say, from voyeurism to rape, as well as an assessment of the likelihood of the offense being or becoming serial in nature.*
>
> *Time Factors: Several factors need to be considered here, and these include the time it took to kill the victim, to commit any additional acts with the body, and to dispose of the body. Additionally, the time of the day or night might also be important as it may provide information on the lifestyle or employment of the offender.*
>
> *Location Factors: Information about where the victim was first approached, and the location of the death and dump sites is similarly important. This may provide insight into whether the offender used a vehicle for transport.*

The third stage is crime assessment, where an attempt is made to reconstruct the sequence of events and victim and offender behaviors. Based on this information and that of the previous stages, decisions are made about the level of organization or disorganization of the offense, so it is primarily during this stage that the application of the typology comes into play. Other considerations include crime scene dynamics, motivation, and considerations of staging.

Stage 4 involves the actual criminal profile and provides insight into the offender's background, physical characteristics, habits, beliefs, values, and preoffense and postoffense behavior (Ressler et al., 1988). Once the profile has been compiled, it can be delivered to the investigative team and integrated into the inquiry by generating suspects and evaluating those already under consideration for their "fit." In a perfect world, this would lead to the final stage, apprehension. If a suspect is apprehended, the authors note that an interview should be conducted to establish the validity of the overall process.

Douglas and Burgess (1986, p. 9) suggest the following seven-step process, which they claim is similar to that used by clinicians in making a diagnosis:

1. Evaluation of the criminal act.
2. Comprehensive evaluation of the specifics of the crime scene(s).
3. Comprehensive analysis of the victim.
4. Evaluation of the preliminary police reports.
5. Evaluation of the medical examiner's autopsy protocol.
6. Development of profile with critical offender characteristics.
7. Investigative suggestions predicated on the construction of the profile.

Adapting the FBI's methodology, the Dutch profiling unit has taken this method a step further, attempting to address some of the concerns raised about the approach. While being staffed in part by profilers trained by the FBI, the unit adopts a more multidisciplinary approach because these profilers also work closely with investigators, psychologists, and legal professionals. Discussing the increasing role of crime analysts within Dutch police organizations, Jackson, van den Eshof, and de Kleuver (1997, p. 107) note the following:

> *This interest led to several initiatives, one of which was the setting up of an offender profiling unit within the National Criminal Intelligence Division of the National Police Agency. The task of that unit was to respond to requests from regional police forces for help and advice with criminal investigations, particularly for those involving serious contact crimes.*
>
> *When the service finally went into operation in September 1991, the unit's guiding principles and work methods bore a strong resemblance to FBI methods. However, from the beginning of the enterprise it was also recognized that to be effective, the unit had not only to be accountable to those it served, namely the Dutch police, but should also be actively involved in the scientific forum. This meant that research, including evaluation studies, should be carried out and the findings made public to ensure critical debate and opportunities for development.*

Thus, instead of just relying on subjective interpretation, intuition, and investigative experience, this unit tests its range of hypotheses about offenders and publishes the results, allowing for transparency in its operations. Ainsworth (2001) suggests this stands in stark contrast to the FBI, which was largely secretive about its work until agents such as John Douglas published their memoirs (Douglas & Olshaker, 1995). These individual biographical accounts may not be a good judge of their success, however (Ainsworth, 2001, p. 135):

> *This openness comes in marked contrast to the FBI's work where, in most cases, public scrutiny only became possible when ex-profilers wrote and published their memoirs....*

> *Even in such cases, the amount of detail which was provided hardly allowed for the scientific assessment of many of the claims. In addition, it seems likely that ex-profilers will speak at length about their successes but be noticeably more reticent about their failures.*

According to Jackson et al. (1997, p. 108), there are two principles guiding the development of the unit, each having consequences for their operations:

1. Offender profiling is a combination of detective experience and behavioral scientific knowledge. Given this perspective, it is not surprising that close links were quickly established with the Behavioral Science Unit of the FBI (as it was then called) and still continue to be maintained. A further consequence of this view is that the unit should be organized on multidisciplinary lines. The team comprises a police officer (trained at the FBI Academy at Quantico) working closely together with a forensic psychologist who is also a qualified lawyer (a further footnote in the chapter states that a second psychologist has joined the profiling unit).
2. An offender profile is not an end in itself, but it is purely an instrument for steering an investigation in a particular direction. Within Dutch police practice, offender profiling is not viewed as a product in itself, but simply as another management instrument to further the work of the detective team. This principle means that the profiler's description of a possible offender must always be coupled with practical advice and suggestions about how to proceed with the investigation at hand.

As noted, this method is the most prevalent today and the reasons for this are many and varied, including its ease of use, the legitimacy afforded the near mythical status of its developers,[2] and the range of literature available on it. Not all of this literature is flattering, and CIA has attracted considerable criticism.

Petherick and Turvey (2012) note a number of general shortcomings with this method, specifically citing problems with its application. Most notably, it is these authors' concern that classifying an offender based solely on the presentation of the crime scene may in some instances lead investigators astray. This is likely to occur when the offender or evidence dynamics change or obscure the physical evidence on which the assessment is made. Crimes involving the use of drugs, those during which the offender is interrupted, anger-motivated offenses, and staged offenses can all change the presentation of the crime scene on which determination of the offender's level of sophistication is made (i.e., whether the offender is organized or disorganized). This may lead the profiler to believe that authorities are dealing with a disorganized offender because of the presentation of the scene when they are actually confronted with the crime of an organized offender.

[2] Jenkins (1994, p. 70) notes that "this meant presenting the FBI's behavioral scientists (the 'mind hunters') as uniquely qualified to deal with the serial murder menace, and this interpretation became very influential. The mind hunter image of the BSU was initially presented in a series of high laudatory media accounts, which reinforced the prestige of the unit as the world's leading experts on serial violence."

A further problem with the method comes from the fact that there is no loading on the factors that make up each offense type. Put another way, there is no instruction on which of the offender characteristics may be of more importance in instances where you have mixed crime scene characteristics. Therefore, it may be a matter of subjects' judgment as to which of the organized and disorganized offender characteristics apply. This introduces a level of subjectivity into the process that may adversely affect the outcome and strain the method's validity.

On a methodological level, the sample size was relatively small (n = 36), not randomly selected, and the interviews relied heavily on self-report. In a small number of cases, the agents conducting the interview could not decide which category the offender fit into, so they were told to force the offender into either the organized or disorganized group (Ressler & Burgess, 1985). Each agent was essentially left to decide which category the offender belonged to, and no inter-rater reliability was conducted to determine if the offender had been correctly classified. With regard to the reliability of the study, it has never been replicated on an international level and so its application outside of the United States may also be questionable (Woodworth & Porter, 2001; Petherick, 2003).

Lastly, it has been noted that few offenders will fit neatly into either the organized or the disorganized category, and that most will fall somewhere between these two extremes (Ressler & Shachtman, 1992; Canter, Alison, Alison & Wentink, 2004; Petherick & Turvey, 2012). In the words of Ressler and Shachtman (1992, p. 180), "As with most distinctions, this one is too simple and too perfect a dichotomy to describe every single case. Some crime scenes, and some murderers, display organized as well as disorganized characteristics and we call those mixed."

Baker (2001) claims that the mixed category is less helpful to investigators. Moving to a continuum may decrease the method's strength in discriminating between types because an offender may change from organized to disorganized and vice versa throughout the course of his or her criminal career. This concern does not only apply to the application of the mixed category though, and this evolution (or de-evolution) represents a general problem with the approach.

In examining the literature on the involvement of FBI profilers in individual cases, there are a substantial number of less than flattering reports. It is not the purpose of this chapter to discuss these in depth, but the interested reader should consult Investigations Subcommittee and Defense Policy Panel of the Committee on Armed Services (1990); Darkes, Otto, Poythress, and Starr (1993); Kopel and Blackman (1997); Fox and Levin (1996); Thompson (1999); and Petherick and Turvey (2012).

Despite having as a backdrop an empirical study from the 1980s, CIA in application is a little more subjective. All told, with these profiles, over three quarters of the sample were given without any justification or justified with personal belief, reflecting the idiosyncratic nature of the method. A greater array of crimes were profiled by the CIA trained profilers with single homicide again being the most prolific (N = 7); followed by serial homicide (N = 4); serial rape and abduction (N = 2 cases each); and rape, stalking, threatening letters, and suicide all being profiled one time each.

From 19 FBI-based profiles there were a total of 312 characteristics offered. Of concern, two-thirds of the sample (65.7%) offered no justification at all for the characteristics given, with only 16.1% (N = 43) of the characteristics being reasoned from the available evidence. What's more, despite wide reference to the FBI's early study that may lead one to believe statistical corollaries play a role, just under 6% (N = 20) employed statistics or research, and about 12% (N = 40) cited the profiler's own opinion or belief as cause. In total, there was a range of 28 characteristics offered, with a minimum of 4 (Profile 28) and a maximum of 32 (Profile 25) characteristics. The mean number of characteristics was 16.4 (SD = 9). In individual profiles, the greatest range was 23 characteristics offered but not justified (Min = 2, Max = 25), while the smallest range was 7 characteristics using statistics or actuarial justification (Min = 1, Max = 8). Despite the seventh stage of the profiling process, discussed by Douglas and Burgess (1986) as revolving around the development of investigative suggestions, only about 16% of the profiles from the CIA method provided this advice. This contradicts the purported goals and philosophies of the method discussed in the literature.

Investigative Psychology

As with CIA, investigative psychology (IP) identifies profiling as only one part of the overall process. The main advocate of this method is David Canter, a British psychologist who promotes a research approach to offender behavior. It is inductive and dependent on the quality and amount of data accumulated (McGrath, 2000). Although many inductive methods suffer from the same problems, Canter employs larger sample sizes than the FBI, continually conducting research and using more rigorous methodologies to expand knowledge (Egger, 1998; Petherick, 2003). Therefore, the conclusions are still inductive, but they are based on more empirically robust evaluations. According to the program's web site, IP provides a:

> *scientific and systematic basis to previously subjective approaches to all aspects of the detection, investigation, and prosecution of crimes. This behavioral science contribution can be thought of as operating at different stages of any investigation, from that of the crime itself, through the gathering of information and on to the actions of police officers working to identify the criminal then on to the preparation of a case for court.*

Canter has gone to great pains to differentiate IP from everyday profiling (Canter, 1998, p. 11):

> *So should psychologists be kept out of the investigation of crimes? Clearly, as the director of an institute of investigative psychology I do think that psychologists have much to offer to criminal, and other, investigations. My central point is to make a distinction between "profiling" and investigative psychology.*

Furthermore, to distinguish between IP and profiling approaches that are more idiosyncratic, Canter (1998, p. 11) notes the following:

> *Investigative psychology is a much more prosaic activity. It consists of the painstaking examination of patterns of criminal behavior and the testing out of those patterns of trends that may be of value to police investigators.... Investigative psychologists also accept that there are areas of criminal behavior that may be fundamentally enigmatic.*

This approach has five main components that provide a theoretical backdrop, commonly referred to as the five-factor model, as being reflective of an offender's past and present: interpersonal coherence, significance of time and place, criminal characteristics, criminal career, and forensic awareness.

Interpersonal coherence refers to the way people adopt a style of interaction when dealing with others (Canter, 1995). Canter believes that an offender will treat his victims in a similar way to that in which he treats other people in his daily activities—that is, there is some consistency in his relationships with others between offending and nonoffending behavior. A rapist who exhibits selfishness with friends, family, and colleagues will also exhibit selfishness with his victims. This belief is not unique to IP, and most profiling approaches rely on the notion of interpersonal coherence in developing offender characteristics (Petherick, 2003).

Because "interpersonal processes gain much of their psychological nuance from the time and place in which they occur" (Canter, 1989, p. 14), the *significance of time and place* also reflects some aspects of the offender's personality. That is, the time and place are often specifically chosen and thus provide further insight into an offender's actions in the form of mental maps. The suggestion here is that "an offender will feel more comfortable and in control in areas which he knows well" (Ainsworth, 2001, p. 199). Two considerations are important here—the specific location and the general spatial behavior, which is a function of specific crime sites (Canter, 1989). Canter (2003) has dedicated an entire work to these aspects, which are largely based on the theory of environmental criminology.

Criminal characteristics provide investigators with some idea about the type of crime they are dealing with. The idea is to determine "whether the nature of the crime and the way it is committed can lead to some classifications of what is characteristic … based upon interviews with criminals and empirical studies" (Canter, 1989, p. 14). This is an inductive component of the approach and, as it stands, is similar to attempts made by the FBI in applying the organized/disorganized typology.

Criminal career suggests that a criminal will behave in a similar way throughout a crime series, although it is acknowledged that there is some room for adaptation and change. This adaptation and change may be reflective of past experiences while offending. For example, a criminal may bind and gag a current victim based on the screams and resistance of a past victim (Canter, 1989). This aspect may reflect an evolution of modus operandi displayed by many offenders who learn through subsequent offenses and continue to refine their criminal behaviors. In addition, the nature and type of precautionary behaviors may provide some insight into the type of contact the offender has had with the criminal justice system.

Finally, *forensic awareness* may show an increase in learning based on past experience with the criminal justice system. A rapist may turn to using condoms in order to prevent the transfer of biological fluids and prevent subsequent DNA analysis. Perpetrators may well be sophisticated in that they will use techniques that hinder police investigations, such as the wearing of a mask or gloves, or attempt to destroy other evidence (Ainsworth, 2000).

Furthermore, there are five characteristics or clusters that are instructive to investigators. These are self-explanatory and include residential location, criminal biography, domestic/social characteristics, personal characteristics, and occupation/education history (Ainsworth,

2000). Although there is not necessarily any greater weighting placed on any of these profile features, Boon and Davies (1993) suggest that residential location and criminal history are most beneficial (again highlighting the emphasis that IP places on crime geography). Even a cursory examination of the literature arising from this paradigm shows a considerable focus on examinations of the offender's geographic behavior. In this way, the method shares many similarities with other approaches to geographic profiling detailed subsequently.

The criticisms of IP parallel those of other inductive approaches but include others that are more unique to the method. Considerable emphasis is placed on the use of statistical procedures in determining offender characteristics, with the most notable being multidimensional scaling or smallest space analysis (SSA). An SSA provides a graphical representation of the relationships between variables, with those that are closely correlated appearing closer together in the plot, and those not correlated being further apart. The specific clustering of variables may also indicate those groups of behaviors that are related, thereby suggesting themes in offending behavior, crime, or offender characteristics.

As with any statistical procedure, it is possible to err in the interpretation of the data. For example, the SSA provides a graphical representation of correlations of every variable to every other variable in a data set. Given different offenders will do similar things with no common motivational origin for the behavior, it may be possible in a given data set to misinterpret or overstate the correlation between two variables. Worse, because the context of the behavior is not established or poorly understood, the subsequent interpretation of the data may be incorrect. Consider the following example: During the course of a sexual assault, a rapist bites the breast of a rape victim in an attempt at foreplay. In another unrelated sexual assault, the rapist bites the victim's nipple as a form of gratification or stimulation, and in yet a third case, the biting behavior is intended to gain victim compliance. The same behaviors are borne of different motivations, mean different things to the offenders, and are intended to serve different functions or fantasy behavior. Simply reducing the variable to "biting" tells us little, if anything.

McGrath (2000) is concerned that predictions about offender behaviors or characteristics may not be applicable to a certain case because of a low baseline of occurrence. As a result, generalizations may or may not apply to a particular case in guiding the conclusion rather than the conclusion being case specific. For a more detailed overview of application, see Canter (2003); Canter, Coffey, Huntley, and Missen (2000); and Snook, Canter, and Bennell (2002). Whatever the criticisms, IP at least introduces a systematic and scientific study of criminal behavior.

Consistent with BEA and CIA profiles, Investigative Psychology most commonly provided assessments of single homicides (N = 3). Arson was the next most frequent (N = 2), followed by one case each of serial homicide, spree homicide, and serial rape.

Investigative Psychology, the profiling approach placing the most emphasis on empiricism, ranked second in terms of the number of statistical generalizations (with 27% of the characteristics relying on the statistics or research for justification). This method ranked highest in terms of the profile characteristics offered without justification (68% overall had no justification). Only about 4% of the characteristics used evidence, and less than 1% used personal belief as a form of justification. These results may have been skewed by the inclusion of a number of profiles from the same source who tended to offer little in the way of grounds for support.

The number of characteristics given in all IP profiles summed 180. The mean number offered was 11.3 (SD = 9.6) and the range for the method was 21 (Minimum = 1, Maximum = 22). Looking at the individual assessments, they ranged between no justification of any description (Profiles 35, 36, 37, and 38) through to extensive justification in profile 40 (approximately 95% of the characteristics were reasoned on statistics or research). Profiles 39 and 41 also weighed in with considerable focus on actuarial justifications, with about 55% and 67% of the characteristics justified statistically. Because one profiler from this sample presented the information without justification, and because some of the assessments were geographic profiles and only provided one characteristic, the profile features were reexamined to determine the degree to which the IP profiles were affected by the inclusion of these baseless conclusions.

Without these geographic profiles (36, 37, and 38), the percentage of characteristics offered without justification falls to 53% (from 68%). Still only 6% of this smaller sample relied on physical evidence, and the reliance on statistics or research rose to 40%. A bare minimum (1%) of characteristics relied on personal belief in their argument.

There was also a large range of profile characteristics deleted from the IP profiles because of their low frequency: Rearing & Development, Social Environment, Finances, Sexual Perversion, Fantasy, Victimology, Victim Lifestyle, Victim Incident, Knowledge of Crime Scene, Knowledge of Methods and Materials, Contradictory Acts, Intent, Staging, Remorse, Point of Contact, Crime Scene Type, Method of Control, Use of Force, Trust of Victims, Use of Weapons, Victim Resistance, Post-offense Behavior, Preoffence Behavior, Sexual Acts, and Leave Town.

Geographic Profiling (Geoprofiling)

Whereas criminal profiling attempts to define a number of characteristics of the offender from his or her actions at the crime (e.g., age, sex, race, and intelligence), geographic profiling focuses on just one aspect of the crime: the offender's likely location. According to Rossmo (1997, p. 161), geographic profiling focuses on the "probable spatial behavior of the offender within the context of the locations of, and the spatial relationships between, the various crime sites." As with criminal profiling, it is not intended to be an investigative panacea but, rather, a tool that assists police and prioritizes search areas (Laverty & MacLaren, 2002; Ratcliffe, 2004; Rossmo, 1997, 2003). Ideally, a geoprofile should follow from and augment a full criminal profile, once done (Rossmo, 1997).[3]

Protagonists identify geographic profiling as a decision support system used to make estimates of the likely geographic region of an offender's home location (Rossmo, 2000), although it may also identify where the offender works (Ratcliffe, 2004) or some other location with which the offender is familiar (referred to as *activity nodes*). Essentially, geographic profiling makes use of the nonrandom nature of criminal behavior, presupposing that most crimes have rhyme or reason to them (Wilson, 2003):

> *Crimes are not just random—there's a pattern. It has been said criminals are not so different from shoppers or even from lions hunting prey. When an offender has committed*

[3] In Rossmo (1997, p. 161), it is noted that "a psychological profile is not a necessary precursor for a geographic profile," but this position later changed.

a number of crimes, they leave behind a fingerprint of their mental map, and you can decode certain things from that. We put every crime location into a computer program and it produces a map showing the most probable areas the police should target.

The provision of geographic profiling software, profiling units, and specialist geoprofilers gives the distinct impression that the approach is scientific and robust, but in reality the theories on which the practice rests are dated and the application of geoprofiling to individual cases has met with serious debate and criticism. For example, the *least effort principle*, which is a core component of Rossmo's approach in the form of the "nearness principle," was first suggested by Zipf in approximately 1950. *Distance decay*, the notion that crimes decrease in frequency the farther away an offender travels from home, has also been around for several decades.

The next section considers some of the theoretical underpinnings of geographic profiling.

The Least Effort Principle

The least effort principle at its most fundamental level suggests that given two alternatives to a course of action, people will choose the one that requires least effort. That is, people will adopt the easiest course of action.

According to Rossmo (2000, pp. 87–88),

When multiple destinations of equal desirability are available, the least effort principle suggests the closest one will be chosen. The determination of "closest," however, can be a problematic assessment. Isotropic surfaces, spaces exhibiting equal physical properties in all directions, are rarely found within the human geographic experience.

As Rossmo suggests, the ability to impose arbitrary concepts of nearness onto crime is made difficult by the fact that our geographic environment is largely nonuniform. This means that not only does the layout of our environment impact on offending decisions but also our physical location in a three-dimensional space will come into play.[4]

The least effort principle may not account for other offense contingencies either, such as the lack of victim availability in certain areas, interrupted offenses, or any other event outside the offender's immediate control. In addition to these constraints, Rossmo (2000) also suggests that a criminal's financial resources are a consideration in his or her journey to crime.[5]

[4]For example, certain types of offenders may not select high-rise buildings for a variety of reasons, and in terms of opportunity factors in crime commission, high-rise buildings may not present the same opportunities because they are not typically thoroughfares. This may be particularly critical in areas such as New York and other major cities where high-density housing is the norm. In rural areas where travel routes are typically straighter and naturally larger, the application of the least effort principle may also be problematic. The caution is not necessarily against the application of these principles generally; rather, applying the same principles in open environments that one may apply in city spaces.

[5]The author is reminded of the burglar who used public transport to get to and from his crime sites and, in an attempt to return to his home base, offered the bus driver a stolen DVD player because he had no cash with which to pay his ticket.

Distance Decay

Distance decay refers to the idea that crimes will decrease in frequency the farther away an offender travels from his or her home (Rengert, Piquero & Jones, 1999; van Koppen & de Keijser, 1997). Distance decay is a geographical expression of the principle of least effort (Harries, 1999) and results when an offender shows a preference for closer crime sites.

This does not mean that crime sites are closely clustered around the offender's home because this would constitute a threat to the offender's anonymity and liberty. Because of this, Rossmo (2000) posits the existence of a comfort or "buffer zone" directly around the offender's home. Within this area, targets are viewed as less desirable because of the perceived risk associated with offending too close to home (Rossmo, 2000). This is confirmed by van Koppen and de Keijser (1997, p. 1), who note that "offenders rarely commit offences on their own doorstep, presumably because the chances of recognition by people who know them are higher."

Distance decay is also affected by opportunity in the same way as the least effort principle. According to Rengert et al. (1999, pp. 428–429), regardless of the degree to which criminals would like to choose the locations of their offenses, they are unable to do so given the lack of opportunities and the random and unpredictable behavior of others, which will often foil even the best laid plans:

> *This is not to deny the "individuality" of criminals; each of them does indeed make separate decisions. However, each decision is made within the framework of constraints. For many criminals, a major aspect of these constraints is represented by distance. In other words, no matter how much one may wish to emphasize "free will" of the individual, in practice, criminals are not free to commit crime anywhere they wish. Their ethnic character may make them stand out in a strange neighborhood, their economic status will determine their access to different modes of transportation, and their past experiences (e.g., school, armed services, and so on) determine the area they have knowledge of. Criminologists can begin to understand the working of these constraints by measuring the distance decay effect exhibited in criminal spatial interaction.*

The Circle Hypothesis

Those involved in geographic profiling seem to be preoccupied with the way in which geometric shapes are suggestive of a criminal's journey to crime. For example, Canter and Larkin (1993) proposed the "circle hypothesis," which was later tested by Kocsis and Irwin (1997) on a sample of Australian rapes, arsons, and burglaries. Snook et al. (2002) tested the utility of the circle hypothesis by giving a circle heuristic to a group of human judges and comparing their results to an actuarial computer-based model, and a similar study was later conducted by Snook, Taylor, and Bennell (2004).

The danger of overlaying arbitrary geometric shapes should be quite obvious, but the appeal of juxtaposing a circle, a square, or a wedge onto a map for a novice might be too

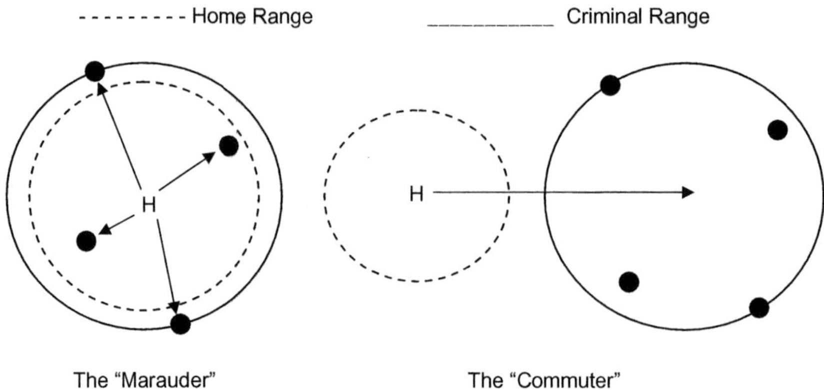

FIGURE 4.1 The marauder and commuter models.

much to avoid. One such example can be drawn from the author's own experience, in which an experienced intelligence analyst, in considering an extensive temporal and geographic crime series, proudly pronounced something like "we found a pattern. If you plot out all of the offenses on a map, you can draw a circle around them!" When questioned at greater length about what this might mean or the implications that it may have for the investigation as a whole, the question was greeted with stunned silence. When asked again what implications this might have, it was pronounced again, though in a more subdued tone, that you could draw a circle around the offenses once they were plotted on a map. This was, apparently, the extent of the revelation about the spatial pattern of the offending. Taken out of context, misinterpreted, or applied inconsistently, the actual meaning of any pattern will be nil.

Canter and Larkin (1993) proposed two types of offending based on the degree to which the offender was proximally tied to his or her home. The marauder hypothesis describes an offender who strikes out from his home location and then returns, with the home being within a circle defined by the two outermost offense locations. On the other hand, a commuter, still operating out of a home base, leaves the general location of this home to offend in a different geographic region, later leaving this area and returning to the locale of his home base. The two models are presented in Figure 4.1.

In Canter and Larkin's (1993) study, there was no support for a commuter model in a sample of 45 sexual assaulters, but in 41 of the 45 cases, the offender's home was located within the circle. Because of this, they suggested there is "strong support for the general marauder hypothesis as being the most applicable to these sets of offenders" (p. 67).

Although the theory seems plausible and attractive, there are a number of issues with the model. First, although Canter and Larkin (1993) identified 87% of offenders as marauders, the decision regarding whether one is dealing with a marauder or a commuter when the offender's home base is not known may still be a matter of luck or educated guess. If the profiler relies on the statistical probability that the offender is a marauder, then the same general cautions apply as those for any inductive method, such as whether the case is statistically anomalous (in the Canter and Larkin study, this would mean that the offender was part of the 13%, or perhaps that the research did not apply in any meaningful way in this community or jurisdiction). In addition, the following points are raised, which may highlight limitations in this particular study (from the Discussion section):

- The base is not at the center of the circle of crimes (this will impact on search areas and population numbers in densely populated areas).
- The eccentricity of the model is important because it may reflect some developmental processes on the part of the offender whereby he or she sometimes travels further from home for offending than at other times.
- As a result, the differences between marauding and commuting could perhaps be explained by increasing criminal skill or confidence.
- The representation of ranges using circles is overly simplistic, and other research has suggested that in the United States, city expansion from downtown areas may be better indicated by elliptical or sectoral patterns.
- The number of offenses per offender in this sample was relatively small.
- It is possible that the information used in the modeling was not an accurate representation of all the offenses committed by the offenders.

Geographic Profiling Computer Systems

In an effort to simplify the processes used in geographic profiling, geographic profilers have developed a variety of computer programs designed to assist in the process of calculating crime site information. Dragnet, developed and offered by the University of Liverpool in the United Kingdom, is advertised as a "geographical prioritization package" that works by using the locations of a series of crimes and prioritizing areas around the offense locations containing the likely location of the offender's home.

Use of the program involves inputting data on the crime sites, which is ostensibly the first stage. This will produce little more than "dots on a plot" or a screen as shown in the figures available on this web site: http://www.i-psy.com/publications/publications_dragnet.php.

Then the analyst produces a priority map as shown in the prioritization map available on the web site. The priorities are dictated by a legend, with the "hotter" colors suggesting high priority and "cooler" colors suggesting low priority. The map can indicate the presence of more than one focus for investigators, which may be suggestive of more than one offender (thus, in this capacity, it could be said that the system has case linkage ability). This figure also shows the prioritization area with the offender's home marked "H." The produced search areas are usually overlaid with a standard street map.

As with many of its computerized counterparts, Dragnet can integrate information about the layout of certain areas, such as city blocks, incorporating a Manhattan metric designed to account for indirect distances encountered in the urban environment. Figure 4.2 shows the standard Euclidian distance, and Figure 4.3 shows a Manhattan metric accounting for streetscapes.

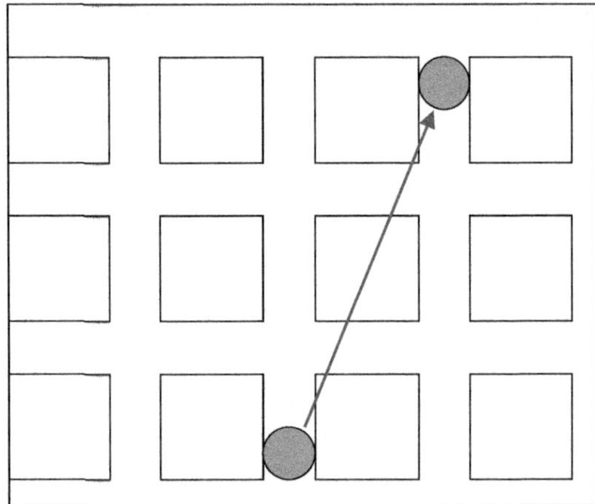

FIGURE 4.2 Euclidian Distances. These are usually point A to point B measurements, or "as the crow flies." This is problematic because it is not an accurate representation of how offenders travel or the layout of the spatial environment.

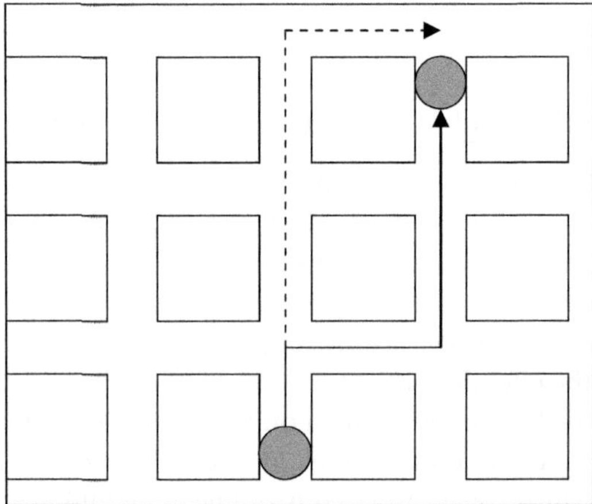

FIGURE 4.3 Manhattan Metrics. This is only a limited solution to the problems of a standard Euclidian distance because of the nonlinear and irregular layout of city spaces and the uncertainty of knowing which route the offender actually took.

Based on his PhD research while at Simon Fraser University, Kim Rossmo developed Rigel Profiler, which is now sold through Environmental Criminology Research Incorporated (ECRI), a company set up to deliver the software. ECRI (2001) states that Rigel:

- Is a system for geographic profiling designed to support serial crime investigations by prioritizing suspects and addresses and enabling investigators to focus their resources on specific locations.
- Uses ECRI's patented Criminal Geographic Targeting (CGT) algorithm and is Java-based for platform independence.

- Supports a variety of GIS and text data sources and can be customized according to customer requirements. Rigel can effectively manage the integration of address and location information, as well as incorporate additional geographic layers (i.e., schools, shops, playgrounds, etc.) that are of interest.
- Is able to extract information from a case linkage system such as ViCLAS. Information can include crime locations, suspect information, case details, and investigator details.
- Presents the results in the form of two- or three-dimensional surface maps called "jeopardies," showing the most probable locations of an offender's residence. At the core of Rigel is the patented algorithm used to derive the output map from the set of input data.
- Enables law enforcement agencies to focus their search efforts on the most likely neighborhoods, thus making optimal use of their resources.
- Is used by leading police agencies and has been used in hundreds of cases throughout the world.

These are not the only programs available for use, although these would be the major systems in use or covered in the literature. The cost of some programs may make their use for either practical or research purposes prohibitive. Other commercial software, such as Microsoft Excel, can provide a similar level of analysis providing one knows how to input the algorithms and structure the output.

Santilla, Zappala, Laukkanen, and Picozzi (2003) conducted a study on the utility of geographic profiling in a series of three rapes in Italy. They found that although there was some limited support for certain distance decay functions, jurisdictions may be unique in travel patterns due to population size, road patterns, and physical geography. Because of this, they claim it is necessary to calibrate the parameters for individual jurisdictions before any attempt to isolate nodes is undertaken. They correctly claim that such calibration would make the "use of an empirical function resource demanding" (p. 51). This may be an insurmountable obstacle in jurisdictions with limited resources, such as funding or computer support, or where there is a lack of expertise. "Flying in" the technology or the expertise may be impossible or unrealistic in many such cases for many of the same reasons.

The practical shortcomings in individual cases have been discussed, but these are extended in a more general theoretical sense, as discussed by Rossmo (2000, pp. 208–209), to the reliability of geographic profiling. He notes that the following considerations may undermine suitability:

- Generally, there should be a minimum of five distinct locations, of the same type, available for analysis. It is usually assumed that the offender has not moved or been displaced during the time period of these crimes, but if this has occurred, then more locations are required. A geographic assessment may be appropriate in cases involving fewer locations.
- Only crime locations that are accurately known should be used. For example, encounter sites may be imprecise if they have to be inferred from last known victim sighting. In some investigations, the locations of certain sites may be completely unknown.
- Analysis of the crime site type with the most locations results in lower expected CGT hit score percentages. Multiple offenses in the same immediate area should not be double

counted. The degree of spatial-temporal clustering must be assessed because crime sites too close in time and space are probably nonindependent events.

- Combining different site types to increase the total number of locations available for analysis can be advantageous when the number of crimes is minimal. However, two potential problems exist with this approach. The first is that locations may be significantly correlated; this is particularly likely when the offender travels directly to the dump site from the encounter site. The second problem occurs when combined crime locations produce a hunting area larger than that found with a single site type, resulting in the possibility of a greater search area, even though the hit percentage is smaller. This problem is most likely to occur if the two crime site areas are incongruent.
- Preference should be given to the crime site type that affords the greatest degree of choice to the offender. Site types with constrained target backcloths[6] tell us little about the criminal. If victim specificity leads to spatial bias, then encounter locations may not be the best profiling option. Similarly, body dump sites in isolated areas may reveal only general detail about an urban killer.

The absence of any of the previous information would seriously impact on the ability of the profiler to accurately assess an offender's geographic behavior. Given the previous considerations, the following points should also be noted:

- The first of Rossmo's points assumes not only that the offender has not moved location but also that the crime series has been accurately linked to the one offender. In some cases, previously unlinked offenses may not be identified as the work of the same offender until some time after the offender is caught. Behaviors indicative of escalation may also foil attempts here because the voyeurism and theft of personal belongings (e.g., underwear) by a serial rapist may go unreported or unnoticed. If the victim is killed, this information may never come to light, and so it is possible that the number of known offenses may not currently, if ever, reach a threshold where a geoprofile is possible. Also, given the previous considerations, it would seem that a profile of a serial criminal early in his or her criminal actions will be largely ineffective.
- In some serial murder cases, the only information police have to go on is the last seen locations. This, in theory at least, makes it difficult, if not impossible, to offer a geographic profile in such cases, unless the profiler chooses to advance without this information. Given Rossmo's warning, this would not be recommended.
- The degree of choice an offender has regarding a crime site may not be known at the time of the geoprofile, if ever; thus, although this would be important to know, it may be impossible to introduce into an analysis. For example, an offender plans to break into an apartment

[6]"Target or victim backcloth is important for an understanding of the geometric arrangement of crime sites; it is the equivalent of a spatial opportunity structure (Brantingham & Brantingham, 1993). It is configured by both geographic and temporal distributions of 'suitable' (as seen from the offender's perspective) crime targets or victims across the physical landscape. The availability of particular targets may vary significantly according to neighborhood, area, or even city, and is influenced by time, day of week, and season; hence, the term structural backcloth is also used" (Rossmo, 2000, pp. 126–127).

> and rape the lone female occupant. Unbeknownst to him, she has visitors and so his attempts are foiled. This crime site may provide the best insight into his behavior, but we would never know because the lack of an opportunity structure prohibited the crime from occurring. A similar lack of opportunity can be seen in the crimes of Berkowitz. On some nights, he would go looking for victims, but failure to find any would see him returning to previous crime sites where he masturbated. It may be that the crimes that would have occurred closest to his home were those that were foiled, and that those farthest away offered the best availability of victims and situations.

Turvey (1999, cited in Petherick & Turvey 2012, pp. 90) expresses similar concerns about the utility and reliability of geographic profiling, including the following:

- This method breaks the same tenet of behavioral-evidence analysis as the others mentioned previously: It takes a single manifestation of offender behavior (offense location selection) and attempts to infer its meaning out of the overall behavioral and emotional context that it was produced in.
- This method is actually employed without the benefit of a psychological profile. Although Rossmo states that he requires a full psychological profile for a competent geographical analysis, he has been known to proceed without one or to construct his own.
- The result of ignoring overall behavioral evidence and case context and not utilizing full criminal profiles, geographic profiling cannot, and does not, distinguish between two or more offenders operating in the same area.
- This method assumes that all cases that are submitted have been positively linked by law enforcement. It does not check the veracity of this or any other information provided by law enforcement.
- This method assumes that offenders most often live near or within easy reach of their offense area.
- Rossmo's dissertation very competently outlines the weaknesses and the shortcomings of the published research on serial murder. Then, his dissertation goes on to base theories regarding geographic profiling, and the CGT software, on those admittedly flawed studies.
- The technology used in CGT is impressive but amounts to only so much scientification. Inferences regarding offender anchor points and spatial behavior must still be drawn by the analyst.

Despite an impressive array of costly computer solutions to the journey to crime problem, it is clear that, although a nice theory, the application of geographic profiling raises more questions than the theories on which it is based answer. As noted by Rengert et al. (1999), the decision where to offend is often outside the offender's control and cannot, as some criminological theories would have us believe, be based strictly on free will. One of the factors in decisions to offend is the distance an offender will have to travel to commit his or her crimes.

It is also instructive to consider the viewpoints of others about specific geographic profiling units. Despite the positive press generated by a number of these, it is evident that not everyone associated with their use regards them so highly. For example, in *Rossmo v. Vancouver (City) Police Board* (2001, at 21 and 38, respectively), the following claims were made:[7]

- A cursory analysis seems to suggest that a choice to extend the contract would not be a good business decision. In short, there is little apparent evidence of enhanced policing outcomes. And establishing the extent and durability of prestige is problematic.[9] It was acknowledged that Rossmo's international celebrity was good for the VPD, but as this comment acknowledges, it is difficult to quantify celebrity and prestige and so actual return to the VPD was difficult to gauge.
  - The question for the Vancouver Police Department and the Police Board is to what degree do we wish to continue what is essentially an international police program. There have been no definitive applications of geographic profiling in the VPD and the department is facing significant budget issues that require decisions on funding priorities.

Understandably, this case generated much media interest in what would, at least on the outside, appear to be the fall from grace of a very public internationally known figure. In "Profiling Section Wasn't Good Value," the Vancouver Sun (2001) reported the following:

> *The contract of a detective-inspector in charge of the city police's geographic profiling section was terminated because the department felt it wasn't getting good value for its money, deputy chief Gary Greer testified Wednesday.*
>
> *The termination had nothing to do with jealousy or the existence of a so-called boy's club on the force, he said in B.C. Supreme Court.*
>
> *"It wasn't cost effective," he said.*
>
> *Kim Rossmo, a 22-year member of the force, is suing for wrongful dismissal after his 5-year contract wasn't renewed last Dec. 31.*
>
> *Greer was an inspector when he recommended that Rossmo's job be one of three positions the police department had to cut to meet budget requirements imposed on city hall.*

Geographic profiling wasn't examined as a distinct method in the research on profiling approaches discussed at other points in this chapter.

Diagnostic Evaluations

As discussed in Chapter 1, much of the earliest profiling work available for reference was by medical doctors, psychiatrists, and psychologists. Indeed, many modern approaches to profiling are heavily grounded in psychological theory and practice. As a generic term for the "as needed" work by mental health practitioners, Wilson, Lincoln, and Kocsis (1997) identify diagnostic evaluations as a form of criminal profiling.

[7]Rossmo was suing the Vancouver Police Department (VPD) for wrongful termination when his contract expired. He lost the suit and has since left the Geographic Profiling Unit.

Although the approach and application of the various profiling paradigms are well enunciated, diagnostic evaluations are less defined, and there are no unified approaches under this "model." Instead, one's education, training, and experience dictate the approach one takes at a given point in time with a given case, with the profile being the result of the clinician's understanding of offenders, personality, and mental illness (Gudjonsson & Copson, 1997).

Representing the ruminations of psychologists and psychiatrists, Jackson and Bekerian (1997) dedicate sections of their work to developmental and clinical issues involved in profiling and also in the application of personality theories to psychological profiling. Boon (1997) explains how psychoanalytic/psychodynamic, learning, dispositional/trait, humanist/cognitive, and alternative/Eastern philosophies may assist in case disposition, and Woodworth and Porter (2001, p. 244) contend that "although the use of psychoanalytic concepts in profiling is rarely seen today, the Mad Bomber prediction remains an interesting highlight in the development of profiling."

Fritzon (2000) discusses a similar application of personality theories to the crime of arson. In examining arsonists, Fritzon suggests that it may be instructive to consider their motives within the framework of needs theories. Two of those considered are Maslow's hierarchy of needs and McClelland's learned needs. The application of Maslow's hierarchy is illustrated here (pp. 162–164):

> *Maslow's theory explains human behavior in terms of a hierarchy of five general needs. The most basic of these are psychological needs, including food, water, oxygen, etc. … In some cases, serious fires can result from these individuals' efforts to stay warm when sheltered … fires which are set for financial gain could also be said to be motivated by physiological need in that food and shelter are usually dependent on financial considerations. … The second level of the hierarchy of needs is safety and security needs. These include a desire for security, stability, and protection. In terms of arson, firesetting, which is motivated by crime concealment, fulfills the need for protection from the undesirable consequences of being caught and convicted of the primary crime. The next level of the hierarchy concerns social needs such as the need for love, affection, and a sense of belonging. Maslow states that individuals who are unable to satisfy this need will feel lonely, ostracized, and rejected. … Their behavior can be seen as resulting from frustration and dissatisfaction of these needs. It may be a way (albeit a dysfunctional one) of restoring the disequilibrium that such frustration causes. … The fourth level of Maslow's hierarch concerns ego and esteem needs, which can be focused either internally or externally. … This category of arson can be seen as an attempt to redress self-esteem by someone who feels they have been wronged. … The final stage of the need hierarchy is the need for self-actualization, which refers to the process of developing our true potential as individuals to the fullest extent. … Arson that is committed by political and extremist groups, such as the Animal Liberation Front, therefore, can be viewed as being motivated by the need for actualization of the particular goals and ideals propagated by that group.*

McGrath (2002, p. 321) provides the following suggestions regarding the psychologist's or psychiatrist's role in profiling:

- Their background in the behavioral sciences and their training in psychopathology place them in an enviable position to deduce personality characteristics from crime scene information.
- The forensic psychiatrist is in a good position to infer the meaning behind signature behaviors.
- Given their training, education, and focus on critical and analytical thinking, forensic psychiatrists are in a good position to "channel their training into a new field."

Although these are obvious areas for forensic mental health specialists to apply their skills, McGrath also notes that any involvement in the profiling process should not be treatment oriented. It is critical that the psychiatrist or psychologist not fall prey to role confusion and descend into treatment advice when acting as a profiler.

Adding to the potential problems this may pose, those conducting diagnostic evaluations seldom have extensive experience in law enforcement or its related areas (Wilson et al., 1997). West (2000, p. 220) provides similar commentary:

> *It has to be conceded that many clinicians, whatever their professional background, do not routinely review crime scene data or witness depositions. ... Instead, the clinical approach ... tends to preclude consideration of more exact details of the offense. All too often it is easier to believe the offender than to read the witness depositions or observe the crime scene. It seems inevitable that such omissions might lead to serious errors in any assessment.*

Because their involvement in profiling tends to be sporadic (Dietz, 1985), the mental health specialist may lose touch with the requirements of a police investigation and therefore offer vague and/or irrelevant suggestions. Ainsworth (2001) suggests that the profile produced by mental health workers may contain statements about the inner workings of the offender's mental processes that will not be directly observable, and that these explanations provided may not be as useful to investigators as those from other approaches. This is referred to as investigative relevance and is discussed elsewhere in this book. The problem may go further than the type of advice offered in diagnostic evaluation profiles and extend into difficulties of getting into police investigations. Canter (1989, p. 13) suggests the difficulty is that "police officers are unlikely to admit psychologists to their investigations unless some mutual trust and reciprocal benefit is expected" and that "it is difficult to make a contribution until some experience has been gained, yet difficult to gain experience until some contribution can be offered."

Despite West's (2000) concern that a profiler may come to believe the offender if given the opportunity to interface directly with the offender, Tamlyn (1999) claims that when the clinician is involved in the investigative phase of a profile, there is usually not an opportunity to directly assess or examine the subject of the analysis, perhaps more an artifact of profiling than diagnostic evaluations specifically. Gudjonsson and Copson (1997) agree, stating that criminal profilers have historically relied on indirect methods such as intuition, psychodynamic theories, behavioral analysis, and statistical reasoning.

With regard to their role, forensic clinicians in the United Kingdom often rely on the good will of their employer to allow them to undertake profiling duties at the potential expense of their employers (Tamlyn, 1999). This means that many will work in their own time and be largely unpaid. It is unlikely that this situation will differ from that of other countries where mental health experts act in the advisory capacity of profilers. In fact, many professionals will perform profiling as an adjunct to their usual duties rather than being employed in this capacity full-time. The reality is that there are very few full-time profilers in any agency throughout the world.

Although diagnostic evaluations are not a unified approach with a clear theoretical framework, Copson, Badcock, Boon, and Britton (1997, p. 16) outline the following principles of clinical profiling:

- Custom made: The advice should not rely on the recycling of some kind of generic violent antisocial criminal stereotype;
- Interactive: At a range of levels of sophistication, depending on the officers' understanding of the psychological concepts at issue; and
- Reflexive: The advice should be dynamic, insofar as every element has a knock-on effect on every other element, and evolving, in that new information must lead to reconsideration not only of the element(s) of advice affected but of the construct as a whole.

They also identify a number of dangers (p. 16):

- There is an imperative to please that must be recognized and overcome, otherwise objectivity will be undermined by tendencies to overinterpretation and unequivocality.
- Close interaction with the officers leaves the profiler open to allegations of improper collusion, such as tailoring a profile to fit a known suspect, or devising some interviewing strategy that is unethical or even unlawful.
- The mass of data that comes out of an interactive and reflexive process means that recording is an extremely difficult and time-consuming business, even to the extent that sometimes a written report never quite emerges.
- The reduction of a mass of data into a summary document—and more especially the failure to produce a summary document—leaves the profiler open to being misrepresented.

There are no specific critiques of diagnostic evaluations in the literature, but these may be easily extrapolated from the approach itself. For example, without a unified approach, the principles involved may not be clearly enunciated, and any attempt to study the efficacy of the approach may be hampered by the inability to reproduce the train of thought that led to particular conclusions. Ainsworth (2001) claims that the profile produced by mental health workers may contain statements about the workings of the offender's mental processes, and that the explanations they provide may not be as useful to investigators as those derived under other methods. Finally, certain aspects of psychological analysis may be difficult to integrate into a police investigation, bringing into question the utility of the profile and the profiler's involvement, such as Brussel's assertion that the "Mad Bomber" suffered from an Oedipal complex.[8]

Diagnostic Evaluations (DE) didn't include any assessments of single homicides, unlike other methods considered. The main focus of DE profiles were spree homicides (2 profiles each) and serial homicides (1 case). One abduction was profiled, as was one bombing, and the "Other" classification was a psychological profile.

Over one half of the DE sample relied heavily on statistical justification, with 60% of the characteristics offered using this reasoning. Interestingly, this method used the most personal belief as a form of reasoning, being nearly 26% of the sample (Mean = 3.4). The reliance on physical evidence was also low, at 5.3% (Mean = <1), with no justification at all offered nearly 9% of the time (Mean = <1).

Fifty percent of the sample of diagnostic evaluations relied solely on statistical judgment in inferring characteristics (Profiles 43–46) though the sample mean was 60.1% for Statistical Justification. The next most common was Personal Belief (26%), while 8.6% were given without any justification and only 5.3% relied on evidence. These results conform intuitively to the philosophy of this approach, as they are anchored in clinical judgment (personal experience and opinion) and research (clinical profiles of personality and mental disorder). Furthermore, it is unlikely that most mental health experts would have had any experience with forensic science, and so it would be expected that evidentiary justifications would be low, which was also supported by the current sample. Of the total number of characteristics offered in DE profiles, there were only four offered (one time each at 12.5%) that used evidence as a form of justification. These were Method of Attack, Use of Weapons, Criminal Skill, and Personality.

A number of characteristics were not offered and so were removed from the analysis. These were Finances, Victimology, Victim Lifestyle, Victim Incident, Offender Risk, Knowledge of Victim, Knowledge of Crime Scene, Knowledge of Methods and Materials, Escalation, Transport, Precautionary Acts, Contradictory Acts, Planning, Forensic Awareness, Intent, Staging, Military History, Hobbies, Point of Contact, Scene Type, Method of Approach, Method of Control, Use of Force, Trust of Victims, Victim Resistance, and Leave Town.

Behavioral Evidence Analysis

In profiling terms, behavioral evidence analysis (BEA) is the most recent of the individual profiling methods. The method was developed by Turvey, and it is based on forensic science and the collection and interpretation of physical evidence and, by extension, what this means about an offender. BEA is primarily a deductive method and, as a result, will not make a conclusion about an offender unless specific physical evidence exists that suggests the characteristic. What this means is that instead of relying on averaged offender types, BEA profilers conduct a detailed examination of the scene and related behaviors and infer from this what offender characteristics are evidenced in the behavior and scene.

[8]Although Freud is undoubtedly one of the fathers of modern psychology and his impact on psychology is considerable, many of his theories have been disputed or discredited because of their questionable basis.

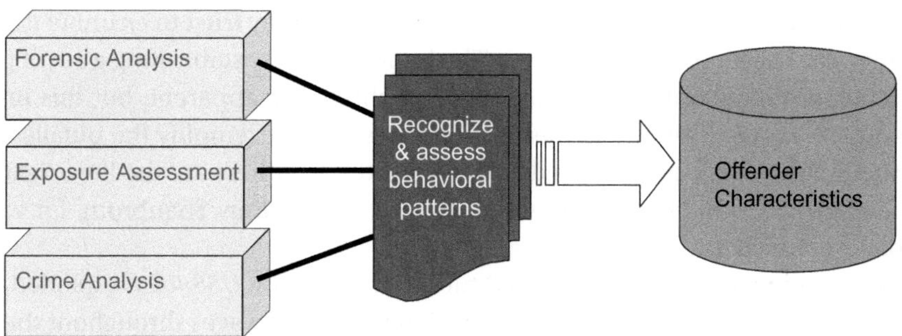

FIGURE 4.4 Stages of Behavioral Evidence Analysis.

The strength of BEA lies in the fact that the profiler works only with what is known; nothing is assumed or surmised (Petherick, 2003), and a great deal of time is spent determining the veracity of the physical evidence and its relationship to the crime. In this way, evidence that is irrelevant or unrelated has little evidentiary value and is not given weight in the final analysis. This assists in maintaining objectivity and leads to a more accurate and useful end product.

Like its inductive counterparts, BEA involves a number of steps, with each building on previous stages to provide an overall picture. These can be represented graphically, as shown in Figure 4.4.

The first stage of BEA is called the Forensic Analysis (EFA) and refers to the examination, testing, and interpretation of the physical evidence. In this stage, all the physical evidence surrounding a case is examined to assess its relevance and determine its overall nature and quality. This step also ensures the probative quality of the evidence should the case end up in court. Ultimately, the EFA informs the profiler what evidence he or she has to base a profile on, what evidence may be missing, what evidence may have been misinterpreted, and what value that evidence has in subsequent analyses. Thornton (2006, p. 37) contextualizes the importance of physical evidence:

> *We are interested in physical evidence because it may tell a story. Physical evidence—properly collected, properly analyzed, and properly interpreted—may establish the factual circumstances at the time the crime occurred. In short, the crime may be reconstructed. Our principal interest is ultimately in the reconstruction, not the evidence per se.... Also, along with the ethos is an ethic—a moral obligation to maintain the integrity of the processes by means of which the reconstruction is accomplished. In short, the ethics of crime reconstruction represents an imperative to "get it right.""Getting it right" involves more than guessing correctly. It necessitates a systematic process. It involves the proper recognition of the evidence, the winnowing of the relevant wheat from the irrelevant chaff, and the precise application of logic, both inductive and deductive. The process is not trivial.*

Because this stage relates to the examination of physical evidence, profilers who are not familiar with or qualified to interpret physical evidence should not undertake this task.

Instead, they should work with trained professionals whom they trust to examine the evidence on which they are basing their conclusions. The importance of establishing a set of given facts from information obtained during an investigation should be apparent, but this information is often assumed as correct without question. Two cases that exemplify the pitfalls of working with information that has been gathered and interpreted by others are the investigation of the explosion aboard the *USS Iowa* and the homicide of Joel Andrew Shanbrom, for which brief explanations are provided.

Early one morning in 1989, the number 2 turret on board the *USS Iowa* exploded, killing 47 of the ship's crew (Thompson, 1999). The explosion sent shockwaves throughout the US Navy, with the subsequent investigation revealing dangerous practices, incompetence, cover-ups, and investigative failures, only some of which were related to the explosion and deaths. Given the magnitude of the disaster, the Navy consulted agents from the FBI's Behavioral Analysis Unit to provide some insight into what it believed were the actions of a suicidal homosexual, Clayton Hartwig.

In an attempt to provide this insight, the FBI agents used a technique known as equivocal death analysis (EDA), essentially another name for a psychological autopsy (a profile of a deceased person). Although the EDA was not responsible for first bringing attention to Hartwig as the person responsible for the explosion, it was most certainly responsible for catalyzing this opinion in the minds of investigators and the naval executive. What followed was a series of events that perpetuated bad judgment and showed just how dangerous it can be to accept at face value information or evidence that one has not collected firsthand: Investigators from the Naval Investigative Service (NIS) started by assuming Hartwig's guilt and then provided this information to the FBI profilers, whose assessment fed this line of thinking back to the NIS and the Navy.

With regard to their analysis, a report of the Investigations Subcommittee of the Committee on Armed Services House of Representatives (1990) noted two important issues with the FBI's analysis (pp. 6–7):

- The procedures the FBI used in preparing the EDA were inadequate and unprofessional. As a matter of policy, the analysts do not state the speculative nature of their analyses. Moreover, the parameters that the FBI agents used, either provided to them or chosen by them, biased their results toward only one of three deleterious conclusions. Further biasing their conclusions, the agents relied on insufficient and sometimes suspect evidence. The FBI agents' EDA was invalidated by 10 of 14 professional psychologists and psychiatrists, heavily criticized even by those professionals who found the Hartwig possibility plausible.
- The FBI analysis gave the Navy false confidence in the validity of the FBI's work. If the Navy had relied solely on the work of the NIS's own staff psychologist—which emphasized that such psychological autopsies are by definition "speculative"—the Navy would likely not have found itself so committed to the Hartwig thesis.

Despite the questionable nature of the EDA process and its methodology, there were more fundamental concerns about the material on which the analysis was based. The following concerns were also raised by the Investigations Subcommittee about the process and results:

- Richard Ault admitted that the Navy had only provided him with fragments of the evidence assembled against Hartwig.
- Ault was asked who wrote the poem "Disposable Heroes," a key piece of information on which Hartwig's alleged homosexuality hinged, and he did not know.
- Asked whether the agents were aware that another gunner's mate told Admiral Milligan that another sailor had written the poem, Hazelwood stated that this was immaterial because Hartwig had the potential to see it.
- The agents were asked if they were aware that David Smith had recanted the testimony used in their EDA, and they claimed they were not sure what he had recanted.
- The agents had relied entirely on the information provided to them by the NIS and had not done any interviews themselves.

There were further concerns about the veracity of the information on which the profile was based (Investigations Subcommittee and Defense Policy Panel of the Committee on Armed Services, 1990, p. 42):

> *The preponderance of material came from interviews conducted and provided to the FBI by the NIS. As the subcommittee found earlier, serious questions were raised about the leading nature or bias introduced in the interviews by the NIS interviewing agents. Some witnesses denied making statements to NIS that are significant to the profile. … In at least one instance, the witness recanted several portions of his testimony, but was still considered a valuable witness.*

Another example stressing the importance of not only establishing a set of facts for oneself but also assessing evidence dynamics is the homicide of Joel Andrew Shanbrom, a school district police officer in California. Shanbrom's wife, Jennifer, claimed that she was upstairs bathing their son when she heard an altercation downstairs between her husband and some (black) men. A profile of the alleged offender was compiled by Mark Safarik of the FBI's Behavioral Analysis Unit.

Safarik's assessment gave considerable weight to the apparent ransacking of certain rooms in the house, including that of the son, Jacob:

> *The dressers and night stands in the master bedroom, Gisondi's room, and Jacob's bedroom had been disturbed.… In Jacob's bedroom, a room clearly identified as a child's bedroom, the dresser drawers were pulled out to give the appearance they were searched. Such a room would not be expected to contain any valuables and this would have been passed over by offender(s) looking for valuables.*

Although police had trouble with Jennifer Fletcher's story from the outset, particularly after discovering significant life insurance policies on her husband, the profile stuck steadfast to its assessment of ransacking. It was not until an expert profiler, in providing trial assistance to the defense, was able to establish through consideration of evidence dynamics that the scene had in fact been altered by a police officer in her search for clothing for Jacob Shanbrom, who was naked and cold from hiding in a bedroom closet with his mother since the alleged homicide. In a postscript to this case, Jennifer and Matthew Fletcher were both charged with the 1998 murder of Shanbrom after facing counts of murder, fraud, and conspiracy (Associated Press, 2002; Blankstein, 2002).

It is also necessary to establish the accuracy and quality of the information that serves as the basis of the profile because of the *evidence dynamics*. This refers to "any influence that changes, relocates, obscures, or obliterates physical evidence, regardless of intent" (Chisum & Turvey, 2008, p. 167). Thus, evidence dynamics may be the result of the offender moving from one room to another during an offense, a bleeding but not yet deceased victim crawling down a hallway, paramedics attending the scene of a violent crime, or firefighters attending a fire scene, among others. However, evidence dynamics is important in the case far beyond the extant circumstances of the crime scene, playing a role from the time the evidence is deposited until the final adjudication of the case (Chisum & Turvey, 2000). To provide some context to the way in which evidence dynamics may alter the physical presentation of crime scene actions, consider the following example from Chisum and Turvey (2000, p. 9):

> *A youth was stabbed several times by rival gang members. He ran for a home but collapsed in the walkway. A photo of the scene taken prior to the arrival of the EMT team shows a blood trail and that the victim was lying face down. Subsequent photos show the five EMTs working on the body on his back. He had been rolled over onto the blood pool. It became impossible for bloodstain patterns interpretation to be used to reconstruct the events leading to the death of the youth.*

The importance of the EFA and establishing a set of facts for one's self should be clear. Although only two cases have been used as examples, there are a litany of others with a similar lack of critical appraisal of the presenting evidence (see also Superior Court of California, 1999).

The other aspect of the forensic analysis that is important and factors in evidence dynamics is crime reconstruction, which involves a determination of the actions surrounding the crime. Popular conceptions of crime reconstruction abound, with some believing the process involves the physical rebuilding of the crime scene in another location. Saferstein (2004) suggests that the reconstruction will support a sequence of events through the observation and evaluation of physical evidence, as well as any statements made by witnesses or those involved with the crime. Rynearson (2002) incorporates "commonsense reasoning" and its use with forensic science to interpret evidence as it resides at the crime scene. Cooley (1999, p. 1), in an excellent paper written while a graduate student at the University of New Haven, suggests that crime scene reconstruction is the foundation of the BEA method:

> *Deductive reasoning, via crime scene reconstruction, can and will provide the profiler with the appropriate information allowing him or her to construct the most logical profile of an unknown offender. This will enable the profiler to supply the requesting agency with investigatively relevant information.*

The second stage of the process, victimology, examines all aspects of the victim, including lifestyle, hobbies, habits, friends, enemies, and demographic features. The information derived through the victimology can help to determine the existence or extent of any relationship between the victim and the offender. Two other related components of the victimology are victim and offender exposure. Victim exposure refers to the possibility of suffering harm or loss by virtue of an individual's personal, professional, and social life (Petherick & Turvey, 2008). This is further partitioned into lifestyle exposure and the exposure present at the moment of victimization, known as incident exposure. As a general rule, exposure can be low, medium, or high, indicating the level of risk a person is at by virtue of the person's personal, professional, and social life. In BEA, just as much time should be spent examining the victim's personality and behavioral characteristics as spent examining the offender.

In the third stage, crime analysis, the profiler determines factors such as the method of approach and attack, the method of control, location type, nature and sequence of any sexual acts, materials used, the type of verbal activity, and any precautionary acts the offender engaged in (Turvey, 2012). Precautionary acts may include wearing gloves or a balaclava, altering one's voice, or wearing a condom. This stage also sets out to determine what type of crime scenes are involved in a criminal event. These include the point of contact; primary, secondary, and tertiary scenes; and the dump or disposal site. For example, a victim with extensive wounds that would have produced a substantial amount of bleeding is found in an area devoid of bloodstains. This is suggestive of the victim being killed elsewhere (a primary crime scene) and then moved to the scene where the body was found (the dump or disposal site).

The final stage is the actual criminal profile, and is called offender characteristics. All the information from the previous stages is integrated and assessed through the scientific method and deductive reasoning to determine what the physical evidence, victimology, and crime scene characteristics collectively argue about the offender. Turvey (2012) argues against offering the profile characteristics of age, sex, race, and intelligence because these are typically assessed inductively and not based on physical evidence.

Although BEA is a method that relies on deductive logic, it cannot be characterized as purely deductive. This is because the process of deduction relies in part on induction, which produces theories that may be tested against the evidence. This is confirmed by Stock (2004, p. 5), who writes, "In the natural order of treatment inductive logic precedes deductive, since it is induction which supplies us with the general truths, from which we reason down in our deductive inferences."

Because of the reliance on physical evidence and the reconstruction of the behavior involved in the criminal event, inductive reasoning will be employed. Wound patterns and victimology are two such examples in which inductions may be used to form the basis of a later deduction. The type of knife used, its width, the length of the blade, and other characteristics of edged weapons have typically been determined through a study of known weapons and their features as well as their associated wound patterns. However, the application of this knowledge to the particular features of a set of wounds present on a victim's body involves the deductive application of this knowledge.

There are no direct criticisms of BEA in the literature, although there is some minor discussion of deductive approaches in general. Most seem to be quite confused by the application of the reasoning (see Chapter 2; Canter, 2004; Godwin, 1999), whereas others provide some cursory discussion of it but seem unsure of how the overall process operates. Holmes and Holmes (2002, p. 7) note that "much care is taken from the examination of forensic reports, victimology, and so forth and the report will take much longer to develop using only this approach." First, the authors seem largely unaware of the finer points of logic, such as induction being a component of and important to the overall process of deduction. The reader is also left with the distinct impression that the thoroughness of the approach (and the subsequent time involved) is pejorative. A final deductively rendered opinion will rely on inductively derived knowledge, although Holmes and Holmes tend to treat both processes as being dichotomous and largely exclusive. This suggests a fundamental lack of overall knowledge of the processes involved in reasoning.

However, McGrath (2000) has identified one critical observation of this method: If the initial premises on which conclusions are based are wrong, then the subsequent conclusions will also be wrong. Given that one of the primary purposes of the forensic analysis is to establish the veracity of the premises, this is not necessarily a problem as long as profilers are aware that it is incumbent on them to establish the basic information on which their decisions are based. If the basis of the premises cannot be established, then this may limit the amount of characteristics that can be offered (because deductive approaches will only derive conclusions on what has been unequivocally established). Beyond these observations, there has been little criticism of this approach.

The most common crime type profiled in the sample of BEA profiles was single homicide (12 cases) followed by serial homicide and mass homicide once each. In 14 BEA profiles there were a total of 166 characteristics offered. Of these 166 characteristics, the majority were given with physical evidence as a justification, in line with the evidentiary underpinnings of BEA. All told, just short of 89% of the profile characteristics (N = 145) used evidence as justification, with just short of 10% (N = 17) of the characteristics not offering any form of justification. Less than 1% of the characteristics used either statistical or actuarial reasoning (N = 1) and about 2% used personal belief (N = 3). This too is in line with the theory of BEA, and the caution against using either research or subjective personal opinion as the basis for profile conclusions.

For the individual profiles, there was a range of 28, with a minimum of 2 (Profile 3) and a maximum of 30 (Profile 9) individual characteristics offered (M = 11.9, SD = 9). Profile 5 had the highest number of characteristics without any justification at all (33%), although this may be misleading without acknowledging that the profile itself only contained three characteristics in total. Profile 7 contained 17 characteristics, of which 16 were justified with evidence; this being the highest number out of the BEA profiles justified in this way (94%).

Conclusion

Although there are commonalities among approaches, such as their goals, they are not as homogeneous as they may appear. Because there are significant shortcomings of some of the approaches detailed herein, anyone looking to invest time and resources in a profile should expend some effort on researching the differences and determining which approach might best serve their needs. Inductive methods, those relying on statistical reasoning or "averaged" offender types, appear to be the most problematic.

In contrast, deductive approaches provide the most potential for an accurate evaluation because of their reliance on examinations of physical evidence and its meaning and also because of the underlying power of deductive reasoning. Add to this the application of the scientific method and this may further strengthen the approach and its promise. Although deductive approaches are not without problems, their potential shortcomings are easily controlled. To be able to determine the approach that may provide the most help to police, more research must be conducted to ascertain not only the accuracy of profiling methods but also the operational utility each has to offer, and users are cautioned to educate themselves about the positive and negative aspects of each school of thought.

Questions

1. Regardless of individual method or author, the definition of criminal profiling is generally uniform. *True or false?*
2. The original study conducted by the FBI took place between _________ and _________.
3. BEA is currently the only profiling method that utilizes deductive logic. *True or false?*
4. Investigative psychology uses _________ _________ analysis in examining crime data.
5. What are the five factors in investigative psychology?
6. List and describe the stages of BEA.
7. List and briefly describe the criticisms of geographic profiling.

References

Ainsworth, P. B. (2000). *Psychology and crime.* Harlow, UK: Longman.

Ainsworth, P. B. (2001). *Offender profiling and crime analysis.* Devon, UK: Willan.

Associated Press. (2002). March 2 Wife of slain man charged. *Las Vegas Review-Journal,* Available at < http://www.reviewjournal.com> Accessed 14.11.05.

Baker, T. E. (2001). Understanding and apprehending America's most dangerous criminals. *Law and Order, 49*(5), 43–48.

Bennett, W. W., & Hess, K. M. (2001). *Criminal investigation* (6th ed.). Belmont, CA: Thompson Learning.

Blankstein, A. (2002). Couple charged in man's shooting: Jennifer and Matthew Fletcher are accused of murder in the 1998 death of her former husband, Joel Shanbrom. Available at <http://articles.latimes.com/2002/mar/01/local/me-arrest1> Accessed 15.11.05.

Boon, J., & Davies, G. (1993). Criminal profiling. *Policing, 9*(8), 1–13.

Boon, J. C. W. (1997). The contribution of personality theories to psychological profiling. In J. J. Jackson & D. Bekerian (Eds.), *Offender profiling: Theory, research and practice.* Chichester, UK: Wiley.

Brantingham, P. L., & Brantingham, P. J. (1993). Environment, routine, and situation: Toward a pattern theory of crime. In R. V. Clarke & M. Felson (Eds.), *Routine activity and rational choice: Advances in criminological theory* (Vol. 5, pp. 259–294). New Brunswick, NJ: Transaction Publishers.

Burgess, A. W., Hartman, C. R., Ressler, R. K., Douglas, J. E., & McCormack, A. (1986). Sexual homicide: A motivational model. *Journal of Interpersonal Violence, 1*(3), 251–272.

Burgess, A. W., & Ressler, R. K. (1985). *Sexual homicides crime scenes and patterns of criminal behavior (Grant No.82-IJ-CX-0065).* Washington, DC: National Institute of Justice.

Canter, D. (1989). Offender profiles. *The Psychologist, 2*(1), 12–16.

Canter, D. (1995). *Criminal shadows: Inside the mind of the serial killer.* London: HarperCollins.

Canter, D. (1998). Profiling as poison. *Inter Alia, 2*(1), 10–11.

Canter, D. (2003). *Mapping murder.* London: Virgin Books.

Canter, D. (2004). Offender profiling and investigative psychology. *Journal of Investigative Psychology and Offender Profiling, 1,* 1–15.

Canter, D., Alison, L. J., Alison, E., & Wentink, N. (2004). The organized/disorganized typology of serial murder: Myth or model? *Psychology, Public Policy, and Law, 10,* 293–320.

Canter, D., Coffey, T., Huntley, T., & Missen, C. (2000). Predicting serial killers' home base using a decision support system. *Journal of Quantitative Criminology, 16*(4), 457–478.

Canter, D., & Larkin, P. (1993). The environmental range of serial rapists. *Journal of Environmental Psychology, 13,* 93–99.

Chisum, W. J., & Turvey, B. E. (2000). Evidence dynamics: Locard's exchange principle and crime reconstruction. *Journal of Behavioral Profiling, 1*(1).

Chisum, W. J., & Turvey, B. E. (2008). An introduction to crime reconstruction. In B. E. Turvey (Ed.), *Criminal profiling: An introduction to behavioral evidence analysis* (3rd ed.). Burlington, MA: Academic Press.

Cooley, C. (1999). Crime scene reconstruction: The foundation of behavioral evidence analysis. Paper presented at the University of New Haven. Unpublished.

Copson, G., Badcock, R., Boon, J., & Britton, P. (1997). Articulating a systematic approach to clinical crime profiling. *Criminal Behaviour and Mental Health, 7,* 13–17.

Darkes, J., Otto, R. K., Poythress, N., & Starr, L. (1993). January APA's expert panel in the congressional review of the USS Iowa incident. *American Psychologist,* 8–15.

Dietz, P. E. (1985). Sex offender profiling by the FBI: Preliminary conceptual model. In M. H. Ben-Aron, S. J. Hucher, & C. D. Webster (Eds.), *Clinical criminology.* Toronto: M & M Graphics.

Douglas, J. E., & Burgess, A. E. (1986). Criminal profiling: A viable investigative tool against violent crime. *FBI Law Enforcement Bulletin, 55*(12), 9–13.

Douglas, J. E., Burgess, A. W., Burgess, A. G., & Ressler, R. K. (1992). *Crime classification manual: A standard system for investigating and classifying violent crime.* New York: Simon & Schuster.

Douglas, J. E., & Olshaker, M. (1995). *Mindhunter: Inside the FBI Elite serial crime unit.* New York: Scribner.

Douglas, J. E., Ressler, R. K., Burgess, A. W., & Hartman, C. R. (1986). Criminal profiling from crime scene analysis. *Behavioural Sciences and the Law, 4*(4), 401–421.

Egger, S. A. (1998). *The killers among us: An examination of serial murder and its investigation.* Upper Sadder River: Prentice Hall.

Environmental Criminology Research, Inc. (2001). What is Rigel? Available at <http://www.geographicprofiling.com/rigel/index.html> Accessed 10.04.09.

Fox, J. A., & Levin, J. (1996). *Killer on campus.* New York: Avon Books.

Fritzon, K. (2000). The contribution of psychological research to arson investigation. In D. Canter & L. Alison (Eds.), *Profiling property crimes.* Aldershot: Ashgate.

Geberth, V. J. (1996). *Practical homicide investigation: Tactics, procedures and forensic techniques* (3rd ed.). Boca Raton: CRC Press.

Godwin, G. M. (1999). *Hunting serial predators: A multivariate classification approach to profiling violent behavior.* Boca Raton: CRC Press.

Godwin, J. (1985). *Murder USA: The ways we kill each other.* New York: Ballantine.

Gudjonsson, G., & Copson, G. (1997). The role of the expert in criminal investigation. In J. L. Jackson & D. Bekerian (Eds.), *Offender profiling: Theory, research and practice.* Chichester, UK: Wiley.

Harries, K. (1999). *Mapping crime: Principles and practice.* Washington, DC: U.S. Department of Justice, Crime Mapping and Research Center.

Hazelwood, R. R., & Douglas, J. E. (1980). The lust murderer. *FBI Law Enforcement Bulletin, 49*(4), 1-5.

Hazelwood, R. R., Ressler, R. K., Depue, R. L., & Douglas, J. E. (1995). Criminal investigative analysis: An overview. In R. R. Hazelwood & A. W. Burgess (Eds.), *Practical aspects of rape investigation: A multidisciplinary approach* (2nd ed.). Boca Raton: CRC Press.

Holmes, R. M., & Holmes, S. T. (2002). *Profiling violent crimes: An investigative tool.* Thousand Oaks: Sage.

Investigations Subcommittee and Defense Policy Panel of the Committee on Armed Services House of Representatives, (1990). *USS Iowa tragedy: An investigative failure.* Washington, DC: U.S. Government Printing Office.

Jackson, J. L., & Bekerian, D. (1997). In J. J. Jackson & D. Bekerian (Eds.), *Offender profiling: Theory, research and practice.* Chichester: John Wiley and Sons.

Jackson, J. L., van den Eshof, P., & de Kleuver, E. E. (1997). A research approach to offender profiling. In J. L. Jackson & D. A. Bekerian (Eds.), *Offender profiling: Theory, research and practice.* Chichester: John Wiley and Sons.

Jenkins, P. (1994). *Using murder: The social construction of serial homicide.* New York: Aldine.

Kocsis, R. N., & Irwin, H. J. (1997). An analysis of spatial patterns in serial rape, arson, and burglary: The utility of the circle theory of environmental range for psychological profiling. *Psychiatry, Psychology & Law, 4,* 195–206.

Kocsis, R. N., Irwin, H. J., & Hayes, A. F. (1998). Organized and disorganized criminal behavior syndromes in arsonists: A validation study of a psychological profiling concept. *Psychology, Psychiatry and Law, 5*(1), 117–131.

Kopel, D. B., & Blackman, P. H. (1997). *No more Wacos: What's wrong with federal law enforcement and how to fix it.* New York: Prometheus.

Laverty, I., & MacLaren, P. (2002). Summer geographic profiling: A new tool for crime analysis. *Crime Mapping News, 5,* 5–8.

Liebert, J. A. (1985). Contributions of psychiatric consultations in the investigation of serial murder. *International Journal of Offender Therapy and Comparative Criminology, 29,* 187–199.

McGrath, M. G. (2000). Criminal profiling: Is there a role for the forensic psychiatrist? *Journal of the American Academy of Psychiatry and Law, 28,* 315–324.

Petherick, W. A. (2003). Criminal profiling: What's in a name? Comparing applied profiling methodologies. *Journal of Law and Social Challenges, June,* 173–188.

Petherick, W. A., & Turvey, B. E. (2008). Victimology. In B. E. Turvey (Ed.), *Criminal profiling: An introduction to behavioral evidence analysis* (3rd ed.). Burlington: Academic Press.

Petherick, W. A., & Turvey, B. E. (2012). Alternative methods of criminal profiling. In B. E. Turvey (Ed.), *Criminal profiling: An introduction to behavioral evidence analysis* (4th ed.). Burlington: Academic Press.

Ratcliffe, J. H. (2004). Crime mapping and the training needs of law enforcement. *European Journal on Criminal Policy and Research, 10,* 65–83.

Rengert, G. F., Piquero, A. R., & Jones, P. R. (1999). Distance decay reexamined. *Criminology, 37*(2), 427–445.

Ressler, R. K., & Burgess, A. W. (1985). Crime scene and profile characteristics of organized and disorganized serial murderers. *FBI Law Enforcement Bulletin, 54*(8), 18–25.

Ressler, R. K., Burgess, A. W., & Douglas, J. E. (1988). *Sexual homicides: Patterns and motives.* New York: Lexington Books.

Ressler, R. K., Burgess, A. W., Douglas, J. E., Hartman, C. R., & D'Agostino, R. B. (1986). Sexual killers and their victims: Identifying patterns through crime scene analysis. *Journal of Interpersonal Violence, 1*(3), 288–308.

Ressler, R. K., Burgess, A. W., Hartman, C. R., Douglas, J. E., & McCormack, A. (1986). Murderers who rape and mutilate. *Journal of Interpersonal Violence, 1*(3), 273–287.

Ressler, R. K., & Shachtman, T. (1992). *Whoever fights monsters.* New York: Pocket Books.

Rossmo, D. K. (1997). Geographic profiling. In J. L. Jackson & D. Bekerian (Eds.), *Offender profiling: Theory, research and practice.* Chichester: John Wiley and Sons.

Rossmo, D. K. (2000). *Geographic profiling.* Boca Raton: CRC Press.

Rynearson, J. (2002). *Evidence and crime scene reconstruction: A guide for field investigations* (6th ed.). Redding, CA: National Crime Investigation and Training.

Saferstein, R. (2004). *Criminalistics: An introduction to forensic science* (8th ed.). Upper Sadder River: Prentice Hall.

Santilla, P., Zappala, A., Laukannen, M., & Picozzi, M. (2003). Testing the utility of a geographical profiling approach in three rape series of a single offender: A case study. *Forensic Science International, 131,* 42–52.

Snook, B., Canter, D., & Bennell, C. (2002). Predicting the home location of serial offenders: A preliminary comparison of the accuracy of human judges with a geographic profiling system. *Behavioural Sciences and the Law, 20,* 109–118.

Snook, B., Taylor, P. J., & Bennell, C. (2004). Geographic profiling: The fast, frugal and accurate way. *Applied Cognitive Psychology, 18,* 105–121.

Stock, G. W. J. (2004). *Deductive logic.* Oxford: Project Gutenberg Press.

Superior Court of California. (1999). *The People of the State of California v. Douglas Scott Mouser,* Available at <http://www.corpus-delicti.com/mouser_101999_prodan_direct.html> Accessed 11.11.05.

Tamlyn, D. (1999). Deductive profiling: A clinical perspective from the UK. In B. E. Turvey (Ed.), *Criminal profiling: An introduction to behavioral evidence analysis.* London: Academic Press.

Thompson, C. C. (1999). *A glimpse of hell: The explosion on the USS Iowa and its cover-up.* New York: Norton.

Thornton, J. (2006). Crime reconstruction: Ethos and ethics. In J. W. Chisum & B. E. Turvey (Eds.), *Crime reconstruction.* San Diego: Academic Press.

Turvey, B. E. (2012). *Criminal profiling: An introduction to behavioral evidence analysis* (4th ed.). Burlington: Academic Press.

Vancouver Sun. (2001). Profiling section wasn't good value, Vancouver police deputy chief says, June 28.

van Koppen, P. J., & de Keijser, J. (1997). Desisting distance decay: On the aggregation of individual crime trips. *Criminology, 35,* 505–515.

West, A. (2000). Clinical assessment of homicide offenders: The significance of crime scene in offense and offender analysis. *Homicide Studies, 4*(3), 219–233.

Wilson, C. (2003). Mapping the criminal mind. *New Scientist, 178,* 47. April.

Wilson, P., Lincoln, R., & Kocsis, R. (1997). Validity, utility and ethics of profiling for serial violent and sexual offenders. *Psychology, Psychiatry and Law, 4*(1), 1–12.

Woodworth, M., & Porter, S. (2001). Historical foundations and current applications of criminal profiling in violent crime investigations. *Expert Evidence, 7,* 241–264.

Wright, J. A., Burgess, A. G., Laszlo, A. T., McCrary, G. O., & Douglas, J. E. (1996). A typology of interpersonal stalking. *Journal of Interpersonal Violence, 11*(4), 487–503.

5 Geographical Profiling: From Pins in Maps to GIS

Gareth Norris

Introduction

Whereas crimes may differ substantially in their *modus operandi*—both within and between the behaviors that signify that crime classification (e.g., rape or burglary)—they must nevertheless be constructed in a physical time and space. Arguments over crimes conducted on the Internet or debates on primary and secondary crime scenes aside, the physical setting for a crime is as real and important as the gun or threatening letter collected as evidence; some would argue that the analysis of these locations is equally important—possibly even more useful—as an investigative tool. Behavioral profiling is not only concerned with the internal motivations and physical characteristics of the offender, but also other patterns of activity, including spatial awareness. Despite some promising research findings that suggest a reasonably high accuracy rate for the technique referred to as "geographic profiling," it seems that there needs to be more information on the other attributes of the offender for it to have a practical application in the field. However, recent developments with Geographic Information Systems (GIS) and what has been termed "predictive policing" have created a resurgence of interest in these principles of spatial behavior.

Theories of Spatial Behavior

The study of criminal geography is almost as old as modern criminology itself; the Chicago School are regarded as pioneers in the analysis of offender's spatial behavior (see Shaw &

McKay, 1942). Following the traditions of Thrasher (1927), they established concepts such as the *Zonal Hypothesis*, which identified particular areas in a city where crime was more likely to be experienced. This theory suggested that although the majority of crime was committed in a few roughly defined areas of a city, there were distinct population characteristics that characterized these zones; recent immigrants and the less financially stable being omnipresent in these high-crime neighborhoods. Focusing their attention on developing a convincing explanation of this phenomenon, they proposed *Social Disorganization Theory* to illustrate the lack of established norms among certain communities as a major factor contributing to their experiences of criminal behavior.

There are many other theories that have been applied to understanding crime in a similar way. For example, *Rational Choice Theory* (see Bennett & Wright, 1984) was originally developed from the analysis of interview data with convicted burglars. The proposal was that when choosing to offend, perpetrators would perform a rudimentary cost-benefit analysis; by weighing the expected reward against the potential cost of offending (i.e., being caught and punished), decisions would be made regarding when and where to commit particular crimes. Similarly, *Routine Activity Theory* (see Clarke and Felson, 1993; Cohen & Felson, 1979) suggests that most crime has three basic elements: a motivated offender, a suitable victim, and the absence of a capable guardian. The authors suggest that the reason inner-city areas have such high crime rates is due to the abundant coexistence of these three elements. The location of potential targets was a key aspect of the decision to offend and formed a significant part of many offenders' daily lives as they sought out the best locations for crime.

The Chicago School's analysis focused primarily on the *ecological* aspects of crime distribution, and it wasn't until some decades later that attempts were made to explain these activities from a more individualized perspective. The work of environmental psychology more generally focuses on the relationship that people have with their physical surroundings; the use of this research in areas such as town planning and crime prevention is well documented (see Crowe, 2000; Newman, 1972). In explaining the specific spatial behavior of criminals, the work of Brantingham and Brantingham (1981) was pioneering in this domain. Their theory proposed that—in executing criminal behavior—offenders would utilize spatial information about an area gained from the knowledge they acquired in their *noncriminal* activities. In other words, offenders would operate in a similar spatial fashion and range as they did when not offending; that is, the places where they worked, socialized, shopped, and so forth, and that this would ultimately be tied to or have a bearing upon their home location. What have become commonly referred to as mental maps (Canter, 1994) are the internal representations of the geography of the external world. Each person's mental map is largely unique; this is not only a result of the different spatial behavior they experience, but also the individual interpretation they apply to it. For example, a car driver's perception of travelling from A to B will be significantly different from that of someone who travels the same journey by train or on foot.

In relation to behavioral profiling, there are a number of points that should also be considered when analyzing spatial behavior. The first is that a person's mental map is reliant on an individual interpretation of the actual distance traveled. Knowledge of a city is likely to be of poor scale; the actual distances are at best an estimate that can be influenced by traveling times, traffic, land makeup, and familiarity. Indeed cities with underground transport systems have been shown to significantly distort a person's mental map in the physical sense, as to the locations of and distances between key landmarks (Rossmo, 2000). Physical barriers, such as major roads and rivers, can also have a major bearing on a person's spatial behavior, presenting a psychological obstacle. People living in north London, for example, will rarely travel south of the river Thames for this very reason (Canter, 1994). The other major consideration is simply the ability a person has to cover distances in the physical sense. Time and money have a major bearing on individual mobility; those lucky enough to own a car seemingly have a major advantage in this respect, although such means of transport is not always so efficient in densely populated areas. Cheap and reliable public transport is also a major factor and often separates rural and urban environments in relation to mobility.

In summary, the ideas and theories on why crime appears in particular places can provide us with considerable information to develop the concept of being able to infer the spatial behavior of the offender from a series of crime scenes. When used in the criminal investigation process, this information can provide an estimate as to the location of an offender's home. However, the problem therein is that geographical profiles (and arguably all profiles) provide, at best, a broad estimation based within a range of acceptable parameters. Unlike the sophisticated technology viewed in the fast-paced TV shows of this genre, it is unlikely to whittle down to a specific address! Hence, a geographical profile will tend to indicate areas of interest, which may be useful in narrowing down the suspect pool.

The Center of Gravity

One of the best examples of the utility of a geographical profile is also one of the first instances that such knowledge was applied (albeit retrospectively) in a criminal case. Peter Sutcliffe, the "Yorkshire Ripper," terrorized the north of England in the late 1970s and early 1980s, culminating in the murder of 15 women. From a geographical perspective, Sutcliffe's crimes were interesting due to both the specificity of his victims and the range of area that he covered. As a lorry driver, Sutcliffe had a large mental map of various areas of northern England as well as the mobility and justification to visit these locations. From an investigative perspective, this range, along with a major anomaly in the form of a hoax confession,[1] gave the police a significant challenge in trying to deploy investigative resources to one identifiable area. Although some of the early crimes surrounded the Bradford area, the series quickly progressed to Leeds, some 20 miles away, and then to the town of Manchester, which is over 50 miles from the first murder. This area is vast and densely populated; as it became more obvious that they were dealing with a highly mobile offender, the police were unable to rule out the possibility that the Ripper

[1]The so-called Wearside Jack was a series of tapes sent to the investigation team claiming to be from the Ripper himself, where he refers to himself as Jack. Linguistic analysis pinpointed his accent to an area further north of the site of the murders and diverted attention away from Sutcliffe for a number of years. Ultimately, this contributed to a number of women losing their lives, and in 2006, John Samuel Humble was sentenced to 8 years in prison for perverting the course of justice. Interestingly, FBI profiler Robert Ressler alleged that he told the UK police the tapes were a hoax in his memoirs published in 1992.

could live in any of these areas. The other important fact was that Sutcliffe was mainly targeting prostitutes (or at least lone women in red-light areas), and as such it cast the assumption that it was highly unlikely the police could either predict where the next victim would be or where the suspect might be from.

Peter Sutcliffe was apprehended quite by chance after a long and exhaustive inquiry that spurred some other vital changes to investigation procedures in the United Kingdom; for example, the HOLMES computer system for major enquires was set up as a result of the *Byford Enquiry* into the operation. During this case review, the police had consulted with the Director of the Home Office Central Research Establishment, Dr. Stuart Kind. Using techniques he had learned serving as a navigator in the Royal Air Force during WWII, Kind analyzed the data on the crime locations to provide an area that he described as the "centre of gravity." In essence, this technique involved calculating the shortest distance between the offences. Kind (1999, p.79–80) described it with reference to his experiences in ordinance during the war:

> *The "centre of gravity" approach can be easily understood, in principle, by imagining some fairly common distribution problems. Imagine the warehouse for a network of supermarkets or the fuel dump for a group of bomber airfields. What are the criteria for positioning the warehouse, or the fuel dump, for minimum travel overall? Nowadays sophisticated computer methods are used to solve such problems but this must not be allowed to obscure the elementary fact that, in principle, the problem is easily conceived in simple mechanical terms. Imagine a map with the individual supermarket positions marked on it. Now visualise choosing a position for the warehouse, by eye, somewhere near the centre of the cluster of supermarkets. Mark all the positions so identified by using map pins. Now join each supermarket position with the warehouse by a piece of taut thread. Measure the total length of thread used. Now choose another position for the warehouse and repeat the exercise. Do this several times. The amount of thread used in each exercise will vary but the warehouse position that uses the least thread lies at the centre of gravity of the cluster of warehouses.*

In the case of the Yorkshire Ripper, Kind assessed this to be near to Bradford, and possibly "Manningham or Shipley" (Kind, 1985, p. 390). After Sutcliffe's apprehension—made quite by chance during a random traffic stop—he gave his address as "6 Garden Lane, Heaton, Bradford" (the town between Manningham and Shipley).

This finding is somewhat remarkable and in retrospect would quite likely have led to an earlier apprehension of Sutcliffe—he had already been questioned a number of times prior to his eventual arrest. Had the police consulted with Kind earlier—and perhaps been more open to the principles that he advocated—the investigation could have been directed toward searching for an offender in that general area. The huge area that Sutcliffe operated in seriously hampered the effective investigation and the follow-up on the millions of leads that were provided to the police. Stuart Kind went on to become one of the United Kingdom's most prominent forensic scientists, and in his own humble biographies recounts his experiences in a range of major investigations (Kind, 1987, 1999). Although his inputs to the Yorkshire Ripper inquiry were received too late to be of use in the apprehension of Sutcliffe, nevertheless his expertise was valued during the *Byford Enquiry* into the investigation, and it put these relatively novel techniques into the police toolkit for large inquiries of this sort.

Kim Rossmo and David Canter

One of the early proponents of modern geographical profiling was Dr. Kim Rossmo, originally a civilian with the Vancouver Police Department. Rossmo is a keen supporter of environmental criminology, having studied with the Brantinghams at Simon Fraser University, British Columbia. He often cites their work alongside *Routine Activity Theory* in relation to his *Criminal Geographical Targeting* (CGT) method of offender geospatial behavior. Included in this theory is an elaborate formula that identifies the spatial behavior of serial offenders and was used in the pilot episode for the US crime drama *Numb3rs*. More recently, Rossmo has applied his analysis of spatial behavior to predators in the animal kingdom and, specifically, the hunting patterns of white sharks in South Africa (Martin, Rossmo & Hammerschlag, 2009).

Returning to the theoretical ideas in relation to offending, Rossmo's models are based upon a range of different theoretical propositions concerning human geospatial behavior, including those mentioned earlier and additional input from wider social perspectives, for example, Hirschi's *Social Control Theory*. Rossmo (1995, p. 224) details this four-step process:

1. Map boundaries delineating the offender's hunting area are first established using the locations of the crimes and standard procedures for addressing edge effects.
2. Manhattan distances (i.e., orthogonal distances measured along the street grid) from every "point" on the map, the number of which is determined by the measurement resolution of the x and y scales, to each crime location are then calculated.
3. Next, these Manhattan distances are used as independent variable values in a function that produces a number that: (a) if the point lies outside the buffer zone, becomes smaller the longer the distance, following some form of distance-decay; or (b) if the point lies inside the buffer zone, becomes larger the longer the distance. Numbers are computed from this function for each of the crime locations. For example, if there are 12 crime locations, each point on the map will have 12 numbers associated with it.
4. Finally, these multiple numbers are multiplied together to produce a single score for each map point. The higher the resultant score, the greater the probability that the point contains the offender's residence.

Rossmo cites a high success rate in actual investigations and research simulations, with the offender usually being in the top 5% search area. Sensibly, the limitations of CGT/geographic profiling are accounted for—particularly those based upon small data series events (i.e., serial crimes with relatively few offenses). It is recognized that "[...] the randomness inherent in most human behavior limits the conclusions that can be derived from a small number of crime sites" (p. 227). Rossmo also identifies a range of investigative considerations/applications, for example, Patrol Saturation (a geographic profile of the Hillside Strangler led the LAPD to send over 200 officers to an area of Los Angeles). The key strength of Rossmo's approach is perhaps the ability to link the theoretical and investigative elements together into a somewhat practical solution for those investigating serial crime, although he is not without his critics (see Rossmo, 2005 and Snook, Taylor & Bennel, 2004).

Rossmo is relatively unique in his belief that geographical profiling is essentially a method in its own right, whereas other profiling theories incorporate spatial information within the overall investigative advice. For example, it is common for the FBI to make assertions to where the offender may be operating from, gleaned from factors such as the availability of a vehicle. Similarly, the clinical profile of Metesky by Brussels (see Chapter 1) correctly deduced that he would reside in Connecticut based largely due to the timing of his offenses and potential travel options. Additionally, as part of the five-factor model developed within the *Investigative Psychology* paradigm, the "significance of time and place" is included as a key variable. Canter and colleagues have since become key players in this research domain and have sought to develop, test, and refine these spatial theories.

One of Canter's first attempts to apply the principles of environmental psychology to the study of crime was in the profile he produced in the Railway Rapist investigation (Canter, 1994). He suggested that the offender would live in the area circumscribed by the first three offenses and also that he would have some knowledge of the railway system in that area. This information would prove to be quite accurate and led to the development of a theoretical model of offenders' spatial behavior (Canter & Larkin, 1993). The circle theory of offending behavior proposed that if a circle is drawn using the two furthest most crime locations as its diameter, then not only would all the crime scenes be located within it, but the location of the offender's home also. Remarkably this was found to be accurate in 85% of the serial rapist cases examined. Two constraints were also proposed on this model, that being the "marauder" and the "commuter" offender typology. Those offenders who were contained within the circle were classified as marauders, as it was assumed that they would travel out in different directions from their home location to commit crime. This contrasted with the commuter, who was more likely to travel to a specific location in order to offend.

Perhaps due to its apparent effectiveness or even its simplicity, the circle theory has stood the test of time with regard to its ability to predict offenders' spatial behavior. There are many recent studies that both cite and test its validity (e.g., Kocsis, Cooksey, Irwin & Allen, 2002). Current directions have now focused on discovering the behaviors that occur *within* the circle and how an offender's activities progress with the crime series. The notion of *distance decay* proposed that as the offenses in a crime series proceed, the actual distance traveled will reduce (see Rossmo, 2000; Canter, 1994). Research into this concept suggests that the first three offenses were often the furthest apart, hence encompassing the remainder of the offenses in a series and the home location. From this discovery it was reasonable to assume that the other offenses in a series would then be closer to home and that as a crime series progressed the locations would become closer to home. Another aspect of this theory was the idea of a *buffer zone*, which would be an area around the home location where the offender wouldn't offend, probably due to factors such as being recognized.

The aim of these models was to enable the police to narrow the search area for an offender. It is obvious that there is considerable utility in being able to focus on a particular neighborhood in search for a suitable suspect, rather than a whole city for instance. As with profiling in general, the predictions that have been inferred from the analysis form a basis on which resources in an investigation can be directed. The geographical profile is unable to provide the exact address of an offender, but coupled with other information will assist in the selection and elimination of suspects in a large pool. For example, a list of vehicle types, of which there may be 500 in a city, could be reduced to 50 with the aid of a geographical profile. From an investigation perspective, this number becomes far more manageable, saving both time and money in the process. Geographical profiling has the ability to direct scarce resources into particular areas.

Application of Geographical Theories

The overall outcome of these research endeavors has resulted in a model of spatial offending behavior that became more accurate at predicting home locations than the circle theory alone; such predictions have formed the basis for statistical analysis of the spatial information in a computer simulation known as a *Geographical Profiling System* (GPS). Research by Canter and his colleagues at the Centre for Investigative Psychology resulted in the development of such a system known as *Dragnet.* This model of GPS utilized the concepts developed in the course of investigations, namely the circle theory, distance decay, and the buffer zone. What resulted was a computer simulation that was able to provide areas that were likely to provide added benefit in the criminal investigation process. By entering coordinates as represented in a series of crime locations, the system provides hot spots that could be indicators of the offender's home location and hence direct resources during an investigation.

Others have also produced simulations similar to Dragnet, most notably Rossmo (1993) and his package named the *Criminal Geographical Targeting* (CGT) model or its commercial name: *RIGEL.* Using algorithms that contribute to applying Rossmo's theory to a computer simulation, it develops a jeopardy surface that will highlight areas that are likely to be of significance to the offender's home location. Rossmo develops the marauder/commuter analysis further to encompass "hunting styles" of offenders, which include both their search and attack methods. The two elements are proposed to affect the encounter and dump sites, respectively, and allow a more subjective analysis of the crime scene locations.

The research and application of geographic profiling has also been prominent in Australia, primarily by Richard Kocsis. Utilizing Canter's circle theory, Kocsis has applied the method to urban and rural burglars in NSW. He discovered the marauder and commuter ratio to be slightly less than the 85% of serial rapists (Canter and Gregory, 1994), with approximately 65% of burglars' homes being located inside the circle circumscribed by their two furthest crimes. This would appear to be of less investigative utility, but still raises some important questions in the analysis *across* criminal activities. Indeed a recent publication has been able to highlight the use of appropriate heuristics to aid in the selection of an appropriate area in the search for an offender (Snook, Canter & Bennel, 2002). Comparing Dragnet with a student's ability to predict an offender's home base indicated that the computer was of significantly greater accuracy. However, when students were later informed of distance decay and the circle theory, their predictions were at a comparable level to Dragnet. This is of particular importance when considering the utility that a computerized system provides, in that there may only be a limit to the accuracy that the theory can provide when identifying a home location.

Whereas some academics and professionals have denounced the need for sophisticated computerized models, recent technology has made the analysis of the spatial behavior of criminals a science in its own right. For example, a recent study by the University of Birmingham[2] used the location information gleaned from a person's Smartphone to make predictions about where they would likely be in preceding days down to a distance of 200 meters. Although the algorithm was initially developed to exploit commercial interests, the researchers believe it may have additional applications, for example, in predicting criminal behavior. Based upon the theory of overlap between the criminal and noncriminal spatial activity that features heavily in all geographical profiling methodologies, police could utilize this information to locate and apprehend suspects just by tracking their mobile device.

What has been termed "predictive policing" has found favor in some law enforcement circles. Exploited in the Tom Cruise movie *Minority Report,* these efforts to preempt offending behavior have been found to have slightly less foretelling ability, but have nonetheless showed some level of early success. The Californian city of Santa Cruz, has been one such example, with reported burglaries down some 19% since the inception of this practice. Using a computer algorithm called PredPol,[3] the basic premise is that crime is concentrated in space and time, with the majority of offenders and victims experiencing repeated involvement. Just as the Chicago School had developed its *Zonal Hypothesis* based upon the concentration of offending in particular neighborhoods, modern systems utilize GPS mapping to provide real-time predictions that enable police patrols to be targeted in specific locations. Unlike the instances in *Minority Report,* the overall premise is to save money by utilizing police resources in an efficient way. It is also unlikely that an individual offender would be apprehended *before* a crime has been committed, as the process appears to be preventative from the standpoint of resource deployment. Academic reviews of these practices are limited and largely inconclusive; one such attempt by McCue and McNulty (2004) suggested that there was predictive capacity in relation to establishing armed robbery, but that it extended to more than simple time–location analysis and needed to include temporal data also. Braga (2005) also suggests that there are some real tangible benefits from targeted policing, without the threat of displacement (simply moving the crime problem on to an adjacent area). Debates continue in this area from within the wider context of Problem Oriented/Community Policing (see Bullock, Erol & Tilley, 2006).

An Investigative Method in Its Own Right?

Geographical considerations are frequently included in profiles as a matter of course and there is debate as to whether the principles of geographical behavior can or should be separated from the wider endeavors of providing investigative advice. Knabe-Nicol and Alison (2011) provide a convincing argument that indeed the cognitive expertise of these profilers is a key factor in the

[2]http://www.birmingham.ac.uk/news/latest/2012/07/16-Jul-12-Do-you-know-where-youre-going--Your-smartphone-soon-will.aspx

[3]www.predpol.com

development of a distinct "profession." Based upon UK research with four dedicated geographical profilers attached to the National Policing Improvement Agency (NPIA), the authors highlight the specific abilities among these individuals to recognize patterns in both spatial and temporal crime data and to use this information to form specific hypotheses about the likely events and offender. Interestingly, the study reports how these geoprofilers were able to provide investigative advice in single-case crimes rather than relying on the analysis of patterns associated with serial offenses as is often the norm. Hence, it appears from the results of this study that there is a level of tacit knowledge that is specific to the endeavors of these individuals, which may be quite different in its scope to the analysis of crime scenes and interpersonal interaction.

Although considerable research has been able to highlight the basic utility of geographic profiling, there is always scope to further test these theories and develop new hypotheses that can give further direction to the study of offender spatial behavior. Attempts have also been made to integrate the crime scene behaviors that are likely to have an influence on the geographical behavior of offenders. Various researchers have indicated that the average distance that an offender will travel varies according to the crime being committed (e.g., Pyle, 1974; Rhodes and Conly, 1981) and other factors such as an offender's age (Nichols, 1980), sex (Rengert, 1975), and race (Pettiway, 1982) are also believed to have a bearing on this journey to offend distance. LeBeau (1987) also differentiates distances according to area type (e.g., industrial or residential). Specifically looking at the crime of rape, Canter and Gregory (1994) found that white offenders traveled further than black, and that those who raped outdoors traveled 2.7 times the distance of indoor rapists. Davies and Dale (1995) also discovered that in their sample of rapists, 29% would offend within one mile of home.

Another significant area of research has focused on what have been referred to as "dump sites," that is, the place where a body was found (and in some instances also where an attack actually took place). Much less emphasis has been applied to other aspects of the overall spatial behavior, for instance, where the actual abduction may have taken place; the so-called *point of first encounter* (PFE). This has the possibility of not only influencing the relationship to the offender's home, but also the link between these locations and the dump sites as proposed by Godwin and Canter (1997). Their analysis of these two separate locations in a crime series indicated that the PFE was likely to surround the offender's home and be significantly closer to it than the dump sites. In turn the dump sites were then likely to be at a greater distance than the offender's home and surround the encounter locations for the sample of 56 US serial killers in the study. This has important implications for the study of serial crimes and it was indicated that PFE was a better indicator than dump sites, certainly in terms of distance and possibly for the understanding of spatial behavior in general. In particular, the notion that recognition and initial interaction of victims was developed during daily activities was proposed, along with the notion that selection of dump sites could be a deliberate attempt to distract from the home location. Godwin and Canter also cite the work of Ford (1991), in that it is imperative to discover where the predator met its prey. Various anomalies were also discovered; for example, it appeared from the data that the ninth and tenth dump sites were on average closer to home. This perhaps provides an indication that offending behavior becomes more integrated with daily life, growing confidence, or simply the risk of transportation.

Studies such as these give a somewhat more subjective analysis to spatial behavior and highlight the possibility of mapping crime scene activities within the more specific geographical profiling paradigms. For example, if a series of indoor and outdoor rapes are linked to one offender, we could utilize the findings of Canter and Gregory (1994) and assume that the indoor offenses will be more likely to be near the offender's home. Warren et al. (1998) applied this method of breaking down the actual activities in a series of rapes, to provide a number of basic assumptions about the offender's spatial activities. For example, those offenders who rape during the day are likely to have a larger buffer (or safety) zone, most probably due to the reduced chance of being seen and/or recognized during the hours of darkness. A similar finding was reported for older offenders. In a comparable fashion to Canter and Gregory (1994), the burglar-rapist who entered a victim's home on average would cover a greater distance to offend, and the same was found for convicted rapists, those who selected white victims, and those who brought restraints to the scene.

Other research has also provided some more specific variations regarding offender's spatial behavior. For example, Warren et al. (1998) were able to provide statistical support for their findings, although they were unable to provide concrete explanations as to why these differences in behavior may occur. For example, the race of an offender may have economic bearing in that African-Americans in the United States are poorer than whites on average, hence influencing their transportation methods. It could be equally as likely though, as Warren et al. suggest, that fear of recognition in a nonblack neighborhood could be just as important. What this study is useful in highlighting is that there is a subjective element to offending behavior that to some extent any geographical profile predictions would be wise to adhere to. Offending behavior is not uniform, and the type and style of offense may have just as important an impact on crime location as an offender's mental map.

But while there would appear to be scope to expand and develop the methods and procedures, there is also be evidence that limitations may have been reached as to how far geographic profiling can develop. Although computerized methods have been hailed as a major breakthrough in spatial analysis and criminal investigation, the work of Snook, Canter, and Bennel (2002) would cast some doubt about the increased utility that these systems provide. Statements such as "there is no substitute for a good theory" or Occam's Razor, "a basic principle of science states that, when multiple explanations for a phenomena exist, the simplest one should be chosen" (Rossmo, 2000, p. 49), could be pertinent to the analysis of geographical behavior. Perhaps the circle theory or Rossmo's CGT system are at the pinnacle of objective scientific analysis in this case. Human geographic behavior may be too sporadic to be able to progress from the basic premises identified in environmental psychology and criminology.

Conclusion

This chapter has highlighted some of the long-standing theories about criminal behavior in the physical environment and also some of the current research and applications that this area of criminal profiling is moving toward. Twenty years ago it probably would have been the realm of science fiction television series and spy genre films that would have been bold to predict where an individual in question would reside. This is especially so for the GPS tools, which are able, to some extent, to emulate human behavior. Although it is unlikely that an actual address would be produced and there are other limitations, this is hardly the point in question. In the majority of investigations, resources are limited; geographical knowledge that can be applied to the direction of these resources is of unquestionable value.

If we accept and compensate for the limitations and areas of fallibility that have been documented in the literature on profiling in general, then geographic profiling can be marketed as a reliable, valid, and highly useful tool at the police's disposal. The very nature of human behavior, especially that with a high emotive content, will be unlikely to conform to a strictly uniform pattern. But by accepting this, in the cases where these patterns do appear that have been proposed in this area, there is a very real possibility of identifying an offender's home location. Whether geographical profiling is seen as a separate method or not, the theoretical underpinnings of this practice are robust and universal, which is somewhat in contrast to the debates and controversies that surround the wider methods. However, it appears that technology might be the key factor that drives the development of spatial crime analysis, and in some respects it will allow the police to create systems that provide investigative support in-house without having to rely on outside expertise.

Questions

1. Which team of researchers created the *Zonal Hypothesis*?
   a. The New York School
   b. The London School
   c. The Melbourne School
   d. The Chicago School
2. Dr Kim Rossmo was originally a civilian with:
   a. The LAPD
   b. The Australian Federal Police
   c. The Vancouver Police Department
   d. New Scotland Yard
3. David Canter first provided geographical profiling advice in the case of:
   a. The Railway Rapist
   b. The Beltway Sniper
   c. The Yorkshire Ripper
   d. The Backpacker Murderer
4. Most offenders will only travel into specific areas to commit crime. *True or false?*
5. Computers can predict an offender's home location better than humans trained in geographical profiling techniques. *True or false?*

References

Bennett, T., & Wright, R. (1984). *Burglars on burglary: Prevention and the offender.* Aldershot, Hants: Gower.

Braga, A. (2005). Hot spots policing and crime prevention: A systematic review of randomized controlled trials. *Journal of Experimental Criminology, 1,* 317–342.

Brantingham, P. L., & Brantingham, P. J. (1981). Notes on the geometry of crime. In P. J. Brantingham & P. L. Brantingham (Eds.), *Environmental criminology* (pp. 27–54). Beverley Hills: Sage Publications.

Bullock, K., Erol, R., & Tilley, N. (2006). Problem-oriented policing and partnerships: Implementing an evidence-based approach to crime reduction. Home Office: Crime Science Series.

Canter, D. (1994). *Criminal shadows.* London: Harper Collins.

Canter, D., & Gregory, A. (1994). Identifying the residential location of rapists. *Journal of the Forensic Science Society, 34,* 169–175.

Canter, D., & Larkin, P. (1993). The environmental range of serial rapists. *Journal of Environmental Psychology, 13,* 63–69.

Clarke, R., & Felson, M. (1993). *Routine activity and rational choice.* New Brunswick: Transaction Publishers.

Cohen, L., & Felson, M. (1979). Social change and crime rate trends: A routine activity approach. *American Sociological Review, 44,* 588–605.

Crowe, Tim. (2000). *Crime prevention through environmental design* (2nd ed.). Boston: Butterworth.

Davies, A., & Dale, A. (1995). *Locating the stranger rapist.* London: Police Research Group Special Interest Series, Home Office. (Paper 3).

Ford, D. (1991). Investigating serial murder: The case of Indiana's gay murders. In S. Egger (Ed.), *Serial murder: An elusive phenomenon.* New York, NY: Praeger.

Kind, S. (1987). Navigational ideas and the Yorkshire Ripper investigation. *Journal of Navigation, 40,* 385–393.

Kind, S. (1999). *The sceptical witness.* Harrogate: Forensic Science Service.

Knabe-Nicol, S., & Alison, L. (2011). The cognitive expertise of geographic profilers. In Laurence Alison & Lee Rainbow (Eds.), *Professionalising offender profiling: Forensic and investigative psychology in practice.* Oxford: Routledge.

Kocsis, R. N., Cooksey, R. W., Irwin, H. J., & Allen, G. (2002). A further assessment of "circle theory" for geographic psychological profiling. *Australian and New Zealand Journal of Criminology, 35,* 43–62.

LeBeau, J. L. (1987). The journey to rape: Geographic distance and the rapist's method of approaching the victim. *Journal of Police Science and Administration, 15,* 129–136.

Martin, R. A., Rossmo, D. K., & Hammerschlag, N. (2009). Hunting patterns and geographic profiling of white shark predation. *Journal of Zoology, 279,* 111–118.

Newman, Oscar. (1972). *Defensible space: Crime prevention through urban design.* New York: Macmillan.

Nichols, W. (1980). Mental maps, social characteristics, and criminal mobility. In D. E. Georges-Abeyie & K. Harries (Eds.), *Crime: A spatial perspective.* New York, NY: Columbia University Press.

Pettiway, L. (1982). Mobility of robbery and burglary offenders: Ghetto and non-ghetto spaces. *Urban Affairs Quarterly, 18,* 255–270.

Pyle, G. (1974). The spatial dynamics of crime. Department of Geography Research Paper 159. University of Chicago Press; Chicago.

Rengert, G. F. (1975). Some effects of being female on criminal spatial behavior. *The Pennsylvania Geographer, 13,* 10–18.

Rhodes, W. M., & Conly, C. (1981). Crime and mobility: An empirical study. In P. J. Brantingham & P. L. Brantingham (Eds.), *Environmental criminology* (pp. 167–188).

Rossmo, D. K. (1995). Place, space, and police investigations: Hunting serial violent criminals. In J. E. Eck & D. L. Weisburd (Eds.), *Crime and place: Crime prevention studies* (Vol. 4, pp. 217–235). Monsey, NY: Criminal Justice Press.

Rossmo, D. K. (2000). *Geographic profiling.* Boca Raton, FL: CRC Press.

Rossmo, D. K. (2005). Geographic heuristics or shortcuts to failure?: Response to Snook et al. *Applied Cognitive Psychology, 19*(5), 531–678.

Shaw, C., & McKay, D. (1942). *Juvenile delinquency in urban areas.* Chicago: University of Chicago Press.

Snook, B., Canter, D. V., & Bennell, C. (2002). Predicting the home location of serial offenders: A preliminary comparison of the accuracy of human judges with a geographic profiling system. *Behavioural Sciences and the Law, 20,* 109–118.

Snook, B., Taylor, P. J., & Bennell, C. (2004). Geographic profiling: The fast, frugal and accurate way. *Applied Cognitive Psychology, 18,* 105–121.

Warren, J., Reboussin, R., Hazelwood, R., Cummings, A., Gibbs, N., & Trumbetta, S. (1998). Crime scene and distance correlates of serial rape. *Journal of Quantitative Criminology, 14*(1), 35–59.

Rossmo, D.K. (1995). Place, space, and police investigations: Hunting serial violent criminals. In J. E. Eck & D. L. Weisburd (Eds.), *Crime and place: Crime prevention studies* (Vol. [illegible]). Monsey, NY: Criminal Justice Press.

6 The Fallacy of Accuracy

Wayne Petherick

Introduction

The defining criterion by which the utility of a particular tool is often judged is its accuracy or sensitivity of detection. We place little faith in that which is inaccurate, or in those things that do not detect what they are meant to. Things are no different in the profiling community, and the most common measure by which a profiler claims utility is how close his or her approximations are to an offender, if one is caught. As will be shown in this chapter, with the craft being the way it is, this is probably the worst possible way to declare one's success.

It has been noted in the preceding chapters that a criminal profile is an estimation (the differences in profiling methods aside) of an offender based on his behavior and interactions with a crime scene and a victim. Typically, the goal is to identify gross personality and behavioral characteristics that may set the criminal apart from other criminals, or from general members of the community.

The defining issue here is that any attempt to describe criminal profiling must include an understanding that it is an attempt to identify gross personality and behavioral types and traits, rather than indicating the guilt of a specific individual. This differentiates the approach as class evidence, where one item can be placed in a group of similar items, rather than individuating evidence, which can differentiate between individuals, even of the same class (Inman & Rudin, 1997). Although profiling belongs to the former group, practitioners often toe the line or clearly exceed the limits of what can be legitimately achieved through the process (*New Jersey v. Fortin* is one such example, discussed by McGrath in Chapter 7, as is the profile prepared in *The Estate of Samuel H. Sheppard v. The State of Ohio*, discussed subsequently). Signature evidence, a common form of profiling evidence, is often used in court to provide a basis for case

Profiling and Serial Crime.

linkage. If it can be shown by a profiler that the crimes of an accused are remarkably similar to other open cases, then these crimes may also be attributed to the same offender, or it may be possible to taint a jury by claiming that a current series of offenses is similar to those an accused has been previously charged with. This speaks to the ultimate issue, usurping the role of the jury and potentially corrupting criminal justice processes.

The confusion as to the ability of a profile to identify a specific person is evidenced in the Criminal Investigative Analysis (CIA) submitted by Gregg McCrary in *The Estate of Samuel H. Sheppard v. The State of Ohio* (Court TV Online, 1999). Although a CIA is based on probabilities, the typical opening caveat in this report was conspicuously absent. Although it was noted throughout the report that "the more time an offender spends at a crime scene the higher the probability that the offender is comfortable and familiar with that scene," and "the totality of this evidence reveals that this crime was, in all probability, not a 'for-profit' or drug-related burglary, nor a sexually motivated crime," the report goes far beyond these statements of probability in closing where it is noted that:

> *The totality of the physical, forensic and behavioral evidence allows for only one logical conclusion and that is that the homicide of Marilyn Reese Sheppard on July 4, 1954 was a staged domestic homicide committed by Dr. Samuel Sheppard. The known indicators for criminal staging as well as the known crime scene indicators consistent with a staged domestic homicide are abundantly present. This evidence not only supports no other logical conclusion, but also significantly contradicts Dr. Samuel Sheppard's testimony and statements.*

This is not only in opposition to other assertions throughout the profile, which are correlations between this case and indicators provided in the *Crimes Classification Manual* (see Douglas, Burgess, Burgess & Ressler, 1992), but far exceeds the certainty with which such a conclusion can be made. In this case, the profiler is attempting to individuate the offender from the evidence. Behavioral evidence simply cannot meet this threshold.

The Fallacy of Accuracy

As criminal profiling methods and techniques permeate the academic and investigative communities, more is being learned about how offender characteristics are developed from the offender's crime scene and behavior. This may be attributed to the rise of a number of independent schools of thought in the criminal profiling community that are challenging long-held assumptions, as well as an increase in the literature about the efficacy of profiling (see Ainsworth, 2001; Horgan, O'Sullivan & Hammond, 2003; Devery, 2010; Norris & Petherick, 2010).

Although there are many areas for improvement in this field, only one will be the focus of this chapter, and that is the fallacy of accuracy. This issue is not only important, but highly relevant to the current development of the field as it speaks directly to the utility of the end product: the final criminal profile.

The fallacy of accuracy encompasses two issues: actual accuracy and utility.

First, we must address the issue of accuracy. When pressed on the witness stand, at professional meetings, or in interviews, some criminal profilers boldly claim 100% accuracy rates, that their methods and analysis are as good as fingerprints and DNA evidence (*New Jersey v. Fortin*, 2000), or that they "haven't been wrong yet" (McKnight, 2000). Other criminal profilers have suggested that accuracy equates to usefulness; if it was accurate, that means it must have been useful and vice versa. Still other criminal profilers argue that if criminal profiling wasn't accurate, they wouldn't get so many requests for it. Would this same argument be accepted if put forth by a psychic? Clearly, none of this reasoning is valid. The only way to determine actual accuracy is to compare a criminal profile to an offender who has been unequivocally convicted of the crime that was profiled (and even under ideal conditions this may be a very subjective process). If this is not being done, then the full extent of a profiler's accuracy is unknown and any claims should be viewed with the appropriate skepticism.

What is often forgotten by zealous criminal profilers is that, as discussed in Hazelwood, Ressler, Depue, and Douglas (1995), a criminal profile, also referred to as a CIA (Cooper & King, 2001), is an investigative tool that is designed only to narrow and define suspect pools. As such, a disclaimer usually precedes the actual analysis such as that discussed in Hazelwood (1995, pp. 176–177):

> *It should be noted that the attached analysis is not a substitute for a thorough and well-planned investigation and should not be considered all inclusive. The information provided is based upon reviewing, analyzing, and researching criminal cases similar to the case submitted by the requesting agency. The final analysis is based upon probabilities. Note, however, that no two criminal acts or criminal personalities are exactly alike and, therefore, the offender may not always fit the profile in every category.*

The caution prescribed by the disclaimer is contextualized in Hazelwood, Ressler, Depue, and Douglas (1995, p. 125), where it is stated that "CIA and profiling should be used to augment proven investigative techniques and must not be allowed to replace those methods; to do so would be counterproductive to the goal of identifying the unknown offender." But what is published in the literature and what is told to the court when expert qualification and testimony are on the line do not always add up. For example, the presence of this caveat (or similar) may be removed from an investigative report that is tendered to the court where the profiler wishes to provide expert evidence. One potential explanation for this is to remove from view any concerns the court may have about the validity or generalizability of the evidence put before it.

This kind of omission is fairly serious and speaks to the reluctance of those in the field to disclose or admit to the shortcomings or limitations of particular methods. What's more, the selectivity with which this caveat is used highlights a more insidious knowledge: that the product is flawed and airing this may prevent subsequent expert testimony. Good scientific practice[1]

[1] It is acknowledged that profiling is not a science (see Muller, 2000; Snook, Taylor, Gendreau & Bennell, 2009; for a brief discussion on the role of science in profiling), but this does not mean that we should not apply scientific principles to our analyses. The argument that profiling is not a science and therefore not bound by the same principles is vapid and used as an excuse for lackluster performance. It is argued that a stricter adherence to a scientific process will make the practice of profiling more accurate and better able to assist the police and courts in their determinations.

involves not only articulating conclusions based on evidence, arrived at from solid analytical reasoning, but also pointing out the limitations of any analysis conducted (see Inman & Rudin, 2001, for a cogent discussion of this point). Profiling should be no different.

But addressing the issue of accuracy is only half of the battle. What help is an accurate profile that cannot be put to good use by anyone?

Next the issue of utility must be addressed. A criminal profile may be entirely accurate, but so general in its characteristics that it is useless to those who need investigative guidance; a common complaint among end users of criminal profiles. For example, the leader of one major serial killer task force criticized the profile developed for the case as lacking utility. As reported in Ebnet (1998):

> *Detectives also say their profile of the killer is of little help. The profile, which agents from FBI headquarters in Quantico, Va., crafted during a winter visit to Spokane, contains little detail. "The first thing (the agents) told us after they gave us the profile is not to use it," Silver said. "You hope it gives you direction. It just doesn't."*

The purpose of a criminal profile is to reduce the suspect pool, not to be so inclusive that it applies to just about everyone. It should be of use to the investigation: something that investigators can put to work, advancing their inquiry. A criminal profile without utility can be a waste of valuable time and resources.

There is a general dearth of literature on this subject, and many individuals and agencies are reluctant to broadcast their accuracy figures, as inaccuracy may be perceived as ineffectiveness. If they are not seen as being effective by those who control funding, then budgets may be cut, positions eliminated, and roles diffused. For this reason, it is often prudent for these figures to be concealed, misplaced, misrepresented, or simply not gathered at all. As stated in Ainsworth (2001, 176), "There have been very few pieces of research which have looked at both the accuracy and usefulness of profiles used in 'live' criminal cases." This small handful of publications or studies examining the accuracy of criminal profiling includes most notably Darkes, Otto, Poythress, and Starr (1993); Homant and Kennedy (1998); Ingram (1998); Torres, Boccaccini, and Miller (2006) for a study on utility and validity; and Snook, Eastwood, Gendreau, Goggin, and Cullen (2007).

The Measure of Success

Jackson, van den Eshof, and de Kleuver (1997) state that the success of profiling can be defined as the number of hits scored by profiles. These authors later go on to suggest that their definition is perhaps too restrictive, and that it should be extended to include the perceived value of advice in relation to investigative suggestions, crime assessment, and interview techniques. This is owing to the fact that the work of their profiling unit "covers a wider scope of assistance than merely producing profiles" (p. 127). It is the opinion of this author, however, that the former definition is not restrictive at all; that it is in fact far too general to be of much use in providing a measurable standard with which to gauge the accuracy of a profile. Rossmo (2000) adopts a qualitative approach to utility, and suggests that for a profile to be useful, it must assist in the investigative decision-making process. He further notes that any suggestions that are vague, general, unworkable, or of low probability are not likely to produce helpful leads. (Rossmo adopts a statistical approach in the profiling process and as such probabilities are all important.) Rossmo's proposal that a profile must assist in the investigative decision-making process is fully supported herein.

Gudjonsson and Copson (1997, p. 73) erroneously state that "if success in profiling were synonymous with accurate prediction, then profilers could claim much success." As this is simply not the case, there must be another yardstick with which to measure the assistance that a profile provides an investigation. Unfortunately, some in the discipline may indeed measure their success in this way, which invariably leads to gratuitous self-promotion and an overinflated sense of utility. Surely Godwin's (1985) assertion in the early days of profiling that nine out of 10 profiles were vapid and likened to a game of blind man's bluff, still applies today. The analogy this author has frequently used is that of the fisherman's net: If one uses a net that is big enough, and casts it over a wide area, surely one has an increased chance of catching fish. However, the size of the net or the width of the cast plays little part in the quality of the fish caught.

Accuracy Rates

Alleged accuracy figures range from the sublime to the ridiculous. While there are a variety of problems associated with determining statistical accuracy, it is clear that many estimates of accuracy are based solely on the "feel good" attractiveness of the profile, and not necessarily on any actual benefit derived from its publication. That is, simply by virtue of having a profile done on a case, investigators may feel it has helped, regardless of whether it is even used during the investigation. This perception of assistance may be further heightened as a function of the complexity of the case, or of a case that falls well outside of the experience of even the most sophisticated investigator. In addition, many investigators already employ a simplified form of profiling in their duties and may indeed arrive at many of the same conclusions. Though they may not know how they arrived at these conclusions (so employ a more intuitive process), the involvement of a profiler might assist in articulating their thoughts. Having a third party reaffirm existing thoughts in this way can be quite reassuring.

In 1981, as part of regular management practices, the FBI conducted a cost–benefit study to determine the value of the service to consumers (Pinizzotto, 1984). In an effort to determine this, 192 end users (of 209 cases) were polled as to the assistance provided by FBI-prepared profiles. The results suggested that only 46% of these crimes had been solved, which amounted to 88 investigations. Of these, it was further determined that they helped focus the investigation in 72% of the cases, helped locate a suspect in 20% of those cases, directly identified a suspect in 17% of cases, and assisted in the prosecution of suspects in 6% of cases. Interestingly, the profile was deemed to be of no assistance to the same degree that it helped directly identify a suspect (17%; Rossmo, 2000).

Pinizzotto (1984) claims that basing their decision on a combination of common sense, logic, intuition, and experience, the BSU has an accuracy rate in excess of 80%. Later, Pinizzotto teamed up with Norman Finkel (Pinizzotto & Finkel, 1990) to assess the outcome and process differences in profiles among groups of profilers, detectives, psychologists, and students. This was assessed using the expert/novice approach (Pinizzotto & Finkel, 1990; Rossmo, 2000) where the skills of qualified investigators are compared to those of neophytes. The results of the study suggest that between the four groups, profilers had the highest mean number of accurate predictions (29.1), with the detectives having the second highest (15.8), psychologists coming in third (10.8), and students with the lowest number of mean accurate predictions (6.3). The finding that profilers are more accurate at profiling than other groups has also been found elsewhere, and, hopefully, should not be that surprising.

In one study in the United Kingdom on the accuracy of profilers, the Coals to Newcastle project (see Gudjonsson & Copson, 1997) found that the aggregate accuracy ratio among all groups studied was 2.2:1 (this means that for each 2.2 correct points, there was one incorrect point). Although individual accuracy rates were also calculated (for example, between clinical and statistical profilers), the point is well illustrated by looking simply at these aggregate scores. Essentially a 2.2:1 ratio suggests that only an approximate 66% accuracy rate can be established.

In cases in which criminal profiling has lead to the apprehension of an offender, there is little explanation as to exactly how it was of help. For example, in the Coals to Newcastle project it was determined that in five out of the 184 cases the criminal profile led to the identification of the offender. Without knowing how such success was defined or established, the full utility of the criminal profile cannot be assessed, nor can successes be studied and replicated. Undoubtedly, the degree to which a profile helps "catch" an offender will also be dictated by the case at hand, with the evidence playing a considerable part. Also, if a prime suspect has already been identified or if there is supporting physical evidence, this may assist in case resolution in spite of the involvement of a profiler.

In examining the degree to which ambiguous statements play a role in the perceived accuracy of a profile, Alison, Smith, and Morgan (2003) conducted two studies. The first employed a bogus profile, though it used a real case with two possible offender outcomes: one genuine and one fabricated (given to two groups of police officers). In this first study, over half of both groups rated the profile as accurate, and despite there being differences between the offenders, neither group showed accuracy ratings that differed between the real and fabricated conditions. In the second study, a genuine profile was employed. Despite being given information on different offenders, over 75% of each sample rated the profile as somewhat accurate, and 50% as generally or very accurate. These researchers suggest that there is a type of "creative interpretation" (p. 193) that occurs when individuals view information that is equivocal in nature. That is, there is a "joint process of selectively noting aspects of the profile that can be easily applied to the offender, ignoring those aspects that are not applicable, and constructing meaning from ambiguity" (p. 193).

But it is not only a matter of whether a profile is accurate or inaccurate. Kocsis and Hayes (2004) conducted research on the perceived accuracy of profiles as adjudged by the profile's author. Fifty-nine police officers from various states in Australia were recruited and provided with a paragraph that gave a minimum amount of information (location of the body, a description of the crime scene, etc.). Participants were then provided with a paragraph, which they were told was a criminal profile written by one of two people. Depending on which condition they were assigned to, the police officers were either told that the author was a professional profiler, or they were told that the author was "someone the investigator consulted" (p. 152). The results of a 2×3 ANOVA showed that the only significant result was that of author label, and those who were told the author was a professional profiler perceived the profile to be more accurate. In short, it is not only the actual content of the profile and its accuracy (whether the profiler correctly stated the offender's age, residential location, etc.), but also whether the author is known to be, or is considered to be, an actual expert in the field. This may be a reflection of a belief structure in that experts should know what they are doing.

Problems

Perhaps the greatest obstacle to objectively examining this issue is the way in which criminal profiles are assessed for their accuracy. Should we simply compare the final profile to the offender once caught? Where do we then stand if the offender is not caught? As stated by Homant and Kennedy (1998, p. 324), "even when the identity of the offender is unambiguously determined, there is still a large subjective element in deciding how well the person fits the profile." Also, providing a criminal profile may only confirm what investigators currently think. If the suspect is later arrested and charged, who then "gets the credit" for accuracy or utility (especially if the profile is merely tailored to fit a suspect rather than painstakingly compiled from a thorough analysis of the crime): the investigating detective, the criminal profiler, or both?

One common method employed in determining the usefulness of profiling are studies of consumer satisfaction. Typically, this involves polling a select group of consumers of criminal profiling and asking questions related to their satisfaction with the results. This is inherently problematic for a number of reasons. First of all, virgin consumers may be so enamored with the information they receive that they inadvertently report their bedazzlement rather than genuine satisfaction. This may be particularly the case where bizarre, novel, or unique information is provided, and this is similar to the concern voiced by Campbell (1976), who stated that police might be more seduced by the academic credentials of the profiler than by the profile itself. This belief reflects that studied by Kocsis and Hayes (2004), discussed earlier. Second, the studies may not consider longitudinal data, opting instead for a cross-sectional design. This would have the effect of providing information on satisfaction with limited cases, in a limited time frame, and possibly from limited sources, potentially biasing results owing to restricted exposure to profiling. Last, a criminal profile in a particularly difficult case may provide the investigators with false hope (or possibly even renewed vigor), subsequently inflating their opinion of the profiling process.

One might argue that the best way to assess the utility of a criminal profile is to count the number of correct characteristics in the profile against the offender once apprehended. This problem could be illustrated in the following way. One criminal profile may contain 10 characteristics, and only be correct on two of them. However, one of these two accurate characteristics leads to the successful identification of the suspect pool, from which an offender is identified through other evidence. In another case, the same criminal profiler offers 10 characteristics and is correct in all of them, though the criminal profile has not assisted in developing or apprehending a suspect. In which case does the profiler have the right to claim success and/or utility? Is it prudent for the profiler to claim an accurate profile in the second case as argument toward his or her overall success? Or is it misleading?

Controlled studies present problems of their own. For example, Kocsis, Irwin, Hayes, and Nunn (2001) attempted to qualitatively assess the differences between the abilities of students, detectives, psychologists, profilers, and psychics. Although the purpose of their study was not to determine the success of profiles per se, the nature of the study was to compare the abilities of these various groups and a measure of their abilities was indeed communicated in terms of their success. In this study, two measures of accuracy were used. First of all, total accuracy was measured and defined as "the total number of questions from … four submeasures … that were correctly answered" (paragraph 7). The second measure used was Pinizzotto and Finkel accuracy, which was constructed using a set of questions similar to those used by Pinizzotto and Finkel (1990).

The study showed that the psychologists identified more of the physical behaviors and offense characteristics than did the police officers, and also that they identified more of the physical characteristics than did the psychics. None of the other characteristics was deemed to be statistically significant. Although the authors note that this casts serious doubt on the utility of profilers in investigations, it is equally likely that this was an artifact of the questionnaire used. For example, a close-ended set of questions was asked rather than letting the participants define their own profile parameters. Under physical characteristics, study participants were asked the offender's age (bracketed to 1–12 years, 13–17 years, 18–25 years, and so forth), build, height, hair color, eye color, and ethnic background. Under offense characteristics study participants were asked questions regarding the distance the offender lived from the crime scene and method of approach, among others. The offender's history and habits were the last category of the questionnaire. Many of these characteristics were not directly inferable by offender behavior, and as a result, would have required a degree of guesswork indicating that the accuracy assessed within this study was questionable.[2] For those characteristics in which only a limited number of options were present (such as sex), guesswork may have indeed played a large role, given that a smaller number of options increases one's chance of accuracy.

It should be clear now that the process is not as simple as many would have us believe.

Suggestions

In search of success and celebrity, some criminal profilers may be too concerned with how accurate their profiles are (no matter how general, inclusive, or subjective), and broadcast this

[2] It is possible that some of the questions such as hair and eye color were intended more for the psychics, but asking the profilers to assess these still places their conclusions outside of the usual realms of profile characteristics.

as evidence of their uncanny ability to identify an unknown offender through their criminal behavior. The activities of a cavalcade of so-called experts in the Washington sniper and other high-profile cases provide relevant examples. Utility may take a back seat.

As a result of the prior discussion, a number of suggestions arise regarding the accuracy of a profile, and subsequent to this, the utility of a method in general and individual profiles specifically. These are easy to consider and implement when embarking on casework, and should become the cornerstone of practice when engaging in operational profiling work. These can be summarized as follows:

1. Establish a clear set of guidelines for the development of the profile.
2. Consider how the profile may actually be used by the consumer.
3. It is perhaps easiest to keep your eye on the prize when it is known exactly what the prize is (what this means is that without some clear direction or goal when preparing a profile, it is easy to fall into the trap of offering vague and irrelevant characteristics instead of relevant suggestions).
4. Be guided by ethical and practical considerations and constraints.
5. Have an enduring commitment to the assistance provided and be accountable for your conclusions.

The first point relates to some of those issues that have been raised earlier in this chapter. This includes discussing what evidence was and was not available, the ways in which this may affect subsequent conclusions, and being clear in outlining what information is required for the type of analysis to be performed. Also, the profiler should inform the end user what reasoning process has been employed in developing the profile.

Consideration of how a profile might be used by the end consumer is paramount to utility. Without thinking about the variety of ways in which a profile may be acted upon, profilers may fall into the trap of providing ambiguous offender characteristics that may confuse rather than aid the investigation. To further highlight this point, consider an example from an oft-cited profiling text (Holmes & Holmes, 2002):

> *The killer is a seriously disturbed individual…The manner in which he cuts the parts of the body shows determination and anger plus making the victim less than a human being: "Not only are you nothing, now you are little bits of nothing." What is especially interesting is that the person has kept, or at least it has not been found, the skin from the neck to the waist. This is the most important part for him. I can see him skinning this body part and wearing it at night around the house where he lives alone.*

This profile comes across as intensely subjective and is full of supposition guided by what the author believes may have occurred. Indeed, if the skin mentioned had not been found, then it cannot be accounted for in any fashion, and the whole basis for the final opinion comes crashing down around its foundation. Last, how would a detective act on this information? Surely, if they found the skin in someone's possession this would leave little doubt they had found the offender (or at least a very viable and strong suspect), but how would they arrive at this point from the information provided? If an investigator cannot act on a characteristic, in data terms it is nothing more than noise, and should be left out.

This brings us to the third point. How then are we to determine what is clutter and what is useful? This answer is very simple and rests only on a determination of what investigators are seeking. Typically, they have some feature of the offense in mind on which they are seeking assistance, and it is this that should become the focus of the profile.[3] This may be a determination of precautionary acts, intent or premeditation, staging, or motive, to name but a few. This will ensure that both the profile and the investigation stay on track.

The well-known medical maxim "Do no harm" may be appropriate for consideration here. Not only must profilers consider the harmful effects that may come about from their involvement, but they must also be constantly vigilant about the practical constraints of their craft; some of these have been discussed at length, either in this chapter or elsewhere within this volume.

Ethics are discussed in Chapter 12, and will therefore not be afforded lengthy discussion here. Suffice it to say that though ethics are absent from many quarters of the area of profiling, this does not absolve a profiler from behaving ethically. When life and or liberty may hang on the words of any expert, then that expert must do his or her utmost to behave properly, and this would include behaving in a responsible and ethical manner. To do otherwise will only serve to bring the field (and the expert) into further disrepute.

Perhaps as a final consideration for developing valid profiles, it should be pointed out that the work of the profiler is not over once the report has been drafted, or even submitted. First, the report should be subject to revision if and when new evidence comes to light. In this way the profile becomes a dynamic document, not one that becomes outdated the minute evidence in a case changes. Also, and perhaps equally important, is that it should be incumbent on the profiler to take time with investigators to explain and detail his or her report, and how best to implement its contents into their investigation. Furthermore, profilers should provide clear indications of how they arrived at their conclusions. There would be no greater shame than to have an investigator presented with a profile whose promise was high, that was then not utilized as a result of confusion over its development or subsequent place within the investigative process.

Conclusion

If we are more concerned with the accuracy of a profile than we are with its investigative utility, we run the very real risk of failing to advance profiling beyond the personality and celebrity of those offering the service. Any criminal profiler who undertakes casework without consideration of the usefulness of his or her end product is disregarding the very reason criminal profiles are constructed in the first place: to assist the investigative community in the identification of personality and behavioral characteristics that distinguish offenders from the general

[3] Some investigators may be seeking full profiles, but this should not be assumed. And it should never be assumed that an individual who is unfamiliar with the area should be fully informed as to what they are after.

offender population and that of the public. It is possible to advance the practice beyond its current state, though to do so practitioners must be cognizant of issues relating to utility and relevance. To ignore these is to remain ignorant of flaws in thinking and practice.

Questions

1. In the study conducted by Pinizzotto, what percentage of profiles were found to be of no assistance?
   a. 46%
   b. 72%
   c. 20%
   d. 6%
   e. 17%
2. The Coals to Newcastle project found that the aggregate accuracy ratio among all groups studied was:
   a. 2.2:1
   b. 1.7:1
   c. 2:1
   d. 4.3:1
   e. 1:1
3. If a criminal profile has 10 offender characteristics in it, and these 10 characteristics prove to be accurate, it could be argued that the profile is useful. *True or False?*
4. Some criminal profilers suggest that accuracy equates to usefulness. *True or False?*
5. The fallacy of accuracy encompasses two issues. These are _________ and _________.

References

Ainsworth, P. B. (2001). *Offender profiling and crime analysis.* Devon, UK: Willan.

Alison, L., Smith, M. D., & Morgan, K. (2003). Interpreting the accuracy of offender profiles. *Psychology, Crime and Law, 9*(2), 185–195.

Campbell, C. (1976). Portraits of mass killers. *Psychology Today, 9,* 110–119.

Cooper, G., & King, M. (2001). *Analyzing criminal behavior.* Ogden: IQ Design.

Court TV Online (1999). State expert's new report implicating Sam Sheppard. Available from <http://www.courttv.com/national/2000/0131/mccrary_ctv. html> Accessed on 28.06.2002.

Darkes, J., Otto, R. K., Poythress, N., & Starr, L. (1993). APA's expert panel in the congressional review of the USS *Iowa* incident. *American Psychologist, January,* 8–15.

Devery, C. (2010). Criminal profiling and criminal investigation. *Journal of Contemporary Criminal Justice, 26*(4), 393–409.

Douglas, J. E., Burgess, A. W., Burgess, A. G., & Ressler, R. K. (1992). *Crime classification manual: A standard system for investigating and classifying violent crime.* New York: Lexington Books.

Ebnet, M. (1998). Spokane officials have few leads on serial killer. *Seattle Times, June 15.*

Godwin, J. (1985). *Murder USA: The ways we kill each other.* New York: Ballantine.

Gudjonsson, G. H., & Copson, G. (1997). The role of the expert in criminal investigation. In J. L. Jackson & D. A. Bekerian (Eds.), *Offender profiling: Theory, research and practice.* West Sussex, UK: Wiley.

Hazelwood, R. (1995). Analysing the rape and profiling the offender. In A. Burgess & R. Hazelwood (Eds.), *Practical aspects of rape investigation* (2nd ed.). Boca Raton, FL: CRC Press.

Hazelwood, R. R., Ressler, R. K., Depue, R. L., & Douglas, J. E. (1995). Criminal investigative analysis: An overview. In A. Burgess & R. Hazelwood (Eds.), *Practical aspects of rape investigation* (2nd ed.). Boca Raton, FL: CRC Press.

Holmes, R. M., & Holmes, S. T. (2002). *Profiling violent crimes: An investigative tool* (3rd ed.). Thousand Oaks, CA: Sage Publications.

Homant, R. J., & Kennedy, D. B. (1998). Psychological aspects of crime scene profiling: Validity research. *Criminal Justice and Behaviour, 25*(3), 319–343.

Horgan, J., O'Sullivan, D., & Hammond, S. (2003). Offender profiling: A critical perspective. *The Irish Journal of Psychology, 24*(1-2), 1–21.

Ingram, S. (1998). If the profile fits: Criminal psychological profiles into evidence in criminal trials. *Journal of Urban and Contemporary Law, 54,* 239–266.

Inman, K., & Rudin, N. (1997). *An introduction to forensic DNA analysis.* New York: CRC Press.

Inman, K., & Rudin, N. (2001). *Principles and practice of criminalistics: The profession of forensic science.* Boca Raton, FL: CRC Press.

Jackson, J. L., van den Eshof, P., & de Kleuver, E. E. (1997). A research approach to offender profiling. In J. L. Jackson & D. A. Bekerian (Eds.), *Offender profiling: Theory, research and practice.* West Sussex, UK: Wiley.

Kocsis, R. N., & Hayes, A. F. (2004). Believing is seeing? Investigating the perceived accuracy of psychological profiles. *International Journal of Offender Therapy and Comparative Criminology, 48*(2), 149–160.

Kocsis, R. N., Irwin, H. J., Hayes, A. F., & Nunn, R. (2001). Expertise in psychological profiling: A comparative assessment. *Journal of Interpersonal Violence, 15*(3), 311–331.

McKnight, K. (2000). Expert's opinion challenged. *Ohio Beacon Journal, April 1.*

Muller, D. (2000). Criminal profiling: Real science or just wishful thinking? *Homicide Studies, 4*(3), 234–264.

New Jersey v. (2000). Fortin, 745A.2d 509, NJ.

Norris, G., & Petherick, W. A. (2010). Criminal profiling in the courtrooms: Behavioural investigative advice or bad character evidence? *Cambrian Law Review, 41*(4), 39–54.

Pinizzotto, A. J. (1984). Forensic psychology: Criminal personality profiling. *Journal of Police Science and Administration, 12*(1), 32–40.

Rossmo, D. K. (2000). *Geographical profiling.* Boca Raton, FL: CRC Press.

Snook, B., Eastwood, J., Gendreau, P., Goggin, C., & Cullen, R. M. (2007). Taking stock of criminal profiling. *Criminal Justice and Behavior, 34*(4), 437–453.

Snook, B., Taylor, P. J., Gendreau, P., & Bennell, C. (2009). On the need for scientific experimentation in the criminal profiling field. *Criminal Justice and Behaviour, 36*(1), 1091–1094.

Torres, A. N., Boccaccini, M. T., & Miller, H. A. (2006). Perceptions of the validity and utility of criminal profiling among forensic psychologists and psychiatrists. *Professional Psychology, Research and Practice, 37*(1), 51–58.

7 Offender Signature and Case Linkage[1]

Michael McGrath

Introduction

Signature can be defined as evidence of behavior at a crime scene not necessary to complete the crime that points to an underlying psychological need of the offender. By implication, the behavior exhibited is distinct enough to allow for the opinion that a single offender (or group of offenders) has committed the crimes where the signature behavior is found.

The concept of signature arose from the need to link cases to a known or unknown offender. Although possessing a certain panache, the term signature is misleading because it implies that it can be used to individualize, when this is usually not the case. In criminal profiling, the signature associated with a crime (and thereby the offender responsible for the crime) is often assumed to be specific to a crime or crime series, when in fact this is often not verifiable. The notion appears to be misunderstood by both laymen and expert criminal profilers, leading to some unsupportable conclusions.

Most profiling methods are inductive in nature, such as the Federal Bureau of Investigation's (FBI) organized–disorganized dichotomy. Such a method offers generalizations that are for the most part investigatively useless. The paradigm was developed from early observations of FBI profilers that were to be codified and validated through a National Institute of Justice grant-funded study of serial killers. The study never validated the paradigm, and in fact the grant was not renewed due to a flawed study design and data collection. Canter et al. (2004) published a study

[1]This chapter is adapted from McGrath, M., "Signature in the Courtroom: Whose Crime Is It Anyway?" *Journal of Behavioral Profiling*, 2001, Vol. 2, No. 2.

reviewing the organized–disorganized paradigm, finding no support for the FBI organized–disorganized style of profiling. One could argue that case linkage aspects of criminal profiling are separate from the organized–disorganized paradigm of crime scene assessment, but this author would argue that the same misunderstanding of basic science and statistics that led to endorsement of the organized–disorganized model would account for the misuse of case linkage in court by FBI-trained profilers.

This chapter will review the forensic concepts of identification and individualization, investigative and probative opinions, and present a case where signature was attempted to be introduced in court.

Identification vs Individualization

In the forensic sciences there is a significant difference between evidence *consistent* with a theory or piece of evidence (i.e., a match) and evidence that is capable of *identifying* a source to the exclusion of all others, allowing for *individuation* of an item, be it a fiber from a carpet or a set of behaviors from a crime scene (i.e., a signature). Signature behavior between crime scenes is more akin to a match or identification than an individuation. It may be more prudent for criminal profilers to refer to the behaviors evident between two crime scenes as matching, or consistent, with each being the result of a single offender(s), as opposed to definitely being related to a single source. If there is definite proof (e.g., DNA) that two crime scenes are connected, that would allow for the opinion that the crime scenes are definitely connected to one offender(s), but then a criminal profiler would not have been needed to arrive at that conclusion.

Kirk (1974, p. 15) makes the distinction well:

> *In the examination and interpretation of physical evidence, the distinction between identification and individuation must always be clearly made … to determine the identity of source (emphasis in original). That is, two items of evidence, one known and the other unknown, must be identified as having a common origin. On the witness stand, the criminalist must be willing to admit that absolute identity is impossible to establish. Identity of source, on the other hand, often may be established unequivocally, and no witness who has established it need ever back down in the face of cross-examination.*
>
> *It is precisely here that the greatest caution must be exercised. The inept or biased witness may readily testify to an identity, or to a type of identity, that does not actually exist. This can come about because of his confusion as to the nature of identity, his inability to evaluate the results of his observations, or because his general technical deficiencies preclude meaningful results…*
>
> *To sum up: accurate identification must rest on a proper basis of training, experience, technical knowledge, and skill, and an understanding of the fundamental nature of identity itself.*

What Kirk (1974, p. 10)—referring to physical evidence—was saying, was that "identification is the placing of an object in a class or a group." If you see a large metal object with four tires moving down the street with exhaust following it, you can be confident of *identifying* it as a motor vehicle. But to know enough of its characteristics to *individualize* it as your own car (i.e., a specific member of a class) that has been stolen requires much more information. In fact, you might see a vehicle having so many characteristics (model, year, color, etc.) in common with your own as to believe it to be your vehicle, only to realize you have *misidentified* the vehicle when the key does not unlock the door. Merely identifying an object does not individualize it.

Thornton (1997) explained the issue by noting that identification consists of placing an item in a particular category. To narrow identity further requires individualization, a categorization that implies uniqueness. Thornton (1997) cautioned that identification does not require uniqueness. Something can be identified as a motor vehicle without resorting to any unique elements that are different from all other motor vehicles. Thornton (1997) further advises that the term identification is often used when what is actually meant is the forensic concept of individuation. Care should be exercised in how one frames one's opinions so that they are supportable and comply with the terminology of the forensic sciences. As terms are often (even by learned professionals) misused, it is wise to explain terms both in report writing and testimony.

While it is possible to separate out linkage analysis (i.e., signature) from criminal profiling, this is a somewhat artificial partitioning of the processes as both rely on a review of behavioral evidence to determine something. In the case of a criminal profile one seeks offender characteristics and victim connections. In case linkage one attempts to find a connection between crimes. That they overlap is obvious; how and where one draws the line between them is not.

As noted by Turvey (2012, p. 408) there:

> *...is a consensus in the literature that behavioral evidence and criminal profiling alone should not be used to individualize a particular person in relation to a particular crime or series of crimes (Burgess et al., 1992; Burgess & Hazelwood, 1995; Holmes & Holmes, 1996; Ingram, 1998). Criminal profiling methods may be used to suggest the type of person most likely to have committed an offense, but not to accuse a specific person.*

The danger is clear. Just as it is not possible to visually individuate a hair sample, behavioral evidence cannot individuate a crime.

Investigative Profiles vs Probative Profiles

Some experts (not limited to criminal profiling by any means) fail to take into account the context in which they offer an opinion. It is possible to offer an opinion that is investigatively helpful but that does not rise to the level of having probative (i.e., court-worthy) value (McGrath, 2000). For example, during the course of an investigation a profiler could opine that behaviors evidenced at crime scene A are consistent enough with behaviors evidenced at crime scene B to warrant advising the investigators that they can (for investigative purposes) assume the two crime scenes are related to one offender, or group of offenders. This opinion or assumption may be helpful in focusing the investigation. A suspect could be developed (either as a result of the profile or otherwise) and tied to crime scene A through DNA evidence, so that there is little factual doubt that the offender was at crime scene A at the time of the crime. No such evidence exists to tie the offender to crime scene B. A year later the profiler might be asked by a prosecutor if he or she could testify in court that the signature (i.e., behavioral evidence) evident at the two crime scenes proves that the crimes were committed by the same person(s). The profiler should not accede to this request.[2] The profiler must make clear that he or she cannot individualize the behavior evidence to the crime scene, although he or she may certainly offer an opinion regarding consistencies and such, making the limits of the opinion clear. The profiler would need to assess the probative value of the initial opinion and decide that either it is probative, or it is not. If not, it is possible that further evaluation may buttress it to the extent that it becomes probative, through further collecting and weighing of behavioral evidence. Unfortunately, this author suspects that this evaluation of court-worthiness too often fails to occur, and an opinion is deemed to be court-worthy by a profiler when it is not.

Contextuality

It is important to understand the context under which an opinion was formed. An analogy is offered from the area of forensic psychiatrist McGrath (2000, n.p.):

> *A psychiatrist in an office may diagnosis a mental illness, prescribe medication and treat a patient for several months. A year later the doctor could be asked in court during a lawsuit or criminal action (not related to the doctor) what the diagnosis was. The doctor (in this author's opinion) must ask if he/she is being asked for a lay (i.e., fact) opinion or an expert opinion. If a lay opinion, the doctor would give the diagnosis in the chart. If an expert opinion, the doctor could (should?) reply that he/she has no opinion, as the patient was never examined for the purpose of testifying in court. The evaluation of the patient would (and should) be markedly different in the two contexts, treatment vs. forensic. The criminal profiler needs to understand the difference between rendering an investigatively helpful profile, vs. a profile written to a level that imparts probative (i.e., court worthy) value.*

It would be the author's contention that most criminal profiles are developed (and appropriately so) to further an investigation with no expectation that the profile would be the subject of (expert) testimony at some future date.[3] As such, the threshold for forming opinions would be less than that required if one were preparing a criminal profile with the intent of it being

[2] Based on behavioral evidence alone. Yet, if there were physical evidence tying the offender to scene B, the profiler would be superfluous and unlikely to be called, unless it is to support a weak case.

[3] In fact, this is a reason many profiles are never written down. Profilers (and prosecutors) have historically not wanted to have a defense attorney attempt to misrepresent an investigative profile as a probative profile in an attempt to "prove" their client could not have committed the crime.

introduced at a trial and providing expert testimony. To have an investigative threshold[4] profile introduced into evidence masquerading as a probative threshold profile becomes problematic. This author would contend that for a profile to have probative value it must clarify the method(s) used to infer the content of the profile and show how this was done. In other words, the profile must explain what was done and how it was done (Baeza et al., 2000). It would further be this author's contention that the issue of whether a profile is investigatively relevant, probative, or both is often ignored.

Signature

Signature is differentiated from *modus operandi* (MO), behaviors necessary for the commission of a crime. It is believed that signature is the expression of underlying needs of the offender (Geberth, 1996) and can be both a way to link crimes and to draw inferences about the psychological needs of the offender. Various authors (Douglas & Munn, 1992; Keppel, 1995) state that MO changes or evolves as the offender gains experience or matures in his or her criminal career. For example, wearing a mask to thwart identification during a robbery would be indicative of MO. The type of mask worn might be a manifestation of signature. Some authors (Douglas & Mann, 1992; Geberth, 1995; Turvey, 1999; Turvey & Freeman, 2012) differentiate between signature aspect and signature. Geberth (1995) identifies the signature aspect as the underlying psychodynamics related to the behavior seen at the crime scene, with the signature behavior being the behavior evidenced at the scene. Douglas and Mann (1992, p. 261) appear to use signature aspect where others would use signature, referring to the "signature aspect, or calling card …" as going "… beyond the actions necessary to perpetrate the crime. It composes a unique and integral part of the offender's behavior while he is committing the offense."[5] They then go on to state (p. 261) that "The core of the offender's ritual will never change. Unlike the MO, it remains a constant and enduring part of the offender. However, signature aspects may evolve." It would appear that the "core" of the ritual they are discussing is really the signature aspect. Douglass and Munn (1992) make one point worth remembering (p. 261): "The signature does not always show up in every crime scene because of contingencies that might arise, such as interruptions or an unexpected victim response." Lack of all parts of an expected signature may have more to do with the circumstances attending a particular offense than with the emotional or psychological needs of the offender.

Turvey (1999) clearly delineates the two "separate but interdependent parts to the concept of signature" (p. 159). These are signature aspect and signature behaviors. The signature aspect is defined as the "emotional or psychological themes" that are satisfied during the offense and the signature behavior is the manifestation at the crime scene of the underlying signature aspect. Turvey (1999) also points out that signature and MO can overlap: "Signature and MO needs may be satisfied by the same behavior … Different offenders do similar things for different reasons … Individual offender behaviors are multi-determined; they can be the result of multiple offender motivations and multiple external influences" (p. 160). Turvey and Freeman

[4]The term threshold is being used in the sense of a level of probity, not as a threshold assessment as described by Turvey (1999).

[5]Note the use of the word unique. This implies an ability to individualize.

(2012) make several important points. One is that mere repetition of a behavior at different crime scenes does not make it a signature behavior. Another is to break signature into active and passive behaviors, with active denoting signature behaviors that are conscious and deliberate and passive signature behaviors being unintentional.

Keppel (1995, p. 670) states that "Unlike the characteristics of an offender's M.O., the signature remains constant. However, a signature may evolve over time." It appears Keppel means the signature aspect remains the same, while the signature behavior(s) may evolve.

New Jersey v. Fortin

Steven Fortin was convicted of murder in the death of a New Jersey woman, Melissa Padilla. At his trial, testimony related to ritualistic and signature crimes was allowed as so-called "other crimes evidence" to link him to a nonfatal sexual assault on a female police officer in Maine. The New Jersey Supreme Court (New Jersey v. Fortin, 2000) ruled that the expert testimony on linkage analysis lacked sufficient scientific reliability, but that other evidence of the crime in Maine that connected it to the defendant could be used. The Court found (New Jersey v. Fortin, 2000):

> *Proposed expert testimony concerning linkage analysis lacked sufficient reliability to establish that same perpetrator committed Maine and New Jersey crimes; although expert possessed sufficient expertise in his field and his intended testimony was beyond the ken of average juror, the field of linkage analysis was not at 'state of the art' such that his testimony could be sufficiently reliable, and there were no peers to test his theories and no way in which to duplicate his results.*

The facts of the case are as follows and are drawn from the court opinion (162 N.J. 517, 745 A.2d 509):

> *Melissa Padilla was murdered on August 11, 1994, in the Avenel section of Woodbridge, New Jersey. Her body was discovered by her boyfriend, lying half inside a sewer or drainage conduit, alongside a roadway. She was wearing a shirt, but no bra, and was naked from the waist down. Melissa's shorts (with the underwear still inside) were found on a nearby shrub. Several items were found scattered near the body: several bags of food, a receipt from a store, an earring, cigarette butts and a dollar bill with blood on it. A bloodstain was found inside the conduit. Melissa had been brutally beaten about the head, leaving her face swollen and bruised, and her nose fractured. Autopsy revealed she had been manually strangled, anally assaulted, and bitten on the left breast, left nipple, and left chin.*
>
> *On April 3, 1995, almost nine months after the death of Melissa Padilla, Maine State Trooper Vicki Gardner stopped to inquire about the status of a vehicle and driver parked on the shoulder of the road. The driver was Steven Fortin, who told the police officer he was having mechanical trouble. The trooper smelled alcohol on Fortin's breath. She called for back up and administered sobriety tests. While sealing the sobriety tests, Fortin seized her by the throat and strangled her until she was semiconscious. While obtunded,*

Gardner was sexually assaulted. As the back up trooper neared, Fortin sped away in his car with Gardner, punching her in the face and swearing at her. She was able to jump from the car, but was dragged for a short distance until freed from the vehicle. Fortin lost control of the car and after it overturned he fled the area on foot, to be apprehended about a mile away at a rest stop. Gardener's face had been severely beaten and her nose was fractured. She had been manually strangled and during the course of the sexual assault had been bitten on the left chin, left nipple, and left breast, and suffered injury from vaginal and anal penetration. The trooper's pants, underpants and bra had been removed in the course of the assault. When recovered in the patrol car, her nylon running pants had her underwear still inside them. Fortin eventually plea bargained in the Maine case.

The Maine State Police contacted the New Jersey police regarding Fortin's[6] *arrest and charges. The New Jersey investigation into Melissa Padilla's murder included information related to Steven Fortin: Fortin lived in the general vicinity of Ms. Padilla at the time of the murder; earlier on the day of the murder, Fortin had argued and fought with his girlfriend*[7]*; later that day his girlfriend noted scratches on Fortin's head, neck and chest; examination of dental molds and the bite marks on Melissa Padilla led to an opinion that Fortin caused the bite marks on her breast, while the other bite marks were less certain and only "could" have been caused by Fortin.*

The State wanted to introduce evidence by former FBI agent Roy Hazelwood as an expert in modus operandi and ritualistic crimes. Hazelwood, by reputation and background, was considered an expert in the field of crime analysis. The defense objected to both Hazelwood's testimony and any evidence of the Maine case being allowed at trial. Hazelwood had reviewed both crimes and determined that the modus operandi of the two crimes showed fifteen consistent MO aspects:

- Both crimes were high-risk.
- Both crimes were committed impulsively.
- Both crimes were committed against females.
- Both victims were fully mature in age.
- Both crimes were committed against victims who crossed the offender's path.
- Both victims were alone when attacked.
- Both attacks took place near well-traveled roads.
- Both attacks occurred during darkness.
- No weapons were used during the attacks.
- Both victims sustained only blunt force trauma.
- Both assaults took place at the point of confrontation.
- Both victims sustained trauma primarily to the upper face with no damage to the teeth.
- Both victims had their lower garments completely removed.
- Both victims were wearing shirts, but their breasts were free.
- Neither victim had seminal fluid in or on her body.

[6] The reason for initially connecting the two crimes was not given.
[7] There is no mention of whether the fighting included any physical assault by either party.

Hazelwood noted that he had never seen the cluster of MO characteristics found in the two crimes in his 35 years in law enforcement, which included having personally investigated over 7000 crimes. Also noted was the fact that that both victims' noses were broken and that their underwear was found intertangled with their outer pants. Hazelwood's report went on to describe the ritualistic or signature aspects linking the crimes. He offered five such items:

- Bites to the lower chin.
- Bites to lateral left breast.
- Injurious anal penetration.
- Brutal facial beating.
- Manual (frontal) strangulation.

Hazelwood testified that he had never seen this combination of ritual behaviors. He had determined that the likelihood of different offenders committing the two crimes was "highly improbable."

On June 3, 1998 the New Jersey (Appellate) Law Division ruling was made on the two issues raised by the defense: the other crimes evidence (the assault on Trooper Gardner) was admissible, but not Fortin's guilty plea. This was based on the fact that it was clear Fortin had committed the Maine offense and the similarity of the crimes was in issue. There was insufficient evidence of Fortin's guilt in the New Jersey case (relying on the bite mark and cigarette butt) and it was felt the two crimes were "similar in kind and reasonably close in time." The probative value of the other crimes evidence was felt to outweigh any prejudicial effect. Hazelwood's testimony and background was reviewed and the Law Division felt he had sufficient expertise to offer his intended testimony and qualified him as an expert on modus operandi and ritualistic behavior. This ruling was appealed and the Appellate Division affirmed on the other crimes evidence with cautions, but reversed on the matter of Hazelwood's testimony. The other crimes evidence had to be "sanitized," presenting only the facts needed to prove identity to the jury.

The Appellate Division decided that the linkage analysis performed by Hazelwood was not sufficiently reliable to be admitted. It was believed to be "ultimate issue" testimony. In other words, if Fortin committed the Maine assault (a known fact) and Hazelwood were to testify that the same person who assaulted the Maine trooper committed the New Jersey homicide, then he has essentially testified that Fortin committed the New Jersey crime. The Appellate court saw Hazelwood's testimony as an application of behavioral science and ruled that his testimony should be evaluated under the test for scientific evidence (i.e., Daubert). The court decided that dissimilarities in the cases and the small sample size (two) separated this evidence from similar evidence admitted in other courts. The defense appealed again to the New Jersey Supreme Court on the issue of allowing other crimes evidence (even if "sanitized") and the State appealed on the exclusion of Hazelwood's testimony.

The Supreme Court of New Jersey on review agreed that Hazelwood's proffered signature testimony should not reach the jury and added some thoughts. Expert testimony needs to meet three thresholds: 1) be beyond the knowledge of the average person (juror), 2) the field in question [here linkage analysis] must be at a level of maturity that an expert's testimony will be "sufficiently reliable," and 3) the expert must have adequate expertise in the field. The court took issue with the second prong of the test, feeling concerned over the scientific reliability of the testimony. Hazelwood is quoted from *The Evil that Men Do*[8] (1998, pp. 177–78) [sic]: "An aberrant offenders' behavior is as unique as his fingerprints, as his DNA—as a snowflake" (p. 231). Hazelwood explained that linkage analysis is different from criminal profiling, as if it was identified as criminal profiling it would be harder, if not impossible, to get his testimony into the courtroom. The reference to DNA, fingerprints, and snowflakes is misleading at best. It is simply not a factual statement and from a scientific perspective it is unclear what one can make of it. Aside from the fact that no one has ever shown that all snowflakes are unique (Thornton, 1997), there is no reason to assume that all offenders exhibit unique behavior. Unfortunately, the court then used the case of the Boston Strangler to show that behavioral scientists were "off target," by creating a profile(s) of the strangler that appeared to be wrong when Albert DeSalvo confessed to the crimes. To date, no one has been convicted of the Boston stranglings and it is far from proven that DeSalvo was the killer. In fact, evidence may exist to show otherwise (Kelly, 1995). In Fortin, the court went on to note:

> *[According to Hazelwood] linkage analysis is a field in which only Hazelwood and several of his colleagues practice. Other experts would be current or former co-workers of Hazelwood's, leading the court to state that there were no peers to test his theories, and thus no way to duplicate his results. The court stated that the current case differed from State v. Code and Pennell v. State, where signature testimony had been allowed. The court made it clear that Hazelwood had not attempted to clothe his testimony in an aura of scientific reliability. He acknowledged that linkage analysis was not a science. It is "based on years of training, education, research, and experience in working on thousands of violent crimes over an extended period." The court further added that while it felt linkage analysis failed to meet the second prong of the test for admissibility, it did serve an investigatively relevant function. As an experienced investigator, Hazelwood could be allowed to testify about similarities between crimes "without drawing conclusions about the guilt or innocence of the defendant."*

The Supreme Court of New Jersey wisely drew the line between an investigatively useful tool (linkage analysis) and a court-worthy opinion. Putting that aside, the author will now examine the evidence offered by Mr. Hazelwood to show that Mr. Fortin committed both crimes.[9]

[8]The reader should note that this work is a trade memoir of Mr. Hazelwood's crime fighting career. It is not a scholarly work. That the court relied on it for anything is troubling.

[9]It is important for the reader to understand that the guilt or innocence of Mr. Fortin in the New Jersey homicide is not at issue in this critique. He may very well have committed both crimes. What is at issue is whether anyone could opine with the degree of certainty required to convict a person of murder that the two crimes were committed by the same person based on the behavioral evidence (MO and signature) alone.

According to Hazelwood, the MO of the two crimes showed 15 points in common. This author would argue that many of these MO points could be considered signature as opposed to MO and that many of these "consistencies" between the crimes can be found in other crimes. To list them as if they somehow convey uniqueness to the two crimes is misleading. Granted, as the list grows it gives the appearance of evidentiary weight, but an examination of the evidence appears to dilute its mass.

1. Both crimes were high-risk.
   It is clear that assaulting the state trooper was high-risk; in fact, it bordered on insane. Fortin knew his license plates and name had been called in to the dispatcher, yet he assaulted the police officer, who was carrying a gun. The Padilla murder occurred at night, near, but off, a well-traveled road. While this could have been a high-risk crime, it could also have been the opposite: a single female, by herself, with no one nearby.
2. Both crimes were committed impulsively.
   This is true for the Maine assault. It is possibly true also for the New Jersey murder, but another approach could be to frame the Maine assault as impulsive and desperate, while the New Jersey crime was one of opportunity.
3. Both crimes were committed against females.
   While certainly true, this tells us nothing and offers little value in connecting a series of (sexual assault) crimes. The fact that two crimes were committed against women would hardly justify connecting them.
4. Both victims were fully mature in age.
   Again, this tells us little. Fully mature is vague enough to cover a very large percentage of the female population. This has no real discriminative value.
5. Both crimes were committed against victims who crossed the offender's path.
   Without further explanation, one is left to wonder why this would be expected to have any significance. For the crime to occur it is necessary that the victims cross the offender's path. Possibly what was meant is that the offender was not out looking for victims but opportunistically assaulted them. It could be argued that this then would simply be the equivalent of point 2 counted twice.
6. Both victims were attacked when alone.
   This fact would fit almost all sexual assaults.
7. Both attacks took place near well-traveled roads.
   It is hard to believe that this has not been encountered before. Yet, there are dissimilarities: One assault occurred essentially on a road, while one occurred off a road.
8. Both attacks occurred during darkness.
   About 46% of all crime occurs from 6 PM to 6 AM, but close to two-thirds of rapes and sexual assaults occur during the same time frame (U.S. Dept. of Justice, 2001). It does not appear that the fact that two sexual assaults occurred at night would offer much discriminative power in connecting the crimes, as most sexual assaults are committed at night. The attack on the trooper may also have been initially precipitated as much by the

need to flee from her (to avoid a DWI arrest) as to instigate a sexual assault. The timing (day vs. night) of the assaults may have had more to do with the isolated location and availability of the victims, rather than the fact that it was light or dark out. While the 15 consistencies are listed, the many inconsistencies between the two crimes are not.

9. No weapons were used during the attacks.
   This is consistent with most sexual assaults. In fact, Bureau of Justice statistics (U.S. Dept. of Justice, 2001) cite the use of a weapon as present in only 6% of all rapes and sexual assaults in 2000. Clearly, lack of a weapon offers little in connecting sexual assaults.
10. Both victims sustained only blunt force trauma.
    One could argue this would follow from point 9.
11. Both assaults took place at the point of confrontation.
    This would seem to be a corollary of points 2 and 5 but is qualitatively different. Again, this would be consistent with many assaults.
12. Both victims sustained trauma primarily to the upper face with no damage to the teeth.
    The fact that both victims sustained trauma to the face may be important, but it may be more indicative of a signature behavior than MO, as the victims were strangled, leading to decreased or no resistance. We are given no information on assaults or sexual assaults in general, where the victim suffers trauma to the face without the teeth being damaged.[10] This author would suggest that this phenomenon is not uncommon.
13. Both victims had their lower garments completely removed.
    Again, one would have to ask how often this occurs in sexual assaults in general. Once again, this author would suggest that it is not so uncommon as to pose uniqueness.
14. Both victims were wearing shirts, but their breasts were free.
    This essentially means that the victim's bras were removed while their shirts were still on. Again, it is hard to view this as a unique feature among sexual assaults in general.
15. Neither victim had seminal fluid in or on her body.
    Any offender using a condom would forge the same scenario. Any offender who failed to ejaculate inside or near the victim could leave the same scenario. Any offender who never attempted to insert his penis into the victim could leave the same scenario. Different offenders, with different motivations (intended or not) for not leaving semen in or on the victim could leave a similar scene.

The reader may at this point feel that this author has succeeded in shaving off some weight from almost each point, but that the totality of the consistent points still persuasively points to a single offender being responsible for both crimes. It would be well then to lump the consistent points together and see how persuasive they are. A helpful turn might be to look at the

[10] Information was drawn from the court record, not from Mr. Hazelwood's report. He may well have included this information in his report, although this author is doubtful. This author was unable to locate published studies dealing specifically with the rate of dental injury accompanying blunt injury to the face by an assailant. Informal consultation with various physicians and dentists led this author to believe that there was little discriminatory value in the fact that two people were assaulted and suffered facial injury without dental injury when attempting to connect the two incidents to a single assailant. Facial trauma without dental injury may be common.

consistencies and judge how likely it is that the assaults were not committed by the same person. One must ask, what is the possibility of two nonrelated sexual assaults sharing the following features: victims female and adult; alone; near a road; at night; offender subdues using physical force with trauma to the face and sexually assaults where he finds the victim; offender took off the victims' pants and bra before assaulting them; and the offender fails to leave semen at the scene. It is hard to believe that only two crimes were ever committed fitting this description.

Hazelwood then presented five ritual or signature behaviors:

1. Bites to lower chin.
   This is likely a signature behavior, offering no clear MO advantage.[11]
2. Bites to the left breast.
   This also is a signature behavior.
3. Injurious anal penetration.
   At first glance this appears to be a signature behavior, but it must be kept in mind that any nonconsensual anal intercourse is likely to cause some injury. Therefore, it may be safer to say the act of anal intercourse is a signature behavior, but withhold judgment on the injury aspect.
4. Brutal facial beating.
   The reader will recall that this was also covered to some degree earlier (points 10 and 12) in MO behavior. It is the brutal aspect that raises this to a signature behavior, but even then possibly only in the face of significant victim resistance.
5. Manual (frontal) strangulation.
   This could be a signature behavior, as there are other ways to kill someone. But it may be an MO behavior to quickly subdue a victim. One must ask, though, what are the chances that a male who wants to kill a woman and has no weapon on him would resort to strangling her? This author would suggest the odds are quite high. It hardly would qualify as unique behavior.

Of the five signature points offered, this author has essentially concurred that the five points are mostly indicative of signature behavior. In fact, this author, while dismissive of the weight of the MO behaviors, would offer that the signature behaviors offer much more hope of connecting the two crimes than the MO aspects, and this author would advise any interested investigating party to review the two crimes with the hope of connecting them to one offender. Yet this author is not satisfied that the available behaviors allow for a probative opinion that the two crimes were committed by the same offender. Part of this hesitation is due to the fact that although the five behaviors can appropriately be presented as signature behaviors, this does not carry the connotation that by signature we mean unique (i.e., individualization). In other words, "I think (or believe) they were committed by the same person" is not the same as "I am willing to testify in court that they were committed by the same person." Put another way, the level of confidence in one's opinion must correlate with the facts and the context in which those facts are found.

[11] One wonders if anyone asked Fortin's girlfriend (or former girlfriends) if he exhibited biting behavior in the past.

Furthermore, if one is to consider the similarities, one must also consider the differences when attempting to connect different crimes to an offender (Turvey, 1999; Turvey & Freeman, 2012). There are several differences between these two crimes that, at the least, would need to be noted:

1. One was a sexual assault; one was a sexual homicide.
2. One involved an extraordinarily high-risk victim: an armed police officer who had already called in the offender's license plate number and name to a dispatcher. The other involved a medium- to high-risk victim.
3. The police officer was not vaginally assaulted. She was anally assaulted. The homicide victim was anally and vaginally assaulted.
4. While both victims were strangled, the homicide victim was killed via strangulation. Strangulation appeared to be used only to subdue (decrease resistance) the police officer. In fact, Fortin stopped strangling the officer when she became semiconscious. The officer had a firearm. Strangling her may have been partly an MO behavior. Once she stopped struggling, he stopped strangling her.
5. While both victims suffered significant facial trauma, Melissa Padilla was beat about the face for no known reason, while Gardner was beat while Fortin was trying to drive away from the crime scene with her in the car with him. He may have been trying to maintain control as she regained consciousness.

Conclusion

Signature in criminal profiling is a concept, not a true signature. It is not a fingerprint, nor the equivalent of DNA evidence. Signature is not capable of individuation. It is one of several assays a profiler or investigator can make to offer an opinion as to whether or not two or more crimes are connected to each other and to a particular known or unknown offender(s). But care should be taken to be cognizant of the contextual aspects of the opinion formed by the criminal profiler or crime analyst. Not all opinions formed for the purpose of furthering an investigation can be assumed to meet the higher threshold necessary before offering such opinions to a court of law.

Questions

1. Define signature.
2. Signature behavior between crime scenes is more akin to a _________ or _________ than individuation.
3. In general, an example of individuating evidence would be:
   a. Modus operandi
   b. Shoe size
   c. Tire impressions
   d. DNA
   e. None of the above

4. It is the contention of McGrath that most profiles are:
   a. Developed to further an investigation only
   b. Developed to assist the prosecutor with interview strategies
   c. Help establish guilt
   d. Developed to assist the prosecutor with trial strategies only
   e. Of little to no value
5. Modus operandi behaviors are those things necessary for the successful completion of the crime. *True or false?*

References

Academy of Behavioral Profiling. (1999). Ethical guidelines. Available online at <http://www.profiling.org/abp_conduct.html>.

Baeza, J., Chisum, W. J., Chamberlin, T. M., McGrath, M., & Turvey, B. (2000). Academy of behavioral profiling: Criminal profiling guidelines. *Journal of Behavioral Profiling, 1*(1)

Burgess, A., & Hazelwood, R. (Eds.). (1995). *Practical aspects of rape investigation* (2nd ed.). New York: CRC Press.

Canter, D., Alison, L. J., Alison, E., & Wentink, N. (2004). The organized/disorganized typology of serial murder: Myth or model? *Psychology, Public Policy, and Law, 10*(3), 293–320.

Douglass, J. E., & Mann, C. M. (1992). Modus operandi and the signature aspects of violent crime. In J. E. Douglass, A. W. Burgess, A. G. Burgess, & R. K. Ressler (Eds.), *Crime classification manual* (pp. 259–268). San Francisco, CA: Josey Bass.

Geberth, V. J. (1995). The signature aspect in criminal investigations. *Law and Order Magazine, 43*(11), 45–49.

Geberth, V. J. (1996). *Practical homicide investigation* (3rd ed.). Boca Raton, FLA: CRC Press.

Hazelwood, R. R., & Michaud, S. G. (1998). *The evil that men do*. New York: St. Martin's Press.

Holmes, R., & Holmes, S. (1996). *Profiling violent crimes: An investigative tool* (2nd ed.). Thousand Oaks, CA: Sage Publications. (As cited in: Turvey, B. E. (2000). Criminal profiling and the problem of forensic individuation. *Journal of Behavioral Profiling*, Vol. 1, No. 2).

Ingram, S. (1998). If the profile fits: Criminal psychological profiles into evidence in criminal trials. *Journal of Urban and Contemporary Law, 54*, 239–266. (As cited in: Turvey, B. E. (2000). Criminal profiling and the problem of forensic individuation. *Journal of Behavioral Profiling*, Vol. 1, No. 2).

Kelly, S. (1995). *The Boston stranglers: The public conviction of Albert DeSalvo and the true story of eleven shocking murders*. New York: Carol Publishing.

Keppel, R. D. (1995). Signature murders: A report of several related cases. *Journal of Forensic Sciences, 40*(4), 670–674.

Kirk, P. L., & Thornton, J. I. (Eds.). (1974). *Crime investigation* (2nd ed.). Malabar, FL: Kreiger Publishing Company.

McGrath, M. (2000). Forensic psychiatry and criminal profiling: Forensic match or Freudian slipup? *Journal of Behavioral Profiling, 1*(1).

New Jersey v. (2000). Fortin 162 N.J. 517, 745 A.2d 509.

Thornton, J. I. (1997). The General assumptions and rationale of forensic identification. In D. L. Faigman, D. H. Kaye, M. J. Saks, & J. Sanders (Eds.), *Modern scientific evidence: The law and science of expert testimony* (Vol. 2) (pp. 1–49). St. Paul: West Publishing Co.

Turvey, B. E. (1999). *Criminal profiling: An introduction to behavioral evidence analysis.* London: Academic Press.

Turvey, B. E. (2000). Criminal profiling and the problem of forensic individuation. *Journal of Behavioral Profiling, 1*(2).

Turvey, B. E., & Freeman, J. (2012). Case linkage: Offender modus operandi and signature, chapter. In B. E. Turvey (Ed.), *Criminal profiling: An introduction to behavioral evidence analysis* (4th ed.). New York: Academic Press.

U.S. Department of Justice. (2001). Bureau of justice statistics: Crime characteristics. Available online <http://www.ojp.usdoj.gov/bjs/cvict_c.htm#time>.

Staged Crime Scenes–Literature and Types

Dr. Claire Ferguson

Introduction

Many things can hamper an investigation. For example, the crime may be a truly random occurrence without links between the victim and the offender, evidence may not be acknowledged or properly collected, and the crime type itself may influence solvability. In other cases still, offenders actively seek to hamper the police investigation in an effort to avoid being caught and going to prison. In fact, the literature on homicide notes that it is not uncommon in many cases of this type for the offender to engage in precautionary acts (Turvey, 2007). According to the criminological literature, precautionary acts (Turvey, 2008, p. 212):

> *...are behaviors that offenders commit before, during or after an offense that are consciously intended to confuse, hamper, or defeat investigative or forensic efforts for the purposes of concealing their identity, their connection to the crime, or the crime itself.*

A few examples include using a mask, clothing, or disguise to conceal physical features of the offender; using a secluded or less traveled location for the offense; using gloves to prevent the transfer of fingerprints or biological fluids; staging the crime scene; and so on (Turvey, 2008).

This chapter details a particular type of precautionary act called staging and will introduce readers to this arena of evidence manipulation that may be employed by offenders to thwart investigative efforts. First, the definitions of crime scene staging will be discussed, followed by staging as it relates to its broader counterpart: deception. Why we lie and how staging is a physical manifestation of deceit will be addressed. Following that, the literature surrounding simulated scenes will be reviewed, with reference to both criminal and death investigations. Finally, a discussion of the author's research into staged scenes will be briefly reviewed, the difference between behaviors carried out at staged legitimate deaths versus illegitimate deaths explained, and case examples given.

Definitions

Staging, or simulating a crime scene, is one of many precautionary acts offenders may carry out in order to distance themselves from a criminal act. The behavior known as crime scene staging or simulation is defined as the deliberate alteration of physical evidence at the location where a crime has actually or allegedly occurred, in an effort to simulate events or offenses that did not occur for the purpose of misleading authorities or redirecting an investigation (Geberth, 2006; Turvey, 2008). For example, after killing a person an offender may relocate the deceased's body into a car, position it as if the victim was driving, and send the car into a body of water to give the impression the victim died in an automobile accident. In such a case, the act of relocating the body, positioning it in the car, and driving it—or otherwise allowing it to roll—into the water would be considered acts of staging.

The easiest way to conceptualize the difference between other precautionary acts and staging is to note that, where a **precautionary act** generally involves taking something away or preventing something from being left at the scene, staging involves an attempt to prevent offender identification by depositing or doing something addition to the criminal act in order to make it appear that something has taken place that has not. It should additionally be acknowledged that staged or simulated scenes are not those involving a family member or loved one of the victim covering or dressing them when they have been found unclothed or in an otherwise embarrassing situation or position despite the contention in some of the literature (Geberth, 2006).[1] The defining factor involved in staged/simulated scenes is the goal behind them, which is to thwart investigative efforts or set the investigation in the wrong direction. It is for this reason that acts committed by a nonoffender after the fact are not considered staging, as the aim of thwarting investigative efforts is absent. This intention is the essence of the difference between other behaviors carried out at the scene and those acts that constitute staging.

[1] See Douglas & Munn, 1992; Douglas & Douglas, 2006; Hazelwood & Napier, 2004; Meloy, 2002. Each of these works and the definitional issues within them will be dealt with in detail in the literature review section.

The next section will attend to the reasoning behind scenes being staged as well as the possible solutions to how these scenes can be identified based on the research on detecting deceit. These theories will provide a basis for how lying through staging is accomplished, how the real nature of the event is hidden, and the personal characteristics and evidence necessary for investigators to readily detect deceptive efforts via staging.

Staging as Deception

Although the connection may seem limited to the uninitiated, the investigation and recognition of crime scenes that have been staged is, for all intents and purposes, a variation of **deception detection**. When investigating a scene that has been manipulated to present as something it is not, investigators are unsure whether they are observing the actual evidence of the crime as it happened, or the evidence of how the offender wished to present the crime (Gross, 1936). For the most part then, the investigator observing a complex crime scene is no different from one observing or conversing with a possibly deceptive suspect. They are both charged with determining whether or not they are being deceived based on the evidence available to them and their interpretation of it. The difference is that much research has been undertaken on how to tell the liars from the truth-tellers when it comes to face-to-face conversations or interrogations (see Bond & DePaulo, 2006; Buckley & Jane, 2001; Caso, Gnisci, Vrij & Mann, 2005; Ekman, 2001; Inbau, Reid, Park, Levine, McCormack, Morrison & Ferrara, 2002; Porter, Doucette, Woodworth, Earle & MacNeil, 2008; Stromwall, Granhag & Hartwig, 2004; Vrij, 2000). Unfortunately, as will be discussed in detail in subsequent sections, those investigators seeking to determine the liars from the truth-tellers based strictly on the physical and behavioral evidence left at a crime scene do not have the luxury of this wealth of literature behind them. Indeed, compared to the detection of deception, there is almost no systematic research on how to determine if a crime scene has been altered to deceive those investigating it. It is these investigators and profilers who are at an extreme disadvantage when attempting to detect deceit in the form of a staged scene, or even understand it after it has been detected. It seems possible that since staged scenes are, in actuality, a physical form of deception and trickery, perhaps the same theories that apply to traditional deception detection could also apply to detecting these scenes. However, those theories that address why and how people lie, as well as how to detect deception, are plagued by their own limitations. These will be touched upon briefly next.

Definition of Deception

According to Mitchell (1986 as cited in Vrij, 2000, p. 5), deception may be defined as "a false communication that tends to benefit the communicator." To this, Vrij (2000) adds that in order for something to be classified as a deception it must also be a deliberate attempt to mislead on the part of the deceiver. Therefore, unknowingly misrepresenting something cannot be classified as lying. The same can be said of staged crime scenes, where the intent behind the act determines whether or not a scene has been staged. A number of behaviors that could be utilized for other goals can also be considered staging if the intention behind them is to evade detection or thwart investigative efforts. For example, moving a deceased's body may be done to facilitate medical intervention in some cases, which would not be considered a deceptive action or staging. In cases in which the body is moved to have the scene present as something alternate to what it really is, this same behavior would be considered deceitful.

Detecting Deception

Whaley (1982, p. 190) contends that any and all deceptive efforts can be found out, regardless of the effort employed by the liar as long as the profiler has the right tools. He explains:

> *The possibility of detecting deception, any deception, is inherent in the effort to deceive. Every deception operation necessarily, inevitably, leaves clues. The analyst requires only the appropriate sensors and cognitive hypotheses to detect and understand the meaning of these clues. The problem is entirely one of technology and procedures and never one of theory.*
>
> *Because everything (whether objects or events) can to some extent be both simulated and dissimulated, deception is always possible. However, because this can never be done to the full extent, counter-deception is also always possible. In other words, incongruent characteristics (clues) inevitably are present in every deception operation. These incongruent [characteristics] form alternative patterns (hypotheses) that themselves are incongruent (discrepant, anomalous, paradoxical) with reality. As there are no paradoxes, no ambiguities, no incongruencies in nature, to detect incongruency is to detect the false.*

Since it is theoretically always possible to uncover deceit, how to detect these incongruities when we know them to be present becomes the challenge. In Vrij's discussions of detecting deceit he proffers the notion that at certain times lying is more difficult for the liar than others, and as such, sometimes detecting deceit is easier for the detective. The ease with which a lie can be uncovered has to do with the complexity of the lie, as well as the consequences of telling the lie. Specifically, Vrij (2000, p. 11) notes:

> *[L]ying is more difficult when the other person has some form of evidence that a person may well be lying ... [l]ying is also more difficult if the other person is suspicious ... Finally a lie is easier to tell when the liar has the opportunity to prepare the lie.*

Although not often touched on in the deception detection literature, Vrij here highlights an important and relevant aspect of uncovering lies: the use of evidence.

Traditionally, the literature maintains there are three ways to determine whether or not someone is being deceitful. However, based on Vrij's discussion, and that of several other authors (Park, Levine, McCormack, Morrison & Ferrara, 2002), it is also possible that there is a fourth method that may be useful. In terms of the first three methods (Vrij, 2000, p. 213):

> *The first is by observing liars' non-verbal behavior such as the movements they make, whether or not they smile or show gaze-aversion, the pitch of their voice, their speech rate,*

whether or not they stutter and so on. The second way is by analysing what is being said [content analysis]. The third way is by examining physiological responses (blood pressure, heart rate, palmar sweating, and so on).

The additional method is the interpretation and analysis of any physical evidence that may betray the lie. That is, through evidence of a person's behavior at the crime scene, as opposed to their face-to-face movements, their speech patterns, and their physiological response during an interrogation, a deceit may be evidenced. As mentioned, this has been mostly overlooked in the deception literature previously, although a few authors have touched on using anomalous evidence to raise suspicion, and then using these techniques to actually detect the lie during questioning. Although this method of deception detection has not been given much attention, many of the principles related to traditional detection efforts also work to improve discovery of a lie based, not on the liars and their behavior in an interrogation, but their prior behavior at a crime scene. One such theory is that related to the motivational impairment effect.

Not all lies carry the same consequences, and therefore not all liars are motivated to pull off the misperception to the same degree. In their study of motivation and detecting deceit, Zuckerman and Driver (1985) determined that the more motivated a liar is to avoid getting caught, the more likely it is his or her behavior will give the lies away. It is this concept that the three previous methods are based on; those with a greater motivation to lie experience stronger emotions (like a fear of being found out), they may think harder than those who are less motivated (because of this fear), and they may try harder to control their behavior. This has been termed the motivational impairment effect (DePaulo, Kirkendol, Tang & O'Brien, 1988), and purportedly allows for a better indication that the person is lying based on verbal, nonverbal, and physiological responses. The motivational impairment effect inherently works in favor of those attempting to detect the deceit, making the lie more obvious in these three ways.

However, it is also possible to expand this motivational impairment to an offender's ability to deceive via manipulating the evidence at a scene. It is possible that those who are thinking harder, and trying harder to cover their tracks, may be more likely to panic after the crime has taken place, or forget their plan (assuming they had one to begin with). By virtue of the fact they are highly motivated to create a scene that did not occur, these individuals may actually leave more evidence of themselves and the real scenario (such as leaving more DNA, footprints, bloodstains, and so on). As explained by Svensson and Wendel (1974, p. 292):

Even when the murderer has carefully planned the crime and taken all imaginable precautions to avoid leaving traces, they are still found. As a rule, the murderer comes to a sudden realization of the terrible results of his deed after the killing. He may then lose his head completely and try to obliterate the evidence of his act, but in his confused state of mind only works against himself by leaving new clues.

Therefore the motivational impairment effect may not just work for detecting deceit in a more traditional fashion, but may also allow for this detection based strictly on the physical evidence available. This effect is important to the current discussion because, for the most part, those who simulate crime scenes often have a lot at stake if the lie is not believed (such as significant time in prison, or the death penalty), and may have gone to great lengths to prepare the lie, thus increasing their motivation to be believed.

Like the determination of deceit in a more traditional sense then, using incongruities left at crime scenes can assist investigators in determining whether or not a scene has been staged. These cues take the form of physical and behavioral evidence, and instead of looking for such things as stuttering, speech rates, and so on, profilers may seek out evidence of paradoxical offender behavior, inconsistencies in the physical evidence, and the like. Undoubtedly though, these incongruities will be similar to more traditional indications of deceit in that they will become more or less obvious based on the time the offender has to prepare the lie (or crime scene), the consequences of the lie, and complexity of the facade they are trying to portray (Vrij, 2000).

Along with the motivation an offender has to be believed, the motivation a profiler has to discover the lie can also have an effect. In terms of the personal characteristics of an investigator necessary to be able to uncover lies, Vrij (2000) remarks that there are several guidelines to keep in mind (adapted from Vrij, 2000, p. 222–225):

> *Be suspicious*
>
> *Lies often remain undetected because observers have too much good faith—too often they assume that people speak the truth. It is essential for a lie detector to be suspicious and to distrust what people are saying. This is sometimes difficult.*
>
> ...
>
> *Be Informed*
>
> *It is easier for the observer to catch a liar if he or she is well informed about the topic of the lie. The more details the observer already knows, the more likely it is that he or she will notice that what the liar is saying is untrue.*
>
> ...
>
> *Watch and Listen Carefully and Abandon Stereotypes*
>
> *There is no typical non-verbal behavior that indicates deception, nor do all liars say specific things or avoid saying certain things. It is therefore not useful to make judgments about deceit on the basis of stereotypical beliefs (e.g. 'liars show gaze-aversion,' 'liars fidget,' 'liars stutter'). Instead, observers should judge each case individually. To look carefully at how someone is behaving and to listen carefully to what they are saying is thus essential.*

Although fairly nonspecific, these guidelines dovetail nicely with the characteristics of a good investigator/profiler that have been offered in the criminology literature, including this text. This fact lends credence to the notion that although previously existing independently, there is much overlap between detecting deceit and generally investigating criminal behavior. It is possible to take from this that deception detection, and the theories and principles that surround it, can be applied to detecting anomalies in the physical evidence at the crime scene, and an additional, and seemingly useful method of deception detection may be to make use of the physical evidence as opposed to, or in addition to, traditional techniques.

Now that staging as a manifestation of deceit has been explained, the criminological and forensic science literature relating to crime scene staging will be addressed, highlighting some of the strengths and weaknesses present therein. It is to this discussion that we now turn.

Staged Crime Scenes: The Literature

Staging and Criminal Investigations

Despite the fact that staged crime scenes are not uncommon (Gross, 1934; Geberth, 1996; Turvey, 2000), there is a paucity of published literature devoted to studying them in many forensic communities (Douglas & Munn, 1992a,b; Geberth, 1996; Gross, 1934; O'Connell & Soderman, 1936; Svensson & Wendel, 1974; Turvey, 2000). In fact, thus far only two published studies (Turvey, 2000; Hazelwood & Napier, 2004) have ever been conducted on staged crime scenes. One attempted to describe them by their common features (Turvey, 2000) while the other asked seasoned law enforcement agents to give their opinion on common indicators (Hazelwood & Napier, 2004). Because they are so few and far between, each of these two works as well as a few others can be discussed in a timely fashion. The following section will discuss these works in detail, as well as the currently unpublished study carried out by the author. For a brief overview of the other anecdotal literature, especially early works relating to crime scene staging, see Turvey (2000).

In their piece on staged scenes in fatal and false report cases, Hazelwood and Napier (2004) canvassed 20 consultants who have testified as experts or worked cases involving staged scenes. The rationale behind this study is in agreement with other authors (for example Geberth, 1996), who opine that staging behaviors are on the rise due to the effect of mass media and the portrayal of forensic techniques therein.[2] Of the 20 consultants surveyed, Hazelwood and Napier (2004) asked how many cases they had worked, how many were staged, and the types of staging commonly found. The authors report (p. 754–755):

> *[T]he 20 law enforcement professionals that participated in the survey reported that in their experience, nonfatal false allegations of sexual assault were the most common form of staging, followed by staging homicides as burglary-related or robbery-related crimes, staging the manner of death, and finally staging the homicides as sexually-related crimes.*

This survey also found that approximately 3% of violent crimes are staged (Hazelwood & Napier, 2004). If these figures are to be trusted, of the 4.9 million nonfatal violent crimes in the United States in 2008 (Rand, 2009), approximately 147,000 would involve elements of staging.

[2] For a detailed discussion of how offenders learn from mass media see Ferguson (2010) or Shelton, Kim, and Barak (2006).

Similarly, of the nearly 17,000 homicides in the United States in 2005 (Fox & Zawitz, 2007), 501 would involve such elements. Although the research design employed here is certainly problematic, if these figures are even remotely accurate they indicate a very large number of criminal acts involving various levels of staging, making the lack of sound research in this area even more disturbing.

In terms of methodology, these estimations were given by the law enforcement consultants over the phone and were based strictly on top-of-the-head memories. They were not asked to go back and review the cases they had worked or make any exact determination of how many involved staging. Because of the use of this specific methodology, availability biases[3] will certainly be an issue in the reliability of these results.

Furthermore, these authors did not address whether and how many of these cases were worked by more than one of the consultants participating. This is an important element of the survey to address as some of the cases included in the results of this study may have appeared more than once. More concerning, the authors note the results of this survey lacked generalizability, as it was designed to "report investigative perceptions" rather than to "provide detailed predictive analyses" (p. 746).

In this discussion, Hazelwood and Napier (2004) endorse a similar definition for staging to that of previous authors such as Douglas and Munn (1992a,b). They note that staging behaviors have one or both of two possible motivations behind them. Staging can be done in order to mislead the investigator as to "a) the manner of death (i.e., homicide, suicide, accident, natural or other), b) the cause of death (i.e., the medical reason for the death), or c) the motive for the original act (i.e., greed, anger-revenge, attention, game playing or other)" and that the motivation behind these goals is either "self preservation" or "embarrassment-shame" (p. 751). The first motivation (self preservation) is that which is typically endorsed in the other literature and here, applying to the perpetrator who wishes to manipulate evidence in order to evade suspicion and capture. The embarrassment-shame motivation is where the offender "is attempting to provide the victim with a degree of dignity or to allow the family to remember the victim in a more generous sense than the original scene would have allowed" (p. 751). This embarrassment-shame motivation is typically not endorsed in other definitions, and is heavily criticized in Geberth (1996), Turvey (2002), and Ferguson (2010). Hazelwood and Napier (2004, p. 753) defend this part of their definition, saying that "when the location has been intentionally rearranged to mislead the investigation as to the means or manner or death, it has been staged, and the classification is certainly applicable". This statement is both confusing and paradoxical. It begs the question, how can an act intended, by definition, to avoid embarrassment or shame for the victim or the family be classified along with criminal behavior of an offender motivated by a desire to pervert the cause of justice? That is, there is no criminal intent behind embarrassment and shame motivations, and therefore this should be treated as a different constellation of behavior. The intention behind staging, by definition, is to thwart the

[3]An availability bias refers to the subjective likelihood of certain events increasing based on one's ability to imagine them. This could be due to having previous experience with such an event (Carroll, 1978). Therefore, having experienced cases involving staging previously, participants in this study may be more likely to judge those events as probable because they have a scenario under which those events could occur available to them.

investigation and evade capture, not embarrassment. The authors further note, "sparing the relatives embarrassment or shame should not enter into the decision on whether to categorise or investigate a scene as staged" (p. 753). This notion is somewhat more agreeable; however, they fail to mention that determining whether an offender or a relative manipulated the scene is of extreme import, as the conclusion will alter the suspect pool for the primary offense dramatically. Therefore this distinction is paramount.

In terms of how to investigate staged scenes, Hazelwood and Napier (2004) provide many recommendations and general commentary similar to that provided by Douglas and Munn (1992a,b) and Douglas and Douglas (2006). They note that an investigator has two main sources of information for any given crime—the scene and the victim. In order to determine whether and what inconsistencies are present, which may indicate staging, they recommend a careful victimology be undertaken. They also postulate that there are three areas where inconsistencies may be discovered: victim-centered, immediate location, and distant locations. They expand (p. 757):

> *The term victim-centered refers to information about the victim (i.e., victimology) and those elements of the crime that directly impact upon the victim (i.e., sexual assault, injuries, clothing disarray, etc.). Immediate location refers to significant facts or conditions present at the scene, near the scene or around the alleged assault location (i.e., forced entry, items taken or destroyed, signs of a struggle, TV on or off, etc.). Finally the term distant locations refers to other geographic locations associated with the crime, such as where the body was disposed of, car disposal site, or even a location where a pseudo victim alleges she was taken.*
>
> *All behaviors and other significant facts about the crime are placed in one of these three categories. The investigator then compares what he observes in and across each category with what he would expect to observe in similar situations, basing those expectations on his education, training and experience. In other words, does what he observes make sense? If the investigator observes inconsistencies, they must be explained.*

This categorization system is reasonable, and may be useful in the conceptual study of these cases. However what is absent is any reference to a proper crime reconstruction being undertaken as well as a wound pattern analysis by a qualified forensic examiner. This is a notable omission, as many of the other authors opining on simulated crime scenes refer to this as being an absolute necessity. Interestingly, this work does include a profile of an offender who stages a crime scene, noting that they are usually someone known to or an intimate partner of the victim and a white male between the ages of 26 and 35. Although based on the "observations of highly trained and experienced investigators" it is unknown exactly how this profile, or the recommendations above for that matter, are meant to be put to use. Both of these elements lack the detail necessary for other examiners to use the recommendations offered here, and therefore they may be of limited value.

Again similar to Hazelwood and Napier (2004) as well as Douglas and Munn (1992a,b), Meloy (2002) also endorses a definition of staging as that involving either alteration of the crime scene by the offender to thwart or confuse investigative efforts, or by someone close to the victim to save them embarrassment, dishonor, or humiliation in a spousal homicide staged as a sexual homicide. Although an interesting case, Meloy provides no empirical data on staged crime scenes, and fails to mention whether he, in fact, investigated the homicide. He does note that in a personal communication with A. Eke (June 2001 as cited in Meloy, 2002, p. 398) he learned that common motivations for staging are "the desire to suggest another unknown perpetrator, a suicide, an accident, death by natural causes or an act of self-defense." Meloy provides no further detail on Eke or her expertise, and fails to note that these so-called motivations are not motivations at all, and that the desire to have the evidence appear as something it is not is inherent in the definition of staging.

Citing Geberth (1996), Keppel and Weis (2004) discuss the rarity of staging as well as posing of bodies. They first differentiate between staging and posing behaviors, and then give case examples and common characteristics of each. Although some of the only empirical research in the area, this piece has several irreconcilable errors.

The first issue with this research is that posing is viewed as discrete from staging behaviors. The authors fail to address the fact that posing a body can be utilized as an element of staging. They note (p. 1310), "Posing is not to be confused with staging, because staging refers to manipulation of the scene around the body as well as positioning of the body to make the scene appear to be something that it is not." Posing is designed to leave the victim in a position that would be considered sexually degrading, and this could be done, according to Keppel and Weis (2004, p. 1310) for one of two reasons: "1) to shock the finder of the body or police investigators, and 2) for the killer's own pleasure." These authors have failed to take note of the fact that posing a body in a sexually degrading position may be used as a way of staging the scene as well (not that an offender could get pleasure out of shocking the finder of the body and police). Failure to recognize this fact may lead to investigators, or the authors themselves, doing exactly what they warn against and confusing staging for posing. Given the stark contrast between the data presented by Keppel and Weis (2004) on the profile of those who commit each of these types of behaviors, this would be a serious misjudgment.

Another problem with this research is the sampling method utilized to gather cases involving staging. Although the authors recognize that staging involves many more behaviors than simply repositioning the body, and in fact may not even involve such repositioning, cases were included or excluded from the sample of staged cases based on the question "did the offender intentionally place the body in an unusual position? (e.g., staged or posed)" (p. 1310). Through this sampling procedure, many cases involving staging where the body was not positioned were surely excluded. The subsequent statements about the infrequency of staging are therefore misled. The authors would be more accurate in stating that cases involving repositioning of the body for the purposes of staging the crime scene may be rare. Despite this major oversight in the sampling approach, these authors inexplicably state "posing a victim's body or staging a murder scene occurs so infrequently that it is unlikely that most violent crime investigators will ever investigate a murder that has been staged or posed." This is contradictory to what other authors have noted pertaining to the commonality of these scenes (Gross, 1934; Geberth, 1996; Turvey, 2000). Perhaps what Keppel and Weis (2004) mean, and what can be shown by the evidence in their research, is that based on their sample from one year in Washington State, posing or repositioning a body for the purpose of thwarting investigative efforts occurs infrequently, or perhaps worse, that a number of staged cases go unnoticed and undetected.

Keppel and Weis (2004) go on to address the characteristics common to cases involving either staging or posing according to their definitions. This is again problematic as the word "staging" is used to describe only those cases in which the offender altered the body as part of his or her efforts to deceive investigators. Furthermore, the characteristics do not take into account that posed bodies may also be staged bodies, and therefore the characteristics may not be discrete but overlapping. Perhaps the most egregious issue with this work is not those addressed earlier, but the statements made about premeditation without any evidence whatsoever. The authors state (p. 1308) that "staging a murder scene requires the killer to spend time before the murder, planning its execution." This is again reiterated at the end of the paper (p. 1311) in that "[placing bodies in unusual positions] requires that the offender spend time planning the events leading up to murder and rearranging the body and crime scene after the victim's death." As mentioned, these statements are not referenced to any previous work or study, and there is no indication where the authors are getting the notion that these behaviors must be planned in advance. This passage not only shows the lack of credible evidence and research pertaining to staging behaviors, but also the inaccuracy of the claims made by those few who are indeed publishing in this area.

Upon identifying the palpable lack of systematic research on staging, Turvey (2000) conducted a preliminary study to identify common characteristics associated with staged crime scenes. The research examined 25 homicide cases in the United States from 1980 to 2000, in which crime scene staging was confessed to, witnessed, or proven with physical evidence. Because of the link between staged crime scenes and domestic homicide, the study compared its findings to those found in similar studies of domestic homicides in the United States (Bureau of Justice Statistics, 1998; Mukherjee et al., 1983).

Turvey's (2000) study found that all offenders had a current or prior family or intimate relationship with their victim. This finding supported Geberth's (1996) hypothesis that crime scene staging is most commonly used to conceal an offender's close relationship with the victim. The research also found that offenders were more likely to stage the homicide to appear as a stranger burglary than any other crime, and in many cases, although staged to appear as a burglary, no valuables were taken by the offender. Offenders used available weapons in about half the cases and were often the people to discover the body. Together these findings illustrate the lack of sophistication that was present in the cases studied, and also highlight the somewhat troubling notion that those involved in law enforcement may be more likely to stage scenes than non-law-enforcement offenders in order to thwart identification (Turvey, 2000).

Although simple and preliminary, this research set the stage for more detailed and exhaustive studies to be conducted in order to more systematically describe staged crime scenes. This research was the first empirical study of this topic conducted, but it failed to address a major area of relevance, that is, the red flags or common characteristics of different types of staged scenes as opposed to all scenes combined. It is important to recognize that those who stage accidents are likely to carry out different behaviors than those who attempt to stage sexual homicides. Undoubtedly, those who attempt to simulate sexual homicides likely manipulate the evidence in different ways to lend credence to the illusion than those who stage suicides. Therefore, it is necessary to separate out the types of staging attempted in order to get a more accurate and specific set of behavioral indicators that can be used as red flags. This will be returned to later, in the section relating to the author's work in this area.

Staging and Death Investigations

Whereas criminal investigators usually determine whether a crime has taken place; who is responsible; and where, when, why and how it happened; they also often rely heavily on the opinions of forensic pathologists, coroners, and medical examiners who determine the manner of death in equivocal cases. However, investigators can often complement the strictly clinical findings with much circumstantial or contextual evidence in order to assist in making such a determination. Therefore, a number of criminal investigative texts have also touched on how to examine equivocal deaths (differentiating between accidents, suicides, homicides, naturals, and undetermined), and will be addressed here.

Medico legal death investigations involve investigating the death of an individual by combining medical, scientific, and circumstantial information in order to determine the cause, mechanism, and manner of death. According to DiMaio and DiMaio (2001, p. 3–4):

> *The cause of death is any injury or disease that produces a physiological derangement in the body that results in death of the individual … the mechanism of death is the physiological derangement produced by the cause of death that results in death … [And] the manner of death explains how the cause of death came about. Manners of death can generally be categorized as natural, homicide, suicide, accident or undetermined.*

Medical examiners' and coroners' offices decide which cases warrant an autopsy being performed, and then perform them. Ordinarily, these are cases involving violent, suspicious, sudden, or unexpected deaths, or those occurring without a physician in attendance (DiMaio & DiMaio, 2001). Medical examiners' offices usually function under a police agency, or the public health system, and the medical examiner is usually an appointed physician with qualifications in pathology and forensic pathology (Edwards & Gatsonis, 2009). A coroner, on the other hand, is usually someone who is elected, at least in the United States. The qualifications necessary to become a coroner are different depending on the jurisdiction (Edwards & Gatsonis, 2009). This can be more or less problematic depending on who the coroner is and their expertise. By and large, coroner systems are fraught with issues regardless of the specific coroner. This is especially relevant to cases involving equivocal deaths, or possible staging, because these cases may involve complex determinations that require advanced forensic knowledge. An unknowing coroner may decide that a death such as this is an obvious suicide or accident and therefore fail to order a body for autopsy in the first place, thus rendering the expertise of the physician who would have carried out the autopsy completely moot.

As alluded to, the circumstances present at the scene are extremely important to the forensic pathologist, medical examiner, or coroner. Nothing happens in a vacuum, and these professionals are therefore charged with rendering not only an opinion on the nature of the injuries to a victim, but also whether they are congruous with the account of the incident given by police, witnesses, or anyone else who may be involved. These incongruities or a lack of correlation between scene information and autopsy findings may become the basis for an opinion that a crime scene has been staged. This may especially be the case in those instances involving manner of death determinations, such as when the scene information indicates an accident but the autopsy reveals homicide. The importance of a qualified, objective, and thorough forensic pathologist/ME/coroner cannot, therefore, be understated in these cases. The necessity of collaboration between criminal investigators and medicolegal investigators is also evident.

Suicides Staged as Homicides/Accidents

Aside from the aforementioned criminological literature that deals directly with homicides that are staged to appear as something else, several other authors have broached the subject from other standpoints, including psychological/psychiatric pathologies (Munchausen Syndrome) and various motivations for suicide. Adair and Doberson (1999), Imajo (1983), and McDowell (1987) have all published case reports that outline and explain suicide cases in which the victims staged their own deaths to appear as murders or accidents. Each author's work will be described, as these cases are certainly relevant to the role a profiler plays. Following this, the problems with defining these cases as "staged" will be addressed.

In his case analysis of a suicide staged to appear as a homicide, McDowell (1987) addresses the issue of Munchausen Syndrome and the pathology that goes along with it that may lead a person to wish to commit suicide while implicating another person or scenario. Munchausen Syndrome is a factitious disorder that involves patients who fake symptoms of various disorders and ailments for psychological reasons as opposed to malingering for monetary gain or some other secondary gain. These individuals enjoy the role of being sick, and will often follow through on receiving serious medical intervention and procedures to "cure" their supposed ailments (Factitious Disorder–Munchausen Syndrome, n.d.). In his treatment of this related area, McDowell (1987) stresses the need for any forensic examiner, be they a medical or law enforcement practitioner or a profiler, to validate complaints objectively and create a critical patient history or victimology.

Although studying suicide by purposeful car accident as opposed to a supposed homicide, Imajo (1983) again stresses the importance of a thorough victimology, including addressing the victim's traumatic situations before death; guilty feelings; self-punishing behaviors; increased or decreased activity, withdrawal, or drinking; weight loss or gain; depression and feelings of worthlessness; physician visits; substance abuse; and mental illness. He also reiterates the problems outlined earlier, that there is very little information available on these types of scenes, people, and how to investigate them. Imajo (1983) notes the importance of publishing more information on this area for medical examiners, although the sentiment clearly rings true for anyone charged with determining what happened at these scenes, including law enforcement and profilers.

Similarly, Adair and Doberson (1999) describe one case involving a suicide staged by the victim to appear as a homicide. They note that cases such as this, although rare, provide a great challenge to medical examiners and police. They further explain the importance of thorough and careful crime scene investigation, so that any elements that may indicate that the victim has put him- or herself in that position can be discerned (in the case used for the report the victim utilized quick-release magician's handcuffs, which gave the impression that he was restrained, but they were actually very easily removed).

While each of the three works explained earlier describe cases in which suicides are "staged" to appear as something else (either homicides or accidents), it could be argued that this term is not appropriate for these instances. Similar to Douglas and Munn (1992a,b), Douglas and Douglas (2006), Hazelwood and Napier (2004), and Meloy (2002), it is clear that these authors are endorsing a definition of staging that is not limited to altering the crime scene in order to thwart or confuse investigative efforts. Instead, these authors are utilizing a much more broad definition, which includes any alteration of the crime scene in order to confuse or mislead anyone viewing the scene. That is, these suicides staged to look like something else may be designed as vengeful acts against others left behind. As stated by Adair and Doberson (1999, p. 1309), "[s] taging a suicide as a homicide, by the victim, may be a final effort by the victim to gain notoriety or exact revenge against friends or family." Cases of this type do not meet the definition of staging utilized herein, as the intent behind these efforts is different, despite them being attempts to deceive through manipulation of crime scene indicators. More importantly, in the cases discussed by Imajo (1983), there may be no staging based on even the broadest definition. Choosing to purposefully get into a car accident may simply have been viewed as an easy and available way to commit suicide, and there may have been no real desire on the part of the victim to have others believe that it was an accident. In fact, in one of the cases cited by Imajo (1983), the victim told someone he was leaving to commit suicide by "roll[ing] his car"; therefore, any expectation of the crash being ruled accidental would be greatly diminished. This highlights the importance of addressing issues related to staging of any type on a case by case basis.

It should now be apparent that aside from the mostly anecdotal case studies presented by the previously reviewed texts, very little work has been done on the subject of staged crime scenes, and more notably, bar a few studies, no intensive systematic research had been conducted on the topic until 2010. This is problematic due to the fact that elements of staging are such a consistent characteristic of criminal modus operandi (MO; Geberth, 1996; Gross, 1934; Turvey, 2000), and because these determinations often necessitate successful collaborations between medical professionals and investigators/profilers. The authors noted earlier, with the exception of Turvey (2000), Hazelwood and Napier (2004), and Keppel and Weis (2004), offer suggestions on how to identify these characteristics; however, these suggestions are based solely on their expertise or the expertise of others, and therefore run the risk of being at best inaccurate and at worst misleading and detrimental to serious criminal investigations. Certainly, more reliable and detailed research is necessary.

The Defects of the Situation

In order to address this lack of research in the area, the author undertook a systematic study of staged crime scenes as part of her doctoral thesis (Ferguson, 2010). This project involved a detailed analysis of 141 cases of homicide wherein some element of the evidence had been staged. From this, general red flags for staging were discovered, as well as those specific to different types of staging that could be used to discriminate between bona fide and simulated cases. Through a detailed analysis of common behaviors, a simple typology was also developed that separates out cases designed to appear as legitimate deaths from those designed to appear as illegitimate. Each of these elements of the research will be described briefly in turn.

Red Flags for Staging

The results of this study suggest that, overall, staged cases were more likely to have multiple victims and/or multiple offenders than general homicides. Firearms were less likely to be used in staged cases than nonstaged, but blunt force or strangulation may be more likely to be used in this sample than in the general homicide sample. Therefore the red flags for all types of staging would be multiple victims and multiple offenders and the use of blunt force or strangulation to cause the fatality. It is possible that these two things are actually not a construct of staging but of domestic homicides in general, since many of the homicides in the staged sample were domestic in nature. However, the Bureau of Justice Statistics (Fox & Zawitz, 2007) indicates that, in fact, the most common weapon in domestic homicides (involving spouses, ex-spouses, boyfriends, and girlfriends) are firearms or knives, and that most cases involve only one offender and one victim. The presence of these two basic characteristics should arouse suspicion in investigators to the fact that the homicide may have been staged. This, coupled with how the scene seemingly presents, will allow investigators to seek out and interpret any evidence of the red flags specific to each type of staging discussed in Ferguson (2010). These findings are of interest to profilers in and of themselves; however, it is also important to make note of the fact that most of the findings here were not predicted by the authors whose work was outlined in detail earlier and in other works (see Turvey, 2000). In fact, very few of the predictions made by the authors opining on staging and the behaviors common to it have been endorsed by Ferguson's (2010) findings.

Perhaps one of the major shortcomings, and the biggest detriment to investigators attempting to detect these scenes, is that many of the previously mentioned works do not discriminate between staging behaviors with different goals. Although grouping all staged scenes together regardless of the goal is counterintuitive, doing so has not been recognized as a major downfall in the past. For the uninitiated student and profiler, it is imperative to acknowledge that scenes staged to appear as legitimate deaths, like accidents, will involve a different constellation of behavior than those staged to appear as illegitimate deaths, such as home-invasion murders. A classification system to categorize the different types of staging behaviors is necessary.

Separating Staging Behaviors by Intent

Although these red flags do exist, and help investigators/profilers determine between staged and genuine scenes, it was also found in the author's research that red flags differ depending on what type of scene the offender is seeking to stage. That is, offenders whose intention was to stage a certain type of scene carried out behaviors that were different to those with other intentions. As such, the importance of separating out each type of staging from the others is highlighted. In that regard, cases may be classified into categories based on the staging behaviors present in the case and the statements the witness made to authorities investigating the death. For example, if the victim's body is placed at the bottom of the stairs and the witness tells police that he or she saw the victim fall down the stairs, but the medical examiner testifies the victim died as a result of a gunshot, the case is classified as a staged accidental death because it is clear the offender is trying to make the scene present as such. Cases can thus be separated based on the aim of the staging, and each type studied in more depth. The most prevalent categories of staging in the author's sample were Burglary/Home Invasion, Suicide, Car Accident, Accidental Death, Sexual Homicide, and Self-Defense Homicide. In the descriptive analysis done in the author's research it was apparent that each type indeed showed differing characteristics, although there was some overlap between them. It is not feasible in this chapter to outline all the red flags and all the differences within and between each type (for such an in-depth discussion see Ferguson, 2010). However, it is of import to acknowledge that staging with different goals takes place with different frequencies and, as such, it is necessary to outline how often various styles of crime scenes were staged in this sample.

The most likely type of staging present in this sample was Burglary/Home Invasion (43.3%). The next most frequent types of scene staged were suicide (12.8%), car accident (12.1%), and accidental death (11.3%). Sexual homicides and self-defense homicides were next most frequently staged, although they were not particularly common (5% and 4.3%, respectively). It should also be noted that an approximately equal number of cases (4.3%) had an unknown goal behind the staging, and the staging behaviors may have been carried out nonspecifically or simply to confuse. Drug-related homicides, executions, and stranger attacks were equally unlikely (1.4% each), and frame-ups, natural deaths, hate crimes, and carjacking/robberies were the least likely, each occurring in less than 1% of cases (0.7% each).

Although every type of staging cannot be discussed in detail, it is possible to broadly discriminate between staged legitimate deaths and staged illegitimate deaths as per the author's study. This discrimination was made based on a Multi-Dimensional Scaling (MDS) technique that was utilized, and indicated that the biggest difference in the actions carried out by offenders at a crime scene depended upon whether they were seeking for the scene to appear as a legitimate death (i.e., where a crime had not occurred) or an illegitimate death (i.e., where a crime had occurred, but they were not personally involved). It is this discriminating factor that made up the final basic typology of staging:

1. Staged Legitimate Deaths
   - A. Suicide/Accident
   - B. Car Accident
2. Staged Illegitimate Deaths

Each type will be discussed in turn, with a case example.

Staged Legitimate Deaths

According to the author's study there are two types of staged legitimate deaths, which present differently. These are staged accidents/suicides and staged car accidents. Staged legitimate deaths, such as staged suicides and accidents, involve not utilizing a weapon in order to inflict the fatal injuries; for example, killing the victim by beating them manually or causing them to fall. In these cases the victim's body is likely to be discovered in his or her own bedroom, and he or she often has injuries that could be considered "pseudo self-injuries," or injuries perpetrated by the offender that are designed to appear as though they were self-inflicted by the victim. The cause of death associated with these types of homicides is often strangulation. These staged suicides or accidents are also correlated with the violence happening during or immediately after a confrontation between victim(s) and offender(s).

The following is a case example of a staged legitimate death (suicide) adapted from *Kenneth KORITTA v The State of* Georgia (1992, No. A92A1325 (424 S.E. 2d 799)). The irrelevant details have been removed, as well as the appellate decisions and legal arguments.

KORITTA v. The STATE of Georgia

Kenneth Koritta was convicted for voluntary manslaughter in the shooting death of Bruce Blankenship. Koritta appeals from the denial of his motion for a new trial, enumerating three errors in the court's charge to the jury.

The evidence adduced at trial established that on the night of February 8, 1991, paramedics responding to an emergency call from appellant's apartments found Blankenship seated on the living room couch with a .38 revolver in his right hand and a bullet wound in the back of his head. Blankenship was pronounced dead soon after he was taken to the hospital.

Appellant was questioned by police several times the next day. He first gave a statement indicating that Blankenship shot himself while appellant was out of the room. Later that day, appellant gave another statement recounting that Blankenship had been visiting at appellant's apartment and drinking alcohol during the afternoon; that appellant came home from work at 6:00 PM and began drinking with him; that Blankenship found appellant's gun hidden in the couch cushions and began toying with and cocking the gun; that appellant tried to wrestle the gun from Blankenship and it fired in the ensuing struggle; and that he staged the suicide scene out of fear and panic. In the third statement, given that evening, appellant said he became angry when he found Blankenship cocking the gun because appellant's son was asleep in a chair in the room and his daughters were in their bedroom; that Blankenship angrily refused appellant's demand to return the gun; that they struggled over the gun and appellant grabbed it; that Blankenship fell forward and appellant fired the gun.

At trial, the medical examiner testified that the physical evidence was most consistent with appellant's third statement, as the condition of the wound suggested the gun had been fired from two to three feet away, but acknowledged the second version could not be completely ruled out. Appellant testified that he found Blankenship playing with the gun, that Blankenship refused his demands to put down the gun, and that appellant then lunged at Blankenship and they struggled. Appellant wrestled the gun from Blankenship and pushed him onto the couch. Appellant testified that as he braced himself for a fight, the gun fired, hitting Blankenship in the back of the head. Appellant testified he did not intend to shoot the gun and had only intended to defend himself in a fight.

Although not a textbook case of a staged suicide according to the red flags identified by the research, this case highlights one important overarching characteristic of staged homicides—a profound lack of sophistication. Unlike Keppel and Weis's (2004) assertions, these behaviors often have very little planning and very few elements to them. In this case the offender simply placed the gun in the victim's hand and subsequently lied to police. This lack of criminal sophistication was certainly noteworthy in the study conducted by the author.

Staged legitimate deaths involving pseudo car accidents present slightly differently. The behaviors include utilizing multiple weapons to inflict the fatal injuries and the cause of death being blunt force trauma. The victims' bodies in these cases are often transported to a location other than the primary crime scene, and they are often discovered with post-mortem mutilation as well as in their own vehicle. Further, the weapons utilized to inflict the blunt force trauma are often opportunistic in nature, or previously available at the crime scene. Weapons in these cases are also more likely to be positioned at the scene. For example, the victim may have died as a result of blunt force injuries from a baseball bat, and the scene is arranged to appear as though they had sustained those injuries after being thrown from a car during an accident.

The following is a case example of a staged automobile accident adapted from *Commonwealth of Massachusetts v. Milton L. RICE* (1998, (692 N.E. 2d 28)). The details presented here are part of the factual summary of the case. The irrelevant details have been removed, as well as the appellate decisions and legal arguments.

Commonwealth of Massachusetts v Milton L. RICE

A jury convicted the defendant of murder in the first degree by reason of deliberate premeditation and extreme atrocity or cruelty and of assault and battery by means of a dangerous weapon. The victim was the defendant's wife.

...

We summarize the evidence before the jury. On August 4, 1993 at approximately 5:50 AM, police officers responded to a report of a car fire on Parker Road in West Barnstable. The car was off the road and contained the charred remains of a body in the front seat. After learning that the car was registered to Milton L. Rice of 120 Buttonwood Lane in West Barnstable, the police proceeded to that address and observed the defendant walking toward them from a wooded pond area behind the house. The police told the defendant that his car had been "in a very serious motor vehicle accident. Somebody had been deceased." He was asked who could have had access to the car. The defendant went inside the house, ostensibly to determine if the victim was at home, and on his return, stated that she was gone and that her bedroom "was a mess." After obtaining the defendant's permission to enter the house, two police officers went upstairs to the second floor bedroom and observed blood on the bedroom furniture, floor, carpet, walls and ceiling. The police officers went back outside and informed the defendant of his Miranda rights. The defendant waived his rights, and also signed a consent form for the search of his home. After being informed of his rights a second time, the defendant stated "My life is over. I screwed up big time. I had a divorce all worked out. She wouldn't go along with it. I hit her with a club. I punched her. I threw her in the car, staged an accident. What's going to happen to me? What's going to happen to my son? I'm an embarrassment to all my friends."

The defendant was also taken to the police station, where, after once again waiving his Miranda rights, he gave a detailed confession.

. . .

An argument ensued, after which the victim went upstairs to the master bedroom at approximately 11:30 PM. The defendant followed her to the bedroom, and then, according to his statement, "snapped," striking her with a club when she was sitting on the bed and looking the other way. She screamed and fought back, hitting him across the bridge of his nose and scratching his eyes. They fell to the floor and continued to struggle. The defendant stated that he hit her with the club seven times, then dropped the club and punched her with his fist. The defendant did not know how long they struggled, but stated that the victim "would not give up." At some point, she stopped moving.

The defendant realized that there was blood everywhere and that he had to clean it up. He carried the victim downstairs and placed her in the front passenger seat of their car, then returned to clean up the blood. After a few attempts to wipe down the walls, he abandoned the clean up and instead tried to disguise the blood by pouring red wine on the stains.

At approximately 4:15 AM, the defendant drove the car containing the victim's body to Parker Road, which was located approximately one-quarter mile from his house. He caused the car to run off the road in an attempt to make it look like the victim's injuries had been the result of a car accident. The defendant stated that he knew the accident was not severe enough to have caused her injuries, but left the car and went home.

After returning home, the defendant gathered items that had too much blood on them to be cleaned, including a pillow and pillow case, a sheet, books, and a latex glove, and placed them in a plastic trash bag with a brick. He threw the bag, along with the sneakers that he had been wearing at the time of the murder into the pond behind his house.

Staged Illegitimate Deaths

Illegitimate deaths that have been staged appear with a different set of behaviors. Those cases that are staged to appear as illegitimate deaths such as the result of a burglary/home invasion or sexual homicide are associated with the offender(s) attempting to organize some sort of alibi for themselves. These cases are also correlated with deaths as a result of firearm injuries, in which the firearm or other weapon is brought to the scene by the offender. Ransacking of the scene is also very common, and more often personal items belonging to the victim are disrupted at the scene, as well as removed. For example, the offender(s) may empty drawers, knock items over, or generally mess up the scene, removing or disrupting personal items but not necessarily valuables. These types of scenes are also correlated with entry and exit points for the offender being staged and the offender often purposely injuring him- or herself as part of the staging effort.

The following is a case example of a staged burglary (*The People of the State of Illinois v. Keith SEAWRIGHT*, 1992, No. 1-90-0935 (593 N.E. 2d 1003)). The details presented here are part of the factual summary of the case. The irrelevant details have been removed, as well as the appellate decisions and legal arguments.

The People of the State of Illinois v. Keith SEAWRIGHT

A jury convicted the defendant, Keith Seawright, of the murder of his wife, Estralita; he was sentenced to 30 years imprisonment followed by a three year period of mandatory supervised release.

Around 8 AM on June 23, 1986, the police were called by the defendant to his home at 262 Arcadia in Park Forest. The police found the defendant's wife, Estralita, in bed; she had been shot twice in the face. She was revived by paramedics but died on the way to the hospital. The defendant subsequently told the police that he conspired with a co-worker, Tim Reynolds to kill his wife and that Reynolds did the killing. After the police investigated and exonerated Reynolds, the defendant confessed that he had shot his wife.

...

The officers [who arrived at the scene of the possible homicide] asked [SEAWRIGHT] what he had done before calling them. The defendant said that he had left for work around 10:30 pm the previous night and worked the 11 to 7 shift at a paper company in Alsip. He left work around 7:10 AM and arrived home approximately 20 or 25 minutes later. He parked in the driveway and used his key to enter the house through the back door. He saw several items of paper scattered about the kitchen and the living room, and all the lights in the house were on. He called to his wife but received no answer. He went into the bedroom and saw his wife lying on the bed. He tried to find her pulse and to wake her. He then went into the living room where he found the phone unplugged; he plugged it into the wall and called the police. He ran next door to get his neighbor; he brought the neighbor back to his house, showed her his wife and told her that he had called for the police and an ambulance.

...

[Detectives] walked up the driveway and observed the exterior of the house and the back yard. They found a shell casing in the driveway and a cassette tape on the air conditioner in the back yard. They found some jalousie window slats on the ground outside the garage, and they also noticed broken glass on the ground outside the garage and through the window in the interior of the garage. There was a sizable opening into the garage. The doors to the garage were locked.

[Detectives] decided to look around the house to try to determine any offender's point of entry. They entered the kitchen and observed that the rear kitchen window was completely open. The screen from the open window was in the back yard near the window; it appeared to have been pushed out from inside the house. [One detective] noticed that the

window on the storm door was loose from its frame. The storm door and the wooden door behind it showed no signs of forcible entry. The windowsill underneath the open kitchen window was clean and free of any marks. The aluminum kitchen sink below the window was free of any scuff marks or shoe prints. The window edge and glass were uniformly dusty with no marks suggesting entry or exit through the window. There was dust on the window and around the frame of the window.

In the living room, [detectives] saw various items, including department store bags and purses, scattered on the floor. The furniture, stereo equipment and television all appeared to be in the proper places. Books, papers, purses, and other small objects were lying on the floor; some of these items were stacked on top of each other. There were no signs of forcible entry on the front door.

In the first floor bedroom they saw a large water bed covered with blood. There was also blood on the floor near the bed. The blood was still in liquid form; some of it had started to coagulate. [Detective] found two shell casings in the bedroom. One on the east side of the bed and one on the west side. There were cosmetics, jewelry, some clothing, a clock radio and a fan on top of the dresser. The drawers in the dresser were closed. There was jewelry hanging out of boxes in the bedroom, but it appeared undisturbed.

...

[Detectives] did not think that the house appeared to have been burglarized.

...

[An evidence technician] examined the upstairs office/bedroom and found a purse lying on the floor. A wallet containing money, credit cards, and a checkbook was on the desk. There was a cosmetics bag on the floor, and its contents appeared to have been poured out onto the floor next to it. ... He noted that the automatic dialing portion of the alarm system had been disconnected from the phone line box.

...

Inside the defendants garage, [an evidence technician] noticed that the switch for the security light outside the garage was in the 'off' position. The light was equipped with a light sensor, enabling it to turn on automatically at night and turn off automatically in the morning; however the switch would have to be in 'on' position for the light to work. He examined the Lincoln Continental parked inside the garage and found that the cover on the steering wheel had been pried away and the turn signal lever had been broken off. He found both of these items in the garbage can in the garage. The ignition system on the car had not been bypassed; therefore it could not have been taken without a key. The car's alarm system had been deactivated.

[The evidence technician] noticed several markings on the car's trunk lock. He removed the lock and submitted it to the crime laboratory for comparison testing, along with a screwdriver he found on the workbench. During his examination of the scene, he recovered approximately 25 latent fingerprint lifts, as well as several footwear impressions.

While [the evidence technician] was examining the house, [the detective] used a key which he found in the house to open the garage. He found broken glass on a workbench underneath the jalousie window, but none of the tools or other items on the workbench appeared to have been disturbed. There were undisturbed cobwebs across the opening of the window. [The detective] said that he did not think anyone could have gone through the window without disturbing the cobwebs.

...

[The detective] also had learned that the security light over the garage turned on every night, but that it did not do so on the night of June 22.

...

In the statement the defendant said that he had shot Estralita twice so that he could collect the money from her life insurance policy. Estralita had incurred a lot of bills, and he needed the life insurance money to pay them. He admitted that he had scattered papers around, pushed the kitchen screen out, pulled the slats out of his garage window and his neighbor's garage window and damaged the car to make it look as if Estralita had been killed during a burglary.

The defendant's second confession is a detailed explanation of how and why he killed his wife. He told of her spendthrift habits, of which the police had no previous knowledge; he suspected her of infidelity; and he contemplated divorce. He told of his attempts before going to work to do things he would not have time to do after shooting his wife: his damage to the car in the garage and the removal of the glass from his garage and from his neighbor's garage. His statement that he used a screwdriver to pry open the trunk of the car is particularly significant because crime laboratory tests taken later disclosed that the screwdriver had, in fact, been used on the trunk. The police could not have known of this fact at the time that the statement was made. Also significant is his statement that after punching out at work, he "drove home fast." He told of scattering papers and "other stuff" and of pulling out the screen in the kitchen "to make it look like a burglary" had occurred.

This case presents an interesting, and very sophisticated, staging attempt by comparison to others the author has studied. Its presentation is designed to illustrate the different behaviors inherent in attempts to stage scenes to appear as crimes versus those staged to appear as legitimate deaths. In order for investigators and profilers to identify and solve any of these cases, it is thus crucial to recognize that staging efforts and common behaviors will be different depending on the aim of the person doing the staging. Therefore, red flags for staging in general, such as those identified in much of the past literature, may not be helpful. Every case needs to be addressed on its own merits and each piece of evidence assessed as to what it would mean if it were legitimately deposited during the crime or was put there intentionally to deceive.

Conclusion

It should now be clear that although little is written about the study of staged crime scenes, being able to identify them accurately is a necessary tool in the arsenal of any good profiler.

Staging can be done to have the scene appear in many different ways, however for the definition of staging to be met the offender must be attempting to evade capture or throw off the investigation. Someone who unknowingly manipulates evidence or does so with any other motivation is not carrying out an act of staging. Profilers need to be explicitly clear on this definition and should now understand the necessity of assessing each case on its merits, rather than how it compares to past cases or those discussed in the literature. This discussion has proven that often the literature is not specific enough to be of assistance for anything other than theory building, and profilers need to be prepared to conclude that the literature does not apply to the case they are working, no matter how much harder that conclusion may make their analysis.

People lie for a variety of reasons, and they may be more or less motivated to be believed based on the consequences of their behaviors. Staging a crime scene to appear as something it is not in order to thwart investigative efforts is a physical manifestation of a lie, which is often combined with more traditional lying to police. If profilers are to discover either of these types of deception they need to be prepared to be skeptical, informed, and energetic. The more information gathered the better when it comes to being able to recognize the ever-present inconsistencies in the evidence and determine their source. With these characteristics the "'grand-blunder,' which the most experienced and crafty criminal rarely fails to commit" (Gross, 1936, p. 433) may be discovered and explained by the profiler.

Questions

1. Redressing a loved one after they have been discovered in women's clothing after a suicide is generally considered staging. *True or false?*
2. Staging is a type of precautionary act. *True or false?*
3. The theory that states that those with greater motivation to lie experience stronger emotions and greater attempts to control their behavior is known as:
   a. Motivational bias theory
   b. Behavior-motivations theory
   c. Behavioral-control theory
   d. Motivational-impairment theory
   e. None of the above
4. Hazelwood and Napier (2004) found that what approximate percentage of crimes were staged?
   a. 3%
   b. 5%
   c. 8%
   d. 9%
   e. This cannot be determined from the data.
5. A psychological disorder in which symptoms are faked to get attention or some other gain is known as __________ __________.

References

Factitious Disorder- Munchausen Syndrome (n.d.) *PsychNet-UK: Disorder information sheet.* Retrieved 5 May 2010 from: <http://www.psychnet-uk.com/dsm_iv/factitious_disorder.htm/>.

Adair, T., & Doberson, M. (1999). A case of suicidal hanging staged as homicide. *Journal of Forensic Science, 44,* 1307–1309.

BJS (1998). Bureau of justice statistics, violence by intimates: Analysis of data on crimes by current or former spouses, boyfriends, and girlfriends. In B. E. Turvey (Ed.), *Criminal profiling: An introduction to behavioural evidence analysis* (2nd ed.). London: Academic Press. 2002.

Bond, C., & de Paulo, B. (2006). Accuracy of deception judgments. *Personality and Social Psychology Review, 10,* 214–234.

Carroll, J. (1978). The effect of imagining an event on expectations for the event: An interpretation in terms of the availability heuristic. *Journal of Experimental Social Psychology, 14,* 88–96.

Caso, L., Gnisci, A., Vrij, A., & Mann, S. (2005). Process underlying deception: An empirical analysis of truth and lies when manipulating the stakes. *Journal of Investigative Psychology and Offender Profiling, 2,* 195–202.

Commonwealth of Massachusetts v Milton L. RICE (1998, (692 N.E. 2d 28)).

de Paulo, B., Kirkendol, S., Tang, J., & O'Brien, T. (1988). The motivational impairment effect in the communication of deception: Replications and extensions. *Journal of Nonverbal Behavior, 12,* 177–202.

di Maio, V., & di Maio, D. (2001). *Forensic pathology* (2nd ed.). CRC Press.

Douglas, J., & Douglas, L. (2006). The detection of staging, undoing and personation at the crime scene. In J. Douglas, A. Burgess, A. Burgess, & R. Ressler (Eds.), *Crime classification manual* (2nd ed.). San Francisco: Jossey-Bass.

Douglas, J., & Munn, C. (1992a). The detection of staging and personation at the crime scene. In A. Burgess, A. Burgess, J. Douglas, & R. Ressler (Eds.), *Crime classification manual.* San Francisco: Jossey-Bass.

Douglas, J., & Munn, C. (1992b). Violent crime scene analysis: Modus operandi, signature, and staging. *FBI Law Enforcement Bulletin,* 1–10.

Edwards, H., & Gatsonis, C. (2009). Strengthening forensic science in the United States: A path forward (National Academy of Sciences 2009). Retrieved 26 June 2012 from <http://www8.nationalacademies.org/cp/projectview.aspx?key=48741/>.

Ekman, P. (2001). *Telling lies: Clues to deceit in the marketplace, politics, and marriage* (3rd ed.). New York: Norton.

Ferguson, C. E. (2010). *The defects of the situation: An examination of staged crime scenes.* Gold Coast: Bond University. (Unpublished doctoral thesis).

Fox, J. & Zawitz, M. (2007). Homicide trends in the United States. Homicide trends in the United States series. Retrieved 17 April 2010 from <http://bjs.ojp.usdoj.gov/index.cfm?ty=pbdetail&iid=966>.

Geberth, V. (1996b). The staged crime scene. *Law and Order Magazine,* 89–92. (February).

Geberth, V. (2006). Practical homicide investigation: Tactics: *Procedures and forensic techniques* (4th ed.). Boca Raton: CRC Press.

Gross, H. (1934). *Criminal investigation.* London: Sweet & Maxwell.

Hazelwood, R., & Napier, M. (2004). Crime scene staging and its detection. *International Journal of Offender Therapy and Comparative Criminology, 48,* 744–759.

Imajo, T. (1983). Suicide by motor vehicle. *Journal of Forensic Science, 28,* 83–89.

Inbau, F., Reid, J., Buckley, J., & Jayne, B. (2001). *Criminal interrogation and confessions* (4th ed.). Gaithersburg: Aspen Publishing.

Kenneth KORITTA v The State of Georgia (1992, No. A92A1325 (424 S.E. 2d 799)).

Keppel, R., & Weis, J. (2004). The rarity of "Unusual" dispositions of victim bodies: Staging and posing. *Journal of Forensic Science, 49*, 1308–1312.

McDowell, C. (1987). Suicide disguised as murder: A dimension of munchausen syndrome. *Journal of Forensic Science, 32*, 254–261.

Meloy, J. (2002). Spousal homicide and the subsequent staging of a sexual homicide at a distant location. *Journal of Forensic Science, 47*, 395–398.

Mitchell, R. (1986). A framework for discussion deception. In R. W. Mitchell & N. S. Mogdil (Eds.), *Deception: Perspectives on human and nonhuman deceit* (pp. 3–4). Albany: State University of New York Press.

Mukherjee, S., VanWinkle, B., & Zimring, F. (1983). Intimate violence: A study of intersexual homicide in Chicago. In B. Turvey (Ed.), *Criminal profiling: An introduction to behavioral evidence analysis* (2nd ed.). London: Academic Press. 2002.

O'Connell, J., & Soderman, H. (1936). *Modern criminal investigation.* New York: Funk & Wagnall.

Porter, S., Doucette, N., Woodworth, M., Earle, J., & MacNeil, B. (2008). Halfe the world knowes not how the other halfe lies: Investigation of verbal and nonverbal signs of deception exhibited by criminal offenders and non-offenders. *Legal and Criminological Psychology, 13*, 27–38.

Rand, M. (2009). Criminal victimization 2008. Bureau of Justice Statistics. Retrieved 24 August, 2010 from <http://bjs.ojp.usdoj.gov/index.cfm?ty=pbdetail&iid=1975>.

Shelton, D., Kim, Y., & Barak, G. (2006). A study of juror expectations and demands concerning scientific evidence: Does the CSI effect exist? *Vanderbilt Journal of Entertainment and Technology Law, 9*, 331–368.

Svensson, A., & Wendel, O. (1974). *Techniques of crime scene investigation* (2nd ed.). New York: American Elsevier.

The People of the State of Illinois v. Keith SEAWRIGHT, 1992, No. 1-90-0935 (593 N.E. 2d 1003).

Turvey, B. (2000). Staged crime scenes: A preliminary study of 25 cases. *Journal of Behavioral Profiling, 1*, 3.

Turvey, B. (2002). *Criminal profiling: An introduction to behavioural evidence analysis* (2nd ed.). London: Academic Press.

Turvey, B. (2008). *Criminal profiling: An introduction to behavioural evidence analysis* (3rd ed.). London: Academic Press.

Vrij, A. (2000). *Detecting lies and deceit: The psychology of lying and the implications for professional practice.* Sussex: John Wiley & Sons Ltd.

Whaley, B. (1982). Toward a general theory of deception. *The Journal of Strategic Studies, 5*, 178–192.

Zuckerman, M., & Driver, R. (1985). Telling lies: Verbal and nonverbal correlates of deception. In A. W. Siegman & S. Feldstein (Eds.), *Multichannel integrations of nonverbal behaviours* (pp. 129–147). Hillsdale, NJ: Lawrence Erlbaum.

9 Investigative Relevance

Dr. Claire Ferguson

Introduction

Criminal profiling is one tool available to investigative agencies that may assist in narrowing suspect pools, linking crimes, providing relevant leads and new investigative strategies, and keeping the overall investigation on track (Turvey, 2008). However, like a flashlight in a darkened room, profiling may not always provide valuable assistance if it shines in the wrong direction or fails to shine at all. In a perfect world, profiles are intended to provide investigators with a set of refined characteristics of the offender for a crime or a crime series that will assist their efforts. In contrast, it could be argued that profiles are not intended to provide information that may be irrelevant, unclear, confusing, or distracting to these efforts. Any information provided within the profile that does not assist in narrowing suspect pools or providing new avenues of inquiry is left open to misinterpretation and is therefore potentially damaging (Turvey, 2008). The degree to which information provided in a profile can actually be utilized by investigators to meet their goals is known as investigative relevance.

This chapter examines whether criminal profiles actually provide the assistance they are meant to provide—that is, whether they are investigatively relevant or whether they are

Profiling and Serial Crime.

distracting and of little value to investigators. This chapter discusses some of the critical issues in investigative relevance and presents the results of research conducted by the author. It is shown throughout that the various types of profiles differ greatly in how much they acknowledge, and strive toward, investigative relevance. Before examining the research on investigative relevance, the goals of profiling and the information used and subsequently provided are examined.

Goals of Profiling and Inputs and Outputs

According to Homant and Kennedy (1998), criminal profiling was originally developed (1) to assist investigators in narrowing suspect pools to smaller, more workable numbers and (2) to provide new avenues of inquiry for investigators to follow. Despite the behavior of some practitioners to the contrary, it is important to note that profiling is not designed to implicate a certain individual as responsible for the crime, nor should it (Muller, 2000). Instead, profiling has more general goals.

Holmes and Holmes (2002) identify four main goals of criminal profiling, which are summarized as follows:

- To provide investigating authorities with a social and psychological evaluation of the offender.
- To narrow the suspect pool.
- To provide a psychological assessment of items found in possession of the offender.
- To provide interviewing and interrogation strategies.

Turvey (2008) similarly identifies a number of goals of profiling, during either the investigation or the trial that may follow. According to Turvey (p. 138), there are five main investigative goals for which identifying characteristics of the suspect pool is of primary importance:

- To reduce the viable suspect pool in a criminal investigation and to help prioritize the investigation for those remaining suspects.
- To assist in the linkage of potentially related crimes by identifying crime scene indicators and behavior patterns (e.g., modus operandi and signature).
- To assist in assessing the potential for escalation of nuisance criminal behavior to more serious or more violent crimes (e.g., harassment, stalking, and voyeurism).
- To provide investigators with investigatively relevant leads and strategies.
- To help keep the overall investigation on track and undistracted.

In the trial phase, in which the offender is already known, the profile is used to assist in the preparation of interviews, hearings, and trials. For the trial stage, there are also five goals (Turvey, 2008, p. 138):

- To assist in the process of evaluating the nature and value of forensic evidence in a particular case.
- To assist in the process of developing interview or interrogative strategy.
- To help develop insight into offender fantasies and motivations.

- To help develop insight into offender state of mind before, during, and after the commission of a crime (e.g., levels of planning, evidence of remorse, and precautionary acts).
- To help elucidate crime scene linkage issues by examining modus operandi and signature behavior.

Although helpful in many crimes, criminal profiling is not always suitable or necessary (Petherick, 2007). Simply requiring that suspect pools be narrowed or strategies be taken to interrogate an offender does not mean that criminal profiling is necessary in any one case. Also, although profiling may be beneficial to one type of case generally, not every case of this type will benefit from it (Petherick, 2007). Homicide is a prime example. Whereas a profile might provide some assistance in a stranger homicide, its use in a domestic homicide, where the link between the offender and victim is usually more clear, may be questionable. Whether or not a profile is called for depends on the goals of the investigating agency, the available evidence, case specifics, and whether a profiler is available. Unfortunately, profiling may also be used in error to "bootstrap" a case when the prosecution case is weak or lacking in physical evidence. In determining whether or not a profiler should be recruited, investigative agencies should first determine what information they can make available to the profiler and what advice they expect in return.

Inputs and Outputs

The quality of any profile is dictated by the information on which it is based; this information is known as the inputs of the profile. Profilers may request many different inputs or materials on which to base their conclusions, including autopsy reports, victim information, witness statements, crime scene photographs, and investigators' reports. Because the quality and quantity of the information available have a direct bearing on the profile, it is incumbent on profilers to ensure they get as much information as possible. In every case, the more available, the better.

Pinizzotto (1984, pp. 33–34) provides the following list of inputs as necessary to produce a complete profile. This list is fairly uniform across most sources. (Interestingly, Geberth, 1996, provides a strikingly similar list of inputs, with almost identical wording. Neither author provides citations for their list, nor an original source.)

1. Photographs of the crime scene: This includes color photos of the victim, enlarged photos of the wounds on the victim's body, various angles and positions of the victim, and complete photos of the entire area of the crime.
2. Neighborhood and complex: This includes racial, ethnic, and social data.
3. Medical examiner's report: This includes photos depicting the full extent of damage to the body, toxicology reports, a report on the presence of any semen, and postmortem wounds.
4. Map of travel prior to death: This includes place employed, residence, and where last seen before the crime scene location.
5. Complete investigative report of the incident: This includes standard report of date, time, location, etc.; weapon if known; investigative officers' reconstruction of the sequence of events; and detailed interviews of witnesses.

6. Background of the victim: This includes age; sex; race; physical description including dress at the time of the incident; marital status/adjustment; intelligence, scholastic achievement, and adjustment; lifestyle and recent changes in lifestyle, personality style, and characteristics; demeanor; residency, former and present, and its relation to the crime scene; sexual adjustment; occupation, former and present; reputation at home and at work; medical history, physical and mental; fears; personal habits, such as the use of alcohol or drugs; social habits; hobbies; friends and enemies; and recent court action.

In their discussion of criminal personality profiling, O'Hara and O'Hara (2003, p. 712) provide a much more vague list of factors to be considered when compiling a profile:

1. The activities of the criminal as evidenced by the arrangement and disposition of materials at the crime scene.
2. The description of the criminal act by witnesses.
3. The background and activities of the victim.
4. Any other detail of the crime that could express the personality of the perpetrator, such as the type and condition of the getaway car.

Once the information has been assessed and an analysis undertaken, the profiler can then move to interpretation and compilation of profile characteristics. These offender characteristics are known as outputs. Despite the various approaches that use similar inputs in constructing a profile, the offender characteristics that make up the final product vary markedly between methods. For example, Turvey (2008) is very conservative in offering offender characteristics and believes that only four characteristics can be argued definitively from the evidence available: knowledge of the victim, knowledge of methods and materials, knowledge of the crime scene or location, and criminal skill.

Taking a far more liberal stance, Ault and Reese (1980) provide a detailed list of characteristics that cover nearly every facet of the offender's past, present, and future behavior, such as sex, age, race, sexual maturity, and probable reaction to police interrogation. Several other authors also support the provision of a large number of potential characteristics of the offender, including Geberth (1996) and O'Toole (2004), who are seemingly of the opinion that the more one knows about the offender, the better. In fact, Geberth provides the following list of 22 factors that can be determined by a profile (pp. 780–781): age, sex, race, marital status, intelligence, scholastic achievement/adjustment, lifestyle, rearing environment, social adjustment, personality style/characteristics, demeanor, appearance and grooming, emotional adjustment, evidence of mental decompensation, pathological behavioral characteristics, employment/occupational history and adjustment, work habits, residence in relation to crime scene, socioeconomic status, sexual adjustment, type of sexual perversion or disturbance (if applicable), and motive. Although it may seem that more information about the offender is better, an excess of information that cannot be used by investigators has the potential to distract the inquiry and may therefore do more harm than good.

From an examination of profiling methods, it can be seen that inductive (nomothetic) methods (Criminal Investigative Analysis [CIA] and Investigative Psychology [IP]) generally argue for a larger number of offender characteristics, whereas deductive (idiographic) methods that focus on individual cases (Behavioral Evidence Analysis [BEA]) offer less. This is most likely because statistical methods compare characteristics of the current crime to a list of many possible characteristics present across a number of past cases, whereas BEA aims to examine the current crime to make conclusions about this offender, at this crime, with this victim, regardless of other similar crimes and criminals (Petherick, 2007).

The previous discussion leads to the question of accuracy, utility, and investigative relevance in criminal profiling. Are more characteristics in a profile more useful to investigators? Do characteristics presented in a profile that prove to be accurate necessarily indicate that a profile was helpful to the investigation? These issues are discussed in the following section.

Accuracy, Utility, and Investigative Relevance

Accuracy and utility were detailed in Chapter 4, but a brief summary of each is provided for the sake of context.

According to Ainsworth (2001, p. 176), not enough research has been done comparing the accuracy and utility of criminal profiles. Despite little research in the area, the issue of accuracy must be discussed because it is generally these criteria that profiles have been measured against in the past (Petherick, 2007). Some profilers have claimed that the accuracy of their profiles is directly related to their usefulness, and that if profiles were inaccurate, then profilers would not be in such high demand (Petherick, 2007). This is a logical fallacy called an appeal to common practice, and it is not an acceptable argument to support the accuracy of criminal profiling. Actual accuracy can only be determined by comparing profile characteristics to offenders after they have been indisputably convicted of the crime that was profiled, and even this process may remain subjective because of the imprecise nature of many profile characteristics (e.g., intelligence). It should also be noted that in many cases in which a profile is written, the profile is used to determine who, specifically, committed the crime and to bootstrap the prosecution's case against the accused to secure a conviction. It is therefore not surprising, considering the profile was used to find the offender, that it is accurate. Any appeal to this argument for accuracy is therefore circular and redundant.

Rossmo (2000) proposes that for a profile to be useful to investigators, it must advance the decision-making process involved in the investigation. He suggests that offender characteristics presented in a profile need to be clear, distinguishable from the general population, probable, and of use in order to assist investigators. This brings about the focus of this chapter—investigative relevance. If a profile is too vague or indiscriminate for an investigator to use, it is not investigatively relevant. In light of this, any attempt to gauge the advantages of criminal profiling should acknowledge that accuracy, utility, and investigative relevance are very clearly linked.

One of the few discussions on investigative relevance is provided by Turvey (2008), who maintains that it is the responsibility of the criminal profiler to demonstrate how the conclusions made in the profile are relevant to the current investigation. Petherick (2007; see also Chapter 4) suggests that investigative relevance is a two-part concept: (1) Profiles must include information that can be acted on by investigators, and (2) profiles must provide information that distinguishes the offender from the general population.

It should also be noted that the relevance of some offender characteristics may be case dependent. Baeza's (1999) discussion of investigative relevance suggests that different profile characteristics will be relevant for different cases, and that characteristics that are the product of guesswork or intuition will never be relevant. Because of this, he highlights the importance of assessing cases on an individual basis. Baeza also maintains that despite the perception that certain offender features are relevant, such as personality characteristics, marital status, education, intelligence, hobbies, personal interests, and transport, these features often do not provide the detail that would be necessary for investigators to act on. It is further noted that simply because an offender characteristic made a list of features that are generally included, this does not mean the characteristic should be included in every case, nor does it guarantee that the feature will be relevant to the current investigation.

In line with this discussion, the profile characteristics adopted in the research discussed next were deemed to be investigatively irrelevant based on any, or any combination, of the following:

1. The characteristic does not discriminate from the general public or offender population. For example, stating that an offender is married or involved in a serious and long-term relationship does not assist investigators in a case because many others in the suspect pool are also married or involved in serious relationships. This fact may be true of an offender, but identifying it does not assist the investigation and may instead distract investigators. These characteristics are therefore not relevant. Other such characteristics are socioeconomic status, whether the offender is employed, education level, whether the offender is a day or a night person, type of preferred dress, social skills, whether the offender has friends or is a loner, what social environments the offender prefers, whether the offender has an automobile and what condition it is in, and the condition of the offender's residence.
2. It is not clear how identifying the characteristic could be acted on by the investigating agency. For example, stating that an offender's mother was the dominant parent may be interesting, or ultimately correct; however, identifying such a characteristic does not allow investigators to further the decision-making process in an ongoing case. Other characteristics that were not included based on this were escalation of emotion; risk of future offenses; whether the offender has a history of sexual problems; whether the offender is known to carry/collect/display weapons and, if so, what type; any recent change in the offender's behavior; and personality type.
3. Stating any such characteristic is redundant. To lessen the chance of wasting crucial investigative time, characteristics should not be offered unless there is substantial and reliable evidence to indicate their presence. However, for certain characteristics, reliable and substantial evidence speaks for itself, and therefore it is not necessary for a profile to restate that such a characteristic is present. For example, a profile will not assist investigators if it makes an educated guess or statistical inference regarding the race of the offender. In order for race to be inarguably inferred, physical evidence or eyewitness

accounts must be present. However, if such evidence is present, it is not necessary for a profile to reiterate what investigators already know. Therefore, profiles should never contain information on such characteristics as the offender's name, age, race, sex, height, weight, whether the offender was under the influence of drugs or alcohol, or whether the offender has any physical abnormalities.

4. The characteristic does not describe the offender but describes his or her behavior during the crime or the crime itself. In order to be relevant, the profile should not only report the behaviors but also make a conclusion about the offender based on these behaviors and how they are reflected in the physical evidence at the scene. Although describing offender behaviors may be helpful in producing a profile, they are not considered offender characteristics. For example, describing the level of planning or control that was apparent in a crime may tell us about the offender and could be evidence of certain offender characteristics, but it is not a characteristic in and of itself. Describing such behaviors illustrates the offender's state at the time of the crime, but it does not go beyond this to make an inference about the offender's traits in general. This does not mean, however, that describing the behavior is unimportant, because this can provide crucial background information and context to the profile.

An Analysis of Investigative Relevance

As discussed previously, there have been many attempts to analyze and evaluate profiling methods and profiles in the past (Ainsworth, 2001; Petherick, 2007). These attempts, however, have generally focused on the accuracy of the profile based on a comparison with apprehended offenders (Pinizzotto & Finkel, 1990) or the perceived usefulness of the profile to the requesting agency (Copson, 1995). Only one study has focused on assessing whether offender characteristics given in profiles are relevant to ongoing investigations and what proportion of characteristics given can actually further the investigation. This study was undertaken as part of the author's master's thesis and is discussed in detail here.

For the purposes of the research, the definition of investigative relevance provided by Petherick (2007) as well as the discussion by Baeza (1999) was utilized. This definition maintains that investigatively relevant characteristics distinguish an offender from the general suspect pool or population and/or must provide enough detail to be acted on by law enforcement. Furthermore, characteristics that are the product of guesswork or intuition are never relevant. Identifying vague characteristics does not allow investigators to further the decision-making process in an ongoing case because, clearly, leaving the decision up to investigators to decide how ambiguous characteristics apply is fraught with problems.

To determine what characteristics fit this concept of investigative relevance, an exhaustive list of offender characteristics was compiled from a number of sources (Ault & Reese, 1980; Geberth, 1996; O'Toole, 2004; Turvey, 2002) as well as from the profiles. Each characteristic was then compared to the definition to determine whether it could be considered relevant. Any characteristic that was the product of guesswork or intuition, which could not be acted on by law enforcement, or could not distinguish from the general population was then eliminated from the list. Upon conducting this examination, two other factors were noted that affected the relevance of offender characteristics. Characteristics were further eliminated from the list if they simply restated what the physical evidence clearly showed without drawing any further conclusions from it or if they described the offender's behavior during the crime without further interpretation. Stated simply, characteristics that provided information that was the product of guesswork, was not discriminating from the general public, which could not easily be acted on by investigators, or which simply restated the physical and behavioral evidence present at the crime scene were not viewed as relevant to an investigation and were therefore excluded from the list. After separating the irrelevant characteristics from the initial exhaustive list, five characteristics remained: Motive, Special Skills or Knowledge of Methods and Materials, Knowledge of or Relationship to the Victim, Knowledge of the Crime Scene or Location, and Criminal Skill/Forensic Awareness. A coding dictionary was prepared to define these five characteristics, which is summarized as follows:

Motive: This is defined as "the physical, psychological, or emotional needs that impel and drive behavior" (Turvey, 2008, p. 276). It may be a general or specific descriptor.

Special Skills or Knowledge of Methods and Materials: This is presented in the profile as being demonstrated in the criminal behavior by a very specific type of knowledge of some special skill, method, or material, such as flying an airplane, the ability to crack a safe, or hacking into a complex computer system.

Knowledge or Relationship to the Victim: Offender behaviors may indicate the offender(s) had knowledge of his or her victim, such as the victim's schedules, routes of travel, and other personal details. Evidence at the crime scene that may indicate that the victim was familiar with the offender includes a lack of forced entry, no signs of a struggle, or lack of defensive wounds.

Knowledge of Crime Scene or Location: This refers to specific knowledge an offender may display of the location where the crime took place. Examples include knowledge of the location of safes and valuables, cleaning products, knowledge of access to remote areas, as well as knowledge of security codes or knowing the exact location in a multiroom dwelling of a specific victim.

Criminal Skill and Forensic Awareness: This is the degree of criminal knowledge an offender displays in committing the crime as well as knowledge of physical evidence and police or forensic procedures. This knowledge could be the result of time spent in prison or experience committing similar crimes. It may also reflect the general intelligence of the offender. Planning, precautionary acts, and deliberate acts to confuse and hamper investigations may reflect criminal skill and forensic awareness.

To assess the investigative relevance of criminal profiling, a number of profiles were collected. These consisted of written profiles from published works such as textbooks, web sites, biographies, and journal articles. Only cases in which complete profile was given were included in the analysis because this provided not only a complete list of characteristics but also the greatest insight into the reasoning on which characteristics were offered. This reasoning was necessary to examine because it allowed for a distinction to be made between those characteristics that were based on evidence and those that were the product of guesswork or intuition. Therefore, incomplete, summarized, or bullet-point profiles were excluded. A total of 59 profiles from four different profiling methods—diagnostic evaluations (DE), CIA, IP, and BEA—were analyzed for this study, drawn from various crime types and locations throughout Australia, Canada, the United Kingdom, and the United States.

Each profile was analyzed to determine the total number of offender characteristics present, how many of these characteristics were relevant as measured against the coding dictionary (i.e., to determine the number of relevant characteristics as a proportion of the total number of overall characteristics), as well as what type of evidence was used to support each characteristic. The types of justification used to code a characteristic were physical evidence, statistics or research, personal opinion or belief, or no justification. In short, each profile was first examined to determine how many characteristics were present. Each characteristic in the profile was then compared against the coding dictionary to determine if it fit the definition of any of the five relevant characteristics. If one of these definitions was met, the characteristic was further examined to determine what justification, if any, was used to support its presentation. This was done for all 59 of the profiles sampled in this study.

Results

The results from the analysis are presented in two sections. The first section involves a qualitative assessment to describe general trends in the data. In the second section, the data are separated based on the methodology employed in the profile in order to perform a comparative analysis on the characteristics and justifications given by each profiling method.

Analysis of Overall Sample

The initial qualitative analysis provided a breakdown of the profiling methodology employed, as well as the mean number of characteristics given in the profiles of each type. A summary of the data is provided in Table 9.1.

CIA profiles comprised the largest proportion of the sample studied at 47%.[1] Profiles that did not fit into any known profiling methodology (referred to as Other) comprised the lowest

Table 9.1 Characteristics Given by Method

Method	Total # of Profiles	% of Total	Mean No. of Characteristics	Standard Deviation
BEA	12	20	8	10
CIA	28	47	25	18
DE	10	17	58	52
IP	8	14	14	13
Other	1	2	6	0
Total	59	100	25	30

[1] All figures were rounded up or down for ease of reporting; therefore, totals may not always equal 100.

Table 9.2 Frequency of Characteristics and Justification Used

	Motive		Methods/ Materials		Knowledge of the Victim		Knowledge of Location		Criminal Skill	
	n	%	n	%	n	%	n	%	n	%
Not Given	25	42	56	95	27	46	33	56	43	73
Given without Justification	11	19	1	2	11	19	9	15	3	5
Given with Physical Evidence	17	29	2	3	9	15	10	17	10	17
Given with Statistics or Research	0	0	0	0	1	2	2	3	1	2
Given with Personal Opinion or Belief	6	10	0	0	11	19	5	9	2	3
Total	59	100	59	100	59	100	59	100	59	100

proportion of the sample at 2%. Due to this, Other profiles were not analyzed further. The mean number of characteristics given in the whole sample was 25. The lowest number of characteristics given was from BEA profiles (Mean = 8, SD = 10) and the highest from DE profiles (n = 58, SD = 52).

The initial analysis also involved assessing the frequencies of characteristics and justifications given in the profiles regardless of the profiling methodology used. A summary of these frequencies and their corresponding proportion of the total is provided in Table 9.2.

As noted, many of the profiles examined (more than 40% for all characteristics) did not give the characteristics deemed investigatively relevant. The offender characteristics Motive and Knowledge of Victim were given in slightly more than half of the sample (58% and 54%, respectively). Knowledge of the Location was given less than half of the time (44%), whereas Criminal Skill was given in approximately one-quarter of the sample (27%). Offender Knowledge of Methods and Materials was rarely given (5%). When Motive was given in this sample, it was most likely to be justified with physical evidence (17 of 34 profiles) and was never justified with statistics or research. Offender Knowledge of Methods and Materials was given in very few profiles (only 3 of 59) and was most likely justified with physical evidence (2 of the 3) and never with statistics, research, personal belief, or opinion. The offender characteristic Knowledge of the Victim was given in 32 of 59 profiles. It was most likely to be unjustified, or justified with personal opinion or belief (11 profiles each), and was unlikely to be justified by statistics or research (1 profile). Finally, when Knowledge of Location and Criminal Skill were given as offender characteristics (in 26 and 16 profiles, respectively), they were most often justified with physical evidence (10 profiles each) and least often justified with research and statistics (2 and 1 profile, respectively).

Analysis of Sample by Method

After the preliminary analysis, the data were separated by method to compare the various profiling approaches. A cross-tabulation was conducted in which the data was analyzed separately to investigate which relevant offender characteristics were given and what type of justification was used to support each characteristic. The results for each profiling method are presented in turn.

Table 9.3 Frequency and Percentage of Characteristics and Justification Used in CIA Profiles

	Not Given		Given without Justification		Given with Physical Evidence		Given with Stats or Research		Given with Personal Belief or Opinion		
	n	%	n	%	n	%	n	%	n	%	Total
Motive	12	43	7	25	5	18	0	0	4	14	28
Methods/Materials	28	100	0	0	0	0	0	0	0	0	28
Victim	9	32	8	29	3	11	0	0	8	29	28
Location	13	46	5	18	5	18	1	4	4	14	28
Skill	22	79	2	7	2	7	0	0	2	7	28

Criminal Investigative Analysis

In this analysis, 28 CIA profiles were analyzed, which comprised nearly half of the total profiles (47%). As mentioned previously, of these 28 profiles, the average number of offender characteristics given was 25, with a minimum of 2 and a maximum of 69 characteristics offered. Table 9.3 presents the analysis of all CIA profiles to illustrate the frequency with which relevant characteristics were given and the justifications used to support these characteristics.

Similar to the overall data in this study, CIA profiles did not offer the relevant offender characteristics in many cases. Motive was given in slightly more than half the profiles (16 of 28), was often unjustified (7 of 16), and was never justified with statistics or research. The offender characteristic Knowledge of Methods and Materials was not given in any of the CIA profiles. Knowledge of the Victim was the characteristic most likely to be present in the CIA profiles (19 of 28), and when it was given, it was often given without justification or with personal belief as justification (both 8 of 19). Knowledge of the Victim was never justified with research or statistics. Knowledge of the Location was given in 15 of 28 profiles and was likely to be unjustified (5 of 15) or justified with physical evidence (5 of 15). It was justified with statistics or research in only one case. Finally, Criminal Skill was given as an offender characteristic in approximately one-fifth of this sample (6 of 28 profiles). When given, it was likely to be unjustified, justified with physical evidence, or justified with personal opinion (2 profiles each), and it was never supported with research or statistics.

Behavioral Evidence Analysis

In this analysis, 12 BEA profiles were examined. These profiles comprised 20% of the total sample. As mentioned previously, the mean number of characteristics given in the BEA profiles studied was 8 (SD = 10), with a minimum of 3 and a maximum of 36 characteristics. Table 9.4 presents a summary of the analysis of the 12 BEA profiles in this sample. This table presents the frequencies with which relevant characteristics were offered and the justifications used to support these characteristics.

Table 9.4 Frequency and Percentage of Characteristics and Justification Used in BEA Profiles

	Not Given		Given without Justification		Given with Physical Evidence		Given with Stats or Research		Given with Personal Belief or Opinion		
	n	%	n	%	n	%	n	%	n	%	Total
Motive	1	8	0	0	11	92	0	0	0	0	12
Methods/Materials	10	83	0	0	2	17	0	0	0	0	12
Victim	5	42	0	0	6	50	0	0	1	8	12
Location	5	42	2	17	5	42	0	0	0	0	12
Skill	5	42	0	0	7	58	0	0	0	0	12

Table 9.5 Frequency and Percentage of Characteristics Given and Justification Used in DE Profiles

	Not Given		Given without Justification		Given with Physical Evidence		Given with Stats or Research		Given with Personal Belief or Opinion		
	n	%	n	%	n	%	n	%	%		Total
Motive	6	60	2	20	1	10	0	0	1	10	10
Methods/Materials	9	90	1	10	0	0	0	0	0	0	10
Victim	7	70	1	10	0	0	1	10	1	10	10
Location	9	90	1	10	0	0	0	0	0	0	10
Skill	10	100	0	0	0	0	0	0	0	0	10

In the BEA profiles, all the relevant characteristics, with the exception of Knowledge of Methods and Materials, were given in more than half of the profiles (Motive = 92%, Knowledge of Victim = 68%, Knowledge of Location = 68%, Criminal Skill = 68%). Physical evidence was most likely used as justification for all relevant offender characteristics. In all 11 profiles in which Motive was given, it was justified using physical evidence. Similarly, physical evidence was used as justification in all seven profiles that gave Criminal Skill as an offender characteristic, both profiles that gave offender Knowledge of Method and Materials, as well as six of seven profiles that included Knowledge of the Victim. Knowledge of the Location was presented in seven of the 12 profiles, and it was justified by physical evidence in five cases and unjustified in the other two cases.

Diagnostic Evaluations

For this study, 10 DE profiles were analyzed, comprising 17% of the total sample. As noted in the results section, the mean number of characteristics given in the DE profiles was 58 (SD = 52),

Table 9.6 Frequency and Percentage of Characteristics Given and Justification Used in IP Profiles

	Not Given		Given without Justification		Given with Physical Evidence		Given with Stats or Research		Given with Personal Belief or Opinion		
	n	**%**	**n**	**%**	**n**	**%**	**n**	**%**	**n**	**%**	**Total**
Motive	6	60	2	20	1	10	0	0	1	10	10
Methods/Materials	9	90	1	10	0	0	0	0	0	0	10
Victim	7	70	1	10	0	0	1	10	1	10	10
Location	9	90	1	10	0	0	0	0	0	0	10
Skill	10	100	0	0	0	0	0	0	0	0	10

with a large range (minimum, 6; maximum, 155). Table 9.5 provides a summary of the analysis of the DE profiles presenting the frequencies with which relevant characteristics were given and the justifications offered in support.

In the 10 DE profiles, the frequency of presentation of the relevant characteristics was less than 40% for each. In fact, Criminal Skill was not present in any of the profiles. Similarly, for Knowledge of Methods and Materials and Knowledge of the Location, only one profile presented the characteristic, and it was not justified. Motive was given in only four profiles, and it was given with no justification in two of these four, whereas physical evidence and personal belief were given as justification in one case each. Knowledge of the Victim was given in three profiles, with justification being evenly split between no justification, research or statistics, and personal belief, with one case each.

Investigative Psychology

This study analyzed eight IP profiles, which comprised 14% of the total sample. The mean number of characteristics given in these IP profiles was 14 (SD = 14), with a minimum of two and a maximum of 39 characteristics. Table 9.6 presents a summary of the analysis of the eight IP profiles, the frequencies with which relevant characteristics were given, and the justifications used to support these characteristics.

Knowledge of Methods and Materials was not given in any of the eight IP profiles. Motive was presented in three of the eight profiles. Of these three, Motive was unjustified in two cases, and it was justified by personal opinion in the remaining case. Knowledge of the Victim was present in two IP profiles, and it was unjustified in one case and justified with personal opinion in the other case. Knowledge of the Location and Criminal Skill were each present in three profiles. When Knowledge of the Location was given, it was unjustified in one case and justified by research or statistics and personal opinion in one case each. When Criminal Skill was given, it was unjustified in one case and justified by physical evidence and research or statistics in one case each.

Discussion

To meet their goals, criminal profiles must offer offender characteristics that will assist the decision-making process in criminal investigations, thereby allowing the investigation to move forward. Profile characteristics that are confusing, unnecessary, distracting, or not detailed enough to be acted on will not allow the goals of profiling to be met and are therefore a waste of time and resources (Baeza, 1999). With that being the case, the current study examined whether the profile characteristics offered in profiles are, in fact, progressing the decision-making process in investigations.

In many practices, there is a major difference between theory and practice. This research also considered whether profiling is, in practice, based on the theories that underpin a particular method (i.e., does IP use research, and does BEA use evidence?). A validation study focusing strictly on investigative relevance has not been conducted on a criminal profiling sample in the past, and this research therefore fills an existing void. Although the background theory of many profiling methods may seem valid, it is crucial to examine whether these are being applied and, if so, to determine whether the approaches are actually helpful. This issue becomes more salient when issues of public safety and miscarriages of justice are factored in.

For the current study, 59 profiles were examined to determine how many offender characteristics were offered, what investigatively relevant characteristics were offered, and what justification was offered to support these characteristics. This information was then analyzed to determine what characteristics were generally offered in profiles as a whole and how the characteristics differed based on the varying methodologies employed by the profilers.

Interpretation of Results

In general, this research found that three of the four profiling methods provided more investigatively irrelevant characteristics than relevant ones, with BEA being the exception. It has been shown in this research that for the most part, there are five characteristics that can be considered relevant to criminal investigations. However, the average number of characteristics given in the current sample was more than 25. Assuming that all five relevant characteristics were present (which was the case in very few profiles), there was still an average of 20 irrelevant characteristics given in these profiles that have the potential to confuse and distract investigators. However, as previously stated, different offender characteristics may be relevant depending on the case and the evidence provided in their support (Baeza, 1999). Therefore, in some of the sample the characteristics given earlier and beyond the relevant five may have been relevant to that case. However, this surely cannot be the case with all of the characteristics given. More important, this analysis showed that in many of the profiles, not only were there a large number of characteristics that were irrelevant but also the five deemed relevant were not provided. Certainly this presents a problem.

For the sample as a whole, more than 40% of the profiles did not offer at least one of the relevant characteristics. This percentage increased to almost 95% for the characteristic Knowledge of Methods and Materials. This illustrates a serious problem in the profiling community because it indicates that as many as 19 in 20 profiles may neglect to include at least one relevant offender characteristic that would assist the investigation. This may be a result of four factors. First, not enough evidence may be presented to the profiler, making it impossible for the profiler to give insight into certain behavior. Second, there is too much reliance on statistical comparison. If a comparison characteristic cannot be found in the chosen data set, that characteristic will not be offered by the statistical profiler. For instance, in the two research-based profiling methodologies (CIA and IP), Knowledge of Methods and Materials was not given in any of the profiles sampled. In the evidence-based BEA, it was offered in nearly 17% of profiles and was always justified with physical evidence. It may be that the research-based approaches' focus on previous cases leads profilers to fail to search for peculiar knowledge of methods and materials in each case. Third, not including one or more relevant characteristics may be due to the types of crimes and criminals that are being profiled. Perhaps the crimes profiled in this sample did not involve any behavior requiring specialized knowledge. Finally, the absence of these characteristics may be a reflection of the inherent lack of attention to detail, as well as the lack of specific knowledge that would be necessary for a profiler to recognize the offender characteristic. In statistical approaches, where the profiler often has little background in behavioral and forensic science, the profiler may be unqualified to conduct the requisite examination of the evidence and therefore unable to discern this characteristic when present. Any one of these four factors, or a combination of them, may explain the tendency to not recognize or include the characteristic. Identifying these elements highlights the need to not only understand the physical evidence and its meaning but also to work from a base of evidence and not just a degree of similarity.

Knowledge of Methods and Materials was not the only characteristic absent from much of the sample. Nearly three-fourths of the profiles did not provide an assessment of Criminal Skill, which may inform the profiler not only of past crimes committed but also of the offender's contact with the criminal justice system. This cannot be explained by an absence of criminal skill given the prevalence of past offending, especially in the case of serial offenders. In fact, any absence of criminal skill and the evidentiary basis for this should be clearly stated by the profiler and not just assumed or surmised. Twice as many BEA profiles offered Criminal Skill than did CIA profiles, and this was always justified by physical evidence when offered. CIA profiles offered this characteristic in only approximately 20% of profiles, and it was usually unjustified, justified with physical evidence, or justified with personal belief. IP offered Criminal Skill in 40% of the profiles, and when offered, it was unjustified, justified with physical evidence, and justified with research and statistics in one case each. This fact is notable because in theory, IP and CIA profiles are research based, and this characteristic is only justified by research in one case between the two methods.

The other relevant characteristics followed a similar pattern as the IP and CIA profiles. The fact that these offender characteristics are rarely justified by research means that it is impossible to trace a line of reasoning employed in producing the characteristics or to question the veracity of both the profile and the research on which they are meant to be based. Most often, all the characteristics in these profiles were unjustified or justified with personal belief (or physical evidence in a small number of cases). In fact, in none of these profiles was research and statistics the most likely justification for any characteristic. This is clearly not consistent with the research-based theories of CIA and IP. In both methods, the current case is compared with research on other similar cases to determine likely offender characteristics based on common characteristics of convicted offenders (Ainsworth, 2001; Ressler et al., 1988). The question that logically follows is that if IP and CIA profilers are not using research to justify these characteristics, what theories (if any) are being employed? Judging by the results, it appears that these methods are more likely to use personal belief as support for offender characteristics, when they employ any justification at all. This practice is not what each method promotes as its basis, also suggesting that these methods are much more idiosyncratic than these profilers claim. This mismatch between theory and practice clearly indicates a problem worthy of further investigation.

Conversely, the BEA method is in theory driven by evidence. The theoretical underpinnings of BEA were supported in this analysis because almost all of the relevant characteristics offered used physical evidence as justification for their inclusion. In fact, all but three characteristics in the BEA profiles used physical evidence as support. This match between theory and practice may suggest that BEA profiles are more likely to meet their intended goals.

By extension, BEA profiles were generally more likely to contain investigatively relevant characteristics. This can almost certainly be attributed to the fact that the characteristics deemed relevant in this analysis parallel those endorsed by BEA as being both necessary and inferable in a criminal profile (Turvey, 2008). As discussed, the list of characteristics deemed relevant in this study was produced after an independent and exhaustive process. A list of many offender characteristics given in criminal profiles was gathered, and each characteristic was then analyzed to determine relevance based on the definition proposed by Petherick (2007) and Baeza (1999). The similarities between the characteristics judged to be relevant and the BEA method are not surprising given that BEA is the only method that defines and strives for investigative relevance and decreasing investigative distractions.

Conclusion

Profiles are designed to assist investigators by narrowing suspect pools and providing new avenues of inquiry. Any information provided within the profile that does not assist in reaching these goals is left open to misinterpretation and is therefore potentially damaging to the investigative effort (Turvey, 2008).

Based on the findings of this study, it is clear that some profiling approaches maintain investigative relevance better than others. It has been illustrated herein that there is a major discrepancy between the theories and practices of research-based profiling methodologies. This issue needs to be addressed before the profiling community can move forward. It is imperative to the integrity of this community that those working within it adhere more strictly to the philosophies of examination they endorse. Simply relying on a statistical average may reduce the credibility of profiling, delay investigations, further endanger the public, and increase the possibility of a miscarriage of justice. Clearly, some individuals are aware of the issues of relevance, making concerted efforts to maintain relevance in every instance, whereas others are not so concerned with their blanket approach. The failure of many to recognize the importance of offering investigatively relevant investigative support is not only irresponsible but also may be unethical. This chapter has exposed such shortcomings, and in so doing it may lend a hand in bringing the importance of investigative relevance to the fore.

The study discussed here is the first of its kind, and it has opened the door for future research to further the criminal profiling process and therefore assist law enforcement in its investigations. It is hoped that in the future, investigative relevance will become the new measure on which profiling practices are gauged. This will further expose the shortcomings of some methods and perhaps bring about a resolution while acknowledging the usefulness of other methods and the assistance they may provide.

Questions

1. Which of the following is not an investigatively relevant characteristic according to Ferguson?
   a. Motive
   b. Knowledge of methods and materials
   c. Knowledge of the victim
   d. Intelligence
   e. Knowledge of the crime scene
2. Which of the following is not one of the goals of profiling according to Holmes and Holmes?
   a. To provide investigating authorities with a social and psychological evaluation of the offender
   b. To narrow the suspect pool
   c. To provide a psychological assessment of items found in possession of the offender
   d. To provide interviewing and interrogation strategies
   e. Identifying the suspect from a suspect pool
3. What does Rossmo argue of the decision-making process as far as profiling is concerned?
   a. That it must assist in the investigative decision-making process
   b. That it must help develop a suspect from the suspect pool
   c. That it must provide a probable list of characteristics
   d. That only criminal investigators should be trained as profilers
   e. None of the above
4. Criminal profiling is only of use in the investigative phase; beyond that, it has no use. *True or false?*
5. More information is not better in criminal profiling. *True or false?*
6. It is the responsibility of the criminal profiler to demonstrate how conclusions are relevant. *True or false?*
7. Inductive methods usually argue for a smaller number of offender characteristics. *True or false?*
8. With regard to investigative relevance, what is the difference between inductive and deductive methods in terms of the characteristics offered?
9. List and describe some of the inputs of criminal profiling.
10. List and describe the common outputs of criminal profiling.

References

Ainsworth, P. (2001). *Offender profiling and crime analysis.* Devon, UK: Willan.

Ault, R., & Reese, J. (1980). A psychological assessment of crime profiling. *FBI Law Enforcement Bulletin, 49*(3), 22–25.

Baeza, J. (1999). *Monterey, CA.* Investigative Relevance Paper presented at the 1st Annual Academy of Behavioral Profiling Meeting.

Copson, G. (1995). *Coals to Newcastle? Part 1: A study of offender profiling.* London: Police Research Group Special Interest Series Paper 7, Home Office.

Geberth, V. (1996). *Practical homicide investigation: Tactics, procedures and forensic techniques* (3rd ed.). Boca Raton, FL: CRC Press.

Holmes, R. R., & Holmes, S. (2002). *Profiling violent crimes: An investigative tool* (3rd ed.). Thousand Oaks, CA: Sage.

Homant, R., & Kennedy, D. (1998). Psychological aspects of crime scene profiling: Validity research. *Criminal Justice and Behavior, 25*(3), 319–343.

Muller, D. (2000). Criminal profiling: Real science or just wishful thinking? *Homicide Studies, 4*(3), 234–264.

O'Hara, C., & O'Hara, G. (2003). *Fundamentals of criminal investigation* (7th ed.). Springfield, IL: Thomas.

O'Toole, M. E. (2004). Criminal profiling: The FBI uses criminal investigative analysis to solve crimes. In J. Campbell & D. DeNevi (Eds.), *Profilers: Leading investigators take you inside the criminal mind.* Amherst, MA: Prometheus.

Petherick, W. A. (2007). *Critical profiling: A qualitative and quantitative analysis of methods and content.* Robina, Queensland, Australia: Unpublished doctoral dissertation, Bond University.

Pinizzotto, A. J. (1984). Forensic psychology: Criminal personality profiling. *Journal of Police Science and Administration, 12*(1), 32–40.

Pinizzotto, A. J., & Finkel, N. (1990). Criminal personality profiling: An outcome and process study. *Law and Human Behavior, 14*(3), 215–233.

Ressler, R. K., Burgees, A. W., & Douglas, J. E. (1988). *Sexual homicides: Patterns and motives.* New York: Lexington Books.

Rossmo, D. K. (2000). *Geographic profiling.* Boca Raton, FL: CRC Press.

Turvey, B. E. (2002). *Criminal profiling: An introduction to behavioral evidence analysis* (2nd ed.). Burlington, MA: Academic Press.

Turvey, B. E. (2008). *Criminal profiling: An introduction to behavioral evidence analysis* (3rd ed.). Burlington, MA: Academic Press.

Metacognition in Criminal Profiling

Barry Woodhouse and Wayne Petherick

Introduction

As with many professions, one of the more serious problems that confronts the profiling community is that of the inept examiner. Deliberately unethical behavior is one thing, but ongoing incompetence because of profiler ignorance is something else entirely. In some instances, ignorance is the result of a metacognitive deficit caused by a lack of study, a lack of training, or a general lack of mental dexterity. In such instances, the profiler will continually do the wrong thing, such as using flawed methods and erroneous logic, because he lacks the ability to recognize his own ineptitude; the profiler cannot perceive when his methods and reasoning are wrong or why, let alone that they should be corrected and how.

Although discussed in Turvey (2008), this chapter represents the first comprehensive review of *metacognition* and how it applies to the field of criminal profiling. It is further acknowledgment that the problem exists and it impacts the profession in a negative manner. This chapter first provides a review of the literature and then reports the results of Woodhouse's research on the subject. This chapter closes with basic recommendations on how to overcome metacognitive deficits.

Metacognition

The practice of criminal profiling varies significantly from its portrayal in the popular media. Although many unfamiliar with the practice view it as a highly credible source of investigative information, Turvey (2008) notes that the field is replete with examples of incompetent assessment and illogical inferences. Unfortunately, many criminal profilers also display a marked inability to learn from their mistakes and continue to use flawed strategies and methods.

Turvey (2008) notes that although errors within criminal profiling may take a number of forms, such as evidence being misinterpreted or conclusions rendered that do not match the evidence as a result of bias or shoddy work practices, these mistakes are sometimes the result of a common underlying deficit in metacognition. This means that many such mistakes result from an individual examiner's inability to know when he or she is wrong and the subsequent failure to correct his or her course in the face of errors when presented with them.

Metacognition is recognized as an established concept in cognitive psychology. It is defined by Mayer (2003) as one's knowledge and awareness of his or her cognitive processes, and it can be traced back to Flavell's (1971) early work on metamemory. Alternate definitions describe metacognition as "knowledge and cognition about cognitive phenomena" (Flavell, 1979, p. 906) and "knowledge and regulation of cognition" (Brown, 1978, p. 77). Simply stated, metacognition can be explained as "learning about learning," and it refers to strategies and understanding we apply to our everyday lives—how some of these structures are sound and result in favorable outcomes, whereas others do not and should be disregarded.

Kruger and Dunning (1999) suggest that metacognitive deficits are evident when individuals fail to alter their behavior, even in the face of evidence that their thinking strategies lead to poor reasoning. Not only do these individuals reach erroneous conclusions and make bad decisions from them, but they lack the competence to recognize them. Kruger and Dunning provide a case example to illustrate the concept (p. 1121):

> *In 1995, McArthur Wheeler walked into two Pittsburgh banks and robbed them in broad daylight, with no visible attempt at disguise. He was arrested later that night, less than an hour after videotapes of him taken from surveillance cameras were broadcast on the 11 o'clock news. When police later showed him the surveillance tapes, Mr. Wheeler stared in incredulity. "But I wore the juice," he mumbled. Apparently, Mr. Wheeler was under*

the impression that rubbing one's face with lemon juice rendered it invisible to videotape cameras (Fuocco, 1996).

This metacognitive deficit has been demonstrated across a number of areas, where participants who scored in the bottom quartile on assessments of humor, logic, and grammar systematically overestimated their own performance and level of ability (Kruger & Dunning, 1999). Individuals who estimated themselves to be in the 62nd percentile rather than the 12th were deficient in metacognitive skill, or ability to distinguish accurate responses from inaccurate ones. It was also shown that by improving participants' skills, there were gains in metacognitive *competence* resulting in improved responses. In essence, Kruger and Dunning showed that incompetent individuals were unable to accurately assess their own level of skill and therefore believed themselves to be performing well, and that some simple instruction about their failures led to an increase in the ability to recognize and subsequently control for them.

Metacognitive Monitoring

The concept of *metacognitive monitoring* (also known as metacognitive competency; see Wang, 1992) posited by Maki, Shields, Easton-Wheeler, and Lowery-Zacchili (2005) can further aid in explaining the ongoing flaws of thinking evidenced in the profiling community. This cognitive process refers to an individual's ability to reflect on and judge his or her own performance and is crucial for overcoming a metacognitive deficit. This is a good place to make clear that the ability to reflect on your own work product (or having others do it for you in the form of honest peer review) is highly underrated and undoubtedly one of the strongest safeguards against metacognitive error.

Metacognitive monitoring (competency) is a crucial aspect of learning. The ability to reflect and exhibit self-regulation over one's thinking has been demonstrated to be one of the prime differences between low-achieving, at-risk students and stronger achievers (Wang, 1992). The inability to appraise oneself robs incompetent individuals of the means to accurately appraise their abilities and usually results in inflated self-assessments. Termed the *above-average effect* by Kruger and Dunning (1999), this phenomenon occurs when individuals believe themselves to be more competent than they actually are. This better than average effect may be a factor, in some instances at least, when an individual overidentifies with an organization he belongs to or works for, or in situations in which an individual's assistance is sought because of his employer or celebrity rather than proven work product. Here, the individual will harness himself with the perception that he is better than he actually is, because if he were not good, there would not be so many requests for his assistance. In reality, there may be no link between the individual's ability and being sought out.

The above-average effect has not previously been examined within profiling but has been demonstrated across a number of other domains. For example, business managers have been shown to consider themselves more competent than a "typical" manager (Larwood & Wittaker, 1977), football players have been shown to believe they have a greater "football sense" than teammates (Felson, 1981), and high school students have been shown to believe they possess more eloquent written expression and leadership ability than their peers (College Board, 1976–1977, as cited in Kruger & Dunning, 1999). These concerns are at issue in the profiling community when individual profilers fail to understand their own intellectual strengths and weaknesses, as well as to grasp and apply basic principles and practice standards of investigative and forensic examination (Turvey, 2008).

The Role of Competence

Competence is the ability to do something, whether it is a simple task or complex analysis, with accuracy, efficiency, and reliability. Competence has an important influence on metacognitive ability. Research in the area of expertise reveals that novices, or those individuals unfamiliar with an area or subject, possess poorer metacognitive skills than their more experienced counterparts.[1]

This suggests that inexperienced individuals tend not to possess the degree or depth of metacognitive ability necessary for accurate self-assessment compared to their more accomplished peers. Inaccurate and subsequently inflated self-assessment in conjunction with the inability to recognize poor performance can lead to an inaccurate assumption of good or competent performance (Kruger & Dunning, 1999). This compounds the metacognitive errors and ensures that more useful and successful strategies are not learned. Kruger and Dunning (p. 1122) explain that not only does incompetence rob individuals of the ability to recognize their poor performance, but also it leaves them with the "mistaken impression that they are doing just fine."

This can be seen in the profiling community where research of the second author reveals that, after an extensive examination of profiles and their content, individual profilers or those adopting the same method can and sometimes do make the same mistake over and over again. This can be seen in total overall work product, and the repetition of a number of flaws between the work product of specific profilers. This suggests that at least some in the community are unaware of their own limitations, and at least some of this would be the result of metacognitive deficiencies.

The Woodhouse Study

The purpose of this study was to explore faults in metacognition. Specifically, the study investigated whether experts and nonexperts are able to discriminate between two profiles: one that contains a number of structural and logical flaws and one that provides a solid evidentiary basis and sound reasoning.

Method

To critically evaluate either profile, participants had to exercise metacognitive skills such as reflecting upon their own level of knowledge and critically evaluating the assertions put forth by the profile's author. This study took a slightly different tact than previous investigations.

[1] For example, Chi, Glaser, and Rees (1982) demonstrated that novices are less accurate than experts in judging the difficulty of physics problems. McPherson and Thomas (1989) also showed that novices were less able than experienced tennis players to accurately evaluate particular strokes in a tennis match.

By examining these two groups, the goal was to assess the level of metacognitive judgment applied in assessing a problem.

It should be noted that the current study was not an attempt to enter into the existing debate relating to profiling methods or to advocate a particular technique or theoretical orientation. Rather, it was performed to gauge the degree to which metacognition plays a role in discriminating between the bad and the good.

In light of previous research on the nature of expertise and the above-average effect, it was hypothesized that

1. Experts would rate their knowledge of criminal profiling higher than nonexperts.
2. Nonexpert participants would not be metacognitively equipped to distinguish between Profile 1 and the evidence-based Profile 2, and they would therefore rate both documents highly, with no significant difference.
3. Experts would rate Profile 2 significantly higher than Profile 1 due to their enhanced metacognitive ability to detect Profile 1's flaws.

Participants

Participants for the study were divided into either an expert or a nonexpert group based on their experience with profiling.

Respondents in the nonexpert sample were drawn from Bond University undergraduate classes unrelated to the area of criminal profiling and consisted of 32 males and 17 females. Ages ranged from 19 to 50 years, with an average age of 26 years ($SD = 5.1$).

The expert sample consisted of Bond University criminology students enrolled in the criminology subjects Criminal Profiling and/or Behavioral Evidence Analysis (BEA). Criminal Profiling, a subject open to both undergraduate and postgraduate students, is an introductory class that canvasses the theoretical backdrop to profiling as well as covering the major profiling methods and their application. BEA is an advanced profiling subject open to both undergraduate and postgraduate students and focuses specifically on the BEA method, providing in-depth coverage of theory and practice. Postgraduate students undertaking the Master of Psychology (Forensics) program were also included because Criminal Profiling is included in their curriculum. Students from the profiling and BEA classes were recruited between weeks 10 and 12 of the semester to ensure that they had time to develop a more discriminating set of skills relating to criminal profiling. The expert sample consisted of 20 males and 30 females, age 17 to 38 years, with an average age of 24 years ($SD = 4.5$).

Materials

Materials for the study consisted of two criminal profiles. The first of these was a fictional profile conducted by a fictional profiler on a fictional case. The second was a legitimate profile compiled using the Behavioral Evidence Analysis method. The fictional profile was used because, on examination, it showed significant flaws in structure and logic and thereby gave a good contrast to the legitimate profile.

Both profiles contained statements informing participants that any identifying information within had been removed or substituted to ensure the anonymity of any parties involved.

Fictitious Profile (Profile 1)

This document was retrieved from the Internet and largely follows a narrative format using inductive logic and intuition, with its conclusions based on a highly idiosyncratic interpretation of the evidence.

This profile is a 3,752-word document detailing the stalking and disappearance of Purity Ariadne Knight, a U.S. college student. The document states the authors are Dr. Maria McManus (retired) and Special Agent Dr. Martin Ballard of the FBI, acting as consultants for the Yoknapatawpha County Sheriff's Department (a fictional department). The profile states that the analysis is based on a thorough review of materials submitted to the PsiCore Consulting Group by Detectives Armstrong and Anderson as well as being a culmination of the education, experience, and intuition of the profilers.

The profile also contains a fairly standard caveat that states "this profile is not a substitute for a thorough investigation, and should not be considered inclusive or wholly accurate." Following this, the evidentiary basis for the profile is noted as "one recording from an answering message and one set of photographs taken by the offender at the victim's residence."

Following the caveat, the profile states that it will "reflect a personality profile type believed responsible for the stalking of victim Knight." The profile then details the subheadings of Victimology, Psycholinguistic Analysis, Voice Stress Analysis, Photographic Evidence Report, Offender Characteristics and Traits, Post Offense Behavior, and Post Offense Victim Behavior, which comprise the majority of the report.

Note that although the fictitious profile provides an opinion relating to both the offender and the victim's state of mind, it is used as a poor example of a profile and contains a number of substantial flaws. A critical evaluation of the document reveals that the authors fail to make clear the full circumstances surrounding the offense and assume the reader has some familiarity with the crime. Furthermore, the conclusions tendered by the report frequently lack any evidentiary basis, relying instead on appeals to the authors' experience and authority.

Finally, the report contains a number of technical errors, such as spelling and grammatical mistakes, as well as confusion relating to the qualifications of McManus, identifying her initially as a psychiatrist and later as a psychologist. Despite these problems and omissions, the profile as presented may appear sufficiently legitimate as to not be immediately identified as factitious.

Behavioral Evidence Analysis Profile (Profile 2)

Profile 2 employed the Behavioral Evidence Analysis method and was compiled as work product for a case already past the trial stage in the United States. By the time this study was conducted, the matter to which the profile relates had been before the courts, meaning that the document was now part of the public record.

Despite being part of the public record, for ethical reasons all identifying information was removed from the document and replaced with generic information about the protagonists.

The location of the crime scene, names of investigative staff, and dates relating to the investigation were also altered to control for potential familiarity with the gross details of the crime such that participants might judge the document on its "accuracy" rather than quality. To preserve some continuity, the county where the crime occurred was not changed.

Profile 2 is 2,700 words in length and details a double homicide. The majority of the document relates to examination of the physical evidence and includes clear descriptions relating to the location, position, and injuries sustained by both victims as well as a number of assessments addressing the offender's behavior. It also details the perpetrator's attempt to destroy evidence by setting fires, explanation and analysis of the crime scene location and features, precautions taken by the perpetrator, and an assessment of the offender's level of planning and motivation.

As per the methodology of BEA (see Chapter 4), Profile 2 contains a detailed reconstruction of the criminal event based on physical evidence. It includes lengthy sections examining the position of each victim within the crime scene and the surrounding environment. The document also assesses the limitations of the available evidence, such as detailing the effects of fire-fighting efforts at the crime scene.

In contrast to Profile 1, Profile 2 is extremely clear in stating the sources of information that contributed to the final report, where this information was obtained, and specifically identifying the agency or examiner for each piece of evidence.

Profile 2 is also far more conservative in the nature of the conclusions it makes, and it specifically cites the evidentiary basis of each inference made. The profile is also clear in explaining the certainty of any conclusions; it provides a list of possible explanations for behavior for which conclusions are equivocal.

Furthermore, Profile 2 clearly defines any terms used. For example, in the Crime Scene Characteristics section, *location type* is defined with citation to the appropriate textual material.

Measures

Both profiles were rated using a 30-item questionnaire asking participants to evaluate their profile across a number of categories. The questionnaire, titled Metacognition in Criminal Profiling (MCP), asked participants to rate the profile according to its technical aspects (e.g., "How would you rate the profile in terms of its correct use of punctuation and spelling?"), use of logic (e.g., "How would you rate the profile in terms of its use of logic?"), applied use (e.g., "How would you rate the profile in terms of its usefulness to investigators?"), use of evidence (e.g., "How would you rate the profile in terms of making clear the evidence that has been examined?"), level of detail (e.g., "How would you rate the amount of background information included within the profile?"), and examination of perpetrator's behavior (e.g., "How would you rate the profile's examination of the perpetrator's level of planning?"). The full MCP is provided in Appendix A.

Responses to question 1 and questions 3 through 27 were scored across a 5-point Likert scale (1 = very bad, 2 = bad, 3 = neither good nor bad, 4 = good, and 5 = excellent). Question 2 ("How often do you believe criminal profiling is used by the authorities or law enforcement agencies?") was scored using a different 5-point Likert scale (1 = almost never, 2 = on unusual cases, 3 = on serious cases, 4 = most serious cases, and 5 = all serious cases).

A total score for the MCP was generated by summing the participant's responses for questions 3 through 27. Higher scores indicated the profile rated higher across the categories outlined previously. The minimum possible score was 24 and the maximum 120.

Cronbach's alpha was calculated to assess the MCP's reliability. For a measure to be considered reliable (i.e., measuring the domain it purports to examine), an alpha of 0.7 or higher is generally required. Analysis revealed the MCP to be reliable ($\alpha = 0.969$).

Question 8 ("How would you rate the profile in terms of making the credentials of the author clear?") was excluded from the analysis because the BEA profile did not include the appendices containing the author's curriculum vitae; therefore, it could not be meaningfully assessed across this criterion.

A short demographic section was also included to obtain the respondent's age, gender, and highest level of completed education. Following this, three questions were added to examine the participant's previous experience with profiling; two of these were rated with a forced choice (yes/no), whereas the third asked respondents to list from where they obtained their knowledge of criminal profiling (TV & movies, Books, Academic study, Professional work, and Other).

The MCP was developed from scratch due to the fact that no parallel instrument exists to measure metacognition in this way. The measure was developed in collaboration with Petherick.

Development of the instrument was undertaken through a number of stages, beginning with an extensive review of the literature. This was reviewed to develop an appreciation of common mistakes and inconsistencies exhibited within written profiles as well as the strengths and characteristics of a good profile. From these facets, a number of consistent themes emerged that were then used to generate a list of items. These potential items (in excess of 50) were then refined and revised until items best reflecting the aims of the study remained. The final 30 items that comprised the MCP were selected to broadly reflect the facets elicited by the literature search, as well as to highlight the strengths and weaknesses inherent within the profiles selected for the study.

Procedure

Once agreement to participate in the study had been obtained, respondents were given an explanatory statement, a randomly selected profile, and a copy of the MCP. Prior to reading the document, participants were made aware that the profile contained some graphic descriptions of crime scenes, and that they were free to withdraw from the study should this cause them discomfort. Completed questionnaires were returned either by placement in an envelope or through a dropbox to ensure participant anonymity.

Results

Overview

The data was analyzed using the Statistical Package for the Social Sciences version 15. Initial exploration of the data was done through an examination of descriptive statistics to obtain a more comprehensive understanding of each respondent's familiarity with criminal profiling. Following this, a one-way analysis of variance (ANOVA) was conducted to test if expert and

Table 10.1 Respondents' Familiarity with Criminal Profiling

	Nonexpert		Expert	
	n	%	*n*	%
Heard of				
No	16	32	2	4
Yes	34	68	48	96
Exposed to				
No	41	82	8	16
Yes	9	18	42	84

nonexpert participants differ significantly in their perceptions of use by law enforcement agencies. A second one-way ANOVA was used to test hypothesis 1 to determine if experts rated their knowledge of profiling significantly higher than nonexperts.

Prior to examining hypotheses 2 and 3, the assumptions for ANOVA were checked (these are provided later). Once the assumptions had been examined, a 2×2 between-subjects factorial ANOVA was conducted.

Descriptive Statistics

Table 10.1 shows the number of participants who have previously heard of (or read about) criminal profiling, as well as those who have been exposed to a written criminal profile prior to participating in the study.

Of the 100 respondents, 82 stated that they had previously heard of criminal profiling, with 51 stating that they had at some point been exposed to a written criminal profile prior to participating in the study.

Contrary to expectation, a more detailed examination of the data revealed that some participants from the nonexpert sample had been exposed to a written profile (18%) in the past, whereas 16% of respondents from the expert sample claimed to have never encountered a written criminal profile.

One-Way Anova

To gain a more comprehensive understanding of the expectancies of participants, a one-way ANOVA was conducted to determine if experts and nonexperts differ in their belief as to how often criminal profiling is utilized by law enforcement agencies. This relationship was significant ($F(1, 98) = 16.93$, $p < 0.001$), revealing that nonexperts believed profiling was used more often ($M = 3.58$, $SD = 0.928$) than did experts ($M = 2.76$, $SD = 1.06$).

Hypothesis 1

A second one-way ANOVA was conducted to examine if experts rated their knowledge of criminal profiling as higher than that of nonexperts. This test was significant ($p < 0.001$), with an

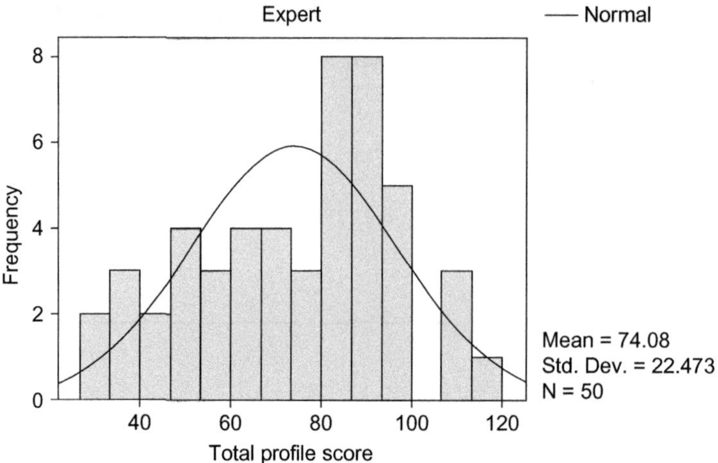

FIGURE 10.1 Distribution of profile score for the expert sample.

examination of the means revealing that experts tended to rate their knowledge of criminal profiling higher ($M = 3.64$, $SD = 0.8$) than did nonexperts ($M = 2.58$, $SD = 0.91$).

2×2 Factorial Anova (Assumptions)

As with all statistical tests, the ANOVA technique contains a number of assumptions that must be met for this type of testing to be considered appropriate. The first assumption, termed independence of observations, essentially relates to the requirement that data be collected randomly. In the case of this study, the assumption was satisfied by the research design, which ensured that the allocation of profiles to each participant within the sample groups was random.

As seen in Figures 10.1 and 10.2, the distributions of total profile score for experts and nonexperts were normal, although a slight degree of positive skew was evident within the expert sample.

Total profile scores for both Profile 1 and Profile 2 also showed symmetrical distributions. These are illustrated in Figures 10.3 and 10.4.

The second assumption of ANOVA, termed homogeneity of variance, was not met for this study. Essentially, ANOVA assumes that each of the samples included in the analysis contains an equal amount of variance, or that each sample group will vary to approximately the same degree. This is measured statistically using Levene's test of homogeneity of variance and was found to be significant ($p = 0.034$). As previously stated, this meant that the assumption was violated; however, ANOVA is considered robust to violations of this assumption, especially when samples are equal in size, as was the case in this study.

If the homogeneity of variance assumption is violated, it is suggested that the level of significance be adjusted from 0.05 to the more conservative level of 0.01. This means that it is more difficult to detect relationships within the data, although when detected, these relationships are more likely to be "real" rather than the result of error. This alteration was performed in this study.

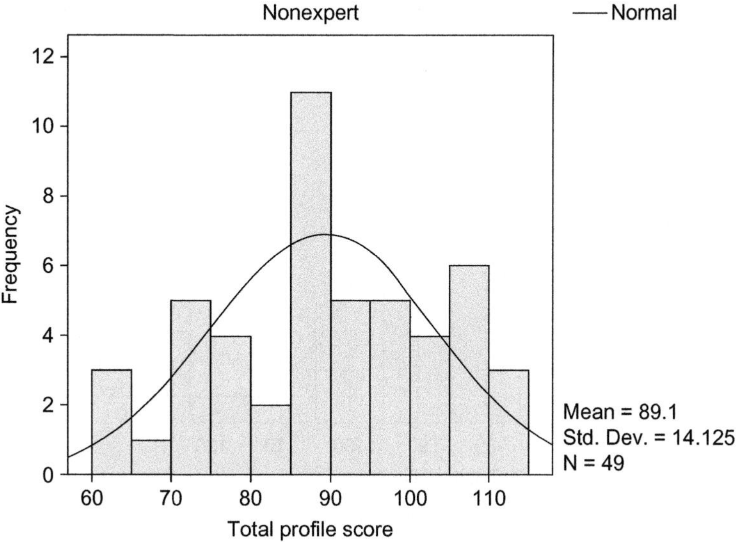

FIGURE 10.2 Distribution of profile score for the nonexpert sample.

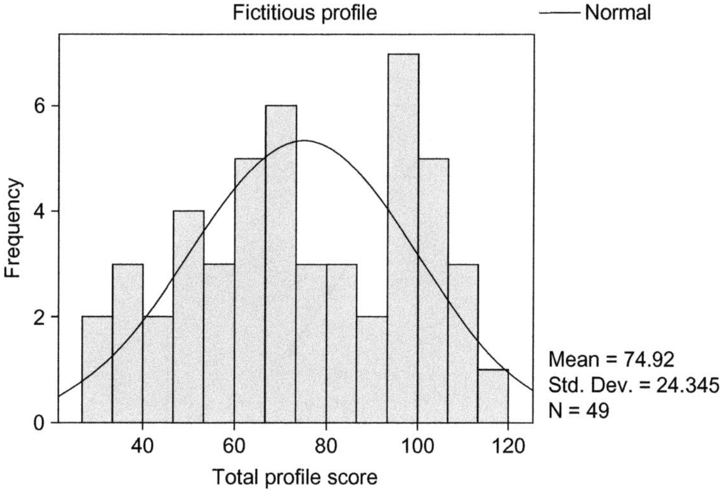

FIGURE 10.3 Distribution of total profile score for Profile 1.

Hypotheses 2 and 3

A two-way between groups factorial ANOVA was conducted to explore how experts and nonexperts rated two different profiles. The interaction effect between the sample group (expert and nonexpert) and profile (fictitious and BEA) was statistically significant ($p < 0.001$).

Due to the interaction effect, follow-up univariate analyses were required to determine if nonexperts rated Profile 1 and Profile 2 differently. A one-way ANOVA was conducted using the split-file

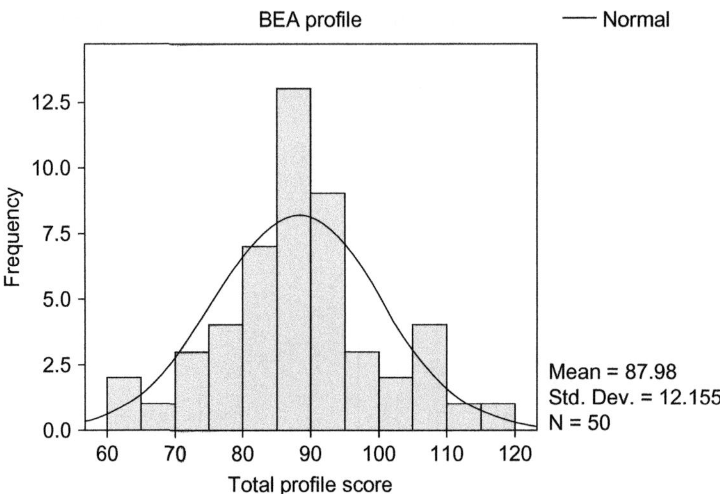

FIGURE 10.4 Distribution of total profile score for Profile 2.

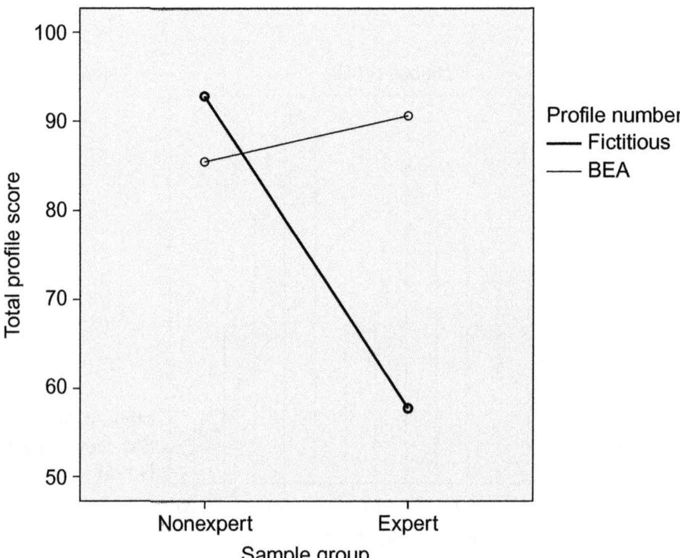

FIGURE 10.5 Expert and nonexpert ratings of Profiles 1 and 2.

procedure, which revealed that nonexperts did not rate the mock profile as significantly different from the BEA profile ($p < 0.001$). The means and standard deviations are outlined in Figure 10.5.

Hypothesis 2, that experts would rate Profile 2 significantly higher than Profile 1, was also examined with a one-way ANOVA. This demonstrated that experts rated the BEA profile ($M = 90.52$, $SD = 12.042$) higher than the fictitious profile ($M = 57.64$, $SD = 17.974$); this relationship was significant ($p < 0.001$). Essentially what this means is that the strength of the relationship observed is greater than what would be expected by chance and therefore can be explained by the fact that experts were able to discriminate between the two profiles.

Discussion

Hypothesis 1, that experts would rate their subjective knowledge of profiling higher than non-experts, was supported. Hypothesis 2, that nonexperts would not distinguish between the profiles, and Hypothesis 3, that expert participants would rate Profile 2 higher than Profile 1, were also supported.

The results from this study support the previous findings in the areas of competency, expertise, and metacognition. The fact that nonexperts were not able to distinguish between a low- and a high-quality profile mirrors the findings of Chi, Glaser, and Rees (1982) and McPherson and Thomas (1989), who found that novices were generally less adept at judging difficulty or success within unfamiliar domains.

Kruger and Dunning's (1999) finding that failing to recognize a poor performance will often lead to the assumption of a good performance is also supported by this research. In failing to recognize the discrepancies within Profile 1, participants rated the document highly, indicating that they considered it to be fulfilling the criteria listed in the MCP. In short, by failing to recognize the profile as a poor example, it was assumed to be insightful.

The fact that nonexperts rated the mock profile higher than the BEA profile further supports the previous findings of Kruger and Dunning (1999). In rating Profile 1 higher than its counterpart, nonexperts clearly demonstrated an inability to subject the document to critical evaluation and exercised a general false assumption that the mock profile was correct in its methodology. The fact that experts were clearly able to distinguish between the two profiles and rate them accordingly demonstrates that this assumption is limited to those unfamiliar with the area.

The above-average effect (Kruger & Dunning, 1999) is also supported, although in a more limited manner, by the current study. Given that the majority of nonexperts were aware of criminal profiling (65%), with only a small number having been exposed to it (18%), the fact that both profiles were endorsed highly suggests that participants had a great deal of confidence in making evaluations. The fact that no significant difference was noted between the ratings of both profiles indicates that nonexpert participants were not metacognitively equipped to make such judgments accurately.

In addition, the ability of the expert sample to accurately distinguish between the two profiles gives further credence to the idea that some regulation of cognition is being exercised. This in turn supports previous investigations into metacognition and competency that have found robust support for the superior abilities of experts (Chi et al., 1982; McPherson & Thomas, 1989; Kruger & Dunning, 1999).

Overall, the current study provides support for the contention that metacognitive deficits are at least partially responsible for the failure to critically evaluate profiles. It appears that consistent with other areas of metacognition, incompetent (nonexpert) individuals overestimate their own ability and fail to exercise regulation of their cognitive processes. In essence, failing to recognize a bad profile will generally lead to the opposite assumption that it is good.

Although it cannot be ruled out that the difference in ability to rate profiles is a result of experts developing a "profiling-specific" skill base and then applying this when required, this would still require the individual to exercise control and self-monitoring over his or her thoughts and therefore would be considered as metacognition. Furthermore, rating Profile 1 across the criteria included in the MCP instrument required little in the way of profiling-specific skills because respondents were provided the categories with which to assess the document.

The fact that many of the flaws contained within Profile 1 were highly transparent also provides a compelling argument against a profiling-specific skill base, as opposed to any effect from metacognition. None of the questions included within the MCP required participants to utilize a prior knowledge base, nor did they need to have an in-depth understanding of the mechanics underlying criminal profiling. Rather, respondents needed to exercise regulation over their cognition when rating their profile against the provided criteria.

It is also possible that the mock profile was granted additional credibility due to the fact that it resembles many media portrayals of profiling. In reading this document and having an alleged ex-FBI agent as one of its authors, participants unfamiliar with the discipline may have believed that these elements added a degree of authority or accuracy to the conclusions. In contrast, the BEA profile contained no information relating to the author's credentials or experience in the area, and it provided less of a basis for speculation relating to the author's professional experience and ability.

Differences between the expert and nonexpert samples' expectations in how commonly profiling is used also highlight the possibility of the media impacting the attitudes of respondents. Experts and nonexperts differed significantly in their belief regarding how commonly law enforcement agencies utilize the services of criminal profilers, with nonexperts believing it to be far more common. Although this illustrates the lack of applied knowledge relating to the discipline between the two subgroups, it may also be indicative of profiling's popularity within the media, and the popular misconception that it is a commonly used tool of law enforcement.

Methodological Considerations

Although the study is considered to be a good introduction to an area that has not previously been researched, it is by its very nature exploratory and therefore contains a number of methodological factors that could be improved in future investigations.

The MCP questionnaire, used in this study to measure the dependent variable, is the primary methodological consideration within this study. Although the measure demonstrated excellent reliability, the questionnaire's high Cronbach's alpha may indicate that some of the items within the measure are redundant. Future investigations may seek to alter the measure to assess a broader range of domains or to reduce the total number of items to minimize redundancy.

The choice of wording for the Likert scale on the MCP (i.e., very bad, bad, neither good nor bad, good, and excellent) may also have influenced participants' responses due to the scale's labeling. Replication of this research would benefit from rewording the responses on the Likert scale to a more neutral tone, thereby reducing the possibility of response bias.

Finally, the study may have benefited from a more accurate measure relating to how respondents attained their knowledge of criminal profiling. Although a question addressing this was included within the MCP, participants often responded multiple times or in an inconsistent manner. For example, participants listed multiple sources from where they obtained their knowledge of profiling, with no indication as to which contributed the most. Therefore, it was not possible to gain a full understanding of how respondents obtained their knowledge of criminal profiling or what impact the media may have had on their expectations. This is especially important because the media is likely to be the greatest source of knowledge for nonexpert participants, and this presentation of profiling is likely to seriously impact their expectancies.

Implications

Given the nature of the study, it is necessary to be somewhat conservative when expanding on the possible implications of the research. It was, however, convincingly demonstrated that nonexperts were not equipped to draw distinctions between good and bad examples of profiling and therefore should not be placed in a position to evaluate such documents. In short, it seems that any evaluation of profiling should be conducted by subject matter experts rather than by nonexperts, even though they may be well educated in other areas. To be perfectly clear on this issue, it could be argued that the skills of an individual schooled in profiling would be more effective and useful than, for example, those of a psychologist or psychiatrist simply because they are behavioral scientists. In other words, profiling skills are domain specific.

It should also be noted that Kruger and Dunning (1999) suggest a relatively simple solution for incompetence. The authors agree with Miller's (1993, p. 4) assertion that "it is one of the essential features of such incompetence that the person so afflicted is incapable of knowing that he is incompetent. To have such knowledge would already be to remedy a good portion of the offense." In practice, it may be that simply informing an individual of his or her relative lack of experience or competence in a given area will be enough to impart positive change.

The study also has important implications for those individuals who are currently working as profilers. Although Turvey (2008) argues that profiling is replete with examples of incompetent assessments and illogical inferences, this study gives some hope in the finding that experts possessed a good ability to critically evaluate profiling documents. This can be seen as providing support for Turvey's contention that metacognitive deficits are responsible for many of the commonly committed errors within profiling.

Although becoming aware of one's own metacognitive deficits is a positive outcome and a partial remedy to future mistakes, this is not enough by itself. While simply highlighting those areas in which one is deficient may be enough to identify a particular problem or problem occasion, overall deficiencies in metacognition may prevent someone so impaired from generalizing this experience to others. In short, metacognitive errors may be prone to repetition, especially in situations that are not identical to those in which prior learning has occurred. Adopting a more rigorous methodology, and applying it consistently with good logic and reasoning, is likely the best remedy to this problem.

This study has demonstrated that nonexperts display a surprising inability to recognize what would be considered by experts to be fairly obvious flaws within a profile. This has serious implications for law enforcement and legal contexts, in which profiling is becoming increasingly popular, yet is likely to be reviewed and utilized by individuals unfamiliar with the area. This study demonstrated that those with some exposure to profiling at a formal level are more discriminating in their assessment of quality than their counterparts. This perhaps calls for a greater level of education among end users of profiling so that they may exercise a similar level of critical assessment. In this way, the quality of work product should improve because consumers will essentially demand it.

Woskett, Coyle, and Lincoln (2007) examined the attitudes of legal practitioners (solicitors, barristers, and crown prosecutors) toward criminal profiling. This research used four vignettes taken from profiles to assess the validity of profiling as expert evidence, with the results showing that on none of the items measured did the opinions reach the positive range. Of interest is the finding that 69% of the lawyers were only partially aware of what is involved in profiling, with 54% stating they are unaware of the different techniques and methods employed by profilers. As such, this study, to determine whether profiling is a valid and probative form of evidence, is putting the proverbial cart before the horse. That is, without a detailed understanding of *what* lawyers know, and *how* they acquired that knowledge, their assessments of profiles may be redundant in light of the findings of the research herein. Having put forward this concern, it should be noted that the legal professionals could likely make a determination as to whether the profile met current legal standards as evidence. However, this would first require the quality of the profile to be assessed, and it is here that metacognition will come into play.

A number of potential remedies arise from the previous discussion that will go some way to addressing the problems of metacognitive impairment. The following list is by no means exhaustive or exclusive, but it is considered a good starting point:

1. Consumers of profiling should do all that they can to inform themselves of the process, and the method that was employed in any given case, rather than relying on uncritical acceptance of the conclusions by virtue of the grandiosity of the profiler or the agency to which the profiler belongs. Profilers should also take time to educate end users in the type of profiling used and in the way the evidence was examined and how the conclusions were formed. To be specific, this means that profiles should contain a full account of the logic and reasoning used in the profile and include a description of the evidence on which the profile is based and how this was factored into the offender characteristics offered.
2. The profiling community as a whole needs to stop engaging in gross levels of intellectual dishonesty. This means that researchers, educators, and practitioners need to be honest and equitable in their accounts of profiling, which is currently not the case. For example, a number of articles and texts that allegedly contain detailed accounts of profiling theory and practice fail to include discussions of any methods other than their own despite extensive literature on them.[2] It is almost as though these authors believe that by not

[2] Or perhaps worse, misinterpret or incorrectly cite the theoretical underpinnings of an approach. Either way, it is a problem of considerable importance.

acknowledging other practitioners and approaches, they can deny their existence and/or utility. Conversely, it may be that in acknowledging these other profiling methods, they run the risk of "making them real," thereby validating any claims other authors make against their own paradigms. A short list of research suffering from this includes Dowden, Bennell, and Bloomfield (2007); Godwin (2002); Canter (2000); and Napier and Baker (2005).[3]

3. More research needs to be conducted in the area of metacognition in criminal profiling. As discussed previously, said research could address any methodological problems with the current research. For example, restructuring the MCP, using a larger sample and including profilers and police investigators, would help determine the extent to which metacognition is a problem. As discussed by Goldsworthy (2001), many police investigators believe that profiling is investigatively relevant, and so inclusion of this sample would be worthwhile.
4. Because profiling could be considered a subdiscipline of behavioral science, it is also necessary to ensure that profilers are trained in the behavioral sciences. This would actually exclude many in the current profiling community who are typically trained under the law enforcement short course model and who hold, at best in many cases, academic qualifications in education, management, law, chemistry, human physiology, and criminal justice (administration).[4] This would ensure that profilers are not only better equipped to understand and interpret complex issues surrounding human, and by extension, criminal behavior but also they will be better equipped to understand any impact this may have on their ability to reach rational and logical conclusions from a given set of facts. This is, however, not a given. As stated previously, it appears that profiling knowledge is domain specific. Consequently, formal education in the behavioral sciences should be tempered with more advanced education in criminal profiling.

Conclusion

This study demonstrated that nonexperts did not possess the metacognitive ability to discriminate between two alternate criminal profiles, one of which provided a solid evidentiary basis, whereas the other was inherently flawed. Profiling "experts" showed a higher level of metacognitive ability and were able to rate each profile appropriately. The study provides support for the contention that metacognitive skills are responsible for the failure to critically evaluate profiles, and that by failing to evaluate a profile, a nonexpert will assume it to be accurate and insightful.

This is important because the end consumers of profiling are typically detectives with little to no exposure to the finer points of theory and practice in criminal profiling and may thus be

[3] Again, this is a short list. A critical examination of the literature reveals the problem to be much more systemic than these few references would have us believe. This would be a project worthy of research for any interested graduate student or doctoral candidate.

[4] Note that many criminal justice programs are housed within social science departments. However, this does not by extension make them social sciences. Many such programs are more concerned with the administrative or procedural side of criminology—that is, the role, structure, and function of the police, courts, and prisons. They may have little, if any, relevance to the interpretation of actual behavior.

inadequately informed to make an educated decision about the quality of any profile. This may be more likely in the case of a serial crime task force, where it is likely a profiler will be called given the repetitive nature of the crime and the greater threat to public safety.

As previously stated, one of the ways to argue for the validity of profiling, or specifically the skills of an individual profiler, is to claim that if the profiler were no good, he or she would not get as much work. This thinking is also faulty because, as this research has demonstrated, nonexperts, many of whom are end consumers, are simply not adept at identifying poor work product. Having these metacognitively impaired individuals decide what is good and bad, and by extension, who is good and bad, is wrong and will most likely lead to the increased perception that all profiling is bad and of little use. This is definitely not the case, and we as a community should be doing what we can to educate and illuminate. In this way, we can help overcome metacognitive deficits, thereby assisting end consumers in their discrimination between good and bad criminal profiles.

Questions

1. Define metacognition.
2. Briefly describe the findings of Kruger and Dunning (1999) with regard to metacognition.
3. List the hypotheses of the current study and whether these hypotheses were supported or not.
4. The study found no difference in the ability to rate the profiles between the expert and nonexpert groups. *True or false?*
5. The incongruity between individuals believing themselves to be capable of recognizing their own errors in thinking and reasoning in the face of sufficient evidence to the contrary is known as __________ __________.

References

Brown, A. L. (1978). Knowing when, where, and how to remember: A problem of metacognition. *Advances in Instructional Psychology, 1,* 77–165.

Canter, D. (2000). Offender profiling and criminal differentiation. *Legal and Criminological Psychology, 5,* 23–46.

Chi, M. T. H., Glaser, R., & Rees, E. (1982). Expertise in problem solving. In R. (1982). Sternberg (Ed.), *Advances in the psychology of human intelligence* (Vol. 1, pp. 17–76). Hillsdale, NJ: Erlbaum.

Dowden, C., Bennell, C., & Bloomfield, S. (2007). Advances in offender profiling: A systematic review of the literature over the past three decades. *Journal of Police and Criminal Psychology, 22,* 44–56.

Felson, R. B. (1981). Ambiguity and bias in the self-concept. *Social Psychology Quarterly, 44,* 64–69.

Flavell, J. H. (1971). First discussant's comments: What is memory development the development of? *Human Development, 14,* 272–278.

Flavell, J. H. (1979). Metacognition and cognitive monitoring: A new area of cognitive developmental inquiry. *American Psychologist, 34,* 906–911.

Godwin, G. M. (2002). Reliability, validity, and utility of criminal profiling typologies. *Journal of Police and Criminal Psychology, 17*(1), 1–18.

Goldsworthy, T. (2001). Criminal profiling: Is it investigatively relevant? *Journal of Behavioral Profiling, 2,* 1.

Kruger, J., & Dunning, D. (1999). Unskilled and unaware of it: How difficulties in recognizing one's own incompetence lead to inflated self-assessments. *Journal of Personality and Social Psychology, 77*(6), 1121–1134.

Larwood, L., & Whittaker, W. (1977). Managerial myopia: Self-serving biases in organizational planning. *Journal of Applied Psychology, 15,* 73–80.

Maki, R. H., Shields, M., Easton-Wheeler, A., & Lowery-Zacchili, T. (2005). Individual difference in absolute and relative metacomprehension accuracy. *Journal of Educational Psychology, 97,* 723–731.

Mayer, R. (2003). *Learning and instruction.* Upper Saddle River, NJ: Pearson.

McPherson, S. L., & Thomas, J. R. (1989). Relation of knowledge and performance in boys' tennis: Age and expertise. *Journal of Experimental Child Psychology, 48,* 190–211.

Miller, W. I. (1993). *Humiliation.* Ithaca, NY: Cornell University Press.

Napier, M. R., & Baker, K. P. (2005). Criminal personality profiling. In S. H. James & J. J. Nordby (Eds.), *Forensic science: An introduction to scientific and investigative techniques* (2nd ed.). Boca Raton, FL: CRC Press.

Turvey, B. (2008). In B. Turvey (Ed.), *Criminal profiling: An introduction to behavioral evidence analysis* (3rd ed.). Burlington, MA: Academic Press.

Wang, M. C. (1992). *Adaptive education strategies: building on diversity.* Brookes: Baltimore.

Woskett, J., Coyle, I. R., & Lincoln, R. (2007). The probity of profiling: Opinions of Australian lawyers on the utility of profiling. *Psychology, Psychiatry and Law, 14*(2), 306–314.

Appendix A: Metacognition in Criminal Profiling Questionnaire

Age:_____

Gender (*Please circle*): male/female

Profile number (*Please circle*): 1/2

Highest level of completed education (*Please check*):

_____ Primary school

_____ High school

_____ University degree

_____ Postgraduate university

Occupation: ________________________

Directions; please read carefully:

The following questions are related to your general knowledge of profiling.

Please circle the most appropriate answer.

1. Have you ever heard of profiling or criminal profiling before? Yes/No
2. Have you ever been exposed to a written criminal profile in the past? Yes/No
3. From where do you get your knowledge of criminal profiling?

TV and movies

Professional work

Books

Academic study

Other: ___________

1. How would you rate your knowledge of criminal profiling?

Very Bad	Bad	Neither Good nor Bad	Good	Excellent
1	2	3	4	5

2. How often do you believe criminal profiling is used by the authorities or law enforcement agencies?

Almost never	On unusual cases	On serious cases	Most serious cases	All serious cases
1	2	3	4	5

The following questions will ask you to rate the profile that you just read.
Please circle the most appropriate answer.

3. How would you rate the profile in terms of its layout?

Very Bad	Bad	Neither Good nor Bad	Good	Excellent
1	2	3	4	5

4. How would you rate the profile in terms of its correct use of punctuation and spelling?

Very Bad	Bad	Neither Good nor Bad	Good	Excellent
1	2	3	4	5

5. How would you rate the profile in terms of its use of logic?

Very Bad	Bad	Neither Good nor Bad	Good	Excellent
1	2	3	4	5

6. How would you rate the profile's overall level of clarity?

Very Bad	Bad	Neither Good nor Bad	Good	Excellent
1	2	3	4	5

7. How would you rate the profile's overall level of detail?

Very Bad	Bad	Neither Good nor Bad	Good	Excellent
1	2	3	4	5

8. How would you rate the profile in terms of making the credentials of the author clear?

Very Bad	Bad	Neither Good nor Bad	Good	Excellent
1	2	3	4	5

9. How would you rate the profile in terms of making its reasoning clear?

Very Bad	Bad	Neither Good nor Bad	Good	Excellent
1	2	3	4	5

10. How would you rate the profile in terms of its usefulness to investigators?

Very Bad	Bad	Neither Good nor Bad	Good	Excellent
1	2	3	4	5

11. How would you rate the amount of background information included in the profile?

Very Bad	Bad	Neither Good nor Bad	Good	Excellent
1	2	3	4	5

12. How would you rate the profile in terms of its level of detail?

Very Bad	Bad	Neither Good nor Bad	Good	Excellent
1	2	3	4	5

13. How would you rate the profile in terms of making the details of the crime clear?

Very Bad	Bad	Neither Good nor Bad	Good	Excellent
1	2	3	4	5

14. How would you rate the profile in terms of describing the crime scene?

Very Bad	Bad	Neither Good nor Bad	Good	Excellent
1	2	3	4	5

15. How would you rate the profile in terms of establishing a clear set of facts surrounding the crime?

Very Bad	Bad	Neither Good nor Bad	Good	Excellent
1	2	3	4	5

16. How would you rate the profile in terms of establishing a time line over which the crime occurred?

Very Bad	Bad	Neither Good nor Bad	Good	Excellent
1	2	3	4	5

17. How would you rate the profile in terms of describing the circumstances surrounding the crime?

Very Bad	Bad	Neither Good nor Bad	Good	Excellent
1	2	3	4	5

18. How would you describe the profile in terms of describing the location where the crime occurred?

Very Bad	Bad	Neither Good nor Bad	Good	Excellent
1	2	3	4	5

19. How would you rate the quality of evidence described in the profile?

Very Bad	Bad	Neither Good nor Bad	Good	Excellent
1	2	3	4	5

20. How would you rate the amount of evidence used to justify the conclusions drawn in the profile?

Very Bad	Bad	Neither Good nor Bad	Good	Excellent
1	2	3	4	5

21. How would you rate the profile in terms of making clear the evidence that has been examined?

Very Bad	Bad	Neither Good nor Bad	Good	Excellent
1	2	3	4	5

22. How would you rate the profile in terms of drawing logical conclusions from the evidence?

Very Bad	Bad	Neither Good nor Bad	Good	Excellent
1	2	3	4	5

23. How would you rate the profile in terms of its examination of the victims?

Very Bad	Bad	Neither Good nor Bad	Good	Excellent
1	2	3	4	5

24. How would you rate the profile's examination of the perpetrator's motivation?

Very Bad	Bad	Neither Good nor Bad	Good	Excellent
1	2	3	4	5

25. How would you rate the profile's examination of the perpetrator's prior criminal history?

Very Bad	Bad	Neither Good nor Bad	Good	Excellent
1	2	3	4	5

26. How would you rate the profile in terms of examining the perpetrator's level of planning?

Very Bad	Bad	Neither Good nor Bad	Good	Excellent
1	2	3	4	5

27. How would you rate the profile in terms of describing the perpetrator's state of mind at the time of the crime?

Very Bad	Bad	Neither Good nor Bad	Good	Excellent
1	2	3	4	5

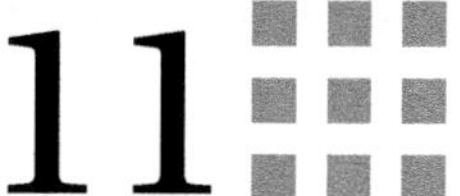

Criminal Profiling as Expert Evidence

Wayne Petherick, David Field, Andrew Lowe, and Elizabeth Fry

Introduction

Profiling evidence has been accepted in courts in the United States in both trial and sentencing phases, but other jurisdictions have been more cautious in their acceptance. For example, courts in the United Kingdom and Australia have been reluctant to introduce profilers as experts, even though profiling has been given some exposure in courts operating at the lower end of the justice system. The reasons for this reluctance are varied but include a lack of uniformity in processes and outcomes, fragmentation of methods, and conflict between profiling organizations and practitioners. In short, there are many methods of profiling, and not all practitioners agree on or accept one way as the best or most suitable.

This chapter addresses criminal profiling as expert evidence. First, some of the issues involving profiling as expert evidence are explored, including the induction-centric nature of the literature, the attitude of courts toward profiling evidence, and some common areas of profiling testimony. Next, a detailed overview of the Frye and *Daubert* rules of evidence in the United States is provided, followed by a thorough examination of the rules of evidence in Australia. The penultimate section discusses the current status of profiling through a number of cases, and at its conclusion, some recommendations are provided that allow for the maximum benefit from profiling evidence.

Criminal Profiling as Expert Evidence

It is important to consider the implications that profiling evidence may have in criminal and civil trials, and the rules and regulations that govern its use, because criminal profiling has a role in trial proceedings (Hazelwood, Ressler, Depue & Douglas, 1999). In doing so, it must be questioned whether profiling can provide relevant information where the probative outweighs the prejudicial value (Petherick, 2000). Probative evidence in profiling is that which provides useful diagnostic information (Davis & Follette, 2002), and it should be objective and supported by factual evidence. On the other hand, evidence is considered to be prejudicial if it leads to a premature judgment or opinion unwarranted by the evidence. Therefore, it is necessary to consider what information in a profile will most assist the court in its determinations. Ormerod (1996, p. 869) suggests that if we rely on the profile as fact, this will be insufficiently relevant at trial. However, if we rely on it as an opinion, "the court may accept the evidence, but will attach to it such weight as is appropriate given the reliability of the opinion."

Because inductive methods, those relying on correlational or comparative reasoning, dominate discourse in this field, there will be an understandable but often dangerous reliance on these methods as pathways to knowledge in court.[1] It is instructive to discuss several works and court decisions and what they have to say about profiling and reliance on statistical databases.

The greater weight of literature on expert evidence covers inductive profiling, and this suggests a lack of awareness that not all profiling methods are equal. First, because psychologists are the professionals most often discussed as giving profiling evidence, it might be assumed that only psychologists can give profiling evidence, an implication that does not augur well for other experts who have made the forensic examination of human behavior their life's work. Second, if only inductive profiling is available for reference in works about expert testimony, does this mean that a deductive model is not likely to be accepted, or is it simply a matter of this method being less prevalent and therefore less well known? Given this, it would seem that there is a definite training need for legal professionals about the differences among profiling approaches and what each has to offer as evidence.

Bartol and Bartol (1994, p. 329) define profiling in much the same way as other authors and note that "to a large extent, the profiling process is dictated by a database collected on previous offenders who have committed similar crimes." The authors also note, citing Pinizzotto

[1] Despite what some in the field would have us believe, the prevalence of an approach is not an analog for utility, nor is it a justification for its continued use.

and Finkel (1990), that profiling is of most use in sexual offenses such as serial rape and sexual homicides because we have a more complete understanding of these offenses. In concluding their discussion, they assert that "profiling based on anything but a strong database … is likely to be plagued by many of the same biases, cognitive distortions, and inaccuracies so characteristic of clinical judgment when predicting dangerousness" (p. 329). In a later work, Bartol (2002, p. 253) again cites Pinizzotto and Finkel (1990) about the use of profiling in sexual offenses and then goes on to state the following:

This is because we have a more extensive research base on sexual offending than we do on homicide. Furthermore, profiling is largely ineffective at this time in the identification of offenders involved in fraud, burglary, robbery, political crimes, theft, and drug-induced crimes because of the limited research base.

McCord's (1987) treatise *Syndromes, Profiles and Other Mental Exotica* treats profiles and profiling as analogous to psychological syndromes (e.g., battering parent profiles and sexual abuser of children profiles). The aim of these profiles is to present evidence that the character of the accused is remarkably consistent to the "typical" profile of certain abuser types. The presentation of this type of evidence is more akin to psychological testimony and is not generally consistent with the overall goal of criminal profiling.

In 1999, in *New Jersey v. Fortin*, the appellate division reversed on the admissibility of profile evidence presented by Robert Hazelwood on the grounds that his linkage analysis was not sufficiently reliable (Turvey, 2000). The appeals court found that those elements of modus operandi cited by Hazelwood (and pivotal in his conclusions) did not demonstrate an unusual pattern; thus, the behavior of the accused (reference) was not in accordance with the standard (behaviors against which to measure the uniqueness of the reference). In determining the reliability of the evidence, it was noted that (New Jersey v. Fortin, 2000):

If the witness can from a reliable database offer evidence that a combination of bite marks on the breast, bite marks on the chin, and rectal tearing inflicted during a sexual attack is unique in his experience of investigating sexual assault crimes, that evidence could help to establish an "unusual pattern."

In addition:

The trial court did incorporate Hazelwood's testimony in its 404(b) ruling, stating that Hazelwood's testimony was persuasive in that Hazelwood had not seen in reviewing 4000 cases this combination of bite marks, anal tears, and brutal facial beatings to a victim. If there was such a database of cases, the witness' premise can be fairly tested and the use of the testimony invokes none of the concerns we have expressed about the improper use of expert testimony.

However, such a database of cases did not exist, unless in the mind of the profiler, and so it becomes difficult, if not impossible, to test the reliability of that database and any conclusions reached. Similar problems are likely to hamper any syndrome evidence passed off as a profile.

Coming from another school of thought, Alison and Canter (1999, p. 25) state the following:

In terms of processes of generating profiles, the procedure of Offender Profiling has taken on two rather different meanings. One is as the presentation of the personal opinion of an individual who has some experience of criminals through interviewing them as part of his or her professional activity. The second is as the development of the area of applied, scientific psychology known as "investigative psychology."

Both of these types of profile construction are inductive.

Freckleton and Selby (2002b) include profiling under the rubric of novel psychological evidence and also only discuss inductive profiling.[2] Furthermore, a good deal of the discussion on profiling as expert evidence revolves around the assessment of personality traits of the unknown offender and how these match with a suspect or how they may be suggestive of the predisposition of the accused to act in certain ways (ergo, similar fact or propensity evidence). The overriding thrust of this discussion is on profiling evidence from psychologists, and Freckleton and Selby's discussion on the future of criminal profiling suggests that "the challenge lies ahead for psychiatrists and psychologists who claim to be able to profile particular kinds of offenders ... to show empirically that certain kinds of crimes are ... committed by persons of a particular psychological makeup" (p. 410).

In the United Kingdom, the most substantial analysis on the admissibility of psychological profiling evidence took place in *R. v. Gilfoyle* in 2001 (Freckleton & Selby, 2002b). In this case, Professor David Canter provided evidence as to the likelihood that a deceased person had committed suicide, an analysis referred to as a psychological autopsy (a profile of a deceased person). The evidence put forth by Canter was largely based on an analysis of the suicide note, which he suggested was not penned by Paula Gilfoyle, the deceased.

The court of appeal declined the evidence, noting that although Professor Canter was an expert (Freckleton & Selby, 2002b, p. 403):

He had never embarked on evaluating suicidality of a deceased person previously and on the basis that "his reports identify no criteria by reference to which the court could test the quality of his opinions: There is no database comparing real and questionable suicides and there is no substantial body of academic writing approving his methodology."

Interestingly, despite Canter's assertion in this case and the degree to which the prosecutors believed that his evidence proved their case was valid, Canter has recently changed tact (Kennedy, 2008):

The pioneer of criminal profiling in Britain has switched sides to say that a man he helped to jail for life for murdering his wife is innocent.

[2]Although not specifically referred to as inductive profiling (most works of this nature do not make the distinction between induction and deduction), you need only consider the nature of the discussion to determine what they are talking about.

Eddie Gilfoyle was prosecuted after David Canter, a psychology professor, told police that his hanged wife's suicide note betrayed signs of having been faked. But research prompted by the case into the difference between genuine and false suicide notes has persuaded Professor Canter that Paula Gilfoyle, 32, was, indeed, the sole author of her final words.

Now campaigners for the jailed husband are hoping to use Professor Canter's analysis of the suicide note as part of a fresh appeal.

On a June evening in 1992, Paula Gilfoyle's body was found hanged in the garage of the home in Upton, Wirral, Merseyside, that she shared with her husband.

Mrs. Gilfoyle, who worked in a local factory, was 8 months pregnant and presented a cheery front to the world. But the long suicide note that she left spoke of a feeling of failure and unhappiness, and hinted at strains in her marriage. She told her husband not to blame himself, and even suggested that the baby was not his. There is an overwhelming feeling of guilt and self-blame in the note.

Friends and relatives refused to believe that she could have killed herself. They insisted that she had no cares and was looking forward to the birth of her first baby. Suspicion soon turned on her husband. Some workmates told police that she had said that her husband, a hospital porter, had persuaded her to write a bogus suicide note as part of a course that he was taking on suicide. No such course existed.

However, Professor Canter points out, in a 10,000-word report on the case, that for the bogus suicide plot to have worked Gilfoyle would have had to persuade his wife to climb a ladder in the garage and allow a noose to be placed around her neck. There were no signs of force on her body.

Gilfoyle has always protested his innocence of what was portrayed as a calculated, evil plot to make his pregnant wife's killing look like suicide.

When Merseyside police began to investigate Mrs. Gilfoyle's death, they consulted Professor Canter, who had been the first psychological profiler to be used by British police and who shared their doubts about the note.

His evidence formed part of the prosecution case, though it was never heard by the jury. He nonetheless believes that it helped to reinforce prosecutors' determination to press ahead against Gilfoyle, who was convicted unanimously of murder in July 1993.

Professor Canter used a technique of linguistic analysis to try to establish whether Mrs. Gilfoyle had composed her note. Police suspected that her husband had dictated it to her. But studies since, including one supervised by Professor Canter, have shown that errors can be produced by using simple word counts as the main basis for deciding authorship.

By chance, a couple of years after the conviction, Professor Canter moved to Merseyside, taking a post at the University of Liverpool. There, he came into contact with Gilfoyle's relatives and eventually met the prisoner himself. "He wasn't that creative an individual," Professor Canter said. The academic then began looking closer into the science of suicide notes.

The most pertinent study was conducted 50 years ago by the founders of the Los Angeles Suicide Prevention Center, Edwin Schneidman and Norman Farberow. The two psychologists, pioneers in suicide prevention, compared genuine suicide notes with artificial ones written by people who had never been suicidal.

Their purpose was to look for ways to stop people taking their own lives. But Professor Canter made a study of those 1950s notes, along with other samples, to seek clues to how a genuine suicide note could be distinguished from an imagined one. It became clear that it is difficult to simulate the elements in a real suicide note. Professor Canter now uses Mrs. Gilfoyle's final handwritten lines, beginning "Dear Eddie" and ending "Goodnight and God bless, love Paula," in his lectures.

"It is my opinion that the suicide note was written, unaided, by Paula Gilfoyle," he said. "That this intention was genuine is difficult to determine, but the way in which the note appears to be the culmination of months of thinking of various possibilities for dealing with her situation, and indicates so directly that Paula could see no other way, is consistent with a very real determination to kill herself."

Gilfoyle's brother-in-law, Paul Caddick, a retired police sergeant who found Mrs. Gilfoyle's body and now runs the miscarriage of justice campaign, praised Professor Canter.

"He is a brave man," Mr. Caddick said. "We are very pleased he has come on to the defense side because he is a man of integrity. Obviously, for a long time, Eddie didn't like him. When he came on to our side he said, 'The bastard, he should've said the right thing in the first place.' But now he realizes it was a dreadful mistake."

Gilfoyle has already lost two appeals against conviction but his new legal team at Birnberg Peirce is preparing evidence to bring before the Criminal Cases Review Commission.

Merseyside Police said: "There was a lot of other evidence heard by the jury and he was convicted on that evidence."

Given the position of Thornton (1997, p. 13) that "induction, not deduction, is the counterpart of hypothesis testing and theory revision," it is of some concern that considerable attention has been given to inductive methods, specifically as this focus relates to the delivery of expert testimony. It is certainly a curious position we find ourselves in when courts that deal in facts prefer a position more aligned to the offering of theories, many of which may not even be supported by the available evidence.

Thus, despite the fact that induction is really the first step in the process of developing a logical argument, it is the dominant style of reasoning in theory, practice, and expert evidence in profiling. Many of the authors discussed previously cite the need for further research and databases on offense types, and although these may have general criminological value, we are also reminded of their frailty and the dangers of using statistical averages when life or liberty may be at issue. If more profilers adopted a deductive approach, then their conclusions would be certain based on known evidence, as opposed to statistical averages, and therefore more suited to forensic practice.

Next, some common areas of expert evidence concerning state of mind, intent, similar fact evidence (also referred to as propensity evidence), and staging are discussed.

State of Mind and Intent

Historically, psychologists or other mental health professionals examined the suspect after his or her arrest using information provided to them by the offender. The problem with this is that information given to the psychologist may not be true and the offender may be in a different state of mind from when the crime was committed—factors that may bias the profiler. Because a profile relies on information usually a level removed from the offender (crime scene photographs, wound patterns, etc.), profilers' analyses may not be as open to bias from this source. Because of this, it may be beneficial for a profiler to interpret the physical evidence and to provide an assessment of the offender—before, during, and after the crime—regarding his or her state of mind and intent.

Any number of behavioral patterns can be evidenced in a crime and can inform the profiler about state of mind and intent. This could include information relating to offense planning (whether low or high), motive, victimological inferences, and whether the offender displayed remorse (referred to as undoing, an attempt to psychologically reverse the criminal event). This type of assessment is important because it may influence decisions regarding offender culpability and sentencing. For example, when considering homicide, if the absence of intent can be proven, then an offender may be found guilty of manslaughter. However, if an offender is found to be fully culpable and intent can be proven, the offender may be convicted of the more serious offence of murder and a harsher sentence may be handed down.

The offender's state of mind is directly related to intent. As indicated by Findlay, Odgers, and Yeo (1999, p. 17), a person has intention for a result when he or she means to bring about that result, or when the person is aware it will likely occur in the course of events. Freckleton and Selby (1999a) state that when intent is an issue, the accused may call expert evidence to establish any abnormal characteristics that may have affected the offender's mental functioning. In some cases, criminal acts such as murder may be ancillary and not the primary intent of the offender (Douglas, Ressler, Burgess & Hartman, 1986), and a crime scene assessment may help to flesh out those intended actions from the unintended and also those acts of criminal behavior from precautionary acts the offender engaged in to escape the attention of the police.

However, in cases in which the mental functioning of the accused is not at issue, evidence on intent may not require the opinion of an expert: "It was said not to be a question of medical science or a question upon which a psychiatrist or any other professionally qualified person has any greater claim to express an opinion than an unqualified person" (Freckleton & Selby, 2002b, p. 179). Readers are cautioned to check local precedent on this issue.

Similar Fact Evidence

Similar fact evidence is often used to suggest that behavior evidenced in a criminal action conforms to the general character of the accused. Attempts have been made in a number of jurisdictions to suggest that because of the character of the accused, he or she is more or less likely to have committed the crime under consideration (Freckleton & Selby, 2002b). It may also describe information from other acts of misconduct by the accused on other occasions, which are similar to the offense currently presented to the court (Field, 2008; McNicol & Mortimer, 1996). Because of its prejudicial nature, similar fact evidence is normally inadmissible unless it is deemed to be directly relevant to the issue before the jury. For similar fact evidence to be allowed, there must be a striking similarity between cases. For example, the fact that in two separate crimes two rapists used a condom is not sufficient grounds on which to link cases. However, two offenders who use exactly the same knot in a ligature and provide an identical script for the victim to read during the assault may be.

In its latest ruling on the subject (Phillips v. R (2006) 225 CLR 303 at 483), the High Court of Australia reaffirmed that the test of admissibility is that "[similar fact evidence] will be admissible only if its probative value exceeds its prejudicial effect ... in other words, that there is no reasonable view of the evidence consistent with the innocence of the accused."

Criminal profiling may assist courts on evidence of similar fact, especially in cases of multi-count indictments, by identifying the existence of case linkage based on behavioral information from the crime scene. Links between cases can also be done using the physical evidence, such as DNA, and in cases where this is present a profiler's opinion may not be warranted. However, it may still be called on if prosecutors want to "bootstrap" a case to help secure a conviction or to increase the severity of the sentence. In these instances, profilers should be careful and heavily weigh up their involvement.

Similar fact evidence is an area also warranting caution because another important consideration is determining exactly when coincidence ceases and clear evidence of case linkage exists. Obviously, this will change depending on the case, and although precedent may provide a guide, it will be up to the individual court to decide if there is a strong nexus of similarity.

Staging

A staged (also called simulated) crime scene is one in which the offender has deliberately altered the physical evidence to obscure the facts, mislead the investigators, and/or direct the investigation away from the most logical suspect (see Chapter 8). This subject will only be discussed here briefly as it is covered in detail by Ferguson elsewhere in this volume.

The concept of the staged crime scene is not new; it was discussed in Hans Gross's seminal work *Criminal Investigation* in 1924. Gross (1924, p. 439) refers to staging as the "defects of the situation":

> *So long as one looks only on the scene, it is impossible, whatever the care, time, and attention bestowed, to detect all the details, and especially note the incongruities: but these strike us at once when we set ourselves to describe the picture on paper as exactly and clearly as possible. ... The "defects of the situation" are just those contradictions, those improbabilities, which occur when one desires to represent the situation as something quite different from what it really is, and this with the very best intentions and the purest belief that one has worked with all of the forethought, craft, and consideration imaginable.*

Gross (1924) touches on two critical points with regard to staging: (1) Staging is a desire on the part of the offender to represent the crime as something other than what it actually is, and

(2) no matter what care the offender takes, staging is usually detectable by those who know what to look for. It is because of experience with a variety of crimes and crime scenes that the profiler may often be called upon to advise the court on aspects of staging (this may not always be a flawless presentation, however, as the case studies discussed later will show).

Although staging is quite well defined in the literature, even with some uniformity, there is some debate about which specific aspects of an offender's attempt to cover up his or her crime constitute staging. Most authors suggest that the identification of staging be limited to those cases involving criminal intent whereby the staging covers another criminal act. However, Douglas and Munn (1992) include in their discussion the purposeful alteration of physical evidence to protect the victim or the victim's family, as might happen with an autoerotic fatality involving fetishism. This definition is inconsistent with other literature on the topic and is not a suitable way to define the topic.

Rules of Expert Evidence

Profiling does have the potential to serve as useful and important evidence in certain trials. However, as in other fields that fall under the title of expert evidence, it must be subject to rules of admissibility.

In the United States, the first rule of expert evidence was established in Frye v. United States (1923), when the results of a lie detector test were offered as evidence (Melton, Petrila, Poythress & Slobogin, 1997; Moenssens, Inbau & Starrs, 1986). James Alphonso Frye was charged with second-degree murder, and he argued that the lie detector test would determine whether his protestations of innocence were true (Frye v. United States, 1923):

> *The opinions of experts ... are admissible in evidence in those cases in which the matter of inquiry is such that inexperienced persons are unlikely to prove capable of forming a correct judgment upon it, for the reason that the subject matter so far partakes of a science, art, or trade as to require a previous habit or experience or study in it, in order to acquire a knowledge of it. ... When the question involved does not lie within the range of common experience or knowledge, but requires special experience or special knowledge, then the opinions of witnesses skilled in that particular science, art, or trade to which the questions relates are admissible in evidence.*

Although the court concurred with the general essence of the rule, it held that the test in question (polygraphy) did not meet the required scientific recognition among physiological and psychological authorities "as would justify the court in admitting expert testimony deduced from the discovery, development, and experiments thus far made" (Frye v. United States,1923).

Essentially, Frye revolves around the general acceptance of expert evidence within the scientific community (Freckleton, 1987; Wood, 2003) in that "the thing from which the deduction is made must be sufficiently established to have gained general acceptance in the particular field to which it belongs" (Rudin & Inman, 2002, p. 183). The main problem with Frye is that it is too generous with testimony that is generally accepted even if its validity has not been scientifically demonstrated, and it is too restrictive of novel evidence that is the result of excellent scientific verification (Melton, Petrila, Poythress & Slobogin, 1997). Newer areas of expertise may be excluded regardless of their utility simply because they are not generally accepted (Melton, Petrila, Poythress & Slobogin, 1997; Moenssens, Inbau & Starrs, 1986). This may be further complicated by standing practices that may be generally accepted but are not necessarily legitimate.

Seventy years later, in 1993, the *Daubert* rule (established in the case of Daubert v. Merrell Dow Pharmaceuticals, Inc., 1993) proposed that the admissibility of evidence should be based on its scientific reliability and validity, its potential for misrepresentation or falsification, its error rate, and whether it has been subject to peer review (Wood, 2003; Wrightsman, Greene, Nietzel & Fortune, 2002). Underwager and Wakefield (1993) suggest that the unanimous ruling of *Daubert* in effect replaces Frye with the Popperian principle of falsification as the key determinant of scientific knowledge. Using *Daubert,* evidence would have to be proven through testing and examination. The criteria for acceptance of such evidence should include the proof of any theories to be offered as opinion evidence, the scrutiny of peer reviews, and the level of acceptance of scientific methods used to reach a conclusion (Melton, Petrila, Poythress & Slobogin, 1997). Technically, *Daubert* applies only in federal jurisdictions, but it has also been adopted by many US states, although several still follow the Frye ruling (Wrightsman, Greene, Nietzel & Fortune, 2002).

Daubert should provide some scope for deductive profiling. This is because the deductive method produces conclusions derived from physical and behavioral evidence such as autopsy and forensic reports, which are themselves valid scientific methods allowed as expert testimony. However, *Daubert* may be less likely to contemplate inductive profiling because the methods used to reach conclusions are based on previous cases and not always on the evidence relating to the case presented in court. This may place too much emphasis on factors outside the boundaries of the case, highlighting the potential for misrepresentation of the facts that may not be valid and reliable.

Australian Rules of Evidence

In Australia, there are essentially five rules of expert evidence that dictate the recognition of expert witnesses and define the scope and limits of their testimony: the expertise rule, area of expertise rule, factual basis rule, common knowledge rule, and ultimate issue rule. Although these rules specifically relate to the Australian legal climate, they apply in a general way in other legal jurisdictions. For example, in both the United States and the United Kingdom (and most other jurisdictions), an expert must not provide evidence on the guilt of a person and, thus, must not speak to the ultimate issue.

In some way, shape, or form, the following rules apply equally across regions.

Expertise Rule

The expertise rule simply states that an expert must be an expert in his or her respective field but not necessarily the leading expert or authority (Freckleton & Selby, 2002a), although an expert must possess a quantity of knowledge superior to most in his or her given area. Because an expert is allowed to testify to what would be considered hearsay for other witnesses, it must be established that the expert possess sufficient knowledge in an area and that this "hearsay" carries some probative value.

This rule questions whether the witness has knowledge and experience sufficient to entitle him or her to be considered an expert who can assist the court. The witness must "possess some specialized knowledge, skill, training, or possibly experience sufficient to enable them to supply information and opinions" (Freckleton, 1987, p. 18). As a result, counsel must establish the witness's ability and competence to comment on the matter presented.

There is little literature addressing the issue of what education and training one must undertake to be considered a criminal profiler. It is expected that profilers would have qualification in the broad area of behavioral science, such as criminology or psychology, as well as a working knowledge of investigations and investigative procedures. However, competency as an expert may also be established through "participation in special courses, membership in professional societies, and any professional articles or books published" (Saferstein, 2004, p. 16), as well as direct occupational experience. Ultimately, whether a person is qualified to give expert opinion is at the discretion of the court after certifying an individual's education and experience is commensurate with the type of analysis to be performed.

Any debate about a person's qualifications to testify as an expert would typically be aired during the voir dire in the absence of the jury or during a pretrial application, when the procedural rules of the relevant criminal jurisdiction provide for such a process. Here, opposing counsel would subject the prospective expert to a grueling examination in which the expert's education, training, and experience would be scrutinized to determine if he or she should be allowed to present his or her opinions to the jury.

In a dated but relevant piece, Wiard (1931a, p. 143) discusses the importance of establishing the qualifications of any expert on which decisions may hang:

> *The counsel, however, has a certain task which he cannot customarily delegate "in toto" to the expert. This involves eliciting the opinions and conclusions of his technical witness in that form in which they may be most convincing, prior to which, however, he must establish, to the satisfaction of the court and jury, the gentleman's ability and integrity. This of course would be very simple were it necessary only to introduce him as witness, call upon him to present his opinions, and allow him to depart without having to offer either any background for his conclusions or to substantiate them by withstanding a cross-examination. However, court procedure does not recognize the capability of a so-called expert merely because his name may be such and such, and the opposing side, of course, will refuse to grant his qualifications under any conditions.*

Area of Expertise Rule

Experts cannot testify on areas that are not a part of a formal sphere of knowledge or profession (Freckleton & Selby, 2002b), whereby others of similar experience and knowledge are able to evaluate their theoretical and operational applications. As profiling has thus far struggled in endeavors to be classified as a profession—let alone other problems within the community—it could be argued that it doesn't represent a formal sphere of knowledge. And the problems of an area of expertise are not just about a formal sphere of knowledge or whether something exists within a profession. For example, Freckleton (1994, n.p.) notes that constructs such as rape trauma syndrome may be discussed in the literature and exist within a formal sphere of knowledge (psychology, psychiatry, etc.), but that these conditions may not be sufficient enough to allow testimony in a court of law:

> *However, the function of these "syndromes" is misapplied when they are set in concrete and used for purposes for which they were never initially envisaged. To allow an expert to put before a jury the inference that because a complainant's behavior is of a certain kind that therefore a crime has or has not been committed is dangerous and ought to be precluded at the least as more prejudicial than probative and in all probability as not emanating from an "area of expertise."*

Factual Basis Rule

The strength of an expert's opinion is related to the factual reliability of the evidence on which the opinion is based. The court will allow expert opinion evidence if the factual basis of that opinion has not yet been established, provided that after further evidence is admitted, the facts on which the evidence is based will be highlighted (Australian Law Reform Commission, 1994). If not, the testimony is still admissible, but the weight of the evidence will decline on direction of the judge (Australian Law Reform Commission, 1994). If the facts on which the expert testimony is based are not established at all, then of course the expert evidence will be worthless (see R. v. Ryan [2002] VSCA 176).

This rule affects criminal profiling in a similar, if not identical, manner to any other expert testimony. The base information of a criminal profile includes, but is not limited to, crime scene photographs, investigators' reports, autopsy documentation, evidence logs, and witness statements (Geberth, 1996). As such, the weight of profiling testimony is only as strong as the underlying evidentiary value of the information provided to the profiler in the case before the court. Testimony may be weighed by the degree to which an opinion is based on evidence or supposition and also on the quality of the interpretation. In addition, the closer the expert is to the facts of the case, whether conducting the crime scene reconstruction if qualified, or indeed whether he or she even visited the scene, the more authoritative the opinion. In particular, it should be noted that expert witnesses frequently give their opinions on the basis of assumed facts given to them by the party commissioning them. The easiest way to neutralize expert opinion is therefore to cast doubt on or disprove the facts on which that opinion is based. Because of this, the profiler is cautioned to independently establish the basic facts on which his or her opinion is based.

In arriving at a profile, the expert witness may be called upon to utilize reports prepared by others, such as autopsy reports, psychiatric assessments, physical examinations, or records from family services, department files. From the prosecutor's point of view, it will be essential to ensure that every document is "spoken to" by an appropriate witness to lay a factual basis for the profiler's assessment. From the profiler's perspective, he or she may occasionally need to admit that the final opinion is based on the facts regarding the accused that are being "assumed," in that the contents of the files and reports on which the opinion is based have been treated as accurate records of the facts.

If the expert witness is prepared to "adopt" previous literature on which his or her report is based, so as to incorporate it within the report, then that previous literature becomes "evidence" as part of his or her final conclusion (PQ v. Australian Red Cross Society [1992] 1 VR 19).

Common Knowledge Rule

This rule precludes the offering of expert evidence on matters that may be considered within the general knowledge or common sense (Freckleton & Selby, 1999b; 2002b). For example, an expert would not be allowed to testify that roads are slippery when wet because this is within common knowledge, but the expert could testify after the mechanical examination of a particular vehicle that it would behave in a particular way on a wet road.

Criminal profilers have "expert knowledge about domains of interrelated procedures" (Bekerian & Jackson, 1997, p. 221), including forensic science, behavioral science, and medico-legal death investigation. In the course of their analyses, profilers examine many offense-specific domains, such as modus operandi and signature, and these procedures are not considered part of general knowledge and common sense of the lay person or practitioners of the law. However, a profiler could not testify to the fact the offender in a given case was a male if it had previously been established that the victim was raped before she was murdered, that there was semen found on the body that did not belong to anyone known to her, and that she was not in a relationship at the time of the offense. These conclusions could be reached without specialist knowledge.

The reasoning behind this rule can be traced back to an opinion expressed by Lord Mansfield in the eighteenth century (Folkes v. Chadd, 1782):

> *The fact that an expert witness has impressive scientific qualifications does not by that fact alone make his opinion on matters of human nature and behavior within the limits of normality any more helpful than that of the jurors themselves; but there is a danger that they may think it does.*

The theme has been adopted and built upon considerably in R. v. Turner (1975). Although accepting that it was permissible to expose eyewitness identification to the challenge of psychiatric analysis of how the human identification process works, Lawton LJ emphasized the general caveat that "psychiatry has not yet become a satisfactory substitute for the common sense of juries or magistrates on matters within their experience of life."

Note, however, that objections of this genre are predicated on the belief that somehow the evidence of behavioralists is being substituted for the "everyday common sense" of the jury as to how people, in their experience, behave in a given situation. As such, it is seen as a challenge to the process whereby the actions of "ordinary" humans are judged by other ordinary humans who make up the jury. This, of course, is not what profiling is about.

The work of a profiler, in the main, is conducted in the context of abnormal behavior. What he or she seeks to bring to the attention of the jury are salient facts that may be adduced about the perpetrator of the particular offense through the perpetrator's behavior. It is sometimes no different from the subconscious process employed by a jury when they are told that an accused battered his wife to death when she confessed to being unfaithful to him. In both cases, the reference is to "known" behavioral characteristics—the difference is that the jury in the case of the wife killer is dealing with a common situation to which they can all relate, if necessary, with the application of a little imagination. In a case in which the profiler is offering assistance, on the other hand, the behavior is not that with which one could expect a jury to be familiar.

Very few jurors, from everyday experience, could form a mental picture of someone who rapes and murders in a ritualistic way, any more than they could conclude from the fact that the hyoid bone of the deceased was fractured that he or she had been manually asphyxiated. Both are areas of scientific conclusion based on observable facts, in respect to which the jury requires assistance from someone who can interpret those facts by means of an acceptable and accredited scientific process.

Ultimate Issue Rule

It is still generally regarded as the basic rule that an expert witness must not seek to decide the ultimate issue before the court (i.e., guilt or innocence) and is usually concerned with whether an expert's contribution will supplant the function of the jury by deciding on this issue for them (Freckleton & Selby, 1999a). However, note that in Australian jurisdictions covered by the Uniform Evidence Law (principally New South Wales, the Australian Capital Territory, and Tasmania and all cases involving federal laws being tried in federal courts), this "ultimate issue" rule has been relaxed to the point of abrogation; see, for example, Evidence Act 1995 (Cth), s. 80.

It is impossible for behavioral evidence from the crime scene to suggest that an accused is guilty or innocent of a crime, although several cases show how some profilers have erroneously tried just that (some of which are discussed later). It is an inferential process that involves an analysis of offender behavior including their interactions with the victim and crime scene, their choice of weapon, and their use of language, among other things (Petherick, 2003), but the profile should not be so specific as to identify a specific individual.

In summary, these five rules of expert evidence serve to promote the reliability of the information being provided to the court by the expert. This is achieved by certifying that the individual has the appropriate education and experience in a "formal sphere of knowledge" to perform examinations that the court cannot do itself. It also ensures the validity of the information forming the basis of the expert's opinion.

The Latest Indications on the Status of Profiling

R. v. Ranger

Many of the issues raised in this chapter were most recently considered by the Court of Appeal for Ontario in R. v. Ranger (2003). The accused was convicted of the first-degree murder of a former girlfriend and the manslaughter of her younger sister. The accused was said to have been unable to accept the termination of the relationship. Both deaths occurred at approximately the same time, and the two bodies were found in the house they shared with their mother. The victims were knifed to death (allegedly by the accused and his cousin), and a curious feature of the case was that although the house gave the appearance of having been ransacked, only three items had been taken. All of these related to the accused's former girlfriend, one of which was a necklace the accused had given to her.

Profile evidence offered by the Crown at trial related specifically to a suggestion that whoever had committed the crimes had "staged" a break and enter to divert attention from his or her connection to the victims. Following a voir dire, the trial judge ruled as follows (R. v. Ranger, 2003):

> *I am satisfied that opinion evidence is needed in this case in the sense that it will likely provide information that is outside the experience and knowledge of the jury. The factual issue of whether a break and entry is authentic or staged is not likely to be a subject within the common knowledge of the jurors. This, of course, is subject to the Crown qualifying the proposed expert as an expert in this particular area.*

In short, the proposed evidence satisfied the first test of relating to an issue outside the likely experience of the average juror and could be admitted provided that (1) the Crown could demonstrate the evidence of the expert was one proceeding from an established and recognized field of specialist study, and (2) the proposed witness was an expert in that field.

The witness offered by the Crown was Detective Inspector Kathryn Lines from the Behavioral Sciences Section of the Ontario Provincial Police, who claimed that criminal profiling was "a behavioral approach to criminal investigation" in which she had considerable experience. Crown counsel confirmed (in answer to a question from the trial judge) that the detective inspector was being offered as "an expert witness in the area of staged crimes," who would confirm that the crime scene had indeed been staged.

Neither counsel made submissions regarding the detective inspector's qualifications as an expert in this area, and the trial judge ruled that she was qualified "to give expert opinion as to staged crimes." Of note, this decision was arrived at despite the fact that the witness conceded during voir dire that there was no independent or objective process in existence against which to test the hypothesis of a "staged crime scene."

Defense counsel expressed concern that the witness's evidence might wander into the area of the alleged motive for the murder and was assured by Crown counsel that this was not his intention. As it transpired, the witness went much further than that.

On three occasions during her examination in chief, Crown counsel was allowed to elicit the witness's opinions regarding the motivations of the likely perpetrator and his or her characteristics. On each occasion, defense counsel objected on the ground that such a question was beyond the scope of what was deemed admissible during the voir dire, and on each occasion he was overruled.

The first occasion concerned the suggestion that the perpetrator of the crime was more interested in the former girlfriend of the accused than her younger sister. Despite the objection that this issue had more to do with the perpetrator's psychology than the staging of the crime scene, the question was allowed and answered in the affirmative. The second objectionable question related to the type of person likely to stage a crime scene, and the witness was allowed to incorporate into her answer a quotation from a crime scene manual, which stated that "it is almost always someone who had some kind of association or relationship with the victim." This despite the predictable objection from the defense that the question and answer amounted to "dime store psychology" that sought to make the accused fit within the class of person likely to commit the offense "through the mouth of an expert witness." The trial judge seemed content to admit the question on the basis that if the break and enter was staged, it rendered it likely that the perpetrator knew the victim. Third, the witness was allowed to testify to the fact that only items belonging to the accused's former girlfriend were missing from the crime scene, and because of this it was concluded that the perpetrator had "a particular interest in the possessions or things related to" her.

When defense counsel began cross-examination, he asked a series of questions designed to suggest that the witness's final opinion was fatally contaminated because she knew what the police investigation team was hoping to conclude. The trial judge brought this line of questioning to a close by reminding the jury that it was their opinion that mattered and not that of either the witness or the police. The Court of Appeal held that defense counsel should have been allowed to continue down that avenue of inquiry, quoting in support one of the caveats of Kaufman (Report of the Kaufman Commission on Proceedings involving Guy Paul Morin, 2003): "Profiling, once a suspect has been identified, can be misleading and dangerous, as the investigators' summary of relevant facts may be colored by their suspicions."

This case clearly demonstrates the danger of allowing the expert to wander outside his or her alleged area of expertise, down the perilous avenue toward the "ultimate issue." It also illustrates how easy it is to allow this to happen.

The initial agreement was that the expert witness would deal only with the issue of whether or not the crime scene had been staged. It was never suggested by the Crown (or contemplated by the trial judge) that she would be allowed to drift into the area of why the crime scene had been staged, even less that she would be allowed to offer an opinion on whether or not the accused met the profile of the likely perpetrator.

Yet this is, according to Ormerod (1996, p. 865), the very work of a profiler, who begins by reconstructing how the crime occurred, on which is based an inference as to why the crime happened, and culminates in an educated guess about the characteristics of the offender. This "what" to "why" to "who" is seen as the nucleus of a criminal profile.

Indeed, it is difficult to imagine any other logical reason for admitting the "what," other than its relevance to the "who." This is the very reason we have criminal trials, and it should have been within everyone's contemplation that the evidence skirted the issue of whether or not the accused was the perpetrator of the crime.

The error committed by the trial judge was that of allowing someone whose expertise was the "what" to answer the "why" and "who" questions. Despite the fact that she had not been deemed qualified to make those extended conclusions, there was a distinct risk that the jury would believe that she was qualified and would not be able to define the moment at which she stepped outside the boundary of what she was qualified to give opinions on. This was all the more dangerous given that (R. v. Ranger, 2003) "expert opinion testimony about 'why' or 'who' usually raises more concerns. These concerns relate to ... the requirement that the evidence be sufficiently reliable to warrant its admission and the requirement that its probative value exceed its prejudicial effect."

In illustrating the distinctions to be made, the trial judge Charron J gave, as examples of the "what," the opinion in an arson that the fire was deliberate rather than accidental and a pathologist's opinion on the likely cause of death. She added that (R. v. Ranger, 2003):

> *The scientific basis for this kind of evidence is usually not contentious. By contrast, attempts to adduce expert opinion evidence and WHY an offense was committed in a particular manner and, more particularly, about WHO is more likely to have committed the offense, that is, the kinds of evidence that I have labeled more particularly as criminal profiling, have generally not met with success, either in this jurisdiction or elsewhere.*

In support of this assertion, Her Honour quoted the Supreme Court of Canada's observation in R. v. Mohan (1994) that "the closer the evidence approaches an opinion on an ultimate issue, the stricter the application of this principle." Charron J adopted the rule that she took to have emerged from Mohan, to the effect that before evidence relating to the disposition of an accused might be admitted via an expert witness, "There must first be something distinctive about the behavioral characteristics of either the accused or the perpetrator that makes a comparison of the two sets of characteristics helpful in determining innocence or guilt."

This confirms some observations that lawyers become very nervous when "disposition" evidence is offered against an accused without proof that he or she has in the past exhibited the characteristics identified in the profile. Even when there is such proof, the Court will be required to be convinced of the scientific reliability of the profile characteristics. As per Sopinka J in *Mohan*, the trial judge should consider the opinion of the expert and whether the expert is merely expressing a personal opinion or whether the behavioral profile the expert is putting forward is in common use as a reliable indicator of membership of a distinctive group. In other words, has the scientific community developed a standard profile for the offender who commits this type of crime?[3]

In *Mohan*, the Court went on to hold that the expert evidence being offered for the defense did not satisfy that test, and therefore:

> *In the absence of these indicia of reliability, it cannot be said that the evidence would be necessary in the sense of usefully clarifying a matter otherwise inaccessible, or that any value it may have had would not be outweighed by its potential for misleading or diverting the jury.*

[3]Again, one can see the fairly ubiquitous reference to inductive profiles despite all of their fallibilities discussed throughout this work and others. An affirmative finding on this basis will satisfy the criteria of relevance and necessity.

In a subsequent case involving criminal profiling, the Supreme Court of Canada again rejected psychiatric evidence for the defense to the effect that the accused did not exhibit the allegedly distinctive personality traits of the perpetrator. This was on the grounds that the profile in question was not sufficiently "standardized." The Court explained that "the requirement of a standard profile is to ensure that the profile of distinctive features is not put together on an ad hoc basis for the purpose of the particular case."[4]

The court in Ranger then reminded itself that the testimony of the expert witness had not been restricted to the simple question of whether or not the crime scene had been staged (the "what" question) but, rather, had drifted into "why" (to redirect the suspicion away from the most obvious suspect) and then "who" ("almost always someone who has some kind of association or relationship with the victim"). The Crown had supported this extension with the argument that this type of profiling had been accepted in both the United States and Canada, an assertion that was rejected by the Court of Appeal.

Also considered was a recent English authority in R. v. Gilfoyle (2001), in which the defense at a murder trial had sought to admit expert evidence from David Canter (this case was discussed previously) of a psychological autopsy of the deceased. Canter's opinion was that the deceased had committed suicide, but this was rejected by the Court of Appeal on the basis that:

> *There is no data base comparing real and questionable suicides and there is no substantial body of academic writing approving his methodology. ... If evidence of this kind were admissible in relation to the deceased, there could be no difference in principle in relation to evidence psychologically profiling a defendant. In our judgment, the roads of enquiry thus opened up would be unending and of little or no help to a jury. The use of psychological profiling as an aid to police investigation is one thing, but its use as a means of proof in court is another.*

Putting together all these strands of authority, the Ontario Court of Appeal in Ranger rejected the evidence of the expert witness because:

> *Criminal profiling is a novel field of scientific evidence, the reliability of which was not demonstrated at trial. ... Her opinions amounted to no more than educated guesses. As such, her criminal profiling evidence was inadmissible. The criminal profiling evidence also approached the ultimate issue in this case and, hence, was highly prejudicial.*

The Estate of Samuel Sheppard v. the State of Ohio

In *The Estate of Samuel H Sheppard v. The State of Ohio*, the state hired retired FBI Supervisory Special Agent Gregg O. McCrary to testify that the crime scene of the homicide of Marilyn

[4]Here is another reference to "standard profiles." Ironically, criminal profiles should be constructed on a specific case with a specific set of evidence to make them valid for that case and its individual context.

Sheppard in 1954 was staged (McCrary, 1999). According to the report, staging is the "purposeful alteration of the crime and the crime scene by the offender. Staging is a conscious effort by the offender to mask the true motive for the crime by altering the crime scene to suggest false motives" (McCrary, 1999, p. 2).

In his report, McCrary (1999) concludes that Dr. Sheppard staged the crime scene to look like a profit- and drug-related burglary with a sexually motivated homicide.

The principal aspects of the case and McCrary's conclusions are as follows. The victim was murdered on approximately July 4, 1954, and her body was found in her bedroom having been severely beaten around the head approximately 25 to 35 times. Marilyn Sheppard was discovered with her pajama top pushed up to expose her breasts and one trouser leg pulled off. The victim's legs were hanging off the end of the bed, with one on either side of the bedpost. From this evidence, McCrary concluded that the crime scene had been staged to give the appearance of a sexually motivated homicide. He based these conclusions on the evidence of overkill, which is generally thought to occur only in crimes in which the offender and victim know each other. Also, there was no physical evidence of sexual activity, and the rage in which the offender killed the victim is inconsistent with the careful removal of the pajamas without ripping them, indicating a stark difference between the two behaviors. McCrary therefore concluded that there was no physical, forensic, or behavioral evidence that this was a sexually motivated homicide, but that it had been staged to give the appearance of one.

Parts of the house had been ransacked, including the drawers of a desk and Dr. Sheppard's medical bag and trophies; however, the damage was minor. The fact that there was a minimal amount of damage to property and that nothing of great value was taken led to the conclusion that the burglary was also staged. The only items taken were money from Dr. Sheppard's wallet and morphine from his bag, although this was based purely on Dr. Sheppard's previous evidence alone. McCrary (1999, p. 2) determined that "in this case it was the victim, not money or goods that were the primary focus of the attack." There were inconsistencies between the homicide and the burglary in that there was evidence of overkill, yet the offender took much care with the property. This suggested to McCrary that the offender had an interest in the condition of the property.

Forensic inconsistencies are apparent when considering the lack of blood found on Dr. Sheppard and the testimony that he did not clean himself at all. According to his testimony, the killer, who would have been covered in blood, touched him after the murder on two occasions. During one of these contacts, the killer took his wrist watch and ring, yet there was absolutely no blood found on Dr. Sheppard beyond a few blood spatters on the watch, later found outside the house. This raised questions not only because the killer would have been covered in blood after such a brutal attack but also because McCrary concluded that the blood spatters on the watch were consistent with impact spatter. This would only have been transferred onto the watch if it was in close proximity to the body of the victim during the attack. Dr. Sheppard also testified that he felt for his wife's pulse, which also means that he should have had a secondary transfer of blood, which then should have been transferred again to the telephone he used to call his neighbors. Dr. Sheppard testified that the killer took his wallet from his trouser pocket, yet there was no blood on his trousers.

The report also argued that this crime would have taken a considerable amount of time to commit. According to McCrary (1999, p. 5), "offenders who spend a great deal of time at a crime scene often have a legitimate reason for being at the scene and therefore are not worried about being interrupted or found at the scene."

This indicated that the offender felt comfortable and familiar at the crime scene. McCrary (1999, p. 8) then goes on to match every aspect of the homicide to the Crime Classification Manual's definition of a staged domestic homicide, before concluding that:

> *The totality of the physical, forensic, and behavioral evidence allows for only one logical conclusion and that is that the homicide of Marilyn Reese Sheppard on July 4, 1954, was a staged domestic homicide committed by Dr. Sheppard. The known indicators for criminal staging as well as the known crime scene indicators consistent with a staged homicide are abundantly present. This evidence not only supports no other logical conclusion, but also significantly contradicts Dr. Samuel Sheppard's testimony and statements.*

After a lengthy voir dire from Dr. Sheppard's attorney, McCrary's evidence was limited only to staging in general and not the Sheppard case, largely because of an affidavit prepared by Turvey (2000). Turvey came to the conclusion that McCrary's evidence should not be admitted for several reasons, including the fact that his determinations were drawn from the definition of staged domestic homicide in the Crime Classification Manual. Although this manual may be considered by some as a useful investigative guide, it is not an adequate base from which to draw conclusions and facts in a court of law. McCrary identified all characteristics of the accused and named the accused as the offender, which violates the ultimate issue rule. McCrary also admitted that he had no experience investigating domestic homicides or blood spatter analysis, rendering those aspects of the evidence outside his area of expertise.

There are also some notable assumptions and inconsistencies in McCrary's report. For example, he stated that Dr. Sheppard testified he was rendered unconscious on the beach but then regained consciousness in the bedroom where the victim was found.

R. v. Klymchuk

Maria Klymchuk was murdered on Easter Sunday, 1998 (unless otherwise stated, all information is taken from R. v. Klymchuk, 2005). The murder occurred in the drive shed located on her property near Bolton, Ontario, where the deceased used to train her dogs. On this particular evening, she had gone out to the shed at approximately 10 PM with one of her dogs. At approximately 11 PM, her husband, Kirk Klymchuk, called 911 reporting that he had found his wife in their driveway with head injuries. He was told to perform cardiopulmonary resuscitation until emergency services arrived. Upon arrival, they were to find Maria Klymchuk dead.

Kirk Klymchuk was interviewed about the matter three times between Easter Sunday and June. In December 1998, he was arrested and charged with his wife's murder.

The Crown's case rested primarily on opportunity, that the accused was home on the night and had access to his wife, and motive, that he was under pressure from his girlfriend, Robin Mays, to leave his wife and children, aged 5 and 2 years.

Mays announced that she was returning to her de facto husband and wanted to end their relationship. Klymchuk called Mays a few days later and stated that his wife agreed to a divorce and that she would announce this to her parents on Good Friday. Klymchuk then called Mays on Friday claiming that there was a delay as his wife was ill. The relationship between Klymchuk and Mays continued after Maria's death, and Mays informed police of their relationship. Telephone conversations between the two were subsequently intercepted. In August 1998, Mays ended their relationship.

It was to become the prosecution's contention that the crime scene was staged, given the appearance that someone had broken into the shed through the window. To assist in this argument, the Crown called Special Agent Allan Brantley of the FBI.

The following is from R. v. Klymchuk (2005):

> *[22] Special Agent Brantley had worked for the FBI for 17 years. He had been trained in and become an expert in what he described as criminal investigation analysis. Agent Brantley testified that criminal investigation analysis is an umbrella designation referring to a number of investigative services offered to police agencies to assist them in their investigations and sometimes offered to the courts as expert evidence. These investigative services included profiling and crime scene analysis. Agent Brantley testified that when performing a crime scene analysis, he was always concerned with whether the scene had been staged or manipulated to create a misleading impression. He defined staging as:*
>
> *The intentional alteration or manipulation of the crime scene by the offender to divert attention away from that individual as a logical suspect and/or to divert attention away from the most logical motive.*
>
> *[23] In response to a long hypothetical, that was rooted in the evidence, Agent Brantley opined that the scene in the drive shed had been staged to make it appear as though there had been a break-in. He emphasized that his opinion was based on the combined consideration of many circumstances and not on any one factor. He testified that there were many "behavioral, forensic, and investigative contradictions" that told him there had not been a real break-in, but rather an attempt to make it appear as though there had been a break-in.*
>
> *[24] The factors referred to by Agent Brantley can be grouped into five categories. First, he opined that the drive shed was a "high-risk" target for a break-in (in the sense that the risk to a burglar of being caught was substantial), and not one likely to be selected by a burglar. This statement of the risk posed to a burglar was based on many considerations, including the ample lighting around the drive shed, the locks on the doors, the alarm system, the presence of dogs in the home, the activity in the area of the home on that evening, the Klymchuks' presence in the home that evening, the close proximity of neighbors, the relative unlikelihood that there would be valuable, easily portable property in the drive shed, and the availability of easier targets in the vicinity.*
>
> *[25] Second, Agent Brantley described Mrs. Klymchuk as at a very low risk to be the victim of crime. She was security conscious, lived in a good neighborhood, and did not engage in any activities, such as drug dealing, that would make it more likely that she would become a victim of crime.*

[26] Third, based on a statistical review of break and enters in the United States and in the 5 years between June 1995 and October 2000 in the area of the Klymchuks' home, Agent Brantley concluded that confrontations between the burglar and the victim were rare, and that in those rare cases where a confrontation occurred, there was seldom any violence directed at the victim. The burglar preferred to flee the scene. Brantley said:

When you consider the incidents where contact is made between a burglar and the resident, when that happens for there to be a confrontation or the offender remains in the area and does not flee immediately, that is very rare. Even more rare is when a confrontation does occur and it turns violent. It is even more rare when that violent confrontation is also murder or homicide.

[27] Brantley testified that his review of the 5 years for which he had statistics of break and enters in the area of the Klymchuk home revealed no other case where a break and enter had resulted in a homicide.

[28] Fourth, Brantley considered the nature of the violence inflicted on Mrs. Klymchuk, the absence of any evidence of sexual assault, or theft from her person, and the indication that the perpetrator had quickly gained control over Mrs. Klymchuk in a confined area as contraindicative of homicide by an unknown intruder.

[29] Fifth, Agent Brantley focused on the window which was the apparent point of entry by the burglar. In Brantley's view, a burglar would not have entered the drive shed through that window. The window was in plain view and there were other, less exposed windows in the drive shed. The cutting of the screen on the window also, according to Agent Brantley, seemed unnecessary to gain entry through the window since the screen could be easily removed. The location of the cut on the screen and the manner in which the cut was made were viewed by Agent Brantley as inconsistent with the screen having been cut by someone who was trying to gain entry through the window. He also noted that the area around the window where the screen had been cut did not show any indications of entry through that window (i.e., fingerprints). Finally, Brantley found it significant that the window had been left open. In his opinion, a burglar would close the window after the burglar gained entry to avoid the risk that the open window could attract someone's attention.

[30] While I will have more to say about parts of this evidence later in these reasons, for the moment I observe that this evidence was all directed at the WHAT question and Brantley's opinion that this was not a break-in, but an attempt to make it appear as though there had been a break-in.

[31] At the end of his examination-in-chief, Brantley gave a series of answers which Mr. Gold contends went beyond the permissible limits of expert evidence of staging. I will quote those questions and answers in full:

Q. Sir, you indicated in this case that one of the factors that you considered as one of the more highlighted ones, and you pointed it out initially, was the apparent maximum human injury or human loss to the minimal property loss, did I understand that as being your evidence?

A. That's correct.

> *Q. What, if any significance, does that have to do from a crime scene analysis point of view?*
>
> *A. It is important in terms of what was the focus of the offender. Was the focus of the offender assault and killing of the victim and was there more time spent accomplishing those acts than any other acts that we assessed at the scene.*
>
> *Certainly we consider what was done to the victim. The numerous forms of trauma and the length of time that that process took. You compare that with the rather minimal movement of that snow blower. Clearly, that the focus in this particular situation was on her and not on that piece of equipment.*
>
> *Q. Is there a name for that sort of focus?*
>
> *A. Well, we would refer to this, because there was no indication of sexual activity or that the sexual parts of the body were traumatized or any semen or sperm or body fluids present and the fact that there was nothing taken from the scene we would describe this or classify this as a "personal cause homicide."*
>
> *Q. And what does a personal cause homicide mean?*
>
> *A. Well, the victim is killed, because of who that victim is, he or she and not necessarily because of what that victim possesses. This generally includes reasons of revenge, anger, elimination of an obstacle to a goal. Those kinds of things are part and parcel to the personal cause homicide.*
>
> *Q. Agent Brantley are you aware of any homicide case that you have been involved with in which staging was found to exist wherein the victim and the offender were strangers?*
>
> *A. I'm aware of none [italics added].*
>
> *[32] The answers quoted above provide Brantley's opinion as to the possible motives for the murder and offer his opinion that there was a prior relationship between Mrs. Klymchuk and her killer. These answers are directed at the WHY and the WHO questions and not the WHAT question. They offer Agent Brantley's opinion that the killer was someone who knew Mrs. Klymchuk and had a personal motive for killing her. That profile of the killer fit the appellant.*

In addressing the expert evidence, the Court applied the decisions of both *R. v. Clark* and *R. v. Ranger* (*Ranger* was discussed previously). From R. v. Klymchuk (2005):

> *[33] In Ranger, the expert was allowed to offer an opinion as to the killer's motive, the existence of a prior relationship between the killer and the victims, and which of the victims was the true target of the killer. This court held that none of that evidence was properly admitted stating at para. 82:*
>
> *Detective Inspector Lines' [the expert] opinions about the perpetrator's likely motivation for staging the crime scene and his characteristics as a person associated with the victims and having a particular interest in Marsha [one of the victims] constituted evidence of criminal profiling. Criminal profiling is a novel field of scientific evidence, the reliability of which was not demonstrated at trial. To the contrary, it would appear from her limited testimony about the available verification of opinions in her field of work that her*

opinions amounted to no more than educated guesses [italics added]. As such, her criminal profiling evidence was inadmissible. The criminal profiling evidence also approached the ultimate issue in the case and, hence, was highly prejudicial.

[34] In Clark, the expert (the same expert who testified in Ranger) was allowed to advance the opinion that the killer knew the victims and was familiar with the residence in which the homicides occurred. In holding that this evidence went beyond the pale of permissible expert evidence of staging, this court said at para. 87:

To the extent that the Detective Inspector's evidence about the phone and the lighting may have conveyed the impression that the offender was someone familiar with the layout of the Tweeds' [the victims] apartment, it was offensive. She was not entitled to testify about the characteristics of the likely offender, characteristics which in this case comfortably fit with the appellant. That constituted criminal profiling evidence [italics added]. As such, for reasons stated earlier, it was inadmissible and should not have been received.

[35] No meaningful distinction can be drawn between Agent Brantley's answers quoted above and the evidence found to be inadmissible in Ranger and Clark. In all three cases, the evidence was offered to identify the killer by reference to the killer's motive and his prior association with the victim(s). In each case, the accused fit the profile of the killer provided by the expert.

[36] There is nothing in the basis of Agent Brantley's opinion that renders it inherently more reliable as expert evidence than the similar opinions rejected in Ranger and Clark. The Crown did not offer any evidence that Agent Brantley's opinions as to the motives and prior connection between the killer and victim of those who stage a break-in in the course of committing a homicide had been or could be tested according to the generally accepted scientific methodology identified in Daubert v. Merrell Dow Pharmaceuticals, Inc. 509 U.S. 579 (1993) and quoted with approval in R. v. J. (J.L.), supra, at 501-502.

[37] Agent Brantley's opinions as to the killer's motive and prior relationship with the victim were not founded on any scientific process of inquiry, but on his own experience as augmented by his review of similar case files and interviews with incarcerated felons. Agent Brantley's experience and review of the other sources led him to conclude that those who staged break-ins as part of a homicide probably had a personal motive for the homicide and probably had a prior association with the victim. Even if those opinions accurately reflect the statistical probabilities that a killer who stages a break-in as part of a homicide has a personal motive for the homicide and a prior relationship with the victim, conclusions based on statistical probabilities can offer no insight as to what happened in a specific case. For example, evidence from a homicide investigator that in his experience, his review of similar cases, and his interviews of killers, 85 percent of spousal homicides (a hypothetical figure) not involving a sexual assault or theft from the victim were committed by the surviving partner, could not be offered as evidence (expert or otherwise) that a specific spousal homicide was committed by the surviving partner. To borrow the words of Charron J.A. in Ranger, Agent Brantley's opinion as to the killer's motive and prior relationship with the deceased were "educated guesses" and not scientifically based opinions. As Charron J.A. indicated, those "educated guesses" can play a valuable role in the

investigation of crime by directing the police to fruitful areas of investigation. They cannot, however, be admitted as evidence under the guise of expert opinion.

[38] The trial judge erred in law in allowing Agent Brantley to give opinion evidence as to the killer's prior relationship with Mrs. Klymchuk and the possible motives for her killing. These errors were compounded by the failure to limit Agent Brantley's opinions as to the WHAT question to evidence based on his examination and reconstruction of the crime scene.

The court took issue with the basis of Agent Brantley's conclusions, specifically citing the probabilistic nature of the opinions and the inherently unreliable nature of discussing average or typical victims and crimes. The following were noted as points of concern:

- There were essentially five factors guiding the conclusion that the crime was staged. These were (1) the drive shed was a high-risk burglary target; (2) the victim was considered a low risk for being the victim of crime; (3) statistics relating to break and enters and the incidence of associated violence; (4) observations of the victim's body and the surrounding areas; and (5) observations of the cut shed window. The first two, it was concluded, are essentially profiling conclusions revolving around whether the victim and the shed were typical targets of a burglary gone wrong. Furthermore, the last two are properly viewed as reconstruction evidence on which an expert could base an assessment of staging.
- There was nothing in Brantley's evidence to suggest that his profile of burglary locations or victims was any more scientific than his profile of those who stage break-ins. The court noted the range of offenders who engage in burglaries, from "drug addled teenagers" to the sophisticated "second story" man. The court further noted that given the differences in offenders, it was their targets that would have much in common.
- Brantley's assessment of the shed as high risk relied on an assumption of the type of offender who would usually commit this type of crime. If the assumption of offender type was removed from the argument, the argument has no validity.
- Brantley's assumption of Maria Klymchuk as a low-risk victim suffered from the same problems as his assumption of the shed being high risk.
- Brantley's assessment required little to no expert knowledge in that the average person could assess the shed as a potential high-risk burglary target (well lit, with dogs in the home, and a burglar alarm).
- The court also noted the problems with applying general information or knowledge to a specific case under consideration: "Statistical evidence of probabilities based on prior similar events, while useful in many disciplines, offers no admissible evidence as to what happened on a specific occasion in a criminal trial."

Given the issues presented by the evidence, the court saw fit to quash the conviction and grant a new trial. In 2008, Klymchuk was convicted of the crime, although it is alleged that questions remain. Makin (2008) reported the following:

A fatigued jury convicted Ontario chiropractor Kirk Klymchuk of second-degree murder yesterday after deliberating for 5 days over whether he had bludgeoned his 27-year-old wife, Maria, to death with an axe on Easter Sunday, 1998.

The verdict ended a legal drama that included three trials—one that resulted in a conviction that was overturned on appeal, one that resulted in a hung jury, and the proceedings that concluded yesterday—over 8 years.

Yesterday's verdict may have reflected a divided jury since the Crown pressed hard for a first-degree conviction on the basis that Mr. Klymchuk stage-managed the crime scene to make it look as if a burglar had killed his wife.

"In my view, this was a miscarriage of justice," defense counsel Tim Breen said shortly after the verdict. "There are many unresolved questions that point to the innocence of my client, and that made this a very suspect case."

Second-degree murder carries a sentence of life imprisonment, with parole eligibility of between 10 and 25 years. Mr. Klymchuk is to be sentenced May 30.

Eight of the jurors made no parole recommendation yesterday. One proposed 10 years, one suggested 12 years, and one recommended 20 years. The 12th juror was discharged for medical reasons early in the deliberations.

The verdict was a particular triumph for prosecutor Eric Taylor and Ontario Provincial Police homicide officers who investigated the case. An acquittal or hung jury would likely have meant the end of Mr. Klymchuk's legal troubles, since it is virtually unheard of for the Crown to attempt to procure a fourth trial.

Should Mr. Klymchuk launch an appeal, it would likely center on defense allegations that investigators failed to convey evidence honestly or falsified it.

In his charge to the jury, Mr. Justice Fletcher Dawson of the Ontario Superior Court specified that were the jury to accept that police dealt with a portion of the evidence dishonestly, the entire investigation could be in doubt.

Ms. Klymchuk, a teacher, was killed in a drive shed behind the couple's suburban home as their children slept nearby. Mr. Klymchuk told police that he went out to check on her before going to bed, and found her bleeding profusely.

In apparent panic, he called 911 and attempted to provide CPR to his blood-drenched wife.

Soon after the killing, police discovered that Mr. Klymchuk had been involved in a torrid, 5-month love affair with Robin Mays, who had moved from Alberta to Brampton to be near him. Just days before Ms. Klymchuk was killed, Ms. Mays had broken off the relationship because Mr. Klymchuk had not left his wife.

Mr. Taylor alleged that the defendant's staging included ripping a window screen in the drive shed, opening the window behind it, and pressing a shoe print onto the window sill.

He said that Mr. Klymchuk also put a snow blower outside the drive shed, as if to suggest that a thief had been in the process of stealing it.

Mr. Breen dismissed the Crown theory as fanciful and full of holes. He said investigators fixed their sights on Mr. Klymchuk almost from the moment he called 911 on the day of his wife's violent death. He also said they paid no attention to hunting down other suspects and even tried to hide evidence that would corroborate Mr. Klymchuk's story of giving the dying woman CPR in an effort to save her life—irrefutable proof of his innocence.

Recommendations

Although it may seem as though this chapter has provided more support for excluding profiling evidence than including it, this was not the aim. In fact, it is our belief that profiling can bring a considerable level of expertise to court proceedings. On this note, and as these recommendations will suggest, we do recommend caution in the way that profiling evidence is applied. If for no other reason, there is nothing more damaging than experts who build their careers as people who speak on demand, doing immeasurable harm to the field in which they are speaking.

The following recommendations are by no means exhaustive but do cover some of the major considerations for experts presenting evidence in court. They are based on the rules of evidence, on legal precedent, and on the past behavior of experts who have given evidence on profiling.

First, although the development of inductive profiles is likely to be more readily understood, and although they may yield results on the odd occasion, it is probable in the long term that they will have a negative impact on the case for profiling in court. Deductive profiling, on the other hand, will be more likely to elicit productive information as long as the profiler explains his or her analysis and conclusions in a clear and concise manner. Furthermore, the profile is a direct extension of the physical evidence, which has been established either by some other expert or by the profiler giving evidence if so qualified. This ensures that the basis of the testimony has also been established and can be accepted by the court.

Second, in line with the expertise rule, it is not unreasonable to expect that experts be just that. Although there are no universal standards for profilers in terms of education, training, and experience, it is imperative that, given the nature of profiling, those providing the service have an adequate level of education and experience in the behavioral sciences, particularly psychology and criminology. As noted by Hans Gross in his seminal work *Criminal Psychology* (1968, p. 1), "Of all disciplines necessary to the criminal justice in addition to the knowledge of law, the most important are those derived from psychology. For such sciences teach him to know the type of man it is his business to deal with."

This should extend beyond coverage of the fundamental principles of psychology (history, application, etc.) and should ideally involve more advanced coursework in this field. Postgraduate study in related areas would ensure that the individual's education is well rounded. This is not to say that the acceptance of an expert rests solely on his or her education, or that this alone should dictate the weight given to an expert's testimony, but it must surely play a considerable role. The general warning given by Kirk (1974, p. 16) is relevant here: "When the liberty of an individual may depend in part on physical evidence it is not unreasonable to ask that the expert witnesses who are called upon to testify, either against the defendant or on his behalf, know what they are doing."

Of utmost importance is the requirement that experts realize the limitations of their own skills. The best expert is not one who continually oversteps the boundaries of his or her trade but one who realizes its limitations and endeavors to operate within these. If something is not discernible from the evidence or the behavior, then one cannot draw conclusions from it. In addition, if something is unknown, experts should refrain from simply filling in the gaps based on what they assume to be the case or what their experience suggests. In the witness box, the expert must not be tempted to stray from the basis on which his or her expertise was deemed to be of assistance to the court: The closer his or her expertise comes to offering an answer to the ultimate issue, the greater the need for constraint.

Next, in accordance with the area of expertise rule, there should be some theoretical basis on which an opinion is formed. For example, a conclusion that an offender rapes elderly women because of a hatred of elderly women formed during his teenage years should be based on more than a "gut feeling" or the simple issue that the victims are elderly. In short, an expert should be able to articulate his or her conclusions and the reasoning behind them. Anyone who cannot articulate an opinion, or provide detailed information on the method used to arrive at one, should be treated with the utmost skepticism and excluded from giving expert testimony.

As discussed by Wiard (1931b, p. 539), caution should be exercised when employing the testimony of experts, with particular care taken to ensure that they adopt the impartiality incumbent upon them as an advisor to the court:

> *If the witness makes statements which are too dogmatic and too general, he thereby lays himself open to more or less successful attack by the opposition and may soon find himself in an unenviable position. The other side should, therefore, note carefully the general complexion of the comments of the witness, in an endeavor to determine whether or not he is making an honest effort to be fair and impartial and offer the benefit of his experience for the general good of the case, or whether he is merely saying certain things, presenting testimony which is colored to suit his employers. Unfortunately, there are so-called expert witnesses who are credited at least, if not actually proven, to be able to take either side of a question and discourse quite learnedly upon it. Such men are usually most dangerous, because they are ordinarily acquainted with the procedure of the courts and can deal in half truths, equivocations, and evasions, to such an extent that it is almost impossible to pin them down to bold misstatements, perjury, or the like.*

The essence of Wiard's cautions should be no different today, and his last concerns are echoed and reinterpreted in a critical discussion by Thornton (1997, pp. 16–17), who notes that occasionally experts may deliberately seek to mislead the court. In Table 11.1, Thornton poses common questions asked of experts, their responses, and the occasionally hidden meanings behind these.[5]

Although it stands to reason that the expert's credentials should be established, regardless of the level of the court, this is not done in all cases. In a bail hearing at the Coroner's Court level, a "behavioral consultant" testified as to the continued danger posed by the applicant. As noted by Crispin J:

[5]Although most experts testify openly and honestly, there can be no doubt that the expertise offered in some instances is questionable, in either its integrity or its purpose.

Table 11.1 Questions by Lawyers with Expert Responses

Question	Answer	Translation
Is this situation unusual?	I have never seen a similar situation.	You don't know what I have seen and what I haven't, so I can say this and get away with it.
What is the basis of your opinion?	My 26 years of experience in the field.	It's really a surmise on my part. I believe it to be true, but I can't really tell you why I think that. It's more of an impression that I have than anything else but I can't say that it's a surmise or a vague impression, could I?
Can you tell us how many cases of this type you have examined?	Many hundreds.	I don't know, and I certainly don't know how many of them would support my current position, and I might not be able to tell even if I went back and pulled the files.
Can you supply us with a list of those cases?	Oh, no, I don't think so. They go back many years.	No way. You don't have any way of smoking those cases out of me, and even if I was ordered to do so, I could come up with plenty of reasons not to comply.
Can you supply us with the raw data on all those cases?	I don't think so. Some of them were when I was employed in my previous job. And some could be on microfilm. And it would take weeks or months to locate all of them.	Not a chance.
Were those cases subjected to independent scrutiny for technical correctness?	All of them were reviewed by my supervisors. I don't have any reason to believe that their review wasn't adequate.	No. And also, now you are going to have to argue with those nameless, faceless supervisors that I have alluded to but haven't identified.

I have no doubt that he gave his opinion honestly but, in my opinion, he was plainly not qualified to express the opinions that he did ... The bulk of this evidence was clearly inadmissible and whilst no objection was taken to it ... I was obliged to conclude that it could be given no real weight.

As a result, some experts are allowed to offer their opinions in a relatively unfettered manner, occasionally doing incalculable damage to the defendant or his or her case.

Even in cases in which the guilt of the accused may not be an issue, the role of the expert in the initial trial may be such that it provides the defense with grounds for appeal at a later date, whereas if not for the expert giving his or her own tainted view of events, the trial would have proceeded within legal constraints, ultimately seeing justice best served. The outcome here may be to see guilty defendants walk free on technicalities raised at appeal. This is also clearly not desirable.

As a final point and observation of those legal professionals who employ consultants to provide an exam of their case, it is similarly not unreasonable to expect they be at least conversant in the language of the area the expert will testify in, and that they possess some working knowledge of how the testimony may relate to or affect their case. Again, Wiard (1931b, p. 540) provides some poignant commentary:

> *It is almost hopeless for a lawyer lacking a scientific education to oppose technical testimony by apparently searching interrogations upon the minutiae of the matters involved. Needless to say, both counsels may be in the same boat in this respect, as was evinced in a recent case in which the writer appeared. This was in connection with a shooting, and the counsel employing the expert witness believed, and practically so stated in court, that all bullets were flaming as they passed through the air. The opposing counsel, on the other hand, believed that automatic pistols were loaded in a manner similar to that employed for the muzzle loading cap-and-ball arms which went out of existence at the end of the Civil War days. One can well imagine that under these conditions the witness, although amused at the continual misstatements of facts, was not in a very enviable position, for most of the questions propounded by both attorneys were based on utter misconceptions of the facts, so that he was in the position of having to disagree with practically everyone concerned.*

Conclusion

Some jurisdictions in the United States have been more receptive in their adoption of profiling than others, whereas Australian and English courts have been more reluctant. The rules of expert evidence in Australia allow for profiling as expert testimony, even if only in a limited manner, perhaps in some lower levels of the criminal justice system. As profiling receives more attention through practical application and academic literature, it stands to reason that it will receive a greater chance of being accepted in court.

It is unlikely that any acceptance will come in a flood, but legal commentators of recent times also scoffed at the acceptance of other forms of evidence that are now commonplace in the courtroom. Providing that courts are suitably judicious in their use of this evidence, and that they ensure that experts are just that, profiling may help clarify behavioral evidence for a judge and jury in the same way that experts have begun clarifying other technical areas such as DNA probabilities.

Questions

1. What is perhaps the most beneficial evidence that profiling offers to criminal proceedings?
   a. Motive and intent to commit the criminal act
   b. Offender state of mind before, during, and after the commission of a crime
   c. Offender modus operandi
   d. Signature analysis and case linkage
   e. Offender residential status

2. List and briefly discuss the areas in which profiling may be used in court.
3. Courts in Australia and the United Kingdom have been very open and receptive to profiling evidence. *True or false?*
4. The rules of expert evidence presented in the chapter are unique to Australia and not utilized in other countries. *True or false?*
5. Gross argued that of all the disciplines necessary to criminal justice, in addition to the law, the most important is psychology. *True or false?*

References

Alison, L., & Canter, D. (1999). Professional, legal and ethical issues in offender profiling. In D. Canter & L. Alison (Eds.), *Profiling in policy and practice.* Aldershot, UK: Ashgate Dartmouth.

Australian Law Reform Commission. (1994). Compliance with the Trade Practices Act 1974: Issues related to court procedure. Available at <http://www.austlii.edu.au> Accessed 12.11.04.

Bartol, C. R. (2002). *Criminal behavior: A psychosocial approach* (6th ed.). Upper Saddle River, NJ: Prentice Hall.

Bartol, C. R., & Bartol, A. M. (1994). *Psychology and law: Research and practice* (2nd ed.). Pacific Grove, CA: Brooks/Cole.

Bekerian, D. A., & Jackson, J. L. (1997). Critical issues in offender profiling. In J. L. Jackson & D. A. Bekerian (Eds.), *Offender profiling: Theory, research and practice.* Chichester, UK: Wiley.

Daubert v. (1993). Merrell Dow Pharmaceuticals, Inc 113 S. Ct. 2786.

Davis, D., & Follette, W. C. (2002). Rethinking the probative value of evidence: Base rates, intuitive profiling, and the "postdiction" of behavior. *Law and Human Behavior, 26*(2), 133–158.

Douglas, J. E., & Munn, C. (1992). Violent crime scene staging: Modus operandi, signature and staging. *FBI Law Enforcement Bulletin, February.*

Douglas, J. E., Ressler, R. K., Burgess, A. W., & Hartman, C. R. (1986). Criminal profiling from crime scene analysis. *Behavioral Sciences and the Law, 4*(4), 410–421.

Field, D. (2008). *Queensland evidence law.* Sydney: Butterworth/NexisLexis.

Findlay, M., Odgers, S., & Yeo, S. (1999). *Australian Criminal Justice* (2nd ed.). Melbourne: Oxford University Press.

Folkes. v (1782). Chadd 3 Doug K. B. 157.

Freckleton, I. R. (1987). *The trial of the expert: A study of expert evidence and forensic experts.* Melbourne: Oxford University Press.

Freckleton, I. R. (1994). When plight makes right: Forensic abuse syndrome. *Criminal Law Journal, 18*(1), 29–49.

Freckleton, I. R., & Selby, H. (1999a). *Australian judicial attitudes toward expert evidence.* Melbourne: Australasian Institute of Judicial Administration.

Freckleton, I. R., & Selby, H. (1999b). *The law of expert evidence.* Pyrmont, Australia: LBC Information Services.

Freckleton, I. R., & Selby, H. (2002a). *The law of expert evidence.* Pyrmont, Australia: Law Book Company.

Freckleton, I. R., & Selby, H. (2002b). *Expert evidence: Law, practice, procedure and advocacy.* Pyrmont, Australia: Law Book Company.

Frye v. United States (1923). Frye v. United States 293 Fed. 1013 1923.

Geberth, V. J. (1996). Practical homicide investigation: Tactics: *Procedures and forensic techniques* (3rd ed.). Boca Raton, FL: CRC Press.

Gross, H. (1924). *Criminal Investigation* (3rd ed.). London: Sweet & Maxwell.

Gross, H. (1968). *Criminal psychology: A manual for judges, practitioners and students.* Montclair, NJ: Patterson Smith.

Hazelwood, R. R., Ressler, R. R., Depue, R. L., & Douglas, J. E. (1999). Criminal investigative analysis: An overview. In R. R. Hazelwood & A. W. Burgess (Eds.), *Practical aspects of rape investigation: A multidisciplinary approach.* Boca Raton, FL: CRC Press.

Kennedy, D. (2008). Hope for prisoner as expert recants on wife's suicide letter. *The Times, February,* 25.

Kirk, P. (1974). *Crime investigation* (2nd ed.). New York: Wiley.

Makin, K. (2008). Man's 3rd murder trial ends with verdict of guilty. *Globe and Mail, May 17.*

McCord, E. (1987). Syndromes, profiles and other mental exotica: A new approach to the admissibility of nontraditional psychological evidence in criminal cases. *Oregon Law Review, 66,* 19–108.

McCrary, G. (1999). Criminal investigative analysis. The Estate of Samuel Sheppard v. The State of Ohio. Available at <http://www.courttv.com> Accessed 22.11.04.

McNicol, S. B., & Mortimer, D. (1996). *Evidence.* Chatswood, UK: Butterworth.

Melton, G. B., Petrila, J., Poythress, N. G., & Slobogin, C. (1997). *Psychological evaluations for the court: A handbook for the mental health professionals and lawyers* (2nd ed.). New York: Guilford.

Moenssens, A. A., Inbau, F. E., & Starrs, J. E. (1986). *Scientific evidence in criminal cases* (3rd ed.). New York: Foundation Press.

New Jersey v. Fortin. (2000). New Jersey v. Fortin 162 N.J. 517, 745 A.2d 509 2000.

Ormerod, D. (1996). The evidential implications of psychological profiling. *Criminal Law Review, 717,* 863–877.

Petherick, W. (2000). Criminal profiling in the Australia legal system. Paper presented at the Academy of Behavioral Profiling General Meeting. Las Vegas, Nevada, October 6-8.

Petherick, W. A. (2003). Criminal profiling: What's in a name? Comparing applied profiling methodologies. *Journal of Law and Social Challenges, 5,* 173–188.

Phillips v. R. (2006). 225 CLR 303 at 483.

Pinizzotto, A. J., & Finkel, N. (1990). Criminal personality profiling: An outcome and process study. *Law and Human Behavior, 14,* 215–233.

PQ v. (1992) Australian Red Cross Society 1 VR 19.

R. v. Gilfoyle 2 (2001). Cr. App. Rep. 57.

R. v. Klymchuk (2005). 203 C.C.C. (3d) 341, 205 O.A.C. 57.

R. v. Mohan 2 (1994). SCR 9, 89 C.C.C. (3d) 402.

R. v. Ranger (2003).178 C.C.C. (3d) 375 (Ont. CA).

R. v. Ryan (2002) VSCA 176.

R. v. Turner (1975). QB 834.

Report of the Kaufman Commission on proceedings involving Guy Paul Morin. (2003). Toronto: Queen's Printer for Ontario. Available at <http://www.attorneygeneral.jus.gov.on.ca/english/about/pubs/morin> Accessed 20.06.05.

Rudin, K., & Inman, N. (2002). *An Introduction to Forensic DNA Analysis* (2nd ed.). Boca Raton, FL: CRC Press.

Saferstein, R. (2004). *Criminalistics: An introduction to forensic science* (8th ed.). Upper Saddle River, NJ: Prentice Hall.

Thornton, J. I. (1997). The general assumptions and rationale of forensic identification. In D. L. Faigman, D. H. Kaye, M. J. Saks, & J. Sanders (Eds.), *Modern scientific evidence: The law and science of expert evidence.* St. Paul, MN: West Publishing.

Turvey, B. E. (2000). Criminal profiling and the problem of forensic individuation. *Journal of Behavioral Profiling, 1*(2), 1–15. Available at <http://www.profiling.org>.

Underwager, R., & Wakefield, H. (1993). A paradigm shift for expert witnesses. *Institute for Psychological Therapies Journal, 5,* 1–18. Available at <http://www.ipt-forensics.com/journal/volume5/j5_3_2.htm> Accessed 21.10.04.

Wiard, S (1931a). The preparation and presentation of expert testimony. *American Journal of Police Science, 2,* 143–147.

Wiard, S (1931b). The cross examination of expert witnesses. *American Journal of Police Science, 2,* 538–542.

Wood, J. (2003). Forensic sciences from the judicial perspective. *Australian Journal of Forensic Sciences, 35*(1), 115–132.

Wrightsman, L. S., Greene, E., Nietzel, T. M., & Fortune, W. H. (2002). *Psychology in the Legal System* (5th ed.). Belmont, CA: Wadsworth.

12

Where to From Here?

Wayne Petherick and Nathan Brooks

Introduction

The history of profiling is easy to trace—after all, it has already been recorded and is available for review (see Chapter 1 by Norris; Petherick, 2003). The future of profiling is another story entirely. Given the nature of the craft and the advances made in recent years, it stands to reason that only further improvements will be made. At least, this should be our hope.

An increase in use at the coal-face is matched by a rise in the number of scholarly works dedicated to the field. Most provide a general overview of profiling (Jackson & Bekerian, 1997; Ainsworth, 2001) with others providing a more in-depth examination of particular methods or issues (Rossmo, 2000). Apart from a few peripheral discussions on practical issues, few dedicate much time to the more pragmatic issues of professionalization, the scientific method, research, ethics, accountability, and education and training.

However, none of these issues should be considered in isolation, and the inter-reliance among many of these topics often makes separate discussion difficult. For example, one could not argue for ethical standards without professionalization, and one cannot argue for professionalization without having standards for education and training. So while the following is composed of a number of separate discussions, they are less discrete domains than their disaggregation would suggest.

This chapter will provide an overview of these areas, specifically as they relate to where profiling is going in the future, and how we might get there. On this issue, Bekerian and

Profiling and Serial Crime.

Jackson (1997, p. 209) provide a decent overview that looks at the future of profiling, where they note that:

> *All profiling techniques focus on behavior; and there is a good deal of diversity in the techniques that are employed. Variation in an area of research is important for scientific progress. However, too much diversity can result in the field becoming fragmented theoretically, and therefore less accessible to application. There are at least three ways in which fragmentation might occur in the area of offender profiling: differences in frameworks, individual differences between profilers, and differences in culture.*

Differences in frameworks, they explain, refers to the debate over the appropriate methodological framework. Perhaps nowhere is this more profound in profiling than the debate between those who adhere to a deductive model and those who would prefer an inductive model. Despite being one of the most fundamental ways that profiling approaches differ, there has perhaps been too much focus on this aspect alone, clouding the issue of logic's role within the profiling process (logic is defined as the science of valid thought; see Bhattacharyya, 1958; see also Chapters 2, 3, 4, and 5 of this work, and as discussed later in this chapter). These differences will not be easily overcome in the immediate future.

Further fragmentation is created when profilers vehemently pronounce the utility of their own method, while at the same time denouncing that of their counterparts. This is not in itself a problem, but when practitioners do not understand the shortcomings of the methods they employ, this does suggest a fundamental and systematic flaw in practice. It is one thing to provide assistance in an investigation and acknowledge the limitations of the methodology; however, it is an ethical and professional violation if the profiler partakes in an investigation and fails to do so.

The purpose of any profile is to assist in the investigation and apprehension of the offender. Unfortunately the discipline has become removed from this purpose and instead profiles appear to be based on the profiler's personal needs, status, connection to sources, and ability to promote their methodology as infallible. Although healthy competition fosters progress, it also affects overall harmony in the community. This infighting may be seen by potential consumers as evidence of profiling's lack of worth, and in some instances, they wouldn't be too far afield.

Individual differences between profilers suggests that no two profilers will produce the same profile where a standard methodology is not used (this is possible, even likely). This is because of differing levels of education, training, and experience, and each brings something different to the table. Whereas one profiler may have keen insight into what motivates a particular offender, another may have similarly keen insight into precautionary acts and staging. In essence, a profile will be the result of a person's experiences, or as Bekerian and Jackson (1997, p. 211) put it, "the act of profiling is personal." In every discipline or field, human variability is likely to have a substantial influence on a given outcome; this is no more so than in criminal investigations. As there are no well-established or universal principles that apply to all crimes or criminals (Canter & Youngs, 2009), human variability will continue to influence offender profiles. Therefore, it is of the utmost importance that a structured and universal methodology is employed by the profiler, particularly with regard to characteristics stated in the profile and the extent to which they apply to the investigation. Until a standardized structured methodology is employed, the discipline will continue to receive and be exposed to criticism, human error, and unreliable work product.

With regard to differences in culture, it is noted that although contemporary approaches to profiling started in the United States, it must be questioned whether and how these differences can be juxtaposed into other cultural and religious groups. The authors note that the differences in offending between countries are distinct in many areas, and this is well documented in the criminological literature (for example, the homicide rate between the United States and Australia, weapon availability, victimological differences). Caution should be exercised when using a statistical model in which research is applied in a culture other than where it was developed (see Canter, 2004 for a discussion of one particular method), and as provided in Alison (2005, p. 251) in a specific analysis, "the report is based on research and investigations conducted in the United Kingdom, Canada, and the United States. Caution must therefore be exercised in interpreting the extent to which these figures transfer to Eastern European cases."

Another such example among many includes (The Medicolegal Society of NSW, undated):

> *The particular problem with some statistical methodologies is that they are also often built around a localized database and localized demographic situations, and it is very difficult to transfer this information from one group or one country to another. In the past we have had experiences where FBI profilers have come up with the view that the perpetrator of a New South Wales crime was a 26 year old black American negro on the basis of the statistical analysis they have done, which is not very likely.*

At the very least, it is incumbent that the analyst check whether the crime statistics they are using even apply in the area in which they are being used. This will ensure that statistical generalizations are valid and relevant, or that there is "ecological validity" in statistical terms.

Professionalization

One way to improve upon profiling is to increase professionalization among those who perform it. This would involve establishing standards of practice and accountability. To provide context for any future approach at professionalization, we must look at what has been done in the past as a guide to how things should be done from this point on.

Given the multiplicity of profiling approaches and the fragmented and often ad hoc approach to profiling that many take, it is unreasonable to suggest that all protagonists settle their differences, form one professional organization, and develop a unified theory of criminal profiling. Although much of the theory and practice involved in criminal profiling is consistent across methods, as are its goals, subtle differences make unification difficult if not impossible. This may, on its face, seem advantageous; however, the differences in individual approaches are beneficial and will help to elevate standards (as discussed by Bekerian & Jackson, 1997, earlier). However, we must not let these differences prevent any further advance in the community, or the very thing that could advance the community may well stop it in its tracks.

Professionalization is one of the greatest obstacles to profiling's advance, and in this domain education and training play a significant role. Essentially anyone can call him- or herself a criminal profiler, regardless of education, training, and experience. This leads to a lack of uniformity in training and education standards, which subsequently affects the work product of those in the community (which may in turn taint the perception of profiling within the investigative communities they serve and the academic communities who research them). For profiling to become recognized as a professional discipline, a code of ethical standards and guidelines that profilers act under and according to must develop. It may be a long time before a universal ethical code is set for the field; however, for the survival of the discipline, ethical standards are the first consideration that must be addressed for professionalization.

Another area that has often resulted in diverse and often unreliable offender profiles is the lack of consensus between those in the field. It is recognized that profilers may often be police officers, criminologists, psychologists, or others with a law enforcement history or involvement. The biggest limitation of this diversity is the lack of communication and professional peer guidance that has likely hampered the industry thus far. For many years peer supervision and case meetings have been a required professional standard set by psychologists and those in the mental health field, a process that allows clinicians to be guided and assisted by a fellow practitioners' expertise, and to offer the same skills to others (Fisher, 2009). Supervision provides a formal format that places expectations on the practicing clinician to abide by professional practice standards. Therefore, for profiling to move from a discipline that has been clouded by misconduct and poor offender profiles, supervision between practitioners in the field must become a mandated requirement.

An example of an attempt at professionalization can be found in the United Kingdom, where a register of profilers is kept with the National Crime Faculty as part of the Association of Chief Police Officers. Part of their function is to act as a regulatory agency for criminal profilers, which is a commendable endeavor and goes a long way toward providing a common standard by which to ensure a profiler's skills. Either a person meets these requirements and can offer a profile, or they do not, and therefore cannot. Although this demands certain standards, it is still a considerable way from a professional organization that serves not only to set such requirements but also to further the field through continued training, education, dissemination of information, and sanctions for those who violate ethical precepts.

The Scientific Method

There can be no doubt that the scientific method should be the cornerstone of any inquiry made, but this is sadly not always the case. Some may even argue that because criminal profiling is not a science, that the scientific method simply does not apply. Given that one can apply the scientific method to many forms of inquiry, and one need not be a scientist to apply the scientific method, this argument does not stand up to scrutiny.

According to Allen (2004):

> *The scientific method is a set of procedures designed to establish general laws through developing and evaluating theories that attempt to describe, explain, and predict phenomena. Hypotheses are made from such theories; the hypotheses are evaluated using objective, controlled, empirical investigations; and conclusions are open to public scrutiny, analysis, and replication.*

Inman and Rudin (2001) agree, stating that the scientific method provides a framework for hypothesis testing, whereby a theory is formulated and measured against the evidence, with the ultimate goal being to falsify the standing hypothesis. Without relying on a process of falsification, one cannot be sure that one's conclusions are sound, or that one conclusion is more likely than any other. As such, it is necessary to falsify all theories regarding offender behavior. Only in this way can we be certain that our conclusions are reflective of the available evidence, and not some *a priori* bias. If the process is repeatedly applied, conclusions should be complete, well informed, and able to stand up to a great deal of scrutiny. Before one can determine a set of hypotheses to test though, premises and formulations must be derived from logical decision making. Any decision related to a profile must be based on a set of heuristic logical principles (McInnerney, 2004). These logical assumptions may not need to prove anything, but rather require the absence of a counter argument or example (Beall, 2010). This may be viewed in terms of logical consequences; an effect or outcome that results in specific implications from attempting to derive a logical assumption.

The scientific method provides a stepwise process that allows us to investigate a particular relationship, and to solve a problem by investigating cause-and-effect connections. This process can be represented graphically, as shown in Figure 12.1.

In some instances, failing to falsify the hypothesis could be owing to an error in the initial data collection. In these cases, we need to return to our original data and ensure that (1) we have collected it properly; (2) that we have collected all the available data; and (3) that it means what we think it means. In other instances, there may be more than one hypothesis or theory that supports the data, which we have initially failed to consider. In these cases, we need to revise our hypotheses to ensure that they adequately capture the complexity of the data held.

However, just because we make meager attempts to falsify our theories it does not mean that the scientific method is being employed. For example, one theory in a profile may be that the victim was high risk, so we should look for evidence that disproves this, such as safety and security procedures taken by the victim or that they have a cautious personality. In the absence of such signs, this theory seems more likely, but this still does not mean it is necessarily correct. We must also develop other theories and try to disprove these by measuring them against the evidence also. At the end of the process, if all theories are tested rigorously and the theory remains that the victim was high risk, then this hypothesis is most likely correct and

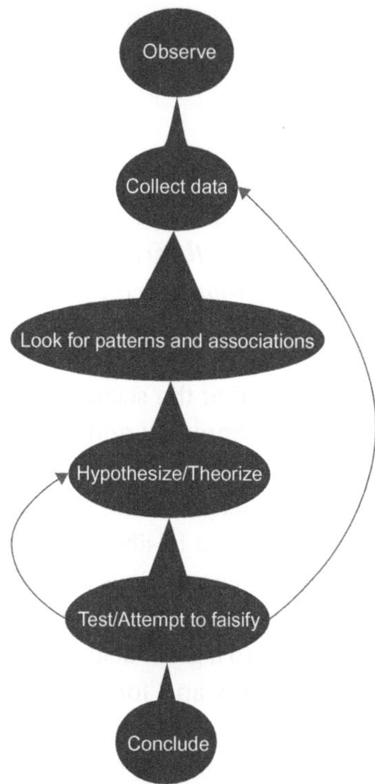

FIGURE 12.1 Steps in investigating a particular relationship using the scientific method.

could be posited with a high degree of confidence. In short, to provide support for a theory, a vigorous attempt must be made to disprove it.

Research

One of the ways to improve a product such as profiling is to conduct research into its effectiveness and the features that have been helpful or detrimental. More research on profiling and the ways it can assist police in their inquiries is also definitely warranted.

Having said that, it should be noted that there are a lot of problems in researching a field such as profiling, and these are outlined in detail elsewhere (see Ainsworth, 2001; Petherick, 2003). Some of the research to date has been somewhat repetitive, unhelpful, or confusing. Perhaps the most common form of research stems from questions about how accurate profilers are (see Gudjonsson & Copson, 1997; Pinizzotto, 1984; Pinizzotto & Finkel, 1990), with the latest variation aimed at determining how accurate profilers are compared to other groups (see Kocsis, Irwin, Hayes & Nunn, 2000; Kocsis, 2001, 2003; Kocsis, Hayes & Irwin, 2002).

Although it may be useful to examine the differences between such groups, what is more instructive is to examine the abilities of practitioners from the different approaches, and for this reason, the research presented in Chapter 4 was conducted. This clarifies a lot of the current confusion about the differences between the methods, such as how a case is approached and how insight is developed through the application of each main paradigm.

As stated, any research on profiling carries with it many potential problems. First of all, laboratory settings lack the same pressures as operational police environments, and the ability to include new tips, leads, and pieces of evidence may not be easy to replicate. Similarly, the dynamics created by the involvement of the media, victims, families and friends of the victim/s, and other contributors are nearly impossible to introduce in a controlled environment in a meaningful way.

When carrying out this research, there are methodological concerns also, such as whether to employ an open-ended approach in which profilers provide all of their opinions based on the supplied information or simply ticking a box corresponding to a predefined template of answers. The first scenario would provide detailed information but may present problems in tabulating the data. In the second scenario, some advice that would otherwise be useful may not be accommodated, because it would fall outside the limits of the study parameters. This would restrict the flow of information and data available on which to base an assessment. Also, a template approach, though trying to capture the essence of profiling, may ask unrealistic questions about the offender, such as the offender's religion or height, which may play no role in related offense behavior or when inferring offender characteristics.

Research conducted into the content and processes involved in profiling (Petherick, 2007) showed a significant number of shortcomings in terms of explaining the reasoning behind the conclusions in the profile, as well as in the background documentation regarding its construction. As an example, the background to the extant case was provided less than half of the time, definitions for any terms used occurred slightly less than one third of the time, and most profiling methods gave little information regarding the documents examined or specific analysis of the evidence. What's more, few of the profiles provided any basis for the conclusions provided. With BEA profiles, 89% of the characteristics in the profiles used physical evidence as justification; CIA profiles offered no justification at all 65.7% of the time; IP profiles, despite their research backdrop, used statistics as justification only 27% of the time; and Diagnostic Evaluations used statistics 60% of the time and personal belief 25% of the time.

A similar research project (Almond, Alison & Porter, 2007) examined the reports of Behavioral Investigative Advisors in the United Kingdom. In short, the study found that, of the sample of 47 reports, there were 805 claims with 96% containing grounds for the claim, though only 34% had any formal support. Further, while 70% were verifiable, only 43% were falsifiable in terms of objective measurement post-conviction. Both pieces of research have illustrated the vast variability in both gross profiling approaches and within and between individual reports.

This research is of vital importance in understanding how profiles are constructed and argued, but it is by no means the final word. More research into these areas needs to be done in order to best understand what each method has to offer and how one particular approach may assist in case resolution. Further development of this understanding will lead to more informed decisions among consumers as to which method may best answer questions about cases in which they seek a profiler's advice.

Ethics

Owing to the fact that profilers come from a variety of backgrounds, one of the areas in which there is definite room for improvement is in the development of ethical standards. Although profiling in its most modern form was developed by those in the medical and mental health professions, and although many of its protagonists are still a part of that fraternity, it is often a practice undertaken by them (and others) outside of their normal duties. In other words, there are few full-time criminal profilers. As a result, some may argue that the ethical guidelines of a practitioner's professional organization do not apply to any work undertaken as a profiler. This is problematic because it may tempt the practitioner to step outside of acceptable boundaries and engage in practices that would otherwise be unacceptable in other areas of their profession.

Ethical behavior is the fundamental obligation to do good, to not harm, to respect others, and to treat all honestly and fairly (Fisher, 2009). Adopting an ethical and moral approach is not only imperative for fundamental personal values but also professional practice. Every profession, regardless of the occupation, requires ethical conduct whether for well being, safety, or legal purposes. The importance of ethics to profiling is profound, particularly when considering the moral judgment and moral behavior of profilers.

Profilers have an enormous responsibility to the community, the organization that they are employed by (generally law enforcement), and often the accused offender. Therefore, any decision or behavior by the profiler must be performed with careful consideration that weighs up the alternatives and the consequences of reaching an outcome. The profiler has an ethical obligation to all parties and anything that does not take into consideration the best interest of these parties poses a risk of placing the profiler in an ethical and moral violation. In the end, it is the profiler's own moral and ethical adherence that will lead to the correct decisions; profilers can be pertinent to as much resources and guidelines as desirable, but ultimately the choice rests with them (Lazarus, 1994).

Ethics are not often at the forefront of individual practice, that is, they do not always guide what an individual does and how he or she does it. Instead, they come into play once an individual has done something wrong and must attempt to mitigate it. Rarely are ethics seen for what they are: a set of rules that dictate appropriate (usually professional) conduct. A profiling approach itself cannot be unethical, nor can conclusions, but the behavior of the individual using the approach or drawing the conclusion most certainly can be (Wilson, Lincoln & Kocsis, 1997). Dempsey (1996, p. 17) highlights the importance of the behavioral component of this definition, which states that "ethics can be defined as the practical normative study of the rightness and wrongness of human conduct." This requirement that ethics be restricted solely to human conduct also constitutes one of the four elements of ethics proposed by Pollock (2007, p. 11–12):

Act: There must be some act to judge.

Only human acts: Ethics are directed specifically at human acts; the acts of lower order animals cannot be considered unethical.

> *Free will: Only behavior stemming from free will and free action can be judged unethical; behavior of individuals that is done under threat is not unethical.*
>
> *Effects on others: Unethical behavior must have some significant effect on other people.*

Sadly, such rules or standards have been absent from the field of profiling for too long, and the behavior of many practitioners within the field has been deplorable because of it. Too often, unethical practitioners will fall back on this lack of standards as an excuse for their misconduct. In addition, some may simply argue that profiling is an inexact tool, nothing more than educated guesswork. So long as this is the prevailing attitude we can expect little in terms of advancement.

This behavior should not be tolerated, nor does it have to be.

One recent and notable example of this is of Richard Walter, a prison therapist who perjured himself while testifying in the trial of Robie J. Drake for two counts of second-degree murder. The facts of the case are as follows (from *Drake v. Purtuondo*, 2003):

> *In 1982, Drake was convicted by a jury in New York State Supreme Court, Niagara County, on two counts of second degree murder for the shooting of a young couple in a parked car in an isolated area near a junkyard. The defense theory was that Drake often used abandoned cars for target practice, that he shot up the victim's car without realizing it was occupied, and afterward in panic stabbed the young man (who was dying), and drove the car to a nearby dump. To aid the prosecution of a crime that was seemingly without motive, the prosecutor at the last minute called to the witness stand a putative expert who testified about a particular syndrome of sexual dysfunction that appeared to account for the particular, gruesome circumstances of the crime.*

The Daily Record (2003) also included the following facts:

> *He fired 19 rounds of ammunition from the semi-automatic rifle. The petitioner claimed he did not intend to kill the victims and only found out they were in the car when he heard a groan from the car. He opened the car door and discovered the two bodies … he then stabbed Rosenthal in a fit of panic because he thought Rosenthal was still alive. The petitioner then drove the car to a secluded spot down the road from the parking lot and he was discovered by two police officers on routine patrol.*

The prosecution conceded that the expert testimony was designed to plug a large hole in their case, namely the issue of intent. The defense was given one weekend to find a psychologist to rebut the prosecution's expert, though they informed the trial judge that try as they might, they were unable to find an expert who had heard of piquerism (a psychological condition ascribed to the accused in which one receives sexual stimulation from cutting, stabbing, slashing, or shooting). Given the time frame and the time of the week, this was probably not unreasonable.

In outlining his qualifications, it was stated of the expert, Mr. Richard Walter, that (Daily Record, 2003)[1]:

> *He had extensive experience in the field of psychological profiling. This included working on 5,000 to 7,500[2] cases over a number of years in the Los Angeles County Medical Examiner's Office; an adjunct professorship at Northern Michigan University and four years as a prison psychologist with the Michigan Department of Corrections. He also stated that he had given expert testimony in hundreds of criminal trials in Los Angeles and Michigan.*

This case has been revisited a number of times, and it was noted by Ewing (2003, p. 84) that:

> *Drake repeatedly appealed the decision, but his conviction was routinely affirmed. He claimed that the psychologist who testified against him had misrepresented his credentials. The Appellate Division of New York's Supreme Court ultimately rejected Drake's appeal, finding that while the expert's credibility might have been adversely affected had the jurors known the truth about his credentials, no legal relief was warranted because nothing indicated that the prosecution was aware that he was misrepresenting his credentials.*
>
> *Acting as his own attorney, Drake next took his appeal to the federal courts. In 2000, the U.S. District Court agreed with the state courts, holding that "There is no reasonable probability that the verdict would have been different had the evidence [of the expert's misrepresentations] been available to [Drake] and used by him to impeach the expert" (Drake v. Portuondo, 2000 U.S. Dist. LEXIS 20296).*
>
> *Not until earlier this year did Drake finally convince a court that the psychologist's misrepresentations might require a new trial (see Drake v. Portuondo, 321 F.3d 338 [2003]). The U.S. Circuit Court of Appeals for the Second District took issue with the purportedly expert testimony, stating that "It is now clear that the expert's qualifications were largely perjured, and that the syndrome, dubbed 'piquerism' is referenced nowhere but in a true-crime paperback."*
>
> *As the court explained: "As the prosecution now concedes, [he] performed no criminal profiling in the Los Angeles County Medical Examiner's Office. According to [his] supervisors there, he was employed as a lab assistant responsible for cleaning and maintaining the forensic lab. There seems to be no record that [he] was ever on the payroll of Northern Michigan University, where he claimed to be an adjunct professor. The Los Angeles County District Attorney's office has found no record of [him] testifying as an expert witness in a criminal proceeding…"*

Specific ethical standards may be difficult to develop as they may apply more (or only) to the organization through which they were developed. As a result, a general code of ethics may

[1] This information has been verified with the trial transcript and is an accurate reflection of the testimony given.

[2] Even using a conservative estimate of 5000 cases during 4½ years, this equates to about 3.04 cases profiled each and every day for the full 4½ year period. This is clearly an unrealistic estimate.

best suit the area. Borrowed initially from Thornton (1997), Petherick and Ferguson (2010, p. 257) provide the following code of ethics for forensic criminologists, modified slightly for use herein to apply to profilers and other types of crime analysts (italics added):

- As a practicing *crime analyst/profiler*, I pledge to apply the principles of science and logic and to follow the truth courageously wherever it may lead.
- As a practicing *crime analyst/profiler*, I acknowledge that the scientific spirit must be inquiring, progressive, logical, and unbiased.
- I will never knowingly allow a false impression to be planted in the mind of anyone availing themselves of my services.
- As a practicing *crime analyst/profiler*, it is not my purpose to present only that evidence which supports the view of one side. I have a moral and professional responsibility to ensure that everyone concerned understands the evidence as it exists and to present it in an impartial manner.
- The practice of *crime analyst/profiler* has a single demand—correctness. It has a single ethical demand—truthfulness. To these I commit myself, totally and irrevocably.
- The exigencies of a particular case will not cause me to depart from the professionalism that I am required to exercise.

To hold only those few wrongdoers responsible for the lack of standards in the field as a whole is also irresponsible. In fields such as profiling, people often chose to do wrong because we as a community or profession allow it. If the tolerance for such behavior declines, so too should the misfeasance. Inman and Rudin (2001) have noted that peer pressure may be the most effective method of ensuring ethical conduct. They also suggest that for peer pressure to work, protagonists must be willing to challenge each other. These authors couldn't agree more.

Accountability

Inherent within any discussion of ethics is the notion of accountability. Although related, it is of sufficient importance to warrant its own discussion. One can be held accountable for one's conclusions, regardless of ethics, just as one can behave ethically but still fail to be held accountable for one's conclusions.

Unlike ethics though, where one can unwittingly breach an ethical guideline, one cannot mistakenly fail to be responsible for one's opinions. Such a failure arises from conscious thought, and accountability for this is currently lacking.

Accountability is the requirement to justify actions or decisions, and may by extension involve a continued responsibility toward one's opinions, thoughts, and conclusions. As such, even the most responsible and ethical of people may refuse to be held accountable for their actions. One may also adopt the position that their lack of accountability stems from the fact that they were only allowed access to a limited amount of the evidence. In such a case, it is incumbent on the profiler, not the client, to point out the limitations of the analysis and not to blaze ahead in spite of it, only to cry foul at some later date. The bottom line is that your conclusions are just that, and you should have a continuing commitment to them. This has been evidenced by some profilers failing to address the "relevance" of their profile to the investigation, an issue addressed by Ferguson in Chapter 9. It would seem that due to such broad interpretations of what an appropriate profile is, many profilers are left unsure or are misguided when providing an analysis. Clearly not a tenable position, as when you take on a case, you take it on as an expert.

One way to make an end run around accountability is to provide a caveat to the effect that the information provided is based on a "best guess" or is not to be taken as accurate and/or reliable. This is paramount to all profiles. It is of great importance that profiles contain a summary of the logical consequences (implications of such decision making) and provide a hierarchy of profile characteristics based on importance and sound hypothesis testing. If characteristics are to be provided based on statistical/theoretical research this must be noted as carrying significantly less weight (greater logical consequence) in the profile. Although caveats are not the antithesis of a good profile, and one should be provided if some part of the information was not provided for assessment, a caveat that highlights the profile's flaws from the onset may be a sign of things to come. For example, the following profile states (Prodan, 1995):

> *The following crime scene analysis was prepared by Special Agent Supervisor/Criminal Investigative Profiler Michael Prodan in consultation with FBI Supervisory Special Agent James Wright and other members of the National Center for the Analysis of Violent Crime (NCAVC), FBI Academy, Quantico, Virginia. This analysis is based upon a thorough review of the materials submitted by your agency and the conclusions are the result of the knowledge drawn from the personal investigative experience, educational background, and research conducted by these crime analysts. It is not a substitute for a thorough, well planned investigation and should not be considered all inclusive. Any information provided is based upon reviewing, analyzing and researching criminal cases similar to the case submitted by your agency. The following analysis is based upon probabilities, noting that no two criminal acts or criminal personalities are exactly alike. Therefore, the offender at times may not always fit the analysis in every category.*

One of the ways that we may assist in upholding accountability in the profession is to insist that all profiles be written down, as this locks the analyst into a position, providing there is no ambiguity, that they cannot back away from at a later date. This way, the content of the profile is irrefutable and accessible. This opens one up for scrutiny in a number of ways, but most importantly it allows for peer review. While relating specifically to laboratory examination, Inman and Rudin (2001, p. 259) warn that "If you did not write it down, you did not do it." Highlighting the importance of documentation to any opinion, this applies equally to profiling.

While some advocate heavily for recording one's thoughts in the form of a written report, others are not so keen to create a record. There are myriad reasons for this, possibly because they do not want to be held accountable in perpetuity, or because they later want to claim success without having their profile call this accuracy into question. There are also legal reasons for not doing so.

But what legal reasoning may there be to preclude a written analysis *in toto*? Perhaps it is, as this author has heard a number of times, that to put one's conclusions in writing does little more than generate *Brady* material. According to *Brady v. Maryland* (1963), a U.S. legal precedent dictating the disclosure of evidence:

> *After the petitioner had been convicted in a Maryland state court on a charge of murder in the first degree (committed in the course of a robbery) and had been sentenced to death, he learned of an extrajudicial confession of his accomplice, tried separately, admitting the actual homicide. This confession had been suppressed by the prosecution notwithstanding a request by the petitioner's counsel to allow him to examine the accomplice's extrajudicial statements. Upon appeal from the trial court's dismissal of his petition for postconviction relief, the Maryland Court of Appeals held that suppression of the evidence by the prosecution denied petitioner due process of law, and remanded the case for a retrial of the question of punishment only.*

In short, a *Brady* violation is one in which the prosecution withholds potentially exculpatory evidence that, if it had been made available to the defense, may have affected the outcome of the trial. In a *Brady* violation, the court may order a retrial.

According to *Strickler v. Greene* (1999), there are three necessary elements for the finding of a *Brady* violation:

> *The evidence at issue must be favorable to the accused, either because it is exculpatory, or because it is impeaching; that evidence must have been suppressed by the State, either willfully or inadvertently; and prejudice must have ensued.*

As for the first, if the profile was constructed using valid methodology and consists of conclusions resulting from a careful and meticulous examination of the physical evidence that point away from the accused, it could be argued that the profile may be favorable to the accused. Of the second, regardless of the intent, if the State is aware that the profile is potentially exculpatory and they fail to turn it over, then it could be considered to have been suppressed. Of the last, prejudice may ensue when, in the absence of information regarding the mismatch between the profile and the characteristics of the accused, the jury may be more inclined to accept the prosecution's contention that the accused is guilty.[3]

This becomes relevant to profiling when, for instance, the prosecution requests a profile of a suspect who has already been arrested and charged and is due to stand trial (or perhaps when the profile is done during the investigation). Should the profile provide characteristics that do not match the defendant, it may be argued by the defense that the mismatch is evidence of the defendant's innocence. As such, the profile may not be surrendered to the defense

[3] It could perhaps be argued that such a profile would be more prejudicial than probative, but this would be a matter for the judge to decide.

as this would be seen to "help" their case. Withholding this information, however, may constitute a *Brady* violation.

If this is in fact the legal reasoning for not writing a profile down, then it would seem that many in the community do not like the idea of accountability, especially when having it may be seen to assist "the enemy" with their case. This speaks of a notion of sides when working as an expert, a position that runs counter to all notions of scientific expert opinion where the first responsibility is to the evidence, not for whatever side the expert feels they are on. Any profiler who subsequently suggests that profiles should not be written down for this specific reason may be knowingly complicit in a *Brady* violation.

As a final point, it should be noted that accountability extends to the report itself and to the utilization of the information contained therein. It is not up to the end users to demonstrate the utility and/or the application of the information to their investigation. Rather, it is up to the profiler to demonstrate its application. As Inman and Rudin (2001, p. 274) note:

> *The scientist must take responsibility for communicating his results and conclusions, using thoughtful wording that clearly conveys the intended meaning of the data. The report should be organized, easy to read, and written in grammatically correct English. In other words, the burden should be on the scientist, not the reader, to ensure that written communication is effective in disseminating the scientist's opinion.*

Education and Training

Another topic that has not been addressed at any length in the literature, and perhaps it is more deserving of some detailed analysis, is the problem with the governance of profiling and the lack of universal training or education standards. This means that virtually anyone can go forth and call themselves a profiler, even without formal training (university or otherwise). This is problematic because profiling is an area in which the behavior of one individual can tarnish the work of others very easily. What's more, anyone can call themselves a profiler after having done little more than reading a number of books on the topic.

The lack of standardized education is sadly evident and widely available from a number of sources. All one has to do is to search the Internet for any number of web sites dedicated to the topic, and it becomes clear exactly how poorly defined this issue is. Some even set a standard and admit that even they do not meet it. The following information is taken from the Sexual Homicide Exchange (http://www.she-dc.com) in answer to the question of education and training standards:

> *There aren't any and by that I mean there are really no established rules and regulations that have been followed with any consensus. Obviously, it is always nice to have as much traditional education as possible. Employers like degrees and if you can get a PhD, more power to you. However, a master's may be perfectly acceptable and a bachelor's will at least give you the ability to say you are college educated. There are very few actual*

criminal profiling programs around although they are starting to surface. Most people chose forensics, psychology, or criminal justice as their degree programs. Some double major along the way and some focus on one aspect like psychology in their undergraduate program and then go on to get a forensics degree for their master's. Some students take police investigative courses or death investigation courses at community college and then go on to a four year university.

Others who want to become profilers join the FBI or the police. Either one of these organizations may offer the possibility of becoming a profiler in the very distant future and neither one can promise you will get the opportunity to actually profile. If you go this route, you need to be willing and interested in other aspects of these jobs in case you never get the opportunity to become involved in profiling.

There are a few of us who did not study profiling in college nor do we have law enforcement backgrounds. We accumulated our knowledge through self-study and research, seminars, and experience.

Regardless of how you gain your knowledge in the field, it is up to your employer or client to determine the suitability of your skills to handle the job.

The extract notes that a PhD is desirable or that a master's degree is perfectly acceptable, but it fails to note what areas might be most useful. For example, whereas a master's in business administration might be useful in running a family business, or a PhD in accounting would be useful for an accountant, neither of these programs do anything for profilers in their rumination of human behavior. In addition, simply possessing a university degree so profilers can say they are educated offers little and is misleading. Again, a bachelor's program may be in an unrelated area (environmental science or liberal arts, for example), and whereas these are useful in their respective trades, they offer little for the development of theoretical and practical skills as a profiler.

So this begs the question: What is an acceptable level of training and education for one to possess to call him- or herself a profiler? As a general rule, university-level training in the social sciences is a must, and some higher degree training in a relevant area is not just desirable but recommended. This would include higher degrees (such as a master's degree) in areas including but not limited to psychology, criminology, and forensic science. This must include a sound ability to understand methodological limitations, interpret statistical information, and critique published research. For the discipline to move forward and be based on considerations of science, it is vital that professionals/profilers are able to determine the requirements for a valid and reliable profile. Knowledge of the investigative procedures used by police may also assist profilers in keeping their information relevant.

But developing this proficiency is about more than reading a few books, taking a few courses, and being able to "talk the talk." Unfortunately, this is exactly what a large amount of profiler education has become, with the short course model being front and center. These courses, as the name implies, are compacted forums usually designed for working professionals who typically cannot take large amounts of time away from their work commitments. They may range from hours to days, and in some cases may be as long as weeks or months.

In profiling, a number of short courses may be taken over a long period of time, which collectively are suggested to impart proficiency in one or a number of areas (crime reconstruction, bloodstain pattern analysis, bomb damage assessment, etc.). The problem is that while these short courses may help one communicate with other professionals in a meaningful way, they do not alone impart expert status. For example, a course on the interpretation of human behavior will be less meaningful if the individual has no behavioral science background. A course on bloodstain patterns will be less meaningful without a substantive understanding of forensic science. This has been discussed by Chisum (2007, pp. 314–317), who also notes a number of problems inherent in short courses:

> *In addition to reading the recommended publications, it is advised that anyone interested in crime reconstruction take a course in bloodstain analysis from a qualified forensic scientist. These courses can be useful for providing certain basic overviews of fundamental concepts. However, depending on the scientific background of the instructor, they may be lacking in certain crucial areas. A true scientist will find that a majority of the short bloodstain classes are lacking with regard to a discussion of accuracy, precision, and significant numbers. Appreciating these deficiencies is the difference between the technician's pedantic understanding of bloodstains and the forensic scientist's interpretive role in the reconstruction of the crime.*
>
> *A great deal of time in these classes will be spent on single drop analyses and the review of basic bloodstain types and terms…*
>
> *These terms will allow you to communicate with other bloodstain analysts and are important for that reason. However, there are mathematics and physics components necessary to make certain bloodstain interpretations. Without this background, the reconstructionist is insufficiently prepared to perform bloodstain pattern analysis. The mathematics are seldom included in short bloodstain classes, and this should be noted by all concerned.*
>
> …
>
> *More important, in actual casework, bloodstains are very seldom limited to a single drop. Consequently, the reconstructionist is concerned not with individual drops but, rather, their overall pattern. The short courses that exist do tend to cover general patterns, and this is perhaps their greatest value. But the approach to interpretation tends to be parochial as opposed to holistic, and it betrays a misunderstanding of the variation that can exist in actual casework. Analysts who are trained to look at and interpret single drops in a rote and technical fashion tend to miss the forest for concentrating on the individual trees with respect to their conclusions.*

This issue has also been canvassed by Cooley (2007, pp. 532–535), reproduced in its entirety[4]:

[4] To be absolutely clear, the discussions by Chisum and Cooley relate specifically to forensic issues, but the problem is no different in other short courses for profilers. Also, many short course profiling models also include those specific courses discussed here.

The CSI–reconstructionist model is too often premised on completing a series of short courses. For instance, many investigators attend 5-day (40-hour) workshops or courses on bloodstain pattern analysis, trajectory analysis, or crime scene reconstruction. Some may even attend advanced 2-week (80-hour) courses in these subjects. Attending these courses does not automatically transform an investigator into a bloodstain or trajectory analysis expert (see Chapter 8). As Stephen Bright, director of the Southern Center for Human Rights and forensic watchdog, explains (as quoted in Wrolstad, 2002, p. 1A):

[W]hat you have in many laboratories are police officers who have been sent up to the FBI training facility in Quantico, Va., and come back after 2 weeks claiming to be experts. ... They tend to embellish, to make statements not supported by science, that often go unchallenged because defendants are poor and don't have the resources to hire independent experts.

...

In their crime laboratory management treatise, Kirk and Bradford (1965, p. 58) scoffed at the notion that examiners or reconstructionists can acquire expert levels of knowledge simply by attending only short or "correspondence" courses:

A degree in science from a college or university ordinarily falls far short of meeting the minimum requirements. Except in the most unusual instances, such a college degree must be considered an essential,[italics added] but not sufficient in itself. Directed laboratory and theoretical work in the field of criminalistics itself is the other essential requirement for the absolute minimum training.

Correspondence and extension courses are occasionally helpful, but generally totally inadequate except as a supplement to sounder training. The student does not learn the subject—he learns a little about it. It does not truly become part of him, either technically or philosophically. For the same reasons, reading of books, however helpful and relevant they may be, is likewise inadequate by itself to meet minimum requirements. The reading and supplementary study should accompany, not replace, the laboratory training. All of this, including the laboratory training, is still inadequate without sound groundwork in basic sciences, such as can be obtained in the colleges and universities.

Again, mastering the many scientific and technical skills needed to properly carry out a reconstructive analysis cannot be acquired in a 2- or 3-week time span. An undergraduate or graduate science degree, combined with broad-based knowledge of the forensic sciences, and a demonstrated proficiency in reconstructing crimes using analytical logic, critical thinking, and the scientific method are essential.

With all of the confusion between both practitioners and authors in the area, it is no wonder that there are many confused students and prospective profilers out there. For this reason, if for no other, the subjects of education and training need to be addressed in a more detailed fashion. Only then might we develop a more critical eye for those who are qualified to carry out the work, and those who are not.

Conclusion

As noted in this chapter, there are many areas that will plague the future of profiling and stifle its future development. The answer to many of the questions posed by the foregoing discussion will not be easily come by, and only continued application will see a resolution to many of these issues. One thing that may assist in this process is for end users of criminal profiling to become more educated, and this text and others like it will, it is hoped, go a long way to ensure that this goal is met. Perhaps when the consumer better understands these issues and the problems thus far, they will start to question approaches and take those they have previously called upon to task in their conclusions.

Questions

1. Ethical standards could be discussed without regard to professionalization. *True or false?*
2. To apply the scientific method, one must be a scientist. *True or false*?
3. The requirements to justify actions or decisions is called ________________.
4. There is an established standard for education and training in criminal profiling. *True or false?*
5. List and discuss the issues in the chapter that are needed for profiling to advance.
6. What are some of the general problems with short courses?

References

Ainsworth, P. B. (2001). *Criminal profiling and crime analysis*. Devon, UK: Willan.

Allen, M. J. (2004). The scientific method: *The Concise Corsini Encyclopedia of psychology and behavioral sciences*. California: John Wiley and Sons, Inc.

Alison, L. (2005). *Forensic psychologists casebook*. Devon, UK: Willan.

Almond, L., Alison, L., & Porter, L. (2007). An evaluation and comparison of claims made in behavioral investigative advice reports compiled by the National Policing Improvements Agency in the United Kingdom. *Journal of Investigative Psychology*, *4*(2), 71–83.

Beall, J. C. (2010). *Logic: The basics*. Hoboken, NJ: Taylor & Francis.

Bekerian, D. A., & Jackson, J. L. (1997). In J. L. Jackson & D. A. Bekerian (Eds.), *Offender profiling: Theory, research and practice*. West Sussex, UK: Wiley.

Bhattacharyya, S. (1958). The concept of logic. *Philosophy and Phenomenological Research*, *18*, 326–340.

Brady v. Maryland. (1963). 373 U.S. 83.

Canter, D. (2004). The organized/disorganized typology of serial murder. *Psychology, Public Policy, and Law*, *10*, 293–320.

Canter, D., & Youngs, D. (2009). *Investigative psychology: Offender profiling and the analysis of criminal action*. United Kingdom: Wiley.

Chisum, W. J. (2007). Reconstruction using bloodstain evidence. In W. J. Chisum & B. E. Turvey (Eds.), *Crime reconstruction*. Boston: Academic Press.

Cooley, C. (2007). Reconstruction in a post-Daubert and post-DNA courtroom. In W. J. Chisum & B. E. Turvey (Eds.), *Crime reconstruction*. Boston: Academic Press.

Daily Record. (2003, February 5). More discovery needed to review expert's statements. Wednesday, February 5, 2003.

Dempsey, J. S. (1996). *An introduction to public and private investigations.* Minneapolis: West.

Drake v. Portuondo. (2003). Docket No. 01-2217, January 31 (321 F.3d 338); argued: September 9, 2002, decided: January 31, 2003.

Ewing, C. P. (2003). False credentials cause extensive fallout. *Judicial Notebook, 34*(7), 84.

Fisher, C. B. (2009). *Decoding the ethics code: A practical guide for psychologists* (2nd ed.). California: SAGE.

Gudjonsson, G. H., & Copson, G. (1997). The role of the expert in criminal investigation. In J. L. Jackson & D. A. Bekerian (Eds.), *Offender profiling: Theory, research and practice.* West Sussex, UK: Wiley.

Inman, K., & Rudin, N. (2001). *Principles and practice of criminalistics: The profession of forensic science.* Boca Raton, FL: CRC Press.

Jackson, J. A., & Bekerian, D. A. (1997). *Offender profiling and crime analysis: Theory, research and practice.* Chichester, UK: John Wiley and Sons.

Kocsis, R. N. (2001). Psychological profiling in murder investigations. *Australasian Science, 22*(1), 26–27.

Kocsis, R. N. (2003). Criminal psychological profiling: Validities and abilities. *International Journal of Offender Therapy and Comparative Criminology, 47*(2), 126–144.

Kocsis, R. N., Hayes, A. F., & Irwin, H. J. (2002). Investigative experience and accuracy in psychological profiling of a violent crime. *Journal of Interpersonal Violence, 17*(8), 811–824.

Kocsis, R. N., Irwin, H. J., Hayes, A. F., & Nunn, R. (2000). Expertise in psychological profiling: A comparative assessment. *Journal of Interpersonal Violence, 15*(3), 311–331.

Lazarus, A. A. (1994). How certain boundaries and ethics diminish therapeutic effectiveness. *Ethics & Behaviour, 4,* 255–261.

McInerney, D. Q. (2004). *Being logical: A guide to good thinking.* Westminster: Random House Publishing.

The Medicolegal Society of New South Wales. (undated). Criminal profiling—A psychiatric confession. Available from <http://www.medicolegal.org.au/index2.php?option=com_content&do_pdf=1&id=133> Accessed on 16.06.08.

Petherick, W. A. (2003). What's in a name? comparing applied profiling methodologies. *Journal of Law and Social Challenges,* June.

Petherick, W. A. (2007). *Criminal profiling: A qualitative and quantitative analysis of methods and content.* Bond University. (Unpublished doctoral dissertation).

Petherick, W. A., & Ferguson, C. E. (2010). Ethics for the forensic criminologist. In W. A. Petherick, B. E. Turvey, & C. E. Ferguson (Eds.), *Forensic criminology.* San Diego: Elsevier Science.

Pinizzotto, A. J. (1984). Forensic psychology: Criminal personality profiling. *Journal of Police Science and Administration, 12*(1), 32–40.

Pinizzotto, A. J., & Finkel, N. J. (1990). Criminal personality profiling: An outcome and process study. *Law and Human Behavior, 14,* 215–233.

Pollock, J. (2007). *Ethical dilemmas and decisions in criminal justice* (5th ed.). Belmont: Thompson Wadsworth.

Prodan, M. (1995). Criminal investigative analysis of unknown subject. 27 February.

Rossmo, K. (2000). *Geographic profiling.* Boca Raton, FL: CRC Press.

Strickler v. Greene. (1999). (98-5864) 527 U.S. 263 149 F.3d 1170.

Thornton, J. (1997). The general assumptions and rationale of forensic identification. In D. L. Faigman, D. H. Kaye, M. J. Saks, & J. Sanders (Eds.), *Modern scientific evidence: The law and expert testimony.* St. Paul, MN: West Publishing.

Wilson, P., Lincoln, R., & Kocsis, R. N. (1997). Validity, utility, and ethics of profiling for serial violent and sexual offenders. *Psychiatry, Psychology, and Law, 4*(1), 1–12.

PART 2

Serial Crime

13 Serial Bullying and Harassment

-Yolande Huntingdon and Wayne Petherick

Introduction

Incidents of school violence such as the Columbine and Virginia Tech shootings have prompted legislators, school administrators, and academics to consider tolerance levels and implications of bullying and harassment. Indeed, a number of studies have found that most school shooters had been bullied and that this victimization had played a significant part in, or had provided the catalyst for, their decision to exact this form of retaliation (Chapell, Hasselman, Kitchi, Lomon, MacIver & Sarullo, 2006). Although spree killings and mass murder are, in reality, at the extreme and exceptional end of the response to these forms of victimization, the more insidious outcomes of bullying and harassment can be profound for victim and offender alike.

Serial bullying and harassment is defined as "the situation where one perpetrator preys on two or more victims, often traversing a broad range of classes and grades to target his/her victims" (Chan, 2006, p. 352). Although this definition is intended to address such offenses in the school/college environment, it applies equally to serial bullying and harassment inflicted by adults in the workplace. Indeed, one in every 17 adults in the United States reports a life long pattern of bullying others, indicative of a high base rate for this form of serial antisocial behavior (Vaughn, Bender, DeLisi, Beaver, Perron & Howard, 2010).

The authors acknowledge the delineation between one bully victimizing one victim, one victim targeted by multiple bullies, and the "serial" form of bullying and harassment (one bully and multiple victims). According to most definitions, victim numbers (mostly accepted as two or more) are generally considered the best yardstick by which to identify an offense as serial (Petherick, 2009). As such, bullying and harassment in its serial form has been identified as a more serious form of menace in terms of frequency of attack, the large number of victims, that serial bullies were found responsible for a significant percentage of incidents, and that these incidents were more likely to be of a physical nature causing injury (Choo, 2006).

Discussions elucidating bullying and harassment are important for a number of reasons. First, the long-term and potentially devastating biopsychosocial outcomes for many victims of chronic abuse by peers require that researchers investigate and shed light into its causes and best practice antibullying strategies. Second, since a small percentage of individuals suffer a large percentage of victimization, whether in the schoolyard or workplace, it naturally follows that preventing revictimization will prevent a large number of offenses (Farrell, 1995). Similarly, a small number of bullies (child and adult) are responsible for the majority of bullying behaviors, with prior aggressive and violent behavior being the greatest predictor of future violent behavior (Farrell, 1995; Mulder, Brand, Bullens & Hjalmar van Marle, 2011).

Research also indicates that bullies are more likely to engage in criminal and antisocial behaviors into adulthood, and that former bullies are heavily overrepresented in crime registers. For instance, longitudinal studies by Olweus (1993a,b, 2011) found that 60% of bullies from grades 6 to 9 had at least one criminal conviction by age 20, and that 40 percent had multiple convictions. These results are supported by Sourander and Klomek (2011), who found that teacher reports of childhood bullying were the strongest predictor of adult criminality.

This chapter will discuss school/college and workplace bullying as well as cyberbullying and harassment. Although the term "harassment" is commonly interchanged and confused with "bullying" it is, in fact, a distinct category in both definition and application. Definitions, characteristics, and features of bullying and harassment will be discussed, such as prevalence, risk and protective factors, high risk victim behaviors, and empirical findings in regard to victim and offender outcomes. Strategies for decreasing incidents and risk of school and workplace bullying and harassment will also be presented.

Bullying in Schools

Serial bullying is defined as aggressive acts characterized by persistent and recurring psychological or physical harm, oppression, or intimidation, wherein a real or perceived power imbalance facilitates distress by, or control of, one person by another (Carr-Gregg & Manocha, 2011; Rigby & Smith, 2011; Woods & Wolke, 2003).

For some time, bullying was seen as a rite of passage, a "fact of life," and a normal phase in the child–adult developmental pathway (Bradshaw, O'Brennan & Sawyer, 2008; Campbell, 2000; Carr-Gregg & Manocha, 2011), a view rarely shared by the vast amount of contemporary literature now devoted to this area in regard to the profound negative and long-term outcomes for victims and offenders alike. Importantly, bullying behavior can be accurately identified and assessed in preschool-aged children, and has been found to be a marker (or risk factor) for aggressive and violent behavior in later adolescence and adulthood (Tremblay, 2000).

Forms of Bullying

Bullying is a subtype of a violent antisocial, rule-breaking pattern of behavior; deliberate in nature, generally unprovoked, and involves a spectrum of actions, varying in intensity, form, and modality (Carrera, DePalma & Lameiras, 2011; Sourander & Klomek, 2011). Bullying behavior refers to any aggressive physical contact, or threat of physical contact including rough "play" (where the intention to harm is disguised as an unintended consequence of game-playing), kicking, pinching, punching, spitting, theft or destruction of belongings, stalking, ignoring, and isolating. Ignoring, isolating, social exclusion, and malicious rumor-spreading have also been defined as relational bullying, whereby the dynamics of peer relationships are manipulated with the intention of inflicting psychological and emotional harm (Bauman & Del Rio, 2006; Crick & Grotpeter, 1995). Verbal bullying can be just as diverse and includes name-calling, teasing, taunting, and threats (Woods & Wolke, 2003).

Prevalence

Since the seminal research conducted by Olweus (1993a,b), a large body of literature has been published and initiatives have been implemented to reduce the incidence of bullying in schools (Rigby & Smith, 2011). Although widely assumed that the prevalence of bullying in schools is increasing, research indicates a decrease (with the exception of cyberbullying, which will be dealt with later in this chapter) in many countries, including the United States, England, Wales, Australia, Spain, and Norway according to data collated and published between 1990 and 2008 (Molcho, Craig, Due, Pickett, Harel-fisch & Overpeck, 2009; Rigby & Smith, 2011).

Nonetheless, recent research also indicates an alarming prevalence of bullying in schools. In the United States it is estimated that almost 30% of students are involved in bullying behaviors (Rose, Monda-Amaya & Espelage, 2011) with almost 15% of students being attacked physically (Rigby & Smith, 2011). These figures parallel Canadian and Australian figures at 34% and 32%, respectively (Carr-Gregg & Manocha, 2011; Craig & Pepler, 2003; Cross, Shaw, Hearn, Epstein, Monks, Lester & Thomas, 2009), but are significantly higher than that found in Japan at 22% (Hilton, Anngela-Cole & Juri, 2009), and Britain at around 10% (Boulton & Underwood, 1992). In one 40-country European analysis, 26% of participating adolescents (n = 53,249) reported involvement in bullying (Craig, Harel-Fisch, Fogel-Grinvald, Dostaler, Hetland, Simons-Morton & Pickett, 2009), with levels of involvement significantly higher in developing countries such as Latin America (Molcho, Craig, Due, Pickett, Harel-Fisch & Overpeck, 2009).

Victim Outcomes

Links have been regularly found between being bullied/victimized and obesity, low self-esteem, and body dissatisfaction (Fox & Farrow, 2009), poor academic performance (Adams & Lawrence, 2011), suicide and suicidal ideation (Bonanno & Hymel, 2010), self-destructive behaviors (Fisher, Cabral de Mello, Izutsu, Vijayakumar, Belfer & Omigbodum, 2011), and various longer term mental health morbidities. Additionally, victims present a high incidence of internalizing difficulties and psychopathologies such as adult antisocial behavior, clinical depression, and anxiety disorders (McEachern & Snyder, 2012; Williford, Bouton, Noland, Little, Kärnä & Salmivalli, 2012). The effects of bullying on the victim, as well as the bully, are often long-lasting and can continue from elementary to high school, on to college, and into the workplace (Adams & Lawrence, 2011; Harvey, Heames, Richey & Leonard, 2006; Scherr and Larson 2010).

Victim Risk Factors

Victimization is generally determined by two factors: accessibility and vulnerability. Efforts to understand the causes of peer victimization have led researchers to focus on behavioral vulnerabilities that may contribute to a child being the target of abuse; the child who is singled out and identified as a suitable victim by an aggressor. In regards to accessibility, most victimization occurs at school, a highly charged and competitive environment where potential bullies can interrelate with a number of suitable victims (Beaty & Alexeyev, 2008).

The playground is the most common setting for bullying, followed by the hallways, classrooms, lunch areas, and toilets (Beaty & Alexeyev, 2008; Siann, Callaghan, Lockhart & Rawson, 1993). Victims have been identified and described by research as generally being of the same age as the bully, but smaller and weaker than their peers and commonly deviate from norms or social and cultural majorities. These variables can include styles of dress, body shape, communication style, ethnicity, social, economic advantage/disadvantage, sexual orientation, and physical or intellectual disability (Craig, Sue, Murphy & Bauer, 2010; Estell, Farmer, Irvin, Crowther, Akos & Boudah, 2009; Harries, Petrie & Willoughby, 2002; Olweus 1997; Scherr & Larson, 2010). Childhood developmental stages determine the methods of bullying, with physical and verbal abuse increasing throughout early childhood and declining in junior high where it is gradually replaced by relational bullying. Relational bullying then increases into adolescence and declines thereafter (Craig & Pepler, 2003; Smith, Cousins & Stewart, 2005).

Victims generally exhibit personality traits and behaviors that predispose them to victimization and indicate that they are less likely than others to be able to defend themselves against physical or psychological attack (Farrell, 1995; Hazler et al., 1997). Victims are commonly lacking self-esteem and are predisposed to a high tendency to self-blame, may cry easily, and be disposed to high levels of anxiety and signs of depression (Farrell, 1995; Hazler, Carney, Green, Powell & Jolly, 1997; Sullivan, Clearly & Sullivan, 2005). Although many male victims commonly enjoy close family relationships (Nickerson, Mele & Princiotta, 2008), children from abusive families and those with authoritarian parents are at the highest risk of being bullied (Swearer & Doll, 2001). Overall, victims of chronic bullying have personality traits more often associated with sensitivity and lack of aggressive tendencies (Olweus, 1999).

Risk Factors for Offending

In regard to bullies, research has supported the traditional bully stereotype as highly aggressive, self-sufficient, and impulsive, not as well integrated as their nonbully peers, but more integrated than their victims (Carrera, DePalma & Lameiras, 2011; Olweus, 1997). Boys are more likely to participate in bullying behaviors and are at higher risk of victimization than girls (De Souza and Ribeiro 2005; Olweus 1999, 2010). Additionally, boys are more likely to exhibit more physical and verbal aggression than their female counterparts, who tend to participate in relational or social aggression, such as hurtful gossip, rumor-mongering, and social exclusion (Carrera, DePalma & Lameiras, 2011; Crick and Grotpeter, 1995).

Bowlby (1969) proposed that individuals develop their own conceptions of self and self-worth based upon early experiences of parenting and caregiving, and that these conceptions of self are carried through into adulthood and directly influence one's adult relationships. In regard to family relationships, bullies have generally been found to have been parented by those with insecure attachment styles and coercive parenting within a negative family environment (Espelage and Swearer, 2010; Nickerson, Mele & Princiotta, 2010; Salmivalli, Lagerspetz, Björkqvist, Österman & Kaukiainen, 1996; Schwartz, Dodge, Pettit & Bates, 1997; Smith, 2004; Swearer and Doll, 2001). The insecure attachment style is characterized by inconsistent, dismissive, and preoccupied parenting (Weiten, 2010) and has been empirically linked with high levels of aggression, expressions of anger, negative relationship outcomes, intimate partner violence, decreased ability to negotiate conflict, and insecurity (a preoccupation with attachment; Miga, Hare, Allen & Manning, 2010). Interestingly, this preoccupation with attachment may well explain the need for the bully to control, dominate, and influence the victim's emotional and psychological state, and further account for a propensity for aggression.

Stephenson and Smith (1988) posit two bullying typologies; the active and the passive (or *anxious*) bully. The former, the most common form of abuser, establishes a direct relationship with the victim and manipulates, coerces, and recruits others to take part; a narcissistic personality type with feelings of entitlement and little capacity for empathy or conscience

(Donnellan et al., 2005; Olweus, 1997; Stephenson & Smith, 1988). In contrast, the passive bully is easily influenced and manipulated by an active leader; a recruit characterized by low self-esteem and confidence and desperate to be accepted by a social group not otherwise accessible (Donnellan et al., 2005). Literature posits a third typology, the "Machiavellian" bully (Vaillancourt, McDougall, Hymel & Sunderani, 2010) who presents high self-esteem, social skills and social status, is noncoercive, and employs charisma and magnetism to achieve his own ends (Donnellan, Trzniewski, Robins, Moffitt & Caspi, 2005).

Pathway from Child Bully to Adult Criminality

Gender plays a significant role in the predictive association between bullying in childhood and adult criminality (Carrera, DePalma & Lameiras, 2011; Sourander & Klomek, 2011). Bullying behavior by girls has not been found to elevate the risk of committing criminal or antisocial acts as an adult; perhaps due to the more covert, indirect and relational bullying styles that are less likely to attract the attention of parents and educators (Carrera, DePalma & Lameiras, 2011; Sourander & Klomek, 2011). Indeed, a study by Yoon and Kerber (2003) found that teachers expressed more sympathy toward victims of physical and verbal abuse and were less likely to intervene in instances of relational abuse such as social exclusion. By contrast, in males there is a strong association between bullying and future antisocial and psychopathological behaviors, a negative life trajectory, and crime, particularly violent crime (Kim, Leventhal, Koh, Hubbard & Boyce, 2006; Olweus, Horne & Staniszewski, 2003; Sourander & Klomek, 2011; Spivak & Prothrow-Stith, 2001).

A seminal longitudinal study conducted in Switzerland (Sourander, Jensen, Ronning, Elonheimo, Niemela & Helenius, 2007) found that bullying behavior was predictive of an antisocial tendency. This finding is supported by Luukkonena, Rialab, Hakkob & Räsänena (2011, p. 106) who noted:

> *Our finding concerning the association of violent crimes with bullying behaviour brings us back to the discussion of the relation of bullying to antisocial personality disorder. As it has been shown earlier that being a bully in childhood increases the risk of later antisocial personality disorder and that antisocial personality disorder is known to be associated with habitual violent behaviour, we suggest that bullying among severely psychopathological adolescents may be a sign of a developing antisocial personality disorder which will manifest itself later in life.*

Indeed, a cohort of 8-year-old frequent bullies, when followed through to adolescence, showed a significantly higher likelihood of being involved in violent and repeated crime as well as property, drunk driving, and general traffic crimes, when compared to nonbullying peers (Feder, 2004; Sourander, Jensen, Ronning, Elonheimo, Niemela & Helenius, 2007). Additionally, Olweus (1978) found that approximately 40% of bullies are convicted of three or more crimes and that 25% of elementary school child bullies had a criminal record and had served time in prison by age 30, as compared to 5% of nonbullies.

As a general life trajectory, child bullies were found to be more likely to drop out of school, work in low-skill employment, be involved in domestic violence, and use harsh, coercive, and corporal punishment on their children. There is a strong multigenerational component to bullying, with children of authoritarian parents who were abusers in school more likely to become bullies themselves (Knafo, 2003).

Studies on Best Practice Interventions

Research suggests the investment of time, money, and resources into evidence-based antibullying programs can lead to safer schools, a more peaceful and academically congenial environment, and provide significant future social and economic benefits for society (Smith, Cousins & Stewart, 2005). Bullying is no longer considered by academics as a simple dyadic interaction between bully and victim, but as phenomena encompassing a much larger social system consisting of peers, the family, and the school. It should come as no surprise, then, that a multitiered combination of individual, class, whole-school, and family interventions has provided the most successful outcomes for tackling school bullying (Olweus et al., 2007; Salmivalli, Kaukiainen & Voeten, 2005). These programs seek to inform and establish rules in regard to bullying behaviors and alter social norms and expectations of conduct for bullies, victims, and bystanders (Bradshaw, O'Brennan & Sawyer, 2008).

Additionally, annual anonymous student surveys have been found to harvest a better understanding of the prevalence and nature of bullying within the specific school environment so that prevention strategies can be tailored and personalized according to particular grades, cultures, or bullying modalities (ASCA, 2005; Bradshaw, O'Brennan & Sawyer, 2008). These school-specific strategies are essential due to the complex and diverse nature of cultural, social, and community contexts. For instance, in an inner-city community it may be normative, adaptive, or protective to respond to threat with physical violence and seen to be essential to belong to a bully-group with an active leader (gang) for survival (Bradshaw & Garbarino, 2004; Solomon, Bradshaw, Wright & Cheng, 2008). Indeed, research has indicated that bullying programs are most effective when tailored in response to school-specific problems and designed collaboratively by school counselors, educators, and administrators (Orpinas, Horne & Staniszewski, 2003).

Since the first national efforts to reduce bullying in Norwegian schools, interventions have focused on systemic change, rather than on the specific bully(s) and victim involved in any one instance (Craig & Pepler, 2007; Olweus, 1991, 1993a,b, 2004). These interventions have underpinned the responsibility of educators, parents, and other significant adults in the children's lives to create positive, respectful, and supportive environments and to be role models, leading by example and refraining from aggressive responses.

Bully–Victim Mediation: A Caution

Just as research has informed and directed many effective antibullying strategies, so too has it advised against potentially inflammatory approaches to dealing with instances of bullying. For instance, some schools have attempted to reconcile abuser(s) and victim by way of face-to-face mediation sessions in an attempt to facilitate a solution to what they perceive as a "problem" between the two (Campbell, 2000). This simplistic solution is incongruent with the plethora of emerging evidence on the etiologies of victim and bully relationships, particularly in regard to the vulnerable nature of the victim, the aggressive and commonly antisocial disposition of the bully who actively pursues a power imbalance, the propensity for manipulation on the part of the bully to present him- or herself as a victim, as well as victimization being largely unprovoked and irrational (Klein & Martin, 2011).

Due to the evidence-based and well-established associations between bullying behaviors and mental health disorders such as depression, conduct disorders, and oppositional defiant disorders (Kumpulainen, Rasanen & Puura, 2001), caution is advised before facilitating group sessions or face-to-face mediations involving youths with likely antisocial tendencies or other psychopathologies, particularly if the mediator is not specifically and appropriately qualified to do so. Furthermore, bullying has been identified as a significant marker for adult antisocial personality disorder (APD), with child bullies being nearly eight times more likely to meet future APD criteria (Kumpulainen, Rasanen & Puura, 2001). APD is characterized by pervasive indifference, disregard for and violation of the rights of others, lack of remorse, and rationalizing having hurt or mistreating others (DSM-IV, 2000) indicating that, at best, victim impact statements may be shrugged off and at worst, may result in continued or escalating victimization.

While the authors are not proposing that all child bullies will grow into adult psychopaths (or develop other similar psychopathologies), there is some benefit in looking at adult psychopathic populations who are placed into similar mediation or counseling environments. In Canada, Marnie Rice and her colleagues (Rice, Harris & Cormier, 1992) found that psychopaths in a prison-based therapeutic community program rated higher in violent recidivism than nonpsychopaths. In other research (Ogloff, Wong & Greenwood, 1990), psychopaths had less clinical improvement, were discharged from programs earlier than their nonpsychopathic counterparts, and had less motivation (with these last two likely being linked). Having individuals with these tendencies, even at a young age, in a face-to-face environment with their victims will likely do more harm than good. This is because they are given the opportunity to learn about the vulnerabilities of others, discover their strengths (to be circumvented at a later time), and find out how to best exploit their weaknesses. Finally, significant to this intervention strategy of requiring that the serial bully hear the victim's impact statement, this first-hand account of the victim's suffering may actually serve to reinforce many bullying behaviors when serial bullying is, by definition, intended to cause harm to the victim and to strengthen the authority of the bully.

Herein lays a dilemma for educators and those charged with deciding the consequences for poor student behavior; how does one decide between a punitive, conciliatory, or restorative approach? How do educators know when a student's behavior indicates the need for more serious psychological evaluations and interventions well beyond the educator's area of expertise? One solution would be to employ a professional, qualified in such matters. As such, this professional would:

- Deal with all instances of behavior management and intervention.
- Facilitate restorative processes (such as restorative conferences, affective statements and restorative circles) between student, teacher, or other stakeholders (see Mirsky, 2011).

- Identify children whose behavior is a result of abuse, neglect, intellectual disability, personality disorder, or mental illness, and refer the student for professional assessment and treatment.
- Design and implement strategies to identify and proactively deal with children at risk of bullying behaviors.
- Develop environmental strategies or modifications to increase surveillance and decrease opportunities for aggression.
- Design, implement, and facilitate whole-school programs to deal with bullying, social and self-esteem development, as well as aggression and stress management.
- Design, implement, and facilitate educational programs for educators and parents.

Workplace Bullying

Workplace bullying is a form of interpersonal aggression identical in both definition and modality to school-based bullying and similarly characterized by its persistence and unequal power relationship (Hoel, Beale & West, 2006; Matthiesen & Einarsen, 2010). Amendments to workplace health and safety legislation to safeguard workers from bullying and harassment and to limit employers' liability reflect the burgeoning economic and social consequences of bullying in the workplace (Connolly, 2006).

Costs to business can include decreases in productivity, increased insurance premiums, absenteeism and turnover, as well as poor mental health and early retirement (Yuen, 2005), and although it is recognized that organizations cannot necessarily be held responsible for individual acts of bullying, they are being held responsible for applying measures that seek to address and minimize the presence of such acts (Rhodes, Pullen, Vickers, Clegg & Pitsis, 2010). Furthermore, juries may find that an organization's conduct, if found to have knowingly employed ineffective antibullying measures, to be unreasonable and therefore deliberately indifferent (Campbell, 2000).

Recognition of workplace bullying as a serious social problem began in the 1970s when US psychiatrist Carroll Brodsky published his pioneering book, *The Harassed Worker* (Matthiesen & Einarsen, 2010). The results of 1000 interviews with people who had filed for workers' compensation claims were examined, with Brodsky recording the outcomes for victims of systematic and prolonged serial bullying by colleagues and superiors (Lutgen-Sandvik, Tracy & Alberts, 2007). Although this publication was later to become a seminal and authoritative reference on the subject, there was little interest in workplace bullying at the time of publication until nursing and medical students' experiences of abuse were published in the 1980s and 1990s (Cox, 1991; Lutgen-Sandvik, Tracy & Alberts, 2007; Sheehan, Sheehan, White, Leibowitz & Baldwin, 1990). Since then, US research into the causes and outcomes of systemic and prolonged hostility and aggression in the workplace has steadily improved, along with recommendations for its prevention (Matthiesen & Einarsen, 2010).

Prevalence

Bullying in the workplace is a widespread and pervasive problem (Martin & LaVan, 2010). One US study encompassing a variety of US workers in various age groups, industries, and locales found that approximately 35% to 50% of US workers experienced one instance of bullying, at least weekly in any 6- to 12-month period, and nearly 30% experience at least two types of bullying behaviors recurrently (Lutgen-Sandvik, Tracy & Alberts, 2007). These results correlate with other studies measuring the prevalence of bullying in the United States as well as the United Kingdom (Hoel and Cooper, 2000; Hoel, Cooper & Faragher, 2001; Keashly and Jagatic, 2000; Keashly and Neuman, 2005; Schat, Frone & Kelloway, 2006). Even at these unacceptable levels, workplace bullying is considered an underrepresented and underanalyzed problem negatively impacting the physical and psychological health of a substantial proportion of workers (Lutgen-Sandvik, Tracy & Alberts, 2007).

Although workplace bullying is a global problem (Martin & LaVan, 2010), research suggests that individualistic cultures that emphasize competition, masculinity, assertiveness, power distance, and individual achievement such as the United States, United Kingdom, and Australia (Hofstede, 2001; Mikkelsen and Einarsen 2001; Zapf & Einarsen, 2003) experience more incidents of workplace bullying when compared to collectivist cultures such as Scandinavia. Indeed, as previously stated, where US estimates of 35% to 50% of workers report experiencing one instance of bullying in any 6- to 12-month period, Scandinavian figures suggest less than 10% of workers experience the same (Lutgen-Sandvik, Tracy & Alberts, 2007; Martin & LaVan, 2010). Similarly, 1.6% of Scandinavian workers report weekly instances of bullying when compared to US figures of 30% to 35% (Lutgen-Sandvik, Tracy & Alberts, 2007; Martin & LaVan, 2010).

The United States and United Kingdom also report higher levels of bullying by managers/supervisors to subordinates (10–38%) than Scandinavian countries where workers experience more bullying behaviors between coworkers (Zapf & Einarsen, 2003). Additionally, bullying occurs at higher levels in the Public Service sector than private enterprise workplaces (Unison, 2000; Hoel, Cooper & Faragher, 2001) and women are more likely to be bullied than men (Bowling & Beehr, 2006).

Subtypes of Workplace Bullying

Matthiesen and Einarsen (2010) have distilled and described a number of significant studies that have identified and categorized particular types of workplace bullying (Table 13.1).

Dispute-related bullying develops from interpersonal conflicts typically triggered by perceptions of wrong doing (Einarsen, 1999). As a result of this perception, the social and work relationship sours and escalates into harsh and personal conflict where one person dehumanizes another, thus paving the way for manipulation, destabilization, and elimination of the opponent (Leymann, 1990; van de Vliert, 1998; Zapf & Gross, 2001). If the target's position becomes perceivably disadvantaged, he or she may become the target of wider bullying from additional aggressors (Matthiesen & Einarsen, 2010; van de Vliert, 1998).

Predatory bullying is nonprovocative, irrational, and unjustifiable, wherein the target has become an unwitting, but suitable, target for victimization. The predator's motive is to demonstrate power and authority over the victim or to coerce the victim into compliance (Einarsen, 1999; Matthiesen & Einarsen, 2010).

Table 13.1 Some Subtypes of Workplace Bullying

1. Dispute-related bullying
2. Predatory bullying
3. Scapegoating
4. Humor-oriented bullying
5. Work-related stalking
6. Bullying of workplace newcomers
7. The judicial derelict (secondary bullying)
8. Retaliation from whistle-blowing

Source: Matthiesen and Einarsen (2010)

Scapegoating occurs in response to stress or frustration on the part of the aggressor(s) resulting from a situation or a source perceived as indefinable, inaccessible, too powerful, or too respected to be taken on, reasoned with, or attacked. This frustration is displaced onto an available and vulnerable "scapegoat" who is seen as receiving his or her "just deserts" as the symbol, representation, or outlet for hostility (Brodsky, 1976; Matthiesen & Einarsen, 2010; Thylefors, 1987).

Humor-orientated bullying may be seen as a less pervasive and more covert aggressive behavior by the bully(s) and occurs when a person becomes the butt of jokes or a target for humiliation, teasing, and ridicule. Of course, good-natured, interpersonal, symmetrical humor equally balanced and reciprocated between employees who share similar status or genuine social acceptance is common and usually encouraged in the workplace. However, if the humor is imbalanced or asymmetrical and the jokes are not repaid or reciprocated, the target may perceive this behavior as aggressive, disrespectful, and as bullying (Matthiesen & Einarsen, 2002; Matthiesen & Einarsen, 2010).

Work-related stalking involves repeated and pervasive forms of communication, physical contact, or behaviors related to the workplace that are intrusive and harassing in nature (Petherick, 2009) and, as such, the target experiences rational fear (Meloy, 1998; Petherick, 2009). Behaviors can include sending gifts, persistent written, telephone, or online communications or messages, waiting for the target outside work or home, and any other unnecessary and repeated forms of contact (Matthiesen & Einarsen, 2002; Petherick, 2009; Matthiesen & Einarsen, 2010).

Bullying of workplace newcomers, otherwise known as "rite of passage" bullying, has been a characteristic of workplaces for centuries as is particularly common in the armed forces and male-dominated workplaces such as mechanical workshops and shipping (Brodsky, 1976; Matthiesen & Einarsen, 2010). This behavior is classed as bullying when the target suffers intense and long-lasting victimization that can lead to long-lasting psychological damage, suicide, or suicidal ideation (Buttigieg, Bryant, Hanley & Liu, 2011; Einarsen, 1999; Matthiesen & Einarsen, 2010).

Judicial derelict occurs when the victim of bullying finds his or her complaints or reports with either retaliatory aggression or passive obstruction from a range of people or systems thought to be places of trust or rescue (Einarsen, Matthiesen & Mikkelsen, 1999; Matthiesen & Einarsen, 2010). Einarsen et al. (1999) categorize this form of overt or covert aggression as secondary bullying, wherein the complainant feels ignored, that there is a lack of concern or responsibility on behalf of the organization, or that further complaints may lead to retaliation such as withdrawal of promotion opportunities or even threat of dismissal.

Retaliatory acts after whistle-blowing occurs when an employee, in good faith, notifies authorities of incidents of wrongdoing, such as unethical conduct or criminal acts (Matthiesen & Einarsen, 2010; Near and Miceli, 1996). Rather than this wrongdoing being investigated or stopped, retaliatory acts after whistle-blowing occurs when the person reporting the misdeed becomes the victim of a process intended to "shoot the messenger" and punish or ostracize him or her. These punishing behaviors can include isolation, dismissal, and sullying the good name of the person within the organization, and perhaps more widely throughout the associated industry or community (Matthiesen & Einarsen, 2010; Near & Miceli, 1996).

Consequences of Workplace Bullying

Workplace bullying can precipitate profound and far-reaching consequences for the victim, the perpetrator, the organization, and wider society (Buttigieg, Bryant, Hanley & Liu, 2011). For the victim, physical outcomes can include headaches, gastro intestinal and sleep disorders, psychological outcomes such as stress, a number of negative mental disorders, and outcomes including suicide (Buttigieg, Bryant, Hanley & Liu, 2011; Einarsen, 1999). Lutgen-Sandvik, Tracy & Alberts (2007) compare workplace bullying to a third-degree burn, which has the capacity to result in deep and permanent damage.

At the organizational level, outcomes of workplace bullying can include increased employee turnover, decreased loyalty and job satisfaction, reduced productivity, high absenteeism, negative impact on the organization's reputation and brand, public backlash, and risk of litigation (Buttigieg, Bryant, Hanley & Liu, 2011; Salin, 2003). Estimates suggest that one-third to one-half of all work-related stress may be ascribed to bullying at work and that stress-responses to bullying contribute significantly to the total working days lost due to sickness (Long, 2002). Consequences of workplace bullying then shift to the society, which proceeds to bear the costs associated with medical support, sickness, unemployment benefits, litigation, and the life-time burden of disease (Buttigieg, Bryant, Hanley & Liu, 2011; Salin, 2003; Vaughn, Fu, Bender, DeLisi, Beaver, Perron & Howard, 2010).

In a study of 45 litigated cases of workplace bullying, Martin & LaVan (2010) identified outcomes of stress, retaliation by employees, reduced productivity, Post traumatic stress disorder, and physical violence. The negative organizational outcomes measured were reduced morale, productivity, and safety as well as increased voluntary turnover.

Perpetrators are similarly susceptible to negative health, legal, and career outcomes of workplace bullying. Adverse consequences for the bully can be the result of social dysfunction, inability to moderate or recognize his or her own inappropriate, aggressive behaviors and responses, or the legal ramifications or hostile responses by coworkers or management. Negative psychological outcomes for bullies have been found in terms of depression, anxiety, post traumatic stress disorder, loss of confidence in their own abilities, and suicidal ideation (Jenkins, Winefield & Sarris, 2011). Additionally, accused bullies are commonly terminated by their superiors and shunned by prospective employers, despite accusations being unsubstantiated (Jenkins, Winefield & Sarris, 2011).

Risk Factors

Martin & LeVan (2010) used Salin's conceptual framework to identify three distinct categories of risk factors within an organization that increased the likelihood or the climate for organizational bullying: precipitating variables, motivating structures, and enabling structures (Table 13.2). Precipitating variables in isolation are not responsible for the act, but are seen to hasten, or bring about the act prematurely. Motivating structures are those conditions that provide reasons for, or impel bullying behaviors, and enabling structures provide the means, conditions, or a conduit by which bullying behavior can occur.

Unlike school-based bullying, some studies have shown little support for a causal relationship between workplace bullying and the personality of the victim (Glaso, Matthiesen, Nielsen & Einarsen, 2007), where other researchers posit a loose link between personality and victim behaviors citing traits such as negative affect, introversion, neediness, instability, and conscientiousness being contributing factors (Einarsen, 1999; Shallcross, 2003). Those at heightened risk, however, have been found to be young employees with little experience or authority, older employees, and newcomers (Buttigieg et al., 2011).

A number of studies have analyzed victim perceptions of bullies, as well as categorized the personality of the bully by measures such as the ICES Personality Inventory (Bartram, 2008) and the IBS Clinical Inventory (Mauger, Adkinson, Zoss, Firestone & Hook, 1980; Seigne, Coyne, Randall & Parker, 2007). These studies suggest the personality of the bully as the major contributing factor to workplace bullying and aggression that includes aggression, hostility, and extraversion and independence (Seigne et al., 2007). Additionally, bullies are usually

Table 13.2 Organizational Variables for Organizational Bullying

Precipitating Variables	Motivating Structures	Enabling Structures
Employees feeling powerless	Politicized climate	Perceived power imbalances
Organizational restructuring/ downsizing	High competition between employees	Low costs/consequences for the perpetrator
Change of management	Disciplinary action for violation of production norms or expectations	Lack of punishment for bullying behaviors
Changes in group composition	Benefits for the perpetrator	Autocratic management style
Reengineering/delegation of control to autonomous teams	Sales/production ranking/ achievement awards	Laissez-faire leadership style
Cost cutting		Bullying accepted as a rite of passage
Promotion of perpetrator		

Source: Martin and LeVan (2010)

egocentric, selfish, and show little empathy or respect for the opinion of others (Seigne et al., 2007). As previously discussed, however, these problematic personality traits are often those deemed the best fit for organizations based in individualistic cultures and workplaces, where high levels of aggressiveness, competitiveness, and achievement are considered most attractive by employees and associated with the ideals of solid leadership and success.

Reducing the Risk of Workplace Bullying

As more companies and organizations implement programs and protocols aimed at reducing and preventing workplace bullying, it has been recognized that few of these have been research- and evidence-based with very few empirical articles published on the issue of prevention since the late 1990s (Mikkelsen, Hogh & Louise, 2011; Ta & Loumis, 2007). Reviews of scientific literature further indicate that many efforts to reduce workplace bullying yield, at best, limited success or even outright failure (Mikkelsen, 2011).

Crucial to the development of any intervention program are the initial foundational structures upon which it is built. Workplaces, like families, neighborhoods and cultures, have their own blend of personalities, idiosyncrasies, objectives, and values. As such, to adopt a once-size-fits-all, or blanket, approach to solving any organizational problem, such as workplace bullying, has little guarantee of success. With this in mind, Mikkelsen (2011) adopted Goldenhar, LaMontagne, Katz, Heaney, and Landsbergis's (2001) three-phase model to research and develop an intervention program found beneficial to the organization for which their study was designed (Mikkelsen, 2011). Furthermore, the intervention was process-orientated, involved multitiered employee participation in its development and implementation, and was based upon the findings of the organization's unique qualitative and quantitative data. This workplace-specific approach suggests its suitability for a number of diverse organizational structures and cultures.

First, the researchers and design consultants established partnerships with and formed local (according to individual branch/department/workgroups) steering committees that included members from all levels of management and staff. Preintervention interviews with these groups tested causal hypotheses and discussed the efficacy of various interventions; interventions that were developed according to empirically based theories on the etiologies and prevention of conflicts and bullying.

Next, the information and knowledge gathered were analyzed in order to recognize group and wider-organization factors that could stimulate success of interventions (such as a participatory approach, building trustful relationships) or alternatively, obstruct the success of interventions (such as poor planning of the interventions or lack of management support). Finally, the interventions were designed and implemented and a process, including timeframe, of measuring success was developed. In Mikkelsen, Hogh & Louise's (2011) experiment, the interventions included classes on bullying and conflict management attended by all levels of staff as well as distribution of newsletters, posters, and pamphlets and steering group interviews and meetings.

Results indicate that participants benefited from the interventions and found the classes in conflict resolution and management as well as group interviews particularly helpful. The authors of the study highlight the importance of a participatory approach to development of interventions by all organizational levels as well as recognizing and discussing stimulating and obstructing factors (Mikkelsen, 2011).

Cyberbullying

Cyberbullying is a form of relational bullying that occurs via electronic and cyberspace mediums, such as Internet web site postings and electronic messaging, intended to cause harm to the victim (Beran & Li, 2005; Lenhart, Purcell, Smith & Zickuhr, 2010). Research shows that computers and the burgeoning growth of the Internet yield substantial benefits for students, particularly in the areas of collaborative learning, social interaction (Li, 2007), research gathering, and information-sharing (Livingstone & Shepherd, 1997). Furthermore, computers in classrooms have been shown to have positive impacts on student learning in all subjects (Li, 2007).

Recent reports of mobile and Internet use, along with studies into social media such as Facebook, Twitter, MySpace, and instant messaging, estimate that access to social networking sites by 12- to 17-year-olds has risen from 55% in 2006 to 73% in 2009 (Lenhart, Purcell, Smith & Zickuhr, 2010; Sontage, Clemans, Graber & Lyndon, 2011). The growth of technology-based learning and social interaction, however, has created new and significant problems that deserve enquiry and attention. Findings suggest that there may be aspects unique to cyberbullying when compared to other forms of traditional victimization, and that a deeper understanding of cyberbullying may result in more effective evidence-based interventions (Sontage, Clemans, Graber & Lyndon, 2011).

Unique Characteristics of Cyberbullying

Bullying online provides some distinct advantages for the perpetrator as well as disadvantages for the victim. For the bully, intentionally aggressive and harmful behaviors have the same potential to frighten and damage the victim, but can be done at a time convenient to the bully, in real-time, at any time, and anonymously (Kirby, 2008). Indeed, under the cover of anonymity, bullies can act more aggressively than they would in face-to-face confrontations as well as avoid the risk of physical injury (Hinduja & Patchin, 2008; Sontage, Clemans, Graber & Lyndon, 2011). Additionally, where face-to-face bullying can be witnessed and moderated by parents, teachers, or peers, cyberbullying can be performed in private, without regulation or consequence (Holt & Keyes, 2004).

Sontage, Clemans, Graber & Lyndon's (2011) study into cyber-aggression found that 40% of adolescent bullies participated *exclusively* in cyberbullying and that 31% engaged in face-to-face *as well as* cyberbullying. Thus, where some adolescents are using cyberspace as an additional outlet for aggressive behaviors, there are others for whom the physical distance, anonymity, or perceivable impersonal nature of cyber-confrontation is preferable. One explanation for this phenomenon may be that, although face-to-face-only and cyber-only aggressors resembled one another in most analyses, including measurements for proactive aggression (goal-oriented, calculated aggression motivated by external reward), cyber-only bullies scored significantly lower (in fact, the same as low/no aggressive participants) on reactive aggression (a response to an external stimulus; impulsive and retaliatory) than those who bully online and in person (Fite & Vitulano, 2011; Sontage, Clemans, Graber & Lyndon, 2011).

As noted, proactive aggression, as a more retaliatory and impulsive form of aggression in response to an immediate threat or frustration, is more likely to be involved in face-to-face aggression. On the other hand, proactive, premeditated, and goal-orientated aggression may be more suited to cyberbullying (Sontage, Clemans, Graber & Lyndon, 2011). Furthermore, cyber-only bullies, though tending to exhibit less aggressive proclivities, may also benefit from being shielded from the immediate emotional suffering of the victim.

Cyberbullying emanates most frequently from relationship problems such as break-ups, jealousy or frustration, ganging up, or perceived personal intrusions or harms (Hoff & Mitchell, 2009). Victims may experience profound negative effects, particularly exacerbated by the relentless "24/7" prevalence, that the bullying can follow them from school, into the home, and social activities via mobile telephones and portable computers, and that perpetrators can hide their identities. Additionally, aggressive tactics in cyberspace are not limited to damaging words or physical intimidation or injury, but can extend to sexual or degrading images able to be shared by or posted to an almost limitless array of web sites, online bulletin boards, or chat rooms.

Although the negative psychological effects generally mirrored those of victims of traditional, face-to-face bullying, online victims report a greater sense of powerlessness and fear, particularly when the identity of the perpetrator is unknown (Hoff & Mitchell, 2009). Online victims were also more likely to believe that victimization would eventually decrease in its own time thus justifying an avoidance strategy on the part of the victim, which, in more cases than not, allowed the victimization to escalate (Hoff & Mitchell, 2009).

Prevalence

US figures estimate that 17% of school children are victims of cyberbullying and 18% are perpetrators (Patchin & Hinduja, 2008), figures significantly lower than Canadian studies estimating victimity at 25% and offending at 17% (Li, 2006). US and UK studies find that girls are more likely to be victims of cyberbullying and that boys are more likely to be the perpetrators (Dehue et al., 2008; Smith et al., 2008; Wang et al., 2009) and that, unlike face-to-face bullying, there seems to be no correlation between age and victimization (Tokunaga, 2010).

Forms of Cyberbullying

Willard (2005) described eight types of cyberbullying:

- **Flaming**: sending angry, rude, vulgar messages to a victim either in private or public domains
- **Harassment**: constantly sending messages that may or may not be offensive, but intended to cause the victim distress
- **Denigration**: sending degrading, untrue, unkind rumors about a victim to others
- **Cyberstalking**: sending harassing, threatening, or intimidating messages

- **Masquerading**: assuming a false identity and sending information to either discredit, embarrass, endanger, or intimidate the victim
- **Trickery**: engaging in trickery or deception to solicit embarrassing information about a victim and then making the information public
- **Outing**: posting personal information about the victim for all to see
- **Exclusion**: intentionally isolating a person, with the intent to cause distress, from a social group by blocking access

Offender Typologies

Similar to face-to-face bullies, cyberbullies are more likely to be victims of bullying, are more likely to have poor relationships with their caregivers, are at higher risk of displaying antisocial behavior and substance abuse, and are more likely to rate highly on Internet use.

Studies have identified four main typologies of cyberbullies (Feinberg & Robey, 2009):

- **Vengeful angel**: takes on the role of the vigilante who protects, defends, or retaliates on behalf of a friend who has been bullied or cyberbullied. This offender does not see him- or herself as a bully, but thinks his or her actions are justified retaliation.
- **Power hungry**: (also known as "revenge of the nerds") exert their authority and strike fear in heart of the victim. These offenders are often victims of face-to-face bullies who, for a variety of reasons (e.g., physical stature) avoid face-to-face bullying, feeling less fearful or more confident in cyberspace.
- **Mean girls**: usually bully out of boredom or for entertainment and torment their victim in social groups.
- **Inadvertent**: do not think about the consequences of their actions and harm or distress is unintentional.

In summary, cyberbullying is a significant problem and may, due to its unique features, present more harm than the more traditional face-to-face bullying modality. These features include the pervasive and consistent nature of cyberbullying, that the offender has the choice of multiple tools such as Internet, phone, text and instant messaging, and has access to the victim at any time and place. Researchers, educators, and parents alike are concerned that this form of bullying is growing more rapidly than adequate responses to it. All stakeholders need to adopt strategies to identify offenders quickly, limit their unsupervised access to the technology, and encourage victims to recognize incidents of cyberbullying and to report to adults if they witness or are targeted by an offender.

Harassment

The terms *bullying* and *harassment* are often used interchangeably but they are distinguishable by both law and definition. Where bullying is widely defined as including aggressive, intentional, persistent, and repetitive acts that cause harm to, or oppression or intimidation, of a victim (Carr-Gregg & Manocha, 2011; Rigby & Smith, 2011; Woods & Wolke, 2003), harassment refers to offensive and discriminatory treatment of one person by another based on the victim's personal characteristics (such as age, race, religion, sexual orientation, disability, gender), as protected by laws of antidiscrimination and equal opportunity (Connolly, 2006; Washington State Department of Labour and Industries, 2011).

Sexual Harassment

Sexual harassment is unwanted behavior of a sexual nature. Acts can be verbal, physical, written, or visual and are severe or pervasive, and denigrate, ridicule, or intimidate the target. Most commonly reported incidents involve men sexually harassing women, but reports do include women sexually harassing men. Sexual harassment can traverse a wide range of behaviors from suggestive comments, lewd looks or gestures, explicit jokes, innuendo and belittling, to sexual assault, indecent exposure, and rape (Cates & Machin, 2012).

The Equal Employment Opportunity Commission (EEOC) recognizes two types of sexual harassment. The most common form, quid pro quo (Latin for "this for that"), occurs when the victim either submits to, or accepts, behavior of a sexually harassing nature, and this rejection or submission forms the basis for employment opportunities or conditions (Cates & Machin, 2012). The second type, *hostile environment,* creates an intimidating, threatening, or offensive environment wherein, if the person tries to stop the behavior, he or she is subjected to distressing consequences such as demotion, termination, or ridicule (Cates & Machin, 2012).

One recent study found that 25% of participating organizations experienced a rise in recent sexual harassment claims and that 37% of these organizations provide yearly workshops and training sessions in regard to sexual harassment (Cates & Machin, 2012).

Racial Harassment

Racial harassment is unwanted behavior based on ethnicity and includes written or verbal insults, threats, or demeaning comments in reference to skin color or racial origins. Behaviors can include racial "jokes," name-calling including nicknames of a racial nature, damage to property including graffiti, and inciting others to commit similar offenses.

Estimates suggest that 98% of ethnic minority groups experience at least one racially harassing event within one 12-month period, and that 66% experience at least one racially harassing event within a two-week period (Buchanan, 2009).

Religious Harassment

Religious harassment is unwanted behavior based on religious beliefs or practices. Like other forms of harassment, religious harassment can encompass a wide range of behaviors such as denigrating the victim's dress or religious views or customs, disallowing leave requests for religious-based holidays or cultural events (when others' religious days are provided for), and uninvited evangelizing or proselytizing (Nimon, 2011).

According to figures provided by the EEOC (2011), religious harassment figures are rising ahead of all other types of discrimination, doubling in the last 13 years, and represents increases in claims by most religious groups across America (EEOC, 2011; Nimon, 2011).

Disability Harassment

Disability harassment is unwanted behavior based on physical or intellectual impairment or disability that creates an exclusionary, intimidating, difficult, hostile, or threatening environment. Although behaviors may not be conscious or deliberate, disability harassment may demonstrate stereotyping and stigmatizing of people with disabilities thus limiting their access to employment opportunity, social groups, or wider social structures (Draper, Reid & McMahon, 2011).

Sexual Orientation Harassment

Harassment of a person based on sexual orientation is a form of discrimination against those who are either known or presumed to be lesbian, gay, bisexual, or transgender (Stacey, 2011). Harassing behaviors include name calling, stereotyping, derogatory or demeaning comments or suggestion by innuendo, exclusionary behaviors, or unwanted disclosures to others of the victim's sexuality. Domains for discrimination can include the workplace, sport or educational arenas, domestic partner insurance, protection from criminal victimization (hate crimes), child adoption, and exclusion of same-sex partners from social events (Stacey, 2011).

U.S. Equal Employment Opportunity Commission

The U.S. EEOC is responsible for enforcing federal laws that make it illegal to discriminate against a job applicant or an employee because of the person's race, color, religion, sex (including pregnancy), national origin, age (40 or older), disability, or genetic information. It is also illegal to discriminate against a person because the person complained about discrimination, filed a charge of discrimination, or participated in an employment discrimination investigation or lawsuit" (EEOC, 2011).

Data compiled by the EEOC include the total number of individual charges filed in the United States per fiscal year in regard to cases of discrimination reported across all types of work situations; hiring, firing, promotions, harassment, wages, and benefits. Figure 13.1 lists charges filed for 2011.

Significant to discussions differentiating and comparing the prevalence and outcomes of bullying verses harassment, are the findings of Russell, Sinclair, Katerina, Poteat, and Koenig's (2012) study of adolescents, which found that the prevalence of harassment based upon bias is more common than nonbiased bullying (35.8% compared to 15.5%, respectively) and that victim outcomes for harassment based on bias were worse.

When outcomes for bias-based harassment were compared against those for nonbias-based bullying, Russel, Sinclair, Poteat, and Koenig (2012) found that bias-based harassment more negatively affected health status, substance use levels, and academic performance and truancy was more likely to involve use of a weapon and damage to property (Russel, Sinclair, Poteat & Koenig, 2012).

Consequently, the importance of identifying the needs and resources required to address the issue of vulnerability resulting from prejudice cannot be overstated. As antibullying and discrimination laws are increasingly employed to protect vulnerable groups, research and empirically based interventions must also work to identify and impact the causes that motivate and maintain this behavior.

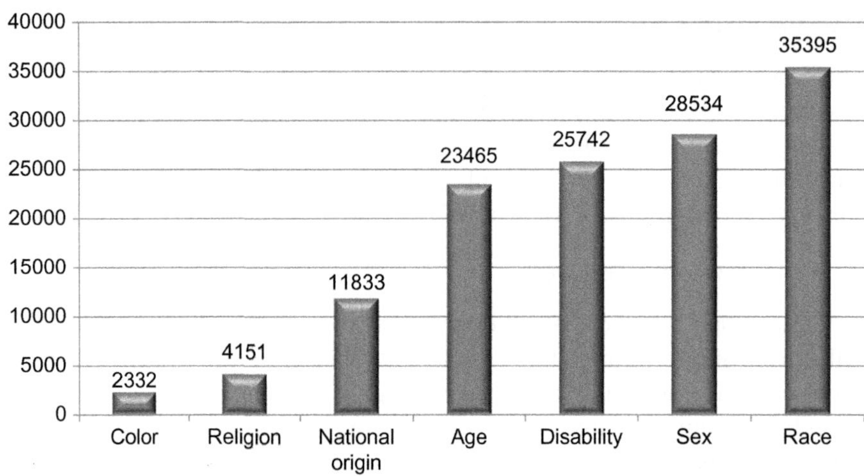

FIGURE 13.1 EEOC Charge Statistics, Fiscal Year, 2011

Bullying, Harassment, and Criminological Theory

Critical to communicating and understanding the main concepts and causes of crime and deviant behavior is good criminological theory (Mazerolle, 2009). Similarly, if one is to design strategies for change, theory is critical to understanding the mechanisms of change, the variables that influence change, and how variables can relate to each other in time and space (Sutton, Cherney & White, 2008). As such, theories of crime, criminal and deviant behavior "represent the building blocks for organising knowledge and are crucial for informing interventions aimed at reducing crime" (Mazerolle, 2009, p. 189).

This section will seek to explain the social phenomena of bullying and harassment and apply three criminological theories; Agnew's (1992) general strain theory (GST) to explain bullying behavior, Sutherland's (1947) differential association theory (DAT) to explain generational and peer-influence on bullying behaviors, and Felson's (1995, 2002) routine activities theory (RAT) to investigate the role of guardianship in reducing bullying behaviors.

General Strain Theory

The key proposition of GST is that strains cause delinquency. Agnew (1992) identified three categories of strain: the failure to achieve valued goals, stressful life events, and the presentation of toxic stimuli to individuals such as emotional and physical abuse, victimization, or discrimination. These strains create negative emotions which in turn influence delinquent, deviant, or criminal behavior (Agnew, 1992). According to GST, these deviant behavioral responses to negative stimuli serve to correct or alleviate negative emotions caused by negative life events (strains) (Agnew, 1992).

Patchin and Hinduja (2011) applied GST to incidents of face-to-face and cyberbullying and found a clear relationship between strain and both kinds of behaviors, with those reporting strains and negative emotions such as anger and/or frustration, as being significantly more likely to be bullies. The authors of this study concluded that "the results from the current work are consistent with much of the previous strain literature and highlight the robustness of the basic GST model in its theoretical applicability to both bullying and cyberbullying" (Patchin & Hinduja, 2011, p. 741).

Building upon the results from this study, the authors suggest several recommendations:

- That schools implement health education programs involving emotional self-regulation strategies for students to help them deal appropriately with interpersonal conflict and friction.
- That parents, caregivers, and educators open lines of communication and create environments of care and empathy where students can vent, discuss ways to deal with conflict, or report offenders.
- According to the contention posited by the GST that strain produces pressure, and that this pressure leads to deviant behavior (to correct or release the pressure caused by negative emotions), that positive outlets for youths' aggression and frustration can be directed to extracurricular physical or mental activities. These activities would also be designed to improve feelings of self-worth and value.

Differential Association Theory

Sutherland's (1947) DAT posits that behaviors, both good and bad, are learned by association with parents, peers, and significant others. Sutherland contends then, that criminal or delinquent behaviors are more likely to occur when an individual associates with delinquent peers or deviant parents who demonstrate a propensity for violating laws or social norms, or exhibit antisocial behaviors and attitudes. The effects of these associations are dependent on frequency, duration, priority, and intensity of these relationships (Sutherland, 1947).

The literature provides abundant evidence of a strong relationship between criminality and association with delinquent peers (Elliott & Menard, 1996; Simons, Wu, Conger & Lorenz, 1994; Warr, 2005) and that juveniles who associate with delinquent peers are more likely to engage in antisocial behaviors and exhibit positive attitudes toward the use of violence (Moon, Hwang & McCluskey, 2011). Furthermore, several studies have examined the relationship between associating with delinquent peers and attitudes toward violence and bullying and found that those who associate with bullies are more likely to engage in bullying, indicating that the DAT is one feasible explanation for bullying as a social phenomenon (Espelage, Bosworth & Simon, 2000; Moon et al., 2011; Pepler & Craig, 1995).

Given the significant support for an association between delinquent-peer association and antisocial behaviors such as bullying, it is rational to suggest that strategies that discourage these negative relationships may reduce the incidence of bullying, particularly if the perpetrators are acting as a group. To this end, studies relevant to preventing delinquent associations may be helpful and suggest that:

- Parental attachment plays an important role in preventing delinquency and determining proclivity for delinquent associations (Spohn, 2012; Warr, 1993) and that positive or negative mothering and fathering were found to be related to adolescents' personal characteristics as well as deviant peer association (Padilla-Walker, Bean & Hsieh, 2011).

- Social competence has a direct relationship on academic success as well as association with delinquent peers, and that educational and parental development of adolescents' social competencies will reduce delinquent-peer involvement, protect at-risk youth from engaging in antisocial behaviors, increase academic success, and initiate a positive life-course (Stepp, Pardini, Loeber & Morris, 2011).

Routine Activities Theory

Felson's RAT framework provides a very accessible and usable guide to link theory and prevention in regards to the issues of face-to-face and cyberbullying and harassment. Felson argues that, for crime to occur, the presence of three elements need to come together in time and space—a motivated offender, a suitable target, and the absence of capable guardianship (see Figure 13.2). In the case of bullying and harassment the target would be the victim, the offender the bully(s), and the guardianship would include educators, parents, and security devices such as cameras and alarms, as well as bystanders. Absence of capable guardianship exacerbates the likelihood of a crime occurring whether it be absent in a neighborhood, a street, or a school (Felson, 1995).

Of particular significance to discussions of reducing incidence of face-to-face and cyberbullying and harassment is the issue of capable guardianship. For instance, Reyns, Henson, and Fisher (2011) found that lack of guardianship (either human, or electronic in the form of profile trackers for cyberbullying) was a greater influence on bullying than suitability of the victim. In addition, cyberbullying and victimization have been found more likely to occur if the computer is in a private place, such as a bedroom, rather than in a common-room such as a lounge room where behaviors have some chance of being monitored (Sengupta & Chaudhuri, 2011).

RAT suggests the efficacy of a proactive, rather than reactive, punitive response to bullying and harassment and offers many practical reductive and preventative strategies such as:

At home:

- Move computers and restrict mobile phone use to common areas in the home such as the kitchen and lounge room.

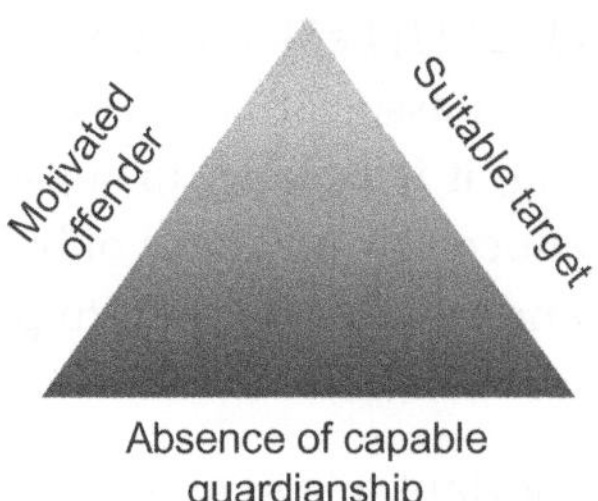

FIGURE 13.2 Felson's crime triangle.

- Ensure parental access and monitoring of social networking sites.
- Do not allow youths to delete browsing histories (if there is no history, it has been deleted).

At school:

- Increase opportunities for surveillance.
- Clearly define boundaries (and preferred use within these spaces), and restrict student access to private and secluded areas, such as classrooms and corridors during recess.
- Create clear sight-lines by trimming trees/hedges that prevent visual observation and install corner-sight mirrors.
- Regularly inspect and monitor toilet blocks during recess times.
- Restrict known offenders to high-visibility supervision areas.
- Create a supervised, calm, and accepting "refuge" for victimized or ostracized children with, perhaps, computer, reading, or music facilities, that they can access at recess times.

Conclusion

This chapter has defined and discussed some key features, characteristics, and strategies for dealing with incidents of bullying and harassment across the domains of school, work, and online. It has highlighted the importance of a continued commitment to providing evidence-based research and theory in dealing with this social phenomenon that has profound negative implications for victim, offender, school, organization, and the wider society. Important themes emerging from this discussion are:

- The importance of theory-driven and evidenced-based approaches to researching and designing environment-specific antibullying and harassment programs.
- The need for appropriately trained and qualified personnel to oversee the development and facilitation of antibullying and harassment protocols.
- The importance of managements' solid commitment to antibullying and harassment programs and strategies and an inclusive development approach (staff/teachers/students/employees).

Finally, if bullying behavior in children is an accurate marker for identifying life-course aggression and violent behaviors, and predictive of significant negative outcomes for the victim, bully, and wider society; and if bullying behaviors can be accurately identified in preschool-aged children, it behooves researchers and policy-makers to identify and address this behavior from the earliest age. As an issue of public health, further research into the development of effective reduction strategies is of profound importance for the safety and well-being of all.

Questions

1. Explain the difference between bullying and harassment.
2. List three reasons for a historical acceptance of bullying.

3. List three examples of relational bullying and explain why this type of bullying may fall under the radar of educators/authorities.
4. Explain Stalin's three distinct categories of risk factors within an organization (precipitating variables, motivating structures, and enabling structures) that increase the likelihood or the climate for organizational bullying. Provide an example of each.
5. List four forms of cyberbullying and provide a definition of each.
6. Apply one criminological theory and explain its utility to the issue of bullying. Provide two recommendations from this theory that may serve to impact bullying in a workplace or a school.

References

Adams, F. D., & Lawrence, G. J. (2011). Bullying victims: The effects last into college. *American Secondary Education, 40(1)*, 4–13. <http://search.proquest.com/docview/921231925?accountid=26503>.

Agnew, R. (1992). Foundation for a general strain theory of crime and delinquency. *Criminology, 30*, 47–87.

American Psychiatric Association. (2000). DSM-IV.

American School Counselor Association, (2005). *The ASCA national model: A framework for school counseling programs* (2nd ed.). Alexandria, VA: Author.

Bartram, D. (2008). Global norms: Towards some guidelines for aggregating personality norms across countries. *International Journal of Testing, 8(4)*, 315–333.

Bauman, S., & Del Rio, A. (02/2006). Preservice teachers' responses to bullying scenarios: Comparing physical, verbal, and relational bullying. *Journal of Educational Psychology, 98*(1), 219–231. ISSN 0022-0663.

Beaty, L. A., & Alexeyev, E. B. (2008). The problem of school bullies: What the research tells us. *Adolescence, 43*(169), 1–11.

Beran, T., & Li, Q. (2005). Cyber-harassment: A new method for an old behaviour. *Journal of Educational Computing Research, 32*(3), 265–277.

Bonanno, R. A., & Hymel, S. (07/2010). Beyond hurt feelings: Investigating why some victims of bullying are at greater risk for suicidal ideation. *Merrill-Palmer Quarterly, 56*(3), 420. ISSN 0272-930X.

Boulton, J. J., & Underwood, K. (1992). Bully/victim problems among middle school children. *British Journal of Educational Psychology, 62*, 73–87.

Bowlby, J. (1969). *Attachment and loss: Vol. 1: Attachment.* New York: Basic Books.

Bowling, N. A., & Beehr, T. A. (2006). Workplace harassment from the victim's perspective: A theoretical model and meta-analysis. *The Journal of Applied Psychology, 91*(5), 998–1012.

Bradshaw, C. P., & Garbarino, J. (2004). Social cognition as a mediator of the influence of family and community violence on adolescent development: Implications for intervention. *Annals New York Academy of Science, 1036*, 85–105.

Bradshaw, C. P., O'Brennan, L. M., & Sawyer, A. L. (2008). Examining variation in attitudes toward aggressive retaliation and perceptions of safety among bullies, victims, and bully/victims. *Professional School Counseling, 12*(1), 10–21. <http://search.proquest.com/docview/213337301?accountid=26503>.

Brennan, B. School bullying: It's time to face facts [online]. Teacher: The national education magazine, Sept 2009: 38–39. Availability: <http://search.informit.com.au.ezproxy.bond.edu.au/documentSummary;dn=043663719462117;res=IELHSS>.

Brodsky, C. M. (1976). *The Harassed Worker*. Toronto, Canada: Lexington Books.

Buchanan, N. L. (2009). Unique and joint effects of sexual and racial harassment on college students' well-being. *Basic & Applied Social Psychology, 31*(3), 267–285.

Buttigieg, D. M., Bryant, M., Hanley, G., & Liu, J. (2011). The causes and consequences of workplace bullying and discrimination: Results from an exploratory study. *Labour & Industry, 22*(1), 117–141. <http://search.proquest.com/docview/964019214?accountid=26503>.

Campbell, W. (2000). Techniques for dealing with student harassment at high school level. *American Secondary Education, 29(1)*, 34. <http://searchproquest.com.ezproxy.bond.edu.au/docview/195184247>.

Carrera, M., DePalma, R., & Lameiras, M. (2011). Toward a more comprehensive understanding of bullying in school settings. *Educational Psychology Review, 23*(4), 479–499. doi:10.1007/s10648-011-9171-x.

Carr-Gregg, M., & Manocha, R. (Mar 2011). Bullying: Effects, prevalence and strategies for detection [online]. *Australian Family Physician, 40*(3) 98–102. Availability: <http://search.informit.com.au.ezproxy.bond.edu.au/documentSummary;dn=806920434455968;res=IELHEA> ISSN: 0300-8495.

Cates, S. V., & Machin, L. (2012). The state of sexual harassment in America: What is the status of sexual harassment in the US workplace today? *Journal of Global Business Management, 8*(1), 133–138. <http://search.proquest.com/docview/993153654?accountid=26503>.

Chan, J. H. F. (07/2006). Systemic patterns in bullying and victimization. *School Psychology International, 27*(3), 352–369. ISSN 0143-0343.

Chapell, M. S., Hasselman, S. L., Kitchin, T., Lomon, S. N., MacIver, K. W., & Sarullo, P. L. (2006). Bullying in elementary school, high school, and university. *Adolescence, 41*(164), 633–648.

Connolly, M. (2006). Harassment, bullying and stress: The legal issues. *Accountancy Ireland, 38*(6), 38–40.

Cox, H. (1991). Verbal abuse nationwide. Part II: Impact and modifications. *Nursing Management, 22*, 66–67.

Craig, W. M., & Pepler, D. J. (2003). Identifying and targeting risk for involvement in bullying and victimization. *Canadian Journal of Psychiatry, 48*, 577–582.

Craig, W. M., Sue, J., Murphy, A. N., & Bauer, J. (2010). Understanding and addressing obesity and victimization in youth. *Obesity and Weight Management, 6*(1), 12–16.

Craig, W., Harel-Fisch, Y., Fogel-Grinvald, H., Dostaler, S., Hetland, J., Simons-Morton, B., et al. (2009). A cross-national profile of bullying and victimization among adolescents in 40 countries. *International Journal of Public Health, 54*, 216–224. doi:10.1007/s00038-009-5413-9.

Craig, W. M., & Pepler, D. J. (2007). Understanding bullying. *Canadian Psychology [PsycARTICLES], 48*(2), 86. <http://search.proquest.com/docview/229302736?accountid=26503>.

Crick, N. R., & Grotpeter, J. K. (1995). Relational aggression, gender and social-psychopathological adjustment. *Child Development, 66*, 710–722.

Cross, D., Shaw, T., & Hearn, L., et al. (2009). *Australian covert bullying prevalence study (ACBPS)*. Perth: Child Health Promotion Research Centre, Edith Cowan University.

De Souza, E. R., & Ribeiro, J. (2005). Bullying and sexual harassment among Brazilian high school students. *Journal of Interpersonal Violence, 20*(9), 1018–1038.

Donnellan, M. B., Trzeniewski, K. H., Robins, R. W., Moffitt, T. E., & Caspi, A. (2005). Low self esteem is related to aggression, antisocial behaviour, and delinquency. *Psychological Science, 16*(4), 328–335.

Draper, W., Reid, C., & McMahon, B. (October 2011). Workplace discrimination and the perception of disability. *Rehabilitation Counseling Bulletin, 55*, 29–37. doi:10.1177/0034355210392792 (first published on December 28, 2010).

Einarsen, S. (1999). The nature and causes of bullying. *International Journal of Manpower, 20(1/2)*, 16–27.

Einarsen, S., Matthiesen, S. B., & Mikkelsen, E. (1999). *Time is a great healer? Health effects after bullying at work*. Bergen, Norway: University of Bergen.

Equal Employment Opportunity Commission (EEOC). Retrieved from <http://www.eeoc.gov/eeoc/newsroom/release/11-27-09.cfm>.

Espelage, D. L., & Swearer, S. M. (2010). A social-ecological model form bullying prevention and intervention: Understanding the impact of adults in the social ecology of youngsters. In S. R. Jimerson, S. M. Swearer, & D. L. Espelage (Eds.), *Handbook of bullying in schools. An international perspective* (pp. 61–72). New York: Routledge.

Espelage, D. L., Bosworth, K., & Simon, T. R. (2000). Examining the social context of bullying behaviors in early adolescence. *Journal of Counseling & Development, 78,* 326–333.

Estell, D. B., Farmer, T. W., Irvin, M. J., Crowther, A., Akos, P., & Boudah, D. J. (2009). Students with exceptionalities and the peer group context of bullying and victimization in late elementary school. *Journal of Child and Family Studies, 18,* 136–150.

Farrell, G. (1995). In M. Tonry & D. Farrington (Eds.), *Building a safer society: Strategic approaches to crime prevention* (19, pp. 469–534). Crime and Justice. (A Review of Research).

Feinberg, T., & Robey, N. (2009). Cyberbullying: Intervention and prevention strategies. *National Association of School Psychologists, 38*(4) Retrieved from <http://www.nasponline.org/publications/cq/pdf/V38N4_CyberbullyingInterventionandPrevention.pdf>.

Fisher, J., de Mello, M. C., Izutsu, T., Vijayakumar, L., Belfer, M., & Omigbodun, O. (03/2011). Adolescence: Developmental stage and mental health morbidity. *International Journal of Social Psychiatry, 57*(1), 13–19. ISSN 0020-7640.

Fite, P. J., & Vitulano, M. (2011). Proactive and reactive aggression and physical activity. *Journal of Psychopathology and Behavioral Assessment, 33*(1), 11–18. doi:10.1007/s10862-010-9193-6.

Fox, C., & Farrow, C. (2009). Global and physical self-esteem and body dissatisfaction as mediators of the relationship between weight status and being a victim of bullying. *Journal of Adolescence, 32*(5), 1287–1301. ISSN 0140-1971.

Glaso, L., Matthiesen, S., Nielsen, M., & Einarsen, S. (2007). Do targets of workplace bullying portray a general victim personality profile? *Scandinavian Journal of Psychology, 48*(4), 313–319. doi:10.1111/j.1467-9450.2007.00554.x.

Goldenhar, L., LaMontagne, A., Katz, T., Heaney, C., & Landsbergis, P. A. (2001). The intervention research process in occupational safety and health: An overview from the national occupational research agenda intervention effectiveness research team. *Journal of Occupational and Environmental Medicine, 43*(7), 616–622.

Harries, S., Petrie, G., & Willoughby, W. (2002). Bullying among 9th graders: An exploratory study. *NASSP Bulletin, 86*(630), 3–14.

Harvey, M. G., Heames, J. T., Richey, R. G., & Leonard, N. (2006). Bullying: From the playground to the boardroom. *Journal of Leadership & Organizational Studies, 12*(4), 1–11. <http://search.proquest.com/docview/203130795?accountid=26503>.

Hazler, R. J., Carney, J. V., Green, S., Powell, R., & Jolly, L. S. (1997). Areas of expert agreement on identification of school bullies and victims. *School Psychology International, 18,* 3–12.

Hoel, H., Beale, D., & West, B. S. (2006). Workplace bullying, psychological perspectives and industrial relations: Towards a contextualized and interdisciplinary approach. *British Journal of Industrial Relations, 44*(2), 239–262.

Hoel, H., Cooper, C. L., & Faragher, B. (2001). The experience of bullying in Great Britain: The impact of organizational status. *European Journal of Work and Organizational Psychology, 10,* 443–465.

Hoel, H., & Cooper, C. L. (2000). *Destructive conflict and bullying at work.* Manchester, UK: University of Manchester Institute of Science and Technology (UMIST).

Holt, M., & Keyes, M. (2004). Teachers' attitudes toward bullying. In D. Espelage & S. Swearer (Eds.), *Bullying in American schools: A social-ecological perspective on prevention and intervention* (pp. 121–139). Mahwah, NJ: Erlbaum.

Hoff, D. L., & Mitchell, S. N. (2009). Cyberbullying: Causes, effects, and remedies. *Journal of Educational Administration, 47*(5), 652–665. doi:10.1108/09578230910981107.

Hofstede, G. (2001). *Culture's consequences: Comparing values, behaviors, institutions, and organizations across nations* (2nd ed.). Thousand Oaks, CA: SAGE Publications. ISBN 978-0-8039-7323-7. OCLC 45093960.

Jenkins, M., Winefield, H., & Sarris, A. (2011). Consequences of being accused of workplace bullying: An exploratory study. *International Journal of Workplace Health Management, 4*(1), 33–47.

Kaiser Family Foundation. Children now. Talking with kids about tough issues. Available at: <www.childrennow.org/nickelodeon/%20new-booklet.pdf>.

Keashly, L., & Neuman, J. H. (2005). Bullying in the workplace: Its impact and management. *Employee Rights and Employment Policy Journal, 8*, 335–373.

Keashly, L., Jagatic, K. (2000). The nature, extent and impact of emotional abuse in the workplace: Results of a statewide survey. Academy of management conference, Toronto.

Kim, Y. S., Leventhal, B. L., Koh, Y. J., Hubbard, A., & Boyce, A. T. (2006). School bullying and youth violence: Causes or consequences of psychopathologic behavior? *Archives of General Psychiatry, 63*, 1035-1041.

Kirby, E. (2008). Eliminate bullying—A legal imperative. *A Legal Memorandum, 8*(2), 1-6.

Klein, A., & Martin, S. (2011). Two dilemmas in dealing with workplace bullies—false positives and deliberate deceit. *International Journal of Workplace Health Management, 4*(1), 13–32.

Knafo, A. (2003). Authoritarians, the next generation: Values and bullying among adolescent children of authoritarian fathers. *Analyses of Social Issues and Public Policy, 3*(1), 199–204.

Kumpulainen, K., Rasanen, E., & Puura, K. (2001). Psychiatric disorders and the use of mental health services among children involved in bullying. *Aggressive Behavior, 27*, 102–110.

Lenhart, A., Purcell, K., Smith, A., & Zickuhr, K. (2010). Social media and mobile internet use among teens and young adults. Retrieved from <http://www.pewinternet.org/Reports/2010/Social-Media-and-Young-Adults.aspx>.

Leymann, H. (1990). Mobbing and psychological terror at workplaces. *Violence and Victims, 5*, 119-126.

Li, Q. (2006). Cyberbullying in schools: A research of gender differences. *School Psychology International, 27*, 157–170. doi:10.1177/0143034306064547.

Li, Q. (2007, July). New bottle but old wine: A research of cyberbullying in schools. *Computers in Human Behavior, 23*(4), 1777–1791. ISSN 0747-5632, 10.1016/j.chb.2005.10.005.<http://www.sciencedirect.com/science/article/pii/S0747563205000889>.

Livingstone, I., & Shepherd, I. (1997). Using the Internet. *Journal of Geography in Higher Education, 21*(3), 435–443. <http://search.proquest.com/docview/214727114?accountid=26503>

Long, J. A. (2002). Taking the BULLY by the horns. *The Safety & Health Practitioner, 20*(2), 30–33. Retrieved from <http://search.proquest.com/docview/200949370?accountid=26503>.

Lutgen-Sandvik, P., Tracy, S., & Alberts, J. (2007). Burned by bullying in the American workplace: Prevalence, perception, degree and impact.* *Journal of Management Studies, 44*(6), 837–862. doi:10.1111/j.1467-6486.2007.00715.x.

Lutgen-Sandvik, P., Tracy, S., & Alberts, J. (2007). Burned by bullying in the American workplace: Prevalence, perception, degree and impact.* *Journal of Management Studies, 44*(6), 837–862.

Luukkonena, A., Rialab, K., Hakkob, H., & Räsänena, P. (2011, April 15). *Forensic Science International, 207*(1–3), 106–110. Bullying behaviour and criminality: A population-based follow-up study of adolescent psychiatric inpatients in Northern Finland <http://dx.doi.org.ezproxy.bond.edu.au/10.1016/j.forsciint.2010.09.012>.

Martin, W., & LaVan, H. (2010). Workplace bullying: A review of litigated cases. *Employee Responsibilities and Rights Journal, 22*(3), 175–194. doi:10.1007/s10672-009-9140-4.

Matthiesen, S. B., & Einarsen, S. (2002). Working, humor and bullying—How to exceed the limits?. In S. Tyrdal (Ed.), *Humor og Helse* (pp. 165–186). Oslo, Norway: Kommuneforlaget. 220–222.

Matthiesen, S. B., & Einarsen, S. (2010). Bullying in the workplace: Definition, prevalence, antecedents and consequences. *International Journal of Organization Theory and Behavior, 13*(2), 202–248. <http://search.proquest.com/docview/763246673?accountid=26503>.

Mauger, P., Adkinson, D., Zoss, S., Firestone, G., & Hook, D. (1980). *Interpersonal behavioural survey.* Los Angeles, CA: Western Psychological Services.

Mazerolle, P. (2009). In H. Hayes & T. Prenzler (Eds.), pp. 189–204.

McEachern, A. D., & Snyder, J. (2012). Gender differences in predicting antisocial behaviors: Developmental consequences of physical and relational aggression. *Journal of Abnormal Child Psychology, 40*(4), 501. doi:10.1007/s10802-011-9589-0. ISSN 0091-0627, 05/2012.

Meloy, J. (1998). The psychology of stalking. In J. R. Meloy (Ed.), *The psychology of stalking: Clinical and forensic perspectives*. London: Academic Press.

Miga, E. M., Hare, A., Allen, J. P., & Manning, N. (2010). The relation of insecure attachment states of mind and romantic attachment styles to adolescent aggression in romantic relationships. *Attachment & Human Development, 12*(5), 463–481. doi:10.1080/14616734.2010.501971.

Mikkelsen, E. G., & Einarsen, S. (2001). Bullying in Danish work-life: Prevalence and health correlates. *European Journal of Work and Organizational Psychology, 10*(4), 393–413.

Mikkelsen, E., Hogh, A., & Louise, B. P. (2011). Prevention of bullying and conflicts at work. *International Journal of Workplace Health Management, 4*(1), 84–100. doi:10.1108/17538351111118617.

Mirsky, L. (2011, 09). Building safer. *Saner Schools Educational Leadership, 69*(1), 45–49. ISSN 0013-1784.

Molcho, M., Craig, W., Due, P., Pickett, W., Harel-Fisch, Y., & Overpeck, M. (2009). Cross-national time trends in bullying behaviour 1994–2006: Findings from Europe and North America. *International Journal of Public Health, 54*, 225–234. doi:10.1007/s00038-009-5414-8.

Moon, B., Hwang, H., & McCluskey, J. (2011). Causes of school bullying. *Crime & Delinquency, 57*(6), 849–877. doi:10.1177/0011128708315740.

Mulder, E., Brand, E., Bullens, R., & van Marle, H. (2011). Risk factors for overall recidivism and severity of recidivism in serious juvenile offenders. *International Journal of Offender Therapy and Comparative Criminology, 55*, 118–135. first published on February 24, 2010. doi:10.1177/0306624X09356683.

Near, J. P., & Miceli, M. P. (1996). Whistle-blowing: Myth and reality. *Journal of Management, 22*, 507–526.

Nickerson, A. B., Mele, D., & Princiotta, D. (2008). Attachment and empathy as predictors of roles as defenders or outsiders in bullying interactions. *Journal of School Psychology, 46*, 687–703.

Nimon, K. (Summer 2011). Religious discrimination. *Annals of the American Psychotherapy Association, 14*(2), 86.

Ogloff, J. R. P., Wong, S., & Greenwood, A. (1990). Treating criminal psychopaths in a therapeutic community program. *Behavioral Sciences and the Law, 8*, 181–190.

Olweus, D. (1978). *Aggression in the schools: Bullies and whipping boys*. Washington: Hemisphere.

Olweus, D. (1991). Bully/victim problems among schoolchildren: Basic facts and effects of a school based intervention program. In D. Pepler & K. Rubin (Eds.), *Development and treatment of childhood aggression* (pp. 409–445). Hillsborough, NJ: Erlbaum.

Olweus, D (1993a). *Bullying at school: What we know and what we can do*. Oxford: Blackwell Publishers.

Olweus, D. (1993b). *Bullying at school*. Oxford: Blackwell Publishers.

Olweus, D. (1997). Bully/victims problems in school. Facts and intervention. *European Journal of Psychology of Education, 2*(4), 495–510.

Olweus, D. (1999). Sweden. In P. K. Smith, Y. Morita, J. Junger-Tas, D. Olweus, R. Catalano, & P. Slee (Eds.), *The nature of school bullying: A cross-national perspective* (pp. 7–27). London, UK: Routledge.

Olweus, D. (2004). The Olweus bullying prevention programme: Design and implementation issues and a new national initiative in Norway. In P. K. Smith, D. Pepler, & K. Rigby (Eds.), *Bullying in schools: How successful can interventions be?* (pp. 13–36). Cambridge, UK: Cambridge University Press.

Olweus, D. (2011). Bullying at school and later criminality: Findings from three Swedish community samples of males. *Criminal Behaviour and Mental Health, 21*(2), 151–156.

Orpinas, P., Horne, A. M., & Staniszewski, D. (2003). School bullying: Changing the problem by changing the school. *School Psychology Review, 32*, 431–444.

Padilla-Walker, L., Bean, R., & Hsieh, A. (2011, October). The role of parenting and personal characteristics on deviant peer association among European American and Latino adolescents. *Children and Youth Services Review, 33*(10), 2034–2042. ISSN 0190-7409, 10.1016/j.childyouth.2011.05.034. <http://www.sciencedirect.com/science/article/pii/S019074091100212X>.

Patchin, J. W., & Hinduja, S. (2008). *Bullying Beyond the School Yard.* California: Corwin Press.

Patchin, J. W., & Hinduja, S. (2011). Traditional and nontraditional bullying among youth: A test of general strain theory. *Youth & Society, 43*(2), 727–751. doi:10.1177/0044118X10366951.

Pepler, D. J., & Craig, W. M. (1995). A peek behind the fence: Naturalistic observations of aggressive children with remote audiovisual recording. *Developmental Psychology, 31*, 548–553.

Petherick, W. (2009). Serial stalking: Looking for love in all the wrong places (pp. 257–281)? In W. Petherick (Ed.), *Serial crime: Theoretical and practical issues in behavioural profiling* (2nd ed.). Burlington, MA: Elsevier Academic Press.

Reyns, B., Henson, B., & Fisher, B. (2011). Being pursued online. *Criminal Justice and Behavior, 38*(*11*), 1149–1169. doi:10.1177/0093854811421448.

Rhodes, C., Pullen, A., Vickers, M. H., Clegg, S. R., & Pitsis, A. (2010). Violence and workplace bullying. *Administrative Theory & Praxis (M.E. Sharpe), 32*(1), 96–115. doi:10.2753/ATP1084-1806320105.

Rice, M. E., Harris, G. T., & Cormier, C. A. (1992). An evaluation of a maximum security therapeutic community for psychopaths and other mentally disordered offenders. *Law and Human Behavior, 16*(*4*), 399–412.

Rigby, K., & Smith, P. (2011). Is school bullying really on the rise? *Social Psychological Education, 14*, 441–455. doi:10.1007/s11218-011-9158-y.

Rose, C. A., Monda-Amaya, L. E., & Espelage, D. L. (2011). Bullying perpetration and victimization in special education: A review of the literature. *Remedial and Special Education, 32*, 114. doi:10.1177/0741932510361247. Originally published online 18 February 2010.

Russell, S. T., Sinclair, K. O., Poteat, V. P., & Koenig, B. W. (2012). Adolescent health and harassment based on discriminatory bias. *American Journal of Public Health, 102*(3), 493–495. <http://search.proquest.com/docview/1001240893?accountid=26503>.

Salin, D. (2003). Bullying and organisational politics in competitive and rapidly changing work environments. *International Journal of Management and Decision Making, 4*(1), 35–46.

Salmivalli, C., Lagerspetz, K., Björkqvist, K., Österman, K., & Kaukiainen, A. (1996). Bullying as a group process: Participant roles and their relations to social status within the group. *Aggressive Behavior, 22*, 1–15.

Salmivalli, C., Kaukiainen, A., & Voeten, M. (2005). Anti-bullying intervention: Implementation and outcome. *British Journal of Educational Psychology, 75*, 465–487. <http://search.proquest.com/docview/216966219?accountid=26503>.

Schat, A., Frone, M., & Kelloway, E. (2006). Prevalence of workplace aggression in the US workforce: Findings from a national study. In E. K. Kelloway, J. Barling, & J. J. J. Hurrell. (Eds.), *Handbook of workplace violence.* Thousand Oaks, CA: Sage.

Scherr, T. G., & Larson, J. (2010). Bullying dynamics associated with race, ethnicity, and immigration status. In S. R. Jimerson, S. M. Swearer, & D. L. Espelage (Eds.), *Handbook of bullying in schools. An international perspective* (pp. 223–234). New York: Routledge.

Schwartz, D., Dodge, K. A., Pettit, G. S., & Bates, J. E. (1997). The early socialization of aggressive victims of bullying. *Child Development, 68*(4), 665–675.

Seigne, E., Coyne, I., Randall, P., & Parker, J. (2007). Personality traits of bullies as a contributory factor in workplace bullying: An exploratory study. *International Journal of Organization Theory and Behavior, 10*(1), 118–132. <http://search.proquest.com/docview/212025637?accountid=26503>.

Sengupta, A., & Chaudhuri, A. (2011). Are social networking sites a source of online harassment for teens? *Evidence from survey data Children and Youth Services Review, 33*, 284–290.

Shallcross, L. (2003) The workplace mobbing syndrome: Response and prevention in the public sector. Paper presented to Workplace bullying: A community response conference, Brisbane, Australia.

Sheehan, K. H., Sheehan, D. V., White, K., Leibowitz, A., & Baldwin, D. C. (1990). A pilot study of medical student abuse. *Journal of the American Medical Association, 263*, 533–537.

Siann, G., Callaghan, M., Lockhart, K., & Rawson, L. (1993). Bullying: Teachers' views and school effects. *Educational Studies, 19*(3), 307–321.

Smith, J., Cousins, B., & Stewart, R. (2005). Antibullying interventions in schools: Ingredients of effective programs. *Canadian Journal of Education/Revue canadienne de l'éducation, 28*(4), 739–762.

Smith, P. K. (2004). Bullying: Recent developments. *Child and Adolescent Mental Health, 9*(3), 98–103.

Solomon, B. S., Bradshaw, C. P., Wright, J., & Cheng, T. L. (2008). Youth and parental attitudes toward fighting. *Journal of Interpersonal Violence, 23*, 544–560.

Sontage, L., Clemans, K., Graber, J., & Lyndon, S. (2011). Traditional and cyber aggressors and victims: A comparison of psychosocial characteristics. *Journal of Youth Adolescence, 40*, 392–404. doi:10.1007/s10964-010-9575-9.

Sourander, A., Jensen, P., Ronning, J., Elonheimo, H., Niemela, S., Helenius, H., et al. (2007). Childhood bullies and victims and their risk of criminality in late adolescence. *Archives of Pediatric and Adolescent Medicine, 161*, 546–552.

Sourander, A., Klomek, A. B., et al. (2011). Bullying at age eight and criminality in adulthood: Findings from the Finnish nationwide 1981 birth cohort study. *Social Psychiatry and Psychiatric Epidemiology, 46*(12), 1211–1219.

Spohn, R. E. (2012). Delinquent friends and reactions to strain: An examination of direct and indirect pathways. *Western Criminology Review, 13*(1), 16–36. <http://search.proquest.com/docview/1017894794?accountid=26503>.

Stacey, M. (2011). Distinctive characteristics of sexual orientation bias crimes. *Journal of Interpersonal Violence, 26*(15), 3013–3032. doi:10.1177/0886260510390950.

Stepp, S. D., Pardini, D. A., Loeber, R., & Morris, N. A. (2011). The relation between adolescent social competence and young adult delinquency and educational attainment among at-risk youth: The mediating role of peer delinquency. *Canadian Journal of Psychiatry, 56*(8), 457–465. <http://search.proquest.com/docview/889145008?accountid=26503>.

Sullivan, K., Clearly, M., & Sullivan, G. (2005). Bullying in secondary schools: *What it looks like and how to manage it?* London: Corwin.

Sutherland, E. (1947). *Principles of criminology*. Philadelphia: J. B. Lippincott.

Sutton, A., Cherney, A., & White, R. (2008). *Crime prevention: Principles, perspectives and practices.* Port Melbourne: Cambridge University Press.

Swearer, S. M., & Doll, B. (2001). Bullying in schools: An ecological framework. *Journal of Educational Psychology, 2*(2–3), 7–23.

Ta, M. L, & Loomis, D. P. (2007). *Journal of Safety Research, 38*(6), 643–650. ISSN 0022-4375.

Thylefors, I. (1987). Scape goats: *About removal and bullying at the work place.* Stockholm, Sweden: Natur och Kultur.

Tokunaga, R. (May 2010). Following you home from school: A critical review and synthesis of research on cyberbullying victimization. *Computers in Human Behavior, 26*(3), 277–287. doi:10.1016/j.chb.2009.11.014. ISSN 0747-5632.

Tremblay, R. E. (2000). The development of aggressive behaviour during childhood: What have we learned in the past century? *International Journal Of Behavioral Development, 24*(2), 129–141.

Unison, (2000). *Police Staff Bullying Report #1117*. London: Unison.

U.S. Equal Employment Opportunity Commission web site (n.d.). Retrieved from <http://www.eeoc.gov/eeoc/statistics/enforcement/charges.cfm>.

Vaillancourt, T., McDougall, P., Hymel, S., & Sunderani, S. (2010). Respect or fear? The relationship between power and bullying behavior. In S. R. Jimerson, S. M. Swearer, & D. L. Espelage (Eds.), *Handbook of bullying in schools. An international perspective* (pp. 211–222). New York: Routledge.

van de Vliert, E. (1998). Conflict and conflict management. In P. J. D. Drenth, H. Thierry, & C. J. J. de Wolff (Eds.), *Handbook of Work and Organizational Psychology, Book 3: Personnel Psychology* (pp. 351–376) (2nd ed.). Hove, East Sussex, UK: Psychology Press.

Vaughn, M. G., Fu, Q., Bender, K., DeLisi, M., Beaver, K. M., Perron, B. E., & Howard, M. O. (2010). Psychiatric correlates of bullying in the United States: Findings from a national sample. *Psychiatric Quarterly*, *81*(3), 183–195.

Warr, Mark (1993). Parents, peers, and delinquency. *Social Forces*, *72*, 247–264.

Washington State Department of Labour and Industries, (2011). Workplace bullying and disruptive behavior. *Safety and Health Assessment Research and Prevention*. Retrieved from <http://www.lni.wa.gov/Safety/Research/Files/Bullying.pdf>.

Weiten, W. (2010). Psychology: Themes and variations: *Belmont* (8th ed.). Wadsworth: Cengage Learning.

Willard, N. 2005. An educator's guide to cyberbullying and cyberthreats. <http://csriu.org/cyberbullying/pdf> (accessed 24.09.05).

Williford, A., Boulton, A., Noland, B., Little, T. D., Kärnä, A., & Salmivalli, C. Effects of the KiVa anti-bullying program on Adolescents' depression, anxiety, and perception of peers. *Journal of Abnormal Child Psychology*. *40*, 2, pp. 289–300, ISSN 0091-0627, 02/2012.

Woods, S., & Wolke, D. (2003). Does the content of anti-bullying policies inform us about the prevalence of direct and relational bullying behaviour in primary schools? *Educational Psychology*, *23*(4), 381.

Yoon, J., & Kerber, K. (2003). Aggression: Elementary teachers attitudes and intervention strategies. *Research in Education*, *69*, 27–35.

Yuen, R. A. (2005). Beyond the schoolyard: Workplace bullying and moral harassment law in France and Quebec. *38 Cornell International Law Journal*, 628. (Yuen, Rachel A).

Zapf, D., & Gross, C. (2001). Conflict escalation and coping with workplace bullying: A replication and extension. *European Journal of Work and Organizational Psychology*, *10*, 497–522.

Zapf, D., & Einarsen, S. (Eds.). (2003). *Individual antecedents of bullying*. London: CRC.

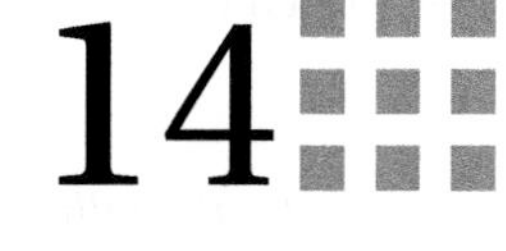

14 Serial Stalking

Looking for Love in All the Wrong Places?

Wayne Petherick

Introduction

In parts of Australia and the United States, stalking legislation is now into its third decade after introduction, even though it is a new classification for an old behavior (Meloy, 1999; Mullen, Pathé & Purcell, 2000). Stalking has emerged as a significant social problem (Mullen, Pathé & Purcell, 2009), and did not simply appear with the inception of "anti-stalking" legislation, but entered the public conscience from a number of media reports involving celebrity victimization (Dressing, Henn & Gass, 2002). Coverage of this victim pool still taints our perceptions and is reinforced in the media, where reference is made to pathological attachments held by the stalkers toward celebrities such as Steven Spielberg, Madonna, Pamela Anderson, David Letterman, or George Harrison (see Fremouw, Westrup & Pennypacker, 1997; Natalie's Nightmare, 2003; Objects of Obsession, 2000; Pearce & Easteal, 1999).

However, contrary to popular belief, it was not risk to celebrities or a number of high profile celebrity deaths at the hands of stalkers that brought about stalking legislation, but a number of domestic homicides where stalking was a precursor. As discussed in Watson (1998):

> *While I was a Municipal Court Judge in Newport Beach in 1990, five women were murdered by ex-lovers, estranged husbands, or would-be suitors. All the victims had restraining orders and were terrified for their lives. Each told friends that they believed they would be killed by the person named in the orders.*

After the killings, there was a feature article about the tragedies. A police officer was interviewed and was asked why their department hadn't taken any steps to protect these innocent victims. He answered that until a crime was committed there was nothing they could do.

Therefore, I drafted the first anti-stalking law in the United States, Penal Code Section 646.9. This section makes it a felony to cause another, or their family, to be in reasonable fear for their safety and carries a state prison sentence.

I presented my idea to then State Senator Ed Royce (R). We went to Sacramento together and made a presentation to the appropriate Senate and Assembly Committees. The law passed and within three years was copied in every state of the United States.

Having had enough time to conduct research and refine laws, "it may no longer be the case that stalking research is in its infancy and that we are feeling our way in the dark" (Sheridan, Blauuw, and Davies, 2003, p. 148).[1] With our general knowledge increasing exponentially, so too does our understanding of different types of stalkers and stalking and how those things may lead to victimization (see Petherick & Ferguson, 2012, for example). With increasing access to and use of communications technologies, other types of stalking have also come to the fore and are presenting problems of their own (Fraser, Olsen, Lee, Southworth & Tucker, 2010). Here, stalkers turn to the Internet and other electronic means in "cyberstalking," and because of a number of recent cases, our knowledge of this crime has been updated yet again. Other examples have introduced yet another variant of the same stalking behavior: the serial stalker, where one offender has a number of victims.

A discussion of serial stalking may seem misplaced; after all, it is by its very nature a crime prone to repetition. That is, in most definitions and legal classifications it is a behavior that must occur on more than one occasion before an offender can be classified as a stalker. This very feature separates stalking from other crimes such as murder and arson, and related offenses such as sexual assault, which may be perpetrated on only one occasion.

This chapter will focus on a number of features of serial stalking. First, general definitions of stalking will be provided before moving onto its incidence and prevalence. The next section will discuss what constitutes a serial crime, such as victim numbers and dynamics, followed by the utility of profiling in stalking matters. Finally, two case studies will be provided as an overview of selected features of serial stalking.

What Is Stalking?

It is necessary to first consider what we mean by stalking, how it is defined, and what behaviors may constitute stalking. According to Sheridan, Davies, and Boon (2001), one of the most prominent questions to arise out of the criminalization of stalking is what exactly constitutes stalking? As with many areas of social inquiry, stalking is defined in a number of ways. Of

[1] While the literature on stalking has seen considerable growth, there is still a lot we do not know or completely understand. As noted later in this chapter, serial stalking is one of these areas.

particular importance here are legal definitions, which draw on the ways that legislatures have defined the behavior, and social science definitions, which rely to some degree on regional legislation to identify criteria being examined as well as providing some understanding of psychopathology.

Stocker and Nielssen (2000) suggest that most commentators tend to draw from legal discourse because the psychiatric literature has been hampered by difficulties in arriving at a definition. In legal terms, some provide comprehensive descriptions of behaviors whereas others apply only broad terms (Sheridan, Blauw & Davies, 2003), though the definitions of stalking remain fairly uniform regardless of the jurisdiction. It is mainly in specific legal requirements, such as the number of individual acts, that they differ. For example, the Protection from Harassment Act (1997) in the United Kingdom simply cites a course of conduct requirement, though it should be noted that it does not actually use the word stalking, nor does it really define harassment (Network for Surviving Stalking, 2012);[2] Section 646.9 of the Californian Penal Code cites "any person who willfully, maliciously, and repeatedly follows or willfully and maliciously harasses another person," whereas the Queensland legislation (section 359 of the Queensland Criminal Code Act 1899) cites behavior "engaged in on any 1 occasion if the conduct is protracted or on more than one occasion."

Meloy (1998) identifies three common provisions in stalking legislation. These are a pattern (course of conduct) of behavioral intrusion upon another that is unwanted; an implicit or explicit threat evidenced in the pattern of behavioral intrusion; and that as a result of these intrusions, the threatened person experiences reasonable fear. Holmes (2001) suggests that from many definitions there are four components of stalking: (1) a deliberate course of action; (2) a repeated course of action; (3) this action causes a reasonable person to feel threatened, terrorized, harassed, or intimidated; and (4) this action actually causes the victims to feel threatened, terrorized, harassed, or intimidated.

According to Mullen, Pathé, and Purcell (2000), the term stalking has come to describe persistent attempts to impose on another various forms of communication or contact. Behaviors associated with stalking include the sending of unsolicited gifts, the ordering or canceling of services on the victim's behalf (pizza, taxi, etc.), threats, loitering near, following, surveilling, and in some cases assault or homicide. Communications include letters, telephone, e-mail, and graffiti. The range of stalking behaviors and communications are limited only by the motivation, innovation, and imagination of the stalker.

Although the behaviors are limitless, what we consider stalking may also include those innocuous behaviors encountered in typical courting scenarios, such as persistent calling, letter writing, or the giving of gifts. Although stalking behavior may manifest as benign gestures meant to represent the stalker's affection, their intrusive behavior causes the victim to react with fear. As a result, in some countries legislators have found it difficult to frame stalking laws because many of the behaviors that constitute stalking are routine, mundane, or harmless (Sheridan & Davies, 2001). This leads to some concern that "the liberty of people to pursue

[2]While relying on the Protection from Harassment Act in the past, the UK will be implementing stalking laws to target this offense. See Johnson & Gordon (2012).

everyday activities or sincerely seek to initiate a relationship may be compromised" (Sheridan, Blauw & Davies, 2003, p. 150).

Stalking behaviors may also escalate into assault, masturbatory fantasies, theft of the victim's belongings (especially underwear and other intimate or personal items), and property damage. Although there is some concordance between courting and stalking, stalking is typically characterized by its duration and persistence. "In the spectrum of actions that lie between surveillance and physical harm, it is probably repeated harassment that defines the difference between stalking and unwanted courtship by a stranger, rejected suitor, or former lover" (Miller, 2001, p. 5).

Miller (2001, p. 5) provides a definition of stalking that is more reflective of legal considerations, in that "stalking is obsessional pursuit, harassment, and intimidation by a person who has or believes he has a significant relationship with the object of his unwanted attention." Not all stalkers have, or believe they have, a relationship with the victim, and although this may be the intended goal of a number of stalkers, this definition potentially excludes cases of stranger stalking.

Sheridan (2001, p. 2) defines stalking as a "series of actions directed at one individual by another that taken as a whole amount to unwanted persistent personal harassment," whereas Wright, Burgess, Laszlo, McCrary, and Douglas (1996, p. 487) define stalking as "the act of following, viewing, communicating with, or moving threateningly or menacingly toward another person." Given that much stalking is covert in nature, such a "movement criterion" would seem obsolete.

When viewing the component behaviors in isolation, stalking is perceptually nonthreatening, though when one looks at the universe of behaviors in a given case, then factors in duration, it is reasonable to see how it constitutes an intrusive and deleterious invasion of private life. To account for this, a definition is put forward in this work that sees stalking as "a constellation of behaviors that may, when considered in isolation, seem innocuous, but when viewed collectively and in the context in which they occurred, constitute a maladaptive and proscribed course of conduct." This definition is useful for a number of reasons. First, it not only acknowledges the broad range of behaviors that constitute stalking, but also identifies their possible innocence when viewed individually. Second, it makes no attempt to explain motive, as any definition would by necessity have to encompass cases borne of desperation, revenge, and sexual stimulation. Last, it emphasizes the maladaptive nature of stalking behaviors when viewed collectively and in the context in which they occurred.

What Makes Something Serial?

This question has a great deal of practical impact on the examination of serial behavior, and in the allocation of investigative resources. It is argued herein that once a case has been identified as the work of a serial offender, the approach taken to case resolution should then undergo a fundamental change, such as the formation of a task force in an extreme case and considerations of public safety. Although much of the literature defining serial crime relates specifically to serial homicide, the same issues apply across the board: victim numbers, dynamics, and investigative difficulties. So although the following discussion will rely heavily on the research on serial homicide, the same general caveats and considerations apply equally to serial stalking, serial rape, serial arson, or any other crime committed by the serial offender.

As the issue is with seriality, we can turn to other related areas for guidance on how to best address the issue of serial stalking. Kocsis (2000) suggests that of the issues plaguing the examination of serial murder, foremost is a lack of consensus on the basic definition of what a serial murderer is. This becomes apparent even if only a cursory examination of the literature is undertaken. Definitions of serial murder typically encompass three areas:

- A defined number of victims.
- A period of time between each offense.
- Offenses occurring in different geographic locations from each other.

By definition alone, it is the inclusion of a "cooling-off" period and the commission of the offense in different geographic locations that distinguishes among serial, spree, and mass murder. Spree killings are "a series of murders connected to one event committed over a time period of hours or days without a break or cooling-off period" (Busch & Cavanaugh, 1986, p. 5) and are characterized by a single murder event over a number of different geographic areas. They murder at least two victims, and the reason for the offense is said to be primarily for the enjoyment of it (Helsham, 2001; Power, 1996). Blackburn (1993, p. 214) claims that "in mass murders, several victims are killed on one occasion, while in serial murders, killings are repeated over an extended period," with mass murder being defined primarily by the length of time over which the murders take place (usually a single temporal event), occurring in the same geographic location (Gresswell & Hollin, 1994). Mass killers are identified elsewhere (Fox & Levin, 1997) as those who kill their victims in one event, who tend to target people they know, often for the purpose of revenge, and use weapons of mass destruction such as high-powered firearms.

The number of victims is typically between two and four, but higher requirements are also identified. Egger's (1984, 1990) definition states that a serial murder has occurred when a second or subsequent murder is committed. Hickey (1991) and Ressler, Burgess, and Douglas (1988) believe a serial murderer claims three or more victims over a period of time. Dietz (1986), however, believes that the victim count should be at least five. Whereas most authors adopt a numerical system, Kocsis (1999, p. 194) is critical of defining serial murder from the perspective of victim numbers:

> *The heart of the problem of definition has been the development of an entrenched association of a minimum victim tally as a criterion for serial murder. Indeed, this apparently simple issue of a minimum victim number to identify the crime as serial murder shows a remarkable diversity within the literature on the topic.... Unfortunately researchers have become absorbed in this debate on minimum victim tally and have overlooked several conceptual problems that exist in defining serial murder on this criterion.*

Kocsis and Irwin (1998) suggest these victim tally definitions be abandoned in favor of definitions that encompass the propensity to reoffend. It should be noted that this too would be problematic owing to a variety of factors outside of the offender's control, such as the intention but not the ability to reoffend (he might be apprehended before his second offense; future offenses might be disrupted; the reasons for the offending, called criminogenic needs, may be addressed). It may further be argued that we consider the motivation and the dynamics of the offense while disregarding the number of victims. Given that motivations are poorly understood and the dynamics of the offense may not become known until sometime later, such an approach could leave some serial offenders uncategorized and undetected. This is clearly not a favorable outcome from a policing or public safety perspective.

With all this talk of utility and futility, a decision must still be made on how to define a serial crime so that it can be accurately identified once committed (an excellent discussion is provided in Turvey, 2008). Whereas some have argued that it is too arbitrary to simply attach a numerical value, others prefer to consider the case dynamics and motivations of the offense. All of these considerations will dictate how we view, identify, and treat the serial criminal. Although not a perfect approach, this author argues that victim numbers are likely the best yardstick we have to define the point at which a criminal becomes a serial offender. Admittedly, although the distinction of serial offending based solely on numerical value is problematic, it is currently the best starting point and is useful in allocating resources, dictating investigative strategies, and identifying other deficiencies in the investigative process that must be overcome (such as motivations and dynamics).

Based on these definitions and the preceding discussion on serial crime, a serial stalker is one who pursues multiple victims over time and location, with this chapter distinguishing between two manifestations of pursuit style. First, the *consecutive* stalker pursues two or more victims in generally different timeframes; that is, they move from one victim to another. This may occur where a pursuit is thwarted for some reason (the victim moves away or seeks assistance with threat management or from the police, or someone else "catches the stalker's fancy") and the stalker moves on to another victim. Second, the *concurrent* stalker pursues two or more victims at the same time. Neither type is mutually exclusive but describes an overall victim targeting strategy. For example, one stalker may identify and pursue a new target before moving on from a current victim.

In one of the few pieces written on serial stalking, Lloyd-Goldstein (2000) defines serial stalking as the sequential stalking of different victims at different times (those that are consecutive in nature as discussed). He also notes that any subsequent victims should not be linked to the original victim to whom the stalker became attached, because in such cases additional victims may simply be friends, family, or coworkers who become entwined in the stalking while assisting the primary target of the stalking. However, in identifying the difference between consecutive and concurrent stalkers, it is noted that "stalkers with multiple love objects on a concurrent basis should be distinguished from true serial stalkers" (p. 178). From this, it is not clear whether a stalker who harasses multiple victims at the same time is considered less of a serial offender than someone who moves from victim to victim.

Although the two case studies presented later represent both consecutive and concurrent pursuit styles, the following example highlights purely consecutive stalking to contextualize the difference (Petherick, 2001):

A 34-year-old female was being stalked by a former intimate. She claims they met while working as volunteers in a community project, and that they had dated for approximately

1 year. It later turned out that he had joined the project simply to get close to her, a modus operandi he had repeated on three previous occasions. She sought help from a number of sources, but all were unable to assist with her situation for a number of reasons. One evening, after stealing a key to her apartment during a previous visit, he let himself in and was found crawling down the hallway of her house with her dog's muzzle clamped in his hand. She called the police and they asserted that, given their prior relationship, a conviction would be problematic at best. It was only after more time elapsed, her physical and psychological functioning continued to decline, and neighbors reported seeing him outside her bedroom window, that she sought other help. At this point she contacted this author, who assisted with threat management. In a fortuitous telephone conversation and subsequent meeting, she found out that this person had done similar things to others who had shown him any form of care and attention. He was not known to stalk a number of people at once, but instead moved from victim to victim at the dissolution of relationships, or when victims sought outside help.

Incidence and Prevalence

It is difficult to disaggregate the number of serial stalkers from the overall number of stalkers represented by various studies on the prevalence of this crime. Until recently, serial stalking had not received any significant coverage in the literature; in fact, a review of several hundred pieces of academic literature on stalking revealed only a handful articles in which the topic was discussed and data presented. This section will first present the general incidence and prevalence of stalking, followed by that of serial stalking.

In Australia, the first extensive community study was undertaken by the Australian Bureau of Statistics (ABS) 1996 study titled Women's Safety[3] (McClennan, 1996). This study found that 2.4% of women over the age of 18 had been stalked by a man in the last 12 months, with 15% having been stalked by a man at least once in their lifetime. Of those polled, 7.5% were still undergoing victimization at the time of the survey. This study showed that women were more likely to be stalked by strangers than by men they knew (this survey only considered stalking cases in which females were the victims and males were the offenders). Purcell, Pathé, and Mullen (2000) conducted a smaller-scale study of their own involving a random selection of 3700 men and women in Victoria. For those who responded positively to the defined forms of harassment, further information was sought about the frequency and presence of fear. Results indicate that 23.4% of the respondents had been stalked at some point in their lives, with 5.8% being stalked in the 12 months prior to the survey. Approximately 10% were subjected to prolonged harassment involving multiple intrusions that lasted at least 4 weeks. Females were far more likely to be a victim of stalking in their lifetimes. Those who were younger were more likely to be stalked, with those aged 18 to 35 making up 31.8% of the sample, whereas the

[3]This study also explored other aspects of women's safety and did not focus exclusively on stalking. It has also been criticized for its findings because of its narrow scope; see Mullen, Pathé, and Purcell (2000).

36- to 55-year age group comprised 27.6% of the participants, and only 14.6% of those over 56 years of age reported being stalked.

In the biggest and most widely cited study in the United States, the National Institute of Justice noted that "survey findings indicate that stalking is a bigger problem than previously thought, affecting about 1.4 million victims annually" (Tjaden, 1997, p. 1). Other reports indicate that 8% of women and 2% of men have been stalked at some time in their lives, which is more than one million women and more than a quarter of a million men (Tjaden & Thoennes, 1998). This study (of 8000 men and 8000 women) also found that most victims are female, that 52% of all victims are aged between 18 and 29, and that women are significantly more likely than men (59% versus 30%) to be stalked by someone with whom they had a prior relationship.

Basile, Swahn, Chen, and Saltzman (2006) conducted further research into the stalking problem in the United States. Their research yielded 9684 interviews (4877 women and 4807 men). Participants were first asked a question about stalking:

> *"Have you ever had someone besides bill collectors or sales people follow or spy on you, try to communicate with you against your will, or otherwise stalk you for more than one month?"*

If they answered in the affirmative, they were then asked:

> *"The last time this happened to you, how serious would you say the stalking was?"*

Participants were limited in their responses to "nothing to be concerned about," "annoying," "somewhat dangerous," or "life threatening."

The results of this survey show for those aged 18 years and above, "4.5% reported that they have been stalked in their lifetime in a way that they perceived to be somewhat dangerous or life threatening" (Basile, Swahn, Chen & Saltzman, 2006, p. 173). Women had a significantly higher rate of victimization than men (7% and 2%, respectively). Those respondents who were never married, separated, widowed, or divorced were at higher risk of being stalked than those who were married or lived as a couple. Those aged 55 years and older or who were retired had a much lower chance of being stalked. It should be noted that there are differences in the rate of stalking than in others reported throughout this chapter. This may be because of the relatively narrow definition of stalking used, or because the 4.5% figure was limited to those who perceived the stalking to be somewhat dangerous or life threatening (so at the extreme end of the spectrum). It may also be owing to the specific use of the term "stalking," which may of itself evoke a particular type of response.

In the United Kingdom the picture is similar. The British Home Office produced a report on the nature of stalking from the British Crime Survey, which showed that 11.8% of adults aged 16 to 59 were the subject of unwanted and persistent attention at least once since age 16 (Budd, Mattinson & Myhill, 2000). They further found that, like their Australian and U.S. counterparts, victims were more likely to be female (73%). Another similarity is that youth tends to elevate one's risk of victimization, with almost a quarter of women aged 16 to 19 and a fifth of women aged 20 to 29 reporting stalking harassment. This is compared with only one tenth of women aged 55 to 59.

University students have also been widely studied as a population to determine their victimization from stalkers. There are a number of reasons why this group may be particularly prone to the attention of persistent harassers. First, the age at which one leaves for university is generally the age at which many people experience their first "adult" relationship, making for a volatile mix of love and love lost on the dissolution of a relationship (some studies have indicated that younger females, typically aged between 18 and 35 [see Purcell, Pathé & Mullen, 2000; Tjaden & Thoennes, 1998] are the most common victims of stalking). Second, for many people, this is their first time away from home, leading to a change in social and familial support networks that may have been relied upon in previous periods of crisis. This may also mark the first serious period of experimentation with alcohol and/or drugs.

In an undergraduate sample from West Virginia, Fremouw, Westrup, and Pennypacker (1997) examined the prevalence of stalking on campus. This study explored two facets of stalking, with the first assessing the behaviors of those who stalk and the second assessing the victims, also taking into account the relationship of the victim to the stalker. Two actual studies were conducted, with the second using a sample of 299 participants and a revised questionnaire, the goal of which was to replicate the first study.

Their findings suggest that stalking among this college population is higher than that indicated by other community samples (indicating a general increase in victimization among this age group). In this study, 44 of the 165 female respondents (26.6%) and 17 of 129 (14.7%) male respondents reported that they had been stalked. In study 2, the rate was somewhat higher, with 35.2% of females and 18.4% of males reporting victimization. A large proportion of females (47% in the first study and 40% in the second) were stalked by someone they had "seriously dated." Males were stalked by someone they had "seriously dated" in about one quarter of the reported instances, or 24%. Interestingly, this study also inquired as to the number of respondents who had themselves stalked another. Only three of 129 males responded in the positive, meaning that either the participants underreported their own stalking behaviors or those individuals responsible for the victimization were outside of the study sample.

Fisher, Cullen, and Turner (2000) also conducted a national survey of stalking among college women in the United States. Their sample was considerably larger than the previous study, with some 4446 respondents completing the survey with a response rate of 85%. Of this sample, 13.1% of females had been stalked at least once since the beginning of the academic year. Of those who had been stalked, 12.7% had been stalked twice, and 2.3% were stalked on three or more occasions. This rate is again higher than some community samples. Nearly all the stalkers were male. In a similar study on student victimization, Coleman (1997) used a sample of 141 undergraduates, with 29.1% responding positively to being stalked. Furthermore, 9.2% of the students stated that this repeated attention was malicious, physically threatening, or fear inducing.

All of these studies tend to suggest that the picture of stalking in English-speaking countries is fairly universal: Young females tend to be victimized more often by typically male offenders that they know or with whom they have had a former relationship. Overall and depending on the study, rates of victimization range from about 8% to approximately 23%. This suggests that stalking constitutes a considerable social problem. But what about serial stalking?

One of the first studies on stalking was conducted by Zona, Sharma, and Lane (1993), studying 74 files from the Threat Management Unit referred largely by the entertainment and mental health community. The findings from this study suggest that stalkers, although all obsessional in their pursuit behavior, could be divided into three main groups. The Erotomanic has a delusional belief that he or she is loved by another, usually of higher social status. The Love Obsessional is similar to the Erotomanic, and there is not usually a relationship between the subject and the victim, except through the media. In the Simple Obsessional group, there is a prior relationship, from acquaintance to lover. In all cases, stalking behavior began after the relationship had gone bad or there was a perception of mistreatment. While not aimed at detecting serial stalking specifically, findings indicate that one member of the Erotomanic group (N = 7, approximately 14%) had pursued another victim prior to the current victim. For the Love Obsessional group, 5 of 32 (15%) had pursued victims previously, whereas none of the Simple Obsessional group (N = 35) had.

In another forensic sample, Harmon, Rosner, and Owens (1995) studied 48 stalkers referred to a forensic psychiatric clinic in New York. These researchers developed their typology along two axes, "one relating to the nature of the attachment between the defendant and the object of their attention, and another relating to the nature, if any, of the prior interaction between them" (p. 189). According to Lloyd-Goldstein (2000), 16 (33%) of the cases in this sample involve multiple victims of harassment, with all being stalked concurrently. Interestingly, within this group there was a fair degree of criminal versatility exhibited, including both more general criminal behavior as well as that aligned with the stalking itself. Aggravated harassment was common in 59% of the sample, followed by criminal contempt (20%), harassment (6%), menacing, assault, and criminal possession of a weapon (3% each), followed by burglary, kidnapping, and attempted rape (2% each).

In developing a stalking typology of use to law enforcement, Boon and Sheridan (2001) examined 124 cases. Their findings indicate that over a third of the victims (48) claimed that their stalker had also targeted at least one other person. Twelve of the 48 serial stalkers had a previous relationship with the victim, and all of these had previously stalked another former partner. Of the 48, the vast majority (44) had stalked others before the victims taking part in the study, with another three stalking others at the same time as those taking part in the study. Although this study does not purport to represent the general population of serial stalkers, the issue is considerably more problematic than we may possibly know if even a fraction of this applies to the larger population of stalkers.

A number of other studies have also found that a sizable proportion of stalkers under study have engaged in repeatedly victimizing targets, with one of the most recent (Malsch, de Keijser & Debets, 2011) being conducted on a Dutch Ministry of Justice database. Malsch and colleagues selected the criminal histories of those found guilty of stalking between 2000 and 2003, including other crimes in addition to the stalking. The sample included all offenders since the inception of the Dutch stalking law, totaling 709 offenders. Analysis of the data showed that 53% of the convicted stalkers recidivated during the observation period. It should be noted that the repeat offending was not limited only to further stalking, but for those who did commit another stalking crime (11% of the sample), they did so most quickly, within 7 months. In total, most new crimes had nothing to do with stalking (58%), though approximately 24% were somehow related to stalking, "such as threat, defamation, the destruction of property and crimes against legal order, and unlawfully entering the home" (p. 8).

In another study drawing on cases from the United States and Canada (drawing on the data of Mohandie, Meloy, McGowan & Williams, 2006), Eke, Hilton, Meloy, Mohandie, and Williams (2011) drew from 312 of the police cases from the original study. Of this, 78 offenders were chosen for follow-up study. Of these, the majority were males (73 cases), with most stalking an adult female with whom they had an intimate relationship (62 cases). Offenders were significantly older than their primary index victims. The majority of offenders committed at least one new reported offense, and recidivists had a mean time at risk of 9.8 months for first reoffense; half of the new offenses occurred within 2 months, while 9% reoffended in less than a day. Stalking recidivism was recorded for 44 of the sample, including criminal harassment, theft, mischief, threats, and harassing phone calls, with a mean time at risk of 11 months, but half occurred within 3 months, and just under a quarter within a 24-day period. Violent recidivism is noted as occurring within 8 months, with just under one quarter occurring within 68 days. These offenses were recorded against the index victim 17% of the time, or against a new partner 35% of the time, suggesting a proportion of these offenses represent displaced aggression.

It is generally difficult to determine how many cases of a given population are serial in nature, as this relies on victim reporting, formal reports being taken, and the cases being appropriately linked. Additionally, stalking frequently presents as a covert crime where the victims may not know that they are being targeted (or perhaps may only have suspicions with no tangible evidence). Add to this victim perceptions ("nothing can be done about it," "it is a private matter," "it is embarrassing," "I don't want to get him in trouble") and underreporting, and it is likely that the previous studies on repeat offending are an underrepresentation of the actual picture of serial stalking.

What Can Be Done about It?

It should be acknowledged that there is a lot that can be done about serial stalking, from counseling of offenders once they are identified to educating potential victims about individual characteristics that predispose someone to stalking behaviors (as discussed in Michele Pathé's book *Surviving Stalking*). Only two things will be discussed here, however: criminal profiling and threat management.

Owing to the repetitive nature of stalking behavior, it is argued that profiling may be suited to the investigation of many stalking scenarios. Profiling is "an inferential process that involves an analysis of offender behavior including their interactions with the victim and crime scene, their choice of weapon and their use of language, among other things" (Petherick, 2003, p. 173). Pinizzotto (1984), Geberth (1996), and Holmes and Holmes (2003) argue that profiling is most suited to those crimes involving psychopathology, and with many stalking scenarios exhibiting signs of pathological behavior, this further reinforces the utility of profiling for this crime.

There is both uniformity and contention in the literature about what information a criminal profiler can provide. Geberth (1996) provides a fairly exhaustive list that will not be replicated in full, but it includes age, sex, race, marital status, scholastic achievement, lifestyle, personality style, emotional adjustment, demeanor, evidence of mental decomposition, and work habits. In discussing the FBI's approach, O'Toole (1999) cites a number of features discernible through a criminal profile. This includes a range of characteristics of the offender and his or her lifestyle, emotional age, level of formal education or training, the offender's ability to relate and communicate with others, prior criminal activity, and feelings of remorse and/or guilt concerning the crime or the victim. Although some authors suggest a broad range of offender characteristics that can be derived from the offender's behavior, others are a little more conservative, suggesting that less is directly inferable from offender behavior.

So exactly what use can profiling be in the assessment of stalking cases? To begin, an examination of the general applications of profiling will be provided followed by a cursory discussion of motive, finishing with applications of threat management. These are by no means the only tools, but they are the ones with which the author has found most success.

It could be stated that there are three broad domains in which profiling may apply to stalking (and by extension serial stalking). These are investigatively, at trial, and then within a clinical context. The first is best characterized as profiling the unknown criminal for the known crime, and the last two as profiling the known criminal for the known crime. Profiling as an investigative tool is perhaps the one with which most people will be familiar, and it is this one that has been the focus of most media and movie attention.

Essentially, it is the profiler's job to help investigators determine the value of the available evidence and what it means about the offender in an effort to ensure the best use of manpower and resources. This may greatly enhance the utility of the investigative effort by preventing already overstretched resources from becoming strained to a breaking point. In cases of serial stalking, a profile may assist in developing suspect pools by identifying the motive or depth of knowledge the offender has about the victim and the various locations in which the behaviors are perpetrated. Owing to the repetitive nature of serial stalking, a profiler may also assist in determinations of case linkage by identifying connections between MO and signature behaviors, thereby allowing for the identification of serial offenders and the allocation of relevant investigative resources. Even though many stalking scenarios are characterized more as psychologically intrusive, many cases will culminate in physical contact or other attempts at harm, and here the profiler may provide insight into the potential for an offender's escalation; this may indicate the likelihood that someone engaging in "Peeping Tom" activities will escalate to stalking focusing on one or more of their victims, or perhaps go even further into crimes of violence. As per points 4 and 5 given earlier, further general assistance may be in the form of leads and strategies for advancing the investigation, or by weeding through irrelevant or distracting information that comes out during the investigative phase (see Chapter 9 in this volume).

At trial, the profiler may help legal counsel (either the defense or prosecution) understand the behavior of the accused with regard to things such as state of mind, intent, remorse, planning, and others. While some of the early proponents of profiling suggest helping the prosecution develop a line of questioning or interview style, it is the opinion of this author that this practice should be avoided. To assist with a line of questioning in this manner means that the profiler has to assume the guilt of the accused, and once they have done this, they are no longer an impartial expert but an advocate. The main idea during the trial is that the opinion of the profiler helps the court to understand complex behavioral issues that manifest in stalking.

Another area where profilers may help the court is in determinations of motive, and this may be done either during the investigation or the trial. Motivation, "any force that activates and gives direction to behavior" (Rockelein, 2006, p. 406), is not strictly necessary for an investigation or prosecution, but as it is one of the six investigative questions (who, what, when, where, how, and why), every attempt should be made to address it. As motive is discussed elsewhere in this work, no further discussion is necessary, though as a final point, understanding motive can also assist with the development of a threat management approach, discussed next.

Where public safety may be an issue, a criminal profile may help identify aspects of the offender's behavior that constitute a clear threat to individual safety; for example, by providing a picture of victim selection and aspects of an offender's modus operandi and to comment on future risk that is suggested by current behavior. Identifying precursor behaviors may assist in identifying crimes that are potentially the work of the same offender but that are not currently regarded as part of a series. For example, "Peeping Tom" or surveillance activities of a stalker may help to build up an overall picture of an offender's geographic behavior or some other aspect such as victim selection and planning.

In an attempt to mitigate the risk to victims of stalking, a profile may also be useful in providing threat management services to victims. Here, a profile is utilized to fill knowledge voids by providing an understanding of aspects of the case such as the motive and intent of the unknown stalker. If the case should require criminal justice system intervention, a profile may also help the police identify a suspect pool and reduce the time to apprehension. As practiced by this author, it involves an adaptation of the techniques of situational crime prevention as discussed by Clarke (1997), Clarke and Homel (1997), and Cornish and Clarke (2003). This approach involves identifying intrusive and harassing behaviors of the stalker, those antecedent and consequent behaviors of the victim, and the environment in which they occurred. Following this, an approach is developed in which aspects of the 25 techniques of situational crime prevention are applied. As an example, repeated attempts by the stalker to contact the victim may be addressed by *Rule Setting* under the broad category of *Removing Excuses*. Here the victim should issue what is commonly referred to as a "letter of noncontact" outlining the invasive and harassing nature of their pursuit (see Pathé, 2003). Another example would be in addressing repeated telephone contacts where the stalker calls simply to hear the victim's voice on her answering machine. A successful approach here might be to have the victim replace her current answering machine message with a generic store-bought one or have a female friend record a plain message for her,[4] which would fall under *Denying Benefits* within the general category of *Reducing Rewards*.

[4]This strategy has been used successfully in a number of cases.

A deductive profile can also help to fill a number of voids in what is currently known to be true, and on which further action must be based. Motive and intent are just two areas that may be unknown at the time of case intake, and not only do they narrow the suspect pool, but their assessment may become an instructive part of any threat management undertaken to assist the victim. In one case (Petherick, 2000), a determination of motive guided the entire threat management process to a successful conclusion by focusing solely on manipulating specific motive-oriented behaviors.

Case Studies

The final part of this chapter will briefly examine two case studies involving serial stalking. The first is from Queensland, Australia, and the second is from New York, in the United States. They both involve a large number of victims over a considerable period of time. For the sake of brevity only selected features of each case will be discussed. These include the number of victims, the duration, victim selection, motivation, and the effect on the victim. The chosen cases are not necessarily representative of the general nature of serial stalkers, but have been selected because of their high number of victims and the amount of information available about them.[5]

Robert Zeljko Vidovich

Investigators first identified a link between victims on Queensland's Gold Coast when new complainants began to recount similar details to detectives (Wilson, 2002a). The crimes of Vidovich spanned three and a half years, with his total known victim count at 52 (there are potentially other victims who never made the connection or who, for one reason or another, didn't receive further harassment and did not reveal their victimization to police). They ranged in age from 16 to 83 years.

The victims reported receiving nuisance and harassing telephone calls during which the caller would first make a generally innocuous claim (such as his accidentally receiving some of their mail). Following this, the caller would propose various forms of sexual activity such as rape or bondage, or he would make comments suggestive of voyeurism. Lingerie also played a significant role in the interactions he had with his victims. The following précis from the Supreme Court of Queensland Court of Appeals sums up the offenses (*R. v. Vidovich*, 2002):

> *The applicant had pleaded guilty to an ex officio indictment charging him with 52 counts on the 9th of May 2002 at the Southport District Court.... The applicant ... was aged between 38 and 42 years over the various times of the offenses. The stalking offenses to which he pleaded guilty were committed over a period of approximately three and a half years from April 1998 to September 2001. There were 52 complainants ranging in age from 16 years to 83 years, most of them being aged between 35 and 50. The offenses ...*

[5] A note of acknowledgment should go out to investigators involved with these and similar cases. They are, by nature, difficult crimes to investigate, and it is often only through dogged detective work that they can be solved.

> *generally they involve the applicant telephoning women, most often at their home, but also at work. The phone calls were made from public phones and motel rooms.... In the calls, he proposed various forms of sexual activity in explicit and demeaning language. He threatened to rape the women the subject of three counts, and impliedly threatened to rape, or indecently assault many of the others. He sent pornographic photographs to eight of the women depicting various sexual acts. The women in the photos looked like the recipients and captions accompanied the photos describing what the applicant wanted to do the recipient. From the conversations he had with some five of the women it was clear that he had been spying on them. In one instance he first made contact with the complainant during her pregnancy. At the time of his last call five months later she was breast feeding at the time but not in public. During the call he made reference to her nipples being full of milk.... The applicant attempted to conceal his identity by adopting accents when speaking to the complainants, using gloves when preparing the obscene materials, disguising his handwriting, using an alias when booking into the motels in which he made calls and calling from public phones. He was arrested by police on the 28th of September 2001. In the course of their search the police found 800 pornographic files on his computer, some of which contained captions referring to some of the complainants and a phone list with 23 names on it. With the exception of two complainants the applicant said the women were not known to him and that he'd selected them randomly from the phone book.*

Vidovich was fairly random in his victim selection, and they did not represent significant others in his life, nor someone he harbored particular grudges against (an often-touted motivation for many stalking scenarios), nor did his victims exhibit similarity to one another; in fact, there appeared to be little if anything connecting his victims at all. Their ages and appearances were generally inconsistent, and no links could be found between them or any facilities or services they used. It would seem that most of them were just unfortunate enough to cross his path.

This randomness begs the questions of how these victims came to be chosen and what features of victimology may have been enticing to their harasser. In reference to the summary from the Court of Appeal, the women in the pornographic images bore striking resemblance to some of his victims, and in "doctoring" these images, he would often use their names and provide some commentary of what he was doing (behavioral evidence suggests he saw himself as the male portrayed in the images) or what he would like to do to them. Others still provided some insight into his perceptions of their "relationship." One manipulated image in which the victim's hair had been computer edited contained the caption, "Oh yes ... so you are a friend of Paul's ... well he won't be home until later tonight." The sentiment of this action was further verbalized by another of his victims in that "he saw each one of us as someone he was having a relationship with" (Margen, 2003). As another example of his misguided perceptions of a relationship, he offered to assist one victim in removing her clothes—specifically, "he was offering to help me get undressed out of my work uniform" (Margen, 2003). So it seems then, at least in some of the cases, that his behavior was *reassurance oriented*, whereby he wanted, or at least fantasized about, some form of relationship he perceived he was having.

Beyond the pornography and letters, it was obvious from an early stage that the offender had also engaged in detailed surveillance of the victims and their homes. It has been suggested that some of their telephone details had been secured by stealing mail from their letter boxes, though this could never be proven by police. One of the victims describes a letter in which Vidovich wrote about her liking for long dresses, specifically citing colors of dresses she owned (Wilson, 2002a). In yet another case, one victim came home from work to find underwear from her washing line neatly folded on her doorstep along with a letter, with other victims receiving similar treatment. For example, in one telephone conversation he recounted details of underwear hanging on her washing line (which was not visible from the street). Others had underwear stolen. During a break-in, one victim had some of her underwear stolen from inside her home, which was subsequently referred to during a later telephone call (Wilson, 2002a).

The effect these intrusions had on the victims is obvious and the reactions of these victims is typical. The breach of their privacy had a distinct impact on their personal, professional, and social lives, and the enduring effects of this victimization will be akin to those of other stalking victims (see Brewster, 1997; Collins & Wilkas, 2000; Hall, 1998; Hills and Taplan, 1998; Meloy, 1996; Pathé & Mullen, 1997). One victim's consternation at being selected can be seen in the comment, "To think that it could happen to anyone, just purely by having your name in a phone book." The loss of security and trust they have experienced is echoed in the following two statements: "You still look over your shoulder, hate answering the phone and don't like being by yourself" and "You certainly don't trust people, you think they are capable of just about anything" (Margen, 2003). One businesswoman claimed, "I had my partner ring me at work during the day to check on things and he would come in and help me lock up my Burleigh business" (Wilson, 2002b). One of Vidovich's victims, who received telephone harassment and letters from him for more than 2 years, told the author, "You don't trust anyone. You treat everyone who walks past like a potential criminal. You just don't know who it is, or who it could be. It might be the mailman, the delivery man, or the guy you buy your food from. You just don't know." This is not an uncommon sentiment among stalking victims.

On apprehension, there was a distinct failure on the part of Vidovich to appreciate the seriousness of the charges. Detective Lithgow recounts, "The day we arrived at his house, he was surprised that it was such an issue," and "This is a person who thought that as a punishment for what he had done, it would be adequate for him to clean out police vans on a weekend rather than go to court" (Margen, 2003). Also noted by prosecutor Mark Whitbread, Vidovich's naïveté about his offenses was almost disturbing. In court, Whitbread claimed Vidovich had asked police, "Why do I have to go to court? I mean, I'll apologize. I'll help you with your cases or something" (Stolz, 2002).

The Vidovich case likely represents the worst stalking case in Queensland, possibly in Australia, and this was something that was factored into the judge's considerations, where it was noted, "It is a case where the protection of the community takes precedence over your rehabilitation" (Wilson, 2002b). Furthermore, the custodial penalty imposed on Vidovich was 4 years for 13 of the cases (at the time 5 years was the maximum penalty allowable), whereas for the remaining cases he was sentenced to 7 years, the new maximum allowable under Queensland law. These sentences were to be served concurrently. In addition to his custodial sentence, he was ordered not to have contact with his victims for the next 10 years and was made liable for damage claims that may escalate into the millions.

Robert D. King

Dating back to 1996, Robert D. King of Yorkshire, New York, harassed and terrorized some 28 women in a stalking campaign that involved numerous instances of harassing telephony during which he would threaten to kill or harm them, usually with a knife. The women lived in different geographic locations including Concord, Sardinia, Holland, Yorkshire, Delevan, Machias, and Arcade (Porter, 1998).

King, 45, made his calls from a variety of phone boxes around the towns where his victims lived. Once the call was answered he would establish the identity of the person he was talking to, often using their first name. As one victim noted, "Once he established that it was me on the phone, he would lower his voice to a whisper and say things like, 'I'm going to stab you with a knife.... Tonight is the night.... I'm going to rape your dead body'" (Marciano, 1998).

For his crimes, King was sentenced to 18 months for aggravated harassment and menacing (King Sentenced to Additional Jail Time, 1998), with another 11 months added (to be served consecutively) by Concord Town Court (King Sentenced, 1998). In addition, he was ordered to undergo a variety of counseling regimes, electronic monitoring, and financial penalties, and many of the victims were issued orders of protection.

As noted previously, one of the most interesting aspects of both cases is the apparent randomness of the victim selection. With regard to King (Porter, 1998):

> *"He had no personal connection to most of the people he called," said Erie County Sheriff's Department Detective Ronald Kenyon, the arresting officer in Concord and Sardinia.... "He got their names from going into a business and looking at name tags or by going through the papers."*

The haphazard selection of victims is perhaps one of the things that makes serial stalking so hard to identify and investigate. Without links between victims, it is hard to know when and in what context they were encountered, or indeed whether there are any links at all. In an effort to overcome this, investigators in the case asked complainants to complete a list of places they frequent, places they shop, and any gym or club memberships.

Regarding his victim selection in New York, King had this to say (Whitcomb, 2004):

> *The women that I called were selected for different reasons, some of them I knew personally, others I selected from public newspapers, and occasionally I would run into them while they were working in a store and remember their name and call them later. All of the women I called were listed in the public phone book, either under their name or their husband's. The women that I remember calling include:*
>
> *A woman who is blonde and works at the [deleted] Department store in Yorkshire. She was chosen when I noticed her working*
>
> *[Deleted] who lives in Delevan, and she was chosen because I know her personally*

I selected [Deleted] from her being in the newspaper

[Deleted] was chosen because I knew of her and she crossed my mind

I do not know how I selected [Deleted], I think I just ran into her and remembered her name

I selected [Deleted] from the newspaper and I also selected [name] at the same time because they were in it together

[Deleted] was chosen from me knowing her from her employment

[Deleted] was selected because I knew her husband and I would see her on the road now and then.

This is just a small number of the victims identified by King. Some were unfortunate enough to know him, and others were unfortunate enough to be known to him by association, whereas still others appear simply to have been in the wrong place at the wrong time.

When detectives searched his premises, a collection of individual pieces of paper were found containing the names and details of a number of other females. Some of these were the complainants in the case leading to the investigation; others reported receiving no phone calls, while still others reported receiving calls prior to the inception of the investigation when no suspect was identified. There can be little doubt that the harassment would have continued if King was not apprehended.

Another interesting feature of both cases is the failure of the offender to accept responsibility for what he had done. Vidovich pleaded with detectives to allow him to make reparations to the victims and the police by washing police vehicles and doing menial chores around the victims' homes. King also failed to appreciate the gravity of his situation. According to prosecutor Joseph E. Dietrich III, "His lack of remorse is disturbing.... It's disturbing that he doesn't think what he did was so very wrong" (Marciano, 1998). However, in a later interview with police, King claimed (Whitcomb, 2004):

> *Yes, I know that there were a couple of times where circumstances may have triggered me to do this that I actually did not carry it out because I know that this is wrong, I am actually glad in some ways that I was caught because now I know for sure that I will never do this again. It has also been brought to my attention the impact that I had on these women and their families, and although I knew what I was doing was wrong, I never realized how much pain I was causing them.... I take full responsibility for what happened, and would like to bear the shame alone.*

The context in which this act of contrition occurred must be kept in mind, and it is not known whether King would have experienced a similar form of remorse outside of an arrest scenario or whether he fought with these feelings during his offending.

Although these two offenders are a veritable geographic world apart, their offenses are remarkably similar. Both offenders employed similar MOs in contacting their victims. Vidovich and King would first establish the identities of their victims before talking, and both made use of the anonymity afforded by public pay phones. Neither seemed to appreciate the seriousness of their offenses, with Vidovich believing his crimes could be mitigated by offering menial services as restitution to the victims and police. Another commonality between each was their sheer number of victims, all being victimized over a similar period of time. This would understandably be a time-consuming activity and speaks to the motivation of each in continuation of the harassment.

Conclusion

Stalking is a new crime but an old behavior that has received increasing scholarly attention over the past decade. With more research and more exposure to cases, we are provided with a deeper and more substantial understanding of many aspects including victim and offender relationships, motivation, dynamics, treatment outcomes, and classifications. With communication technologies providing the stalker with a new medium through which to carry out harassment, the number of victims and the exact sequence and nature of their harassment, it is argued, provide another variant that is the subject of this chapter: serial stalking. In one pursuit type, the consecutive stalker will pursue one victim after another, whereas in concurrent cases the offender will pursue multiple victims during the same approximate time period. This type of stalking has not yet been the subject of much academic study, which would be understandably difficult given the inability to link the crimes of the one offender, its covert nature, victim perceptions, reporting styles, and the inability to keep track of an offender once attentions subside. Repeat victimization from one stalker poses a significant obstacle to law enforcement charged with the investigation of such offenses, and only through a deeper understanding of the dynamics of these offenses will our appreciation of individual offenses improve.

Questions

1. One reason why legislators have had trouble framing legal sanctions is because:
   a. The identity of stalkers is never known before they are apprehended
   b. Most stalkers know the law and operate within the bounds of the law
   c. Most of the behaviors constituting stalking are routine, mundane, or harmless
   d. Stalkers never leave evidence that they could be prosecuted for
   e. None of the above
2. The Australian Bureau of Statistics found what percentage of respondents in their study would be stalked at some time in their life?
   a. 7%
   b. 9%
   c. 15%
   d. 16%
   e. 24%
3. Which of the following is not one of the goals of the investigative phase of criminal profiling?
   a. Assist in the linkage of related crimes
   b. Assess the escalation of nuisance behaviors

c. Provide investigators with relevant leads and strategies
d. Keep the overall investigation on track
e. Develop insight into offender motive and intent before, during, and after the crime

4. Generally, there are two main ways in which profiling might assist an investigation. *True or false?*
5. What are the three common provisions of stalking legislation according to Meloy?

References

Basile, K. C., Swahn, M. H., Chen, J., & Saltzman, L. E. (2006). Stalking in the United States: Recent national prevalence estimates. *American Journal of Preventative Medicine, 31*(2), 172–175.

Blackburn, R. (1993). *The psychology of criminal conduct.* Chichester, UK: Wiley.

Boon, J. C. W., & Sheridan, L. (2001). Stalker typologies: A law enforcement perspective. *Journal of Threat Assessment, 1*(2), 75–97.

Brewster, M. P. (1997). An exploration of the experiences and needs of former intimate stalking victims. West Chester University, [proposal no. 5-8432-PA-IJ].

Budd, T., Mattinson, J., & Myhill, A. (2000 October). *The extent and nature of stalking: Findings from the 1998 British Crime Survey.* Home Office Research, Development and Statistics Directorate. [Research Study 110].

Busch, K. A., & Cavanaugh, J. L. (1986). The study of multiple murder: Preliminary examination of the interface between epistemology and methodology. *Journal of Interpersonal Violence, 1*(1), 5–23.

Clarke, R. V. (1997). *Situational crime prevention: Successful case studies* (2nd ed.). New York: Harrow and Heston.

Clarke, R. V., & Homel, R. (1997). A revised classification of situational crime prevention techniques. In S. P. Lab (Ed.), *Crime prevention at a crossroads.* Cincinnati: Anderson.

Coleman, F. L. (1997). Stalking behaviour and the cycle of domestic violence. *Journal of Interpersonal Violence, 12*(3), 420–432.

Collins, M. J., & Wilkas, M. B. (2000). Stalking trauma syndrome and the traumatized victim. In J. A. Davis (Ed.), *Stalking crimes and victim protection: Prevention, intervention, threat assessment and case management.* Boca Raton, FL: CRC Press.

Cornish, D. B., & Clarke, R. V. (2003). Opportunities, precipitators and criminal decisions: A reply to Wortley's critique of situational crime prevention. In M. Smith & D. B. Cornish (Eds.), *Crime prevention studies* (Vol. 16). New York: Criminal Justice Press. [Theory for Situational Crime Prevention].

Dietz, P. (1986). Mass, serial and sensational homicides. *Bulletin of the New York Academy of Medicine, 62,* 477–491.

Dressing, H., Henn, F. A., & Gass, P. (2002). Stalking behavior—An overview of the problem and a case report of male to male stalking during delusional disorder. *Psychopathology, 35,* 313–318.

Eke, A. W., Hilton, N. Z., Meloy, J. R., Mohandie, K., & Williams, J. (2011). Predictors of recidivism by stalkers: A nine-year follow-up of police contacts. *Behavioral Sciences and the Law, 29,* 271–283.

Egger, S. A. (1984). A working definition of serial murder and the reduction of linkage blindness. *Journal of Police Science and Administration, 12*(3), 348–357.

Egger, S. A. (1990). *Serial murder: An elusive phenomenon.* New York: Praeger.

Fisher, B. S., Cullen, F. T., & Turner, M. G. (2000 December). The sexual victimization of college women. *National Institute of Justice Bureau of Justice Statistics Research Report.*

Fox, J. A., & Levin, J. (1997). Serial murder: Popular myths and empirical realities. In A. Thio & T. C. Calhoun (Eds.), *Readings in deviant behavior* (3rd ed.). Boston: Pearson.

Fremouw, W. J., Westrup, D., & Pennypacker, J. (1997). Stalking on campus: The prevalence and strategies for coping with stalking. *Journal of Forensic Sciences, 42*(4), 666.

Geberth, V. J. (1996). Practical homicide investigation: Tactics: *Procedures and forensic techniques* (3rd ed.). Boca Raton, FL: CRC Press.

Gresswell, D. M., & Hollin, C. R. (1994). Multiple murder. *The British Journal of Criminology, 34*(1), 1–15.

Hall, D. (1998). The victims of stalking. In J. R. Meloy (Ed.), *The psychology of stalking: Clinical and forensic perspectives*. London: Academic Press.

Harmon, R. B., Rosner, R., & Owens, H. (1995). Obsessional harassment and erotomania in a criminal court population. *Journal of the Forensic Sciences, 40*(2), 188–196.

Helsham, S. (2001). The profane and the insane: An inquiry into the psychopathology of serial murder. *Alternative Law Journal, 26*(6), 269–273.

Hickey, E. (1991). *Serial murderers and their victims*. Pacific Grove: Brooks Cole.

Hills, A. M., & Taplin, J. L. (1998). Anticipated responses to stalking: Effect of threat and target-stalker relationship. *Psychiatry, Psychology and Law, 5*(1), 139–146.

Holmes, R. R. (2001). Criminal stalking: An analysis of the various typologies of stalkers. In J. A. Davis (Ed.), *Stalking crime and victim protection: Prevention, intervention, threat assessment, and case management*. Boca Raton, FL: CRC Press.

Holmes, R. R., & Holmes, S. (2003). *Profiling violent crimes: An investigative tool* (2nd ed.). Thousand Oaks, CA: Sage.

Johnson, W., & Gordon, G. (2012). New anti-stalking laws expected. *The Independent, 8th March.*

King sentenced to additional jail time, counseling, probation. (1998, August 27). Arcade Herald.

Kocsis, R. N. (2000). The motives of the serial murderer. *Queensland Police Journal, January/February.*

Kocsis, R. N., & Irwin, H. (1998). The psychological profile of serial offenders and a redefinition of the misnomer of serial crime. *Psychiatry, Psychology and Law, 5*(2), 1–10.

Lloyd-Goldstein, R. (2000). Serial stalking: Recent clinical findings. In L. Schlesinger (Ed.), *Serial offenders: Current thoughts, recent findings*. San Diego: Academic Press.

Malsch, M., de Keijser, J. W., & Debets, S. E. C. (2011). Are stalkers recidivists? Repeated offending by convicted stalkers. *Violence and Victims, 26*(1), 3–15.

Marciano, J. (1998, August 6). *Man jailed for making threatening calls*. Buffalo News.

Margen, D. (2003). *A current affair*. Australia. Au: Nine Network. [Pg 141].

McLennan, W. (1996). *Women's safety Australia*. Canberra: Australian Bureau of Statistics. [ABS Catalogue No. 4128.0].

Meloy, J. R. (1996). Stalking (obsessional following): A review of some preliminary studies. *Aggression and Violent Behaviour, 1*, 147–162.

Meloy, J. R. (1998). The psychology of stalking. In J. R. Meloy (Ed.), *The psychology of stalking: Clinical and forensic perspectives*. London: Academic Press.

Meloy, J. R. (1999). Stalking: An old behavior, a new crime. *Forensic Psychiatry, 22*(1), 85–99.

Miller, M. C. (2001, March). *Stalking*. The Harvard Mental Health Letter.

Mohandie, K., Meloy, J. R., McGowan, M. G., & Williams, J. (2006). The RECON typology of stalking: Reliability and validity based upon a large sample of North American stalkers. *Journal of Forensic Sciences, 51*, 147–155.

Mullen, P. E., Pathé, M., & Purcell, R. (2000). Stalking. *The Psychologist, 13*(9), 454–459.

Mullen, P. E., Pathé, M., & Purcell, R. (2009). *Stalkers and their victims* (2nd ed.). Cambridge: Cambridge University Press.

Natalie's nightmare. (2003, March 14). Gold Coast Bulletin.

Network for Surviving Stalking. (2012). England - Wales criminal law. Available from: <http://www.nss.org.uk/advice/england-wales-criminal-law/> Accessed on 21.05.12.

Objects of obsession. (2000, 20 November). Who Magazine.

O'Toole, M. E. (1999). Criminal profiling: The FBI used criminal investigative analysis to solve violent crimes. *Corrections Today, 61*(1), 44–47.

Pathé, M. (2003). *Surviving stalking.* Cambridge, UK: Cambridge University Press.

Pathé, M., & Mullen, P. E. (1997). The impact of stalkers on their victims. *British Journal of Psychiatry, 170,* 12–17.

Pearce, A., & Easteal, P. (1999). The domestic in stalking: Policing domestic stalking in the Australian Capital Territory. *Alternative Law Journal, 24,* 4.

Petherick, W. A. (2000). Case number 0700.

Petherick, W. A. (2001). Case number 0601.

Petherick, W. A. (2002). Stalking. In B. E Turvey (Ed.), *Criminal profiling: An introduction to behavioural evidence analysis.* London: Academic Press.

Petherick, W. A. (2003, June). What's in a name? Comparing applied profiling methodologies. *Journal of Law and Social Challenges,* 173–188.

Petherick, W. A., & Ferguson, C. E. (2012). Understanding victim behavior through offender behavior typologies: *Fifth annual australian and new zealand critical criminology conference proceedings.* Cairns: James Cook University. [July 7–8].

Pinizzotto, A. J. (1984). Forensic psychology: Criminal personality profiling. *Journal of Police Science and Administration, 12*(1), 32–40.

Porter, D. (1998, March 26). Local man arrested for threatening phone calls made to over 28 women. *The Springville Journal.*

Power, D. (1996). Serial killers. *The Criminologist, 20*(2), 94–102.

Purcell, R., Pathé, M., & Mullen, P. E. (2000). The incidence and nature of stalking victimization: *Presented at the Australian institute of criminology stalking.* Sydney: Criminal Justice System Responses Conference. [7–8 December].

Ressler, R. K., Burgess, A. W., & Douglas, J. E. (1988). *Sexual homicides: Patterns and motives.* Lexington, MA: Lexington Books.

Roeckelein, J. E. (2006). *Elsevier's dictionary of psychological theories.* San Diego: Elsevier Science.

R. v. Vidovich. (2002). QCA 422 (10 October 1902)

Sheridan, L. (2001). Stalking. *Journal of Interpersonal Violence, 16*(2), 151–158.

Sheridan, L., & Davies, G. M. (2001). What is stalking? The match between legislation and public perception. *Legal and Criminological Psychology, 6*(3), 3–17.

Sheridan, L., Davies, G., & Boon, J. (2001). The course and nature of stalking: A victim perspective. *The Howard Journal, 40*(3), 215–234.

Sheridan, L. P., Blauuw, E., & Davies, G. M. (2003). Stalking: Knowns and unknowns. *Trauma, Violence and Abuse, 4*(2), 148–162.

Stocker, M., & Nielssen, O. (2000). Apprehended violence orders and stalking: *Presented at the australian institute of criminology stalking.* Sydney: Criminal Justice System Responses Conference. [7–8 December].

Stolz, G. (2002, May 10). *Porno stalker jailed for seven years.* The Courier Mail, Brisbane, Queensland.

Tjaden, P. (1997, November). The crime of stalking: How big is the problem? *National Institute of Justice Research Preview.*

Tjaden, P., & Thoennes, N. (1998, April). Stalking in America: Findings from the national violence against women survey. *National Institute of Justice and the Centers for Disease Control and Prevention: Research in Brief*

Watson, J. M. (1998). First anti-stalking law in the country. Available from: <http://www.smartvoter.org/1998jun/ca/or/vote/watson_j/paper1.html>. Accessed on 22.05.2012.

Whitcomb, T. (2004). *Personal Communication.* July 20.

Wilson, T. (2002a, May 10). Saved from sex stalker. *Gold Coast Bulletin*

Wilson, T. (2002b, May 10). Evil stalker can count the years. *Gold Coast Bulletin*

Wright, J. A., Burgess, A. G., Laszlo, A. T., McCrary, G. O., & Douglas, J. E. (1996). A typology of interpersonal stalking. *Journal of Interpersonal Violence, 11*(4), 487–503.

Zona, M. A., Sharma, K. K., & Lane, J. T. (1993). A comparative study of erotomanic and obsessional subjects in a forensic sample. *Journal of Forensic Sciences, 38*(4), 894–903.

15

Serial Rape

Alicia Jenkins and Wayne Petherick

Profiling and Serial Crime.

Introduction

A topic surrounded by misconceptions, rape is a complex, emotionally charged, and often misunderstood act. Serial rapists potentially create a climate of fear in communities, and media attention to occurrences of sexual assault and rape has increased community awareness of such predators. In an effort to understand these offenders and provide greater public safety, more emphasis needs to be placed on understanding the origins of the behaviors and the motivations that drive these offenders. To explore the issue of rape effectively, both the offender and the victim need to be addressed.

This chapter examines the characteristics of both the victim and the offender in rape and serial rape by exploring a variety of offender typologies. Further, it defines serial rape and how it differs from nonserial rape and sexual assault. Finally, elements of the investigation and investigative techniques are explored in addition to evolutionary perspectives, psychopathology, and issues of forensic awareness.

Rape and Sexual Assault

There are a multitude of definitions for rape and sexual assault, both legally and culturally. According to Section 347 of the Criminal Code of Queensland:

> *Any person who has carnal knowledge of a female without her consent or with her consent if it is obtained by force, or by means of threats or intimidation of any kind, or by fear of bodily harm, or by means of false or fraudulent representations as to the nature of the act, or, in the case of a married women, by personating her husband, is guilty of a crime, which is called rape.*

In early English common law, rape was defined as a man obtaining sexual intercourse by force and without a woman's consent. As early as 1769, English law explained that rape was "the carnal knowledge of a woman forcibly and against her will." This definition has not disappeared over time, with the Uniform Crime Reports of the FBI defining rape in the same manner (Anderson, 2005).

For the purpose of this chapter, Easteal's (1993) definition will be used, where rape is defined as penetration of the mouth, vagina, or anus by any part of the attacker's body, or by an object used by the attacker without the consent of the victim. It should be noted that the source of penetration, object of penetration, gender of perpetrator and victim, and definition of consent varies greatly across jurisdictions (Gannon, Collie, Ward & Thakker, 2008). Groth (1979) further identified rape as an aggressive act, the physical act of which constitutes a discharge of anger, frustration, or resentment.

By comparison, sexual assault is defined as a physical assault of a sexual nature directed toward another person who does not consent, consents through intimidation or fraud, or is legally deemed incapable due to youth or incapacity (Australian Institute of Criminology, 2010). The Australian Bureau of Statistics (1996) defines sexual assault as a criminal offense including any sexual activity carried out against the will of the victim through the use of violence, coercion, or intimidation, even if penetration is not the end result. To sum up, the difference between rape and sexual assault is whether there is actual penetration.

Serial Rape and Rapists

Although the adjective "serial" has been used only more recently to describe an individual whose crime is repetitive, such offenders have likely been present since antiquity. Conceptually, serial rape refers to two or more rape offenses committed by the same offender with a cooling off period between offenses. Repetitive and compulsive offenders, especially those suffering some form of psychopathology, may undertake their crimes in such a way as to elude law enforcement and the understanding of mental health professionals. An associated problem is that the courts and legal officials view the issue as a criminal problem, with the offense and the offender are virtually inseparable, rather than a clinical disorder with common denominators. A problem with this purely legal approach is that it often fails to take into account the degree of dangerousness posed by the offender, the likelihood that the offender will reoffend, or commit a related but more heinous crime. Although crime rates on the whole appear to have declined, serial crimes may be increasing (Schlesinger, 2000), so understanding these offenses may be more critical now than at any other time in the past.

Date Rape

Date rape is a controversial and ambiguous crime, with much debate regarding the definition and prevalence in the past 20 years. While the term rape has largely been replaced in Australian legal terminology with the term sexual assault (Russo, 2000), date rape is identified as a type of sexual assault where the victim and the offender are in, or have been in, some form of personal social relationship. This may range from a first date to an established relationship. Date rape is nonaggravated, nonconsensual sex that rarely involves physical injury, or the explicit threat of physical injury, but may involve the use of drugs or excessive levels of alcohol

Table 15.1 Australian Female Victims of Sexual Assault by Relationship to Offender, in a 12-month Period (1995–1996) and Since Age 15

	In the Past 12 Months		Since Age 15	
Relationship	**Number**	**%**	**Number**	**%**
Known to the Victim				
Current Partner	12 400	8.7	37 300	4.8
Previous Partner	16 500	11.5	176 500	22.8
Boyfriend/Date	23 800	16.6	215 500	27.8
Other Known Man	44 400	31.1	259 400	33.5
Total	97 100	67.9	688 700	89
Unknown to Victim	45 800	32.1	85 400	11.0
Total	142 900	100.0	774 100	100.0

to overcome a victim's defenses. Problematically, because it does not always involve physical injury, and because physical injury is often the only criterion that the act is nonconsensual, what is really sexual assault is often mistaken for seduction. The enforcement of the new laws on sexual assault have done nothing to resolve this problem (Pineau, 1989).

The term date rape has no legal standing and in Australian literature is also often penned relationship rape. The Australian Bureau of Statistics (1996) Women's Safety Survey includes the category "boyfriend/date" in its estimate of the incidence of sexual assault. Here, 16.6% of all sexual assaults are committed by a boyfriend or date (see Table 15.1). Literature on the subject (ABS, 1996; Easteal, 1993) has revealed the complexity of date rape: It is difficult to define, to measure, and to prevent. Because of this, the extent of date rape worldwide is currently very difficult to estimate, and will remain so unless appropriate changes are made in the collection of sexual assault statistics. To compound the problem, date rape, as mentioned earlier, may involve the use of alcohol or other drugs that have a negative effect on memory. This may obscure details about the crime such as the location, what actually happened, or worse, in providing details of the offender or offenders. This may be particularly problematic for the identification of serial offenders and the linkage of their crimes. In order to prevent date rape, measures should be directed toward adolescent men and women, at stages when they begin having intimate relationships, especially in understanding the underlying causes of sexual violence and the inadequate response of the criminal justice system, where they are linked to attitudes about sexuality and gender roles that disadvantage serve to women.

Characteristics

The Crime

Unfortunately there appears to be little statistical evidence around serial rape and there is no way of knowing what proportion of sexual assaults/rapes are in fact the work of serial rapists. Due to this, statistical evidence available of crime characteristics (location, time, weapon involvement) remains predominately focused around individual cases.

Between the period of January 1991 and June 1992, 450 incidents of rape and sexual assault were reported to Queensland police (Moran, 1993). Of these cases, nearly 8% of all attacks involved the use of a weapon while for the same period in South Australia, 28.8% of all cases involved the use of a weapon. From these reports, knives were the most common weapons used, accounting for more than 50% of all attacks. Other weapons reported to police included firearms, wire, wood, hammers, and scissors.

Data from Queensland, Victorian, and South Australian studies indicate that attacks occur predominately in residential dwellings or private homes, accounting for more than 60%, whereas attacks reported outdoors accounted for only 22%. These figures support Hazelwood and Warren's (1989) study on serial rapists, where it was found that 50% of all offenses were committed in the victim's home. Despite this, it has been revealed that only 12% of women feel unsafe in their own home at night, whereas 45% of women feel unsafe walking outside at night (Office of the Cabinet, 1992), suggesting that community understanding of, and attitudes toward, the risk of sexual offenses may be sorely misplaced.

In relation to time of offense, studies revealed that a large majority (74.9%) of attacks occur between the hours of 6 PM and 6 AM. There is also a noticeable jump in attacks occurring over the weekend period, between Friday and Sunday, with the remainder being distributed evenly over the remaining weekdays. Of incidents reported over an 18-month period in three of Australia's largest states, one third occurred in the summer months, with the next highest being spring and autumn, accounting for 23.1%, followed by winter (Moran, 1993).

When looking at the characteristics of the crime itself, identifying the number of scenes is also useful. The potential sources of tangible information that lead to an apprehension when the victim and offender are strangers is dependent upon the offender's approach and the number of separate and distinct scenes or locations in the offense (LeBeau, 1987). This may be a result of the "spread" of evidence between scenes, especially where all scenes are not identified, or perhaps when the scene can be used to provide further investigative information such as forensic evidence or ownership.

It has been suggested that rape occurs in scenes, with the three main scenes being the initial meeting place, the crime scene, and the after scene. The first scene is where the offender meets the victim, the crime scene is where the actual attack takes place, and the after scene is where the offender leaves the victim (LeBeau, 1987). Table 15.2 represents the core scene typology, displaying the three main scenes with the inclusion of two added scenes: victim residence and offender residence.

The Offender

Information about the known characteristics of offenders is vital for the effective assessment and treatment of sexual offenders. In a study using Queensland police reports (Moran, 1993), a number of variables relating to the offender were identified, showing that the highest proportions of offenders were aged between 17 and 25 years, representing nearly 40% of all identified offenders. A general trend in data is noticeable; as age increased, the number of offenders in the older age brackets decreased. The majority of offenders were born in Australia, accounting for 73.5%; the

Table 15.2 Number of Rape Scenes and Definitions

Number of Scenes	Definitions
One	Victim residence, offender residence, meeting place, crime scene, and after scene are all at the same location.
Two	Victim and offender residences are separate but the rest of the crimes take place in one of the residences.
Three	Victim and offender residences are separate and a third scene assumes the role of the crimes scene and after scene.
Four	Victim and offender residences are separate, third location is a meeting place, and the fourth is the crime scene. The after scene will be any one of the previous locations.
Five	All scenes have separate locations.

second highest group of offenders were born in the United Kingdom and Ireland. Generally rapists tend to be characterized by low socioeconomic status; however, incarcerated rapists appear similar on a range of sociodemographic variables to the general prison population. In relation to the offender's employment status, offenders were almost equally employed and unemployed at the time of committing an offense, with students, retirees, and pensioners accounting for a small percentage of offenders. Examination of police reports further revealed offenders with previous charges against them. Over 58% of offenders had some level of police history, including 4% of offenders with previous charges for sexual offenses. In addition, offender's general propensity for violence is evidenced in the likely use of violence in their sexual offenses.

Offender Typologies

A typology is a grouping of items based on shared similarities, with a rapist typology grouping the offenders on characteristics such as motivations (Groth, Burgess & Holstrom, 1977).

Groth (1979) first presented the idea that the act of rape essentially has three main components—power, anger, and sadism—producing three rapist types. While these are discussed at length elsewhere in this volume, they will be discussed briefly here since they apply to sexual offenses.

Power Rapist

One pattern of rape involves power as the dominant factor motivating the offender. The power rapists show less aggression in both sexual and nonsexual situations than other kinds of rapists, because it is not the offender's desire to harm the victim (Hazelwood, 2009), but to possess their sexuality and to achieve sexual submission. Sexuality is a mechanism through which the offender compensates for feelings of inadequacy and further serves as a way to exert control. Such offenders entertain obsessional thoughts and masturbatory fantasies about sexual conquest, and since the act is a test of competency, the offense brings with it a combination of excitement, anxiety, and anticipated pleasure. Offenses of this nature can either be premeditated—the offender searches for the victim with clear intent—or opportunistic—a situation presents itself and the offender unexpectedly finds he or she has access to a victim, which activates propensity for sexual assault.

There are two types of power rapists, the Power Reassurance rapist and the Power Assertive rapist. The Power Reassurance offender has low self-esteem and commits an offense in an attempt to stabilize his or her self-esteem. The offender orchestrates the situation and the victim in such a way that rejection is not an option (Groth et al., 1977). The Power Assertive offender also has low self-esteem and the offense is intended to stabilize this through domination. Fantasy plays a minor role in these crimes, with the rapist being responsible for date, spousal, or acquaintance rape as well as stranger rape (Hazelwood, 2009). In instances where the offender knows the victim, the relationship can also be used as a means to satisfy immediate needs without any thought to how events will affect the victim. In short, the victim is merely the conduit through which the offender expresses virility.

Anger Rapist

This type of rapist is considered unpredictable and is characterized by physical brutality (Hazelwood, 2009), with rage displayed in these assaults ranging from verbal abuse to murder. Unlike the power rapist, anger rapists use far more force than is needed to simply overpower the victim and achieve sexual penetration. Relative to other types of assaults, these tend to be brief, with the amount of violence being excessive even when the victim does not resist. Should the victim resist, the level of aggression would only intensify. Anger rapists want to degrade and humiliate their victims, and they do so by displacing their anger. Such assaults tend to be spontaneous or impulsive rather than premeditated. The experience is one of conscious rage, whereby the offender uses the act as an outlet by expressing fury both verbally and physically; basically sex becomes the weapon.

This broad type has two subtypes: Anger Retaliatory and Anger Excitation. Anger Retaliatory, also known as Revenge, is a category where hostility is expressed toward women (Groth et al., 1977). Often, the assault occurs because the offender has had an argument with a female in his life and the rape is seen as a punishing act, leaving the offender to feel as though his cause has been justified. While Anger Excitation may be the least common, the excitation offender is most brutal with his attacks and has a greater capacity to kill his victims. These attacks are prolonged and can possibly involve a variety of apparatus.

Sadistic Rapist

Sadistic rape is the third pattern, where both sexuality and aggression become fused into a single psychological experience known as sadism. A sexual transformation of anger and power occurs so that aggression itself becomes eroticized (Groth, 1977). An offender's motivation is to achieve sexual gratification through causing mental and physical pain and suffering. An increase in violence usually correlates with an increase in arousal. Sadistic rapists are opportunistic, attacking suddenly with their attack often involving a kidnapping. Sadistic rapists will act out their fantasies symbolically, with bondage and torture, giving the offense a bizarre and ritualistic quality (Groth, 1979).

The Victim

In 2011 the Australian Bureau of Statistics revealed that more females than males were victims of sexual assaults, accounting for 85% of all cases. A report comparing Queensland, South

Australian, and Victorian rape data found that victims aged 25 years and younger accounted for 83%, 76%, and 70%, respectively. Queensland therefore has a greater number of younger victims, figures that are in keeping with the high percentage of intra-family rapes, as discussed later. In instances where marital status was recorded, it was identified that a vast majority of victims (79%) were single, with women in relationships totaling 14%. Similar statistics are reported for both South Australia and Victoria. It should also be noted that marital rape has only been included in the definition of rape in Queensland since 1989, and this could have an effect on the number of married or de facto women reporting rapes to police.

Relationship between Offender and Victim

A number of studies (Australian Bureau of Statistics, 2005; Moran, 1993) have shown that for individual rape cases, approximately 65% of the time, some relationship exists between the victim and the offender. In Queensland alone from January 1991 to June 1992, 44.6% of rapes were committed by friends or acquaintances and 24% by family members, being a relative or a spouse or de facto. In 2011 male victims were more likely to identify that they were assaulted by a stranger than female victims. From available Australian data, in comparison to other states and territories, Queensland has a high proportion of intra-family rapes. However, this could be attributable to the charging process; in some cases family members will be charged with rape instead of incest to increase the probability of a conviction. Research indicates that the majority of intra-family rapes involves victims aged 16 years and under, and victims of rape by an acquaintance or friend were equally in the 16 years and under and the 17 to 25 age bracket. Older victims were more likely than younger victims to be attacked by a stranger, with approximately 45% of victims aged over 40 reporting being raped by a stranger and 18% of victims aged 25 to 40 being raped by a stranger. In a study specifically of serial rapists (Hazelwood & Warren, 1989) it was found that 85% of victims were unknown to the offender. This differs greatly from individual rape cases, where the majority of victims were known to the offender.

Prevalence and Reporting

Prevalence rates are an indication of the number of individuals who have been raped at any time in their lives. Although no federal estimates are available, individual researchers have estimated prevalence based on victimization surveys. It has been estimated that 14% to 25% of women have been victims of sexual assaults (Koss, 1993). A National Women's Study revealed that 13% of adult females had been a victim of a completed rape. Within the 12-month period following the initial study, there were an additional 683,000 victims of completed rapes. Kilpatrick, Edmunds, and Seymour (1992) found that in a 2-year period in the United States more than 1.1 million women were raped. On the whole, this is equivalent to one in every six females and one in every 33 males. It should also be noted that every two minutes, someone in the United States is the victim of sexual assault (Rape, Abuse and Incest National Network, 2009).

Sexual assault remains one of the most underreported crimes, with the extent of nondisclosure being estimated as high as 68% (Burgess & Marchetti, 2009). Several reasons have been identified for nondisclosure (Acierno, Resnick & Kilpatrick, 1997):

- Fear of retribution, especially if the victim is known to the offender.
- Fear of having a stigma attached from being a victim of rape.
- Fear of blame for the attack.
- History of negative outcome following previous disclosure.
- Lack of encouragement to discuss abuse.
- Fear of psychological consequences of disclosure, including anxiety or depression from revisiting the event.

A complex interaction exists between various ideational and structural components of a culture that produces such underreporting, high prevalence, and inadequate responses to rape; Figure 15.1 demonstrates these interactions. According to research comparing the reporting rates of three major Australian cities, over 12% of rapes in Queensland are not reported for two or more years after the event; this is considerably higher than the other two states (Moran, 1993). Due to the significant level of underreporting, The Rape, Abuse and Incest National Network (2009) has estimated that 97% of all rapists will never spend a day in jail. Of those sexually assaulted in 1995 (Bureau of Justice Statistics, 1996), only 32% of incidents were reported to police. Further to this, Burgess and Holstrom's study (1986) revealed that more than 50% of cases were reported by someone other than the victim. Victims of sexual

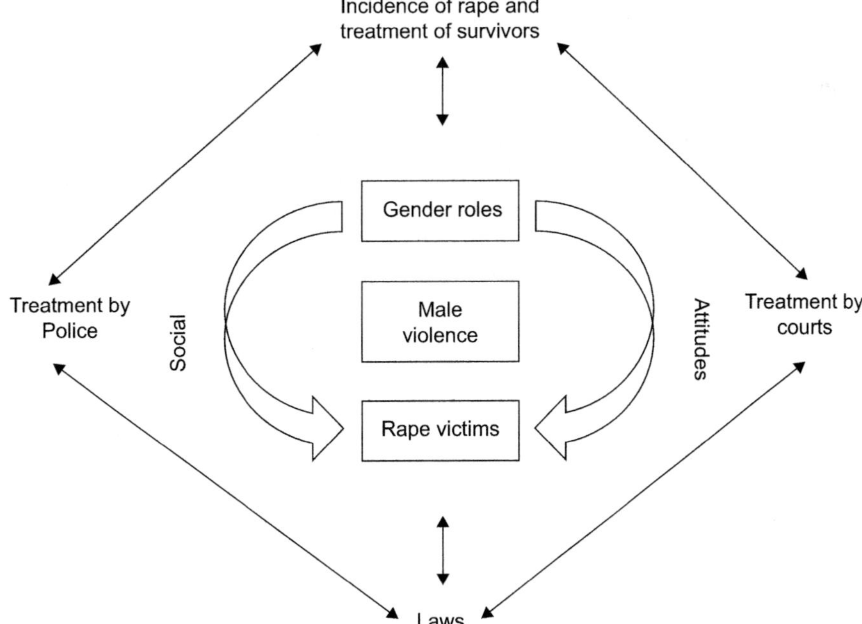

FIGURE 15.1 Societal variables that contribute to rape incidence and treatment of survivors.

abuse suffer mostly in silence, actively avoid recalling their trauma, and do not volunteer information about their traumatic experience. As a result of this a majority of victims who sustain rape-related mental or physical problems obtain effective treatment.

Evolutionary Perspectives

Sex offenders use force or the threat of force to obtain sex. Examining the cause of such behavior from an evolutionary perspective may seem unusual, even objectionable, however might still prove useful (Wilson, Daly & Scheib, 1997). Many social scientists studying criminal behavior have, in the past, ignored or misunderstood evolutionary theory. However, as it is accepted that humans are a product of evolution, there appears to be no valid reason for not exploring the evolutionary perspective when looking at criminal behavior. A step to understanding what evolutionary perspective might contribute to the understanding and prevention of serial rape is to classify the misunderstandings surrounding the evolutionary perspective.

The Naturalistic Fallacy

According to Moore (1903) the naturalistic fallacy is the view that what ought to be is defined by what is, and especially by what is natural. Scholars have continuously rejected the naturalistic fallacy on the grounds that any claim that rape was favored by "natural" selection or was the result of a "natural" desire for sex was equivalent to claiming that rape is justifiable. The fact is that rape is well documented in many species (Palmer & Thornhill, 2000), and probably cannot occur without some sexual arousal on behalf of the rapist. In saying so, this is by no means a justification or excuse for committing the act.

Genetic Determinism

Along with the naturalistic fallacy, there is also the mistaken view that evolutionary explanations are based on the assumption that behavior is genetically determined, meaning fixed by genes alone and not alterable without altering those genes. According to Gray (1997), evolutionary explanations are taken simply to imply that our behavior is programmed by our genes and therefore is natural. "Biological" and "genetic" are often inaccurately equated, resulting in the concept of genetic determinism remaining popular. In reality, every living thing is, by definition, biological; however, everything biological is the result of interactions of environmental factors and genes. This interaction between genes and environmental factors is incredibly intimate. Instead of accepting that behaviors are unalterable, a greater understanding of this intimate relationship could lead us to conclude that changing one or more developmental causes can alter behaviors.

Proximate vs. Ultimate Causation

Rape as a product of evolution is often dismissed because rapists are rarely ever motivated by a desire to reproduce; this argument confuses both ultimate and proximate levels of causation.

Proximate causes of behavior operate over a short term, equating to immediate causes of behavior. They are concerned with how such developmental or physiological mechanisms cause something to happen, whereas ultimate explanations are concerned with why particular proximate mechanisms exist in the first place (Palmer & Thornhill, 1997). These two levels of explanation are not alternatives, but complements. The relationship between proximate and ultimate explanations has been widely misunderstood by critics of the evolutionary perspective and its role in the explanation of rape. To say that rape has not evolved because rapists are not motivated by a conscious desire to reproduce confuses the proximate level of immediate motivation with the ultimate level of reproductive consequences during our evolutionary history.

Evolutionary Perspective: A Contribution

Contributions of the evolutionary perspective to serial rape can be elevated by avoiding misunderstandings about the theory. In the case of serial rape, our evolutionary history is directly related to the questions in Table 15.3. An evolutionary perspective can contribute to a greater understanding of rape by helping to answer these questions.

Evolutionary Explanation of Rape

Two likely explanations exist for the ultimate cause of human rape. The first is that rape may be an adaptation that was favored by selection because it increased male reproductive success. The second notion surrounds rape as a by-product of other psychological adaptations, including greater sexual arousal and desire for sexual variety, to name a few (Palmer, 1991).

Although questions still remain about the ultimate causes of rape, an evolutionary approach can help identify proximate causes of rape that may lead to lowering the frequency of occurrences. It could be also interesting to note that ultimate causes of rape may lie in the evolution of proximate mechanisms that govern sexual behaviors and emotions. Finally, recognizing the environmental factors that are an immediate cause of rape can lead to greater success in its prevention.

Table 15.3 Contribution of Evolutionary Perspective

Why are males usually the rapists and females (usually) the victims?
Why do young males rape more than older ones?
Why does rape occur in all known cultures?
Why are young females more often the victims of rape than older females?
Why is rape more frequent in some situations (war) than others?
Why does rape still occur among humans?
Why have attempts to reform rape laws met with only limited success?
How can rape be prevented?

Source: Palmer & Thornhill, 1997

Psychopathology

Although it is not unusual for psychopathologies in rapists to clearly fit into diagnostic criteria, studies have been unable to draw definitive conclusions from personality inventories and their ability to identify a typical rapist profile. Most methods examining the prevalence of psychopathologies in rapists involve self-report personality tests. Because of this, it is difficult to ascertain the true prevalence of psychopathologies. Rates of diagnosable psychiatric disorders appear generally low in rapists but are higher than that observed in child molesters. In this instance, it is imperative to compare the similarities and differences between rapists and child molesters since rapists are typically treated side by side with the "generic" sex offender (Gannon et al., 2008).

Paraphilias

According to the DSM-IV-TR (American Psychiatric Association, 2000), a paraphilia diagnosis is reliant upon repeated and powerful sexual fantasies, sexual urges, or behaviors that involve unusual objects, activities, or situations. Despite reference to paraphilias such as pedophilia, rape is omitted from the DSM, and this has been widely disputed (Gannon et al., 2008). The absence of an official diagnosis of rape leaves clinicians in a conundrum, as clinical diagnosis is required by civil commitment law and government agencies. Further to this, it does not allow for appropriate classification, assessment, and treatment of rapists (Marshall, 2007).

Personality Disorders

Most interest has been focused on determining psychopathic traits and levels of psychopathy in relation to personality disorders. It has been estimated that diagnosable psychopathy in rapists stands somewhere between 40% and 50%, in comparison to 10% to 15% for child molesters (Hare, 1999). These results are supported by a number of other studies that agree that rapists are generally more psychopathic than child molesters. Another domain related to personality disorders that has been explored is interpersonal characteristics. In relation to rapists, they are found more socially competent, less anxious, and more likely to be in an intimate relationship than child molesters. It should be noted however that despite these findings, rapists are more likely to hold hostile sexual beliefs towards women (Polaschek & Gannon, 2004).

Neurobiological Impairment

Impairment of neurobiological functioning is another factor that can be used to distinguish between rapists and other offenders, by looking at structural deficit or neurotransmitter or hormone imbalance (Gannon et al., 2000). There are two main approaches used to determine a link between sexual aggression and neurobiological impairment, including neuroimaging to assess the structural quality of the brain and neuropsychological testing to detect anomalous brain deficits. Abnormalities within the temporal part of the brain have been detected particularly in sadistic rapists by using neuroimaging techniques (Aigner et al., 2000). Neuropsychological testing is more frequently used but has been hampered by the use of comparisons of mixed groups of sexual offenders with nonsexual offenders. Findings in general showed that overall, sexual offenders showed more abnormalities in the temporal region of the brain affecting memory and auditory and speech skills.

Theories of Rape

An essential basis for assessment and treatment of rapists is an understanding of etiological theories available to explain sexual aggression (Ward, Polaschek & Beech, 2006). These theories are referred to when constructing a case formation or a theoretically driven model representing an offender's problems, the underlying mechanisms, and their interrelationships. Case formation also specifies how the symptoms are generated by psychological mechanisms and provides a basis for determining treatment by tailoring interventions to the specific needs of the offender. Ward and Hudson (1998) conceptualized sexual offending literature as having three main types of theory: single factor, multifactor, and micro theories.

Single-Factor Theories

Single-factor theories, as the name suggests, refers to theories that attempt to explain sexual aggression as the result of a single underlying cause (Ward & Hudson, 1998).

Psychodynamic Theory

Freud's (1905/1953) work gave us one of the earliest explanations of rape. Freud believed that sexual aggression originates from a serious form of psychopathology within the offender that originated in childhood and is extremely resistant to treatment. Although this theory was not empirically validated, Freud's psychodynamic theory did draw attention to the need to understand sexual aggression.

Feminist Theories

Feminist theories view rape as a manifestation of core male patriarchal values and paternalism. Brownmiller (1975, p.6) asserted that rape is "a conscious process of intimidation by which all men keep all women in a state of fear." In other terms, rape and the fear it incites is one of many ways some men exert control over women. Feminist theorists are interested in the societal attitudes and values that support rape and they derive their evidence from macro-level observations of legal and social systems. However, a problem with feminist theories is that they do not account for the fact that some offenders are oblivious to the harm they have caused their victim and may not actually consciously use rape to intimidate females.

Evolutionary Theory

This theory unifies evolutionary theory with some psychological theories to explain the causal ancestral mechanisms that appear to drive rape. Evolutionary theory minimizes the importance of cultural influences and social learning on mental development, and because of this it has been suggested that this model alone cannot shed light on the most effective clinical treatment for rapists. For more information on evolutionary theory see earlier.

Socio-Cognitive Theories

Interest in socio-cognitive theories and methods to explain and understand rape has dramatically increased in recent decades. Three main components underlie a socio-cognitive understanding of rape (Hollon & Kris, 1984):

- Memory content and structure: Offense-supportive beliefs and how they are structured in schemas.
- Cognitive processing: Mechanisms that rapists use to process information in the social world.
- Cognitive products: End thoughts and beliefs that result from the interactions between cognitive content, structures, and processes.

In 2000, Ward constructed a theoretical framework, termed implicit theories, to explain sexual offenders, the beliefs that support their offense, and how these are structured in memory. It was proposed that rapists hold any combination of implicit schemata including women as sexual objects, women are dangerous, entitlement, and uncontrollability. It was hypothesized that these implicit schemata develop in childhood and by the time an individual reaches adulthood, these structures are highly resistant to change. Self-report measures generally support implicit schemata. Polashek and Gannon (2004) found all implicit schemata present in offenders' accounts of their crimes, with women as sexual objects, entitlement, and women are dangerous occurring 70%, 68%, and 65%, respectively. Socio-cognitive theories of rape appear to be substantiated by empirical work, however, an important premise is the presence of rape supportive cognition, to be entrenched by young adulthood. This makes it difficult to account for men who do not show apparent sexual aggression until later adulthood.

Multifactor Theories

These theories combine a number of single-factor theories to explain the interactions and casual relationships that are believed to create a favorable environment for sexual offending (Ward & Hudson, 1998).

Confluence Model of Sexual Aggression

The confluence model of sexual aggression is unique for two reasons; it is one of the earliest models to provide a multifactorial perspective of rape, and as the theory evolved it attempted to reconcile feminist, socio-cultural, and evolutionary perspectives (Gannon et al., 2008). Malamuth (1986) suggested that mate selection pressures resulted in specific and contrasting selection strategies. He suggested that for men, little investment or certainty of paternity existed, however, women must ensure that the male is not only genetically sound but also willing to share the burden of child rearing. Malamuth (1986) further hypothesized that a male's sexual aggression comes from their sexual efforts being thwarted, and this will in turn result in coercion and general domination over females to increase reproductive success.

Four basic principles form the basis of Malamuth's model:

- Sexual aggression is the product of a confluence of risk factors.
- These factors will predict aggression toward women, not men.

- These factors will explain other dominating and aggressive behaviors toward women.
- An individual's likelihood of engaging in sexually aggressive behavior is to some extent shaped by environmental and socio-cultural factors.

Although the model explores relative topics to sexual aggression, it is highly complex and there is a lack of explanatory depth and internal consistency. Due to this, it is unlikely the model can be made coherent enough to aid the formation of treatments for incarcerated rapists.

Integrated Theory

Four factors make up Marshall and Barbaree's (1990) integrated theory:

- Biological
- Developmental
- Socio-cultural
- Situational

Strengths of the model include that it has been progressively improved and empirically relates all four elements to sexual offending. Integrated theory initially hypothesized that male hormonal activity causes influxes in aggressive impulses, which are naturally associated with sexual activity and that this is related to the first factor, biological. As with other theories it was suggested that adverse childhood experiences play a significant role—more specifically, decreasing a male adolescent's ability to control the impulses controlling sexual aggression. The integrated theory has strengths in the area of empirical adequacy and research, however, a gap in the theory is its inability to explain offender heterogeneity.

Integrated Theory of Sexual Offending

The integrated theory of sexual offending (ITSO) is the most recent and unites theories mentioned earlier into one explanatory model of sexual aggression. Ward and Beech (2005) base the theory on the notion that sexual aggression stems from three causal factors:

- Biological factors
- Proximal factors
- Distal ecological niche factors

and three neuropsychological systems associated with assorted brain structures:

- Motivation-motion: cortical, limbic, and brain-stem structures
- Action-control: frontal cortex, thalamus, and basal ganglia
- Memory-perception: posterior neo-cortex and hippocampal formation

The model follows the notion that the motivation-motion system plays a role in allowing our values to influence our choices and behaviors; the action-control system enables an offender to plan, execute, and appraise planned actions; and the memory-perception system processes received stimuli and constructs representations of the stimuli. A clear strength of the ITSO is its creation of a union between various theoretical models of sexual aggression. Because of this, potential benefits exist for assessment and treatment methods. In contrast, there are some apparent gaps in the explanations of the core mechanisms producing sexual aggression.

Micro Theories

Micro theories are descriptive theories derived from an analysis of the offense data and the offenders' accounts of their behavior. These theories specify how offending occurs in terms of cognitive, behavioral, volitional, and contextual factors (Ward & Hudson, 1998). Micro theories, as the name implies, examine the issue at the level of the offender, looking for individual causes and explanations for crime and delinquency.

The Investigation

The Crime Scene

In any investigation of serial offenses the crime scene is of prime importance, and often in a rape case is the common ground between offenses. Rossmo (1997) suggests that the focus of any police investigation is the evidentiary content of a crime scene. It has also been said that the final outcome of an investigation rests on thorough investigative work conducted at the crime scene. According to Keppel and Walter (1999), several outcomes are possible from a crime scene assessment:

- Determining the physical, behavioral, and demographic characteristics of the unknown offender.
- Developing post-offense behavior of the offender and strategies for apprehension.
- Developing interviewing once the offender is apprehended.
- Determining the signature of the offender.
- Determining where evidence may be located.

To achieve any of these outcomes, the information for analysis differs. Typically, this information comes from police investigative files, which include reports, statements, crime scene diagrams, photographs, and videotapes of crime scenes.

Scientific Testing

Evidence ascertained from crime scenes falls into two main types of biological scientific testing. These categories include conventional systems and DNA profiling.

Conventional Systems

A forensic biologist analyzes exhibits from individuals related to an offense, and he or she can also examine and collect various biological substances from crime scenes for testing and analysis. Such exhibits may include articles of bedding, clothing, and motor vehicles or external areas that have been identified as the possible crime scene. Most testing at scenes is of a presumptive nature and requires confirmation in the more controlled environment of the laboratory, while others such as blood stains may be interpretative and provide assistance to field investigators.

Techniques that provide biochemical and immunological evidence are crucial to linking an offender to an offense. This evidence includes blood, semen, hair, saliva, and vaginal secretions to name a few. Other substances including urine and feces are often seen more as corroborative evidence. Conventional systems are imperative to discriminating between potential rape suspects, giving investigators the ability to exculpate individuals from further scrutiny. In one serial rape case in Victoria, at least 20 suspects were eliminated from the inquiry by using conventional methods (Schlesinger, 2000). In general, the conventional methods are cost-effective and the results are obtained rapidly, thus proving to be a substantial investigative tool.

DNA Profiling

DNA profiling has seen a continuous state of flux since its introduction and has been utilized because of the inability of conventional methods to distinguish adequately between individuals. A traditional method associated with DNA profiling is Restriction Fragment Length Polymorphism (RFLP). Small fragments of DNA are analyzed by applying electric current; the fragments separate, leaving behind a pattern similar to a barcode when visualized through X-ray film. This technique is time consuming and requires a large sample, and in response to this, new technology has been developed that allows smaller samples to be profiled at a lower cost and in a shorter time. A new DNA profiling technique using Polymerase Chain Reaction (PCR) is an integral part of the procedure. DNA is prepared from samples and amplified to provide a workable number of copies of the original. Although the PCR method is more easily interpreted, contamination in samples such as vaginal secretions from rape cases can occur, meaning that evidence collected for analysis must be highly accurate (Sheslinger, 2000).

Despite the benefits of forensic investigations, Strom and Hickman (2010) have explained several problems with the reliance on forensic evidence. Substantial backlogs exist with forensic evidence as more evidence is collected and submitted than is possible to analyze, evidence is not being processed due to a lack of a suspect, and in some instances not all evidence is submitted for analysis, with approximately 18% of all rape cases having unanalyzed forensic evidence.

Investigative Techniques

Several issues need to be considered by investigators when conducting an investigation into serial offenses. In most rape cases the identity of the perpetrator is unknown and investigators are faced with the task of identifying the offender before solving the case. When investigating serial rapes, the investigators must rely on a number of techniques, including case linkage and criminal profiling.

Case Linkage and Linkage Blindness

Case linkage is practiced by police around the world and involves linking crimes together to form of series on the basis of behavioral similarity and distinctiveness (Woodhams & Labuschange, 2011). Case linkage assists in a number of ways including efficient deployment of resources and increases in evidence from related crimes. Two assumptions are required to link crimes together on the basis of behavior: offender consistency and offender distinctiveness.

That is, that the offender must display a degree of consistency when committing offenses, and their offenses must be distinct enough to differentiate between two perpetrators (Bennell & Canter, 2002). Case linkage on many occasions has proved successful. Yokota et al. (2007) were able to assign sex offenses to an offender on the basis of similar modus operandi or method of operation. Canter et al. (1991) investigated how accurately crime pairs could be classified linked or unlinked; of the 66 crime pairs, 85% were classified correctly.

Despite these successes, Rossmo (1997) proposes that a problem with case linkage is when linkage blindness occurs, or the inability of the investigators to notice connections between crimes and offenders. Linkage blindness can occur when a crime series is not being recognized and when there is a lack of forensic evidence.

Criminal Profiling

Criminal profiling is an investigative tool designed to assist investigative efforts and describes the process of inferring distinctive personality characteristics of offenders (Turvey, 2008). It involves the analysis of offender behavior and their interactions with the victim and the crime scene (Petherick, 2003). It is not the goal of the profiler to specify an individual who committed a crime, however it is their responsibility to provide suggestions that are investigatively relevant to help law enforcement develop a variable suspect pool in unsolved crimes (Turvey, 2008). This is done by providing new areas of inquiry or narrowing the suspect list.

Petherick and Turvey (2008) have identified two main phases of profiling. One is the investigative phase, which entails seven primary goals and involves discriminating features of the unknown offender for the known crime.

1. Evaluate the nature and value of forensic and behavioral evidence to a particular crime or series of related crimes.
2. Reduce the variable suspect pool in the criminal investigation.
3. Prioritize the investigation into remaining suspects.
4. Link potentially related crimes by identifying crime scene indicators and behavior patterns.
5. Assess the potential for escalation of nuisance criminal behavior to more serious or violent crimes.
6. Provide investigators with investigatively relevant leads and strategies.
7. Help keep the overall investigation on track and undistracted by offering fresh insights.

The second phase is the trial phase, which has five primary goals, and involves providing information about a crime or series of crimes for which there is a suspected offender.

1. Evaluate the nature and value of forensic and behavioral evidence to a particular crime or series of related crimes.
2. Develop interview or interrogation strategies.
3. Help develop insight into offender fantasy and motivations.
4. Develop insight into offender motive and intent before, during, and after the commission of a crime.
5. Link potentially related crimes by identifying crime scene indicators and behavior patterns.

There are no limits to the application of profiling, although it is noted that profiling is suited to crimes involving psychopathology, psychological dysfunction, or crimes of a sexual nature such as rape, due to the greater degree of interaction between the victim and the offender (McCann, 1992).

Forensic Awareness

Crimes are committed these days in more innovative ways as offenders are more aware of forensic techniques, causing them to destroy or clean up evidence (Stevens, 2008). As a result, the criminal justice system is attempting to find more effective ways of apprehending the offenders. A strategy for investigating violent crimes, such as rape, involves the analysis of forensic evidence. This process has developed significantly in more recent decades, due partly to technological progress (Beaver, 2010). It has been suggested that this newly developed forensic awareness stems in part from TV shows like *Law and Order* and *CSI*, and that a serious aspect of the availability of these shows is the knowledge they provide to potential criminals (Beauregard & Bouchard, 2010).

When committing a rape, there are many chances for evidence to be left behind, from skin cells under the victim's nails to semen when the rapist ejaculates. Despite this, there appears to be an increasing trend of a lack of forensic evidence at crime scenes. More specifically, it has been noted that offenders are increasingly wearing gloves to avoid leaving fingerprints, using tape to seal envelopes to avoid leaving DNA, and even using bleach, which destroys DNA, to clean up blood (Stevens, 2008). Davies and Dale (1995) also noted that offenders traveling longer distances to commit a crime may be an indicator of forensic awareness, in addition to moving a victim's body to delay detection.

In a study by Beauregard and Bouchard (2010), aspects of forensic awareness were explored in relation to 72 offenders, averaging five rape offenses each. The study revealed that in more than 50% of the offenses forensic awareness was observed, particularly in relation to identification protection. Table 15.4 demonstrates these findings.

Table 15.4 Descriptives for a Sample of Rape Events (n = 222)

Variables	% (n)
Conceal his identity	44.1 (98)
Wear gloves	15.3 (34)
Wipe semen	6.8 (15)
Prevent his face from being seen	32.9 (73)
Lie about his name	1.4 (3)
Wear a condom	1.8 (4)
Do not ejaculate in or on the victim	0.5 (1)
Make victim comb/shave her pubic hair after assault	0.5 (1)
Make victim shower after assault	0.5 (1)
Forensic Awareness (Total)	55.9 (124)

Conclusion

Serial rapists constitute only a small proportion of the overall total of rape offenders, however, because their crimes are considered particularly heinous they invoke a great deal of fear and disgust. The exact incidence of serial rape will remain unknown as the crime continues to go underreported for a variety of reasons. Serial rapists present a difficult and unusual challenge to law enforcement officers, because the crime is considered rare and is difficult to investigate effectively, and because offenders develop a greater sense of forensic awareness.

Understanding the behavioral characteristics and typologies of a rapist are key to unraveling the mind of an offender, and continued application of case linkage and criminal profiling and the development of DNA investigation will only aid investigators to a greater degree in the future.

Questions

1. Explain the differences between sexual assault and rape.
2. Name the three offender typologies coined by Groth in 1979.
3. Most sexual assaults and rape attacks occur in a familiar environment. *True or false?*
4. Name two of the six main reasons stated by Acierno, Resnick, and Kilpatrick (1997) for nondisclosure.
5. Four factors make up Marshall and Barbaree's 1990 integrated theory of rape: biological, developmental, socio-cultural, and___________.
6. An investigative tool designed to assist investigative efforts, which describes the process of inferring distinctive personality characteristics of offenders, is known as ____________ ____________.

References

Acierno, R., Resnick, H. S., & Kilpatrick, D. G. (1997). Prevalence rates: Case identification and risk factors for sexual assault, physical assault, and domestic violence in men and women. *Behavioral Medicine, 23*(2), 53–64.

Aigner, M., Eher, R., Fruehwald, D., Frottier, P., Guttierez-Lobos, K., & Dwyer, S. M. (2000). Brain abnormalities and violent behavior. *Journal of Psychology and Human Sexuality, 11,* 57–64.

American Psychiatric Association. (2000). *Diagnostic and statistical manual of mental disorders (text revision).* Washington: APA.

Anderson, M. J. (2005). All American rape, 79, pp. 625–644.

Australian Bureau of Statistics. (2011). Victims of crime. <www.abs.gov.au> Accessed 14.06.2012.

Australian Bureau of Statistics. (1996). *Women's safety Australia.* Canberra: Australian Bureau of Statistics. (cat. no. 4128.0).

Australian Bureau of Statistics. (2005). Annual Report 2005-2006. <www.abs.gov.au> Accessed 12.06.2012.

Beauregard, E., & Mouchard, M. (2010). Cleaning up your act: Forensic awareness as a detection avoidance strategy. *The Journal of Criminal Justice, 38,* 1160–1166.

Beaver, K. M. (2010). The promises and pitfalls of forensic evidence in unsolved crimes. *Criminology and Public Policy, 9,* 405–410.

Bennell, C., & Canter, D. (2002). Linking commercial burglaries by modus operandi: Tests using regression and ROC analysis. *Science and Justice, 42,* 1-12.

Brownmiller, S. (1975). *Against our will: Men, women and rape.* New York: Simon & Schuster.

Bureau of Justice Statistics, (1995, 1996, 1998). *National crime victimization survey.* Washington, DC: Department of Justice.

Burgess, A. W., & Holmstrom, L. L. (1986). *Rape: Crisis and recovery.* Newton, MA: Awab, Inc.

Burgess, A. W., & Marchetti, C. H. (2009). Contemporary issues. In R. R. Hazelwood & A. W. Burgess (Eds.), *Practical aspects of rape investigation: A multidisciplinary approach* (4th ed.). Boca Raton, FL: CRC Press.

Canter, D., Heritage, R., Wilson, M., Davies, A., Kirby, S., Holden, R., et al. (1991). *A facet approach to offender profiling* (Vol 1). England: University of Surrey.

Davies, A., & Dale, A. (1995). *Locating the stranger rapist (Special Interest Series: Paper 3).* London: Police Research Group, Home Office Police Department.

Easteal, P. W. (1993). Rape prevention: Combating the myths: *Proceedings of without consent: Confronting adult sexual violence.* Australian Institute of Criminology. October 27–29, 1992.

Freud, S. (1905/1953). Three essays on the theory of sexuality. In J. (1905/1953). Strachey (Ed.), *The standard edition of the complete psychological works of Sigmund Freud* (Vol 7). London: Hogarth Press.

Gannon, T. R., Collie, R. M., Ward, T., & Thakker, J. (2008). Rape: Psychopathology, theory and treatment. *Clinical Psychology Review, 28,* 982–1008.

Gray, R. (1997). In the belly of the monster: Feminism, development systems and evolutionary explanations. In P. Gowaty (Ed.), *Feminism and evolutionary biology.* New York: Chapman & Hall.

Groth, A. N. (1979). *Men who rape: The psychology of the offender.* New York: Plenum Press.

Groth, A. N., Burgess, A. W., & Holstrom, L. L. (1977). Rape: Power, anger and sexuality. *American Journal of Psychiatry, 134*(11), 1239–1243.

Hare, R. D. (1999). Psychopathy as a risk factor for violence. *Psychiatric Quarterly, 70,* 181–197.

Hazelwood, R. R. (2009). Analysing the rape and profiling the offender. In R. R. Hazelwood & J. Warren (Eds.), *The serial rapist: His characteristics and victims* (pp. 18–25). FBI Law Enforcement Bulletin.

Hazelwood, R. R. & Burgess, A. W. (2009). *Practical aspects of rape investigation: A multidisciplinary approach* (4th ed.). Boca Raton, FL: CRC Press.

Hazelwood, R. R., & Warren, J. (1989). *The serial rapist: His characteristics and victims.* FBI Law Enforcement Bulletin. 18–25.

Hollon, S. D., & Kriss, M. R. (1984). Cognitive factors in clinical research and practice. *Clinical Psychology Review, 4,* 35–76.

Keppel, R. D., & Walter, R. A. (1999). Profiling killers: A revised classification model for understanding sexual murder. *Journal of Offender Therapy and Comparative Criminology, 43*(4), 417–437.

Kilpatrick, D. G., Edmunds, C. N., & Seymour, A. K. (1992). *Rape in America: A report to the nation.* Arlington, VA: National Victim Center and Medical University of South Carolina.

Koss, M. P. (1993). Detecting the scope of rape: A review of prevalence research methods. *Journal of Interpersonal Violence, 8,* 198–222.

LeBeau, J. (1987). Patterns of stranger and serial rape offending: Factors distinguishing apprehended and at large offenders. *Journal of Criminal Law and Criminology, 78*(2), 309–329.

Malamuth, N. M. (1986). Predictors of naturalistic sexual aggression. *Journal of Personality and Social Psychology, 50,* 953–962.

Marshall, W. L. (2007). Diagnostic issues, multiple paraphilias, and comorbid disorders in sexual offenders: Their incidence and treatment. *Aggression and Violent Behavior, 12,* 16–35.

Marshall, W. L., & Barbaree, H. E. (1990). An integrated theory of sexual offending. In W. L. Marshall, D. R. Laws, & H. E. Barbaree (Eds.), *Handbook of sexual assault: Issues theories and treatment of the offender.* New York: Plenum Press.

McCann, J. (1992). Criminal personality profiling in the investigation of violent crime: Recent advances and future directions. *Behavioral Science and the Law, 10*(14), 475–481.

Moore, G. (1903). *Principia ethica.* Cambridge: Cambridge University Press.

Moran, A. (1993). Patterns of rape: A preliminary Queensland perspective: *Proceedings of without consent: Confronting adult sexual violence.* Australian Institute of Criminology. October 27–29, 1992.

Office of the Cabinet: QLD. (1992). Women's experience of crimes of personal violence: A gender analysis of the 1991 Qld crime victims survey. QLD: The Unit.

Palmer, C. (1991). Human rape: Adaptation or by-product? *Journal of Sex Research, 28,* 365–386.

Palmer, C. T., & Thornhill, R. (2000). Serial rape: An evolutionary perspective. In L. B. Schlesinger (Ed.), *Serial offenders: Current thought, recent findings.* Boca Raton, FL: CRC Press.

Petherick, W. A. (2003). What's in a name? Comparing applied profiling methodologies. *Journal of Law and Social Challenges,* 173–188. June.

Petherick, W. A., & Turvey, B. E. (2008). Behavioural evidence analysis: Ideo-Deductive method of criminal profiling. In B. E. Turvey (Ed.), *Criminal profiling: An introduction to behavioural evidence analysis* (3rd ed.). San Diego: Academic Press.

Pineau, L. (1989). Date rape: A feminist analysis. *Law and Philosophy, 8*(2), 217–243.

Polaschek, D. L. L., & Gannon, T. A. (2004). The implicit theories of rapists: What convicted offenders tell us. *Sexual Abuse: A Journal of Research and Treatment, 16,* 299–315.

Rape, Abuse and Incest National Network. (2009). Statistics. <www.rainn.org.statistcs> Accessed 20.06.2012.

Rossmo, D. (1997). Geographic profiling. In J. Jackson & D Bekerian (Eds.), *Offender profiling: Theory, research and practice.* Chichester, UK: Wiley.

Russo, L. (2000). Date rape: A hidden crime: *Trends and issues in crime and criminal justice.* Australian Institute of Criminology. 157.

Schlesinger, L. B. (2000). *Serial offenders: Current thought, recent findings.* Boca Raton, FL: CRC Press.

Stevens, D. J. (2008). Forensic science, wrongful convictions, and American prosecutor discretion. *The Howard Journal, 47,* 31–51.

Strom, K. J., & Hickman, M. J. (2010). Unanalyzed evidence in law-enforcement agencies: A national examination of forensic processing in police departments. *Criminology and Public Policy, 9,* 381–404.

Turvey, B. E. (1996). Behaviour evidence: Understanding motives and developing suspects in unsolved serial rapes through behavioural profiling techniques. <www.corpus-delicti.com/rape> Accessed 20.06.2012.

Turvey, B. E. (2008). *Criminal profiling: An introduction to behavioural evidence analysis* (3rd ed.). Boston: Academic Press.

Ward, T., & Beech, T. (2005). An integrated theory of sexual offending. *Aggression and Violent Behaviour, 11,* 44–63.

Ward, T., & Hudson, S. M. (1998). A model in the relapse process of sexual offenders. *Journal of Interpersonal Violence, 13,* 700–725.

Ward, T., Polaschek, D. L. L., & Beech, A. R. (2006). *Theories of sexual offending.* Chichester, UK: Wiley.

Wilson, M., Daly, M., & Scheib, J. (1997). Femicide: An evolutionary psychological perspective. In P. Gowaty (Ed.), *Feminism and evolutionary biology.* New York: Chapman & Hall.

Woodhams, J., & Labuschagne, G. (2011). A test of case linkage principles with solved and unsolved serial rapes. *Journal of Police and Criminal Psychology, 27*(1), 85–98.

Yokota, K., Fujita, G., Watanebe, K, Yoshimoto, K., & Wachi, T. (2007). Application of the behavioural investigative support system for profiling perpetrators of serial sexual assaults. *Journal of Behavioural Science and Law, 25,* 841–856.

16

Understanding Serial Sexual Murder

A Biopsychosocial Approach

Robert J. Homant and Daniel B. Kennedy

Introduction

Serial killers are not exclusively a product of the twentieth century. In fact, history suggests that they have always been with us. From the fifteenth-century castle of horrors of Gilles de Rais and the nineteenth-century London streets of Jack the Ripper to the depredations of Green River Killer Gary Ridgway in the United States, profoundly flawed individuals have visited awful fates on innocent human beings (Newton, 2000; Schechter, 2003). Of the many types of serial killers, nothing challenges our view of human nature so much as the behavior of the serial sexual sadistic killer. This individual kills not out of necessity or for convenience but for the very satisfaction of killing. Furthermore, he or she gains satisfaction from the pain and terror of the victim, a satisfaction that arouses, enhances, or even consummates the killer's sexual pleasure. One test of our knowledge of human behavior—indeed of ourselves—is our ability to put ourselves in the place of others and, by empathizing with their feelings, to understand their thoughts and behavior. Serial sexual sadistic killers, then, raise a special challenge to understand what went wrong. Is it possible that "there but for the grace of God go I"? Could anyone develop into a serial sexual killer—given enough time and the "right" circumstances?

We agree with the point raised by Levin and Fox (2008) that most serial killers actually appear to be quite normal. That is, many of their traits fall well within the normal range of behaviors: the ability to dehumanize others, to compartmentalize behavior, to act friendly and charming, to adopt normal social roles, and to take satisfaction in having power over others. Nevertheless, there are some critical differences that place serial sexual killers beyond the pale. Although they may well be able to empathize with their victims, this empathy is devoid of any inhibiting sympathy that would interfere with their enjoyment of a victim's utter humiliation and terror. Furthermore, this lack of sympathy is not a mere blocking of all feeling because it is accompanied by positive sexual arousal that seems to be directly fueled by the victim's pain.

In this chapter, we explore the phenomenon of *serial killing* in general before focusing specifically on the serial sexual sadistic killer. We review the main theories that have been offered to explain such behavior and the evidence that has been put forth to support these theories. Finally, we suggest some new directions for theory and research in the area of serial sexual killing.

Defining Serial Killing

There is fairly good consensus that serial killing is one of three main types of multiple homicide, which may be simply defined as the killing of three or more people, by either an individual or a group acting in concert. Multiple homicides are generally classified as mass, spree, or serial. With mass murder there are three or more homicides occurring at the same time. In spree killing, the homicides are spread out as to time and/or location but form a more or less continuous series of actions: There is no appreciable "cooling-off period." With serial killing, the same person (or persons) commits three or more murders with a cooling-off period intervening.

Our definition of a serial killer raises two minor issues that should be dealt with here. The first concerns the cooling-off period. Holmes and Holmes (1998) suggest 30 days as the minimum period for distinguishing spree from serial killing. There is sometimes a gray area here, such as, for example, when a serial killer such as Ted Bundy starts to decompensate and kills with increasing frequency, perhaps with only a few hours separating events. Researchers, however, are free to designate some arbitrary period, such as 24 hours, to separate spree from serial killing. The main point is that the first killing has temporarily satisfied whatever motives are driving the killer, and the subsequent killings are part of a separate sequence of behaviors. The second issue concerns the number of killings required for someone to be considered a serial killer. It should be noted that multiple and serial killing are not legal terms; thus, Egger (1984) requires only two killings, whereas other authors have required as many as four (Hickey, 2002; Hodge, 2000) or even five (Dietz, 1986; Myers, 2004). Three killings seem to be required in the most popular operational definition of serial killing since they are enough to provide a pattern within the killings without being overly restrictive. This is not to say that someone who has "only" killed twice does not "qualify" as a serial killer. Indeed, someone who has only killed once may well be a serial killer, psychologically speaking, who simply has not yet acted on his impulses or has lacked the opportunity (perhaps being arrested after the first homicide). Insisting on three separate homicides simply lends more assurance that a given person is a suitable example of a serial killer, and we follow that approach in this chapter.[1]

Types of Serial Killers

Various researchers have proposed typologies of the serial killer. In general, these typologies try to identify the dominant motive of the killer. For example, those who kill three or more times for purely practical or instrumental reasons, such as witness execution, might be expected to have certain traits in common that would distinguish them from those serial killers who kill for revenge or out of anger and, in turn, from those who kill "for the fun of it."

As early as 1886, von Krafft-Ebing (1886/1965) distinguished three types of homicide that occurred in connection with rape and could include serialists: accidental (the unintended consequences of use of force), witness elimination, and lust murder (or sexual sadism). A century later, another typology was proposed by Dietz (1986), based primarily on his clinical experiences and requiring five separate killing incidents to be considered a serial killer. Dietz's types are:

- Psychopathic sexual sadists. (enjoy killing; not psychotic)
- Crime spree killers. (using "spree" more in the sense of a criminal career as exemplified by Bonnie and Clyde)
- Functionaries of organized criminal operations. (contract killers)
- Custodial poisoners and asphyxiators. (e.g., caretakers of the disabled)
- Supposed psychotics. (who may be mentally ill/hallucinating or just malingering)

Holmes and DeBerger (1988) proposed four basic types of serial killer:

- Visionary. ("God wants me to eliminate some evil")
- Mission oriented. ("I want to rid the world of prostitutes," etc.)
- Hedonistic. (for pleasure in the killing itself)
- Power control. (for a sense of dominance)

In a revision of this typology, Holmes and Holmes (1998) describe six categories of serial killer. Three of these—vision, mission, and comfort—seek to accomplish nonsexual goals. The main difference between the visionary and the mission killer appears to be that the visionary is psychotic (e.g., voices tell him to rid the world of prostitutes), whereas the mission killer acts on an ego-syntonic belief ("I want to make the world a better place by ridding the world of prostitutes"). The comfort killer, on the other hand, is more rational, killing because of reasonably anticipated gains, the payoff to a contract killer being an extreme example. The remaining three types all combine sexual and aggressive motives.

[1]The debate concerning numerosity continues. Myers (2004) cites a variety of authors who propose definitions of serial murder that would include two, three, four, or even five victims. See other discussions on the issue throughout this book.

Lust and thrill killers seem to differ mainly in how fantasy is used and whether or not they need a live victim. The power/control type, although described as nonsexually motivated by Holmes and Holmes (1998), still uses sex as one of the means of obtaining dominance. Because lust, thrill, and power/control all involve rape and other forms of sexual assault combined with torture, mutilation, and such, they all appear to be subtypes of sexual sadistic killing. We later return to the issue of distinguishing sadistic from nonsadistic serial sexual killing.

Some observers, however, believe that the Holmes and DeBerger typology suffers from conceptual overlap in certain areas and have suggested minor revisions.[2] Using the Holmes and DeBerger typology as a basis, Levin and Fox (2008) suggested three main types, each with two subtypes:

- Thrill, subdivided into sexual sadism and dominance. (depending on how directly sexual arousal is linked to victim pain)
- Mission, subdivided into reformist and visionary. (depending on whether auditory hallucinations are present)
- Expedience, subdivided into profit and protection. Both profit and protection reflect basic criminal activity: In profit, the criminal gains directly from the murder, as in a professional hit man or someone taking over assets or an inheritance. Protection refers more to a criminal killing someone in order to eliminate a potential witness.

In a separate publication, Fox and Levin (1998) offer yet another typology based even more closely on the motivation of the offender. Five motives are specifically mentioned: power (including sadism), revenge, loyalty, profit, and terror. These motives may also underlie mass murder and presumably spree killing as well. In short, it seems that serial homicide may occur for any of the diverse motives that have fueled murder throughout human history.

Furthermore, there is certainly nothing in theory that would preclude a person from killing one time out of revenge, following this up with killing a witness to a crime, and then evolving into a hit man. Fox and Levin (1999) maintain, however, that the sexual sadist is the most common of all types of serial killer. Whether or not this is the case, it is the serial sexual sadist that has certainly generated the most attention.

Besides distinguishing among serial killers based on their motivation, several other distinctions have been noted, including travel patterns, victim acquisition techniques, and attack strategies. For example, some serial killers are "place specific" and kill in their homes or other special places (e.g., Brudos, Gacy, and Dahmer), others kill in a general area or region (e.g., Bianchi and Buono, and Williams), whereas still others travel widely to murder (e.g., Bundy and Lucas). Serial killers may also stay in their immediate neighborhoods as marauders or travel some distance as commuters to forage for victims (Canter & Larkin, 1993; Godwin & Canter, 1997; Hickey, 2002; Holmes & Holmes, 2002).

Rossmo (1997) uses hunting analogies to explain victim acquisition: hunter (searches from home), poacher (searches from another location), troller (any opportunity), and trapper

[2] In an empirical study of serial killers' crime scenes, Canter and Wentink (2004) found some support for Holmes and Holmes' (1988) broad categories but were unable to distinguish "power or control" from lust and thrill killings.

(careful plan). He further identifies three attack methods as raptor, stalker, and ambusher. Beauregard, Proulx, Rossmo, LeClerc, and Allaire (2007) further refine this into three scripts, which are in turn subdivided into five tracks. Hazelwood and Burgess (1999) described three attack modes as blitz, con, and surprise. The blitz is a sudden attack similar to Rossmo's raptor method. The con is a trick or involves a lure and corresponds roughly to Rossmo's ambusher. Finally, surprise involves sneaking or stealth, such as when a victim wakes up to find a rape murderer in her bedroom.

Organized vs. Disorganized Serial Killers

Although all the foregoing distinctions may prove important for pursuing and understanding the serial killer, the distinction that has received the most attention is that of the organized versus the disorganized serial killer (Ressler, Burgess, Douglas, Hartman & D'Agostino, 1986).

Ressler et al. (1986) compiled extensive data on 36 sexual killers, 25 of whom qualified as serial killers. Based on the offender's background and personality, his behavior during the crime, victim characteristics, and the various crime scenes, each offender was classified on approximately 357 variables.[3] Using these variables, Ressler et al. described two types of offenders and their crime scenes. The *organized offender* is intelligent and socially competent. His criminal behavior is more likely to be precipitated by stress, and he is likely to show significant planning prior to the offense, as shown by traveling to the crime scene, bringing a weapon or other instruments, careful victim selection, and so on. In contrast, the *disorganized offender* is of relatively low intelligence and poor social adjustment. His crime seems to take himself as well as his victim by surprise. He frequently must kill the victim prior to his sexual release to maintain control over the victim. The crime is likely to be committed close to the offender's home, the weapon is something usually acquired on site, and the scene is in disarray. The body is left exposed at the scene or only poorly hidden. The crime is unlikely to have been planned or rehearsed through fantasy.

Originally intended to apply only to serial sexual killers, the distinction between organized and disorganized crime scenes and offenders has been enthusiastically embraced by many in law enforcement and has been extended to other forms of serial criminal behavior, such as arson (Kocsis, Irwin & Hayes, 1998), as well as to single, or nonlinked, crime scenes (Canter, Alison, Alison & Wentink, 2004).

The distinction between organized and disorganized crime scenes made good intuitive sense, and one study found adequate reliability among profilers in classifying crime scenes

[3] All of the serial sexual killers studied by Ressler et al. (1986) were males, as is the case with all of the studies cited here. The female serial killer, however, has not been neglected in case studies and typologies (Hickey, 2002; Holmes & Holmes, 1998; Keeney & Heide, 1994; Silvio, McCloskey & Ramos-Grenier, 2006). Serial killing is unusual for female serialists. When it does occur, it is typically a matter of killing husbands or lovers for money or revenge rather than in connection with sexual arousal. An exception might be the case of Carol Bundy, who allegedly used trophies from her murders in subsequent sexual rituals (Holmes & Holmes, 2002, p. 152). Kelleher and Kelleher (1998) classify Aileen Wuornos as a "sexual predator." An active prostitute, Wuornos used sex to lure seven men to their deaths, but it is debated as to whether she experienced sexual arousal in doing so (Myers, Gooch & Meloy, 2005). Cases of females who act as partners to male sexual sadists are more common (Cooper, 2000).

as organized, disorganized, or mixed (Ressler et al., 1985). One criticism of this early work, however, was that there was no independent test of whether the disorganized elements in the crime scene were correlated with any general (noncrime scene) behavioral characteristics of the offender (Homant & Kennedy, 1998). Ressler et al. (1986) had originally derived their concepts of what constituted organized and disorganized by examining offenders and crime scenes more or less simultaneously (i.e., the offenders and their characteristics were known to those classifying the crime scene characteristics). Thus, there was never any clear evidence that crime scenes tended to cluster as organized versus disorganized, or that the individual elements that make up the operational definition of organized were more likely to co-occur.

To subject the organized/disorganized distinction to a cross-validating test, Canter et al. (2004) analyzed data on 100 crime scenes involving sexual homicide that were linked to 100 different serial killers. Canter et al. found that features indicating an organized crime scene were highly common and found in all 100 crime scenes. As these authors point out, this makes sense in that the killers in their sample were at least able to perpetrate three sexual killings before being caught; thus, some planning and organization must have occurred.

More important, Canter et al. (2004) found that the presence of one disorganized element did not affect the probability of other disorganized elements occurring. Rather, certain elements of disorganization tended to occur together. Canter et al. therefore proposed that all crime scenes involving serial sexual homicide involve both organized and disorganized elements, with the disorganized elements clustering into one of four subtypes, which they labeled mutilation, sexual control, plunder, and execution. These four subtypes represent different ways that the perpetrator is motivated to exploit the victim. Perpetrators who do not need a live victim, for example, behave differently from those who do. Offenders driven to mutilate the victim are going to show the highest frequency of so-called disorganized factors. Although this means that the offender's personality does in some sense determine the nature of the crime scene, the data did not suggest clear patterns. Rather, Canter et al. concluded that contextual factors in the interaction between offender and victim, rather than individual traits, play an important role in determining the nature of the crime or crime scene. Such a model is much more in keeping with the general social psychological finding that traits are at best loose clusters of behavior that do not lead to highly consistent, predictable patterns (Alison, Bennell, Ormerod & Mokros, 2002; Homant & Kennedy, 1998).

In summary, although we do not believe that the research of Canter et al. (2004) requires the immediate abandonment of the organized/disorganized distinction, it does mean that much more attention needs to be paid to the checklist of elements thought to make up this dichotomy and to whether there are meaningful correlations between the occurrences of elements said to indicate one type or the other.[4] Only when the concepts are more clearly operationalized will it make sense to search for the more important correlation between crime scene type and an offender's noncriminal (lifestyle) behaviors and characteristics.

[4]Turvey (2002) was an early critic of the organized versus disorganized dichotomy. Most crime scenes are mixed, for example. Also, disorganized crime scenes can be staged or they can be drug or anger induced. Organized characteristics do not automatically suggest a psychopathic offender. For these and other reasons, Turvey suggests that investigators and profilers purge themselves of any oversimplified expectations before entering a crime scene.

Incidence of Serial Killing

Two issues arise concerning the frequency of serial killing. One issue is how common it is. If serial killing is fairly common, then this suggests that relatively normal personalities are quite capable of committing serial homicide. Conversely, to the extent that it is a rare phenomenon, one would look for highly unique factors that result in someone becoming a serial killer. A second issue concerns changes in the frequency of serial killing, over either time or place. Changes over time, especially relatively short periods of time such as a few decades, suggest the importance of social factors, at least for understanding the changing rates, whereas differences based on location suggest cultural or subcultural forces at work.

Studies of incidence rates for serial killing are complicated by whether one takes into account all forms of serial killing, such as a criminal having committed two or three instrumental homicides over a long career, or whether one is focused more narrowly on sex- or thrill-related homicides. Authors also vary in terms of the amount of evidence they require for considering a homicide the work of a serial killer, with some requiring specific evidence of linkage (if not evidence linking the homicides to a specific killer) and others seeming to attribute not just unknown perpetrator killings but also missing persons to the work of hidden serial killers. One of the more extreme estimates of serial killing in the United States in modern times was approximately 5000 people per year, which could amount to more than 20% of homicides during the 1980s.

Most authors, however, derive much more conservative figures. Hickey (2002) suggests the figure could be as low as 49 to 70 per year, whereas Fox and Levin (2005) suggest that approximately 120 to 180 Americans were slain annually during the serial murder peak years of the 1980s. Quinet (2007), after adjusting for the possible victimization of reported and unreported missing persons, and of the identified and misidentified dead, has revised upward the Fox and Levin estimate of serial murder victims each year. Her series of elaborate calculations suggests a minimum of 362 annual serial murder deaths and an upper limit of approximately 2012 such victims.

The foregoing frequency estimates generally attempted to identify the number of known and unknown serial sexual killers operating at a given time and then estimated the number of victims these killers were likely to have. Holmes and Holmes (2002) argued that there are approximately 100 serial murderers active in the United States, down from an earlier estimate of 200 (Ferguson, White, Cherry, Lorenz & Bhimani, 2003). McNamara and Morton (2004) examined every known killing in Virginia during a 10-year period. Multiple sources were examined to try to establish linkages among approximately 5183 homicides. Twenty-eight homicides—one-half of 1%—were found to be the work of six serial sexual killers.[5] If this rate should prove generalizable to the entire country, it would indicate approximately 75 victims per year of serial sexual homicide. Out of a population of approximately 300 million, this is certainly rare enough to suggest that it may take a quite unusual combination of variables to produce a serial sexual killer.

[5] Pallone (2000) and Meloy (2000) both cite evidence that fewer than 1% of murders reported each year in the United States are sexual homicides, let alone the result of serial sexual killers.

Regardless of how many serial sexual killers there are, is their number increasing relative to the population? Are some areas and times more likely to produce serial killers? Hard data are extremely difficult to come by, but certainly cases of serial killing can be found throughout the world and from various historical periods. Capp (1996, p. 21) finds evidence that "serial murders were just as common in 17th-century England as they are today," although his examples are not sexual homicides. von Krafft-Ebing (1886/1965) found numerous cases of lust murder in nineteenth-century Germany, and Peter Lorre came to fame as a movie actor in the (silent) German film *M*, portraying a serial murderer of children in 1920s Berlin. Newton (2000) lists numerous cases of a variety of types of serial killers throughout the world during the past two centuries.

Missen (2000) finds a general increase in serial killing over time (1860–1995) that is more or less consistent with industrialization/urbanization. Fox, Levin, and Quinet (2008) show that the number of known serial killers active in the United States from 1900 onward closely parallels the total homicide rate. In other words, serial killing increases at approximately the same rate as crime in general, especially violent crime. More significantly, however, when known cases of serial killing are examined, *sexual* serial killers are found to make up an increased percentage of U.S. serial killers. This suggests to Missen that some contributing factors can be found in current social trends (e.g., increased child abuse of all types).[6]

Serial Sexual Sadistic Killing

Although we do not mean to dismiss visionary, mission, and comfort serial killers, to use the Holmes and Holmes (1998) typology, it seems that mainstream theories of crime can easily account for comfort killers, and theories of psychopathology can account for visionary and mission killers.[7] At this point, then, we focus on understanding the serial sexual sadistic killer. First, a few definitional points are in order.

When we previously reviewed the hedonistic subtypes proposed by Holmes and Holmes (1998), we noted that the lust, thrill, and power/control types all combine sexual assault with physical and/or psychological torture of the victim. In this sense, at least, all three might be considered sadistic killers. In the Holmes and Holmes model, however, the link between torture of the victim and sexual arousal for the perpetrator is most clearly spelled out in the lust

[6]Whether there is truly an increase in the per capita rate of serial sexual killing is arguable. Better communications and forensics greatly affect law enforcement's ability to detect the work of a serial killer, especially one who is mobile. The point is more than academic: A stable rate supports the theory that causes are rooted in basic human nature—biology—whereas a variable rate implicates social psychological factors. Missen found the distribution of serial killing across states to be largely consistent with population and crime rates. However, Missen did point out some significant exceptions that he believed needed to be explained. DeFronzo, Ditta, Hannon, and Prochnow (2007) found that California had a rate of 18.6 male serial killers per 10 million residents, whereas Pennsylvania had a rate of 3.4. DeFronzo et al. identified various cultural factors that may account for differences in the rates of serial killing among the states. We return to this point later.

[7]It is important to distinguish the terms psychopathology and psychopathy. A psychopath may be said to possess psychopathy (extreme antisocial tendencies), whereas a mentally ill person has psychopathology (e.g., a severe mood disorder). See Lykken (1995) and Schlesinger (1980) for a discussion of the often confusing and inconsistent use of terms such as sociopath, psychopath, and antisocial personality disorder.

murderer. Although it may be important to draw distinctions based on the way that sadists torture their victims and whether sexual arousal precedes torture (perhaps in anticipation), accompanies torture, or follows afterward, we are satisfied that all three subcategories qualify for the term *sexual sadist.*

This raises the issue, however, of whether all serial sexual killing has a sadistic element. We believe that sexual killing should be understood in the context of rape and other assaultive sexual offenses, and thus typologies of rape become very relevant for understanding sexual killing. One of the most prominent rape typologies was originally proposed by Groth, Burgess, and Holmstrom (1977). In a widely cited application of this original typology, Hazelwood (1999) distinguished four main types of rape: power assertive, power reassurance, anger retaliatory, and anger excitation. Using this system, Keppel and Walter (1999) examined the frequency with which each category accounted for the 2476 sexual murderers they found in the Michigan prison system.

In anger excitation rape, a planned sexual assault and homicide are designed to inflict pain on the victim and thereby bring satisfaction to the perpetrator. Whether or not the actual death of the victim is intended, the infliction of pain is integral to the offender's ego and sexual satisfaction. By their analysis, only 7% of the cases fit this category. The major difference in anger retaliatory rape–homicide is that there is a more specific anger-arousing stimulus; the victim is seen as responsible, in reality or symbolically, for some more or less specific affront to the perpetrator. This, too, could be considered a sadistic rape in that the acting out of the anger leads directly to the perpetrator's sexual satisfaction. Keppel and Walter found anger retaliatory to account for 34% of the Michigan sexual murderers. With power reassurance rape–murder, the rapist killer is seen as acting out a conquest fantasy. The victim's lack of compliance is seen as both angering and panicking the offender. The resulting homicide is seen as overkill (unintended). However, Keppel and Walter continue: "Because the incomplete sexual assault does not validate his sexual competency, he will often explore … sex … postmortem.… Consequently, there is sometimes mutilation of the body.… The postmortem activities and ritualisms can satisfy and reinforce him" (p. 425). In other words, sexual failure leads to anger arousal, which leads to homicide and mutilation, which leads to postmortem arousal. Perhaps this is not sadism in a technical sense, but there is still a fusion of sex and aggression. Power reassurance accounted for 21% of the Michigan sexual murderers. Finally, the power assertive rapist rapes to reassure himself of his masculinity. He does not have the conscious intent to traumatize the victim, but when his power and control are challenged, he may become violent. "Although violence … may have been severe, there is generally no mutilation of the body; that would be perverse in his mind" (p. 421). This type, which seems to show the least evidence of sadism, was found to account for 38% of the Michigan sexual murderers.[8]

[8]Myers, Husted, Safarik, and O'Toole (2006) argue that the sexual sadist is not "angry" at his victim because anger is an unpleasant feeling and the sadist enjoys acting out his or her extreme aggression against the victim. They further explain that although aggression arousal may enhance sexual feeling, the biology of anger arousal is such that it diminishes or even eliminates sexual arousal. We agree that the uninhibited acting out of hostile aggressive impulses is affectively different than normal anger, which has an aspect of inhibited aggression to it and in that sense is usually negative affect (Homant, 1980).

In summary, if one holds to a strict construction of the concept of sexual sadism—deliberate pain to the victim as a necessary and anticipated part of the offender's sexual arousal—then serial sexual sadistic rape-murder becomes an even more rare phenomenon. However, if the term may be used for all of those cases in which harm to the victim appears to contribute to the offender's satisfaction, then most sexual murders seem to involve sexual sadism. Could one have a serial sexual murderer who is not sadistic? Perhaps, but if rape-murder is repeated three times, we suspect that the homicide is part of the attraction and not simply some instrumental elimination of a witness.

A related consideration is whether all sadists are sexual sadists. One of the authors had an inmate client with a history of spanking young children. Although the client readily admitted to sadistic tendencies—that is, taking pleasure in spanking the children—he denied any sexual implications. After significant probing, however, he admitted to masturbating soon after a few of the spanking episodes. The point is that much behavior that may seem "merely sadistic" probably has an underlying sexual element, although we concede the possibility of a nonsexual sadism.[9]

An Illustrative Case

Numerous authors have presented detailed case histories of some of the more infamous serial sexual killers, such as Ed Gein (loosely the model for *Psycho*'s Norman Bates as well as Hannibal Lecter), Ted Bundy, John Wayne Gacy, and Kenneth Bianchi. Newton (2000) and Schechter (2003) present case summaries outlining the basic facts known about hundreds of serial killers, most of them sexual killers. Rather than repeat details of cases that can be found elsewhere, we introduce here a case that has not been covered in the academic literature, although it is described to some extent on Internet web sites devoted to serial killers. Our information comes from police reports, mental health reports, and court depositions that were generated in connection with an ensuing lawsuit. We call our subject "Robert." Names and places have been altered to avoid possible distress to victims' families. As in all such case histories, our confidence in the accuracy of various facts varies greatly from one to the other, but we are confident that the following reconstruction is essentially accurate.

Robert committed a series of five sexual assaults during a 14-month period. Three of the victims were killed and two were raped but escaped death. Robert committed his first sexual assault/murder when he was 17 years old, which is young for a serial sexual killer.[10] Robert was

[9]We do not wish to raise a semantic argument here. By definition, sadism can mean either "the association of sexual satisfaction with the infliction of pain on others" or, more simply, "delight in cruelty" (Morris, 1969). Obviously, if the first meaning is adopted, the term sexual sadist is a redundancy. In its sexual meaning, sadism is a paraphilia (Abel & Osborn, 1992)—a linking of the sex drive to an object or activity not normally considered sexual. In labeling various sexual deviations, sadistic killing has sometimes been referred to as erotophonophilia (Money, 1990). The *Diagnostic and Statistical Manual of Mental Disorders* (*DSM-IV-TR*; American Psychiatric Association, 2000) only refers to sexual sadism, which it describes as sexual excitement linked to a victim's pain or humiliation, or simply to dominance over the victim (consenting or nonconsenting).

[10]Myers (2004) details six case histories of serial sexual murderers who committed at least two of their homicides before they were 18 years old; the cases are of interest precisely because they are rare.

born and raised in a midsized city of a mid-Atlantic state. He was biracial, normally taken for white. His black–Hispanic father and white mother quarreled frequently, with his father occasionally assaulting his mother and possibly Robert as well. The father had a history of alcohol abuse and had served a 7-year prison term for manslaughter a few years before the start of his relationship with Robert's mother. Robert described his mother as the disciplinarian of the family, who would occasionally give him a whipping with a belt. His parents divorced when he was 3 years old, after which he was raised by his mother. He saw his father only occasionally and came to idealize him. Robert had an older brother who also served prison time. This brother converted to Islam while in prison, as Robert also did after his own eventual incarceration.

Robert's school record indicates that he was in trouble at the age of 6 years. Impulsiveness, mood swings, and fighting are specifically noted. A juvenile arrest record begins at age 9 years. During an 8-year period, Robert is arrested 13 times and adjudicated delinquent on six occasions. Three times he is placed in a juvenile home, where fighting with teachers is noted. Most of the arrests were for property crimes, and as a teenager he has a reputation as a burglar. Robert says that he started drinking at age 9 years, and during one juvenile home intake he says that he had been high almost every night during the previous 2 years. His intelligence was variously noted as average and above average. All in all, Robert's childhood would qualify him as a "life-course persistent" delinquent, which is thought to have genetic predispositions (Moffitt, 1993).

When Robert is 17 years old, he has still another burglary charge lodged against him and is awaiting a juvenile court hearing. Probably, he is angry at the prospect of being institutionalized again; perhaps he feels that he might as well do something noteworthy while still a juvenile. It is probable that he begins stalking some women in his neighborhood. The stalking is not overt. It amounts mostly to taking note of their behavior and where they live. The women have in common that they are white and overweight, and probably they are all older than Robert. It is probable that they remind Robert of his mother in various ways, at least subconsciously.

One night, Robert follows one of the women, Jane, to her apartment. Jane is approximately 29 years old and has a history of mild mental illness. She is staying in an assisted living complex approximately four or five blocks from Robert's home. Looking through a window, Robert observes her getting ready for bed. Impulsively, he tears a screen out of the front window and enters the apartment. He confronts Jane in the back of the apartment, but Jane escapes into a different room where she begins pounding on the wall and screaming. An upstairs neighbor hears the commotion but does not get involved. Robert turns the television up very loud to cover the noise of the continuing assault but succeeds mainly in calling more attention to the noise. Nevertheless, the upstairs neighbor does nothing, and Jane receives approximately 37 blows to the head, the first few of which would have killed her. It was unclear whether Robert had carried some sort of club with him, or grabbed some convenient object from the apartment; in any event, the murder weapon, thought to be something like a baseball bat, was never found. After Jane dies, Robert rifles through her bedroom dresser and retrieves a pair of her shorts. He returns to the dead body and proceeds to masturbate over it, ejaculating into the shorts as the television continues to blare loudly. Finally, he leaves through the back door and walks, while still covered with Jane's blood, across a field.

Robert's behavior fits the pattern of a disorganized killer, specifically a plunderer in the Canter et al. (2004) reformulation. He engaged in a blitz attack, showed "overkill," had poor control of the victim, and literally got blood all over the room as well as all over himself. His sexual release was after the victim died, and he (carelessly) left ejaculate behind. There was, however, some planning because he apparently stalked his victim, picked a location where people were unlikely to come to each other's aid, probably brought a weapon with him, and carried it away. Perhaps he might be classified as a "mixed" rather than a disorganized offender. In terms of Ressler, Burgess, and Douglas's (1988) rape classification system, we think he best illustrates the anger retaliatory rapist. We believe that Jane represented some hated aspect of his mother, whom Robert blamed for the loss of his idealized father.

Despite the trail of evidence that might have pointed to Robert and ended his career after one killing, the police focused their attention on a fiancé who had recently broken up with Jane. Meanwhile, Robert was again adjudicated delinquent based on the pending burglary charge and sent to a juvenile institution where he stayed for approximately 8 months. His record in the institution was fairly good—a trend that has been noted of other serial sexual killers.

A few weeks after release from the juvenile institution, now age 18 years, Robert returns to the site of his first killing. It is now approximately 6:30 on a midsummer morning, not a time he is ordinarily up and about. He is driving his mother's blue Tempo. Cruising the neighborhood, he notices a 13-year-old girl on a bicycle delivering newspapers. He stops by the curb, waiting. As she approaches, he releases the trunk latch, jumps out of the car, overpowers the girl, and forces her into the trunk of the car. Although this is still a high-risk blitz attack that could easily have been noticed by any number of people, Robert has shown some development in his technique. He is able to spirit the girl out of the neighborhood before anyone realizes anything is amiss. It is several hours later before the girl's parents are aware that she did not report to school that day, and a search is begun. Her abandoned bicycle is found close to the abduction site, someone reports having seen a blue car drive off down a road to a nearby park, and the park is searched. A trail of blood leads from a parking area down a hillside. The body is quickly found, carelessly covered by last year's leaves. The girl has been raped and then stabbed 22 times. Although a killing is a rare event in this area, the police do not connect the killing with Jane's unsolved murder from approximately 8 months previous and only a few blocks away. Robert, in the meantime, proceeds to live a reasonably normal teenage life in that he has a girlfriend and hangs out with friends. He continues to drink heavily and uses drugs occasionally.

Approximately 6 weeks later, Robert selects his third victim. He follows a woman to her house, which is within a few blocks of his own residence, slightly closer to his home than the locations of the two killings. After dark, Robert breaks into the house and proceeds quietly to the upstairs bedroom. He is surprised to see that the woman is sleeping with her boyfriend. He decides he had better not confront two people. Back downstairs, he pokes around to see if there is anything worth stealing. He encounters the woman's 5-year-old daughter and hesitates only briefly. Grabbing some towels and dirty clothing from the floor of the laundry room, he jumps on the sleeping girl, smothering her with the clothes as he proceeds to vaginally rape her. She is able to put up only minimal resistance before passing out and perhaps this saves her life. The next morning, she is found unconscious but still alive. She was unable to tell anything of what happened to her, but it was determined that she had been raped. With three sexual assault victims, two of them dead and the third almost having been killed, within approximately eight blocks of each other and within less than 1 year, police and community now begin to think in terms of a serial killer.[11]

Approximately 1 month later, Robert selects his fourth victim, again a large (possibly overweight) white woman whom he follows home. She is having trouble sleeping that night and hears someone moving about in the house. Concerned about a possible serial killer in the area, she decides to exit the house quickly. Robert has picked up a knife from the kitchen, but he is surprised when she quickly exits the bedroom, and he drops the knife. He catches her trying to get out the front door and tries to trap her inside. Nevertheless, she escapes to the front yard. It is approximately 4 AM. Robert follows her to the front yard and pins her to the ground while proceeding to rape and simultaneously strangle her. She manages to bite him and to cry out just before passing out. A light comes on next door and Robert breaks off the assault and flees, possibly thinking that the victim is dead. He learns from the paper the next day that there is a living adult victim who can potentially identify him.

Either because he is afraid of being identified or because he is enraged that his victim survived, Robert feels compelled to return and finish the job. On at least two different occasions, he stakes out the house but does not get the opportunity to assault the victim. On one of these occasions, he is actually in the house again when he sets off a newly installed burglar alarm. Frustrated by his failure, Robert stakes out a new territory approximately 2 miles from his home and the sites of his first four victims but within a few blocks of where he once lived as a child. Again, he follows an overweight white woman home and breaks into her house. The woman's adult children and a grandchild are sleeping upstairs while Robert assaults the woman in her downstairs bedroom. Some loud fans help muffle the sounds during the warm late summer night. This time, Robert is successful in raping and then strangling the woman to death. He has clearly progressed to a more organized killer, leaving a much neater crime scene, methodically strangling his victim during or after intercourse, and slipping away without anyone knowing there had been an intruder—although this was still a highly risky rape-murder.

Encouraged by this success—or still not able to accept his previous failure—Robert decides to try one more time to kill his fourth victim. During the middle of the night, he breaks a window and enters her house. He is surprised to find a police officer waiting for him. The officer has been staying in the house for the past several days, expecting one more attempt. Even now, Robert's luck holds. He succeeds in running past the officer, is missed by two pistol shots, and exits the back of the house, setting off the burglar alarm but getting away successfully.

[11] Robert's crimes were eventually linked by DNA evidence. Other than DNA and geographic proximity, there was little to link Robert's first three crimes. Two involved breaking and entering the victim's home, but one was a street abduction. Two victims were described as heavyset, but one was a small child. One victim was bludgeoned, one was stabbed, and one was strangled. In short, there was little consistency in terms of modus operandi, signature, or victimology. This is consistent with the finding of Bateman and Salfati (2007) that any behaviors that were consistent across crime scenes were too common to be discriminatory among serial killers.

However, Robert has cut himself breaking the window and the officer calls the local hospitals and tells them to be on the alert for someone seeking treatment for a cut. Robert does go to a hospital and is finally caught.

Robert consistently maintained his innocence while sitting calmly through two trials. He refused to follow his lawyers' advice that he testify in his own defense. He showed no emotion when he was found guilty and sentenced to death on all three murder counts. Several years later, an appellate judge threw out two of the death penalties because the jurors had not been properly instructed during the penalty phase of the trial. The third death penalty remains in effect and Robert is on death row with a stay of execution while federal court appeals continue.

In summary, Robert engaged in five sexual assaults during a 14-month period, 8 months of which he spent in a juvenile institution. In addition, there were three other attempts to return and kill the victim of the fourth assault. His victims were all female and white, but they varied in age from 5 to almost 50 years; the youngest girl was no doubt a secondary target. In the first assault, his sexual release was postmortem, but in the remaining assaults he completed vaginal rape while the victim was still alive. All of the assaults took place on the offender's (and victim's) home turf. Several methods were used: a club, a knife, smothering, and manual strangulation. His control of the victims and the crime scenes was minimal: He left hair, semen, or blood at every site; he was noticed by someone other than the victim during three crimes (first, second, and fourth crimes) and was at risk of detection during the other two crimes.

Why did Robert commit his crimes? Does the fact that he had the presence of mind to break off his fourth assault when a neighbor turned on a light or that he knew enough to return to kill that possible victim-witness mean that he had "control" of his behavior and should be held legally responsible? Unfortunately, Robert continues to maintain his innocence and has no interest in psychotherapy. His conversion to Islam apparently has satisfied any need for redemption that he may have felt. Hints at possible causes, however, abound. His father was a killer—perhaps there was a genetic predisposition to aggression. There is a hint of physical child abuse—perhaps there was frontal lobe damage, although his above normal IQ suggests more of a bottling up of some sort of rage. Perhaps the early separation from his father left him feeling abandoned and angry. Perhaps his early exposure to alcohol and drugs weakened whatever cognitive restraints he may have had. Perhaps his mixed racial identity played a role, as he identified with his (partly) African-American father and felt rejected by his peer group (if, for example, they disparaged blacks in his presence, thinking of him as white). Perhaps his juvenile institutionalizations exposed him to sexual abuse and further alienated him from society. Perhaps his early career as a burglar gave him the experience of power as he went through the personal belongings of sleeping victims. Perhaps the underwear of sleeping women especially excited him with a sense of power and control. Perhaps this in turn led to rape fantasies—fantasies that were shattered by the resistance of his first victim, Jane, until her brutal destruction restored his sense of potency and established a new behavioral theme for him.[12] As with most serial killers, we do not lack for possible causes; there are more than

[12]Schlesinger and Revitch (1999) might suggest that Robert's early burglaries were sexually motivated, perhaps to find a victim, or were sexually stimulating in and of themselves. Robert's sexual murders might also be classified as "acute catathymic" homicides (Schlesinger, 2004).

enough possibilities. The task is to identify those that are operative in a given case and then to integrate them into a coherent model.

Theories of Serial Sexual Sadistic Killing

There has been no shortage of attempts to explain the behavior of serial sexual killers, most of whom are seen as sadists and psychopaths. Many authors get caught up in the issue of whether such killers should be seen as evil versus sick (Knight, 2007; Wilson, 2003), slated for execution and a one-way ticket to Hell or sympathetically confined, perhaps in the hope of rehabilitation, perhaps only awaiting one more development in the knowledge of brain chemistry. Are they themselves not also victims—of society, of bad parenting, or of a capricious gene? Although such philosophical musings can lead to lively debate, they probably do not help understand (let alone apprehend) even one such person. How, then, do we account for individuals who are so perverse as to find their sexual pleasure at the often unspeakable demise of others? Most theorists, in their effort to account for such extreme behavior, have found it necessary to implicate a wide variety of variables. It has become common to organize these variables at the biological, the psychological, and the sociological levels. The theorist's task, then, becomes to show systematically how these three levels interact to produce the serial sexual killer.

Basic Studies

Most studies of serial killers, by necessity, have relied on small samples, with perhaps a dozen or so people interviewed by the researcher. Those researchers with government connections have often been able to achieve sample sizes in the 30s or 40s.[13] Researchers who have gone beyond this have generally had to rely on case files or even media accounts that are very uneven in terms of the quality and quantity of information from case to case. A good example of such case files is the Missen Corpus of Serial Killer data at the University of Liverpool (Canter, Coffee, Huntley & Missen, 2000). Generalizations across "all" serial sexual killers (even limited to a narrow definition of sadistic killers) are extremely difficult because of the limited nature of the data. Recent studies tend to rely on enlarged databases, but comparisons across studies are difficult because of the high overlap in cases used for obtaining data (see, for example, Kraemer, Lord & Heilbrun, 2004; Morgenbesser, 2008).

One of the best of the early studies for extensiveness of detail on sexual sadists was conducted by Dietz, Hazelwood, and Warren (1990). Every case studied by the National Center for the Analysis of Violent Crime between 1984 and 1989 that showed a clear element of sexual sadism was included (there is some unclear overlap here with the subjects studied by Ressler et al., 1986). This resulted in a sample of 30 cases on which there was extensive, although varied, documentation. All were male; all but one were white. Although all had engaged in intentional torture of their victim(s), only 73% were known to be murderers, and 57% qualified as

[13] According to Beasley (2004), the FBI, through its National Center for the Analysis of Violent Crime, is expanding its database by reviewing case files and conducting additional in-depth interviews of serial killers.

serial murderers (three or more killings). An additional 9% were suspected of being serial killers. A few findings are used here to illustrate the strengths and weaknesses of this study.

Dietz et al. (1990) report that 30% of their sample had an incestuous involvement with their own child. This seems like a very high figure, and its importance might lie in pointing to a psychodynamic (perhaps Oedipal) origin to the subjects' sadistic rage. But what of the other 70%? It may be that they also had incest-related problems that simply did not surface. Twenty percent of the sample reported that they had been victims of child sexual abuse. Are these the same as the incest abusers, or are they part of the 70% who did not report committing incest? Are these rates of incest and sexual abuse high in comparison to those for other types of violent offenders? This too cannot be answered because no comparison group data is given. Mitchell and Aamodt (2005) explored the child abuse history of 50 serial sexual ("lust") killers. There was a record of at least some abuse in 68% of the cases. Compared to general population norms, the serial sexual killers were much more likely to have been abused psychologically (50% vs 2%), physically (36% vs 6%), and sexually (26% vs 3%).

In addition to their abuse history, the following findings from Dietz et al. (1990) also seem worth noting. A significant number were married (43%) and/or had established reputations as solid citizens (30%); most (57%) had no arrest history prior to the instant case. Drug abuse was fairly high (50%), suggesting either a loss of inhibition or an attempt to self-medicate. A variety of sexual deviance was noted, including cross-dressing, indecent exposure, and wife sharing, in addition to the incest and child sexual abuse noted previously. An intriguing finding was "excessive driving," which was noted for 40% of the sample despite being a variable that would not normally be thought of in the context of sexual homicide. One subject explained his excessive driving as expressing a need for freedom—to go wherever he wanted with no one telling him what to do.

In terms of their criminal behavior, the majority were clearly organized, with 93% showing careful planning. The victim was usually approached using a con or pretext, such as an offer of help or asking directions (90%); only three subjects (10%) preferred a blitz or surprise approach. Thirty-seven percent had the assistance of a partner. Sixty percent of the offenders kept a victim captive for more than 24 hours (and up to 6 weeks). Most offenders (87%) were described as unemotional and detached during the offense. A wide variety of sadistic behaviors were engaged in, both physical and psychological. Sexually, oral (73%) and anal (70%) penetration were more common than vaginal (57%). Dietz et al. (1990) attribute this to the high percentage of offenders with a history of homosexual activity (43%). However, "sexual dysfunction" during the offense was also noted for 43% of the offenders, and this may have played a role in their preferred sexual activity. Or, it may simply be that oral and anal penetration both provide the offender with a greater sense of power over the victim. Ligature (32%) and manual (26%) strangulation were the most common causes of victims' deaths ($N = 130$), but gunshot (25%) and stabbing (10%) were also common. In short, Dietz et al. provide a great deal of heuristic data that are difficult to interpret. The study does not distinguish serial sexual killers from single murderers (Kraemer et al., 2004) and other violent offenders, but it does bring out the variety within sexual killers.

Research by Quinsey, Harris, Rice, and Cormier (1998), although not directly involving serial killers, provides some important data for understanding the psychology of the serial sexual killer. They studied hundreds of violent offenders over a 25-year period. Besides treatment considerations, one of their main goals was predicting risk of recidivism (repeat violence). A subset of their violent offenders was made up of violent sexual offenders, a group whom they studied to develop the Sex Offender Risk Appraisal Guide (SORAG). Myers, Husted, Safarik, and O'Toole (2006) argue that serial sexual killers are primarily a type of sex offender, and they recommend a new *DSM* classification, specifically "sexual sadist, homicide type," thus implying the direct relevance of research on all sadistic rapists. Whereas power and control concerns may be pleasurable and useful in the commission of the rape–murder, sadistic sexual gratification is paramount.

Quinsey et al. (1998) report on a series of studies that used "phallometry" to measure the sexual arousal of convicted rapists to tape recordings of various sexual encounters. This research built on earlier work by Malamuth (1981) that classified subjects as either rape prone or unlikely to rape based on self-reports about their likelihood of committing a rape if they knew they could never be caught. A fairly large subset (35%) of a college male sample was identified as rape prone. Malamuth found that rape-prone subjects did show a different pattern of sexual arousal than the unlikely-to-rape subjects; namely, the rape-prone subjects were more likely to show sexual arousal to a rape scenario than to a consensual sexual encounter. However, rape-prone subjects were more aroused by a rape scenario in which the victim herself became sexually aroused and stopped resisting. With a "victim abhorrent" scenario, in which the victim was clearly distressed throughout the rape, the rape-prone subjects showed a somewhat lower level of arousal, though still much higher than the unlikely-to-rape subjects. A reasonable interpretation of the Malamuth research is that rape proneness is a relatively common characteristic among males, but sadistic rape makes up a small subset of rape proneness.

The Quinsey et al. (1998) studies differ from Malamuth's (1981) earlier research in that convicted rapists were used, most of whom had been involved in violent rapes. Over a number of variations in research methodology, one result stands out. Convicted rapists were found to have a different pattern of sexual arousal than did offenders convicted of nonsexual offenses. Rapists were more aroused by listening to rape scenarios than by a consenting sex scenario, with nonsex offenders showing the opposite pattern. More important, this difference was most clearly found when the rape scenarios portrayed "graphic and brutal rape stimuli" (Quinsey et al., 1998, p. 124). Finally, rapists as a group showed sexual arousal to an audiotape depicting nonsexual violence toward a woman but not to a tape depicting similar violence toward a male (all rapists were heterosexual). These findings do not mean that all rapists prefer brutal rape to rape with minimal force, but they do suggest that many, if not most, rapists are not deterred by victim distress and that some rapists, at least, might find that distress arousing. Interestingly, Quinsey et al. found no social skill differences between rapists and nonsex offenders; the rapists, however, did score lower than other offenders on a self-report measure of empathy. The empathy measure, in turn, was correlated with individual differences in arousal to the rape scenarios.

Quinsey et al. (1998) also found that the single best predictor, by far, of violent sexual recidivism was psychopathy, as measured by Hare's (1991) Psychopathy Checklist–Revised (*PCL-R*). Based on Hare's (1993) theory of the *psychopath,* the PCL-R measures a number of personality and background factors of the individual (extensive background information or interviewing is necessary). The 20 subscales of the PCL-R measure two correlated factors thought to characterize primary and secondary psychopaths. The first factor focuses on such characteristics as cruelty; the absence of feelings such as love, empathy, or guilt; egocentricity; and exploitiveness. In combination, these characteristics lead to the selfish and remorseless use of others. The second factor includes such traits as impulsiveness, sensation seeking, and lack of socialization (delinquent and criminal behavior) and accounts for the unstable and antisocial lifestyle of the psychopath. It is debated as to whether the psychopath represents a distinct personality disorder as opposed to an extreme version of the antisocial personality or perhaps an extreme impulse control disorder (Quinsey et al., 1998; Wiebe, 2003; Zuckerman, 1999).

However it is defined, psychopathy as measured by the PCL-R has proven to be highly predictive of repetitive violent sexual offenders, and psychopaths have been described as "polymorphously perverse" (Meloy, 2002). Hundreds of convicted sex offenders were scored on the SORAG, for which the PCL-R was the main component. Those offenders whose scores placed them in the highest risk category had 100% recidivism for a new violent offense during a 7-year follow-up. In contrast, sex offenders with the lowest SORAG scores had only a 7% recidivism rate (Quinsey et al., 1998, p. 244). The entire SORAG measured 13 variables besides psychopathy (PCL-R). Most of these variables, however, merely reemphasized factors already included in the concept of *psychopath*, such as a disrupted home life, poor school adjustment, a criminal history, early age at first offense, and high alcohol use. The one new variable was phallometrically measured deviant sexual arousal (penile arousal to depictions of violent rape). When combined with this measure of deviant sexual arousal, the PCL-R was highly predictive of repeat violent sexual offenses. The Quinsey et al. research did not include serial sexual killers; however, it does not seem to be much of a conceptual leap to argue that findings on repeat violent sexual offenders would be even more true of the serial sexual killer.

Identifying the serial sexual killer as a psychopath with an additional problem related to deviant sexual arousal opens up a plethora of research on the psychopathic personality in general. Most conclusions, however, can be summed up as viewing psychopathy as an extreme form of egoism lacking in impulse control and having a biological predisposition (or "diathesis") that combines with various childhood trauma or other stressors. Zuckerman (1999) summarizes the research on the biological predisposition to antisocial personality and psychopathy. It is thought that this predisposition may be either genetic or nongenetic (e.g., brain injury or developmental biochemical disorders). Insofar as genes are implicated, it must be stressed that no researchers have identified a "psychopath gene." All geneticists agree that no gene has a one-to-one link to behavior; rather, genes create potentials or tendencies that require specific environmental circumstances for a specific behavior to occur.

Zuckerman (1999) cites a number of twin and adoption studies that support both a biological and an environmental contribution to antisocial personality disorder and, by extension, to psychopathy. A reasonable generalization from these studies is that when the subjects come from a fairly homogeneous socioeconomic background, biology accounts for more of the variance than environment; conversely, when child-rearing practices are very heterogeneous, environment accounts for more of the between-person variance in criminal behavior. A prenatal variable, alcohol exposure via the mother' drinking, was also identified as contributing to childhood aggressiveness and conduct disorder. The implication is that exposure to alcohol in the fetal period may affect frontal lobe development, which in turn suggests loss of impulse control. Likewise, there is evidence that maternal rejection, perhaps linked to a difficult birth, may result in early neglect, which in turn may play a role in poor neurological development.

Numerous studies have identified various hormones (e.g., testosterone) and neurotransmitters (e.g., serotonin) as playing a role in emotional arousal and impulsiveness. Although no specific hormone differences have been linked consistently to specific arousal and behavioral characteristics of psychopaths, a number of studies have shown that criminals identified as psychopaths show lower fear-arousal responses and probably a lower overall emotional arousal. This low arousal, in turn, is thought to be a key factor in the trait of sensation seeking. Where psychopaths differ from normal sensation seekers is in their lack of inhibition toward distress, in turn thought to be connected to their lack of empathy/sympathy (Zuckerman, 1999). The combination of low fear arousal, low empathy, and high need for stimulation would certainly fit the serial sexual killer's linkage of victim pain with his own sexual arousal.

Zuckerman's (1999) theory of psychopathy is that the genetic or at least physiological predisposition interacts with the early family environment to produce the adult criminal psychopath. While conceding that there seem to be cases of a full-blown psychopath emerging from a healthy environment, Zuckerman argues that a truly healthy environment is more likely to produce someone with adjustment difficulties that fall short of serious criminal behavior. The emerging psychopath can be fairly well predicted at an early age, with children at risk for antisocial personality and psychopathy being identified as early as age 3 years. The key factors in the family environment are antisocial behavior in the father and (low) nurturance in the mother. Early school failure is both a result of the developing psychopathic personality and a cause of further delinquent and criminal behavior.

In summary, the bulk of the research that we have reviewed has been done on convicted sex offenders and on general criminals, often using the diagnosis of psychopath to establish a subgroup of more dangerous, high-frequency offenders. We believe that serial sexual killers constitute a more extreme group of sexual psychopaths, one that is not profoundly different from the violent sexual offenders studied by Quinsey et al. (1998) nor from many of the psychopaths in the studies reviewed by Zuckerman (1999). Furthermore, the general findings on psychopaths and psychopathic sex offenders have been supported by more clinically based observations of serial sexual killers (Egger, 2002, 2003; Norris, 1988).

Based on case reviews, clinical observations, and evidence similar to that reviewed previously, a number of different theories of sexual serial killers have been proposed. We briefly review three of them for their similarities and differences.

Hickey's Trauma Control Model of the Serial Killer

According to Hickey (2002), there are multiple paths to becoming a serial killer. The predispositions to serial killing can be biological, psychological, sociological, or any combination thereof. No combination of predispositions, however, is likely to produce a serial killer unless some event or series of events, called traumatizations, occur during the person's development. For Hickey, relevant traumas include such things as child abuse (sexual or physical), home life disrupted by death or divorce, ostracism in school, and profuse images of violence (actual or media based). These traumatizations are experienced by many who do not become serial killers, but for those who have a significant vulnerability or predisposition, the effect of the traumas is to create feelings such as rejection, mistrust, confusion, and anxiety, leaving the person unable to adapt to additional stresses. Stresses now have a multiplicative rather than an additive effect. A combination of stresses and negative emotional reactions can lead to a number of responses, both adaptive (help seeking) and maladaptive (from anorexia to suicide). For some reason, however, the evolving serial killer externalizes the blame for his feelings of distress and uses attacks on others as a way of restoring or maintaining self-esteem. Hickey (p. 109) notes the following:

> *In an effort to regain the psychological equilibrium taken from them by people in authority, serial offenders appear to construct masks, facades, or a veneer of self-confidence and self-control. The label of psychopath, given to most serial killers, may actually describe a process of maintaining control of oneself, of others, and of one's surroundings.*

Various facilitators, such as alcohol or drugs, pornography, and fantasy, then operate to reduce inhibitions and lead to killing, which Hickey believes would usually happen eventually even without the facilitators. Although a killing may fulfill a fantasy and restore a sense of control, this satisfaction eventually wears off, leading to a new killing to reestablish the positive feelings that followed the first one. Differences in the nature of the early traumatizations presumably influence the manner of serial killing (e.g., victim preference, ritualistic behaviors during the killing, or degree of sexualization).

The strength of Hickey's (2002) model is that it provides a framework broad enough to encompass many different types of serial killing, not simply sexual sadistic killing. Also, it does not try to put the serial killer into some narrow classification. Even two sexual sadistic killers might have no particular background variable in common. The nature of their predispositions, their traumas, their adult stressors, and their facilitators may vary greatly from each other, yet their behaviors could be quite similar. Of course, some might find this lack of specificity frustrating, but we see nothing wrong with the idea that there might be multiple routes to the same behavior. If we were to point to a weakness in Hickey's model, it would be the lack of distinction between predispositions and traumas. Because the predispositions can be psychological and sociological as well as biological, it is not clear why child abuse is an example of a trauma and (postnatal) brain damage a predisposition since child abuse may be the cause of the brain damage. Also, it is not clear where traumatizations end and various stresses and facilitators begin. One could just as easily have provided a long menu of contributing factors and argued that a wide variety of combinations could produce a serial killer. Thus, given sufficient social psychological factors, there may be cases in which no physiological diatheses are needed.

The Motivational Model

Ressler et al. (1988) offer what they term a "*motivational model*" that is specific to sexual homicide (see also Burgess, Hartman, Ressler, Douglas & McCormack, 1986). Data supporting the theory was based on the same 36 convicted sexual killers used in the Ressler et al. (1986) study of organized versus disorganized killers that was reviewed previously. The authors describe their approach as "law enforcement" rather than psychological, meaning that they are attempting to develop a model of the serial sexual killer that would be especially useful for the crime scene profiler. Although the model is not closely tied to established psychological theories, the influence of Erik Erikson's developmental conflicts and Albert Bandura's social learning theory seems evident.

Ressler et al. (1988) describe five components that shape the personality of the serial sexual killer. First, the child is born into an ineffective social environment. This refers primarily to parents who ignore or even accept the typical cognitive distortions of the young child or actively encourage distortions through their own antisocial behavior. The child is met with a combination of unrealistic expectations, lack of emotional support, and discipline that is either absent, harsh, or inconsistent. Within this ineffective environment, the child then faces both the normal and perhaps the nonnormative crises of childhood: difficulties at various tasks, witnessing or experiencing violence, and so on. During these formative events, there is a lack of support from his environment, which results in the child retreating into fantasy in the face of these stresses: "Aggressive fantasies, aimed at achieving dominance and control, emerge" (p. 71). This retreat into fantasy leads to a failure to bond to the child's adult caretaker and then to interpersonal failure. The unsupportive environment and the failure to adjust to the formative events combine to form patterned responses: a set of negative personality traits supported by a cognitive structure or belief system. These traits are likely to include autoeroticism and lying (because of the social isolation and reliance on fantasy) and belief in dominance and revenge. These patterned responses then reveal themselves in various negative actions toward others/self, such as cruelty to animals, fire setting, and stealing, which evolve into burglary, arson, abduction, and eventually rape and murder. The actions escalate because of the operation of a feedback filter: This essentially refers to cognitive reinforcements and adjustments (rationalizations) made to fit the behavior into the individual's fantasy system.

The motivational model, which is developed by Ressler et al. (1988) over six pages and illustrated in subsequent chapters, reads well, and the foregoing summary does not do it full justice. We believe that the strength of the model lies in its depiction of how a seemingly normal, lovable child can develop into a sadistic "monster" as a result of not-uncommon socialization processes. It is suggestive of a sort of "butterfly effect." That is, a relatively small distortion in development, causing a retreat into fantasy, is not corrected because of inadequate parenting, and this gradually leads to a deep-rooted psychopathic personality. In some ways, this is also a weakness of the model. It would seem to be unable to account for serial sexual killers who emerge from apparently normal family backgrounds, or for those who are highly socially adept and seen as assets to their community until their mask is removed. To be sure, Ressler et al. (1988) make allowances for the socially skilled serial killer, but this part of the model seems a bit ad hoc: They know that there are such cases, so they simply assert that the individual can be superficially sociable (without explaining how these social skills can be developed in the context of the person they describe). This ad hoc nature of the model surfaces in other ways as well. It is asserted that sexual killers "are aroused primarily by high levels of aggressive experience and require high levels of stimulation" (p. 74), but there is no real explanation for this. Elsewhere in the model, it seems to be that tension reduction through fantasy is what motivates the sexual killer. The fact that the model has been developed de novo, as it were, makes it difficult to determine what established psychological constructs are being relied on and thus how the pieces fit together.

Arrigo and Purcell: Lust Murder as a Paraphilia

Both Ressler et al. (1988) and Hickey (2002) explain the behavior of the serial killer as a result of the interaction between stressful events and a vulnerable personality. The Hickey model is somewhat broader in that it attempts to account for all serial murderers and pays much more attention to biological predispositions. Ressler et al. do not deny possible biological predispositions but focus much more narrowly on personality development specific to the sexual killer. Arrigo and Purcell (2001) narrow the focus still further, specifically to those sexual killers for whom the anticipated killing is clearly a key factor in the sexual arousal, as opposed to either the acting out of simple anger or the instrumental elimination of a witness. Arrigo and Purcell's goal is to add to the motivational model of Ressler et al. and Hickey's *trauma control model* by integrating the concept of a paraphilia to account specifically for the lust murderer. As indicated previously, a paraphilia is sexual arousal to a nonsexual object or behavior. Paraphilias are sustained by fantasies typically reinforced by masturbation. In the case of extremely deviant paraphilias, facilitators or disinhibitors, such as pornography or alcohol, are typically present. Arrigo and Purcell's basic task is to explain how the paraphilia of extreme sadism (or erotophonophilia) becomes established in the serial killer.

Arrigo and Purcell (2001) cite Money's (1990) claim that all paraphilias, especially sexual sadism, are due to a brain disease. The concept of disease here is not meant metaphorically, as in "mental" illness, but means that actual centers and pathways in the limbic system malfunction in the transmission of sexual and aggressive impulses: Messages of attack are linked with messages of arousal and mating. Both the trauma control and the motivational models suggest that paraphilias would result from unresolved traumatic life events early in adolescence. Low self-esteem and lack of attachments have caused the youth to become dependent on fantasizing. Anger over repeated rejection and failure is a common element of the youth's fantasy life. As the youth's sexual feelings arise with puberty, he experiences the same social rejection and failure. Because he has already learned that fulfillment in fantasy is safe, it is only natural that he would turn to fantasy to fulfill sexual desires. The difference now, however, is that with masturbation and release, primary positive reinforcement is present for the fantasies (pp. 23–24):

> *Compulsive genital stimulation enables the individual to experience a sexually satisfying result. The person fantasizes and rehearses the paraphilia … to the point of orgasm. This is a conditioning process in which the deviant eventually loses all sense of normalcy.… As the nature and content of the fantasy become increasingly violent and sexual, the paraphilias progress in intensity and frequency.*

The remainder of Arrigo and Purcell's integrated model relies on the trauma control and motivational models to show how escalation proceeds to more intense fantasies and then spills over into compulsive action.

Arrigo and Purcell (2001) should be credited with two significant contributions. They have shown how two prominent models of serial killing are compatible, and they have greatly elaborated on the nature and dynamics of the sadistic fantasies that drive the serial sexual sadistic killer. We also point to two limitations, however. First, the nature of the "brain disease" underlying the paraphilia is not at all clear. Their citing of Money (1990) makes it seem as if a real, ultimately observable structural problem underlies the erotophonophilia. Their examples, however, seem to follow the motivational model's idea that a physiologically normal person could develop into a sadistic serial killer given the right developmental conditions. Perhaps those developmental conditions may be said to produce deviant neural pathways, but the issue, if not the answer, needs more clarification. Second, it does not seem that this model would account for the case of "Robert" reviewed previously. Although it is certainly possible that Robert was acting out a fantasy, it seems more likely that he was acting on unconscious impulses, at least during his first sexual murder. It is more so the organized sexual murderers who report conscious sadistic fantasies (Ressler et al., 1986). One possibility is the idea of "unconscious fantasies," but this would hardly fit the model put forth by Arrigo and Purcell. Another solution is to relegate Robert to the category of "displaced anger murderer" (Groth et al., 1977), but it seems likely to us that Robert's brutal behavior was connected directly to his sexual arousal. In summary, Arrigo and Purcell have supplied a compelling description of how rape-murder fantasies function as paraphilias, but this may apply to only some sexual killers.

A rival viewpoint to that of Arrigo and Purcell (2001) should also be mentioned. Marshall and Barbaree (1990) present a general model of sex offenders that is based on the biological normalcy of the link between sex and aggression in males. For Marshal and Barbaree, a major developmental task is to learn to inhibit aggression in a sexual context. To some extent, this is a distinction that does not make a difference. The same factors that the previous models point to as leading to the fusion of anger and sex (child abuse, poor attachment, and low self-esteem) are seen by Marshal and Barbaree as interfering with the learning of inhibitions. This does make their model somewhat simpler, however. Rather than having to account for the origin of sexual sadism, it may be the natural consequence of failure to achieve a satisfactory relationship with the opposite sex.

Sociological Factors

The theories of sexual sadistic killing reviewed previously have been primarily biopsychological. Although they have not ignored social factors, such factors have been primarily seen as a source for trauma and conflict that shape the developing personality. Thus, in the case of Robert presented previously, racism is suggested as one source of self-esteem or identity problems that Robert may have had. Interaction with the school system and the juvenile justice system further shaped his personality. His involvement in burglary likely facilitated his fantasizing about sexual encounters with occupants and then gave him his first opportunity to act out his anger. Likewise, Zuckerman's (1999) theory of psychopathy and Hickey's (2002) trauma control model emphasize school experiences and other sources of problems that shape the sexual serial killer. Although important, these variables are "social" mainly in the sense that they are part of the human environment that shapes personality. DeFronzo et al. (2007), however, stress that we need to look at macro-level social variables to have a more complete picture of serial killing.

DeFronzo et al. (2007) examined a sample of 151 male serial killers, the vast majority of whom were sexual predators. Derived from the work of Rossmo (2000), the sample represented all known male serial killers active in the United States from 1970 to 1992. DeFronzo et al. found significant variations in the per capita incidence of serial killers from state to state. The purpose of their research was to account for this variation using two macro-level variables. They first distinguished between a "cultural" and a "structural" variable. The cultural variable that they used was Wolfgang and Ferracutti's (1967) subculture of violence. The structural variable was the opportunity for potential serial killers to obtain victims and escape apprehension, a key aspect of Cohen and Felson's (1979) routine activity theory. DeFronzo et al. argue that although biological and psychological forces may shape the personality of potential serial killers, the environment must still facilitate the expression of that personality. A pre-homicidal personality raised in a subculture supportive of aggressive acting out would be more likely to adopt behavioral patterns involving killing. Likewise, a sexual sadist living in an area characterized by anonymity and by many vulnerable people living alone would have more opportunity to act out his fantasies. Using a variety of proxy measures for each of these variables at the state level, DeFronzo et al. found that variations in the strength of the subculture of violence among the 50 states were highly predictive of the number of serial killers who had been born or socialized in each state. Likewise, the availability of vulnerable victims coupled with an environment of anonymity was highly predictive of the number of serial killers active in any given state. Of course, it is possible that sexual serial killers migrate to areas where it is easier to act out their fantasies, but for most of the cases reviewed in the DeFronzo et al. study, the killer was active in the state where he was socialized.

Future Directions

Based on our review of the literature and our own casework, we posit a number of directions that future research may be expected to take. It is well accepted that there are significant differences between sexual and nonsexual serial killers. It may also be useful, however, to distinguish serial killers on other dimensions, as a comparison case study by Wolf and Lavezzi (2007) illustrates. For example, there may be significant differences between adolescent and adult serialists, males and females, same-sex and mixed-sex team killers, heterosexual and homosexual killers, and such categories as chronic family killers and medical murderers. Furthermore, serialists may differ based not only on who they are but also on whom they murder. For example, killers of elderly females (Groth, 1978; Muram, Miller & Cutler, 1992; Safarik, Jarvis & Nussbaum, 2000) may differ from killers of children, same sex or otherwise. Murderers of prostitutes may differ from killers of gay youth, and interracial murderers may differ from intraracial murderers (Walsh, 2005). Serial murder by health care professionals, in itself highly diverse in methods and motives, presents a markedly different picture from sexual serial killing (Yorker et al., 2006). We can foresee theorists one day establishing a killer–victim matrix that will address these distinctions and determine their significance.[14]

As we learn more about such notorious serial killers as Gary Ridgway (Guillen, 2007; Prothero & Smith, 2006), Dennis Rader (Beattie, 2005; Douglas & Dodd, 2007), and Jeffrey Dahmer (Strubel, 2007), the more apparent it becomes to us that childhood trauma theories are, in themselves, insufficient to explain their depredations. Even "normal" families will have their child-rearing quirks; the early socialization experiences of Ridgway, Rader, and Dahmer, however, were simply not so traumatic as to explain the profundity of their evolving perversions.[15] The neuropsychiatric basis of paraphilia and paraphilia-related disorders, as well as the contribution of autism spectrum disorders to the etiology of serial murder, will receive increasing scientific attention in the future (Briken, Habermann, Kafka, Berner & Hill, 2006; Haskins & Silva, 2006; Schwartz-Watts, 2005; Silva, Leong & Ferrari, 2004).

Thus, we believe that the paraphilic nature of serial sexual murder has been reasonably established (Arrigo & Purcell, 2001; Lee, Pattison, Jackson & Ward, 2001, White, 2007). In keeping with this, we speculate that this brutal act may one day be understood as a perversion of courtship. Freund and colleagues (Freund, Scher & Hucker, 1983; Freund & Seto, 1998) have analyzed courtship as comprising four phases, each with its unique paraphilia. Thus, the initial phase of courtship, finding a partner, has the corresponding paraphilia of voyeurism. Likewise, the second phase, affiliation, is perverted by exhibitionism; the third phase, touching, by frotteurism; and the fourth phase, copulation, by preferential or compulsive rape. We believe that erotophonophilia can therefore be seen as a particularly virulent subset of this fourth phase of courtship.[16]

Whereas some theorists approach serial murder from a broader, social structural perspective involving alienation and cultural legitimation of violence (DeFronzo et al., 2007; Leyton, 1986), many researchers are turning to more biological and genetic origins. We expect, for example, that future integrated models will blend genetic predispositions (Brennan & Raine, 1997; Money, 1990; Morrison & Goldberg, 2004; Raine, 1993) and hypersexuality (Ellis, 1991; Krueger & Kaplan, 2001) with the neurological insult and anger stemming from child abuse (Pincus, 2001) to one day explain the violent fantasies (Meloy, 2000) so often associated with

[14]More complex typologies give rise to the possibility of finding a better fit between offender and crime scene characteristics. We agree with Canter and Wentink (2004), however, that it is critical that typologies of crime scenes be developed more empirically—that is, without trying to make them "fit" some a priori offender typology.

[15]Although some scholars continue to emphasize the role played by poor parenting in the creation of the serial killer (Levi-Minzi & Shields, 2007), we are mindful of the confirmation bias wherein investigators find what they are looking for (Prothero & Smith, 2006; Rossmo, 2006) and the self-serving nature of the recollections of serial killers of their abuse as a child. After all, it benefits the murderer to emphasize his exculpatory victimization as a child in the hope of avoiding execution.

[16]We further speculate that a fifth phase of courtship, separation, can be identified. If so, then stalking may come to be seen as a perversion of the normal phase of mate separation. Stalking, of course, is not unrelated to serial sexual homicide, just as many paraphilias are known to be interrelated (Abel, Becker, Cunningham-Rathner, Mittelman, & Rouleau, 1988; Krueger & Kaplan, 2001; Lehne & Money, 2003).

sadistic serial killers. As the complexities of deviant sexual behavior become more widely known to theorists, the contributions of fixated, regressed, primary, secondary, replacement, cumulative, and collateral paraphilias to serial sexual murder will be magnified (Myers, et al., 2007; White, 2007). Theories centering too narrowly on self-esteem and the adverse impact of early social experiences will be modified accordingly.

We also expect theorizing to continue to be based on increasingly popular evolutionary paradigms. Evolutionary psychologists and criminologists have already explained crime generally (Ellis, 1998; Ellis & Walsh, 1997; Quinsey, 2002) and psychopathy (Pitchford, 2001), sociopathy (Mealey, 1995), homicide (Daly & Wilson, 1988), stalking (Brune, 2002), and rape (Thornhill & Palmer, 2000) particularly. In applying the insights of evolutionary criminology specifically to serial sexual killers, there are two distinct paradigms that may emerge. It might seem evident, for example, that serial sexual killing should be seen as a vestigial pathology—that is, a maladaptive deviation that is simply difficult to eradicate. Given its seeming persistence, however, it is tempting to speculate that there might be some adaptive advantage that leads to the selection of those genetically based traits that underlie serial sexual killing. It will be interesting to note whether the selectionist paradigm can help explain the serial killer or whether the existence of this phenotype is better defined by evolutionary psychiatry (Nesse, 1984; Stevens & Price, 1996), as primarily a vestigial pathology or a by-product of other sexual adaptations.

Conclusion: Understanding the Serial Sexual Killer

How far have we come in our ability to understand the serial sexual sadistic killer? Do we know why some individuals get so much pleasure and satisfaction from inflicting pain on others that it becomes their preferred method for sexual arousal and release, driving them to overcome taboos against killing, and in most cases eventually subjecting themselves to life in prison or execution?

Although the unmasking of a serial killer is often met with astonishment and disbelief by those who know him or her, it seems that any time there is the opportunity for detailed inquiry into the person's background, one or more explanations for his or her deviance arise. On the physiological level, there may be genetic abnormalities, a genetic predisposition to becoming a psychopath, brain injury such as frontal lobe damage (perhaps as a result of physical child abuse), or compulsive masturbation or other evidence of hypersexuality. On the psychological level, that same child abuse may have scarred the personality. There may be severe attachment disorder, child sexual abuse, highly conflicted family relations, antisocial or borderline personality disorder, psychosis, substance abuse, and any number of developmental disorders. On the sociocultural level, there may be high exposure to violence and misogyny, poverty, alienation, overemphasis on masculine role taking, gangs and criminal groups that give status for both homicide and dominating women, or simply an environment that presents a number of suitable and unguarded victims. If any theorist's favorite construct is not found in a given case, it may simply be that no one looked for it. Perhaps in most cases one will find the interaction of factors from all three levels of personality formation, whereas in a few cases one particular factor, pushed to an extreme, may be sufficient. Perhaps the use of fantasy combined with rationalization and gradual drift into deviance is enough for a moderately unhealthy personality to become a full-fledged serial sexual killer. If anything, we have too many explanations rather than too few.

Several questions, however, remain unanswered. Are there sufficient differences in the etiology of various serial sexual killers so that meaningful deductions about their individual personalities and lifestyles can be made from their crime scene behavior? Can such a person control his fate? Does he remain morally responsible for his choices, in the sense that society is correct in expecting him to control his deviant impulses, even if he may not be responsible for the deviant desires in the first place? More important, how early in the developmental process does the potential sexual killer need to be identified in order for there to be a reasonable hope of prevention?

Questions

1. von Krafft-Ebing originally described how many types of homicide that occurred in connection with rape?
   a. 2
   b. 3
   c. 4
   d. 5
   e. 7
2. Which three of the Holmes and Holmes typology seek to address nonsexual goals?
   a. Vision, mission, sadist
   b. Vision, sadist, comfort
   c. Vision, mission, comfort
   d. Mission, sadism, comfort
   e. Lust, thrill, power/control
3. Missen found a general decrease in the number of serial killers over time. *True or false?*
4. The classification that has received the most attention is the organized/disorganized serial killer. *True or false?*
5. Select one of the theories of serial sadistic sexual killing and outline its major components and problems.

References

Abel, G. G., Becker, J. V., Cunningham-Rathner, J., Mittelman, M., & Rouleau, J. L. (1988). Multiple paraphilic diagnoses among sex offenders. *Bulletin of the American Academy of Psychiatry and Law, 16*, 153–168.

Abel, G. G., & Osborn, C. (1992). The paraphilias: The extent and nature of sexually deviant and criminal behavior. *Clinical Forensic Psychiatry, 15*, 675–687.

Alison, L., Bennell, C., Ormerod, D., & Mokros, A. (2002). The personality paradox in offender profiling. *Psychology, Public Policy, and Law, 8*, 115–135.

American Psychiatric Association, (2000). *Diagnostic and statistical manual of mental disorders* (4th ed.). Washington, DC: American Psychiatric Association. Text revision.

Arrigo, B. A., & Purcell, C. E. (2001). Explaining paraphilias and lust murder: Toward an integrated model. *International Journal of Offender Therapy and Comparative Criminology, 45,* 6–31.

Bateman, A. L., & Salfati, C. G. (2007). An examination of behavioral consistency using individual behaviors or groups of behaviors in serial homicide. *Behavioral Sciences and the Law, 25,* 527–544.

Beasley, J. (2004). Serial murder in America: Case studies of seven offenders. *Behavioral Sciences and the Law, 22,* 395–414.

Beattie, R. (2005). *Nightmare in Wichita: The hunt for the BTK strangler.* New York: New American Library.

Beauregard, E., Proulx, J., Rossmo, K., LeClerc, B., & Allaire, J. (2007). Script analysis of the hunting process of serial sex offenders. *Criminal Justice and Behavior, 34,* 1069–1084.

Brennan, P., & Raine, A. (1997). Biosocial bases of antisocial behavior: Psychophysiological, neurological, and cognitive factors. *Clinical Psychology Review, 17,* 589–604.

Briken, P., Habermann, M. A., Kafka, M. P., Berner, W., & Hill, A. (2006). The paraphilia-related disorders: An investigation of the relevance of the concept in sexual murderers. *Journal of Forensic Science, 51,* 683–688.

Brune, M. (2002). Erotomanic stalking in evolutionary perspective. *Behavioral Sciences and the Law, 21,* 83–88.

Burgess, A. W., Hartman, C. R., Ressler, R. K., Douglas, J. E., & McCormack, A. (1986). Sexual homicide: A motivational model. *Journal of Interpersonal Violence, 13,* 251–272.

Canter, D., Alison, L. J., Alison, E., & Wentink, N. (2004). The organized/disorganized typology of serial murder: Myth or model? *Psychology, Public Policy, and Law, 10,* 293–320.

Canter, D., Coffey, T., Huntley, M., & Missen, C. (2000). Predicting serial killers' home base using a decision support system. *Journal of Quantitative Criminology, 16,* 457–478.

Canter, D., & Larkin, P. (1993). The environmental range of serial rapists. *Journal of Environmental Psychology, 13,* 63–69.

Canter, D., & Wentink, N. (2004). An empirical test of Holmes and Holmes's serial murder typology. *Criminal Justice and Behavior, 31,* 489–515.

Capp, B. (1996). Serial killers in 17th-century England. *History Today, 46*(3), 21–27.

Cohen, L. E., & Felson, M. (1979). Social change and crime rate trends: A routine activity approach. *American Sociological Review, 44,* 588–608.

Cooper, A. J. (2000). Female serial offenders. In L. B. Schlesinger (Ed.), *Serial offenders: Current thoughts, recent findings* (pp. 263–288). Boca Raton, FL: CRC Press.

Daly, M., & Wilson, M. (1988). *Homicide.* New York: Aldine.

DeFronzo, J., Ditta, A., Hannon, L., & Prochnow, J. (2007). Male serial homicide: The influence of cultural and structural variables. *Homicide Studies, 11,* 3–14.

Dietz, P. E. (1986). Mass, serial, and sensational homicides. *Bulletin of the New York Academy of Medicine, 62,* 477–491.

Dietz, P. E., Hazelwood, R. R., & Warren, J. (1990). The sexually sadistic criminal and his offenses. *Bulletin of the American Academy of Psychiatry and Law, 18,* 163–178.

Douglas, J., & Dodd, J. (2007). *Inside the mind of BTK: The true story behind the thirty-year hunt for the notorious Wichita serial killer.* San Francisco: Jossey-Bass.

Egger, S. A. (1984). A working definition of serial murder and the reduction of linkage blindness. *Journal of Police Science and Administration, 12,* 348–357.

Egger, S. A. (2002). *The killers among us* (2nd ed.). Upper Saddle River, NJ: Prentice Hall.

Egger, S. A. (2003). *The need to kill.* Upper Saddle River, NJ: Prentice Hall.

Ellis, L. (1998). Neo-Darwinian theories of violent criminality and antisocial behavior: Photographic evidence from nonhuman animals and a review of the literature. *Aggression and Violent Behavior, 3*, 61–110.

Ellis, L. (1991). A synthesized (biosocial) theory of rape. *Journal of Consulting and Clinical Psychology, 59*, 631–642.

Ellis, L., & Walsh, A. (1997). Gene-based evolutionary theories in criminology. *Criminology, 35*, 229–276.

Ferguson, C. J., White, D. E., Cherry, S., Lorenz, M., & Bhimani, Z. (2003). Defining and classifying serial murder in the context of perpetrator motivation. *Journal of Criminal Justice, 31*, 287–292.

Fox, J. A., & Levin, J. (1998). Multiple homicide: Patterns of serial and mass murder. In M. Tonry (Ed.), *Crime and justice: A review of research* (pp. 407–455). Chicago: University of Chicago Press.

Fox, J. A., & Levin, J. (1999). Serial murder: Popular myths and empirical realities. In M. D. Smith & M. A. Zahn (Eds.), *Homicide: A sourcebook of social research* (pp. 165–175). Thousand Oaks, CA: Sage.

Fox, J. A., & Levin, J. (2005). *Extreme killings: Understanding serial and mass murder*. Thousand Oaks, CA: Sage.

Fox, J. A., Levin, J., & Quinet, K. (2008). *The will to kill: Making sense of senseless murder* (3rd ed.). Boston: Pearson.

Freund, K., Scher, H., & Hucker, S. (1983). The courtship disorders. *Archives of Sexual Behavior, 12*, 369–379.

Freund, K., & Seto, M. C. (1998). Preferential rape in theory of courtship disorder. *Archives of Sexual Behavior, 27*, 433–443.

Godwin, M., & Canter, D. (1997). Encounter and death: The spatial behavior of U.S. serial killers. *Policing, 20*, 24–38.

Groth, A. N. (1978). The older rape victim and their assailant. *Journal of Geriatric Psychiatry, 2*, 203–215.

Groth, A. N., Burgess, A. W., & Holmstrom, L. L. (1977). Rape: Power, anger, and sexuality. *American Journal of Psychiatry, 134*, 1239–1243.

Guillen, T. (2007). *Serial killers: Issues explored through the Green River murders*. Upper Saddle River, NJ: Pearson.

Hare, R. D. (1991). *The revised psychopathy checklist*. Toronto: Multi-Health Systems.

Hare, R. D. (1993). *Without conscience: The disturbing world of the psychopath among us*. New York: Guilford.

Haskins, B. G., & Silva, J. A. (2006). Asperger's disorder and criminal behavior: Forensic-psychiatric considerations. *Journal of the American Academy of Psychiatry and Law, 34*, 374–384.

Hazelwood, R. (1999). Analyzing the rape and profiling the offender. In R. Hazelwood & A. W. Burgess (Eds.), *Practical aspects of rape investigation: A multidisciplinary approach* (pp. 155–181) (4th ed.). Boca Raton, FL: CRC Press.

Hazelwood, R., & Burgess, A. (1999). The behavioral-oriented interview of rape victims: The key to profiling. In R. Hazelwood & A. Burgess (Eds.), *Practical aspects of rape investigation* (pp. 139–154). Boca Raton, FL: CRC Press.

Hickey, E. W. (2002). *Serial murderers and their victims* (3rd ed.). Belmont, CA: Wadsworth.

Hodge, S. (2000). Serial killing. In J. Siegel, G. Knupfer, & P. Saukko (Eds.), *Encyclopedia of forensic sciences* (pp. 1317–1322). San Diego: Academic Press.

Holmes, R. M., & DeBerger, J. (1988). *Serial murder*. Newbury Park, CA: Sage.

Holmes, R. M., & Holmes, S. T. (1998). *Serial murder* (2nd ed.). Thousand Oaks, CA: Sage.

Holmes, R. M., & Holmes, S. T. (2002). *Profiling violent crimes: An investigative tool* (3rd ed.). Thousand Oaks, CA: Sage.

Homant, R. (1980). A theoretical model of anger and aggression. *Corrections Today, 42*, 32–36.

Homant, R. J., & Kennedy, D. B. (1998). Psychological aspects of crime scene profiling: Validity research. *Criminal Justice and Behavior, 25*, 319–343.

Keeney, B. T., & Heide, K. M. (1994). Gender differences in serial murder: A preliminary analysis. *Journal of Interpersonal Violence, 19,* 383–399.

Kelleher, M. D., & Kelleher, C. L. (1998). *Murder most rare.* New York: Dell.

Keppel, R. D., & Walter, R. W. (1999). Profiling killers: A revised model for understanding sexual murder. *International Journal of Offender Therapy and Comparative Criminology, 43,* 417–437.

Knight, Z. (2007). Sexually motivated serial killers and the psychology of aggression and "evil" within a contemporary psychoanalytic perspective. *Journal of Sexual Aggression, 13,* 21–35.

Kocsis, R. N., Irwin, H. J., & Hayes, A. F. (1998). Organized and disorganized criminal behavior syndromes in arsonists: A validation study of a psychological profiling concept. *Psychiatry, Psychology and Law, 5,* 117–131.

Kraemer, G. W., Lord, W. D., & Heilbrun, K. (2004). Comparing single and serial homicide offenders. *Behavioral Sciences and the Law, 22,* 325–343.

von Krafft-Ebing, R. (1965). In F. S. Klaf (Ed.), *Psychopathia sexualis.* New York: Bell. Trans. (Original work published 1886).

Krueger, R. B., & Kaplan, M. S. (2001). The paraphilic and hypersexual disorders: An overview. *Journal of Psychiatric Practice, 7,* 391–403.

Lee, J., Pattison, P., Jackson, H., & Ward, T. (2001). The general, common and specific features of psychopathology for different types of paraphilias. *Criminal Justice and Behavior, 28,* 227–256.

Lehne, G. K., & Money, J. (2003). Multiplex versus multiple taxonomy of paraphilia: Case example. *Sexual Abuse: A Journal of Research and Treatment, 15,* 61–72.

Levi-Minzi, M., & Shields, M. (2007). Serial sexual murders and prostitutes as their victims: Difficulty profiling perpetrators and victim vulnerability as illustrated by the Green River case. *Brief Treatment and Crisis Intervention, 7,* 77–89.

Levin, J., & Fox, J. A. (2008). Normalcy in behavioral characteristics of the sadistic serial killer. In R. N. Kocsis (Ed.), *Serial murder and the psychology of violent crimes* (pp. 3–14). Totowa, NJ: Humana Press.

Leyton, E. (1986). *Hunting humans: Inside the minds of mass murderers.* New York: Pocket Books.

Lykken, D. (1995). *The antisocial personalities.* Hillsdale, NJ: Erlbaum.

Malamuth, N. M. (1981). Rape proclivity among males. *Journal of Social Issues, 37*(4), 138–157.

Marshall, W. L., & Barbaree, H. E. (1990). An integrated theory of the etiology of sexual offending. In W. L. Marshall, D. R. Laws, & H. E. Barbaree (Eds.), *Handbook of sexual assault: Issues, theories, and treatment of the offender* (pp. 257–275). New York: Plenum.

McNamara, J. J., & Morton, R. J. (2004). Frequency of serial sexual homicide victimization in Virginia for a 10-year period. *Journal of Forensic Science, 49,* 529–533.

Mealey, L. (1995). The sociobiology of sociopathy: An integrated evolutionary model. *Behavioral and Brain Sciences, 18,* 523–599.

Meloy, J. (2000). The nature and dynamics of sexual homicide. *Aggression and Violent Behavior, 5,* 1–22.

Meloy, J. (2002). The "polymorphously perverse" psychopath: Understanding a strong empirical relationship. *Bulletin of the Menninger Clinic, 66,* 273–289.

Missen, C. G. (2000). Serial murder in the United States, 1860–1995. In L. S. Turnbull, E. H. Hendrix, & B. D. Dent (Eds.), *Atlas of crime: Mapping the criminal landscape* (pp. 155–161). Phoenix: Oryx Press.

Mitchell, H., & Aamodt, M. G. (2005). The incidence of child abuse in serial killers. *Journal of Police and Criminal Psychology, 20,* 40–47.

Moffitt, T. E. (1993). Adolescent-limited and life course persistent antisocial behavior: A developmental taxonomy. *Psychological Review, 100,* 674–701.

Money, J. (1990). Forensic sexology: Paraphilic serial rape (biastophilia) and lust murder (erotophonophilia). *American Journal of Psychotherapy, 44,* 26–36.

Morgenbesser, L. I. (2008). Sexual homicide: An overview of contemporary empirical research. In R. N. Kocsis (Ed.), *Serial murder and the psychology of violent crimes* (pp. 103–117). Totowa, NJ: Humana Press.

Morris, (1969). In W. Morris (Ed.), *The American heritage dictionary of the English language 1969*. Boston: Houghton Mifflin.

Morrison, H., & Goldberg, H. (2004). *My life among the serial killers: Inside the minds of the world's most notorious murderers*. New York: Morrow.

Muram, D., Miller, K., & Cutler, A. (1992). Sexual assault of the elderly victim. *Journal of Interpersonal Violence, 7*, 70–76.

Myers, W. (2004). Serial murder by children and adolescents. *Behavioral Sciences and the Law, 22*, 357–374.

Myers, W., Bukhanovskij, A., Justen, E., Morton, R., Tilley, J., Adams, K., et al. (2007). The relationship between serial sexual murder and autoerotic asphyxiation. *Forensic Science International, 176*, 187–208.

Myers, W., Gooch, E., & Meloy, J. R. (2005). The role of psychopathy and sexuality in a female serial killer. *Journal of Forensic Sciences, 50*, 652–662.

Myers, W., Husted, D. S., Safarik, M. E., & O'Toole, M. E. (2006). The motivation behind serial sexual homicide: Is it sex, power, and control, or anger? *Journal of Forensic Sciences, 51*, 900–907.

Nesse, R. (1984). An evolutionary perspective on psychiatry. *Comprehensive Psychiatry, 25*, 575–580.

Newton, M. (2000). *The encyclopedia of serial killers*. New York: Checkmark Books.

Norris, J. (1988). *Serial killers*. New York: Anchor Books.

Pallone, N. (2000). Foreword. In L. Schlesinger (Ed.), *Serial offenders: Current thought, recent findings*. Boca Raton, FL: CRC Press.

Pincus, J. (2001). *Base instincts: What makes killers kill*. New York: Norton.

Pitchford, I. (2001). The origins of violence: Is psychopathy an adaptation? *Human Nature Review, 1*, 28–36.

Prothero, M., & Smith, C. (2006). *Defending Gary: Unraveling the mind of the Green River killer*. San Francisco: Jossey-Bass.

Quinet, K. (2007). The missing missing. *Homicide Studies, 11*, 319–339.

Quinsey, V. L. (2002). Evolutionary theory and criminal behavior. *Legal and Criminological Psychology, 7*, 1–13.

Quinsey, V. L., Harris, G. T., Rice, M. E., & Cormier, C. A. (1998). *Violent offenders: Appraising and managing risk*. Washington, DC: American Psychological Association.

Raine, A. (1993). *The psychopathology of crime: Criminal behavior as a clinical disorder*. San Diego: Academic Press.

Ressler, R. K., Burgess, A. W., Depue, R. L., Hazelwood, R. R., Lanning, K. V., & Lent, C. (1985). Violent crime. *FBI Law Enforcement Bulletin, 8*, 1–32.

Ressler, R. K., Burgess, A. W., & Douglas, J. E. (1988). *Sexual homicides: Patterns and motives*. New York: Lexington.

Ressler, R. K., Burgess, A. W., Douglas, J. E., Hartman, C. R., & D'Agostino, R. B. (1986). Serial killers and their victims: Identifying patterns through crime scene analysis. *Journal of Interpersonal Violence, 1*, 288–308.

Rossmo, K. (1997). Geographic profiling. In J. Jackson & D. Bekerian (Eds.), *Offender profiling: Theory, research and practice* (pp. 159–175). Chichester, UK: Wiley.

Rossmo, K. (2000). *Geographic profiling*. Boca Raton, FL: CRC Press.

Rossmo, K. (2006). Criminal investigative failures: Avoiding the pitfalls. *FBI Law Enforcement Bulletin*, 1–19 (September).

Safarik, M., Jarvis, J., & Nussbaum, K. (2000). Elderly female serial sexual homicide. *Homicide Studies, 4*, 294–307.

Schechter, H. (2003). *The serial killer files*. New York: Ballantine.

Schlesinger, L. (1980). Distinction between psychopaths, sociopaths, and antisocial personality disorders. *Psychological Reports, 147,* 15–21.

Schlesinger, L. (2004). *Sexual murder: Catathymic and compulsive homicides.* Boca Raton, FL: CRC Press.

Schlesinger, L., & Revitch, E. (1999). Sexual burglaries and sexual homicide: Clinical, forensic and investigative considerations. *Journal of the American Academy of Psychiatry and Law, 27,* 227–238.

Schwartz-Watts, D. M. (2005). Asperger's disorder and murder. *Journal of the American Academy of Psychiatry and Law, 33,* 390–393.

Silva, J. A., Leong, M. D., & Ferrari, M. M. (2004). A neuropsychiatric developmental model of serial homicidal behavior. *Behavioral Sciences and the Law, 22,* 787–799.

Silvio, H., McCloskey, K., & Ramos-Grenier, J. (2006). Theoretical consideration of female sexual predator serial killers in the United States. *Journal of Criminal Justice, 34,* 251–259.

Stevens, A., & Price, J. (1996). *Evolutionary psychiatry: A new beginning.* New York: Routledge.

Strubel, A. (2007). Jeffrey Dahmer: His complicated, comorbid psychopathologies and treatment implications. *The New School Psychology Bulletin, 5,* 41–58.

Thornhill, R., & Palmer, C. (2000). *A natural history of rape: Biological bases of sexual coercion.* Cambridge, MA: MIT Press.

Turvey, B. (2002). *Criminal profiling: An introduction to behavioral evidence analysis* (2nd ed.). San Diego: Academic Press.

Walsh, A. (2005). African Americans and serial killing in the media: The myth and the reality. *Homicide Studies, 9,* 271–291.

White, J. H. (2007). Evidence of primary, secondary, and collateral paraphilias left at serial murder and sex offender crime scenes. *Journal of Forensic Sciences, 52,* 1194–1201.

Wiebe, R. P. (2003). Reconciling psychopathy and low self-control. *Justice Quarterly, 20,* 297–336.

Wilson, P. (2003). The concept of evil and the forensic psychologist. *International Journal of Forensic Psychology, 1,* 1–9.

Wolf, B. C., & Lavezzi, W. A. (2007). Paths to destruction: The lives and crimes of two serial killers. *Journal of Forensic Science, 52,* 199–203.

Wolfgang, M., & Ferracutti, F. (1967). *The subculture of violence.* London: Social Science Paperbacks.

Yorker, B. C., Kizer, K. W., Lampe, P., Forrest, A. R. W., Path, F. R. C., Lannon, J. M., et al. (2006). Serial murder by health care professionals. *Journal of Forensic Sciences, 51,* 1362–1371.

Zuckerman, M. (1999). *Vulnerability to psychopathology: A biosocial model.* Washington, DC: American Psychological Association.

17 Serial Arson

Ross Brogan

All truths are easy to understand once they are discovered; the point is to discover them!
—Galileo Galilei

Introduction

Arson is a universal problem, and although the psychological motivation behind the arsonist's behavior is discussed in numerous texts and reference materials, questions about why arsonists set fires, and what they get from doing it, are still common. These are, of course, difficult questions to answer (unless you think like an arsonist).

Arson is a generic term used for the setting of a deliberate, malicious fire to damage property, generally that of another person (Dempsey, 1996; Bennett & Hess, 2001). With arson for fraud, however, the target is usually the property of the arsonist, who is seeking to gain an advantage, usually from an insurance policy. With regard to the evolution of an arson definition, DeHaan (2007, p. 648) states the following:

> *English common law, on which most American law is based, defines arson as the willful and malicious burning of the dwelling house of another. This made arson a crime against the security of habitation (because loss of habitation could well cost the lives of its*

dwellers by exposure to weather or enemies). It required certain elements to be present—the structure had to be a dwelling, it had to belong to another, and it had to be burned as a deliberate or intentional act. As the common law concept of arson became inadequate, statutory law (passed by government bodies) expanded the definition to include other buildings and property. By omitting the dwelling or occupancy requirement, other property such as shops, factories, prisons, public buildings, forests, fields, boats and cars are now included in most arson statutes.

The definition will also depend heavily on the criminal statutes of the country or area in which the fire is lit; in some states of Australia, it is referred to as arson, whereas in others it is termed "malicious damage by fire/explosion." In Scotland, it is officially referred to as "willful fire-raising," and in the United States there are very fine parameters used to define what actually constitutes an arson event. Arsonists are quite often referred to in texts on psychiatry or psychology as "malicious fire-raisers" or "fire-setters," among other common terms.

A prime example of the difficulties faced by arson investigators is contained in a California newspaper article titled "The Life and Death of a Serial Arsonist" (2007). The article tells the story of a typical family man, married with adult children, who was charged with setting fires over a 3-year period. His wife said:

There was nothing in his past suggesting he could be an arsonist. He had no interest in firefighting, no fascination with the many campfires they enjoyed over the years, no recognizable twist of personality that hinted at arson. The whole thing makes so little sense that I can't help but think that investigators made a terrible mistake.

Unfortunately, the investigators not only had convincing physical evidence but also had obtained a taped admission from the husband as to his guilt. Investigators had tracked his vehicle by sight and by GPS locator, and they had carried out surveillance to gather the evidence that eventually led to his arrest and charges. No people were injured in any of the fires, but it soon became evident that the fire-lighting activity was escalating and it was becoming too dangerous to allow it to continue. He was arrested with the prospect of charges in relation to 46 fires.

In continuing discussions with the accused, there was no explanation offered for his actions, no recognizable motive or reasoning behind why he had acted this way. Given his background, investigators were baffled by why he had set so many fires—and why he had set fires at all. While in jail awaiting trial, the accused took his own life, leaving a message for his family: "I'm sorry I let you down and ruined your lives." No plausible explanation was ever obtained for his actions or motivation in setting so many fires ("The Life and Death," 2007).

One difficulty faced by arson investigators and researchers is that our understanding of the fire setter's behavior is still developing. Dickens, Sugarman, Ahmad, Hofberg & Tewari (2007) conducted a study on the gender differences among adult arsonists using data collected from the West Midlands (United Kingdom) Psychiatry Service during a 24-year period. This study sampled 167 adult arsonists, of which 129 were male and 38 female. Data showed that female arsonists had a history of sexual abuse, whereas males had a more varied criminal background, with associated substance abuse problems. The study found significant gender differences among the arsonists studied, suggesting that different treatment may be required for males and females. These differing treatment requirements suggest that, for gender at least, fire setting behavior serves different needs. It stands to reason that the arson investigator would be well served in understanding these needs, which demands training and education directed toward this goal.

Arson is also a difficult crime to investigate because of its destructive nature (Saferstein, 2004), and this also calls for a great deal of training and knowledge on the part of those who seek to research the act and catch the actor. With regard to training of investigators, the following comment on the reason for effective training is provided in the training manual for fire investigators trained through Charles Sturt University (Jacobson & Brogan, 2004, p. 4):

> *To effectively confront the issue of arson it is important that fire investigators have a sound appreciation of the reasons why people commit this offense. It is also useful for investigators to be aware of the latest developments in the psychological research that might provide additional tools to assist in the detection, investigation, and apprehension of arsonists.*

The investigation of fires involves not only arson but also accidental and natural fires (e.g., those that occur through lightning and spontaneous self-heating). Fire services rely on an accurate appraisal of how and where a fire started for many reasons, the most important of which is that this assists their objective of protecting the community from the ravages of fire:

- Fire safety legislation relies on accurate fire statistics to determine building safety regulations, placement of fire safety exits, and placement of sprinklers and hoses to protect the occupants (if the determination of the cause is incorrect, the statistics are incorrect; if the statistics are incorrect, the safety rules may be incorrect).
- The placement of fire stations and specialized fire engines relies on efficient response times to reach areas of greatest risk to the community. The quicker the fire engine arrives, the less damage will occur to the property and the fewer injuries to the community. Accurate statistics assist with effective placement of fire stations.
- If fires continually occur in electrical appliances or machinery or involve similar items, an accurate cause determination may find a fault in that item that can be rectified and eventually make for a safer community.
- If the fire is determined to be incendiary, or a deliberate case of arson, the police can be involved early and evidence collected to prove who might have been involved. The earlier a criminal investigation is started, the better the chance of success—either catching the offender or deterring the criminal activity.

The investigation of a fire is conducted by operational fire officers attending the fire in the first instance, making determinations on cause based on their observations and knowledge of fire behavior. If the task of fire cause determination proves beyond their knowledge, experience, and capability, there are generally specialist fire investigators[1] in fire service units with greater knowledge and expertise capable of attending to a more detailed examination of the scene to make an expert determination of the fire's cause.[2] According to the Australian Institute of Criminology (2008), approximately 280,000 vegetation fires were analyzed in a study of fire statistics from 18 Australian fire and land management authorities. The study concluded that for all vegetation fires for which a cause was recorded, 50% were considered deliberately lit. It was also found that different agencies have differing thresholds for classifying the cause of the fire, and although it became clear that a fire starting from a natural event is rare, a vast majority of fires are related to human causes (Australian Institute of Criminology, 2008).

Once the fire is determined to be deliberate or incendiary in nature (and therefore arson), police service resources are generally brought in to assist or take over the investigation. Specialist police forensic officers, trained to collect and preserve evidence, assist with the scene examination, collection, and documentation of physical evidence.

Evidence samples are collected and sent to selected laboratories for forensic examination or analysis. This evidence and the sampling results then become part of an overall brief of evidence, compiled by trained police detectives from arson squads for presentation in criminal or civil hearings. Insurance companies also have a vested interest in the outcome of the investigation because of insurance policies covering the fire damage. They will often have their own trained forensic investigators or contract specialists from private fire investigation companies to conduct independent investigations into the origin and cause of the fire. Occasionally, all three bodies (fire, police, and insurance) work together on a case to pool their resources and data or information.

To provide central control for directing efforts to combat arson, the government in the United Kingdom has established the Arson Control Forum. The Forum provides the strategic direction to the government-led arson control/prevention program and was established to address the many facets of the menace of arson. To this point, the Forum has:

- Issued improved guidance on investigating fires.
- Published research into what motivates the arsonist.
- Commissioned research aimed at achieving more arson prosecutions.

A document on arson control written by the Forum and commissioned by the Office of the Deputy Prime Minister details what is required when faced with an arson problem. Under "Establishing the Need," it states the following (Arson Control Forum, 2003):

> *All deliberate fire reduction strategies must start with an analysis of local fire problems and an appraisal of the communities' needs. This can then be addressed by the provision*

[1] It is interesting to note that in most states of the United States, fire investigation is conducted by specialist officers called fire marshals. These marshals are fire officers sworn as police officers. They carry weapons; have powers of arrest, search, and seizure; and carry the fire matter through to the court system, conducting the investigation from start to finish.

[2] Throughout the world, there are many different ways in which fire and police services conduct specialist fire investigations. The methodology of conducting an investigation does not vary—it is a well-recognized and accepted method. It is the makeup of the investigating authority that changes.

of the required methodology and resources in terms of finance, personnel, and the construction of partnerships.

The strategy should revolve around four proven strands, which stem from the collection of statistical data that can be accurately analyzed to provide evidence in terms of need, response, and effect. These data, with the addition of time and cost elements, will provide a valuable tool in supporting the strategy. The four strands are:

- Prevention
- Education
- Detection
- Investigation

The primary aim of the strategy should be to reduce deliberate fires, with attempts to reduce arson attacks by 10% by March 31, 2010.

Clearance rate in this crime is generally low; for example, in the United States approximately 100,000 arsons are reported to the police each year, but only 15% of these are solved (Dempsey, 1996). Deliberately lit fires are on the increase throughout the world, but it is not just the number of fires that is a problem. One data set suggestive of the increase in arson is from the Arson Control Forum (2004). The data for the period 1994–2003 demonstrate the following:[3]

- In the past decade, there have been approximately 2.4 million deliberate fires in the United Kingdom.
- Arson involving vehicles has doubled in those same 10 years.
- These fires caused 32,000 injuries and 1200 deaths.
- In an average week, there are 2100 arson fires resulting in two deaths, 55 injuries, and a cost to society of 40 million pounds sterling or 72 million euros.

Further statistics available from the British Government/British Insurers Association Arson Prevention Bureau (2004) show the following:

- Each week, 20 schools are damaged or destroyed by arson.
- Each week, there are 2213 arson attacks in the United Kingdom.
- Each week there are 53 injuries and two deaths.
- Each week, four churches or places of worship are damaged or destroyed.
- Teenagers (10- to 17-year-olds) comprise 40% of those prosecuted or cautioned for arson offenses.
- Arson fires have doubled since 1991.
- Vehicle arson has tripled since 1991.

These statistics suggest a much worse problem than the data from the Arson Control Forum.

[3] Statistics from the 2006 report do not show a great deal of difference from these figures.

In New South Wales (NSW), Australia (which contains the largest population mass of all states in the country), fire statistics show the following for the years 2006 and 2007 (New South Wales Fire Brigades, 2008):

- 138,021 incidents were attended as fire calls.
- 33,118 of these proved to be actual fires.
- 32.92% were bush and grass fires.
- 23.3% were building fires.
- 14.9% were mobile property fires (cars and other vehicles).
- 28.8% were rubbish and other fires.
- Of all actual fires, 39% were attributed to arson causes.

Incendiary/arson causes were the second highest cause allocated to building fires.

Since 1988, the state government of NSW has established several committees and inquiries examining the problem of arson, with recommendations made and implemented over the ensuing years in an effort to reduce the problem. As recently as 2002 and 2003, there were Federal Committees of Inquiry into the large bush fires that ravaged many states and the Australian Capital Territory (ACT) during those years. In the ACT, the McLeod Inquiry resulted in many changes to government bodies and emergency services and the way they handle emergencies. To date, no organization in Australia (similar to the British Arson Control Forum) has been formed as a result of any of the inquiries, although these did bring about changes to the way in which fire and police authorities conduct their fire investigations and evidence-gathering techniques.

Although the exact number of serial arsonists is not known, from my experience with arson, a certain number of fires occur in a community that are lit by the same person or persons, and these fires can be documented and determined to be serial in nature by the astute fire investigator. Until several fires of the same type occur, one cannot determine that the fires are due to serial involvement; determination of serial fires relies on accurate cause determination, accurate documentation, and efficient evidence collection and interpretation.[4]

Methodology of Fire Investigation

To successfully conduct a fire investigation, one must follow a recognized methodology to ensure that all facets of the investigation have been covered adequately. The National Fire Protection Association's (NFPA, 2008) document No. 921 provides a basic methodology for fire investigation that is recognized in most countries throughout the world and followed by professional fire investigators. It states the following (p. 16):

> *A fire or explosion investigation is a complex endeavor involving skill, technology, knowledge, and science. The compilation of factual data, as well as an analysis of those facts,*

[4]I use the word "interpretation" because the determination of serial fires is reliant on the investigator's intimate knowledge and experience of fire scenes to inspect a fire-damaged object and interpret what it was before the fire caused it to melt, decay, or become blackened. Once the investigator has determined what it was, the interpretation has to be made as to how this object was involved in the fire cause.

> *should be accomplished objectively and truthfully. The basic methodology of the fire investigation should rely on the use of a systematic approach and attention to all relevant details.*

The systematic approach recommended in the text employs the scientific method. This approach is not only desirable when carrying out any analytical process but also necessary for a successful conclusion to the investigation.

The scientific method recommended by NFPA 921 (NFPA, 2008) contains the following steps:

- Recognize the need (identify the problem).
- Define the problem.
- Collect data.
- Analyze the data (inductive reasoning).
- Develop a hypothesis.
- Test the hypothesis (deductive reasoning).
- Select the final hypothesis.[5]

Note that NFPA 921 (NFPA, 2008) is a guide only and not a standard; therefore, it is used to guide people conducting fire investigations. NFPA 1033 (NFPA, 2009) is a standard. As a standard, the document details qualities and knowledge required of a person to fulfill the necessary qualifications to carry out the role of a professional fire investigator. Both documents are well recognized and have been adopted by many fire authorities throughout the world.

Specialist fire investigators must be highly trained and knowledgeable in all aspects of firefighting tactics and fire service operations, fire behavior, fire science, materials behavior, building construction, the effects of fire on buildings and building materials, and physical evidence collection and preservation. They must also be able to apply this vast amount of knowledge to writing expert reports and giving testimony on these findings and theories in a court of law or before any other inquiry. In addition to these qualities that are necessary for a successful investigation to be conducted, the investigator needs to be well read in aspects of human behavior related to fires and fire setting. All these are areas of special significance when determining a motive for the fire starting, along with how it was lit and where.

Jacobson and Brogan (2004) cite Prins (1994) when discussing the motivation of fire setters and arsonists. The following quotation regarding motive relates to the requirement for a fire investigator to have specialist knowledge not only of investigative procedures but also of the behavioral aspects of arson (Jacobson & Brogan, p. 142):

> *Prins contends that fire as a phenomenon has always played an important and significant part in human history. It has been put to many uses, the least of which is fire's use as a destructive force. This destructive capacity however is only too evident in today's world with everyday reports of fire, bombings, and incendiarism. Fire, as a phenomenon, has*

[5]It is vital that the final hypothesis be able to withstand rigorous scrutiny in the courtroom.

held, and continues to hold, a fascination every bit as powerful as that evoked by life and death. To successfully operate in this environment it is essential that one understands the complex nature and behavior of people who use fire for destruction and the motives behind their behavior.

When serial arson is suspected, it is imperative that an investigation be conducted into every case in which the suspect is allegedly involved. The details of each of the fires and the findings of the investigator must be thoroughly documented to accurately record the serial nature of these crimes and establish that the fires are in fact linked.

First, the investigator must inspect the fire scene, investigate the circumstances of each fire, and establish that each is a deliberate fire. Once arson has been established, scrupulous attention must be paid to the effective, efficient, and legal gathering of relevant evidence that will prove arson has been committed. Second, there must be a concerted effort to establish evidence that proves involvement by the person suspected as the serial arsonist. Evidence must be available to show that this person has been directly involved in each case. Third, there must be evidence showing a direct link between the person of interest and each of the arson fires that constitutes the serial activity. Without a direct link to a particular person, one may be able to prove serial arson activity but not who the serial arsonist actually is. This is the objective of the exercise.

When serial arson is suspected, it is usually prudent to set up a specialized task force. Guidance on how this is done is provided by the Arson Control Forum (2003); under the heading "Detection," there are several areas of interest that should be taken into consideration:

- A police presence is advised and considered essential.
- Fire and police personnel should be involved in any interviews because it has been found that most young suspects will talk to a firefighter, and not a police officer, in a street location.
- A highly visible vehicle is a valuable tool.
- Training in cognitive interviewing skills is a distinct advantage, as is a background in fire behavior.
- Best practice should be established with the investigation; this should include all available investigative sources being at the scene at the same time—fire investigator, police forensic, police, canine accelerant detector, and so on.

The text contains one piece of advice classified as essential for success: "Training for firefighters in crime scene management and preservation is essential, as it is possible that vital evidence can be missed during the early stages of an incident" (Arson Control Forum, 2003, p. 18).

A similar document published by the US Federal Emergency Management Agency (FEMA,1989) details ways in which to form an arson strike force. This document also mentions the following benefits of an arson strike force (pp. 4–5):

- Greater productivity with existing resources
- Better interagency coordination and cooperation
- Stronger prosecutions

The Arsonist

It is important to note that most classification systems provide a starting point only, and that we should be cautious in the application of rigid typologies. Canter and Almond (2002, p. 11) state the following:

> *It is recognized by psychologists that assigning individuals to one of a few "types" is likely to be very crude and that any such classification process can only be approximate. However, in order to develop a strategy for dealing with arson some attempt must be made to identify the different forms it can take in order to facilitate the targeting of appropriate policies and interventions. It is important to develop a framework that will reduce ambiguities and provide a way of distinguishing between the acts of arson and that takes account of both the characteristics of the arsonist and the property that is the target.*

Table 17.1 provides the proportion of property and vehicle arson for 2000 (Canter & Almond, 2002, p. 11). It is interesting to note the view of Canter and Almond of the "malicious" type (p. 14):

> *It is often assumed that arson is a crime against property. However, it does share some of the characteristics of personal or violent crimes in often being an attack against a person or group of people. Put simply, fire is sometimes used as a weapon.*

This proposition is also supported by Turvey (2008).

Some motives can be multifaceted or obscure in their reasoning. A newspaper article relating to arson in Israel discusses a fire set by a suspect who used gasoline and spray paint in an attempt to both destroy and deface a synagogue. It was considered by local police authorities that this might have been the same person who lit other fires in synagogues prior to this event. On the prior occasion, the perpetrator informed police his actions were in protest of religious women wearing wigs because some rabbis had ruled that wigs were immodest and that women must use cloths to cover their hair ("Serial Arsonist," 2008).

A useful online resource for fire investigators is interFIRE Online (http://www.interfire.org), which provides training, education, and resources for investigators to improve their skills. An article titled "The Study of Serial Arsonists" (2008) contains information compiled by a team

Table 17.1 Arson by Type and Quantity, 2000

Type of Arson	Property	Vehicle
Youth disorder	36%	39%
Malicious	25%	3%
Emotional expression	27%	13%
Criminal	13%	45%
Total Fires	32,200	70,800

from the Federal Bureau of Investigation's (FBI) National Center for the Analysis of Violent Crime (NCAVC) (Sapp et al., 2004). The study was conducted in an attempt to find solutions to problems confronting police authorities, such as serial arson, which had reached epidemic proportions throughout the United States. The research was conducted and the project planned and implemented with several goals in mind. In relation to this, Sapp et al. state that "these goals are based on the belief that any understanding of the typology of arsonists, particularly typological classification based on motivations, may enhance investigative efforts and provide a focus for intervention efforts" (p. 2).

Some interesting results came from the NCAVC study, some of which are mentioned in the case studies detailed later in this chapter (Sapp et al., 2004). Regarding methods of setting fires, the study found that almost all the arsonists used "unsophisticated" methods, which included available materials such as trash, paper, gasoline, and, most commonly, matches or cigarette lighters for the ignition source (see the "Hurricane Harry" case study discussed later). It was noted that few used any sort of handmade device to light their fires, and nearly half left some kind of evidence that could have been used to link them with the fire (p. 3). Regarding mobility, the study found that 61% walked to the scene and 70% of the fires were set within a two-mile radius of their residence. Almost all fires were found to have been lit within an area that the arsonist was familiar with, suggesting that the arsonist was comfortable with these surroundings. The study also showed that few owned motor vehicles and most set fires in their own neighborhood (p. 3).

In 2006, Edwards and Grace conducted an analysis of data, based on New Zealand arson statistics, to test Canter and Larkin's 1993 "circle theory of environmental range for offending by serial arsonists." The offenders were classified as marauders or commuters, depending on whether or not their home base was within the criminal range circle. Their study did not reliably differentiate between characteristics applicable to either marauders or commuters, and they stated, "Overall, these results suggest that the criminal range circle may provide only limited information for predicting the home base of serial arsonists in New Zealand" (p. 1; see also the case studies in this chapter, with the exception of "Sean Broom").

Another issue arising from the NCAVC study is that approximately one-third of the serial arsonists remained at the scene to watch the fire and the subsequent commotion. This proved useful in setting the parameters for investigation into the "city" arsonist, who was thought to be within the crowd watching the fires that he had lit. Approximately one-fourth leave the scene and go to another location from where they can observe the results of their fire and the firefighters fighting it.

Case Studies

During more than 20 years as a fire investigator, I have been involved with a number of serial arsonists: investigating their fires and ensuring the evidence was gathered to prove their arson and their particular involvement with each fire. This has also involved assisting other investigators with the same goals and assisting investigating police officers in compiling a brief of evidence in these serial offenses. Later involvement with some cases has also included attending court and presenting evidence to show the results of the fires and the direct links between them.

The following case histories are provided to illustrate some of the methods used by arsonists and some of the traits displayed that in some cases were used to apprehend and convict them. I was involved in all of these cases in some way, and the facts are from my personal files maintained over many years.[6]

The "City" Arsonist

The "city" arsonist was so named because of the location of his fires, all set within the central business district of the city of Sydney.

Twenty-six-year-old Gregory Alan Brown—a white Caucasian male—started lighting fires in 1987 within the buildings of the inner-city business district. It has since become known that he started lighting fires when he was only 12 years old, admitting that he set fire to the garage of the house next door to where he lived with his adopted parents. This was apparently the start of his criminal career. It was also revealed that he was a bed wetter when he was young. Brown was described as borderline retarded, having suffered brain damage at an early age. There are also indications that he was a drug and alcohol abuser.

Within the city area, the fire service attends a great number of calls directly related to automatic fire alarms, many proving to be false alarms. Many hours of fire service time are spent attending these calls, day and night, with the firefighters becoming frustrated at not seeing any actual fires. Because of the high risk involved with fires in inner-city buildings, old buildings, densely populated areas, and high-rise buildings, the fire service responds with a large number of fire engines and firefighters. Rarely do fires actually break out (compared to the percentage of false alarm calls), and when numerous fires occur, it becomes a topic of animated discussion, drawing much attention. This was the case with the fires attributed to Brown.

Fires were lit in businesses, offices, and commercial buildings throughout the city. They invariably occurred in morning or afternoon peak hours, when many people were moving about the city. As a result, they drew large crowds, with large numbers of fire engines, police vehicles, and ambulances that attended. The fires were located in exit stairs, exit passages, and public access areas of these buildings and were almost always lit using trash or discarded items found in these areas. The fires were set beneath a fire sprinkler or in an area covered by a fire detector where they would be discovered and reported to the fire service immediately (usually by an automatic alarm system). Because of their location beneath a fire sprinkler, they were easily contained and did not spread to become a hazard. Also because of their location, the fires would produce a great deal of smoke once the sprinkler activated. Immediate and rapid response by the fire engines contributed to early intervention in these fires, stopping their progress and ensuring the safety of the building occupants. The fires achieved one main aim, and it was suspected that the arsonist was seeking attention. The large emergency service attendance, large crowds, and evacuation of buildings caused havoc in the city center at peak

[6] I recognize several people in the Acknowledgments who were also involved with these cases, in many cases playing much more important roles than I did.

periods of the day. Minor injuries occurred, mainly from smoke inhalation, although no serious injuries occurred until one of the fire events in 1989.

On September 17, 1989, a fire occurred in the "Downunder" backpackers hostel in the suburb of Kings Cross, this time taking the lives of six tourists who were trapped inside the building by a fire lit in the entry foyer, preventing safe exit from the building. Most of the victims were trapped in their rooms, unable to escape the smoke and toxic gases rising up through the single stairway from the foyer. In this instance, no fire sprinklers were fitted to the building to hold the fire in check or automatically alert the fire service.

Because of the serial nature of these fires and the research suggesting that this person was probably remaining at the scene, standing in the crowd watching the results of his handiwork, the fire and police services made a concerted effort to apprehend the suspect. Undercover operatives from the police worked throughout the city areas where the fires were occurring, hoping to catch the offender in the act. Fire service investigators transferred to inner-city fire stations and responded with fire crews on the first call to fires, carrying video cameras and videotaping the crowd in case a familiar face was sighted at a number of fire scenes. However, all these attempts were fruitless and frustrating.

Within a short period of time after the 1989 tragedy, Brown was arrested and charged with the arson resulting in the fatalities. As a result of ongoing investigations into all the fires, he was eventually charged with lighting approximately 158 fires and the murder of six victims. Brown confessed to his involvement in the fires and participated in a drive-around with police to show them where the fires had been lit. He was found guilty of manslaughter and convicted of his crimes; he was sentenced to 18 years in jail. After his conviction in NSW, he was charged in Victoria with a multitude of fires in the St. Kilda area (a suburb of Melbourne). These charges resulted in his conviction and a sentence of 12 months.

"Hurricane Harry"

From early 1993 to late 1995, a series of fires occurred in a southern suburb of Sydney. These fires involved motor vehicles, trash bins, houses, fences, grass, stacked tires, and other small items. Each of the fires was determined to have been deliberately lit, and a pattern started to emerge in relation to these fires, all in close proximity to each other. Similar evidence was located at many of the fires, which began to suggest they were all lit in the same manner.

A suspect emerged and further investigation revealed certain facts about him and the fires that were lit. This suspect was a 51-year-old male of slight build, unemployed, unshaven, who had an appearance similar to a "homeless" individual (although he did in fact have his own residence). He had a prior history of criminal activity for unauthorized entry to property with intent, and the police nicknamed the suspect "Hurricane Harry."

Fires kept occurring and the pattern that emerged showed that the arsonist either was very fast on his feet (to get around such a wide area in a short period of time) or had some form of transportation. The fires were all linked, and several were lit in a very short period of time, usually in a geographically circular pattern (the last fire was always very close to where the suspect lived). Plastic soft drink bottles containing paper of different types, determined to have been used to start the fire, were found at many fire sites. Once the pattern was discovered, it became vital for the police to try to get to the suspect's address first, before he returned from starting fires; unfortunately, he was extremely fast and apparently wily, and he was never caught returning to his residence at these times.

On one occasion, this suspect was caught entering a property by police. He was carrying a bag that was found to contain advertising leaflets, papers, plastic soft drink bottles, and plastic carry bags—all that one would need to start a fire. No fire was started in this case, and police had no evidence to arrest him.

After this incident, the fires appeared to cease and no further serial activity came to the attention of fire or police authorities. The suspect was never arrested and charged with any of the fires because of the lack of sufficient evidence.[7]

Sean Broom

Sean Broom is a white Caucasian male who was 34 years old at the time of his sentencing in 2003.

Between May 1999 and August 2000, approximately 16 fires occurred in a wide area across the suburbs of Sydney. These fires involved motor vehicles, caravans, tire storage premises, factories, warehouses, and other properties in industrial areas. One thing these fires had in common was that at each fire the attending fire brigades would be met by a male person who then informed them of the whereabouts of the fire and, in some cases, assisted them in finding it. One of the early fires involved a factory where fiberglass swimming pools were manufactured; this was the largest of the fires, causing more than $1 million in damage.

This individual had a prior criminal history of lighting fires (or at least being caught for it) but continued with his activities. One of the main pieces of incriminating evidence was the fact that recordings of the emergency phone calls made to the fire brigade reporting these fires were proven by voice recognition to be the voice of Sean. He had not only lit fires to bring the fire brigade to his area but also was one of the first to phone in the emergency call to ensure that the fire brigade arrived at the correct address. Fire officers gave descriptions of a male observed at the scene of many of the fires, who met them on arrival and was very helpful in assisting them to find the fires, which were usually in remote locations.[8]

On one occasion, Campbelltown Fire Station attended three fires in the same street, during the same night, all involving motor vehicles or caravans in an industrial area, and all were considered to be deliberately lit. In each case, they were met by the same male person who

[7] During unusually high bush fire activity throughout the suburbs of Sydney and in the rural areas of the state in December 2001 and January 2002, I worked on Police Strike Force "Tronto," established to investigate the high incidence of arson reported with these fires. One fire being investigated in a national park close to the southern suburbs of Sydney came to my attention when a report from a fire officer came to my desk. This report contained a description of a male person observed acting suspiciously at one of the fires by an eyewitness—male, approximately 50 years of age, thin, unshaven, with the appearance of being homeless, and riding a bicycle.

[8] I was involved in the investigation of many of the fires suspected as being this person's work. The main thrust of the investigations was to obtain eyewitness accounts and descriptions of this male from attending firefighters. Once obtained and compared, the descriptions linked him to the other fires.

showed them the location of each fire. He also informed them that he had made the emergency call regarding each fire. The firefighters considered his actions suspicious because this was an industrial area late at night and it would be unusual for anyone to be in the area at this time, even more so when this occurred on three separate occasions. The fire brigade investigator was summoned to look into the incidents, and this led to police involvement for further investigation.

The fire brigade investigation unit alerted police to the possibility that a serial arsonist was at work in several areas. It was amazing that these areas were linked to just the one person, and police investigations revealed that, in all, the fires covered a distance of travel across Sydney of approximately 70 km involving five separate suburbs.

During initial investigations by police, the suspect maintained his innocence, but once charged and confronted with court appearances, he pleaded guilty to many of the fires. In 2003, he was sentenced to serve 4 years and 9 months for his crimes. The reason behind this activity has not been revealed, but it could be theorized that this arsonist was looking for personal recognition and kudos, in his own distorted way, for summoning and assisting the fire brigade, thereby helping the community.

Cameron Burgess

Cameron Burgess is the most stereotypical arsonist I have encountered in my career, for many reasons. He was approximately 20 years of age and had been (prior to Christmas 2001) under surveillance by the police for suspicion of lighting fires in the bush in the southern part of NSW in a town called Albury. After several months, he left Albury and went to a village north of Sydney named Dooralong. Here, he again came to the attention of the police for lighting fires in the bush. After a short period, he left Dooralong and went to stay with relatives in a village west of Sydney, within the Lapstone area of the Blue Mountains. It was Christmas when he came to Lapstone, and therefore midsummer in Australia. This particular summer had been very dry as a result of a long drought in the southern states, and high-strength hot winds were drying the bush areas across the state. Many bush fires were starting to cause fire authorities concern.[9]

During the short period between Christmas Eve 2001 and mid-January 2002, an unusually large number of bush fires raged across the state of NSW, stretching firefighting resources to the limit. Many fires were found to be deliberately lit, and evidence existed to show that serial arsonists were involved in many cases. New South Wales Fire Brigade (NSWFB) statistics indicated in excess of 1000 fires attended during this period—just those involving grass, bush, and vegetation and just those fires attended by NSWFB resources. Rural fire services, National Parks staff, and other services attended many more. As a result of this unusual activity and the threat that serial arsonists posed to the community, the NSW government formed a police strike force to investigate the fires and charge and prosecute any offenders caught through the

[9]In Australia, the term bush is used to refer to areas containing trees, scrub, high vegetation, shrubs, and large amounts of vegetation. In other countries, these would be referred to as forests, woodland, wildland, etc. In fact, all the areas outside the major cities are referred to as "the bush," meaning unsettled areas, not necessarily areas containing vegetation. It is from this term that Australians refer to fires in vegetation as bush fires.

mechanism of these investigations. The strike force was called "Tronto" and consisted of NSW police detectives, forensic specialists, and NSWFB and rural fire service members (Strike Force Tronto still exists today, reforming when the need arises because of serial arson activity).

Burgess had been a member of the rural fire service in Albury, a volunteer association formed to assist with bush fires in areas not covered by established fire services. When he came to Lapstone, he joined the local volunteer brigade. At this time, because of extreme weather and fire conditions, the local fire services were on high alert.

Being associated with Police Strike Force Tronto, I became aware of investigations into fires in the Lapstone area and an adjoining area named Glenbrook. When notified that police were conducting a surveillance operation on a suspect in the area of Lapstone and Glenbrook, I was particularly interested because of my knowledge of members of the local fire brigade. Burgess had become a person of interest because of the number of calls he had made to the fire brigade communications center, and apparently he had been making regular calls to report fires in the Lapstone area. Not only had they been able to recognize the phone number from Burgess' personal phone,[10] he also identified himself when calling. This information had been provided to investigating police.

Burgess's modus operandi (MO) was to light a fire in a remote area of the bush near his home. He would then call the fire brigade to report the fire's location. On arrival of the fire brigade, he would show them where the fire was and, on many occasions, he would depart and return soon after clothed in his volunteer firefighting uniform.

In *The Australian*, journalist Martin Chulov (2004) said the following about Burgess in a piece titled "Firebugs in Fire Engines":

> *Peter Cameron Burgess is a textbook example. In early 2002 Burgess was a 20-year-old loner with good parents and a penchant for action games. He told his lawyer his life had become mundane. He wanted to be just like the New York firemen who months before he had seen as the heroes of September 11. Later that year and in early 2002, he became the face of pyromania in regional NSW, an immature, attention-seeking drifter, who was single-handedly responsible for many of the fires that scorched the state—in Albury, the Blue Mountains, and the NSW Central Coast.*

John Laycock, Assistant Commissioner of Police in NSW and Commander of Strike Force Tronto, was quoted in Chulov's article as saying that Burgess's repeated offending was typical of many of the people Tronto had put before the courts: "The thing we have found is that they don't stop lighting fires until they are caught.... They become very serial in nature."

One of the "good" things about Burgess's MO was that, if true to predictions based on research on his type of behavior, he would only light a fire that would stay small and not get out of control (of course, this is in a perfect world, and fire is an unpredictable entity). His MO was to light a fire, call the fire brigade, greet them on arrival, and show them the location of the fire.

[10] Modern communications centers for police and fire brigades are fitted with technology that recognizes telephone numbers from calling handsets.

According to research, he was looking for attention and wished to be viewed as a hero to the community. Thus, if the fire got larger than he wanted, likely someone else would see it and report it. If this happened, the adulation that followed was not likely to be forthcoming, so he would remain vigilant at the fire scenes.

In 2002, Peter Cameron Burgess was charged and convicted of 26 counts of "maliciously damaging property by fire" and three counts of "false representation" (false alarm calls). He pleaded guilty to the charges and was sentenced to a two-year custodial sentence.[11]

Firefighters and Arson

Chulov (2004) discusses the multitude of fires throughout NSW that have been described by police as being deliberately lit by Rural Fire Service (RFS) volunteer firefighters, stating, "A NSW police investigation team estimates that close to one in five of the bushfires to have blazed across NSW during the past 3 years was lit by an RFS volunteer." Further discussion on the matter brought RFS Commissioner Phil Koperberg into the debate. Quoted on the matter, he stated, "I am not surprised by it, but I am disappointed. If you look at any large fire service anywhere on the planet you will find the same problem in the same way that large corporations attract embezzlers."

Chulov's (2004) article contains a list of arsonists and their crimes, including the following:

- Joshua Brook: Malicious damage to property by fire (18 counts).
- Petar Belobrajdic: Intentionally cause fire and be reckless as to its spread (16 counts). The result of this was community service and custodial bonds totaling 6½ years.
- Martin Melbourne: Malicious damage to property by fire (5 counts). Melbourne received a 10-month suspended sentence.
- David Mills: Intentionally cause fire and be reckless as to its spread (7 counts) and set fire to property (3 counts).
- Michael Richardson: Malicious damage to property by fire (8 counts). Richardson was sentenced to 400 hours of community service.

Throughout the world, this is a particular problem given the sheer number of volunteer firefighters, although fire services are attempting to eliminate this problem when recruiting new staff. A representative of the New South Wales Police Service (Laycock) notes that "police are working closely with the RFS, who are also very keen to eliminate these people from their ranks" but also remains doubtful about "whether the firebug vetting process can ever be foolproof" (Chulov, 2004, p. 12).

After the tragic September 11, 2001, terrorist attacks in the United States, the US government instituted a new department to oversee security throughout the country—the Department of Homeland Security. Because firefighters are usually the first emergency service workers to attend any terrorist event, a need arose for screening of those firefighters to

[11] Burgess was released from prison after serving his custodial sentence, moved away from NSW, and currently resides in another state of Australia.

ensure security of scenes. In a thesis on the screening of firefighter candidates, Pope (2006, p. 1) stated,

> *While billions of dollars are spent on buying new homeland security equipment to enhance response and training the workforce to use it, little time and attention has been paid to whom we are choosing to perform the mission.*

Pope considered that it was essential, and critical, for the success of the Homeland Security mission that the fire services in the United States had "a sound workforce, mentally and physically prepared to manage the new challenges they will confront" (Abstract).

A Special Case: John Leonard Orr

John Orr was a dedicated fire investigator and career fire officer, attached to the Glendale (California) Fire Department. He had wanted to be a police officer but had failed in his efforts to join.[12] Orr has become one of the most recognized serial arsonists of our time, even if only by his peers (and the communities of Southern California where he lit his fires). Orr's fires have also been the subject of much popular media coverage, including a documentary on the Odyssey Channel and a special program on US Court TV titled *The Firestarter—John Orr* (2004).

Throughout the 1980s and 1990s, Los Angeles was plagued by a series of fires that caused millions of dollars of damage and killed four people. The serial arsonist clearly knew what he was doing. Forensic investigators realized he was employing time-delay incendiary devices so he could flee before the fires erupted. From the January 1987 fires, investigator Marvin Casey recovered a single fingerprint and developed a theory that the fires were somehow connected to local firefighter conferences. The fingerprint, however, did not match any of the attendees. Two years later, another string of fires was set during another arson investigators' conference. A comparison of the attendance rosters at both conferences produced 10 common names, but no one matched the fingerprint from the previous fire.

In 1991, an arson task force was formed and began working with Casey. With advanced fingerprint technology, the forensic team finally identified the culprit and realized it was one of their own—John Orr, a fire captain and renowned arson investigator. A search of Orr's residence revealed videos of fires that Orr had set before the fire trucks arrived. Also found was a manuscript titled "Points of Origin," which provided details of many fires under investigation, including information only the culprit could know.

The manuscript found in Orr's home related the story (supposedly about a fictitious character) of a fire investigator turned arsonist who was lighting fires across an area of Southern California. Police and prosecutors used the content of the manuscript against Orr in his trial because it matched with uncanny accuracy the fires that were attributed to Orr.

He would set fires using an incendiary timing device (typically a cigarette with a rubber band wrapped around the end wedged in a matchbook) in stores during business hours. He would also set other fires in the same manner in an effort to draw firefighters to small fires. At the same

[12]John Orr's story is subject of a book, *Fire Lover,* by Joseph Wambaugh (2002).

time, another larger fire set in another area would not be attended as quickly, thereby becoming fully involved very quickly. This MO reached epic proportions at a fire set in an Ole's Home Improvement Store, which was set in a display area containing block foam products. The fire spread so quickly that four people were trapped inside, with all losing their lives despite the desperate efforts of attending firefighters. This fire was one of three set on that day. John Orr attended all three.

Ironically, the investigator who initiated the investigation into Orr's fires and assisted in his arrest and conviction was one of his former students. Orr was arrested, charged, and convicted of his crimes. He is currently serving four life terms in a California state penitentiary, with no possibility of parole. Orr was also charged with setting fires in brush (bush/forest) country around the same area and convicted of many of these fires, with one causing millions of dollars worth of damage when it destroyed 67 homes in the College Hills area. There are indications that after he was arrested, bush fires dropped by 90% in the area.

Conclusion

It is quite clear that arson is a huge problem, a universal problem that has no state or country boundaries, and serial arson is "a problem within a problem." The solution is a "team-based effort," as stated by the FBI, FEMA, and the UK-based Arson Control Forum. In addition to this is the necessity for continued research into the psychological aspects of arson and arsonist activity, which will support the physical investigation conducted by fire investigators and forensic examiners, the ongoing investigative efforts of detectives, and the prosecution of those offenders in the courtroom. The overall objective is to stop arson, and particularly serial arson activity, to provide a safer community.

Fire investigators in particular need to be ever vigilant in their fire scene inspections and ongoing investigations into fires occurring in their areas of responsibility. Patience and perseverance are the key factors where there is suspicion of arson, and especially when serial arson is suspected. Without the initial identification of serial activity by the fire investigator in the early stages of the offense, the offender will continue his or her activity until it leads to a serious fire or, worse, a fire fatality.

Taking an open-minded approach to all fire scenes cannot be overemphasized. The approach should be that each fire is a separate, unique incident; there should be no bias regarding the origin and cause of the event. Once the physical inspection has been conducted and evidence gathered, if evidence indicates a link between this and other fire events, then an effort should be made to pursue this avenue of investigation. It should be accepted that this single event could be part of a series of events, linked by physical evidence, methods of ignition, people, motives, and circumstance.

Acknowledgements

I thank the following police officers for their contributions to the case histories contained in this chapter: Detective Sgt. Thomas (NSW Police, Camden), Detective Senior Constable Parish (Sydney South Region Arson Unit, NSW Police), Detective Sgt. Horne (Hurstville Forensic

Services, NSW Police), Sgt. Green (NSW Police Strike Force Tronto), Inspector Jacobson (NSW Fire Brigades), and Inspector Powell (NSW Fire Brigades Fire Investigation Unit).

Questions

1. The study by Dickens et al. (2007) showed that there were significant gender differences in the fire-setting crimes of males and females. *True or false?*
2. List and briefly describe some of the reasons why fire services rely on an accurate appraisal of how and where a fire started.
3. NFPA 912 contains a basic methodology for fire investigation recognized in countries throughout the world. *True or false?*
4. The definition of arson depends heavily on the jurisdiction in which the crime occurs. *True or false?*
5. What about the case study on John Orr is of interest and why?

References

ACT government inquiry into the operational response to the (January 2003). bushfires. 2003. Available at <http://www.cmd.act.gov.au/publications/archived_publications/mcleod_inquiry> Accessed on 12.06.08.

Arson Control Forum (2003). Working Together: How to Set Up an Arson Task Force. Office of the Deputy Prime Minister: London

Arson Control Forum (2004). Annual Report. Office of the Deputy Prime Minister: London.

Arson Control Forum (2006). Annual Report. Office of the Deputy Prime Minister: London Available at <http://www.crimereduction.homeoffice.gov.uk/arson/arson8.htm> Accessed 16.06.08.

Arson Prevention Bureau (2004). Key facts—Key facts about arson. Available at <www.arsonpreventionbureau.org.uk> Accessed 12.06.08.

Australian Institute of Criminology (2008, March 6). *Bushfire arson bulletin (No. 51).* Canberra: Australian Institute of Criminology.

Bennett, W. W., & Hess, K. M. (2001). *Criminal Investigation* (6th ed.). Belmont, CA: Wadsworth.

Canter, D., & Almond, L. (2002). The burning issue: Research and strategies for reducing arson. Office of the Deputy Prime Minister: Arson Control Forum. London.

Chulov, M. (2004). August 23 Firebugs in fire engines. The Australian.

DeHaan, J. D. (2007). *Kirk's Fire Investigation* (6th ed.). Upper Saddle River, NJ: Prentice Hall.

Dempsey, J.S. (1996). An Introduction to Public and Private Investigations West: Minneapolis

Dickens, G., Sugarman, P., Ahmad, F., Edgar, S., Hofberg, K., & Tewari, S. (2007). Gender differences amongst adult arsonists at psychiatric assessment. *Medicine, Science and the Law, 47*(3), 233–238.

Edwards, M., & Grace, R. (2006). Analysing the offence locations and residential base of serial arsonists in New Zealand. *Australian Psychologist, 41*(3), 219–226.

Federal Emergency Management Agency, United States Fire Administration (1989). *Establishing an arson strike force (Report No. FA-88).* Emmitsburg, MD: Federal Emergency Management Agency, United States Fire Administration.

Jacobson, G., & Brogan, R. (2004). *Fire investigation training manual [electronic resource].* Sydney, Australia: Charles Sturt University.

The life and death of a serial arsonist. CN&R Newsreview, 2007. Available at <http://www.newsreview.com/chico> Accessed 12.06.08.

National Fire Protection Association 2008 NFPA 921: A Guide to Fire and Explosion Investigation. National Fire Protection Association: Battery March Park, Quincy, MA. Available at <http://www.nfpa.org>.

National Fire Protection Association (2009). *NFPA 1033: Standard for Professional Qualifications for Fire Investigator*. Battery March Park, Quincy, MA: National Fire Protection Association.

New South Wales Fire Brigades 2008 2006/07 Annual Report. New South Wales Government: Sydney.

Pope, C. M. (2006). *A model strategy and policy for screening firefighter candidates.* Monterey, CA: Naval Postgraduate School.

Prins, H. A. (1994). *Fire-raising: Its motivations and management.* New York: Routledge.

Saferstein, R. (2004). *Criminalistics: An Introduction to Forensic Science* (8th ed.). Upper Saddle River, NJ: Prentice Hall.

Sapp, A. D., Huff, T. G., Gary, G. P., & Icove, D. J. (2004). A motive based offender analysis of serial arsonists. Interfire. Available at <http://www.interfire.org/features/serialarsonists/Motive_based/cover.asp> Accessed 23.11.04.

Serial arsonist who hit 3 synagogues may have struck again. Haaretz Newspaper 2008. Available at <http://www.haaretz.com> Accessed 12.06.08.

The study of serial arsonists (2008). Interfire Online Available at <http://www.interfire.org>. Accessed 12.06.08.

Turvey, B. E. (2008). *Criminal Profiling: An Introduction to Behavioral Evidence Analysis* (3rd ed.). Burlington, MA: Academic Press.

Wambaugh, J. (2002). *Fire Lover*. New York, Harper-Collins.

18 Motivations: Offender and Victim Perspectives

Wayne Petherick and Grant Sinnamon

Introduction

Motivation comes from the Latin root *mot, to move,* along with the term emotion, and applies to any force "that activates and gives direction to behaviour" (Roeckelein, 2006, p. 406). It is perhaps for this reason that we may describe a movie, television show, novel, or story as moving when we associate with it on an emotional level.

Despite some slight variation among theorists, occasionally owing to a misunderstanding of exactly what motive refers to, there is relative uniformity as to what the motives that impel criminal behavior are. Most, for example, agree that there are anger needs that are fulfilled in many violent crimes, and many argue for profit needs that are usually fulfilled through property and other crime resulting in some kind of material gain. But not all agree on the balance, and most definitely not on the terminology, that should be used.

As the reader will be aware, this work is broken into two main parts. The first part dealt primarily with a form of crime analysis called criminal profiling, including history, the different types of profiling approaches, the theories on which they are based, case linkage, and staging, among others. The second part dealt with different types of serial crime including harassment and bullying, stalking, rape, murder, and arson. Given the format, the present chapter may seem a little misplaced, but there is a method to this madness.

Motive is one of the many different aspects of the offender's behavior that profiling can help to identify, understand, and therefore explain. It could be said then, that any discussion on motive would be best placed within the profiling section of this book. However, motive is also a core aspect of both victim and offender behavior, and in the case of the serial criminal (or victim), may indeed go a long way to explaining why any individual will find themselves in the same situations over and over again. Given this duality, the authors have decided that this chapter on motivation therefore best serves as a capstone to this book on serial crime rather than as a section in either of its two parts.

Motive: A Pathways Perspective

One of the most accepted theoretical aspects of motivation is its determinant heterogeneity and evanescence across the lifespan (see Maslow, 1942). That is, with rare exception, there are numerous and changing influences that shape the developing human, including the way our parents respond to us, the treatment of us by our siblings and friends, environmental impacts such as trauma and toxicities, and through our core biology, usually referred to as temperament. In short, any given person is a culmination of various biological and life experiences, and while certain factors may aggravate or mitigate the development of certain personality traits, no one influence, or combination of influences, represents an inflexible developmental outcome. This complex interplay is discussed by von Hentig (1948, p. 3) in his seminal work *The Criminal and His Victim:*

> *Crime is the product of many forces.... To stress the significance of hereditary traits is generally regarded as fatalistic; sound optimism and vital strength turn bravely to the social foundations of delinquency. We assume that constitutional factors are rigid and fixed.... But hereditary characters are not immutable, nor is group life exempt from hampering and immobilizing limitations. We must not forget, moreover, that what we call diathesis—predisposing traits or characters—are only reaction patterns waiting in readiness, dormant and unforeseen, to come into play by stimuli from outside.*

The purpose of this section is to provide a general theory of motivation, from which a theory of criminal motivation can be drawn (and in the second, a theory of victimization). Some aspects of development are predictable and proceed according to certain rules; other aspects are dynamic and experienced by some and not others. This would include physical and emotional abuse, exposure to drugs, and other factors that may contribute to later offending or victimization.

The following model provides an understanding of the various influences that each individual goes through from birth into adulthood, starting with emotional development, self-esteem formation, personality formation, and the formation of personality disorder (if relevant to a particular individual developmental pathway). From here, motivation will be discussed.

Emotion

Even though emotion is a daily or moment-by-moment occurrence (Strongman, 2003), it is a somewhat elusive concept to discuss, especially insofar as it is defined. Indeed, research for this chapter included two texts that, purportedly, provided an in-depth coverage of the *psychology of emotion*, yet both failed to provide even a rudimentary definition for that which was the subject of discussion. Perhaps this is because, as Yarrow (1979, p. 951) points out, "we have used the term emotion as if it had a self-evident validity, as if it were a concept so simple as not to require definition," or it may be that the vast array of emotions and their measurement do not lend themselves well to a unified pattern of study. Whatever the reason, it is necessary to understand them, at a fundamental level at least, to grasp personality and motivation formation because it is the core state that forms the basis of development of all other states to be discussed.

While an understanding of emotion must be provided, this chapter will not go into detail regarding the relevant brain structures, regulation, or the role of alcohol, drugs, and other factors involved in altering emotive processes.

As a testament to the complexity of the issue, Kleinginna and Kleinginna (1981, p. 355) studied 92 definitions and nine skeptical statements of emotions, and classified them according to 11 categories based on key phenomena and theoretical basis. From this review, they provide the following comprehensive definition:

> *Emotion is a complex set of interactions among subjective and objective factors, mediated by neural/hormonal systems, which can (a) give rise to affective experiences such as*

> *feelings of arousal, pleasure/displeasure; (b) generate cognitive processes such as emotionally relevant perceptual effects, appraisals, labeling processes; (c) activate widespread physiological adjustments to the arousing conditions; and (d) lead to behavior that is often, but not always, expressive, goal directed, and adaptive.*

An important consideration here is *introspection*, or the degree to which one can identify, understand, and appreciate one's emotional state. It is introspection that allows us to think deeply about how we feel, and to identify maladaptive negative emotions in an effort to change. Indeed, introspection is a precursor to change, and without it any attempt at change may be largely unsuccessful. This does not mean, however, that all introspection has emotional valence. Further, introspection is not an inherent part of being, and without clear and valid guidance during formative years, may be retarded in development, or may not develop at all. This is discussed by Branden (2001, p. 68), who states that:

> *Competence at introspecting and identifying one's own mental processes has to be acquired; it has to be learned. Most people have not formed the habit of seeking to account to themselves for the reasons of their beliefs, emotions, and desires; consequently, when they do attempt it, they frequently fail—and do not persevere.*

Literature supports the notion that emotions serve a foundational purpose, particularly in paving the way for personality (Cohen, 2008, p. 478):

> *The last decade has been a very fertile one for increasing convergence on models of personality development, arising in particular from evolving conceptions of the origins and role of personality. These newer models present personality as arising from the combination of basic and universal emotions and emotion-related experiences.... Six emotions are considered to be basic because they are unlearned and universal (although varying in strength across individuals) and "preempt consciousness". These are interest, joy/happiness, sadness, anger, disgust, and fear. Interest and joy/happiness are functional at birth and the others are functional within the first 2 years.*

Emotions are powerful motivators in and of themselves, with the ability to provoke further emotional responses or stimulate biological processes promoting physical activity (the affective state of fear stimulates various biological processes, producing the catecholamine epinephrine [adrenaline] and the neurotransmitter norepinephrine [noradrenaline]). They are also critical in the development and formation of self-esteem, as the emotional condition dictates how we feel about ourselves and, by extension, self efficacy, the belief we have about our own abilities.

Self-Esteem

There are both implicit and explicit links between emotion and self-esteem, which are likely far less unidirectional than one might infer from the way this model is presented. While we cannot have "how I feel about me" without "how I feel," it is possible that once we have developed a foundational understanding of our place and position relevant to internal and external factors (known as self-schemas), that this perception can impact and shape our emotions. That is to say that this is a bidirectional relationship in which our emotional experiences help shape our self-esteem and, once formed, our self-esteem becomes a determinant of our emotional bias (this can be seen in the relationship between self-esteem and self efficacy, where a success in a behavioral event bolsters our self efficacy, in turn bolstering our self-esteem). From a developmental perspective, however, we must understand that emotions must precede our feeling of self, even though in later life the relationship is somewhat more complex. The nature and power of self-esteem is perhaps best captured by Branden (2001, p. 109) in the following:

> *There is no value-judgement more important to man—no factor more decisive in his psychological development and motivation—than the estimate he passes on himself.*
>
> *This estimate is ordinarily experienced by him, not in the form of a conscious, verbalized judgment, but in the form of a feeling, a feeling that can be hard to isolate and identify because he experiences it constantly: it is part of every other feeling, it is involved in his every emotional response.*
>
> *An emotion is the product of an evaluation; it reflects an appraisal of the beneficial or harmful relationship of some aspect of reality to oneself...*
>
> *The nature of his self-evaluation has profound effects on a man's thinking process, emotions, desires, values, and goals. It is the single most significant key to his behavior. To understand a man psychologically, one must understand the nature and degree of self-esteem, and the standards by which he judges himself.*

Self-esteem could be described, in its most basic form, as how we feel about ourselves. It is entirely a mental component of being, though there are various behavioral expressions that can be used to identify the level of self-esteem possessed by an individual. These include, among others, attention seeking, sexual promiscuity, and addictive or destructive behaviors. However, this base definition may be far too simplistic for what is, in reality, a very complex phenomenon, the impact of which is considerable, dynamic, and occurs over the life course.

Harter (1999) argues that self-esteem is the culmination of the personal evaluation of our overall worth as an individual. In this definition then, self-esteem may be more than simply what we feel about ourselves; it may also be an evaluation of ourselves based on perceptions of our position relative to others. In addition, self-esteem also includes the self-schemas and beliefs we hold about ourselves, the place we hold (or believe we hold), and perceptions of our ability to operate in our environment (Livesly, Jang & Vernon, 1998). The latter may also be referred to as self efficacy, which Resnick (2008) defines as a judgment of capabilities that allows us to organize and execute courses of action.

The role self-esteem plays in personality and motivation formation is widely discussed and debated in the literature, as are its various forms. Ostrowsky (2010) provides a useful overview on whether low or high self-esteem leads to criminal behavior, suggesting low self-esteem may lead to violence when the individuals are protecting themselves from feelings of inadequacy, or where they want to make themselves feel powerful and omnipotent. It is argued that high self-esteem, on the other hand, may lead to violence when a narcissistically inflated view of the self creates conflict with another who challenges that viewpoint. Donnellan, Trzesniewski, Robins, Moffitt, and Caspi (2005) explored the link between self-esteem, aggression, antisocial behavior, and delinquency. This study found that low self-esteem was consistently correlated with externalizing problems (that may lead to antisocial behavior) and aggression.

Presenting self-esteem as either high or low may be over simplifying the way in which beliefs about the self are manifest in the personality. A low self-esteem may present as high, where superficial grandiosity masks deep feelings of inferiority (Bosson, Lakey, Campbell, Zeigler-Hill, Jordan & Kernis, 2008). This is referred to as the "mask model" of narcissism. In other circumstances, high self-esteem may be both an accurate representation of the emotional state of the individual (this is referred to as secure self-esteem; see Zeigler-Hill, 2006), or it may be a gross distortion of the emotional state, in a situation whereby self-esteem is manifestly high but susceptible to insult (this is referred to as fragile self-esteem; see Zeigler-Hill, 2006).

In addition to levels of self-esteem, there are also temporal dimensions to consider, with Crocker and Park (2006) stating that self-esteem can be state or trait based. State-based self-esteem is transient or episodic and fluctuates according to circumstance. State-based self-esteem may be influenced, in a positive or negative way, by internal processes such as low serotonin levels (see Sylvester, 1997) or external factors such as conflict, criticism, praise, or the receipt of good fortune. In contrast, trait-based self-esteem is more stable and enduring and relates to the base level of self-worth that underpins self-schemas. Trait-based self-esteem is considered to be at the core of psychological well-being and resilience. While individuals with a good (or healthy) trait-based self-esteem may suffer episodic blows, they are generally able to "bounce back" from such trauma because they recognize that these slights do not generally represent who they are, or diminish their overall self-worth. In short, they can see past any short-term suffrage and appreciate the bigger picture. It is trait-based self-esteem that has been the primary focus of the research literature (Crocker & Park, 2006).

The importance of self-esteem is more than simply how an individual feels. It plays a significant role in offending and victimization. Self-esteem is a central factor in many of the motivations discussed later in this chapter, and may indeed be instructive in how these motivations form. For example, paranoia proneness, a central feature of the personality aberration narcissism, is common in those with low self-esteem (Warman, Lysaker, Luedtke & Martin, 2010), also common in both Power Assertive and Anger Retaliatory motives.

Personality

The general area of research referred to as personality theory is as plagued by definition and interpretation as the self-esteem research discussed previously. This is perhaps because personaligy often defies measurement and cannot always be directly observed. On this issue, Rockelein (2006, p. 468) suggests:

> *The definition of the term personality itself seems to be so resistant to a consensual-agreement statement, and so broad in usage, that most psychology textbooks (other than*

> *textbooks on personality theories) use it strategically as the title of a chapter and then expound on it without incurring any of the definitional or positivistic responsibilities attached to it.*

Millon, Grossman, Millon, Meagher, and Ramnath (2004, p. 2) discuss the etiology of the term and provide some brief discussion of its nature:

> *The word personality is derived from the Latin term persona, originally representing the theatrical mask used by ancient dramatic players. As a mask assumed by an actor, persona suggests a pretence of appearance, that is, the possession of traits other than those that actually characterize the individual behind the mask. Over time, the term persona lost its connotation of pretence and illusion and began to represent not the mask, but the person's observable or explicit features.*

Because the personality develops not only in line with temperamental factors, but also in line with a number of other situational and experiential factors, it is argued herein that personality largely develops, with temperament as a base or coping mechanism to our environment. This is supported by Rothbart (2007, p. 207), who notes:

> *Concepts of temperament are necessary to understand the origins of personality development. Temperament describes the initial state from which personality develops and links individual differences in behavior to underlying neural networks. Temperament and experience together "grow" a personality, which will include the child's developing cognitions about self, others, and the physical and social world, as well as his or her values, attitudes, and coping strategies.*

And again by Cohen (2008, p. 479), on the interplay of factors that bring about personality differences:

> *Over time, the basic positive and negative emotions are gradually replaced by emotional schemas in which cognitive frames, appraisals, and attributions develop out of the individual's emotional experience and replace the basic emotions as predominant motivators. These "motivators" may be seen as temperament in early childhood, in a period in which it may be normative that biological differences may have a dominant influence. With increasing age, the schemas combine these emotional states in relatively common/correlated patterns but more-or-less uniquely across individuals, based on genetic and experiential combinations. Thus, personality differences develop from combinations of individual genetic-based differences in the relative strength of these emotions and life experiences that shape the nature of the individual's schema regarding self, others, and the world they live in.*

In instances where there is significant trauma, with or without underlying biological roots, personality aberrations surface. These tend toward extremes of "normal" personality characteristics, and in some cases are so extreme the individual may be diagnosed as suffering from a personality disorder.

Personality Disorder

Given the current debate surrounding personality disorder inclusions and exclusions in the next edition of the Diagnostic and Statistical Manual of Mental Disorder (DSM; 5th edition), this work will draw only on that information in the fourth edition without getting too heavily involved in speculation of what may or may not survive the next incarnation. In short, there is much debate about what might and might not be included, without any concrete knowledge of this until the publication committee makes its final decision.

All individuals have "quirks" of personality. For some, humor is a coping mechanism developed to help overcome feelings of anxiety or depression, while a natural caution of strangers or strange situations may have an evolutionary purpose helping protect our physical or psychological being. Others still have an enviable level of confidence in their abilities, but at what point does this confidence become grandiosity that may be representative of a narcissist personality?

Personality disorders are coded in the DSM-IV-TR as Axis II disorders, which represent deeply rooted problems that are difficult to treat or modify (American Psychiatric Association, 2000; Gertzfeld, 2006). In answer to the earlier question as to where personality stops and personality disorder starts, it may be where disorders of the personality produce features that are maladaptive, inflexible, and cause adjustment problems or personal distress (Gertzfeld, 2006; Oltmanns & Emery, 2011). The Axis II personality disorder classifications are broken down into three clusters. The first, Cluster A, includes Paranoid, Schizotypal, and Schizoid, with individuals being viewed as odd or eccentric. The second, Cluster B, includes those conditions where the individual is seen as being dramatic, emotional, or erratic, and includes Antisocial, Borderline, Histrionic, and Narcissistic. The final cluster, Cluster C, includes those who are often anxious or fearful. Avoidant, Dependent, and Obsessesive-Compulsive disorders fall under this category (American Psychiatric Association, 2000).

Motivation

Every individual, including criminals and victims, will have motives for the entire range of their behavior. These motives may not make sense at the time or be clearly and easily identifiable and inferable. The task, whether profiling or dealing with serial crime, is to understand the theoretical basis of a variety of motivations, know how they manifest at a crime scene and in behavior, and be able to convey this information to any audience, informed or not. This may sound simple, but given the vast array of influences on motive, and the similarly vast array of confounds at the crime scene and in their inference, it is often difficult, or in some cases impossible, to meaningfully infer their presence and influence.

The determination of motive is not absolute. A great many variables come into play in any given situation, such as offender state of mind, victim behavior and response, environmental variables, physical determinants (such as trauma and neurobiology), and alcohol and other drugs as some examples. All of these have the potential to impact on the analysis and interpretation of the ascribed motive. To complicate matters, motives are usually inferred from crime scene evidence, victim and offender behavior, or a confession from the criminal, which may be inherently unreliable because a confession may be self-serving, or there may be little appreciation of the cognitive milieu that led to the offense.

As a result, an important consideration in the determination of motive is *insight*, which refers to the ability of an individual to identify and understand the true nature of a situation. As with other aspects of functioning, insight is multifaceted and can operate on a number of levels based on the degree of appreciation individuals have regarding their particular circumstances. Individuals who rate high on insight may understand both the emotional quality of their behavior and the circumstances that placed them within a given situation. Another individual who rates low on insight may fail to comprehend either the emotional quality of his or her behavior or the circumstances. Another still may fail to comprehend the circumstances, but not understand his or her emotional origins. An important aspect of insight is introspection, discussed previously.

Insight is perhaps one of the greatest determinants then as to whether an individual will become a serial criminal. This is discussed in a therapeutic context by Grant (2001, p. 8):

> *The interest and ability to understand the causes and meanings of one's behavior, thoughts, and feelings are thought to be important variables mediating the outcome of directed, purposeful change.... Furthermore, an understanding of one's behavior, thoughts, and feelings is important in nontherapeutic domains of change because purposeful directed behavior change per se is facilitated by insight.*

While it is not the job of the analyst to understand the deep and historical roots of behavior, it is important to consider insight as it applies to confessions or descriptions provided by offenders as they may not only be self-serving, they may also be only a partial or a completely misunderstood accounting of actions. Insight therefore becomes important when unraveling the often complex reckoning of the crime as provided by the victim or the offender.

Trauma

We each experience trauma as a routine part of life, either as psychological blows or as actual physical harm. These traumas can range from the slight (being told that a joke wasn't that funny), to the extreme (a motor vehicle crash, workplace accident, or the death of a loved one). All of these experiences have the potential to impact on motivation, and on subsequent behavior and cognition. For some, emotional trauma may be more significant and enduring than physical trauma, and so caution must be exercised when attaching weight or significance to the nature of the trauma-inducing event itself.

One set of definitions for trauma is (Merriam-Webster, 2011):

- **a.** an injury (as a wound) to the living tissue caused by an extrinsic agent.
- **b.** a disordered psychic or behavioral state resulting from severe mental or emotional stress or physical injury.
- **c.** an emotional upset.

These aspects of trauma are more than suited to our purposes here, therefore an aggregate of this definition will be employed for this chapter. Here trauma will be defined as "any physical or psychological insult or injury that effects emotional or behavioral inhibition or exhibition."

Mayou & Farmer (2002, p. 426) provide this perspective:

> *Minor trauma is a part of everyday life, and for most people these injuries are of only transient importance, but some have psychiatric and social implications. Most people experience major trauma at some time in their lives.*
>
> *Psychological, behavioral, and social factors are all relevant to the subjective intensity of physical symptoms and their consequences for work, leisure, and family life. As a result, disability may become greater than might be expected from the severity of the physical injuries.*
>
> *Psychological and interpersonal factors also contribute to the cause of trauma, and clinicians should be alert to these and their implications for treatment.*

This model is similar to that of Ronel (2011, p. 1210), who describes the *criminal spin*, which is:

> *An event or set of events that present a process of escalation in criminal behavior accompanied by a criminal cycle of thinking or corresponding emotions. We can discern a spin when there is a sudden, rapid, or gradual acceleration of behavior that is considered criminal. The process operates as an almost inevitable chain of events, one linked to the next, in the generation of criminal behavior, which continually intensifies.*

In summary, the role of trauma must be moderated according to its nature and severity, as well as internal and external moderating and mediating factors such as temperament, emotional state, coping strategies, insight, temperament, or any other contributing factors.

The Motivational Typologies

Typologies are groupings of like objects on the basis of shared characteristics. They are commonly used within the social sciences to take large groups of individuals and break them down into more discrete categories for the purpose of understanding. A typology can be based on almost any measure, such as a psychometric typology of child abusers (Beech, 1998), typologies of stalkers (Wright, Burgess, Laszlo, McCrary & Douglas, 1996; Mullen, Pathé & Purcell, 2009), and an assessment and intervention typology among victims of stalkers (Roberts & Dziegielewski, 1996), among others.

Most criminological typologies are crime or situation specific, and there are few if any so-called "unified theories" that can explain all instances of criminal behavior. This section will provide an overview of several common typologies, including their theoretical basis, intended purpose, and the overlap.

Nicholas Groth, a clinical psychologist who worked in sex offender programs in Connecticut and Massachusetts, published a seminal work titled *Men Who Rape* in 1979, which was a culmination of experiences with over 500 offenders (see Groth, 1979). Here, Groth presented the idea that rape has three main components: power, anger, and sadism. In a Power offense, sexuality is an expression of conquest, while in Anger rape sexuality is a hostile act. In Sadistic rape, anger and sexuality become fused and the offender receives sexual gratification from pain and suffering.

Prior to his 1979 publication, Groth collaborated with Ann Burgess and Lynda Holmstrom in 1977 to research 133 convicted rapists, with another sample of 146 [alleged] rape victims who presented to a Boston hospital with the claim that they had been raped. This typology is premised on the notion that there are identifiable themes that can indicate the motive behind the crime (Groth, Burgess & Holmstrom, 1977, p. 1240):

> *One of the most basic observations one can make about rapists is that they are not alike. Similar acts are performed for different reasons or different acts serve similar purposes. Our clinical experience with convicted offenders and with victims of reported sexual assault has shown that in all cases of forcible rape three components are present: power, anger, and sexuality. The hierarchy and interrelationships among these three factors, together with the relative intensity with which each is expressed and the variety of ways in which each is expressed, may vary, but there is sufficient clustering to indicate distinguishable patterns of rape.*

In this publication, Groth and colleagues suggested a more detailed typology than that which appeared in *Men Who Rape*. Here, there are two general axes, each with two subtypes. The first axis, Power, refers to offenders who seek "power and control over his victim by means of a weapon, physical force, or threat of bodily harm" (Groth, Burgess & Holmstrom, 1977, p. 1240). Power has two further subtypes: In Power Reassurance rapes, the offense is an effort to resolve doubts about his masculinity and adequacy. This offender wants to put the victim in a subjugated role where she cannot refuse or reject him. A Power Assertive offender regards rape as "an expression of his virility and mastery and dominance" (Groth, Burgess & Holmstrom, 1977, p. 1240). This offender also feels inadequate, but he feels entitled to take what he wants, or that the rape is a way of keeping women in line.

In Anger Rape, the offender "experiences anger, rage, contempt, and hatred for his victim by beating her, sexually assaulting her, and forcing her to perform or submit to additional degrading acts" (Groth, Burgess & Holmstrom, 1977, p. 1241). The Anger type also has two subtypes. The first is Anger Retaliatory where rape is an expression of hostility and rage held toward women. The primary motivation here is revenge. The second subtype is Anger Excitation, where the offender "finds pleasure, thrills, and excitation in the suffering of his victim. He is a sadist and his aim is to punish, hurt, and torture his victim. His aggression is eroticised" (Groth, Burgess & Holmstrom, 1977, p. 1242).

While there are discrete categories within this classification, the authors suggest that sexuality is used to express issues of power and anger, and that all three exist to varying degrees within any one case. The motive therefore will be determined by the degree to which each coexists.

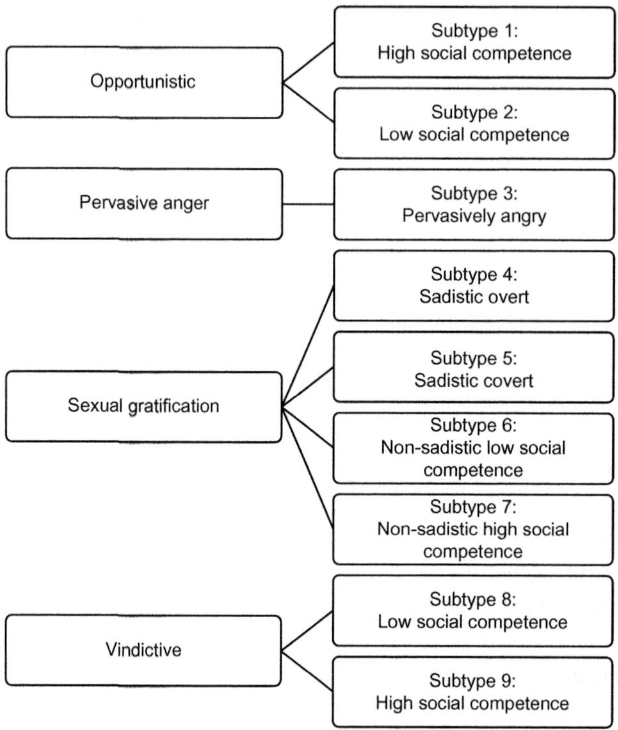

FIGURE 18.1 Subtypes of rapists.

The Massachusetts Treatment Center, Rapist Typology Version 3 (MTC: R3) is based loosely on the Groth typology, in that Groth's provided the same four types that were the basis of the MTC: R1 (Knight, Warren, Reboussin & Soley, 1998), with further revision taking place up to the current version. This typology was developed based on data drawn from three samples: the first of 116 of repeat rapists from the Behavioral Sciences Unit (BSU) of the FBI, a second smaller sample of 25 previously gathered rapists from the BSU, and a third sample of 254 rapists from the MTC itself.

This research also found four types of rapist: Opportunity, Pervasive Anger, Sexual Gratification, and Vindictiveness. As with Groth, Burgess, and Holmstrom (1977), there are subtypes, represented in Figure 18.1.

For the Opportunistic types (Subtypes 1 and 2), the crimes are impulsive, predatory acts, controlled by situational and contextual factors (victim availability, etc.) rather than sexual fantasy or aggression (unless otherwise stated, the information drawn for this section is from Knight, Warren, Rebousin & Soley, 1998). This division is based on the level of social competence and the developmental stage at which their impulsivity manifested.

For the Pervasively Angry type (Subtype 3), the primary motivation is a generalized and nonspecific aggression that invades all areas of the offender's life. These Pervasively Angry offenders usually have long histories of antisocial behavior of which rape is just one type, and there are usually high levels of expressive aggression (expressive aggression is a response to situations that induce anger such as insults, assaults, or failures, where the goal is to make the victim suffer; see Salfati, 2000).

In the MTC: R3, there are four types (Subtypes 4, 5, 6, and 7) where the motivation is deemed to be sexual, that is, the offender has some form of sexual preoccupation. These can be either Sadistic (Subtypes 4 and 5) or Non-sadistic (Subtypes 6 and 7). In Subtypes 4 and 5 there is a fusion of sexual and aggressive feelings; in Subtypes 6 and 7, the preoccupation is characterized by dominance needs, or by feelings of inadequacy. The Sadistic types are divided by whether their violent fantasies are physically expressed (the Overt type) or exist as fantasies only (the Muted type). The Non-sadistic types are distinguished on the basis of their social competence, with Subtype 6 being low and Subtype 7 being high.

The final type is known as Vindictive, and like their Non-sadistic counterparts, they are distinguished on the basis of their social competence (being either low or moderate, respectively). This offender is a misogynist, and their attacks are intended to be both physically harmful and humiliating.

While these typologies relate specifically to sexual assault, Mullen, Pathé, and Purcell (1999, 2009) present a typology that is similar on many fronts to both the previous types and that of Hazelwood (2009), presented later. The original study was based on 145 stalkers referred for forensic treatment. Five types were identified: Rejected, Intimacy Seeking, Incompetent, Resentful, and Predatory.

In Rejected stalking, "the rejected partner begins to stalk after their partner has attempted to end the relationship, or indicated that they intend to end the relationship" (Mullen, Pathé & Purcell, 2009, p. 69). The aim of the stalker is to either take revenge for the rejection or to try to reestablish the relationship. In Resentful stalking, the initial motivation is retribution, and the harassment is designed to frighten and harass the victim. This type may be likely to persist because of the sense of satisfaction that comes about from the power and control the stalker feels over the victim (Mullen, Pathé & Purcell, 2009, p. 76).

Intimacy Seekers and Incompetent Suitors "in combination, account for the majority of stranger stalkers" (Mullen, Pathé & Purcell, 2009, p. 82). Both types are attempting to establish a relationship with the target of their unwanted affectations, though neither necessarily knows how to go about it legitimately. The authors note that, while there are marked similarities in these two types, there are sufficient differences to warrant separate identification.

The final type, the Predatory stalker, was the least in number in Mullen, Pathé, Purcell, and Stuart (1999). This type is usually preparing for a sexual attack and is more likely to have paraphilias and previous criminal histories, usually for sexual offenses (Mullen, Pathé & Purcell, 2009). It may be said that, though the least in number, this type is among the most dangerous, as they are "more likely to assault their victims than all other categories of stalker, except the Rejected" (p. 111).

While not purporting to be a typology as such, Gudjonsson and Sigurdsson (2004) examined the relationship between criminal motivation and personality. They used a self-designed Offending Motivation Questionnaire (OMQ), with a factor analysis revealing four motivational factors for offending (Compliance, Provocation, Financial, and Excitement, though a fifth was added to include those wherein the offender had not considered the consequences of their actions), for offenses ranging from traffic and theft to violence and criminal damage. The five types and their factor loadings are (Gudjonsson & Sigurdsson, 2004, p. 75):

> *Compliance: Seven items had salient loadings on this factor. This reflects the offense being committed in order to please a peer or because the person felt pressured into it by another person.*
>
> *Provocation: Four items loaded on this factor. The highest loadings involved taking revenge, losing control and self-defense.*
>
> *Financial: Three items loaded saliently on this factor and it reflects a financial or a monetary need as the explanation for the offense.*
>
> *Excitement: Four items loaded saliently on this factor. Here the motive was for excitement or fun.*
>
> *Consequences: Three items loaded on this factor. This factor relates to the extent to which the participant failed to consider the consequences of his or her actions.*

It should be noted that while there is significant concordance between some of these factors and other typologies throughout this chapter, some of these "types" are not related to motive at all but are instead aligned more with contextual offense elements. For example, feeling pressured into something is not a motive, but the psychological backdrop that leads someone to capitulate to pressure may well be. Also, failing to consider the consequences of one's actions is not a motive, but consideration of the factors that lead up to that could well be (being so angry that you didn't have time to stop and think).

These typologies are among the most common for their intended purposes, and this section will now move on to that presented by Hazelwood (2009), which represents the first significant adaptation to the original typology developed by Groth, Burgess, and Holmstrom (1977) and Groth (1979), and is presented in *Practical Aspects of Rape Investigation*. While Hazelwood (2009, p. 103) suggests "he has found these types to be accurate in describing more than 4,000 rape cases on which he has consulted," it has been suggested that they are good general motivational typologies than can describe the vast majority of criminal behavior (this position was advanced for the first time by Turvey in 1999). This will be the position taken herein, by using the Hazelwood adaptation as a base, with some minor modification. Obviously, as the following discussion is taken from a work on rape, some reference as follows will be made to behaviors common in sexual assault, but the reader is cautioned to remember that these types will also apply thematically in a more general sense.

Unless otherwise stated, all of the following information is taken from Hazelwood (2009).

Power Reassurance

This offender is driven by a relational fantasy and feels that the victim is special because of it. There is no intent to punish or degrade, and they are the least likely to physically harm their victim since this would shatter the illusion that the relationship was somehow wanted or consensual. The attack is intended to restore diminishing feelings of masculinity, and power is achieved by taking power away from the victim.

Victim selection may be based on geographic location, and this type of offender may target several victims in advance, on the chance that attacks are not, for one reason or another, successful. The Reassurance-Oriented offender is more likely to target vulnerable victim types in an effort to increase the chance of success of the attack. This could include those who are alone, who are with small children, or the elderly. Reassurance-Oriented offenders are likely to apologize for the attack, and may even try to contact the victim at a later point in time to arrange another "date."

Power Assertive

The core emotional mechanisms that underlie Reassurance and Assertive behavior are largely the same: Both offenders feel inadequate and both seek affirmation about their masculinity and worth. The Reassurance-Oriented offender tries to establish a relationship with the victim, and in this way hopes to shore up their low self-worth. In short, if someone else can see them as worthwhile, then they may be able to view themselves as worthwhile also. Not so with the Assertive offender.

Also known as Entitlement, these offenders try to make themselves feel better by making others feel bad. They rape, assault, or stalk to assert their dominance and masculinity. They take simply because they can, because they see it as their right or prerogative. It is of no consequence to this offender whether the victims are hurt; they are merely an object to be used for gratification.

While their Reassurance counterpart may show empathy for the victims, inquiring about their welfare, comfort, or feelings, the Assertive offender is not concerned about the victim's welfare in any form. Moderate to excessive force may be used in controlling the victim, and the attacks will occur at any time and location that is convenient and safe. Clothing may be ripped and torn, and sexual dysfunction may be present.

Anger Retaliatory

Less common, but more violent (Hazelwood, 2009), the Retaliatory offender is striking out against a victim or victim population for wrongs that have either occurred or that they believe have occurred against them. In sexually based offenses, sex is the vehicle through which the offender punishes the victim (Groth, Burgess & Holmstrom, 1977). It is not necessarily a motive in itself (indeed, the only classification in which sex is the primary goal is that of Opportunistic, discussed subsequently), but is simply a tool employed against a victim in a punishing way. The Retaliatory rapist does not want to include the victim or want their input. They will use excessive levels of force, even beyond that needed to gain control over a victim, or that required to get compliance.

The victim may be immediately subdued on encounter, depriving them of any ability to defend themselves. As this type of attack usually has a cathartic component, they tend to be brief in duration, and will last only as long as the negative emotional energy that prompted it.

However, because of this, offenders may be prone to repeat whenever they feel angry again. These attacks can occur at any time and place, as dictated by the offender's anger at a given point.

Offenders hate the target (individual or group) against whom the offense is committed and will hold them accountable for real wrongs, or misplace their aggression as would happen in the case of a perceived wrong. The main difference between this type and the Pervasive type is the focus of the anger: In Pervasive offenses there is no individual or target group and the offender is generally angry about their lot in life. In the Retaliatory type, the focus is an individual or a group that has either done something wrong or that the offender believes has done something wrong. In stranger cases, this may make the determination of motive difficult.

Pervasively Angry

While not appearing in the original Groth (1979), Groth, Burgess, and Holmstrom (1997), or Hazelwood (2009) typologies, the introduction of a Pervasively Angry type as presented in the MTC: R3 makes intuitive sense. The rationale for including this type here is that not all anger-related offenses are the result of revenge or the offender feeling the need to retaliate for real or imagined wrongs.

For the Pervasively Angry type, the offense is the manifestation of anger not directed at a specific target, group, or institution, but results from cumulative life stresses in any or all aspects of being. This anger is global and undifferentiated. The victims of this type of crime have done no more wrong than the target of a stray bullet: They were simply at the wrong place, at the wrong time.

Gang and Opportunistic

Hazelwood (2009) introduced the previous types to explain those contexts in which individuals act in concert with others, or where the sexual offense is pursuant to another crime, such as burglary. The Opportunistic type will not be discussed at further length; suffice to say that these offenses occur in concert with another crime. As such, opportunity is a contextual element only.

The classification of Gang is not in itself a motive but rather a label used for a group, one that usually has some unified purpose in action. Some gangs are involved in drug distribution, loan sharking, money laundering, other standover tactics, or in more a more diffuse array of criminal activity.

In any given group, there will be a variety of reasons for membership that run the full gamut of those discussed in this section. For example, an individual who has low self-esteem and a subsequent need to belong (i.e., is Reassurance Oriented) may seek out a gang in order to provide emotional support that is lacking in other aspects of his or her life (Alleyne & Wood, 2010); another may seek out membership because the gang itself espouses a philosophy that is concordant with their own (such as may be seen in hate groups that peddle anti-Semitic and "white power" agendas); while another still may be Pervasively Angry, and use the group as a platform to legitimize behavior that is more acceptable within a group where antisocial behavior is more normative (research has found that antisocial attitudes are predictive of gang membership, see Egan & Beadman, 2011). In other instances yet, a person may become a gang member for the monetary gains that may arise from the associated illegal activities of the group. This may be more of an issue in countries or jurisdictions with a lower general socioeconomic profile (61% of respondents in a survey in Nigeria report coming from a below-subsistence level, with another 35% respond that they were just managing; see Salaam, 2011). In short, each member will have his or her own motivation for joining a gang and in continuing its mission.

Profit

The motivational label of Profit may be a little misleading as it implies some form of tangible increase in financial situation. This most certainly will not be the case with many offenders who are doing their level best simply to get by. This may be especially true in the case of the drug-addicted offender who steals what is necessary to operate at a level of subsistence that could hardly be described as opulent. Moreover, profit also implies that the offense may yield actual cash. Considering again the case of the drug-addicted offender, goods are likely to be stolen, exchanged for actual money, which is then passed along to a dealer or intermediary for more drugs. Possession of the actual money will be largely fleeting, and most certainly will not imply cash-on-hand at any given moment.

Perhaps a more suitable descriptor would be Materialism, more accurately reflecting the attempt to secure materials, either for continued possession or for sale to redeem cash for a variety of purposes.

The Victim's Perspective

The previous section provided an overview of the pathways model of emotions, self-esteem, personality, and motivations and discussed this in the context of offending behavior. The motivational typologies of Groth (1979), Groth, Burgess, and Holmstrom (1977), and Hazelwood (2009) were presented as a base to understand the motivation behind the offense of rape, and in other crimes in a more general sense.

While the previous discussion related to offender behavior, it should be noted that the presented typologies are actually a fitting representation of general motivational dynamics, and as such they apply not only equally to victims but also as descriptors of more common or everyday behaviors. This is because criminals (and victims) experience the same depth and breadth of emotions and needs as all others, and so it should not be surprising that their behavior serves many of the same needs. It is usually in the execution of these behaviors and the choices they make that they differ.

The victim's role in the criminal event cannot be understated, and without the ability to account for their emotions, actions, and the subsequent consequences, any understanding of the crime will be incomplete. Along with the offender and the location of the crime, the victim constitutes at the least a mathematical proportion and a large part of the human element of the offense. As stated by von Hentig (1948, p. 383), "crime, for the most part, is injury inflicted on another person. Setting aside felonies directed against fictitious victims, the state, order, health, and so forth, there are always two partners: the perpetrator and the victim."

Although the pendulum has swung the other way from earlier attempts to understand the crime by looking only at the offender, more attention is being paid to victims and their characteristics. There are, however, still few attempts to develop a unified theory of victim motivation, though there are a number of attempts at providing typologies in specific domains of victimization. These include sexual harassment (Holcomb, 2008), the nonreporting of sexual offenses (Weiss, 2011), domestic violence (Johnson, 2008), and relationship subtypes among victims of stalking (Pathé, Mullen & Purcell, 2001).

This next section will present a view of motivation from the perspective of the victim through the offender motivation typology, with slight modification. This typology can be applied to victim behavior in all crimes and contexts, with a few exceptions. It can even be used to understand behavior of those who have not yet suffered harm or loss. As the victim constitutes part of the criminal event, it is necessary to understand the evolution and presentation of any behavior that puts someone in harm's way.

Theoretical Background

In *The Criminal and His Victim*, von Hentig (1948) proposes two broad classifications for victims. The first, general classes of victims, is based largely on demographic and ethnographic features, while the second, psychological types, is based on mental or emotional factors that contribute toward victimization. The victim types discussed are:

- *The Young*: Younger individuals are usually weaker in terms of their physical and social standing, and are thus most likely to be victims of attack. This period of life is seen to be the most dangerous period of life, and survival is usually ensured by older, protective parties such as parents.
- *The Female*: The female, like the young, are seen to be the weaker of the species, and so laws relating to chastity and the family are "meant to be a protective device against the superior physical force or the neglect of the male" (p. 407).
- *The Old*: The aged are handicapped in many ways, including a decrease in physical capacity as well as the mental infirmity that may accompany an increase in years.
- *The Mentally Defective and Other Mentally Deranged*: This group includes the feebleminded, the insane, drug addicts, and alcoholics. They lack the ability to detect warning signs, and thus make good victims.
- *Immigrants, Minorities, Dull Normals*: There is an inherent disadvantage to being an immigrant, a minority, or a "dull normal," with the handicap extending from everyday social life into conflicts.

From these general classes, von Hentig proposed broad psychological types:

- *The Depressed*: This group includes those who are afflicted with any of the psychoses, and the clinical picture can be both chronic or temporary.
- *The Acquisitive*: This group includes all those who are seeking to acquire wealth or goods, who are therefore particularly prone to cons or manipulation.

- *The Wanton*: The wanton includes those who are driven by sexual desire, such as the case with rapists or seducers.
- *The Lonesome and the Heartbroken*: The lonely may be particularly susceptible, with loneliness weakening critical faculties.
- *The Tormentor*: Usually found in family tragedies, the tormentor (perhaps a psychotic or alcoholic) will become a victim of retaliatory violence after years of torture of loved ones.
- *The Blocked, Exempted, or Fighting Victim*: This describes the individual who has become so enmeshed in a losing situation that attempts to defend oneself are pointless. This may include victims of blackmail, among others.

Like von Hentig, Benjamin Mendelsohn[1] created a victim typology most akin to a scale of culpability. This is perhaps unsurprising given that Mendelsohn was a lawyer:

- *Completely Innocent Victim*: Victims who do nothing to contribute to their victimization.
- *Victim Due to Ignorance*: The victim does something that puts him or her in harm's way without realizing.
- *Voluntary Victim*: This includes those who attempt suicide, or are otherwise engaging in dangerous behavior.
- *Victim More Guilty than the Offender*: The victim provokes the criminal event in some way, such as being verbally or physically abusive.
- *Most Guilty Victim*: Provokes the attack initially, but becomes the victim, such as the home invader who gets shot by the occupant.
- *Simulating or Imaginary Victim*: The person who falsely claims to be a victim of crime.

Mendelsohn was to later revise his typology based on a reimagining of his definition of victimization and culpability (Wilson, 2009). This new typology incorporates all domains of victimity and is not restricted to those involving criminal elements. This taxon includes (1) victims of crime; (2) victims of oneself (i.e., suicide and other self-destructive behavior); (3) victims of antisocial behavior from the environment (various political forces, genocide, etc.); (4) victims of technology (i.e., medical testing); and (5) victims of natural disasters (i.e., earthquakes, hurricanes, and famine).

Later, in 1967 Steven Schafer proposed his own set of victim types. Like Mendelsohn, Hungarian-born Schafer was a lawyer who took an interest in victims while noting their omission from his father's criminal law books (Wilson, 2009). Schafer was to propose a typology mirroring Mendelsohn's in that it provides a scale of victim responsibility for the act, in what was the first textbook on victimology written in the English language (see Schafer, 1977). The seven victim types are (Schafer, 1977a; Wilson, 2009):

- *Unrelated Victims.* These victims had no relationship with their offenders prior to the crime. For these victims, the criminal was entirely responsible for the decision to commit a crime; they were entirely innocent.

[1] Mendelsohn was the first person to coin the term "victimology," and he is therefore considered the father of modern victimology (Wilson, 2009).

- *Provocative Victims.* The behavior of these victims caused their offenders to react so that a crime occurred; thus, these victims shared a significant amount of the responsibility for the crime.
- *Precipitative Victims.* These victims did something inappropriate because of where they were, how they were dressed, the way they acted, or what they said; thus, their responsibility was only negligible.
- *Biologically Weak Victims.* These victims had physical characteristics that made them obviously vulnerable to their offenders; thus, they had no responsibility for the crime. Examples are the young, the old, the sick, or the handicapped.
- *Socially Weak Victims.* These victims had social characteristics that made them vulnerable to their offenders; thus, they had no responsibility for the crime. Examples are the isolated, immigrants, or minorities.
- *Self-Victimizing Victims.* These victims engaged in deviant and criminal behaviors in which they were partners with the offenders; thus, these victims were totally responsible. Examples are prostitutes, drug users, drunks, and gamblers.
- *Political Victims.* These victims were persons who opposed those in political power and were abused so as not to upset the offender's political dominance. Thus, they are not responsible for their victimization.

All of these early attempts at victim typologies have one thing in common: They are laden with value judgments about the victim's role or culpability within the criminal event. This can be seen in Schafer's own words from 1977a (p. 27):

> *In a way, of course, the victim is always the cause of crime, even if the target is immaterialistic, such as intellectual integrity, the freedom of religion, the interest of public health, or the safety of the nation. There are no crimes without victims, and, necessary, the existence of the victim himself, or something material or immaterial that belongs to him, is what makes the crime potential and may actually produce the criminal result. However, as it often happens, the victim not only potentializes the crime, but precipitates it.*

It would, however, be unfair to characterize these taxonomies as aiming the full weight of responsibility on the victim, and even Schafer (1977b, p. 46) admits there are instances in which the victim is not at all culpable for the harms or losses they suffer:

> *The manager of the bank, for example, is not related to the bank robber, nor is the owner of a burglarized house; these and others are selected by the criminal as victims only randomly or by situational considerations of the planned crime, thus the criminal is supposed to carry the full responsibility.*

The broad context of von Hentig, Mendelsohn, and Schafer's typologies will be provided in the next section on victim precipitation.

Victim Precipitation

Marvin Wolfgang first employed the term victim precipitation to explain those situations in which the victim initiated the actions, which ultimately led to their harm or loss. Precipitation has since been expanded, encompassing any provocation or facilitation of the crime by the victim (Timmer & Norman, 1984). Despite the value judgments of early theorists, understanding victim precipitation and the context in which the crime occurred is critical if analysts are to fully understand and appreciate what happened and why. While understanding this context is not about blame, it certainly can change the perception of the victim as a passive, unwilling, and non-complicit party to any offense. Today, it is thought that the vast majority of homicides are victim precipitated (see Pesta, 2011).

Precipitation takes one of two forms (Siegel, 2008). In the first type, the victim has characteristics that somehow evoke a response from the attacker. This may be in the form of an actual attribute (if the victim is introverted or emotionally withdrawn), it may be symbolic (the victim belonging to a particular group), or imagined (an erroneous belief about attitude or philosophy). This is known as passive precipitation.

In the second type, the victim takes more of an active role and engages in some actual behavior that brings about a sanction. This may happen where the victim, is posturing against the offender or making verbal threats, and may include physical assault. Depending on the nature of the interaction and the type of force involved, it may be difficult to differentiate between the victim and the offender.

Between 1948 and 1952, Marvin Wolfgang conducted a study of homicide records in Philadelphia, finding that over a quarter of those homicides involved some element of victim precipitation (Doerner & Lab, 2005). Controlling for age, race, sex of the victim, and the offender, Wolfgang examined factors such as the presence of alcohol, weapon used, location and time of the offense, victim-offender relationship, and elements of victim precipitation (Hepburn & Voss, 1970).

Later, Curtis (1973, 1974) reported that, in the United States, 22% of all clearances and 14% of non-clearances were precipitated, and Pesta (2011) found that in Ohio between 1977 and 2008, 18% (n = 35) of homicides were victim precipitated. Other research has examined the rate of victim precipitation in rape (Amir, 1971), pedophilia offenses (Virkunnen, 1975), homicides (Voss & Hepburn, 1968; Sobol, 1997), intimate partner violence (Muftić, Bouffard & Bouffard, 2007), and in suicide by cop situations (Klinger, 2001; Parent & Verdun-Jones, 1998). Regardless of the crime type, it would appear then that precipitation plays a significant role and so must be fully understood, despite opposition to precipitation as a type of victim blaming (see Timmer & Norman, 1984).

In any criminal event, the relationships and culpabilities involved will be varied and complex. And the degree to which the victim plays a role will change depending on the crime type, the situation and context, the offender's motivation, involvement of alcohol and other drugs, and any other number of factors involved. Commenting on the complexity of the relationships involved, von Hentig (1948, pp. 383-384) states:

> *That the relationships between perpetrator and victim are much more intricate than the rough distinctions of criminal law. Here are two human beings. As soon as they draw near*

> *to one another male or female, young or old, rich or poor, ugly or attractive - a wide range of interactions, repulsions as well as attractions, is set in motion. What the law does is to watch the one who acts and the one who is acted upon. By this external criterion a subject and object, a perpetrator and a victim are distinguished. In sociological and psychological quality the situation may be completely different. It may happen that the two distinct categories merge. There are cases in which they are reversed and in the long chain of causative forces the victim assumes the role of determinant.*

As it is possible for a criminal to repeat offend (known as recidivism), it is also possible for victims to be subject to repetitions of the acts perpetrated against them (of the same or a different nature). As discussed by Wolfgang and Singer (1973, p. 391):

> *Victim recidivism would appear to be a reasonable term to refer to the repetition of victimization as a counterpart to criminal recidivism in reference to repeating crime by offenders.*
>
> ...
>
> *There are undoubtedly many private homes, commercial establishments, owners of automobiles who have suffered repeated, often similar forms of victimization. Some persons have been robbed beaten, or raped more than once, perhaps several times. Carriers of a subculture of violence who are prepared to respond with physical aggression on slight stimuli of provocation share the value of violence and are likely to be victim recidivists, as they are criminal recidivists.*

Despite a significant theoretical base, and a number of studies providing data on the prevalence of precipitation, not all theorists are convinced by its history (Polk, 1997, provides one such critical overview).

Victim Motivation Typology

The typology proposed herein for understanding the emotional and psychological milieu of victimization is that provided by Petherick and Ferguson (2012) and discussed in Petherick, Sinnamon, and Jenkins (2012). This is based on the work of Groth, Burgess, and Holmstrom (1977), Groth (1979), and Hazelwood (2009), with some slight modification in order to be applicable to victimization and understanding victim types. These are largely a reflection of the offender typologies discussed in the preceding chapter, as applied to the behavior of victims.

The following types capture the vast majority, if not all, of the types of needs and wants that victims experience. It should be noted before presenting this typology that, as with the offender types, there are no absolute boundaries between each type, and it is possible for one victim to exhibit characteristics of more than one type. It is also possible for a victim to start as one type, and through a process of experience, adaptation, and change, move between types as dictated by their experiences and their willingness (or ability) to learn from past mistakes that placed them in risky situations. As discussed at the start of this chapter, insight and introspection will play a role here.

There are inherent differences between some of the behaviors of victims and offenders, such as the use of force or coercion (Petherick & Ferguson, 2012). Too much focus on the behavioral intricacies of a particular situation can distract us from the actual motives in a case though, and we are therefore best served by looking at the underlying themes that the behavior is intended to serve, or in understanding why a particular target was chosen, rather than a pedantic reliance on behavioral cues. Angry behavior, for instance, could *prima facie* appear to be either pervasive, retaliatory, or self-preservative. Until the context is established through an understanding of the constitutional elements, only a preliminary understanding of motive can be established.

Given that victims can move between types in the same general timeframe, and between types over time, a valid question to arise is "what purpose is there in classifying motives?" The answers to this question are (Petherick & Ferguson, 2012):

- Provisioning crime prevention techniques requires a detailed understanding of the psychological state of the victim.
- Threat management, as a form of crime prevention, requires a detailed understanding of the psychological state of the victim.
- Victim's services need to develop an accurate accounting of the psychological state of the victim.
- Understanding motivations provides context to victim precipitation.
- Investigating any given crime will enable a more complete understanding of the circumstances involving missing persons.
- Providing victims with insight into behaviors that place them in harm's way with a view to reducing or eliminating behaviors, potentially reducing criminal and other victimization.
- From a mental health point of view, understanding the motivational backdrop will assist in designing effective therapeutic interventions.

With these in mind, this chapter will now turn to the typology. Unless otherwise stated, all of the following information is taken from Petherick & Ferguson (2012).

Reassurance-Oriented Victims

Reassurance-Oriented victims have low self-esteem and attempt to restore this by establishing relationships and engaging in behaviors that are intended to restore their self worth. An individual's judgment in his or her abilities and actions, referred to as self efficacy (Resnick, 2008), is low and a direct reflection of his or her lack of a sense of skill or aptitude. They tend to feel inadequate and may perform poorly in social interactions. These individuals have sometimes been victimized previously, perhaps repeatedly, because they feel that is their lot in life, or that they are somehow deserving of emotional or physical abuse. By extension, their need for companionship and to feel a sense of worth through being in relationships may lead them to place more emphasis on their partner's needs, neglecting their own as a result. Because they tend to be subservient in nature, they may passively precipitate events.

Victims who are reassurance oriented have a poor self image, doubt their appearance, and may not have much confidence in their social abilities. They are likely to be repeat victims as, over time, they become so acculturated to violence or abuse that they come to accept it as part of being. The personal cost of any trauma, physical or psychological, is seen to be less than the emotional cost of being alone. In extreme cases, these victims may develop avoidance as a compensatory mechanism to fend off abandonment.

Where psychopathology is present, victims may suffer from disorders where self-esteem is a factor, as self-esteem is also a key component of this type. Disorders potentially include Borderline Personality Disorder, Dependent Personality Disorder, Avoidant Personality Disorder, and Histrionic Personality Disorder.

Assertive-Oriented Victims

Assertive-oriented victims also have low self-esteem. The assertive victim, compared to the reassurance oriented, externalize this lack of self worth, acting out against others. These individuals make others feel bad so that they may feel better about themselves. Because of this, events may be actively precipitated by aggressive interactions that cause stress and frustration in others.

Developing largely from compensatory mechanisms to make themselves feel better, they repeatedly push their own agenda and impart their will on others. This will often lead to them developing a reputation of being unpleasant to be around. Small or trivial matters will become grossly inflated as they engage in a battle of the wills in an attempt to get their own way.

Because of the personality features of the assertive victim, they may suffer from Narcissistic Personality Disorder when pathology is present.

Anger-Retaliatory Victims

Anger-retaliatory victims operate out of revenge and may harbor a great deal of anger against individuals, groups, or organizations. They may be the victim of actual wrongs against them, they may project their beliefs about an unjust situation onto others, or others may be blamed for personal inadequacies or failures ("it is my boss's fault I didn't get my promotion because he doesn't like me"). As the basis for this type is anger, they may act impulsively whenever their anger is sufficient.

Events tend to be actively precipitated because of their aggressive responses to others, or because they engage in actively sabotaging the opportunities of others because they perceive they have wronged them in some way. Because their behavior may be the result of perceived wrongs, these individuals may present as being highly paranoid. As a result, retaliatory behavior may be concordant with disorders where paranoia is a feature, such as Paranoid Personality Disorder or Borderline Personality Disorder, or with passive-aggressive personality features.

Pervasively Angry Victims

As with the preceding type, pervasively angry victims have a great deal of rage, but this tends to be generalized rather than focused on an individual, organization, or group. This anger is pervasive in the sense that it runs throughout most aspects of the victim's life and can be seen in other domains of action such as home life, family life, social life, or work life. They, too, may have a reputation of being unpleasant to be around.

The main difference between this type and the retaliatory type is the focus of the anger. Retaliatory victims are focal to an individual, group, or institution whereas pervasively angry victims generalize their anger to other situations. Apart from this, other features are the same as for the Retaliatory type.

Excitation-Oriented Victims

This type is the most difficult to adapt from the offender types as it refers to a sadist; that is, an individual who experiences sexual gratification from the pain and suffering of another. While engaging in this behavior may increase the chance for victimization, characterizing this type only as one where sexual gratification is at play may be problematic. To be able to adapt this victim behavior, it is therefore necessary to slightly modify the main theme of the behavior in terms of the needs served. Because of the hidden nature of excitation behavior, and a subsequent lack of understanding and knowledge of its prevalence, this type is most likely to be the least encountered or identified.

For victim motivations, excitation can take one of two forms. The first is sadism, and the second is masochism. Sadism is directed externally, while masochism is directed internally, though both conditions can coexist. According to the DSM-IV-TR (American Psychiatric Association, 2000, p. 573), sexual sadism involves:

> *Acts (real, not simulated) in which the individual derives sexual excitement from the psychological or physical suffering (including humiliation) of the victim.... Others act on the sadistic urges with a consenting partner (who may have Sexual Masochism) who willingly suffers pain or humiliation. Still others with Sexual Sadism act on their sadistic sexual urges with nonconsenting victims. In all of these cases, it is the suffering of the victim that is sexually arousing. When Sexual Sadism is severe, and especially when it is associated with Antisocial Personality Disorder, individuals with Sexual Sadism may seriously injure or kill their victims.*

Where stranger victims are involved, active precipitation homicides may occur when the nonconsenting partner fights back.

Sexual masochism, where the individual derives pleasure from inflicting pain on themselves, involves (American Psychiatric Association, 2000, p. 572):

> *Acts (real, not simulated) of being humiliated, beaten, bound, or otherwise made to suffer.... Others act on the masochistic sexual urges by themselves (e.g., binding themselves, sticking themselves with pins, shocking themselves electrically, or self-mutilation) or with a partner. One particularly dangerous form of Sexual Masochism called "hypoxyphilia", involves sexual arousal by oxygen deprivation obtained by means of chest compression, noose, ligature, plastic bag, mask, or chemical (often a volatile nitrite that produces temporary decrease in brain oxygenation by peripheral vasodilation).*

In those cases where sexual masochism is involved, the individual is at risk of death by their own hand. The mechanism by which this comes about could be hypoxia (partial oxygen deprivation), anoxia (total oxygen deprivation), or in other cases, where cutting, slashing, or piercing may occur (or other forms of self harm).

While sexuality plays a component in other forms of excitation behavior, not all excitation behavior is sexual in nature. Within the context of victimization, self harm can be a form of negative affect regulation (see Klonsky, 2006). Here, self harm as a form of physical pain moderates psychological pain for which there is little insight.

Materially Oriented Victims

A materially oriented victim pursues some form of material benefit, such as money, goods, accommodation, or others. This category is identified as Profit in the offender motivation types, but this label may be a little misleading given not all things procured actually bring a profit or contribute to wealth creation. In fact, it may be all some individuals can do just to get by on a day-to-day basis. This category involves those cases where someone stays with a controlling partner because they cannot afford to survive on their own, among others.

These victims may also engage in activities such as prostitution or drug dealing, which can increase their risk of harm or loss. On the promise of a "quick buck," they can also fall prey to all manner of frauds or scams. Their untenable financial situation can be the result of bad financial decisions, controlling or dominating partners (who demand financial control), or when a lack of education inhibits employment sufficient to meet financial commitments. This would also include those cases where individuals have gambling or drug habits.

Self-Preservation-Oriented Victims

A preservation-oriented victim engages in behavior that is intended to restore some kind of imbalance of power, especially in situations where their own lives, or the life of another (usually in their care) is threatened. This may occur when a mother kills an angry and threatening father to protect her children, or when a victim of domestic violence kills a partner in his or her sleep.

Not all preservation-related behaviors include killing others for their own or others' protection. In some cases, a preservation-oriented victim will remain in an abusive relationship because his or her life has been threatened should they choose to leave. In this instance, staying is preservative since leaving almost guarantees harm or loss.

Typologies and Disordered Personality

Motivation and personality are inextricably linked and are modulated by a third dimension of self-esteem (Petherick, Sinnamon & Jenkins, 2012). In the case of personality, it is self-esteem that is pivotal in shaping personality characteristics, perceptions, and the self-schemas that underpin the way we interpret our experiences. In the case of motivation, it is the pursuit of self-esteem that is linked to motivation, desire, and one's goals (Donnellan, Trzesniewski,

Robins, Moffit, & Caspi, 2005; Crocker & Park, 2006). As a result, motivational typologies must be considered in light of the combined forces of self-esteem, personality, and motivation (Petherick, Sinnamon & Jenkins, 2012). Because the ultimate goal is to develop predictive capacity, it is important to recognize that there is a strong concordance between the emotional dimensions of motivation and personality and behavioral expression.

In commentaries of victim and perpetrator typologies, the personality disorder figured prominently. Five common elements of disordered personality serve this association: (1) self-esteem that is either low or high but fragile; (2) emotional negativity bias and lack of capacity to modulate emotional expression; (3) high-risk, anti-social, self-serving, or differentially reinforced behavioral tendencies; (4) an unwillingness or incapacity to accurately assess and mitigate risk; and (5) unwillingness or incapacity to moderate behavior responses.

In this way, the personality disorder–serial victim precipitation relationship occurs through a natural synergy between distorted and poorly modulated emotional processing and the lack of ability (whether through incapacity or poor choices) to assess risk and inhibit behavioral options likely to result in adverse outcomes. Numerous studies have shown that this functional inability to interpret environmental and circumstantial risk, and to moderate the emotional responses that provide motivational valence and ultimately behavior choice, are highly characteristic of a number of personality disorders that are recognized as concomitant properties of victim typologies and serial precipitative behaviors (Petherick, Sinnamon & Jenkins, 2012).

Just as in commentaries of victim typologies, commentaries on criminal motivation also carry a message of strong concomitance, in this case, between the disordered personality and recidivistic violence. This relationship occurs almost by default given criminality and pathological personality characteristics are both defined by their relative deviance to the social norm. As with serial precipitation, violent recidivists often have personality disorders in which there is a distinct lack of capacity to assess risk and willingness to follow elementary social norms. Instead, the disordered personality pursues self-preservation motives with little reflection on the moral ethos. Furthermore, some of the socially deviant behavioral traits of certain subclassifications of the personality disordered are essentially possible because personal motivation and behavior are not subject to the same empathic modulation as others. To this end neuroimaging studies have shown reduced functional activity in the regions of the brain that mediate empathy, sentience, and the ability to feel guilt or remorse—that is the right medial prefrontal cortex (Raposo, Vicens, Clithero, Dobbins, & Huettel, 2011; Seitz, Nickel, & Azari, 2006).

To understand the relationship between typologies and personality disorders it is imperative to fully appreciate the extent to which emotion, motivation, and behavior are inextricably linked as a cause–effect functional progression:

- Emotion, the first link in the chain, drives a number of psychological and physiological factors that relate to perception and desire.
- Our perception of the situation and our desire to effect a change to the situation results in a level of motivation to act on this desire.
- The valence of our motivation (i.e., the direction of our desired outcome) provides the choices for our behaviors.

- A confluence of contextual factors such as social norms and expectations, psychological capacity (capacity to modulate autonomic and emotional arousal, control behavioral impulses, rationally consider the circumstances, options and consequences, etc.), physical abilities, previous experience, and environment determine the ultimate course of action taken.

Behavior then is ultimately the result of the complex interplay between the motivation generated by our emotions and the specific personal context created by a situation in light of previous experience, conditioning, and physical capacity.

To predict victim risk through behavioral factors alone is largely unsuccessful. This is not to say that we cannot firmly state that a particular behavior is high risk. Indeed we can confidently state that certain behaviors are high risk and those that succumb to specific adverse outcomes are more likely to have been engaged in specific behaviors than others. For example, there is a correlation between risk of assault and choosing to walk home through a bad neighborhood alone at three o'clock in the morning. However, it is also true to say that nine times out of ten, choosing to walk home alone early in the morning, although a risky behavioral choice, does not always result in an adverse outcome. In this way, gross behavioral choices provide little predictive value for individual victim risk assessment.

Similarly, physical capacity provides only limited predictive value. Even when faced with physical barriers, if the motivation is sufficient, an individual will engage in an attempt to achieve that which is desired. Criminal case files are littered with examples of individuals who engage in precipitative behaviors despite an obvious lack of physical capacity to countenance their actions. For example, it is not uncommon for a physically smaller male or a female to behave aggressively toward a physically larger adversary and, although they initiate the interaction, end up as the victim of a violent exchange.

Of far greater predictive value is the dimension of psychological capacity. The capacity to modulate emotional responses, inhibit impulsive behavioral urges, accurately assess the environment and its associated hazards, and rationally reflect on situationally specific circumstances before making behavior choices provides the core basis for avoiding the risk of becoming a victim in the majority of forms of person-to-person malfeasance.

Therefore, in order to predict victim risk it is important to understand the psychological dimensions of the cause-and-effect chain in which victim precipitation is nested. Ultimately our emotions and our psychological ability to modulate them through the higher-order cognitive capacity for rational contemplation determines what we do (or attempt to do) and how we do it. It is in this way that disordered personality and associated neurofunctional characteristics are implicit in motivating and enabling serial victim precipitation.

Similarly, serial perpetrator behavior is the result of the emotional factors that govern motivation and the previous experiences and associated attitudes that underpin beliefs about what behavior choices are available and appropriate in order to achieve a desired outcome. In the case of serial perpetrators, emotions and the ability to modulate them continue to be an important element in the process of motivation, desire, and controlling impulsive behaviors. Additionally, the lack of empathy that is often a characteristic of violent serial offenders plays an important role in the behavioral choices that are perceived as available to achieve an outcome. In this way emotions establish motivation and then the lack of social affiliation brought about through a lack of empathic reasoning allows the perpetrator to commit violence against others with little or no remorse or guilt. This lack of empathy often reveals itself early in life through poor bonding, lack of friendships, and, as the curiosity of childhood colludes with low empathetic reasoning, cruelty to animals.

Remarkable self-esteem is a characteristic of a disordered personality and is therefore also an important factor in both serial crime and victim precipitation. This would appear to be logical given that perceptions (including perceptions of self) are a significant element of the emotion–motivation connection. The way we perceive ourselves both as a general concept of self and in context-specific circumstances influences our desire to bring about a change in those circumstances. If we perceive that our self-esteem/self-worth is under threat then we will want to protect it. This in turn will drive our motivations and determine our behaviors in accordance with the emotion-motivation-behavior chain of cause and effect. General self-esteem drives motivation and situational self-esteem (known as self efficacy—our perception and beliefs about our value and abilities in the context of a specific situation) and determines the way in which we populate our list of behavioral choices that we believe to be available to us in order to attain our objective.

Depending on the nature of the personality disorder, self-esteem may be remarkably low or remarkably high (Hedrick & Berlin, 2012; Pastwa-Wojciechowska, Kazmierczak, & Blazek, 2012; Roberts & Huprich, 2012). Remarkably high self-esteem may be characterized by elevated narcissistic traits or it may be very tenuous and subject to an underlying fragility. Remarkably low self-esteem is characteristically associated with feelings of self-loathing. The presence of one of these three patterns of self-esteem is an important predictive element in how an individual may perceive his or her environment, be motivated to react to the threats inherent in that perception, and ultimately how he or she will respond behaviorally.

Personality Disorders

There are 10 recognized personality disorders that cluster into three categories of characteristics and symptoms. As stated previously, personality disorders are classified as Axis II disorders in the DSM-IV-TR (American Psychiatric Association, 2000). General symptoms of disordered personality include emotional dysregulation, inability to maintain positive relationships, social isolation, angry outbursts, suspicion and lack of trust, inability to delay gratification, poor impulse control, and there is often a history of alcohol and/or substance abuse. The thoughts and behaviors of those with personality disorders are characteristically considered odd, eccentric, melodramatic, overly emotional, anxious, and/or fearful. Many signs and symptoms of specific personality disorders "bleed" into one another and it is often difficult to proffer an accurate diagnosis that could not be differentially provided by another clinician.

At the end of the day associating specific perpetrator or victim typology with specific subclassifications of personality disorder can be a difficult task given the often arbitrary nature of diagnostic classification as well as the individual differences between those diagnosed. The following offers some guide as to how the emotion-motivation-behavior chain in disordered personality may relate to specific typologies.

Personality Disorders and the Victim and Perpetrator Motivation Typology

Reassurance-Oriented Victims and Perpetrators

Reassurance-Oriented victims and perpetrators are likely to have disordered personality characteristics that come from either the cluster "B" or cluster "C" disorder categories. Cluster "B" personality disorders are characterized by thoughts and emotions that are dramatic and overly emotional. The disorders that are likely to be associated with reassurance-oriented types from this cluster are Borderline and Histrionic Personality disorders. These two disorder subtypes are vulnerable because of their characteristic low self-esteem, impulsivity, need for attention and approval from others, and excessive and extremely volatile emotionality. These characteristics combine with poor predictive capacity in sufferers. This means that they are unable to interpret their surroundings and assess the risk that may be present. Combined with emotional volatility and need for approval, these individuals are at an extremely high risk for precipitative behaviors. Finally, these individuals are also unlikely to learn from their experiences and are therefore prone to repeating behaviors, thereby placing themselves repeatedly into situations likely to result in their becoming a victim of crime.

Cluster "C" personality disorders are characterized by thoughts and behaviors that are anxious and fearful. In this group it is the Avoidant and Dependent Personality disorders that are most likely to fall within the Reassurance-Oriented typology. These personality subtypes are often in the Reassurance-Oriented type as they are at high risk for codependent relationships in which they will submit themselves to another and remain even in the face of extreme adversity and abuse. Feelings of inadequacy and the need to obtain esteem through others combined with timidity, shyness, submissiveness, and high tolerance for abuse means these individuals often place themselves in situations where they are at high risk for personal violence.

For reassurance-oriented victims, it is fear that primarily motivates behavior. The fear of disappointing another and of being rejected or betrayed presents a major threat to an already low self-esteem. Reassurance-Oriented victims have such a low self-esteem that they must seek approval from outside of themselves through others, thereby placing themselves at an elevated risk of exploitation, harm, or loss. They are highly motivated to find this approval and therefore may not be in a position to evaluate the potential cost associated with the chosen method of seeking to obtain it.

The perpetrator who is reassurance oriented is similarly driven by the need for approval from others. For the Borderline and Histrionic personalities, impulsiveness, volatility, and an inability to modulate the fear of rejection can result in aggressive outbursts and violence toward others when they feel emotionally or physically threatened. The result can be violent crimes committed against others or against property. For Avoidant and Dependent personalities, reassurance-oriented acts are committed out of a desire to win or retain the approval and acceptance of others. Common crimes in this group include acts such as theft, prostitution, or acting as a drug courier.

Assertive-Oriented Victims and Perpetrators

Assertive-oriented victims and perpetrators, similar to the reassurance-oriented types, are motivated by a desire to restore self-esteem through others. The two typologies differ in the emotional content that drives the motivation. While it is fear that drives the behavior of the reassurance-oriented victim, the assertive-oriented victim is motivated primarily by an unarticulated anger. The anger is largely a product of the belief that they are better than others and so deserve more than they have, that they are "owed" something by others (or by society) and that, in some way, they are not receiving the recognition they deserve.

In this way they are motivated to "restore" threats to their already low self-esteem through obtaining accolades from others. Alternatively they will attempt to restore the threats to self-esteem through the emotional domination of others. That is to say they will deliberately set out to make others feel worse about themselves in order to make themselves feel superior. This overly emotional, melodramatic, and extremely intense personality is characteristic of the cluster "B" personality types. Victims and perpetrators of the assertive-oriented type are likely to present with traits that are highly characteristic of the Narcissistic Personality disorder subtype.

The hyper-emotional and dramatic characteristics of the cluster "B" personality disorder subtypes are expressed in a dominating and aggressive manner in the narcissistic personality. The individual with this personality subtype that becomes involved in criminal acts, either as victim or perpetrator, is likely to have a high but fragile or low self-esteem. The narcissistic personality who fits into the assertive-oriented type is usually engaging in compensatory behaviors in which they are attempting to dominate others and be the focus of attention. The belief that they are better than others is not supported by the low or fragile self-esteem and therefore behaviors are fueled by the need to repair the incongruence. This occurs through fantasies about power, success, or their own attractiveness to others and results in a "blurring" of reality in which exaggerations of personal achievements, success, and talents are made. The confused reality creates further need for praise and admiration from others and results in increased demand for recognition. In turn, the narcissistic personality often makes these high-maintenance demands while failing to recognize or acknowledge other people's feelings and emotions.

The aggression, selfishness, and personal agenda-driven attitudes of the narcissistic personality can result in criminal behaviors aimed at obtaining what is believed to be rightfully theirs (e.g., material gain that it is believed will make them more respected by others). These characteristics may also result in precipitative behaviors that provoke aggressive or retaliatory responses in others, making them highly susceptible to being a victim of violent crime.

Anger Retaliatory Victims and Perpetrators

Cluster "A" and "B" type disordered personality feature prominently in Anger Retaliatory types. In the personality disorder, retaliatory motivation comes from an exaggeration and distortion of the circumstances surrounding events or perceived events. Cluster "A" retaliatory types are likely to fall within the sphere of the Paranoid Personality type. For these individuals distorted thoughts focus on the beliefs that they have been wronged in some way. The presence of usually low self-esteem combined with paranoia results in an externalization of the blame onto others (whether an individual [e.g., sibling], a group of people [e.g., a parenting group, members of a religious or ethnic group], or an institution [e.g., a government or financial institution]). The theme of the beliefs is that "others" are deliberately preventing them from obtaining some desired object or outcome. Events are interpreted with this paranoid bias and therefore they often see conspiracy in the actions of those around them. For the Paranoid personality, being faced with a conspiracy in which those around you are deliberately acting to prevent you from achieving your goals often results in extreme anger. The lack of capacity to modulate anger responses and inhibit impulsive urges can then lead to acts of retaliation, which they initiate and are the aggressor (perpetrator) but in which they may also become the victim when those they pursue are better equipped to respond.

Cluster "B" Retaliatory types are likely to fall within the sphere of Borderline and Narcissistic Personality disorders. As with the Paranoid personality, the Borderline and Narcissistic Personality types have very poor capacity to modulate anger responses, assess risk, and to control impulses. They are usually found in already volatile relationships that, when combined with their unstable mood, fear of rejection, and impulsiveness, provide a high risk environment for violence. In this way, when these personality types feel threatened they may attempt to "shoot first" as a method of retaliating for the wrong that they believe is going to be done to them. In the event that a wrong is done to them they are likely to retaliate impulsively without regard to risk.

While paranoid and narcissistic types externalize blame to others and seek retaliation accordingly, borderline types are more likely to internalize blame, creating an intense self-loathing. Retaliatory behavior then occurs because the Borderline personality blames the other person for "making" them feel that way.

Pervasively Angry Victims and Perpetrators

Pervasive anger may be a feature of Paranoid Personality disorder (cluster "A") or any of the cluster "B" personality subtypes (Antisocial, Borderline, Histrionic, or Narcissistic). The key element is that the disordered personality develops with a schema that generalizes negativity bias in an aggressive manner. Fault can be found everywhere and "other" is used as a convenient place to direct internal anger that cannot be modulated or rationalized. This form of cognitive distortion is common in the aforementioned personality disorders. Anyone or anything can become the focus of aggressive attention. These personality types will initiate violent exchanges as a means of exerting control and reestablishing self-esteem or may damage property if it is a contextually appropriate displacement of their anger. As potential victims these types are at very high risk for precipitative behaviors as they will often present as confrontational even in pedestrian encounters with others, thereby provoking aggressive responses in return.

Excitation-Oriented Victims and Perpetrators

A complex and challenging typology, excitation-oriented types are more likely to exhibit traits from cluster "B" or "C" personality subtypes. In cluster "B" it is clearly the antisocial personality that may be most predisposed. The antisocial personality, with a lack of empathic reasoning toward others, is emotionally able to place themselves in situations where the pain or suffering of others is secondary to the pleasure obtained by self. Sadomasochistic encounters whether consensual or nonconsensual may therefore appeal. While they are more likely to become perpetrators in this scenario, they are also at risk of becoming a victim.

In cluster "C" personality subtypes, it is the dependent personality that is most likely to be associated with excitation-oriented types. A strong desire to obtain approval from others may result in the dependent personality placing themselves in relationships of unequal power in which they are subservient to others. A sadistic partner may entice a dependent personality into increasingly sadomasochistic "play" and the dependent personality may acquiesce due to fear of being rejected and a desire to be accepted. Increasingly violent "play" may move into abuse if the dependent personality cannot (by fear or physical incapacity) extricate themselves from the escalation. The greatest risk occurs when the dependent personality encounters the antisocial personality. In this case the victim–perpetrator relationship is epitomized.

An additional risk can also come from those whose personality characteristics result in low levels of emotionality and reward stimulation. In this case cluster "A" personality characteristics such as those associated with Schizoid or Schizotypal Personality disorder may be associated with the excitation-oriented type. Altered perceptions and distorted reality may combine with limited emotional expression to motivate a desire to experience greater affect. This can lead to self-harming behaviors as well as thrill-seeking encounters with others. A lack of capacity to assess and mitigate risk makes these personality subtypes potentially at high risk to inflict significant harm on others (perpetrator) as well as become the victim of others, if they pursue these forms of experiences.

Materially Oriented Victims and Perpetrators

All personality subtypes are susceptible to this typology. Low or fragile self-esteem, distorted perceptions, paranoia, fear, a need for instant gratification, poor impulse control, needs arising from alcohol and/or substance abuse, anger and feelings of missing out, or that others are preventing you from obtaining objects or outcomes, fear of rejection, and need for approval can all bring about this motivation. A perpetrator may use criminal means to obtain material gain whether through theft, violence, or illicit commercial dealing (drug dealing, gambling, prostitution). A victim may be materially oriented if they allow themselves to remain in a violent or abusive relationship in order to be "cared" for by the perpetrator, or in the pursuit of "easy money," may fall prey to scams and fraud.

Self-Preservation-Oriented Victims and Perpetrators

As with materially oriented types, all personality subtypes may be identified with the self-preservation-oriented type. Self-preservation is a fundamental survival instinct and, in cases where an individual is impaired in his or her capacity for social reasoning and risk assessment, the natural desire for self-preservation can result in a variety of scenarios in which behavior may be precipitative. This may be in the form of passive precipitation in which the behaviors allow the individual to become a victim. For example, Dependent personalities may allow themselves to become embroiled in an abusive relationship or Avoidant personalities may socially isolate themselves and therefore be at risk for assault. Precipitation may also be active and the behaviors may be such that the individual courts the potential for becoming a victim. This may include someone with Borderline or Paranoid personality characteristics attempting to retaliate for a wrong (or perceived wrong) committed against them without due consideration for the inherent risk associated with the behavior. Active precipitation may also occur when an individual with antisocial, narcissistic, or schizotypal characteristics engage in specific behaviors that provoke responses from others.

Similarly the motivation for self-preservation can result in the commission of a variety of criminal behaviors aimed at restoring some kind of injustice (real or perceived), or protecting the well-being of self or others. These forms of motivation are particularly high risk for cluster "A" personality types who may perceive the world through thick lenses of paranoia, or through distorted and delusional schizotypal perceptions, or cluster "B" narcissistic types whose elevated beliefs about self worth and expectations of praise, admiration, and material reward may promote aggressive pursuit of these goals.

Conclusion

This chapter has presented motivations from the perspective of both the offender and the victim, and proposed a pathways model to explain how these motivations come to be through complex and dynamic interactions with their environment and peers, based on foundational biology. First, emotions play a role and set the stage for the development of self-esteem, how we feel about ourselves, and self efficacy, how we feel about our ability to operate within our environment. Our personality develops as a coping mechanism to help us in our environment with our particular circumstances, and in cases of extreme personality aberrations, personality disorders will arise. Within and between these factors, motivations, the physical or psychological needs that drive behavior, emerge.

As presented herein, there is significant concordance between the motivational types and the characteristics of many of the personality disorders. There is also very strong anecdotal support for this application, and there is ongoing empirical research looking at establishing a clearer picture of the degree of overlap between personality disorders and the motivational types and establishing the factors and characteristics of each type.

Questions

1. According to the pathways model, individual development occurs in the order of __________, __________ __________, __________, and __________.
2. Our temperament is rigid and inflexible, and our biology will predict who we are and what we do. *True or false?*

3. The personality disorder characterized by chronic fears or abandonment and rejection is known as __________ __________ disorder.
4. The ability to identify and understand the true nature of a situation is known as:
    a. Insight
    b. Introspection
    c. Motivation
    d. Temperament
    e. Any of the above is suitable.
5. Which of the following is not one of the personality disorders?
    a. Borderline personality disorder
    b. Narcissistic personality disorder
    c. Passive-aggressive personality disorder
    d. Histrionic personality disorder
    e. Antisocial personality disorder

References

Alleyne, E., & Wood, J. L. (2010). Gang involvement: Psychological and behavioral characteristics of gang members, peripheral youth, and nongang youth. *Aggression and Violent Behavior, 36*(6), 423–436.

American Psychiatric Association. (2000). *Diagnostic and statistical manual of mental disorders (4th ed. text revision)*. Washington: American Psychiatric Association.

Amir, M. (1971). *Patterns in forcible rape*. Chicago: University of Chicago Press.

Beech, A. R. (1998). A psychometric typology of child abusers. *International Journal of Offender Therapy and Comparative Criminology, 42*, 319–339.

Bosson, J. K., Lakey, C. E., Campbell, W. K., Zeigler-Hill, V., Jordan, C. H., & Kernis, M. H. (2008). Untangling the links between narcissism and self-esteem: A theoretical and empirical review. *Social and Personality Psychology, 2*(3), 1415–1439.

Branden, N. (2001). *The psychology of self-esteem: A revolutionary approach to self-understanding that launched a new era in modern psychology*. San Francisco: Jossey-Bass.

Cohen, P. (2008). Child development and personality disorder. *Psychiatric Clinics of North America, 31*, 477–493.

Crocker, J., & Park, L. E. (2006). The costly pursuit of self-esteem. *Psychological Bulletin, 130*(2), 392–414.

Curtis, L. A. (1973-1974). Victim precipitation and violent crime. *Social Problems, 21*, 594–606.

Doerner, W., & Lab, S. (2005). *Victimology* (4th ed.). Ohio: Andersen Publishing.

Donnellan, M. B., Trzesniewski, K. H., Robins, R. W., Moffitt, T. E., & Caspi, A. (2005). Low self-esteem is related to aggression, antisocial behavior, and delinquency. *Psychological Science, 16*(4), 328–335.

Egan, V., & Beadman, M. (2011). Personality and gang membership. *Personality and Individual Differences, 51*, 748–753.

Gertzfeld, A. R. (2006). *Essentials of abnormal psychology*. New Jersey: John Wiley & Sons.

Grant, A. M. (2001). Rethinking: Psychological mindedness: Metacognition, self-reflection, and insight. *Behavior Change, 18*(1), 8–17.

Groth, A. N., Burgess, A. W., & Holmstrom, L. L. (1977). Rape: Power, anger, and sexuality. *American Journal of Psychiatry, 134*(11), 1239–1243.

Groth, A. N. (1979). *Men who rape: the psychology of the offender*. New York: Plenum Press.

Groth, A. N., Burgess, A. W., & Holmstrom, L. L. (1977). Rape: Power, anger, and sexuality. *American Journal of Psychiatry, 134(11)*, 1239–1243.

Gudjonsson, G. H., & Sigurdsson, J. F. (2004). Motivation for offending and personality. *Legal and Criminological Society, 9*, 69–81.

Harter, S. (1999). *The construction of the self: A developmental perspective*. New York: Guilford Press.

Hazelwood, R. R. (2009). Analysing the rape and profiling the offender. In R. R. Hazelwood & A. W. Burgess (Eds.), *Practical aspects of rape Investigation: A multidisciplinary approach (4th ed.)*. Boca Raton, FL: CRC Press.

Hedrick, A. N., & Berlin, H. A. (2012). Implicit self-esteem in borderline personality and depersonalization disorder. *Front Psychol, 3*, 91. doi:10.3389/fpsyg.2012.00091.

Hepburn, J., & Voss, H. L. (1970). Patterns of criminal homicide: A comparison of Chicago and Philadelphia. *Criminology, 8(1)*, 21–45.

Holcomb, W. R. (2008). A victim typology of sexual harassment. *Psychological Reports, 103(3)*, 819–826.

Johnson, M. P. (2008). *A typology of domestic violence: Intimate terrorism, violent resistance, and situational couple violence*. New Haven, CT: Northeastern University Press.

Kleinginna, P. R., & Kleinginna, A. M. (1981). A categorized list of emotion definitions, with suggestions for a consensual definition. *Motivations and Emotions, 5(4)*, 345–379.

Klinger, D. A. (2001). Suicidal intent in victim-precipitated homicide: Insights from the study of "suicide by cop". *Homicide Studies, 5*, 206–226.

Klonsky, E. D. (2006). The functions of deliberate self injury: A review of the evidence. *Clinical Psychology Review, 27(2)*, 226–239.

Knight, A., Warren, I., Reboussin, R., & Soley, J. (1998). Predicting rapist type from crime scene variables. *Criminal Justice and Behavior, 25(1)*, 46–80.

Livesly, W. J., Jang, K. L., & Vernon, P. A. (1998). Phenotypic and genetic structure of traits delineating personality disorders. *Archives of General Psychiatry, 55*, 941–948.

Maslow, A. (1942). A theory of human motivation. *Psychological Review, 50*, 370–396.

Mayou, R., & Farmer, A. (2002). Trauma. *British Medical Journal, 325*, 426–429.

Millon, T., Grossman, S., Millon, C., Meagher, S., & Ramnath, R. (2004). *Personality disorders in modern life* (2nd ed.). New Jersey: John Wiley and Sons, Inc.

Mullen, P. E., Pathé, M., & Purcell, R. (2009). *Stalkers and their victims (2nd ed.)*. Cambridge: Cambridge University Press.

Mullen, P. E., Pathé, M., Purcell, R., & Stuart, G. W. (1999). Study of stalkers. *The American Journal of Psychiatry, 156(8)*, 1244.

Muftić, L. R., Bouffard, L. A., & Bouffard, J. A. (2007). An exploratory analysis of victim precipitation among men and women arrested for intimate partner violence. *Feminist Criminology, 2*, 327–346.

Oltmanns, T. F., & Emery, R. E. (2011). *Abnormal Psychology* (7th ed.). Boston: Pearson.

Ostrowsky, M. K. (2010). Are violent people more likely to have low self-esteem of high self-esteem? *Aggression and Violent Behavior, 15(1)*, 69–75.

Parent, R. B., & Verdun-Jones, S. (1998). Victim-precipitated homicide: Police use of deadly force in British Columbia. *Policing, 21(3)*, 432–448.

Pastwa-Wojciechowska, B., Kazmierczak, M., & Blazek, M. (2012). Self-esteem and styles of coping with stress versus strategies of planning in people with psychopathic personality disorders. *Med Sci Monit, 18*(2), CR119–124. [doi: 882467 [pii]].

Pathé, M., Mullen, P. E., & Purcell, R. (2001). Management of stalking victims. *Advances in Psychiatric Treatment, 7*, 399–406.

Pesta, R. (2011). *Provocation and the point of no return: An analysis of victim-precipitated homicide.* Thesis submitted in partial fulfillment of the degree of Master of Science in the Criminal Justice Program, Youngstown State University, July, 2011.

Petherick, W. A., & Ferguson, C. E. (2012). Understanding victim behavior through offender motivational typologies. Conference Proceedings of the 5th Annual Australian and New Zealand Critical Criminology Conference, Cairns 7 - 8 June, 2011.

Polk, K. (1997). A reexamination of the concept of victim-precipitated homicide. *Homicide Studies, 1*(2), 141–168.

Raposo, A., Vicens, L., Clithero, J. A., Dobbins, I. G., & Huettel, S. A. (2011). *Social Cognitive Affective Neuroscience, 6*(3), 260–269.

Resnick, B. (2008). Theory of self efficacy. In M. J. Smith & P. Liehr (Eds.), *Middle range theory for nursing.* New York: Springer.

Roberts, A. R., & Dziegielewski, S. F. (1996). Assessment typology and intervention with the survivors of stalking. *Aggression and Violent Behavior, 1*(4), 359–368.

Roberts, C. R., & Huprich, S. K. (2012). Categorical and dimensional models of pathological narcissism: The case of Mr. Jameson. *J Clin Psychol, 68*(8), 898–907. doi:10.1002/jclp.21894.

Roeckelein, J. E. (2006). *Elsevier's dictionary of psychological theories.* San Diego: Elsevier Science.

Rothbart, M. K. (2007). Temperament, development, and personality. *Current Directions in Psychological Science, 16*(4), 207–212.

Salaam, A. O. (2011). Motivations for gang membership in Lagos, Nigeria: Challenge and Resilience. *Journal of Adolescent Research, 26*(6), 701–726.

Salfati, G. (2000). The nature of expressiveness and instrumentality in homicide: Implications for offender profiling. *Homicide Studies, 4*, 265–293.

Schafer, S. (1977a). The victim and his functional responsibility. *Criminology, 5*(3), 25–29.

Schafer, S. (1977b). *Victimology: The victim and his criminal.* Reston: Reston Publishing Company, Inc..

Seitz, R. J., Nickel, J., & Azari, N. P. (2006). Functional modularity of the medial prefrontal cortex: Involvement in human empathy. *Neuropsychology, 20*(6), 743–751.

Siegel, J. (2008). *Criminology: The core* (*8th ed.*). Belmont: Wadsworth.

Sobol, J. J. (1997). Behavioural characteristics and level of involvement for victims of homicides. *Homicide Studies, 1*, 359–376.

Strongman, K. T. (2003). *The psychology of emotion: From everyday life to theory* (5th ed.). West Sussex: Wiley.

Sylwester, R. (1997). The neurobiology of self-esteem and aggression. *Educational Leadership, 54*(5), 75–79.

Timmer, D., & Norman, W. H. (1984). The ideology of victim precipitation. *Criminal Justice Review, 9*(2), 120–126.

Turvey, B. E. (1999). *Criminal profiling: An introduction to behavioral evidence analysis* (*1st ed.*). London: Academic Press.

Virkunnen, M. (1975). Victim-precipitated pedophilia offences. *Criminology, 15*(2), 175–180.

von Hentig, H. (1948). *The criminal and his victim.* New Haven, CT: Yale University Press.

Voss, H. L., & Hepburn, J. R. (1968). Patterns in criminal homicide in Chicago. *The Journal of Criminal Law, Criminology and Police Science, 59*(4), 499–508.

Warman, D. M., Lysaker, P. H., Luedtke, B., & Martin, J. M. (2010). Self-esteem and delusional proneness. *Journal of Nervous and Mental Disorders, 198*, 455–457.

Weiss, K. G. (2011). Neutralizing sexual victimization: A typology of victims' non-reporting accounts. *Theoretical Criminology, 15*(*4*), 445–467.

Wilson, J. K. (2009). *The Praeger handbook of victimology*. Santa Barbara, CA: Praeger.

Wolfgang, M. E., & Singer, S. I. (1973). Victim categories of crime. *The Journal of Criminal Law and Criminology, 69*(*3*), 379–394.

Wright, A., Burgess, G., Laszlo, T., McCrary, O., & Dougles, J. E. (1996). A typology of interpersonal stalking. *Journal of Interpersonal Stalking, 11*(*4*), 487–502.

Yarrow, L. J. (1979). Emotional development. *American Psychologist, 34*(*10*), 951–957.

Glossary

Above-average effect: When individuals believe themselves to be more competent than they actually are.

Accuracy rate: The statistical representation of the accuracy of a profile, usually judged by the number of points that match the offender once caught.

Appeal to common practice: A logical fallacy stating that because most people engage in a particular practice, this provides evidence for the practice.

Area of expertise rule: States that experts cannot testify on areas that are not part of a formal sphere of knowledge or profession.

Arson: A generic term used for the setting of a deliberate, malicious fire to damage property, generally that of another person.

Behavioral consistency: The theory that offenders will behave consistently between the offenses they commit.

Behavioral evidence analysis: A deductive profiling method based on the collection and interpretation of physical evidence and the application of deductive logic.

Thomas Bond: A police surgeon who provided an ad hoc profile of Jack the Ripper, a serial murderer from Whitechapel, in the late 1800s.

James Brussel: A New York-based psychiatrist who provided the profile of the Mad Bomber of New York, George Metesky, in the 1950s.

Buffer zone: The area around the home base where the offender is unlikely to engage in criminal acts, usually through fear of being recognized.

Bush: An area containing trees, scrub, high vegetation, shrubs, and large amounts of vegetation.

David Canter: A British psychologist who provided the profile of the Railway Rapist, John Duffy, for Scotland Yard and later developed investigative psychology.

Circle theory: A term coined by David Canter to describe the range of an offender's spatial activity, whereby the two furthest offenses dictate the diameter of the circle and in 80+% of cases will also contain the suspect's home.

Common knowledge rule: States that an expert cannot give opinions on matters that may be considered within the general knowledge or common sense.

Competence: The ability to do something with accuracy, efficiency, and reliability.

Concurrent stalker: A stalker who pursues two or more victims at the same time.

Consecutive stalker: A stalker who pursues two or more victims in generally different time frames.

Consumer satisfaction: The usually subjective degree to which consumers of profiling state that a profile assisted with the investigation.

Criminal Investigative Analysis (CIA): A blanket term used by the FBI and FBI-trained profilers that incorporates profiling, indirect personality assessment, equivocal death analysis, and trial strategy.

Criminal profile: An attempt to provide personality and behavioral clues of an offender based on the offender's behavior and the evidence he or she leaves behind.

Criminal profiling (also known as offender profiling, psychological profiling, offender analysis, behavioral profiling, or just "profiling"): An investigative practice that was initially developed to provide behavioral advice to police investigations and has become synonymous with the crimes of the serial killer.

Cyberbullying: Acts of bullying that occur via electronic mediums such as mobile telephone technologies, Short Messaging Services (SMS), e-mail, social networking, or other outlets.

Date rape: Sexual assault whereby the victim and offender are in, or have been in, some form of personal or social relationship.

***Daubert* ruling:** Proposed that the admissibility of evidence should be based on its reliability and validity, its potential for misrepresentation or falsification, its error rate, and whether it has been subjected to peer review.

Deception: A false communication that benefits the communicator.

Deduction: Where the conclusion is made certain by the supporting evidence or premises.

Diagnostic evaluation: A general term for the profiling work of psychologists and psychiatrists done on an ad hoc basis.

Disorganized offender: An offender who may be psychotic and makes no attempt to clean up the crime scene, remove evidence, hide the body, among others.

Distance decay: The theory that crimes will decrease in frequency the further away an offender travels from his or her home base.

Emotion: A complex state that dictates how we feel about ourselves, others, and our environment.

Environmental criminology: The study of criminal behavior according to physical space and time.

Ethics: The normative study of the rightness or wrongness of human behavior.

Expertise rule: States that an expert must be an expert in his or her respective field, although not necessarily the leading expert.

Factual basis rule: States that the strength of an expert's opinion is related to the factual reliability of the evidence on which the opinion is based.

Fallacy of accuracy: The flawed assumption that accuracy is the best way to gauge the quality of a profile.

Frye ruling: Revolves primarily around the general acceptance of expert evidence within the scientific community.

Geographic profiling: A profiling method that focuses on the probable spatial behavior of the offender as a function of the locations of various crime sites.

Geographic profiling system: The use of computer software to create suspect prioritization maps.

Harassment: Offensive and discriminatory treatment of one person by another based on the victim's personal characteristics.

Homology assumption: A theory stating there is concordance between the behavior of two offenders and their subsequent demographic characteristics.

Identification: Recognition of an item's membership to a class of similar items or objects.

Individualization: Recognition of the characteristics of an item or object that limits its origin to one source to the exclusion of all others.

Incidence: The extent or frequency of a particular occurrence.

Induction: Where the conclusion is made likely by the supporting evidence or premises.

Inputs of the profile: The information or evidence on which a profile is based.

Insight: The ability to identify and understand the true nature of a situation.

Intent: The desire to bring about a certain outcome.

Interpersonal coherence: A type of behavioral consistency, where offenders are theorized to behave consistently between their criminal and noncriminal behavior.

Introspection: The degree to which we can identify, understand, and appreciate emotional states.

Investigative profiles: Evidence at a crime scene that may be used to dictate the allocation of investigative resources.

Investigative psychology: An inductive profiling method developed by David Canter based on psychological principles and research into various offense types.

Investigative relevance: The degree to which a profile actually assists in the investigative decision-making process.

Walter Langer: A psychiatrist who was asked by the Office of Strategic Services to provide a profile of Adolf Hitler, including his future actions.

Least effort principle: Given two alternative courses of action, people will choose the one that requires the least effort.

Logic: The science of valid thought and the process of argumentation.

Cesare Lombroso: An early anthropometrician who attempted to infer criminality from bodily features.

Marauder and commuter: Typologies of offender spatial behavior; the former are people who branch in a number of directions from their home base and the latter travel to a specific area to commit crime.

Medico-legal death investigation: Investigation of the death of an individual by combining medical, scientific, and circumstantial information in order to determine the cause, mechanism, and manner of death.

Metacognition: The knowledge and awareness one has of his or her own cognitive processes.

Metacognitive monitoring: An individual's ability to reflect and exhibit self-regulation over one's thinking.

Modus operandi (MO): Those behaviors necessary for the successful completion of the crime.

Motivation: Any force that activates and gives direction to behavior.

Motivational model: A theory of sexual homicide that attempts to explain the developmental progression of a serial murderer.

Munchausen's syndrome: A factitious disorder where individuals fake symptoms of various disorders in order to get sympathy or some other gain.

Non sequitur: An argument in which the conclusion does not follow logically from the premise(s).

Organized offender: An offender who may be psychopathic and is literally organized in his or her offense behavior, cleaning up the crime scene, removing weapons and evidence, and attempting to hide the body, among others.

Outputs of a profile: The conclusions given about offender characteristics based on the inputs.

PCL-R: The Psychopathy Checklist–Revised, which measures a number of personality and background factors of the individual to assess the presence or degree of psychopathy.

Personality: The observable or explicit features of an individual that characterize his or her being.

Personality disorder: Aberrations of personality that are maladaptive, inflexible, and cause adjustment problems or personal distress.

Posing: Leaving the victim in a position that is considered to be sexually degrading.

Precautionary act: Any act committed before, during, or after the event to help the offender get away with the crime.

Predictive policing: The use of spatial and temporal analysis of past crimes to predict potential areas of future criminal activity and often used to direct police resources into specific areas.

Premise: The evidence, information, or reasons that support the main claim of an argument.

Prevalence: The total number of cases of a disease or occurrence in a population at a given time.

Probative evidence: Evidence that is court worthy, objective, and supported by factual evidence that is diagnostically accurate.

Probative profiles: Evidence at a crime scene that has probative value such as to suggest two crime scenes or evidence items are the same.

Problem of case linkage: A problem of induction where case linkage is premised on the theory of behavioral consistency.

Problem of relevance: A problem of induction where the relevance of the literature used to provide an average for reference is not known.

Problem of reliability: A problem of induction where the profiler will not know whether he or she is dealing with a statistical average or a statistical anomaly.

Problem of trait reliance: A problem of induction where simplified trait descriptions are offered to describe how the offender will behave when found, based on the offender's crime scene behavior sometime in the past.

Psychopath: An individual with a personality disorder characterized by a pervasive disregard for the welfare of others, a callous lack of remorse, and a grandiose sense of self-worth.

Rape: Nonconsensual intercourse, including penetration of the vagina, anus, or mouth by both foreign or digital objects.

Rapist typology: A grouping of offenders based on shared characteristics, such as motivation.

Red flags: Inconsistencies in the evidence that warrants further investigation.

Kim Rossmo: Developed Criminal Geographic Targeting and is an advocate for geographic profiling.

School-based bullying: Aggressive acts that vary in form and intensity and occur within an educational institution.

Scientific method: A systematic way to investigate how or why something works through observation, theorizing, and experimentation.

Self-efficacy: A personal belief about one's abilities to execute a course of action.

Self-esteem: An emotional state that governs how we feel about ourselves.

Serial arson: Two or more deliberate, malicious fires lit by the same person or group.

Serial killing/murder: The killing of two or more people by an individual or a group acting in concert.

Serial rape: Two or more rape offenses committed by the same offender.

Sexual assault: Physical assault of a sexual nature directed toward a nonconsenting individual, or where consent is achieved through fraud or intimidation.

Signature: Evidence of behavior at a crime scene, not necessary to complete the crime that points to an underlying psychological need of the offender.

Similar fact evidence: Evidence based on the degree to which the behavior in a crime conforms to the general character of the accused.

Staging: The deliberate alteration of the physical evidence to obscure the facts, mislead investigators, and/or direct the investigation away from the most logical suspect.

Staging: Any act by an offender intended to thwart the investigation or to distance him- or herself from the criminal act.

Stalking: A repeated pattern of intrusion and harassment involving various forms of communication and physical contact.

State of mind: The psychological state of the offender at the time of the crime, including planning, spontaneity, anger, sadism, remorse, and intent.

Temperament: Predispositions, usually biological, that set the stage for the development of personality, character, and other traits.

Howard Teten and Pat Mullany: FBI agents who started profiling in the FBI in the 1970s.

Threat management: A targeted approach utilizing the 25 techniques of situational crime prevention to reduce or prevent crimes such as stalking.

Theories of rape: Etiological principles available to explain sexual aggression for the purpose of assessment and treatment of offenders.

Trauma: A physical or psychological injury that causes harm.

Trauma control model: A theory of serial killing where traumatizations coupled with predispositions provide the developmental context for serial homicide.

Brent Turvey: A forensic scientist from the United States who developed the deductive profiling method called behavioral evidence analysis.

Typology: A clustering or grouping of types based on shared or similar characteristics.

Typologies: A classification designed to provide an understanding of types based on shared characteristics.

Ultimate issue rule: States that experts cannot give opinions regarding the ultimate issue of guilt or innocence.

Workplace bullying: Aggressive acts that vary in form and intensity and occur within the professional workplace environment.

Index